**BLACKSTONE'S**
## The Pensions

BLACKSTONE'S GUIDE TO

# The Pensions Act 2004

Martin Jenkins, Martin Poore, Helen Dodds,
Asmah Baig, Kate Hainsworth, Kate Byers,
David Brabbs, Pat Abeysekera, and Debbie Don

OXFORD
UNIVERSITY PRESS

# OXFORD
UNIVERSITY PRESS

Great Clarendon Street, Oxford OX2 6DP

Oxford University Press is a department of the University of Oxford.
It furthers the University's objective of excellence in research, scholarship,
and education by publishing worldwide in

Oxford New York

Auckland Cape Town Dar es Salaam Hong Kong Karachi
Kuala Lumpur Madrid Melbourne Mexico City Nairobi
New Delhi Shanghai Taipei Toronto

With offices in

Argentina Austria Brazil Chile Czech Republic France Greece
Guatemala Hungary Italy Japan Poland Portugal Singapore
South Korea Switzerland Thailand Turkey Ukraine Vietnam

Oxford is a registered trade mark of Oxford University Press
in the UK and in certain other countries

Published in the United States
by Oxford University Press Inc., New York

© Dickinson Dees Pensions Law Team 2005

The moral rights of the authors have been asserted

Crown copyright material is reproduced under Class Licence
Number C01P0000148 with the permission of HMSO
and the Queen's Printer for Scotland

Database right Oxford University Press (maker)

First published 2005

All rights reserved. No part of this publication may be reproduced,
stored in a retrieval system, or transmitted, in any form or by any means,
without the prior permission in writing of Oxford University Press,
or as expressly permitted by law, or under terms agreed with the appropriate
reprographics rights organizations. Enquiries concerning reproduction
outside the scope of the above should be sent to the Rights Department,
Oxford University Press, at the address above

You must not circulate this book in any other binding or cover
and you must impose this same condition on any acquirer

British Library Cataloguing in Publication Data
Data available

Library of Congress Cataloging in Publication Data

Blackstone's guide to the Pensions Act 2004/Martin Jenkins . . . [et al.].
  p. cm.
  Includes bibliographical references and index.
  ISBN 0-19-928190-4 (alk. paper)
  1. Great Britain. Pensions Act 2004. 2. Pension trusts—Law and
legislation—Great Britain. 3. Pensions—Law and legislation—Great Britain. 4.
Insurance, Pension trust guaranty—Great Britain. I. Title: Guide to the
Pensions Act 2004. II. Title: Pensions Act 2004. III. Jenkins, Martin.
  KD3132B55 2005
  344.4101'252—dc22
                                                                    2005009599

ISBN 0–19–928190–4   978–0–19–928190–9

1 3 5 7 9 10 8 6 4 2

Typeset by RefineCatch Limited, Bungay, Suffolk
Printed in Great Britain
on acid-free paper by
Biddles Ltd., King's Lynn

# Foreword

I am delighted to have been asked to contribute this Foreword and to associate myself with this timely work by Dickinson Dees. Their pensions expertise has earned them a national reputation.

Having 'shadowed' the Act from its birth pangs to Royal Assent, I regret that it is still so flawed. If its aim was to protect and encourage final salary schemes in the future, then I believe it will certainly fail.

It also brings with it a myriad of new regulations—some of them still being introduced and debated as I write this! Whilst I welcome the new Regulator, we have at the same time established a complex and over-bureaucratic system for overseeing pensions.

One point of principle that Ministers maintained throughout was that the new Pension Protection Fund could not be retrospective, and that was something we accepted. You cannot insure your house against fire when it has already burned down! But unbelievably the Government has recently announced that in certain circumstances the PPF can indeed be retrospective.

This arises because of the inadequacy of the Financial Assistance Scheme designed to help those people who have lost pensions rights before the PPF starts operating. The £400 million provided by the Treasury is plainly inadequate for the purpose—hence no doubt the desire to shift some of the liabilities forward into the new PPF. There is also much anecdotal evidence that some schemes are staggering on, hoping to collapse into the arms of the PPF when it opens its doors.

All this is worrying for well-run schemes and sponsoring employers. They are already facing a period of several years paying a flat-rate levy to finance the PPF. So for that time at least, the good will find themselves subsidizing the bad. This is the so-called 'moral hazard' problem. Our attitude throughout has been—based on the advice we had from the US—that there should be a proper risk-based levy from the outset.

Another issue which caused the Government much grief was the 'anti-avoidance' provisions. In the end, concessions were made to venture capitalists and others. But it remains to be seen how workable those parts of the Act will prove to be in practice.

There has been much misleading talk about the Act providing a 'guarantee'. It does nothing of the sort. There is a 'cap' on payments, and only 90% is payable to people who are not yet retired. The indexation rules have been changed; and there is a power to cut benefits.

A concern I expressed during the Bill's passage was the 'professionalization' of trustees. This may be workable for large schemes, but not necessarily for smaller ones. And for the first time the qualifications required for the job are spelled out on the face of the Act.

I have severe doubts whether this complex legislation will in the event cause any defined benefit schemes to reopen to new entrants, let alone encourage any employer to start a new one. The Pensions Act 2004 has the law of unintended consequences written all over it.

Nigel Waterson MP
Shadow Pensions Minister
*March 2005*

# Preface

The Pensions Act 2004 finally received Royal Assent on 18 November 2004, after over ninety hours of debate in Parliament and more than 650 amendments. The discussion went right to the wire, and it was a very real possibility that the Bill would fail to become law, through lack of parliamentary time, until the last day of debate before the new parliamentary session.

Notwithstanding the effect that the numerous amendments have had upon the quality of drafting, indeed Baroness Hollis agreed during committee stages that certain provisions were 'technically defective',[1] the Dickinson Dees Pensions Team has been kept on its toes tracking these changes. We would like to thank all those involved for their hard work.

We would particularly like to thank those involved in writing the chapters: Pat Abeysekera, Asmah Baig, David Brabbs, Kate Byers, Helen Dodds, Debbie Don, and Kate Hainsworth.

We would also like to thank Edward Smith and his team of proof readers: Lizzie Blanchard, Lucy Cook, Gavin Ellison, Sarah Frost, Suzie Kemp, Dean O'Connell, Mike Patterson, Aine Smith, and Christine Stewart—as well as the manager and staff of Stereo Bar for their services once the task was complete.

Caroline Bilinski, Kathryn Cowen, Emma Hall, Lucy Herbert, Claire Jenkins, and Vicky Renwick provided invaluable secretarial support.

Martin Jenkins  
Martin Poore  
*Newcastle*  
*February 2005*

---

[1] *Hansard*, HL Grand Committee, col 112 (13 October 2004).

# Contents—Summary

| | |
|---|---|
| TABLE OF CASES | xix |
| TABLE OF STATUTES | xx |
| TABLE OF SECONDARY LEGISLATION | xxvii |
| TABLE OF EUROPEAN LAW | xxviii |
| TABLE OF ABBREVIATIONS | xxix |
| COMMENCEMENT TABLE | xxxi |
| 1. INTRODUCTION | 1 |
| 2. THE PENSIONS REGULATOR | 9 |
| 3. THE PENSION PROTECTION FUND | 31 |
| 4. FRAUD COMPENSATION | 69 |
| 5. GATHERING INFORMATION | 77 |
| 6. REVIEWS, APPEALS, AND MALADMINISTRATION | 83 |
| 7. SCHEME FUNDING | 89 |
| 8. FINANCIAL PLANNING FOR RETIREMENT | 95 |
| 9. MISCELLANEOUS PROVISIONS | 99 |
| 10. FINANCIAL ASSISTANCE SCHEME | 143 |
| 11. CROSS BORDER ACTIVITIES WITHIN THE EUROPEAN UNION | 147 |
| 12. STATE PENSIONS | 153 |
| APPENDIX 1. The Pensions Act 2004 | 161 |
| APPENDIX 2. Useful Addresses | 512 |
| APPENDIX 3. Useful Web References | 518 |
| INDEX | 521 |

Visit the Blackstone's Guide Series website: www.oup.com/uk/law/practitioner/bgseries

# Contents

| | |
|---|---|
| TABLE OF CASES | xix |
| TABLE OF STATUTES | xx |
| TABLE OF SECONDARY LEGISLATION | xxvii |
| TABLE OF EUROPEAN LAW | xxviii |
| TABLE OF ABBREVIATIONS | xxix |
| COMMENCEMENT TABLE | xxxi |

| | |
|---|---|
| 1. INTRODUCTION | 1 |
|   A. Implementation Timetable | 1.07 |
|     1. April 2005 | 1.08 |
|     2. September 2005 | 1.14 |
|     3. April 2006 | 1.17 |
|   B. Commentary | 1.24 |
| 2. THE PENSIONS REGULATOR | 9 |
|   A. Introduction | 2.01 |
|     1. Origin | 2.01 |
|     2. Remit and Operation | 2.02 |
|     3. Commentary | 2.04 |
|   B. Structure and Organization of the Regulator | 2.07 |
|     1. Chairman | 2.08 |
|     2. Non-executive Committee | 2.09 |
|     3. The Determinations Panel | 2.12 |
|   C. Provision of Information and Notices | 2.16 |
|     1. Regulator's Annual Report | 2.16 |
|     2. Provision of Information, Education, and Assistance | 2.17 |
|   D. Powers in Relation to the Conduct of Pension Schemes | 2.21 |
|     1. Closure and Winding Up | 2.21 |
|     2. Freezing Orders | 2.25 |
|     3. Powers in Relation to Trustees | 2.28 |
|     4. Pension Liberation | 2.31 |
|   E. Moral Hazard Provisions | 2.32 |
|     1. Rationale | 2.32 |
|     2. Overview | 2.34 |
|     3. Contribution Notices | 2.35 |

|  |  |  |
|---|---|---|
| 4. Financial Support Directions | | 2.40 |
| 5. Restoration Orders where there are Transactions at an Undervalue | | 2.48 |
| F. Registration and General Powers | | 2.52 |
| 1. Maintenance of the Register | | 2.52 |
| 2. Information Held | | 2.53 |
| 3. Inspection and Assimilation of Data | | 2.55 |
| 4. Scheme Returns | | 2.56 |
| 5. Register of Prohibited Trustees | | 2.59 |
| 6. Notifying the Regulator | | 2.61 |
| 7. Information Gathering | | 2.65 |
| 8. Reports | | 2.77 |
| G. Codes of Practice | | 2.78 |
| 1. Issue of Codes | | 2.78 |
| H. Exercise of Regulatory Function | | 2.81 |
| 1. Procedure | | 2.81 |
| 2. Standard and Special Procedures | | 2.83 |
| I. The Pensions Regulator Tribunal | | 2.88 |
| **3. THE PENSION PROTECTION FUND** | | **31** |
| A. Introduction | | 3.01 |
| 1. Origins of the PPF | | 3.03 |
| 2. Green Paper and White Paper proposals | | 3.05 |
| 3. Outstanding Concerns | | 3.07 |
| 4. Role and Function of the PPF | | 3.08 |
| B. The PPF Board—Establishment and Functions | | 3.09 |
| 1. Establishment | | 3.09 |
| 2. Procedure | | 3.17 |
| 3. General Provision about Functions | | 3.25 |
| 4. Non-executive Functions | | 3.27 |
| 5. Financial Matters | | 3.29 |
| 6. Administration Levy | | 3.33 |
| 7. Annual Reports | | 3.36 |
| C. Summary of PPF Procedure | | 3.38 |
| 1. Eligibility | | 3.39 |
| 2. Qualifying Conditions | | 3.40 |
| 3. Assessment Period | | 3.42 |
| 4. Valuation | | 3.43 |
| 5. Assumption of Responsibility | | 3.44 |
| D. Effect of Employer's Insolvency | | 3.45 |
| 1. Duty to Notify Insolvency Events in Respect of Employers | | 3.47 |
| 2. Insolvency Event, Insolvency Date, and Insolvency Practitioner | | 3.48 |
| 3. Notices Confirming Status of Scheme | | 3.50 |

|   |   |   |
|---|---|---|
| | 4. Board Approval of Notices Under Section 122 and Duties where Section 122 is not Complied with | 3.53 |
| | 5. Circumstances in which a Notice Becomes Binding | 3.55 |
| E. | Eligible Schemes | 3.58 |
| F. | Duty to Assume Responsibility for a Scheme | 3.60 |
| | 1. Employer Insolvency | 3.62 |
| | 2. Applications and Notifications | 3.65 |
| | 3. Protected Liabilities | 3.69 |
| G. | The Assessment Period | 3.70 |
| | 1. Duration of the Assessment Period | 3.71 |
| | 2. Restrictions on New Members, Contributions, and Benefits | 3.73 |
| | 3. Directions | 3.77 |
| | 4. Restrictions on Winding Up, etc | 3.80 |
| | 5. Board to Act as Creditor of the Employer | 3.84 |
| | 6. Payment of Scheme Benefits | 3.85 |
| | 7. Reviewable Ill Health Pensions | 3.87 |
| | 8. Valuation of Assets and Liabilities | 3.93 |
| H. | Refusal to Assume Responsibility for a Scheme | 3.95 |
| | 1. Anti-avoidance | 3.96 |
| | 2. Cessation of Involvement with a Scheme | 3.98 |
| I. | Reconsideration | 3.100 |
| J. | Closed Schemes and Winding Up | 3.104 |
| | 1. Closed Schemes | 3.105 |
| | 2. Winding Up | 3.107 |
| | 3. Further Provisions Applying to Closed Schemes | 3.112 |
| K. | Payment of Compensation | 3.118 |
| | 1. Assumption of Responsibility for a Scheme | 3.118 |
| | 2. Effect of a Transfer Notice | 3.121 |
| | 3. Pensions Compensation Provisions | 3.123 |
| | 4. Discharge of the Board's Liabilities | 3.138 |
| | 5. Equal Treatment | 3.140 |
| | 6. Relationship with Fraud Compensation Regime | 3.141 |
| L. | The Fund | 3.143 |
| M. | The Levies | 3.145 |
| | 1. The Initial Levy | 3.146 |
| | 2. The 'Risk-based' Levy | 3.149 |
| | 3. The 'Scheme-based' Levy | 3.150 |
| | 4. Calculations of the Levies and the 'Levy Ceiling' | 3.151 |

## 4. FRAUD COMPENSATION    69

|   |   |   |
|---|---|---|
| A. | Introduction | 4.01 |
| B. | Cases where Fraud Compensation Payments can be made | 4.05 |

|   |   |
|---|---|
| 1. Eligible Schemes | 4.07 |
| 2. Relevant Date | 4.08 |
| 3. Prescribed Offences | 4.09 |
| 4. The Circumstances Set Out in Section 182(2), (3), and (4) | 4.10 |
| 5. The Application and the Authorized Period | 4.15 |
| C. Fraud Compensation Payments | 4.18 |
| D. Interim Payments | 4.23 |
| E. Interaction with the Pension Protection Fund | 4.25 |
| F. Fraud Compensation Fund | 4.28 |
| G. Fraud Compensation Levy | 4.30 |

## 5. GATHERING INFORMATION — 77

| | |
|---|---|
| A. Introduction | 5.01 |
| B. Requirement to Disclose Information to the Board | 5.02 |
| C. Powers of the Board to Obtain Information | 5.03 |
| 1. Notices Requiring Provision of Information | 5.03 |
| 2. Entry of Premises | 5.04 |
| D. Penalties | 5.08 |
| 1. Refusal or Failure to Supply Information | 5.08 |
| 2. Issue of Warrants | 5.11 |
| 3. Provision of False or Misleading Information | 5.15 |
| E. Disclosure of Information by the Board | 5.18 |
| 1. Restricted Information | 5.18 |
| 2. Provision of Information to Members of Schemes and Others | 5.23 |
| 3. Reports | 5.28 |

## 6. REVIEWS, APPEALS, AND MALADMINISTRATION — 83

| | |
|---|---|
| A. Introduction | 6.01 |
| B. Investigation of Complaints by the Board | 6.05 |
| 1. Review of Board Determinations | 6.05 |
| 2. Complaints of Maladministration | 6.15 |
| C. The PPF Ombudsman | 6.19 |
| 1. Establishment | 6.19 |
| 2. References to the PPF Ombudsman | 6.26 |

## 7. SCHEME FUNDING — 89

| | |
|---|---|
| A. Introduction | 7.01 |
| B. Statutory Funding Objective | 7.04 |
| C. Statement of Funding Principles | 7.07 |
| D. Agreement of the Employer | 7.11 |

|  |  |
|---|---|
| E. Advice to the Actuary | 7.13 |
| F. Powers for the Regulator | 7.14 |

## 8. FINANCIAL PLANNING FOR RETIREMENT     95

|  |  |
|---|---|
| A. Introduction | 8.01 |
| B. Legislation | 8.04 |
|    1. Retirement Planning | 8.04 |
|    2. Provision of Information | 8.05 |
|    3. Use of Information | 8.06 |
|    4. Combined Pensions Forecast | 8.09 |
|    5. Provision by Employers of Information and Advice to Employees | 8.14 |

## 9. MISCELLANEOUS PROVISIONS     99

|  |  |
|---|---|
| A. Introduction | 9.01 |
| B. Trustee Obligations | 9.03 |
|    1. Introduction | 9.03 |
|    2. New Trustee Duties | 9.04 |
|    3. Investment Principles | 9.08 |
|    4. Power to make Regulations Governing Investment by Trustees | 9.13 |
|    5. Borrowing by Trustees | 9.16 |
|    6. Requirement for Knowledge and Understanding of Trustees | 9.17 |
|    7. Requirements for Member Nominated Trustees and Directors | 9.29 |
| C. Employer Obligations | 9.45 |
|    1. Introduction | 9.45 |
|    2. Pension Protection on Transfer of Employment | 9.46 |
|    3. Consultation by Employers | 9.62 |
| D. Scheme Modification | 9.77 |
|    1. Introduction | 9.77 |
|    2. New Provisions on Modifications of Pension Rights | 9.79 |
|    3. Areas of Concern | 9.90 |
| E. Pension Disputes | 9.100 |
|    1. Introduction | 9.100 |
|    2. New Dispute Resolution Requirements | 9.101 |
|    3. Requirement for Dispute Resolution | 9.106 |
|    4. Persons with an Interest in the Scheme | 9.115 |
|    5. Minimum Requirements for the Dispute Resolution Procedure | 9.118 |
|    6. Background to new Requirements in Relation to the Pensions Ombudsman | 9.122 |
|    7. Appointment of Deputy Pensions Ombudsmen | 9.124 |
|    8. Jurisdiction of the Ombudsman | 9.133 |
|    9. Investigations—the Ombudsman and Group Actions | 9.138 |
| F. Scheme Design and Regulatory | 9.143 |
|    1. Categories of Pension Scheme | 9.143 |

| | | |
|---|---|---|
| 2. Payment of Surplus to Employer | | 9.147 |
| 3. Restrictions on Payment into Occupational Pension Schemes | | 9.150 |
| 4. Activities of Occupational Pension Schemes | | 9.155 |
| 5. No Indemnification for Fines or Civil Penalties | | 9.159 |
| 6. Short Service Benefit | | 9.161 |
| 7. Early Leavers | | 9.164 |
| 8. Safeguarding Pension Rights | | 9.170 |
| 9. Voluntary Contributions | | 9.174 |
| 10. Payments by Employers | | 9.176 |
| 11. Deficiency in Assets of Certain Occupational Pension Schemes | | 9.183 |
| 12. Annual Increase in Rate of Pensions | | 9.188 |
| 13. Revaluation | | 9.196 |
| 14. Contracting Out | | 9.198 |
| 15. Stakeholder Pensions | | 9.205 |
| **10. FINANCIAL ASSISTANCE SCHEME** | **143** | |
| A. Introduction | | 10.01 |
| B. Framework Provisions for the FAS | | 10.08 |
| C. Practical Issues | | 10.15 |
| **11. CROSS BORDER ACTIVITIES WITHIN THE EUROPEAN UNION** | **147** | |
| A. Introduction | | 11.01 |
| B. Legislation | | 11.03 |
| 1. UK Scheme, European Employer—Conditions UK Scheme must Satisfy | | 11.03 |
| 2. UK Scheme, European Employer—General Authorization of UK Scheme | | 11.05 |
| 3. UK Scheme, European Employer—Authorization for Particular European Employer | | 11.07 |
| 4. UK Scheme, European Employer—Notification by Host State of Legal Requirements | | 11.11 |
| 5. UK Scheme, European Employer—UK Trustees to Act in Accordance with Host State's Legal Requirements | | 11.13 |
| 6. UK Scheme, European Employer—Ringfencing of Assets | | 11.15 |
| 7. European Scheme, UK Employer—Duties of Regulator | | 11.16 |
| 8. European Scheme, UK Employer—Restrictions on Disposal of UK-held Assets of European Scheme | | 11.23 |
| C. Commentary | | 11.29 |
| **12. STATE PENSIONS** | **153** | |
| A. Introduction | | 12.01 |
| B. Legislation | | 12.04 |
| 1. Persons Entitled to more than one Category B Pension | | 12.04 |

| | |
|---|---|
| 2. Deferral of State Pensions | 12.07 |
| 3. Lump Sum Alternative | 12.12 |
| 4. Choice of Pension Increments or Lump Sum | 12.16 |
| 5. Pension Increments | 12.17 |
| 6. Lump Sum | 12.19 |
| 7. Options for Spouse | 12.23 |
| 8. Consequential Amendments | 12.27 |
| 9. Disclosure of State Pension Information | 12.31 |
| 10. Claims for State Pensions Following Termination of Reciprocal Agreement with Australia | 12.32 |
| C. Commentary | 12.34 |
| APPENDIX 1. Pensions Act 2004 | 161 |
| APPENDIX 2. Useful Addresses | 512 |
| APPENDIX 3. Useful Web References | 518 |
| INDEX | 521 |

# Table of Cases

AMP (UK) v Barker [2001] Pens LR 77 ................................................................... 9.17

Beckmann v Dynamco Whicheloe Macfarlane Ltd Case C-164/00 [2002] ECR
I-4893 ........................................................................................................... 9.47, 9.59

Edge v Pensions Ombudsman [1999] 4 All ER 546 ................................................. 9.139

Imperial Group Pensions Trust Limited v Imperial Tobacco [1991] 1 WLR 589 ...... 9.64

Lansing Linde v Alber [2000] OPLR 1 ................................................................... 9.17

Marsh & McLennan Companies UK Ltd v Pensions Ombudsman [2001]
OPLR 221 ............................................................................................................ 9.139

Martin v South Bank University Case C-4/01, unreported ............................... 9.48, 9.59

Pitmans Trustees v The Telecommunications Group plc [2004] 32 PBLR ................. 9.10

R v Pensions Ombudsman ex parte Britannic Asset Management Ltd [2002]
90 PBLR ............................................................................................................. 9.135

# Table of Statutes

Child Support, Pensions and Social
   Security Act 2000 .. 1.27, 9.122, 9.123
   s 42 ................................................ 8.12
   s 54 ............... 9.138, 9.139, 9.140, 9.141
Companies Act 1985 ......................... 3.49

Finance Act 2004 .......... 1.02, 1.22, 9.145,
                                            9.148, 9.155
Financial Services and Markets
   Act 2000 ...................................... 3.31

House of Commons Disqualification
   Act 1975 ...................................... 6.23
Human Rights Act 1998 ................... 3.24

Income and Corporation Taxes
   Act 1988 ................................... 9.147
Insolvency Act 1986 .......................... 3.49
   s 95 ................................................ 3.48

Matrimonial Causes Act 1973
   s 21A ............................................ 3.75

Northern Ireland Assembly
   Disqualification Act 1975 .......... 6.23

Pension Schemes Act 1993 ....... 1.27, 3.58,
                  3.134, 3.139, 8.05, 9.100, 9.122,
                         9.135, 9.198, 9.200, 11.14
   s 1 ................................................ 9.143
   s 10 .................................... 3.139, 9.192
   s 12A ............................................ 9.56
   s 21 .............................................. 9.202
   s 47 .............................................. 3.134
   s 71 .............................................. 9.161
      (3) ............................................ 9.161
   s 84 .................................... 9.196, 9.197
   ss 101AA–101AI ......................... 9.164
   s 111 ............................................ 9.174
   s 111A ......................................... 9.177

s 145 ............................................. 9.124
   (4C) .......................................... 9.125
ss 145–152 ................................... 9.122
s 145A .......................................... 9.127
   (3) .............................................. 9.128
   (4) .............................................. 9.129
   (5) .............................................. 9.130
   (6) .............................................. 9.131
s 146 ............................................. 9.136
   (4) .................................. 9.133, 9.137
   (4A) ............................... 9.133, 9.134
s 148 ............................................. 9.138
s 149 ............................................. 9.138
s 151 ............................................. 9.138
s 181(1) ........................................... 3.58
Pt IV ............................................. 9.164
Pt X ................................... 9.122, 9.139
Pensions Act 1995 ... 1.24, 1.27, 2.30, 3.03,
               3.04, 3.145, 4.01, 9.29, 9.31, 9.32,
                     9.35, 9.40, 9.100, 9.103, 9.114,
                                            9.188, 9.197
   s 3 .................................................. 2.70
   s 7 .......................................... 2.29, 2.81
      (5A) .......................................... 2.29
   s 8 .................................................. 2.29
   s 10 ..... 2.68, 2.70, 3.76, 3.89, 8.18, 9.11,
                      9.41, 11.04, 11.13, 11.15, 11.21
   s 11 ...................... 2.05, 2.07, 2.21, 2.27
      (3A) .......................... 2.21, 3.80, 3.86
   ss 16–21 ....................................... 9.30
   s 23 ................................................ 2.81
   s 35 ..................................... 9.08, 9.09
   s 36 ..................................... 9.13, 9.15
      (2) ............................................. 9.13
      (9) ............................................. 9.15
   s 36A ............................................ 9.16
   s 37 .................................... 9.147, 9.148
   s 49 .................................... 2.78, 9.179
   s 50 ........ 1.14, 9.101, 9.106, 9.111, 9.115
      (1) ............................................ 9.107

| | |
|---|---|
| (2) | 9.102, 9.107 |
| (3) | 9.107 |
| (4) | 9.108 |
| (5) | 9.109 |
| (6) | 9.110 |
| (7) | 9.111 |
| (8) | 9.112 |
| (9) | 9.107, 9.113 |
| (10) | 9.114 |
| s 50A | 9.106, 9.115 |
| (1) | 9.115 |
| (3) | 9.117 |
| s 50B | 9.110, 9.118 |
| (2) | 9.118 |
| (3) | 9.119 |
| s 56 | 3.58 |
| s 62 | 3.140 |
| ss 62–66A | 11.14 |
| s 67 | 2.78, 9.77, 9.78, 9.79, 9.90, 9.91, 9.92, 9.93, 9.94, 9.95 |
| ss 67–67I | 9.79 |
| s 67A | 9.80 |
| (8) | 9.93 |
| s 67B | 9.81, 9.82 |
| s 67C | 9.82 |
| s 67D | 9.82 |
| (5) | 9.96 |
| s 67E | 9.86, 9.95 |
| s 67F | 9.87 |
| s 67G | 9.88 |
| s 67H | 9.88 |
| s 67I | 9.89 |
| s 72B | 2.81 |
| s 73 | 2.23 |
| s 75 | 3, 2.34, 2.35, 2.36, 2.37, 3.74, 3.84, 9.21, 9.183, 9.184, 9.187 |
| s 75A | 9.187 |
| s 88 | 9.179 |
| s 91 | 9.173 |
| (5) | 9.173 |
| s 111 | 9.174 |
| s 124(2) | 3.139 |
| s 125 | 9.146 |
| s 126 | 12.01 |
| s 162 | 9.192 |
| s 252 | 9.150 |
| s 253 | 9.153 |
| s 254 | 9.153 |
| s 279 | 9.193 |
| s 280 | 9.195 |
| Sch 4 | 12.01, 12.14 |
| para 6 | 12.10, 12.11 |
| Pt 1 | 11.14 |
| Pensions Act 2004 | 1.01, 1.06, 1.07, 1.24, 2.02, 2.03, 2.04, 2.28, 3.38, 7.01, 7.03, 9.03, 9.51, 9.104, 9.105, 9.111, 9.122, 11.14 |
| *see* Appendix 1 for full text | |
| s 2 | 2.08 |
| s 8 | 2.09 |
| (4) | 2.09 |
| (8) | 2.09 |
| s 9 | 2.12 |
| s 11 | 2.16 |
| s 12 | 2.17, 2.77 |
| s 13 | 1.29, 2.07, 2.18, 2.81 |
| s 14 | 1.29, 2.07, 2.19, 2.81 |
| s 15 | 2.19 |
| s 16 | 2.19 |
| s 17 | 2.19 |
| ss 18–21 | 2.07, 2.31 |
| s 22 | 1.29, 2.05, 2.21 |
| s 23 | 2.05, 2.07, 2.25 |
| s 24 | 2.26 |
| s 25 | 2.27 |
| ss 33–37 | 1.30, 2.28 |
| s 35 | 9.08 |
| s 36 | 2.30 |
| s 38 | 2.35, 3.143 |
| (3) | 2.39 |
| ss 38–42 | 2.34 |
| ss 38–58 | 1.29, 2.05, 2.33 |
| s 42 | 1.28, 2.04, 2.81, 2.84 |
| ss 43–50 | 2.34 |
| s 44 | |
| (2) | 2.42 |
| (3) | 2.41 |
| s 45 | 2.45 |
| s 46 | 1.28, 2.04, 2.81, 2.84 |
| s 50 | 2.34 |
| s 51 | 2.34 |
| s 52 | 3.143, 3.144 |
| ss 52–54 | 2.34 |
| s 55 | 3.143 |
| ss 55–58 | 2.34 |
| s 59 | 2.52 |

| | | | |
|---|---|---|---|
| s 60 | 2.52, 2.53 | s 93 | 2.81 |
| s 61 | 2.55 | (3) | 2.82 |
| s 62 | 2.56 | s 94 | 2.82 |
| (4) | 2.56 | s 95 | 2.83 |
| s 63 | 2.57 | s 96 | 2.84 |
| ss 63–65 | 2.72 | (3) | 2.84 |
| s 64 | 2.57 | (6) | 2.84 |
| s 65 | 2.58 | s 97 | 2.85 |
| s 66 | 2.59 | (2) | 2.85 |
| s 67 | 2.59, 9.88 | (5) | 2.85 |
| s 69 | 2.61, 2.78 | s 99 | |
| (2) | 2.61 | (1) | 2.86, 2.87 |
| s 70 | 2.64 | (4) | 2.87 |
| s 71 | 2.64, 2.73 | s 100 | 1.34, 2.15 |
| (2) | 2.64 | s 101 | 2.81 |
| (7) | 2.64 | ss 102–106 | 1.34 |
| (8) | 2.64 | s 103 | |
| s 72 | 2.65, 2.67, 2.69 | (7) | 2.89 |
| (3) | 2.65 | (8) | 2.89 |
| ss 72–75 | 2.72 | s 104 | 2.90 |
| s 73 | 2.66, 2.68 | s 105 | 2.90 |
| s 74 | 2.68 | s 106 | 2.91 |
| s 75(2) | 2.67 | (5) | 2.91 |
| s 76 | 2.68, 2.71 | ss 107–220 | 1.34 |
| (5) | 2.68 | s 108 | 3.10 |
| (6) | 2.68 | s 110 | 3.25 |
| (7) | 2.68 | s 111 | 3.19, 3.26 |
| s 77(6) | 2.69 | s 112 | 3.27 |
| s 78 | 2.70 | (5) | 3.27, 3.36 |
| (2) | 2.70 | (7) | 3.28 |
| s 79 | 2.65 | (8) | 3.28 |
| (2) | 2.65 | s 113 | 3.29 |
| s 80 | 2.72 | s 114 | 3.30 |
| (2) | 2.72 | s 115 | 3.31, 4.28, 4.29 |
| s 81 | 2.72 | s 116 | 3.32, 3.33 |
| s 82 | 2.76 | s 117 | 3.33 |
| (4) | 2.73 | s 119 | 3.36 |
| s 83 | 2.75 | s 120 | 3.47 |
| s 84 | 2.76 | s 121 | 3.48 |
| (2) | 2.76 | (5) | 3.48 |
| s 85 | 2.76 | s 122 | 3.50, 3.53, 3.54, 3.55, 3.56, 9.186 |
| s 89 | 2.77 | (2)(a) | 3.62, 4.11, 4.17 |
| s 90 | 2.78 | s 123 | 3.53 |
| (4) | 2.79 | s 125(1) | 3.55 |
| (5) | 2.79 | s 126 | 2.62, 3.58, 3.148, 4.14 |
| ss 90–92 | 2.07 | (2) | 3.64 |
| s 91 | 2.80 | s 127 | 3.60, 3.66, 3.69, 3.118 |
| (5) | 2.80 | (3) | 3.62 |

## Table of Statutes

| | |
|---|---|
| s 128 .. 3.60, 3.65, 3.66, 3.68, 3.69, 3.118 | (5) ............................................. 3.135 |
| s 129 ..................... 3.67, 3.93, 4.13, 4.17 | (6) ............................................. 3.135 |
| (1) ........................................ 3.65, 3.71 | s 167 ............................................. 3.136 |
| (5)(a) .................................. 3.65, 3.71 | s 168 ............................................. 3.137 |
| s 130 ................................... 3.68, 9.186 | s 169 ..................................... 3.19, 3.138 |
| (2) ................................................. 4.13 | s 170 ..................................... 3.19, 3.139 |
| s 133 ................ 3.73, 3.75, 3.76, 3.113 | s 171 ............................................. 3.140 |
| s 134 ......................... 3.77, 3.110, 3.113 | s 172 ..................................... 3.141, 4.25 |
| s 135 ................................................. 3.83 | s 173 ..................................... 3.29, 3.143 |
| s 136 ................................................. 3.82 | s 174 ............................................. 3.146 |
| s 137 ..................................... 3.84, 3.113 | s 175 ......................... 3.25, 3.148, 9.174 |
| s 138 ................................................. 3.99 | (2) |
| s 140 ................................................. 3.88 | (a) ............................................. 3.149 |
| ss 140–142 ..................................... 3.87 | (b) ............................................. 3.150 |
| s 141 | s 177 ............................................. 3.153 |
| (2) ............................................... 3.137 | s 178 ............................................. 3.156 |
| (3) ................................................. 3.90 | s 179 ............................................. 3.158 |
| s 143 ........................... 3.93, 3.94, 3.118 | s 180 ............................................. 3.159 |
| s 144 ................................................. 3.92 | s 181 ............................................. 3.160 |
| s 146 ............................. 3.63, 3.96, 3.98 | s 182 .. 3.141, 4.05, 4.07, 4.23, 4.24, 6.15 |
| s 147 ............................. 3.63, 3.97, 3.98 | (2) ........................ 4.10, 4.11, 4.12, 4.17 |
| s 149 ................................................. 3.72 | (2)–(4) ................................. 4.05, 4.17 |
| (2) ................................................. 3.98 | (3) ........................................ 4.10, 4.13, 4.17 |
| s 150 ................................................. 3.99 | (4) ........................................ 4.10, 4.14, 4.17 |
| s 151 ............ 3.100, 3.102, 3.105, 3.109 | (6) ................................................. 4.16 |
| (2) ........................................ 3.105, 3.109 | s 183(2) ......................................... 4.14 |
| (3) ........................................ 3.105, 3.109 | s 184 ............................................. 4.27 |
| s 153 ............................................. 3.104 | s 185 ........................... 4.18, 4.21, 4.29 |
| (2) ............................................. 3.109 | s 186 ................................. 4.18, 4.29 |
| s 154 .............. 2.81, 3.108, 3.110, 3.113 | s 187 ................................. 4.26, 4.29 |
| (2) ................ 3.72, 3.86, 3.108, 3.109 | s 188 ............................................. 4.28 |
| (5) ........................................ 3.86, 3.117 | s 189 ..................................... 3.25, 3.29 |
| (8) ............................................. 3.110 | s 190 ............................................. 5.02 |
| s 155 ............................................. 3.113 | s 191 ............ 3.19, 5.03, 5.08, 5.10, 5.11 |
| ss 155–159 ......................... 3.106, 3.112 | s 192 ........................ 5.04, 5.10, 5.11 |
| s 156 ............................................. 3.114 | s 193 ................................. 5.08, 5.09 |
| s 157 ............. 3.114, 3.115, 3.116, 3.117 | s 194 ................................................. 5.11 |
| s 158 ............................................. 3.118 | s 197 ................................................. 5.22 |
| (3) ............................................. 3.118 | s 198 ................................................. 5.22 |
| s 159 ..................................... 3.109, 3.117 | ss 198–203 ................................. 5.21 |
| s 160 ................. 2.52, 3.72, 3.117, 3.118 | s 199 ................................................. 5.22 |
| s 161 ............................................. 3.121 | s 200 ................................................. 5.22 |
| (7) ............................................. 3.122 | s 201 ................................................. 5.22 |
| s 162 ..................................... 3.19, 3.123 | s 203 ................................................. 5.23 |
| s 163 ..................................... 3.19, 3.131 | (1)(a) ......................................... 3.19 |
| s 164 ............................................. 3.133 | (2) ................................................. 5.25 |
| s 165 ............................................. 3.134 | (3) ................................................. 5.26 |
| s 166 ..................................... 3.19, 3.135 | (6) ................................................. 5.27 |

xxiii

| | |
|---|---|
| s 205 | 5.28 |
| s 206 | 3.53, 6.05 |
| (2) | 6.06 |
| (3) | 6.07 |
| (4) | 6.08 |
| (5) | 6.08 |
| s 207 | 3.53, 6.09, 6.26 |
| (1) | 6.10, 6.13 |
| (5) | 6.13 |
| s 208 | 6.15 |
| (3)(b) | 6.33 |
| (5) | 6.18 |
| s 209 | 6.19 |
| (4) | 6.19 |
| (7) | 6.19 |
| s 210 | 6.20 |
| (4) | 6.21 |
| s 211 | |
| (1) | 6.23 |
| (2) | 6.23 |
| (3) | 6.24 |
| s 212 | 6.25 |
| s 213 | 6.26, 6.39, 6.41 |
| (3) | 6.28 |
| (4) | 6.28 |
| s 214 | 6.33, 6.39, 6.41 |
| s 215 | 6.39 |
| s 216 | 6.41 |
| s 217 | 6.40 |
| s 218 | 6.42 |
| s 219 | 2.81 |
| s 221 | 7.04 |
| ss 221–233 | 2.78 |
| s 222 | 7.05 |
| s 223 | 7.07 |
| s 226 | 7.08 |
| s 227 | 7.09 |
| s 228 | 7.10 |
| s 229 | 7.07, 7.11, 7.13 |
| s 230 | 7.13 |
| s 231 | 7.14 |
| s 234 | 8.04, 8.05 |
| s 235 | 8.05 |
| (3) | 8.05 |
| s 236 | 8.06 |
| s 237 | 8.11 |
| (2) | 8.12 |
| (3) | 8.12 |

| | |
|---|---|
| (4) | 8.13 |
| s 238 | 8.14, 8.19 |
| (3) | 8.17 |
| (4) | 8.17 |
| s 239 | 9.143, 9.144 |
| s 241 | 9.35, 9.36, 9.43, 9.44 |
| ss 241–243 | 9.30 |
| s 242 | 9.36, 9.40, 9.42, 9.43, 9.44 |
| s 243 | 9.43, 9.44 |
| s 244 | 9.08, 9.10 |
| ss 244–249 | 9.04, 9.06 |
| s 245 | 9.13 |
| s 246 | 9.16 |
| s 247 | 9.18, 9.24 |
| ss 247–249 | 1.30, 2.66, 2.78, 9.17 |
| s 248 | 9.24 |
| s 249 | 9.25 |
| s 255 | 9.156 |
| s 256 | 9.159 |
| s 257 | 9.46, 9.52 |
| s 258 | 9.46, 9.55, 9.60 |
| s 259 | 9.67, 9.74 |
| (2) | 9.74 |
| ss 259–261 | 9.94 |
| s 260 | 9.72, 9.74 |
| s 261 | 9.73, 9.75 |
| s 262 | 2.78, 9.79 |
| s 263 | 9.161, 9.162 |
| s 264 | 9.164 |
| s 265 | 9.170 |
| s 266 | 9.173 |
| s 267 | 9.174 |
| s 269 | 9.179 |
| s 270 | 2.23 |
| s 271 | 9.183 |
| s 272 | 2.24, 9.183 |
| s 273 | 9.104, 9.106 |
| s 274 | |
| (1) | 9.124 |
| (2) | 9.124 |
| (3) | 9.127 |
| (4) | 9.132 |
| (5) | 9.132 |
| s 275(1) | 9.133 |
| s 276 | 9.138 |
| s 277 | 4.22 |
| s 278 | 9.189, 9.190 |
| s 281 | 9.196 |

## Table of Statutes

| | |
|---|---|
| s 282 | 9.199 |
| ss 282–284 | 9.204 |
| s 283 | 9.200 |
| s 284 | 9.202 |
| s 285 | 9.206, 9.207 |
| s 286 | 3.02, 10.03, 10.08 |
| (2) | 10.09 |
| (4) | 10.13 |
| (5) | 10.14 |
| s 287 | 11.03, 11.04 |
| ss 287–295 | 11.01 |
| s 288 | 2.81, 11.03, 11.05, 11.07 |
| s 289 | 2.81, 11.03, 11.07, 11.08 |
| (2) | 11.08 |
| (a) (ii) | 11.03 |
| (3) | 11.09 |
| (4) | 11.10 |
| s 290 | 11.11 |
| (1) | 11.03 |
| (2) | 11.12 |
| s 291 | 11.13 |
| (2) | 11.14 |
| s 292 | 11.15 |
| s 293 | 2.81, 11.16 |
| (2) | 11.17 |
| (3) | 11.18 |
| (4) | 11.19 |
| (5) | 11.20, 11.21 |
| (8) | 11.22 |
| s 294 | 11.23 |
| (3) | 11.25 |
| (4) | 11.26 |
| (6) | 11.28 |
| s 295 | 11.08 |
| s 296 | 12.02, 12.06 |
| s 297 | 12.02, 12.10, 12.35 |
| (1) | 12.12 |
| (2) | 12.12 |
| (3) | 12.14 |
| (4) | 12.15 |
| s 298 | 8.10, 12.31 |
| s 299 | |
| (1) | 12.32 |
| (2) | 12.32 |
| (3) | 12.33 |
| (4) | 12.33 |
| s 300 | 2.02 |
| s 302 | 4.28 |

| | |
|---|---|
| s 306 | 1.23 |
| Sch 1 | |
| para 11 | 2.12 |
| para 20 | 2.10 |
| para 21 | 2.10 |
| Sch 2 | 2.14 |
| Sch 3 | 2.73 |
| Sch 4 | 2.88 |
| Sch 5 | 3.11 |
| Part 3 | 3.17 |
| para 16 | 3.17 |
| para 17 | 3.18 |
| para 18 | 3.18 |
| Part 4 | 3.21 |
| Part 5 | 3.22 |
| para 26 | 3.23 |
| para 27 | 3.23 |
| para 29 | 3.24 |
| Pt 1 | 3.12 |
| para 2 | 3.12 |
| para 3 | 3.13 |
| para 4 | 3.14 |
| Sch 6 | 3.121 |
| Sch 7 | 3.90, 3.123, 3.124, 3.129, 3.130, 3.137 |
| para 3 | 3.88 |
| para 34 | 3.133 |
| Sch 9 | 3.53, 6.05, 6.06, 6.08 |
| Sch 10 | 8.07 |
| para 1 | 8.07 |
| para 2 | 8.08 |
| para 3 | 8.08 |
| Sch 11 | 12.10, 12.15 |
| para 4 | 12.16, 12.29 |
| para 5 | 12.17, 12.29 |
| para 6 | 12.18 |
| (1) | 12.1 |
| (2) | 12.18 |
| para 7 | 12.19 |
| para 8(1) | 12.20, 12.29 |
| para 9 | 12.23 |
| para 10 | 12.24 |
| para 11 | 12.25 |
| para 12 | 12.26 |
| para 14 | 12.27 |
| para 15 | 12.28 |
| para 17 | 12.30 |
| para 18 | 12.30 |

| | |
|---|---|
| para 19 | 12.22, 12.30 |
| paras 20–22 | 12.30 |
| para 24 | 12.30 |
| para 25 | 12.30 |
| para 26 | 12.30 |
| para 27 | 12.30 |
| Pt 2 | 12.30 |
| Pt 1 | 5.01, 11.03 |
| Pt 2 | 6.08 |
|    Chap 1 | 3.10 |
|    Chap 2 | 3.45, 5.24 |
|    Chap 3 | 3.136, 4.10, 4.14, 5.24, 5.25 |
|    Chap 4 | 4.01, 4.14, 5.24 |
|    Chap 5 | 5.01 |
|    Chap 6 | 6.01 |
| Pt 4 | 8.01, 8.02, 12.31 |
| Pt 5 | 9.01, 9.30, 9.45 |
| Pt 7 | 11.01 |
| Pt 8 | 12.02, 12.32 |
| Social Security Act 1989 | 9.172 |
|    Sch 5 | 9.171 |
| Social Security Act 1990 | 9.122 |
| Social Security Act 1998 | |
|    s 3 | 8.07 |
| Social Security Administration Act 1992 | 12.30 |
|    s 122D | 8.08 |
| Social Security Contributions and Benefits Act 1992 | 12.04 |
|    s 43 | 12.05 |
|       (3) | 12.06 |
|    s 55 | 12.10, 12.13 |
|    s 55C | 12.10, 12.13 |
| s 62(1) | 12.30 |
| s 83 | 12.18 |
| s 83A | 12.18 |
| s 84 | 12.18 |
| s 122(1) | 12.30 |
| s 176 | 12.30 |
| Sch 5 | 12.15 |
|    para 1 | 12.17, 12.29 |
|    para 2 | 12.29 |
|       (5)(b) | 12.18 |
|    para 3A | 12.20, 12.29 |
|    para 3B | 12.20, 12.21, 12.29 |
|    para 3C | 12.23 |
|    para 4 | 12.24, 12.29 |
|    para 5 | 12.29 |
|    para 7A | 12.25 |
|    para 7B | 12.25 |
|    para 7C | 12.26 |
|       (1) | 12.26 |
|       (2) | 12.26 |
|    para 8 | 12.27 |
|       (4)–(6) | 12.27 |
|    para A1 | 12.29 |
|    para A1(4) | 12.16 |
| Sch 5A | 12.28, 12.30 |
| Superannuation Act 1972 | 6.24 |
|    s 1 | 6.24 |
| Welfare Reform and Pensions Act 1999 | 1.27, 9.194, 9.206, 9.207 |
|    s 2 | 2.81 |
|    s 33 | 11.14 |
|    s 50(2) | 12.30 |
|    Pt 1 | 11.14 |

# Table of Secondary Legislation

Information and Consultation of
 Employees Regulations 2004
 (SI 2004/3426) ............................ 9.75

Occupational Pension Schemes
 (Contracting out) Regulations 1996
 (SI 1996/1172) ............................ 9.64
Occupational Pension Schemes
 (Disclosure of Information)
 Regulations 1996 (SI 1996/1655) ... 9.64
Occupational Pension Schemes
 (Internal Dispute Resolution
 Procedures) Regulations 1996
 (SI 1996/1270) .......................... 9.101
 reg 8 ............................................ 9.112
Occupational Pension Schemes (Member-
 Nominated Trustees and Directors)
 Amendment Regulations 2002
 (SI 2002/2327) ............................ 9.33
Occupational Pension Schemes (Member-
 Nominated Trustees and Directors)
 Regulations 1996 (SI 1996/1216) ... 9.32
Occupational Pension Schemes (Minimum
 Funding Requirement and Actuarial
 Valuations) Regulations 1996
 (SI 1996/1536)
 reg 28 ............................................ 3.58

Occupational Pension Schemes (Pensions
 Compensation Provisions)
 Regulations 1997 (SI 1997/665) .. 4.07
 reg 3 .............................................. 4.09

Personal and Occupational Pension
 Schemes (Pensions Ombudsman)
 Regulations 1996 (SI 1996/2475)
 reg 1(2) ....................................... 9.135
 reg 2(1) ....................................... 9.135

Social Security (Australia) Order 1992
 (SI 1992/1312) .......................... 12.03
 Art 3(3) ....................................... 12.33
 Art 5(2) ....................................... 12.33
 Sch 3 ........................................... 12.03
Social Security (Australia) Order
 (Northern Ireland) 1992
 (SI 1992/269) ............................ 12.03
 Sch 3 ........................................... 12.03

Transfer of Undertakings (Protection of
 Employment) Regulations 1981
 (SI 1981/1794) .......... 9.46, 9.47, 9.48,
 9.51, 9.52, 9.54
 reg 5 .............................................. 9.46
 reg 7 .............................................. 9.46

# Table of European Law

Directive 1977/187 Acquired Rights
    Directive [1977] OJ L61/26 ....... 9.46, 9.50
Directive 2002/14 on informing and consulting employees ................. 9.75
Directive 2003/41 on the activities and supervision of institutions for occupational retirement provision [2003] OJ L235/10 ............ 7.01, 9.06, 9.12, 11.01
    Art 6(a) ........................................ 11.22
    Art 7 ............................................. 9.155
    Art 12 ........................................... 9.09
    Art 18
        (1) ................................................ 9.13
        (2) ................................................ 9.16
    Art 19(3) ..................................... 11.28
    Art 20 ......................................... 11.16
        (4) ............................................. 11.17
        (5) ............................................. 11.03
        (8) ............................................. 11.12

European Convention on Human Rights
    Art 8 ............................................. 8.03
    Art 10 ........................................... 8.03

Treaty of Rome
    Art 5 ........................................... 9.157
    Art 141 ....................................... 3.140

# Table of Abbreviations

| | |
|---|---|
| 1995 Act | Pensions Act 1995 |
| 2004 Act | Pensions Act 2004 |
| AVC | Additional Voluntary Contribution |
| CSPSSA 2000 | Child Support, Pensions and Social Security Act 2000 |
| DWP | Department for Work and Pensions |
| ECJ | European Court of Justice |
| EU | European Union |
| Acquired Rights Directive | Council Directive 1977/187 as amended by Council Directive 1998/50 |
| EU Pensions Directive | Council Directive 2003/41 on the activities and supervision of institutions for occupational retirement provision |
| Explanatory Notes | Explanatory Notes to accompany the Pensions Act 2004 (11 February 2005) |
| FAS | Financial Assistance Scheme |
| FCF | Fraud Compensation Fund |
| FSA | Financial Services Authority |
| FSMA 2000 | Financial Services and Markets Act 2000 |
| Green Paper | The Pensions Green Paper, *Simplicity, Security and Choice: Working and Saving for Retirement* (Cm 5677, 2002) |
| GMP | Guaranteed Minimum Pension |
| ICE Regulations | Information and Consultation of Employees Regulations 2004 |
| ICTA 1988 | Income and Corporation Taxes Act 1988 |
| IDRP | Internal Dispute Resolution Procedure |
| LPI | Limited Price Indexation |
| MCA 1973 | Matrimonial Causes Act 1973 |
| MFR | Minimum Funding Requirement |
| MND | Member Nominated Director |
| MNT | Member Nominated Trustee |
| Myners Review | Myners Review of Institutional Investment in the UK (March 2001) |
| NAPF | National Association of Pension Funds |
| OPRA | Occupational Pensions Regulatory Authority |
| PBGC | Pension Benefit Guaranty Corporation |
| PCB | Pensions Compensation Board |
| PMI | Pensions Management Institute |
| PPF | Pension Protection Fund |
| PSA 1993 | Pension Schemes Act 1993 |

## Table of Abbreviations

| | |
|---|---|
| Regulator | The Pensions Regulator established under Part 1 of the Pensions Act 2004 |
| Regulatory Impact Assessment | Regulatory Impact Assessment (on the Pensions Bill 2004) published by the DWP on 12 February 2004 |
| RPI | Retail Prices Index |
| SFO | Statutory Funding Objective |
| TUPE | Transfer of Undertakings (Protection of Employment) Regulations 1981 (SI 1981/1794) |
| WRPA 1999 | Welfare Reform and Pensions Act 1999 |
| White Paper | The Pensions White Paper, *Simplicity, Security and Choice: Working and Saving for Retirement: Action on Occupational Pensions* (Cm 5835, 2003) |

# Pensions Act 2004—Commencement Table

| LEGISLATIVE CONCEPT | COMING INTO EFFECT |
|---|---|
| *The Pensions Regulator (the Regulator)* <br> The Regulator will replace the current Occupational Pensions Regulatory Authority (OPRA). The Regulator will have substantially more powers to intervene. | 6 April 2005 |
| *Pension Protection Fund (PPF)* <br> The PPF is designed to meet benefits to members (at a predetermined level) where the sponsoring employers providing defined benefit schemes become insolvent after 5 April 2005. | 6 April 2005 |
| *Limited Price Indexation (LPI)* <br> These provisions change the regulations governing the indexation of pensions from 6 April 2005. | 6 April 2005 |
| *Pension Protection on Transfer* <br> These provisions seek to ensure that employees with access to occupational pension provision prior to business transfer will have a prescribed level of pension provision following the transfer. | 6 April 2005 |
| *Financial Assistance Scheme (FAS)* <br> The FAS is designed to provide some benefits to employees whose pension scheme is wound up with an insolvent employer before 6 April 2005. | 6 April 2005 |
| *Statutory Order on Winding up* <br> The new provisions are designed to bring the priorities on winding up in line with the PPF. The liabilities which would be met by the PPF will be given a higher priority. | 6 April 2005 |
| *Internal Dispute Resolution Procedures* <br> These new provisions will simplify the current complicated procedures under s 50 of the Pensions Act 1995. | 23 September 2005 |
| *Scheme Specific Funding* <br> This will replace the current Minimum Funding Requirement (MFR) and will bring in a new *Statutory Funding Objective and Statement of Funding Principles* (analogous to the current Statement of Investment Principles). | 23 September 2005 |
| *Member Nominated Trustee Procedures* <br> Termination of provisions to opt-out of the MNT procedures by employers under the Pensions Act 1995 and introduction of simpler procedures. | 6 April 2006 |
| *Trustees' Knowledge* <br> The provisions will require trustees to be conversant with the scheme documentation, pensions law, investment, and funding principles. | 6 April 2006 |

| | |
|---|---|
| *Scheme Amendments and Employer Consultations* <br> There will be a duty on the employers intending to make changes to the pension scheme to consult with the employees beforehand. | 6 April 2006 |
| *Scheme Modification* <br> These provisions seek to provide relaxation to the procedures that apply to modification of pension rights. | 6 April 2006 |
| *Transfer Option for Early Leavers* <br> Schemes will be required to offer a transfer option to members leaving the scheme with at least three months' membership. | 6 April 2006 |
| *Contracting Out Provisions* <br> These provisions seek to provide relaxation of restrictions on contracted out benefits. | April 2006 |

## COMMENCEMENT ORDERS

| | | |
|---|---|---|
| The Pensions Act 2004 (Commencement No. 1 and Consequential and Transitional Provisions) Order 2004 (SI 2004/3350) | This brings into force provisions of the Act relating to the establishment of the Pensions Regulator and the Board of the Pension Protection Fund. The Order also makes a few amendments relating to the Pensions Compensation Board. <br><br> No consultation period. | 17 December 2004 |
| The Pensions Act 2004 (Commencement No. 2, Transitional Provisions and Consequential Amendments) Order 2005 (SI 2005/275) | This brings into force the appointed dates for the coming into force of the various provisions of the Act. | Various appointed dates as set out in Pts 1 to 7 of the Schedule to the Order, relating to various provisions of the Act, including: <br> (a) dates for the purpose only of conferring power to make regulations or orders, as the case may be, and <br> (b) dates for all other purposes. |
| The Pensions Act 2004 (Commencement No. 3, Transitional Provisions and Amendment) Order 2005 (SI 2005/695) | This Order makes further provision for the coming into force of various provisions of the Act, including s 300(1) which provides for the dissolution of OPRA and s 300(2) which provides for the transfer of property, rights and liabilities from OPRA to the Pensions Regulator on that day. | Various appointed dates. |

# 1
# INTRODUCTION

| | |
|---|---|
| A. Implementation Timetable | 1.07 |
| B. Commentary | 1.24 |

The Pensions Act 2004 represents a major rewriting of the pensions law landscape in the UK. It is being introduced at a time when the voluntary occupational pension regime is under severe strain. Despite the substantial nature of the legislation—and it grew extensively due to Government proposed amendments during its progress in Parliament—it is clear that there are more changes on the way. **1.01**

The Finance Act 2004 will from April 2006 sweep away a huge number of restrictions on scheme design and operation under the current Inland Revenue limits regime. The Government claims this will 'mean far greater individual choice and flexibility about when and how much to save in a pension. And . . . will reduce administrative burdens on employers and pension providers alike.'[1] **1.02**

Further reforms are planned however. An Independent Pensions Commission was established by the Pensions Green Paper with a brief: **1.03**

To keep under review the regime for UK private pensions and long-term savings, taking into account the proposals in the Green Paper, assessing the information needed to monitor progress and looking in particular at current and projected trends in:
– the level of occupational pension provisions;
  – trends in employer and employee contributions;
  – trends in coverage of occupational pension;
– the level of personal pension savings, including:
  – take-up of stakeholder and personal pensions;
  – contributions to stakeholder and personal pensions; and
– the levels of other saving:
  – financial assets, for example Individual Savings Accounts, housing, businesses, savings, and other assets of partners.

On the basis of this assessment of how effectively the current voluntarist approach is developing over time, to make recommendations to the Secretary of State for Work

---

[1] *Simplifying the Taxation of Pensions: Increasing Choice and Flexibility for All* (HM Treasury/Inland Revenue, December 2002).

## 1. Introduction

and Pensions on whether there is a case for moving beyond the current voluntarist approach.[2]

**1.04** It was envisaged that the Commission's investigation of the long-term structure of private pension provision might take some two or three years to conclude. It was anticipated that its first substantive recommendations would be issued by summer 2005.

**1.05** An initial report analysing the challenges facing the voluntary UK pension provision regime was published in October 2004.[3]

**1.06** In addition, such initiatives as the Employer Task Force on pensions[4] are to provide additional commentary and recommendations. The Act, therefore, is not intended to be the last word and needs to be viewed in this context. Trustees, employers, and other stakeholders need to be prepared for further structural reform to UK pension provision.

### A. IMPLEMENTATION TIMETABLE

**1.07** The Act covers a wide range of legislative objectives. It will be implemented in phases. The present implementation timetable is set out below.

#### 1. April 2005

**1.08** *Pensions Regulator*—A new Pensions Regulator will take over from the existing Occupational Pensions Regulatory Authority having wider powers than its predecessor to step in where pension schemes are in difficulties.

**1.09** *Pension Protection Fund*—A pensions safety net funded by a levy on occupational pension scheme membership. The PPF has its origins in the recommendation made to the Goode Committee on Pension Law Reform in 1993 for a central discontinuance fund. This proposal had been put forward by the National Association of Pension Funds but was ultimately rejected in favour of alternative measures which eventually came into legislative effect as the Minimum Funding Requirement.

**1.10** *Limited Price Indexation (LPI)*—Indexation of defined contribution pension arrangements is no longer required and for defined benefit pension arrangements the ceiling on pension increases under LPI is reduced from 5% per annum to 2.5% in respect of benefits accruing after 6 April 2005.

**1.11** *Pension Protection on Transfer*—New provisions will seek to ensure that employees with access to occupational pension provision, prior to business transfer, have a prescribed level of pension provision following that transfer.

---

[2] *Independent Pensions Commission Work Plan* (DWP, June 2003).
[3] *Pensions: Challenges and Choices. The Turner Report: First Report of the Pensions Commission* (12 October 2004).
[4] Also set up following the Pensions Green Paper.

# Implementation Timetable

*Financial Assistance Scheme*—This is designed to provide some benefits to employees whose pension scheme is wound up with an insolvent employer before April 2005, ie to give some measure of protection to those in situations prior to the implementation of the Pension Protection Fund (PPF).   1.12

*Statutory Order of Winding Up*—New provisions are designed to bring the priority order on winding up of a scheme in line with the new PPF. Broadly, the liabilities which would be met by the PPF will be given a higher priority.   1.13

## 2. September 2005

*Internal Dispute Resolution Procedures*—These new provisions will simplify the current complicated procedures required under s 50 of the 1995 Act.   1.14

*Scheme Specific Funding*—This will replace the current minimum funding requirement with a new Statutory Funding Objective (SFO) and a Statement of Funding Principles.   1.15

*Cross Border Pensions*—A more relaxed regime permitting employees to switch between EU employers whilst remaining in the same pension arrangement.   1.16

## 3. April 2006

*Member Nominated Trustees*—Termination of provisions allowing an 'opt-out' (or employer alternative arrangement) of the member nominated trustee (or member nominated director, as the case may be) requirements and implementation of simpler procedures in relation to the same.   1.17

*Trustees' Knowledge and Understanding*—Provisions requiring trustees to be conversant with their scheme documentation and to demonstrate an understanding of pension law and investment and funding principles.   1.18

*Scheme Amendments and Employer Consultation*—Implementation of a duty on employers intending to make any changes to the pension scheme to consult with the employees and others affected beforehand.   1.19

*Scheme Modification*—Provisions to relax procedures relating to the modification of pension rights.   1.20

*Transfer Options for Early Leavers*—Schemes will be required to offer a transfer option to members leaving the scheme with at least three months' membership.   1.21

*Miscellaneous Provisions*   1.22

(a) Contracting out—minor modifications to the contracting out regime;
(b) Surplus—minor changes to the provisions on return of pension surplus to any employer; and
(c) Additional Voluntary Contributions (AVCs)—removal of the legal requirement for an occupational pension scheme to provide an accompanying AVC facility designed to fit in with the implementation of the relaxations on

# 1. Introduction

freedom of pension contribution introduced by the new tax simplification regime under the Finance Act 2004.

**1.23** Many provisions of the Act will have overriding effect against any conflicting pension scheme provisions or practices (s 306).

## B. COMMENTARY

**1.24** A trustee or employer reading the Act for the first time might be forgiven for perhaps being encouraged by the fact that a great deal of the provisions appear familiar. Terms of the Act on such matters as, for instance, creation of a Pensions Regulator, member nominated trusteeship, and even the new statutory funding standard each build upon (or replace) comparable provisions in the 1995 Act.

**1.25** What will be unfamiliar, however, is the Pension Protection Fund (PPF). The PPF is intended to:

- provide protection (within specified limits) for pension rights under a defined benefit arrangement when an employer becomes insolvent;
- allow the trustees or managers of the scheme to apply to the PPF for assistance if it appears to them that the sponsoring employer is unlikely to continue as a going concern;
- assume responsibility for the pension fund in question to ensure, as far as possible, that the statutory protected liabilities are duly paid; and
- be funded by a levy on pension schemes (subject to some exceptions).

**1.26** The operation of the PPF is likely to have a major effect on employers and pension funds. After an initial period, for instance, the levy will be adjusted for perceived risk of employer default (or underfunding generally). The precise basis of this assessment and the operation of the levy remain to be finalized in regulation. The 'moral hazard' legislation, allowing the Pensions Regulator to impose a contribution notice where there has been an attempt to subvert the legislation, and a financial support direction where a pension scheme is left underfunded, will also have a significant impact on how employers view pension funding.

**1.27** Rather than consolidating existing legislation, the Act builds on the current provisions (albeit some of the existing legislation will be repealed). Trustees, employers, and other stakeholders will now be required to tip-toe through an array of guidance, codes of practice, and legislation (the latter including the Pension Schemes Act 1993, the Pensions Act 1995, the Welfare Reform and Pensions Act 1999, and the Child Support, Pensions and Social Security Act 2000). The Government has warned that it intends to introduce more than one hundred different sets of regulations to implement the various provisions of the

Act. Any suggestion, therefore, that the Act promotes simplicity is likely to ring hollow.

**1.28** Despite Government claims to the contrary,[5] the Act does not provide any substantial new incentives for employers to offer occupational pension schemes. Whilst there is no carrot, however, there does appear to be a stick. The legislation makes it much more difficult for an employer to withdraw from an existing pension arrangement. Regulations made in association with the Act will extend the protection of the debt on employer (on the buy-out basis) to centralized schemes applying to more than one employer. When one employer leaves the group, the debt in relation to the pension deficit represents a proportion of the assets calculated on the buy-out rather than, as now, the Minimum Funding Requirement (MFR) basis. The Regulator will be responsible for the moral hazard provisions under which it will have power to impose financial support directions on groups of companies and associated businesses where a pension scheme is left insufficiently supported. In addition, the Regulator will be able to demand immediate payment where an attempt is made to avoid liabilities altogether; this part of the legislation has been subject to substantial amendment in Parliament. The key consideration was providing a degree of certainty to employers and investors. The legislation now includes facility for a clearance procedure (ss 42 and 46) on group reorganization and company disposals and provisions allowing transactions to proceed where there are bona fides and the changes are not designed to subvert the operation of the PPF.

**1.29** Essential to the legislation is the role of the Pensions Regulator. With an annual budget of just £23 million (compared to OPRA's £17 million per annum) the Regulator will have very wide responsibilities indeed. These responsibilities will include:

(a) *Provision of information and education*—The Regulator is to be responsible for providing information, education, and assistance to pension schemes and employers in relation to the legislation, responsibilities of each party, etc;

(b) *Powers to intervene*—The Regulator is required to be pro-active in identifying concerns and can issue 'improvement'[6] or 'third party'[7] notices to prevent breaches of pension legislation or remedy the underlying causes of breaches which have already occurred. In addition to this the Regulator has power to recover unpaid employer contributions, to enforce the operation of the statutory funding objective, a schedule of contributions or a statement of funding principles. It also has the power to modify schemes to ensure that benefits promised can be paid, and, in certain circumstances, direct the

---

[5] Pensions Green Paper, paras 32 and 33.
[6] Section 13.
[7] Section 14.

winding up of a scheme where it is clear this is the only course available to protect members' interests[8]; and

(c) *Moral hazard*—As has been seen, the Regulator is also responsible for the operation of the moral hazard legislation designed to protect the PPF.[9]

1.30 As if this list is not enough, the Regulator also oversees the arrangements whereby trustees must achieve a reasonable level of knowledge and understanding of pension requirements applicable to them.[10] This provision is part of the Regulator's general jurisdiction over pension trustees. It has broadly similar powers to its predecessor to suspend or permanently remove trustees where required. Unlike its predecessor, however, the Regulator will also be responsible for appointing an independent trustee in insolvency situations.[11] Prior to the implementation of the Act, this appointment was made by the insolvency practitioner where, as is common, an independent trustee is required on corporate insolvency.

1.31 A key factor in the decision to establish a new Pensions Regulator appears to have been the Pickering Report.[12] This proposed a 'new kind of regulator' which would 'have the authority to intervene in a pro-active way where it feels that is necessary and having the skills and knowledge to identify any bad practice or potentially criminal activity at an early stage'.[13]

1.32 Arguably, however, being 'pro-active' and selective as to where to inquire and where to apply a 'lighter regulatory touch' is inconsistent with the huge remit and responsibilities the Act imposes on the Regulator. Pickering did not envisage this wide role and, indeed, suggested that 'regulation should be kept to a minimum'.[14]

1.33 The report also identified that for any regulator to act selectively and pro-actively would require skill and knowledge. This will represent a significant resource challenge if the Regulator is to operate as envisaged.

1.34 The Regulator will also face a significant challenge to ensure it is able to discharge conflicting obligations. On the one hand, it has a duty to protect the PPF and on the other to assist trustees of underfunded pension arrangements to maximize protection of pension benefits. For example, it will be in part the responsibility of the Regulator to assist with the assessment of cases for entry to the PPF.[15] At the same time the Regulator has responsibility to the trustees to ensure the best protection of the members' pension rights.[16] The Regulator will

---

[8] Pensions Act 1995, s 11 amended by s 22 of the 2004 Act.
[9] Sections 38 to 58.
[10] Sections 247 to 249.
[11] Sections 33 to 37.
[12] *A Simpler Way to Better Pensions*, An independent report by Alan Pickering (July 2002).
[13] ibid at 1.19.
[14] ibid at 1.14.
[15] Sections 107 to 220.
[16] Section 100.

separate the work of its staff and the Determinations Panel will be responsible for considering a wide range of key decisions. Decisions and actions of the Regulator can be appealed to the Pensions Regulator Tribunal.[17] Nevertheless the division of responsibilities here may prove difficult to administer in practice. The Act will not be able to operate effectively if the Regulator is unable to meet this challenge either through insufficient resource or expertise.

---

[17] Sections 102–106.

# 2
# THE PENSIONS REGULATOR

| | |
|---|---|
| A. Introduction | 2.01 |
| B. Structure and Organization of the Regulator | 2.07 |
| C. Provision of Information and Notices | 2.16 |
| D. Powers in Relation to the Conduct of Pension Schemes | 2.21 |
| E. Moral Hazard Provisions | 2.32 |
| F. Registration and General Powers | 2.52 |
| G. Codes of Practice | 2.78 |
| H. Exercise of Regulatory Function | 2.81 |
| I. The Pensions Regulator Tribunal | 2.88 |

## A. INTRODUCTION

### 1. Origin

**2.01** The starting point for consideration of the role of the Pensions Regulator ('the Regulator') is the December 2002 Green Paper, *Simplicity, Security and Choice: Working and Saving for Retirement*.[1] In the Green Paper, the Government commented that the existing regulator (OPRA—established under the 1995 Act) was not operating as effectively as it should. The reason for this failing was that OPRA's statutory remit required it to be reactive rather than pro-active.[2] The Green Paper measures proposed a new kind of regulator[3] which would not be required, like its predecessor, to become bogged down with numerous minor infringements of legislation. Instead it would be a pro-active body whose investigative effort is focused on schemes in which there is a higher risk of fraud, bad governance, or maladministration. The Green Paper proposals also

---
[1] Cm 5677 (December 2002).
[2] ibid at Ch 4, para 65: 'OPRA can react when problems have happened but not always anticipate problems and intervene proactively.'
[3] ibid at para 66.

identified that the new Regulator would have an educative and information gathering role.

## 2. Remit and Operation

2.02 These key objectives for the new Regulator are reflected in the terms of the 2004 Act. It is clear, however, that the Regulator (which will replace OPRA under s 300) is, in fact, to have a very wide role indeed in supporting the various elements of the new pensions regulatory regime. In its educative and information gathering role, for instance, the Regulator will be responsible for maintaining the Pensions Registry and for issuing codes of practice and guidelines. It will also have a responsibility to support trustees and managers of pension schemes. Whilst the PPF will be maintained by its Board, it is clear that the Regulator has a key role in ensuring the Fund is not abused and, in particular, in relation to the 'moral hazard' provisions.

2.03 In addition, of course, the Regulator also has powers and responsibilities to identify and step in where pension schemes are in difficulties. The 2004 Act introduces provisions allowing the Regulator to order the freezing of accrual of benefits or winding up of the scheme, and the removal of trustees and appointment of an independent trustee.

## 3. Commentary

2.04 One concern is that the Regulator's proposed targeted and pro-active approach may be blunted somewhat by its very broad range of responsibilities for the new regulatory regime. Like its predecessor, OPRA, the Regulator will be maintained by a levy on occupational pension schemes. Its wide remit, however, in supporting the various elements of the 2004 Act, calls into question whether it will in fact need far greater resources in order to fulfil its responsibilities. One example of the Regulator's wider role, in relation to the so-called 'moral hazard' legislation, is that there is to be some form of clearance procedure on corporate acquisition, disposal, or reorganizations (ss 42 and 46). This facility alone is likely to require a very considerable resource of time and expertise. Yet it forms only a small part of the remit of the new Regulator.

2.05 Another concern is the extent to which the various elements of the Regulator's responsibilities might conflict. So, for instance, the Regulator has a responsibility to step in where a pension scheme is in difficulties and try to provide appropriate support. In doing so, it is able to use its powers to order the winding up of the scheme in question (s 22 by amendment of s 11 of the 1995 Act) or to suspend accrual under a 'freezing order' (s 23). At the same time, however, the Regulator has a central role in protecting the operation of the PPF through the 'moral hazard' and related provisions (ss 38–58). It can also refer cases for consideration of entitlement to benefit under the PPF.

Notwithstanding the separate role of the Determinations Panel, the Regulator may find it difficult to reconcile such potentially conflicting demands. 2.06

## B. STRUCTURE AND ORGANIZATION OF THE REGULATOR

The principal powers of the Regulator are: 2.07

(a) Providing 'information, education and assistance' to pension schemes, and their various stakeholders including the issue of codes of practice (ss 90–92);

(b) Issuing 'improvement notices' where there has been a breach of legislative requirements (s 13), codes of practice or undertakings provided to the Regulator, and 'third party notices' to any party responsible (in part or whole) for such a breach (s 14);

(c) Issuing 'freezing orders' to prevent a winding up beginning or further benefits building up under a scheme while a full investigation is carried out (s 23);

(d) Requiring the winding up of a scheme where necessary (s 11 of the 1995 Act as amended);

(e) Issuing restraining or seeking restitution orders where 'pension liberation' (by unauthorized or bogus transfers) has taken place (ss 18–21); and

(f) Investigating and making directions in relation to compliance with pensions legislation in response to representations, whistle blowing, and other referrals.

### 1. Chairman

The Regulator will have a Chairman appointed by the Secretary of State (s 2). The Chairmanship is to be an independent role—so he or she must not be drawn from the staff of the Regulator (or be Chair of the PPF). The Regulator will also have a chief executive and a board. 2.08

### 2. Non-executive Committee

(a) *Functions*

The Regulator is to have a non-executive committee (s 8). The committee will consist of (a) the Chairman of the Regulator (who also chairs the non-executive committee); and (b) other non-executive members of the Regulator. Certain functions which relate to the Regulator are specified as dischargeable only by the non-executive committee (s 8(4)) or by any sub-committee established by the non-executive committee (s 8(8)). 2.09

The functions of the non-executive committee are: 2.10

(a) To review whether internal financial controls of the Regulator are sufficient;

(b) With the approval of the Secretary of State to determine the terms and conditions of remuneration of the Chief Executive; and

(c) Any further functions delegated by the Regulator (under para 20 of Sch 1).

Power to delegate may be limited by separate regulation (para 21 of Sch 1).

(b) *Remit*

2.11 The remit of the non-executive committee was significantly limited at a relatively advanced stage of parliamentary debate. The Pensions Bill envisaged a non-executive committee which would review and comment upon the strategic direction of the Regulator, and the functions and efficiency of its Chief Executive. The committee would also assess whether the Regulator was meeting its objectives and targets and whether it was reporting on progress sufficiently and accurately. In debate on the Bill, however, these broader functions were removed. Now, in essence, the non-executive function is to maintain internal controls on the Regulator and not to assist with its external role.

## 3. The Determinations Panel

(a) *Structure and remit*

2.12 The Regulator will establish a committee called the Determinations Panel (s 9) whose members will be appointed by a separate appointments committee (para 11, Sch 1).

2.13 It is the role of the Determinations Panel to carry out the various functions of the Regulator by making the relevant decision regarding the particular issue(s) in question. It appears, therefore, that it is for the staff of the Regulator to make investigations and gather evidence in relation to the various responsibilities of the Regulator for the conduct of pension schemes. The regulatory staff will then refer the matter to the Determinations Panel for a decision.

(b) *Reserved regulatory functions*

2.14 The list of 'reserved regulatory functions' for which the Determinations Panel is responsible to make decisions upon is very extensive indeed (see Sch 2). The list includes the:

(a) Power to appoint, remove, or suspend trustees and deal with consequential matters;

(b) Power to give directions in relation to the conduct of a pension scheme including closure, validity of any modifications, winding up, etc;

(c) Issue of restraining, repatriation, or freezing orders and matters ancillary thereto; and

(d) Issue of a contribution notice or financial support direction and issues ancillary thereto.

2.15 In carrying out its various functions the Regulator is required to consider and balance the impact on the members directly affected and the interests generally of the membership of the scheme (s 100). It is clear from the legislation that the duties and responsibilities of the Regulator and its Determinations Panel are very considerable indeed. It will be a challenge to ensure that the separation here of the investigative and information-gathering role of the regulatory staff from the decision-making role of the Panel does not add considerably to the bureaucracy and delay in carrying out the regulatory functions under the legislation.

## C. PROVISION OF INFORMATION AND NOTICES

### 1. Regulator's Annual Report

2.16 The Regulator will make an annual report to the Secretary of State (s 11). This report is required not just to provide a summation of the activities, expenditure, and deliberations of the Regulator over the year, but also an evaluation of the effectiveness of the Regulator so that the Secretary of State can judge its efficiency and progress. In a sense, the report can be viewed as covering those matters which the Pensions Bill attributed originally to the role of the non-executive committee. Accordingly, the report will also include an assessment of the 'strategic direction' of the Regulator, the steps taken to scrutinize the performance of the Chief Executive and review of the Regulator's objectives and targets.

### 2. Provision of Information, Education, and Assistance

2.17 An important part of the Regulator's role is as a provider of 'information, education and assistance as it considers appropriate' to those responsible for the administration of pension schemes or advising trustees and managers of the same (s 12). The Regulator is also separately authorized to provide such services to employers responsible for occupational and stakeholder pension schemes in the workplace.

(a) *Improvement notices*

2.18 The Regulator will have power to issue an 'improvement notice' where there has been a contravention of pension legislation (s 13). The notice will require the person(s) in question not only to remedy the breach but also to take such appropriate action as the Regulator identifies is necessary to prevent a recurrence of the breach. The directions in the improvement notice may make reference to relevant codes of practice and other guidance issued by the Regulator. The notice may also offer a choice of remedies or preventative steps including, presumably, inviting the person(s) responsible to put forward their own proposals. The objective appears to be that, unlike its predecessor, the Regulator will not simply record and, where appropriate, penalize breach of legislation, but instead try to direct and improve both policy and governance of the pension scheme in question.

(b) *Other powers and obligations*

2.19 The Regulator also has power to issue a 'third party notice' where it appears that the contravention was wholly or partly the result of a failure of another person (such as a scheme adviser) to act appropriately (s 14). The Regulator has the power to apply to court for an appropriate injunctive remedy where there is a reasonable likelihood of misuse or misappropriation of pension assets and to seek restitution as appropriate (ss 15 and 16). In relation to unpaid employer contributions, the Regulator has the power (s 17) effectively to step into the shoes of the trustees or managers of the scheme in question and enforce payment of the same (possibly under the relevant schedule of contributions).

2.20 Clearly this contrasts with the approach of the Regulator's predecessor, where the employer and/or trustees might be penalized in relation to a failure to pay contributions on time. It was not necessarily part of the remit of the then regulator to take on responsibility for assisting enforcement of unpaid contributions. Nevertheless, it must be recognized that this wider remedial role will require significant resources. In particular, skilled and experienced personnel will be required to evaluate the great variety of situations which arise in practice and determine, or make a recommendation on, the appropriate course from the numerous powers and provisions available to the Regulator.

## D. POWERS IN RELATION TO THE CONDUCT OF PENSION SCHEMES

### 1. Closure and Winding Up

2.21 As with its predecessor, OPRA, the Regulator has a statutory power to direct the commencement of winding up of a pension scheme. However, the Regulator also has a significantly more extensive armoury of powers than were available to OPRA. The power to wind up itself (s 22) is expressed in broadly similar terms to that which applied to OPRA under 1995 Act (s 11). However, the circumstances where the power to wind up can be applied are much wider. In particular, whereas OPRA had the power to wind up an occupational pension scheme in certain circumstances but only on application by the trustees, managers, employer, etc of that scheme, the Pensions Regulator can be more pro-active (new s 11(3A) of the 1995 Act) and order an occupational pension scheme to be wound up to limit a claim on the PPF.

2.22 It is important to note in this context that the Act makes a number of changes to the operation of winding up of occupational pension schemes generally in particular in relation to defined benefit arrangements.

First, s 270 of the Act amends s 73 of the 1995 Act to vary the priority order. 2.23
Effectively this change will operate to apply a new funding priority order for
securing of benefits as follows:

(a) Benefits already secured by contracts of insurance taken out prior to 6 April
1997 and which cannot be surrendered;
(b) Benefits equivalent to those which would apply if the PPF took over
responsibility for the scheme (see chapter 3 below);
(c) Benefits from Additional Voluntary Contributions (AVCs lose their priority
if they are used to secure additional final salary benefits on an added years
basis for instance); and
(d) Other benefits under the terms of the scheme.

Secondly, for schemes with more than one employer, s 272 provides that when 2.24
an employer leaves a multi-employer scheme, the amount of a debt payable in
such circumstances can be calculated on the full buy-out basis, although an
alternative calculation may be available where arrangements are in place to
support the scheme in the future.

## 2. Freezing Orders

In addition to the power to wind up a scheme, the Regulator may make a 2.25
'freezing order' in relation to a defined benefit arrangement (s 23). A freezing
order may direct that for the duration of the order the following terms may be
varied or suspended:

(a) Admission of new members;
(b) Payments and contributions to the scheme;
(c) Accrual and payment of benefits;
(d) Transfers, buy-out payments, etc; and
(e) Issue of statements of entitlement.

A freezing order may be applied to enable the Regulator to assess a situation 2.26
fully, prior to deciding whether it is appropriate to wind up the scheme in question. The order will override a requirement, for instance, to pay contributions
or benefits which might otherwise apply under the terms of the scheme.
Nevertheless, application of such an order will not prevent:

(a) Any increase in benefit which would otherwise normally accrue (unless the
order specifically states the contrary); or
(b) Giving effect to any ear-marking (also known as a pension attachment
order) or pension sharing order on divorce (s 24).

The freezing order appears intended to be a temporary measure and will not 2.27
normally exceed three months in duration. In any event, the order can only be

extended to last up to six months in total (s 25). The Regulator has the power to revoke a freezing order if its terms are no longer required or, in effect, vary its extent by issue of a new freezing order introducing the changes the Regulator deems appropriate from the terms of the previous order. If an order is made under s 11 of the 1995 Act for the winding up of the scheme, this may take effect from the end of the period covered by the freezing order or, if the Regulator decides it is appropriate (and in particular, if necessary to protect members' interests), with immediate effect. In relation to a freezing order and any ancillary orders thereto, the Regulator is required to notify, as soon as reasonably practicable, the trustees, managers, and employer in relation to the scheme in question. The notification (or the freezing or related order as the case may be) may direct for the due notification to members of the scheme.

### 3. Powers in Relation to Trustees

2.28 The Regulator has broadly similar powers (ss 33 to 37 amending the 1995 Act) to its predecessor (OPRA) to:

(a) Disqualify a person from acting as a trustee of an occupational pension scheme;

(b) Prohibit a person from acting as a trustee of a particular named scheme; and

(c) Make a suspension order—requiring a person to cease to act as a trustee during the period of the suspension (usually while an investigation is taking place).

2.29 Like its predecessor, the Regulator has the power to appoint new trustees where required. However, in addition to the powers (ss 7 and 8 of the 1995 Act) already in existing legislation, the Regulator has an additional power (s 7(5A)) to appoint a trustee where the trustees, members, or the employer in relation to a pension scheme request the same. In making the appointment the Regulator is also able to direct that the trustee thus appointed be provided with fees and expenses paid by the relevant employer, out of the resources of the pension scheme funds or by a combination of both of these methods.

2.30 Section 36 amends the provisions of the 1995 Act in relation to appointment of statutory independent trustees in the circumstances of corporate insolvency. Broadly, instead of the insolvency practitioner having a duty to appoint an independent trustee, this requirement is passed to the Regulator. The Regulator may appoint an independent trustee in relation to a scheme from a register of trustees which it will maintain. In order to qualify to be an independent trustee, the appropriate person needs to demonstrate that it has no interest in the assets of the employer nor any interest in the scheme (other than in its position as trustee).

## 3. Pension Liberation

In addition to its other responsibilities, the Regulator is given a role in combating what the Act refers to as 'pension liberation' (ss 18 to 21). This (apparently positive sounding) process is the term given by the statute to bogus transfers of pension entitlement designed to encash pension rights in breach of tax legislation. In relation to 'pension liberation' activity, the Regulator will be able to make a 'restraining order', effectively freezing an account or other deposit which holds liberated pension money. In addition, the Regulator may make a 'repatriation order' requiring return of the money in question to the transferor pension arrangement and appropriate consequential provisions. An example of such consequential provision may relate to the benefits to be provided by the scheme in respect of the 'repatriated' amounts.

2.31

## E. MORAL HAZARD PROVISIONS

### 1. Rationale

The introduction of the PPF brings with it a concern that relevant stakeholders (in particular employers and shareholders) might seek to offload unwanted pension liabilities onto the Fund. Accordingly, the Government was anxious to introduce accompanying legislation to protect the Fund. The so-called 'moral hazard' provisions of the Act are intended to assist in this regard.

2.32

The provisions were described by a Government spokesman in the following manner:

2.33

> Mitigating the risks of moral hazard is one of the biggest challenges we face in introducing the PPF. It is a challenge we must address if we are to safeguard the integrity and sustainability of the fund and avoid placing an unfair burden on responsible levy payers . . . we know from the experience of the Pension Benefit Guaranty Corporation in the US and, regrettably, from some of the cases which have come to light in this country that we cannot assume that all employers take their pension promise to their employees seriously. We are not naïve to the fact that the advent of the PPF could be seen to provide an even greater incentive for unscrupulous employers to dump their pension liabilities, under the assumption that the PPF will pick up the tab.[4]

The relevant provisions are set out in ss 38–58.

### 2. Overview

The provisions fall into four parts—namely:

2.34

(a) *Contribution notices* (ss 38 to 42)—These allow the Regulator to require provision of a payment to an occupational pension scheme by a person who

---

[4] *Hansard*, HC Standing Committee, col 768 (27 April 2004).

has been involved in a deliberate act (or omission) calculated to avoid pension liabilities. The payment is calculated by reference to provisions applicable in relation to the debt on employer imposed by s 75 of the 1995 Act.

(b) *Financial support directions* (ss 43 to 50)—These allow the Regulator to direct that connected or associated persons to an employer put in place arrangements to guarantee or otherwise support that principal employer's pension liabilities where it is apparent that the principal employer itself is insufficiently resourced to do so. Again, the payment is calculated by reference to the basis applicable under s 75 of the 1995 Act (debt on employer provisions).

(c) *Restoration orders* (ss 52 to 54)—These are orders for return of assets where a transaction at an undervalue has occurred causing loss to a pension scheme.

(d) *Supplementary provisions* (ss 50, 51, 55 to 58)—The supplemental provisions provide useful ancillary powers (including in relation to relevant insolvency legislation) and identify how the various measures should interact.

### 3. Contribution Notices

(a) *Requirement to pay*

2.35 Section 38 (which is stated to relate to 'Avoidance of Employer Debt') allows the Regulator to issue a notice of a liability on a person who was or is an employer in relation to a defined benefit pension scheme or connected or associated with an employer, former employer, etc to pay a specified sum. In order to issue a contribution notice the Regulator must be of the opinion that the person has been a party to an act or deliberate omission the main purpose of which was to prevent either recovery of some or all of any s 75 debt on an employer which might otherwise have applied, or to prevent such a debt arising (or reduce its amount) 'otherwise than in good faith'; and that it is reasonable to impose the liability accordingly.

(b) *Sum required*

2.36 The amount that may be imposed can be up to a full notional 'buy-out' basis debt, calculated as if a s 75 debt had been triggered at the time of the act or failure. The Regulator may issue notices to more than one party to an act or failure, and may decide to apportion any contribution between those persons or make the contribution a joint and several liability between parties.

(c) *Imposing liability*

2.37 There are a number of protections included to ensure that the Regulator does not exercise its powers inappropriately. These are:

(a) The Regulator will need to be of the opinion that a 'main purpose' of the act in question was to avoid the s 75 debt. It will need to be able to demonstrate that it has reasonable grounds for that opinion. In practice it may prove far from straightforward to establish that the purpose of some act or series of measures was to seek to limit pensions liability.

(b) Where the act (or failure) involves preventing a debt arising or reducing its amount, the Regulator must also be satisfied that there was absence of good faith. This again may prove to be a significant hurdle in practice to imposition of a contribution notice. The Regulator's published guidance in this area and the first 'test case' occasions where liability is to be imposed are likely to be scrutinized carefully.

(c) The Regulator can only impose liability if it is of the opinion that it is reasonable to fix that liability on that particular person for the amount concerned. There are specific factors listed which the Regulator must take into account in assessing this question of reasonableness, including:
   (i) The degree of involvement of the person(s) in the act or failure;
   (ii) The degree of control of the person(s) over the employer;
   (iii) Whether the person(s) had/have any particular connection with the pension scheme (for example is a former participating employer or employs former scheme members);
   (iv) Whether the act or failure has been notified to the Regulator; and
   (v) The financial position of the person concerned.

(d) *'Party' to an act or deliberate failure*

**2.38** Being a 'party' is defined as including those who have knowingly assisted in the act or failure. This may, for example, include a parent company who has directed the employer to take the action concerned. The party must have knowledge of the act or deliberate failure itself, but not presumably of the precise objective behind the act, deliberate failure, etc. As stated, in addition to being a 'party to' the act or deliberate failure, the person must also be connected or associated with the employer in question.

(e) *Application and time limits*

**2.39** The provision applies to acts or failures occurring or commencing on or after 27 April 2004. In respect of acts or failures after that date, liability can be imposed by the Regulator during a limitation period of up to six years. When the Pensions Bill provisions were first published a number of groups raised concerns as to the breadth of the powers the Regulator would have on contribution notices. A number of amendments were made in relation to such issues. One concerned group were insolvency practitioners worried that their duty to maximize the viability of an employer and generally to act on behalf of creditors might come into conflict with the new Act. One aspect of the wording of the Act therefore is that the Regulator cannot impose a contribution notice on an insolvency practitioner acting in accordance with his functions as such (s 38(3)).

## 2. The Pensions Regulator

### 4. Financial Support Directions

(a) *Policy*

2.40 The Regulator will have power where the sponsoring employer is (a) 'insufficiently resourced' or (b) a 'service company' to require other associated companies to enter into arrangements to support the pension scheme in the future. This could include imposition of joint and several liability within a group.

2.41 'Insufficiently resourced' means that, if a buy-out basis debt had arisen on a particular day, the employer would not have been able to pay a specified proportion of it; but another member of its group could. The proportion is to be defined in regulations (s 44(3)).

2.42 'Service company' means a group company whose turnover is solely or principally derived from the provision of services to other members of the group (s 44(2)).

2.43 The policy intent in both instances is to seek to avoid groups putting pension liabilities in shell or weak entities which can easily be jettisoned, when the rest of the group is healthy.

2.44 As with contribution notices, the Regulator will need to be satisfied that imposition of the financial support direction is reasonable, having regard to such matters as the Regulator considers to be relevant to the person or persons potentially subject to the financial support direction including:

(a) The relationship with and in particular the degree of control over the relevant employer which the person(s) had;

(b) The value of any benefit received from the employer;

(c) Any connection the person(s) had with the pension scheme; and

(d) The financial circumstances of the person(s) in question.

(b) *'Financial support'*

2.45 There are a number of specific arrangements listed which may be approved by the Regulator, namely:

(a) Adoption of joint and several liability for pensions liabilities across the group;

(b) For the top holding company to take the liabilities; and

(c) Funding arrangements (such as bank guarantees) (s 45).

(c) *Connected/associated persons*

2.46 The Regulator may identify any connected/associated persons against whom to issue the direction. Any one of those persons (or indeed anyone else) may put in place the arrangements covered by the direction. In any event, each of the recipients of the direction will be responsible for ensuring that an arrangement is set up in accordance with the terms of the direction and remains in place.

2.47 If arrangements are not put in place within the time limit imposed by the

Regulator, or if an arrangement subsequently lapses or becomes inappropriate (for example, because the holding company for the group changes), the Regulator can impose a contribution notice on any of the persons to whom its first notice was issued. The maximum amount of the liability is essentially calculated in the same way and in the same terms as that for contribution notices as described above. The Regulator must again, however, apply a reasonableness test when deciding whether to impose liability (and if so how much), and again there are specific factors to be taken into account which are broadly the same as those applicable for contribution notices, but also include the degree of control that person (or those persons) had over whether the arrangement lapsed or not.

### 5. Restoration Orders where there are Transactions at an Undervalue

In respect of transactions at an undervalue (defined in similar terms to insolvency legislation), provisions will allow the Regulator to issue an order to restore the position of a scheme where a transaction at an undervalue involving the scheme has occurred on or after 27 April 2004 and within two years prior to the employer entering into insolvency. 2.48

Essentially, any transaction which represents a 'poor deal' for the scheme during this period can be reopened. An order can only be made against any person who holds the proceeds of the transaction or has received a benefit from it. Person(s) in receipt of the relevant assets or benefit in good faith and for appropriate value will not be subject to an order. There is a presumption of good faith but this will be reversed for those connected to the employer and/or trustees. 2.49

As with a financial support direction, there is provision in the legislation for the imposition of a contribution notice where the restoration order is not complied with. 2.50

The Regulator can either require specific assets to be returned to the scheme or direct that an amount be paid to restore the financial position of the scheme. 2.51

## F. REGISTRATION AND GENERAL POWERS

### 1. Maintenance of the Register

The Regulator must compile and maintain a similar register of schemes to that maintained by its predecessor under s 59 of the Act. The extent to which occupational and personal pension schemes must register will be prescribed by regulations. The register must record the most recent 'registrable information' (as defined in s 60) available to the Regulator. It must also record any notice received by the Regulator that the scheme is to be wound up or to cease to be registrable, and any copy notice received under s 160 where the Board of the PPF assumes responsibility for a scheme. The information in the register may be recorded in 2.52

any way the Regulator considers to be appropriate and the register itself may consist of a number of separate sections.

### 2. Information Held

2.53 Section 60 sets out the 'registrable information'. This includes:

(a) The name and address of the scheme;

(b) The full names and addresses of its trustees and its status in relation to the admittance of new members, whether or not further benefits may accrue or further contributions be paid; and

(c) Whether it has active members and the categories of benefits which are payable.

2.54 In the case of occupational pensions, the register must record the number of members on the last day of the scheme year ended most recently, or the day when the scheme became registrable, whichever is the later. Other information can be required by regulation.

### 3. Inspection and Assimilation of Data

2.55 Regulations will provide for such matters as (a) arrangements for inspection of the register; and (b) dissemination of information derived from the register (s 61).

### 4. Scheme Returns

2.56 Where a scheme is registrable, the trustees or managers are responsible for notifying the Regulator of that fact and for providing the registrable information before the end of the 'initial notification period' (s 62), effectively three months from the date of the establishment of the scheme, or the date that the scheme becomes registrable (if later). If there is a change in the registrable information in relation to a scheme the trustees or managers must notify the Regulator as soon as reasonably practicable of the change and provide the updated information (s 62(4)).

2.57 The Regulator is under a corresponding duty to issue return notices to trustees or scheme managers (s 63). The return date for an initial scheme return must fall into the period of three years from the date on which the Regulator receives notice that the scheme is or has become registrable or from the date when the Regulator becomes aware of the scheme, whichever is the earlier. A subsequent return will have a return date within three years of, but not less than one year after, the return date of the previous notice. By virtue of s 64 the trustees or managers, who have been duly notified in this way, are required to provide the return to the Regulator on or before the return date.

2.58 Section 65 provides some additional guidance on the issue and form of return notices. The notice must be in writing and is treated as having been issued on the date when it is sent to the trustees or managers. The return date must be specified in the return notice and must fall after the end of twenty-eight days from the date of issue. The Regulator will be entitled to specify the form of any information provided under the return and a notice must specify the type of information required. For registrable schemes the return notice must request all 'registrable information' (see para 2.53 above) and may require further information to be provided if this is reasonably required by the Regulator for the exercise of its functions.

## 5. Register of Prohibited Trustees

2.59 It is also the Regulator's duty to maintain, in whatever manner it sees fit, a register of all prohibited persons in accordance with s 3 of the 1995 Act (s 66). Information on this register may be provided in the Regulator's reports, but must not be disclosed to the public except as provided by the terms of s 67. This provision states that:

(a) The Regulator must make the register available for inspection in person and without notice during normal working hours at its principal office (at least); and

(b) A request for information as to whether or not a person appears on the register must be responded to promptly and in a reasonable manner.

2.60 The Regulator may publish a summary of the prohibitions register so long as the information provided contains the name and title of the person prohibited, their date of birth, and the nature of the prohibition. The Regulator should publish three separate lists: one for general prohibitions, one for prohibitions in relation to classes of schemes, and one for prohibitions in relation to particular schemes. The published summary should not identify any of the schemes in relation to which the persons named are prohibited and should not disclose any other information from the register. A person must not appear in the published summary if there is a review of the decision to make the prohibition order pending or if this is likely to be applied for. Nor must such a person be identified on the register itself.

## 6. Notifying the Regulator

(a) *Prescribed events*

2.61 Under s 69 the trustees or managers (or other persons as prescribed by regulation) in relation to a scheme are responsible for notifying the Regulator in writing as soon as is reasonably practicable of a prescribed event in relation to the scheme or one of its sponsoring employers (s 69(2)).

**2.62** It is 'eligible schemes' (as defined in s 126), ie those within the purview and which are potential claimants upon the PPF who may be subject to this notification requirement.

**2.63** The categories of 'prescribed events' which may need reporting upon must await regulation but clearly are likely to refer to significant change in the financial status of the scheme or a sponsoring employer.

(b) *Breaches of the law*

**2.64** The trustees, managers, administrators, employers, professional advisers, or other persons involved in advising the trustees or managers of an occupational pension scheme are under a duty to report in writing to the Regulator where they have reason to believe that an administrative requirement imposed by law is not being complied with (s 70). Making such a report will not be considered a breach of any other duty, and failure to report will result in civil liability under s 10 of the 1995 Act. In addition, under s 71, the Regulator may issue a notice to the trustee, manager, employer, or administrator requiring them to provide information relevant to the Regulator's functions. Such a 'report notice' will require that a person must be nominated or approved by the Regulator with the necessary skills to report on the matters concerned (s 71(2)). The notice may require the report to be provided in a specified form and by a particular date. Any costs must be met by the person to whom the notice is issued but the notice may require a third party to reimburse the whole or part of the costs. Failure to comply with a report notice will result in civil liability (s 71(7) and (8)). If the assistance of a third party is required the Regulator may enforce this by applying for an injunction.

## 7. Information Gathering

(a) *Provision of information*

**2.65** The Regulator may require by way of written notice that a person produce any document or information specified in that notice (s 72). The information or document requested must be relevant to the Regulator's functions. A document is defined (by s 79) as including information recorded in any form. There is a requirement on the producer to ensure that the document is in a legible form (s 79(2)). Any document requested must be provided as specified in the notice (s 72(3)).

(b) *Inspection of premises*

**2.66** The Regulator also has powers (under s 73) to inspect premises in relation to an occupational (or stakeholder) pension scheme. An inspector may enter such premises to investigate a wide range of requirements to comply with pensions legislation including, for instance, whether the trustees' obligation to demonstrate appropriate knowledge and understanding (ss 247 to 249) is being met. Premises are liable to inspection only if there are reasonable grounds to believe that members are employed there, relevant documents are stored there, or the administration of the pension scheme in question is carried out there. The premises may be those of the employer if the purpose of the inquiry relates to the performance of the employer's obligations under the relevant legislation.

An inspector for the purposes of the legislation may make such examination and inquiry as may be necessary for the purpose of the investigation. Any person on the premises may be required to produce documents relevant to compliance with the pertinent legislation (s 75(2)). The inspector may then take copies of such documentation, take possession of it, or take any other steps necessary to preserve it. The legislation does not specify at whose expense the documents might be copied or otherwise recovered. Such costs may not be inconsiderable. It would appear, however, that the Regulator (under s 72) could require that this expense is met by the relevant scheme or employer. The inspector may also require electronically stored information to be downloaded or put into hard copy and may examine any person on the premises. 2.67

Section 76 qualifies and supplements the powers somewhat by stating, for instance, that a private dwelling (not used for business purposes) will not be liable to inspection. It is also provided that in the case of any failure to comply with legislation which would result in a civil penalty under s 10 of the 1995 Act, an investigation into such compliance for inspection for the purposes of ss 73 and 74 counts as valid grounds. An inspector it appears must attend in person (although it also appears that an inspector could be a corporation attending via a representative) but can be accompanied by any other persons as he considers appropriate (s 76(5)). Documents may be retained if they are relevant to legal proceedings until the end of those proceedings, otherwise documents may be retained for a period of up to twelve months (s 76(6) and (7)). This may be extended by a further twelve months. 2.68

(c) *Failure to comply*
The penalties for failing to comply with an investigation are serious. It is an offence to refuse or neglect to provide information or documents duly requested under s 72. Any intentional delay, obstruction of an inspector, or neglect or refusal to produce a document duly required under the legislation is also an offence. It is specifically provided that an offence under these provisions can attract a fine and/or a maximum of two years' imprisonment on conviction on indictment (s 77(6)). 2.69

(d) *Warrants*
Section 78 allows the Regulator to apply to a Justice of the Peace for a warrant if there are reasonable grounds for believing that there are relevant documents on any premises which if required for production would not be so produced and which might be tampered with or destroyed, hidden, etc. A warrant may also be applied for where there are reasonable grounds to consider that an offence has been committed or some misuse or misappropriation of assets relating to a 2.70

## 2. The Pensions Regulator

pension scheme is likely to occur. Where it appears on the same basis that an act or omission has occurred subject to a penalty (s 10 of the 1995 Act) or where there is a likelihood of prohibition as a trustee (s 3 of the 1995 Act) then a warrant may be applied for. It is assumed that the Regulator will not seek a warrant as a matter of routine but only in exceptional cases. The warrant authorizes the inspector to enter premises with force if necessary, search the premises, take possession of documents or take other steps to preserve them, take copies of documents, download information, and to cross-examine any person to obtain an explanation of events in question (s 78(2)). A warrant cannot be issued in relation to documentation issued by an employer to meet its obligations to provide general information on pensions and saving for retirement. The inspector may be accompanied if necessary.

2.71 The protocol for retention of any documents or other materials obtained via a warrant is as provided by s 76 (see para 2.68 above).

(e) *Providing false information*

2.72 Knowingly (or recklessly) providing materially false or misleading information is an offence if it is purportedly being provided in compliance with a statutory obligation to supply information (whether by way of a scheme return (ss 63 to 65) or on request (ss 72 to 75) (s 80)). This is deemed to include a situation where the provider knows that the information will be relied upon by the Regulator in carrying out its statutory business. The penalty will be a fine on summary judgment or a fine and/or a maximum of two years' imprisonment on indictment (s 80(2)). For the avoidance of doubt, it is provided that any information held by the Regulator may be used by it for the exercise of any of its functions (s 81).

(f) *Confidentiality*

2.73 The Regulator is under a duty to keep 'restricted information' confidential. 'Restricted information' is defined as any information relating to a person obtained in the course of the Regulator's duties unless it is already a matter of public record or is contained in a list or other form where the individual in question is not identifiable (s 82(4)). Neither the Regulator nor any person receiving such information from the Regulator may disclose restricted information to any other person. There are exceptions to this requirement in relation to:

(a) Issue of a request for a report notice (s 71);

(b) Information provided to an overseas pension regulator or similar body;

(c) Disclosure properly occurring to enable the Regulator to carry out its functions or those of the Board of the PPF;

(d) Disclosure to a supervisory authority as specified in Sch 3 such as the Pensions Ombudsman or the Bank of England;

(e) Disclosure to the Secretary of State or Inland Revenue where this is in the interest of the members of the scheme in question; and

(f) Disclosure for taxation purposes.

These are broad exceptions. Nevertheless the fact remains that the Regulator must proceed with some care and ensure that information is stored carefully and used only for the specific purpose relevant to the Regulator's function or that of another relevant government agency.

The definition of restricted information is extended by s 83 to include information supplied to the Regulator by a foreign counterpart body.

The restrictions on disclosure under s 82 above do not prevent the Regulator from disclosing restricted information where this is necessary to assist the Regulator in the discharge of its functions (s 84). For example, restricted information may be disclosed for the purposes of obtaining professional advice (s 84(2)) or to assist the PPF in the discharge of its functions (s 85).

## 8. Reports

The Regulator may choose to issue a report on a particular case or issue as appropriate (s 89). The Regulator may do this, for instance, in discharge of its obligations to provide education and information to trustees, managers, employers, etc (s 12).

## G. CODES OF PRACTICE

### 1. Issue of Codes

The Regulator may issue codes of practice on any relevant matter in order to give practical guidance on the exercise of any functions under the pensions legislation or in relation to standards of conduct and practice generally (s 90). The Regulator must also issue codes of practice on the following areas:

(a) What constitutes a 'reasonable period' for compliance with a request, etc;
(b) The notification of a matter as required by the Regulator (s 69) or of a breach of the law (section 70);
(c) Discharge of duties in relation to scheme funding (ss 221 to 233);
(d) Requirement for member nominated trustees (ss 241 to 243);
(e) Knowledge and understanding requirements for trustees (ss 247 to 249);
(f) Failure to pay contributions on time (under s 49 of the 1995 Act);
(g) Scheme amendments (under s 67 of the 1995 Act as amended by s 262 of the 2004 Act); and
(h) Other prescribed purposes including as provided by regulation.

Failure to observe the codes of practice is not of itself a breach of a direct legal responsibility (s 90(4)), but the fact of the breach is admissible as evidence in any legal proceedings including proceedings before the Pensions Ombudsman or the Board of the PPF (s 90(5)).

2.80 The codes of practice must go through a consultation process before publication (s 91). The Secretary of State must approve a code prior to publication and present it to Parliament (s 91(5)).

## H. EXERCISE OF REGULATORY FUNCTION

### 1. Procedure

2.81 The Regulator is required to devise a procedure as to how its 'regulatory functions' are to be exercised (s 93). 'Regulatory functions' covers a wide range of activities including:

(a) The power to issue improvement and third party notices (ss 13 and 14);

(b) Provision of clearance statements or related notices (ss 42 and 46);

(c) Issues reserved for the Determinations Panel (see para 2.14 above);

(d) The power to revoke any order, notice, or determination (s 101);

(e) The power to wind up a scheme in certain circumstances (s 154) or give directions regarding a winding up (s 72B of the 1995 Act);

(f) The power to backdate the winding up of a scheme (s 219);

(g) Decisions in relation to European-wide pension provision (ss 288 to 289 and 293);

(h) Refusal to register a stakeholder arrangement (WRPA 1999, s 2);

(i) The power to appoint a trustee (s 7 of the 1995 Act) or an independent statutory trustee (s 23 of the 1995 Act); and

(j) Such other functions as shall be prescribed.

2.82 The Determinations Panel must decide on the procedure to be followed by it in relation to its decision-making (s 93(3)). There will be a requirement for the Regulator to publish the agreed procedures (s 94).

### 2. Standard and Special Procedures

2.83 The Regulator must comply with either the standard or the special procedure where the Regulator is carrying out the exercise of its functions (s 95). The standard procedure, as the term implies, is the approach commonly to be adopted. It provides for (a) the giving of notice ('warning notices') to parties affected and (b) the opportunity for those parties to make representations and to have these representations considered.

2.84 Notice of determination must then be provided for containing details of the right to refer the decision to the Pensions Regulator Tribunal (s 96). The

Regulator must determine the form and content of warning notices and determination notices and the manner in which these are to be given. Time limits must also be set. Where the standard procedure applies, a determination may be referred to the Tribunal by any person receiving notice of the determination or by any other person directly affected by it (s 96(3)). This will not apply in the case of clearance statements issued under ss 42 or 46. Where the determination was to exercise a regulatory function this may not be exercised during the referral period or indeed generally until disposal of any referral. Certain determinations are exempted from this restriction (s 96(6)).

2.85 The special procedure (s 97) applies to cases where the Regulator considers it necessary to exercise regulatory functions immediately as a result of a potential risk to the interests of the members or to the value of scheme assets if a warning notice were issued. Where the special procedure is applied, the Regulator may dispense with the warning notice and representations (s 97(2)). A combination of both standard and special procedure may be adopted, such as in a case where the Regulator has issued a warning notice and heard representations but then subsequently decides that it is necessary to apply the special procedure to take action immediately because there appears to be a risk to the members' interests or scheme assets. The special procedure may only be applied to certain functions (listed in s 97(5)), which include 'restraining', 'freezing', and 'prohibition' orders and appointment and removal of trustees (including an independent trustee).

2.86 The special procedure must include the giving of notice of the determination to exercise a regulatory function ('determination notice') which must include details of the requirement that the Regulator review the determination (under s 99(1)) and the right for the person(s) affected to subsequently refer it to the Tribunal.

2.87 The recipients of a determination notice must be entitled to make representations in relation to the determination before it is reviewed under s 99(1) and these representations must be properly considered. The review is compulsory and must be carried out by the Determinations Panel of the Regulator as soon as is reasonably practicable. A notice must be given in accordance with s 99(4) on review by the Regulator (the 'final notice') and this must contain details of the right to refer to the Tribunal.

## I. THE PENSIONS REGULATOR TRIBUNAL

2.88 An independent Pensions Regulator Tribunal is being set up. It will deal with referrals by persons dissatisfied with the decision of the Regulator. The lay members of the Tribunal will be drawn from those selected by the Lord Chancellor's department as having appropriate experience (Sch 4).

2.89 The Regulator is required to act in accordance with the Tribunal's decision on a particular matter. The Tribunal can also make recommendations on issues of

## 2. The Pensions Regulator

procedure followed by the Regulator or the Determinations Panel (s 103(7) and (8)).

**2.90** There is a right of appeal on a point of law from the decision of the Tribunal to the Court of Appeal (or in Scotland, the Court of Session) (s 104). The Tribunal must give its permission for an appeal or, if this is refused, the permission of the Court of Appeal (or Court of Session) must be obtained. In an interesting innovation, there is provision (s 105) for the Tribunal itself to decide to look again at its own decision either by review or a formal rehearing and re-determination by the same or by a differently constituted Tribunal. For this reason the chairman's panel and lay panel will need to be sufficiently populated to allow for a new Tribunal to be constituted in reasonable time.

**2.91** The Lord Chancellor's department may propose regulations on a 'Legal Assistance Scheme' in relation to proceedings before the Tribunal (s 106). This may allow for persons appearing before the Tribunal to be assisted or represented by individuals or organizations familiar with the relevant criteria including legal responsibilities of the Tribunal. It appears that the costs of the legal assistance scheme will be funded by the Lord Chancellor's department (s 106(5)).

# 3
# THE PENSION PROTECTION FUND

| A. Introduction | 3.01 |
| B. The PPF Board—Establishment and Functions | 3.09 |
| C. Summary of PPF Procedure | 3.38 |
| D. Effect of Employer's Insolvency | 3.45 |
| E. Eligible Schemes | 3.58 |
| F. Duty to Assume Responsibility for a Scheme | 3.60 |
| G. The Assessment Period | 3.70 |
| H. Refusal to Assume Responsibility for a Scheme | 3.95 |
| I. Reconsideration | 3.100 |
| J. Closed Schemes and Winding Up | 3.104 |
| K. Payment of Compensation | 3.118 |
| L. The Fund | 3.143 |
| M. The Levies | 3.145 |

## A. INTRODUCTION

**3.01** The Pension Protection Fund (PPF) is being introduced from April 2005 with the aim of compensating members of defined benefit and hybrid pension schemes in the event that their employer becomes insolvent and the pension scheme is left underfunded. The new arrangements are to be funded by a levy payable by eligible schemes and are the centrepiece of the Government's pension reforms outlined in the White Paper. Over one third of the 2004 Act (114 sections and 5 Schedules) is devoted to the various aspects of the scope and functions of the PPF, and its creation is by far the most substantial change to the regulation of occupational pension provision introduced by the new legislation.

**3.02** Much of the debate concerning the effectiveness (or otherwise) of the Government's pension strategy has concerned the basis of the PPF as a vehicle for safeguarding pension benefits. Moreover, a significant number of the

### 3. The Pension Protection Fund

amendments to the Bill during its passage through Parliament related directly or indirectly to the nature and status of the PPF. In particular, the so-called 'moral hazard' powers of the Regulator (see chapter 2 above) are a specific attempt to protect the PPF system from abuse. In addition, the outline provisions for the establishment of a 'financial assistance scheme' under s 286 (see chapter 10 below) reflect concerns that the new compensation provisions will not be retrospective and hence will do nothing to alleviate the position of members of occupational pension schemes already in wind up who stand to receive substantially less than their full entitlement.

**1. Origins of the PPF**

3.03 The creation of the PPF reflects a gradual decline in confidence in the system of occupational pension scheme provision over the last few years. Faith in the capacity of these arrangements to deliver their promised benefits has been undermined by a number of high profile scheme failures where members have lost all or the majority of their pension entitlement on the insolvency of the sponsoring employer. This has been coupled with the accusation that workers have not been advised of the risks attaching to defined benefit occupational pension schemes and have been misled by material published by government departments, as well as by their own scheme literature, into believing that such benefits were guaranteed, as opposed to dependent on the ability of the employer to meet any funding shortfall. Much has also been made of the contrast between the position of private sector workers and those in the public sector whose benefits are ultimately underwritten by the taxpayer. The general situation was further compounded by the statutory priority order introduced by the 1995 Act which favoured pensioners to the detriment of other scheme members regardless of their length of service.

3.04 The 1995 Act introduced a raft of measures designed to improve member protection including the creation of OPRA, the establishment of the Pensions Compensation Board (PCB) (to assist members of schemes whose funds have been misappropriated through fraud, etc), a requirement for member nominated trustees and internal dispute procedures, and statutory minimum funding requirements. However, although regarded as significant new provisions at the time, the increasing gap between scheme experience (both in terms of declining investment returns and improving mortality) and the minimum funding levels prescribed by the 1995 Act has meant that these requirements have proved an inadequate mechanism for ensuring the security of member benefits. It is also worth reflecting in this context that the 1995 Act was drafted in a climate where many schemes were well funded and a key concern was to restrict the ability of employers to raid pension scheme surpluses rather than to apportion responsibility for scheme deficits.

# Introduction

## 2. Green Paper and White Paper Proposals

3.05 The Green Paper issued in December 2002 set out a number of options for strengthening member protection, including the possibility of a change in the priority order for distribution of assets on a pension scheme wind up, the creation of a new category of creditor in insolvency proceedings (placing pension schemes ahead of other unsecured creditors), some form of central fund for the purchase of annuities, and an insurance scheme or central discontinuance fund. Following consultation, the White Paper in June 2003 brought forward a more concrete series of measures through which the Government intended 'to improve the security of pension scheme benefits and ensure much greater confidence that pensions that have been promised will be delivered'.[1] The related measures included a requirement for solvent employers who choose to wind up their pension schemes to meet pension promises in full and a revised priority order on scheme wind up.

3.06 The PPF was at this stage presented as a compensation scheme 'to guarantee members a specified minimum level of pension when the sponsoring employer becomes insolvent',[2] with much of the detail of the system and procedures still to be developed. The Government did, however, pay particular attention to views expressed by some respondents to the consultation about the risk of 'moral hazard'. It was suggested that a key danger would be the possibility of an employer choosing to fund the scheme at a particularly low level, or the trustees adopting a high risk investment strategy, because of the existence of the compensation scheme. Equally, it was felt that there was a possibility of directors putting a company into insolvency to avoid the pension debt. The White Paper concluded that payment of a risk-related premium to the new compensation scheme would discourage underfunding or dubious investments, whilst a cap on the pension compensation payable would discourage key decision-makers (who would thereby suffer a significant reduction in pension) from pursuing the insolvency route save where this was unavoidable.[3] The subsequent 'moral hazard' amendments to the Regulator's powers (described in chapter 2 above) have introduced some further disincentives to a deliberately engineered insolvency.

## 3. Outstanding Concerns

3.07 Nevertheless, many substantial concerns and unanswered questions remain in relation to the operation of the PPF. Some of the key issues are as follows:

(a) The Government has consciously adopted the model of the Pension Benefit

---

[1] White Paper, Ch 2, p 9.
[2] ibid at p 3.
[3] ibid at pp 10 and 11.

### 3. The Pension Protection Fund

Guaranty Corporation (PBGC), which provides a similar discontinuance compensation fund in the United States, and claims in the White Paper to have learned lessons from the American experience. However the PBGC is billions of dollars in deficit as a result of a number of substantial company failures and it is unclear how the PPF would cope with the collapse of a major UK employer and its pension scheme.

(b) Despite the 'moral hazard' clauses, there remains the possibility that the employer and trustees may manipulate the formal insolvency of the business or the wind up of the pension scheme to take advantage of the PPF.

(c) The interaction between the PPF funded by the levy and the Financial Assistance Scheme currently funded exclusively by the Government/taxpayer is likely to prove controversial and problematic for the future, particularly whilst resources available to the latter scheme remain limited.

(d) According to the Government, the PPF offers 'insurance-style cover financed by a premium'.[4] The actuarial profession in particular has expressed serious reservations about this insistence on characterizing the compensation fund as an 'insurance' scheme, when it plainly lacks the guarantees one would normally associate with that type of arrangement.

(e) The essential function of the PPF will be to take on the assets and liabilities of underfunded pension arrangements. As such, it is difficult to see how it can avoid having a substantial deficit of its own from inception. Moreover, it is likely that the lack of a government guarantee will mean that, ultimately, the levy will need to increase or the amount of compensation payable will need to be reduced in order to control that shortfall.

(f) Finally, the rules in relation to qualification for compensation threaten to be overly complex and bureaucratic to administer. The convoluted framework of notices, assessment periods, appeals, and reconsiderations, combined with excessively detailed benefit calculation procedures arguably provides neither simplicity nor certainty for scheme members.

### 4. Role and Function of the PPF

**3.08** The role of the PPF as enacted includes not only assessing qualification for and administering payment of pensions compensation where employers are insolvent and the pension scheme is underfunded, but also responsibility for paying compensation to members of both money purchase and defined benefit schemes in the event that scheme assets are lost through fraud or misappropriation (a function currently carried out by the Pensions Compensation Board). This

---

[4] Final Report for House Libraries, *Insolvent Pension Wind-up—Report on Numbers Affected* (DWP, June 2004).

latter role is examined in chapter 4 below. The remainder of this chapter concentrates on the establishment and functions of the PPF Board, together with a detailed examination of the procedure for entering into the PPF arrangements, the treatment of such schemes during the statutory assessment period, the method of calculation of pension compensation payments under the Act, and the funding of the PPF through a system of levies. Subsequent chapters focus on the far-ranging information gathering powers granted to the PPF, and the procedure for reviews, appeals, and treatment of complaints of maladministration.

## B. THE PPF BOARD—ESTABLISHMENT AND FUNCTIONS

### 1. Establishment

**3.09** The PPF will be managed by a Board, whose main responsibilities will be to pay out pension and fraud compensation, determine the amount of the annual levy to be imposed on schemes, and oversee the investment strategy of the PPF. In essence many of the obligations and powers of the Board can be regarded as equivalent to those imposed upon the trustees of a large self-administered pension scheme with similar requirements in relation to record-keeping, preparation of annual accounts, reports and regular valuations, together with restrictions on its ability to borrow and give security.

**3.10** Chapter 1 of Pt 2 of the Act provides for the establishment of the Board of the PPF (referred to throughout the Act as 'the Board') and sets out the details of its composition and role. Section 108 states that the membership of the Board is to consist of a chairman, a chief executive, and at least five other 'ordinary members'. There are restrictions on who may be appointed to these posts:

(a) The chairman cannot be appointed from the staff of the Board, or be the chairman of the Regulator;

(b) There will be a maximum number of ordinary members, which will be prescribed by regulations;

(c) At least two ordinary members must be appointed from the staff of the Board;

(d) A member of staff of the Regulator or its Determinations Panel cannot also be a member of the Board; and

(e) A majority of the members of the Board must be non-executive members in order to comply with corporate governance guidelines. 'Executive' members of the Board include the Chief Executive and the ordinary members appointed from the staff of the Board. Any other Board members are classed as 'non-executive' members.

### 3. The Pension Protection Fund

3.11 Schedule 5 of the Act sets out in greater detail the provisions regarding:

(a) The appointment of members;

(b) The terms of appointment, tenure, and remuneration of members;

(c) The appointment of the Chief Executive and other staff;

(d) The proceedings of the Board;

(e) Its accounts; and

(f) The status and liability of the Board, its members, and staff.

3.12 Part 1 of Sch 5 provides further information on the membership of the Board. Under para 1, the chairman of the Board is to be appointed by the Secretary of State. Under para 2, the first five ordinary members of the Board are to be appointed by the Secretary of State and thereafter appointments will be made by the Board. If at any point there are less than five ordinary members, the Secretary of State must appoint enough new members to bring the number back up to five. The validity of any proceedings of the Board is not affected by any vacancies or other difficulties appointing members of the Board.

3.13 Under para 3, the Secretary of State will determine the terms of appointment of the chairman and the ordinary members appointed by him. For ordinary members appointed by the Board, the chairman (with the approval of the Secretary of State) will determine the terms and conditions if the member is a non-executive member, and the Chief Executive will determine the terms and conditions in the case of an executive member.

3.14 Paragraph 4 sets out provisions for the tenure of members of the Board. The chairman and any ordinary members must hold and vacate office, and resign or be removed from office, in accordance with the terms of their appointment. If the chairman ceases to hold office or becomes a member of staff of the Board, he must cease to be a member of the Board. Similarly, where a non-executive member becomes a member of the staff of the Board, or where an executive member ceases to be a member of staff of the Board, he must also cease to be a member of the Board.

3.15 The staff of the Board will consist of the Chief Executive, whose primary role is to ensure that the functions of the Board are exercised efficiently and effectively, together with other employees of the Board who may be appointed by the Board, with the approval of the Secretary of State as to numbers. There is also provision for the Secretary of State to make additional staff (for example on secondment from the DWP) and other facilities available to the Board if appropriate.

3.16 The table below summarizes how members of the Board are appointed and how their terms and conditions are determined:

## The PPF Board—Establishment and Functions

|  | Initial appointment by | Subsequent appointments by | Terms and conditions set by | Remuneration set by |
|---|---|---|---|---|
| **Chair** | Secretary of State | Secretary of State | Secretary of State | Secretary of State |
| **Chief Executive** | Secretary of State | Board with approval of Secretary of State | Secretary of State | The Secretary of State on initial appointment and on subsequent appointment by the Board (through the committee established to discharge the non-executive functions) and with the approval of the Secretary of State |
| **Non-executive Board members (other than Chair)** | Secretary of State | Board | Secretary of State for first appointment; Chair with the approval of the Secretary of State for subsequent appointments | Secretary of State |
| **Executive Board members (other than Chief Executive and other employees)** | Secretary of State | Board | Secretary of State for first appointment; Chief Executive for subsequent appointments | Board (through the committee established to discharge the non-executive functions) and with the approval of the Secretary of State |
| **Other staff** | Board with Secretary of State approval as to numbers | Board with Secretary of State approval as to numbers | Chief Executive | Chief Executive |

## 2. Procedure

Part 3 of Sch 5 sets out further details regarding the proceedings of the Board and the delegation of its functions. Under para 15, the Board is entitled to establish committees and sub-committees for any purpose. Members of these committees and sub-committees need not necessarily be members of the Board, and members of a sub-committee do not have to be members of the committee. However, members of the committee established to discharge the non-executive functions and its sub-committee *do* have to be members of the Board, and if such a sub-committee includes non-committee members, those members must not be executive members or other staff of the Board. Under para 16, the Board

3.17

has the power to determine its own procedure and the procedure of any of its committees or sub-committees (including quorum).

**3.18** Paragraphs 17 and 18 set out the Board's powers of delegation. The Board has the power to delegate any of its functions to the executive members of the Board, members of the Board's staff and any of its committees and sub-committees. However, the non-executive functions of the Board can only be exercised by the committee established to discharge the non-executive functions (see para 3.27 below).

**3.19** The Board can make arrangements to delegate the following functions:

(a) The pension compensation provisions under s 162;

(b) Adjustments to be made under s 163 where the Board assumes responsibility for a scheme;

(c) The duty to notify the Inland Revenue in relation to Guaranteed Minimum Pensions under s 165;

(d) The duty to pay scheme benefits unpaid at the assessment date under s 166;

(e) The discharge of liabilities in respect of compensation or money purchase benefits under ss 169 and 170;

(f) The issue of notices requiring provision of information under s 191;

(g) The provision of information to members of schemes, etc under s 203(1)(a); and

(h) Supplementary powers under s 111, so far as that section relates to any function conferred by or by virtue of any provision mentioned in paras (a) to (g).

**3.20** Where the Board delegates any of these functions, the provisions relating to the supply of false or misleading information and the disclosure of information to or by the Board will apply to the person delegated to. The non-executive functions of the Board cannot be delegated, as these functions have to be discharged by the committee established to carry out the non-executive functions or its sub-committees. Where the Board's functions are delegated, the person who exercises the function on behalf of the Board also has the power to give a review decision in respect of any reviewable matter arising from the exercise of that function.

**3.21** Part 4 of Sch 5 sets out the requirement for the Board to keep proper accounts and records and to prepare a statement of accounts for each financial year. Each statement of accounts must contain an actuarial valuation of the PPF and comply with any accounting directions given by the Secretary of State with the approval of the Treasury. A copy of the statement of accounts must be sent to the Secretary of State and the Comptroller and Auditor-General before the end of August in the financial year following that to which the statement relates. The Comptroller and Auditor-General has to examine, certify, and report on each statement of accounts and lay a copy of the statement and report before both Houses of Parliament.

## The PPF Board—Establishment and Functions

3.22　Part 5 of Sch 5 sets out provisions regarding the status and liability of the Board. It confirms that the Board is not a servant or agent of the Crown and does not enjoy any status, privilege, or immunity of the Crown. In other words, the Board is independent from the Crown, the property of the Board does not belong to the Crown, nor is the Crown liable to meet any of the liabilities of the Board.

3.23　Paragraphs 26 and 27 make legislative amendments to disqualify members of the Board from membership of the House of Commons or the Northern Ireland Assembly and to allow the chairman and staff of the Board to join the Civil Service pension arrangements.

3.24　There is provision at para 29 to exempt the Board, members of the Board, its committees and sub-committees, or members of its staff from any liability for anything which is done in the exercise of the Board's functions. The Chief Executive and members of the committee established to discharge the non-executive functions and sub-committees are also exempt from any liability incurred in the discharge of their duties. The exoneration from liability is limited to the extent that the act or omission must be committed in good faith and it does not prevent an award of damages in respect of an act or omission that is a breach of the Human Rights Act 1998.

### 3. General Provision about Functions

3.25　Under s 110 of the Act the Board is required to hold, manage, and apply two funds to be known as 'the Pension Protection Fund' and 'the Fraud Compensation Fund'. The provisions for funding these two schemes via a levy are set out in ss 175 and 189 of the Act.

3.26　Section 111 gives the Board powers to do anything which will facilitate, or is incidental or conducive to, the exercise of its functions. This gives the Board the power to carry out the various administrative functions necessary for any public body.

### 4. Non-executive Functions

3.27　Under s 112, the Board must set up a committee to discharge non-executive functions on its behalf. Only non-executive members of the Board are entitled to be members of this committee. The relevant non-executive functions are: to keep under review the Board's internal financial controls; to secure the proper conduct of its financial affairs; and to determine the terms and conditions of remuneration of the Chief Executive, any Board staff who are also executive members of the Board, and other prescribed employees. Under s 112(5), the committee established under this section must prepare a report on the discharge of its non-executive functions for inclusion in the Board's annual report to the Secretary of State.

3.28　Members of any sub-committee of the committee can include people who are

### 3. The Pension Protection Fund

not members of the committee, but must not include people who are executive members or other staff of the Board (s 112(7)). Under s 112(8), the committee established to discharge the non-executive functions has the power to delegate any of its duties, including the duty to prepare the report, to any of its sub-committees.

#### 5. Financial Matters

3.29 Section 113 of the Act gives the Board the power to invest funds 'for the purposes of the prudent management of its financial affairs'. When exercising this power in relation to the PPF, the Board is required to take into account the interests of individuals who are or may be entitled to compensation and the effect of the exercise of the power on the rate of the levy. When exercising this power in relation to the Fraud Compensation Fund (FCF) regard must be had to the interests of members of schemes to which s 189 (Fraud Compensation Levy) applies, and the effect on the level of any levy to be imposed under s 189. The Board must appoint a minimum of two fund managers, which for these purposes is 'an individual who or firm which is appointed by the Board to manage the fund maintained under s 173 (the Pension Protection Fund)'. In each case, the Board must be satisfied that the individual or firm appointed has the appropriate knowledge and experience for managing the investments of the PPF.

3.30 Under s 114 the Board is required to prepare and maintain a written statement of investment principles. The statement should follow the prescribed form and content and must be reviewed and revised as often as may be prescribed.

3.31 Section 115 gives the Board the power to borrow funds from a 'deposit taker' in order to exercise its functions and to give security for any money borrowed by it, but places restrictions on its borrowing powers. The Board is not allowed to borrow money if this would exceed its 'borrowing limit', which will be determined by the Secretary of State. 'Deposit taker' has the meaning ascribed to it under the Financial Services and Markets Act 2000. Effectively, the section gives the Board powers to borrow and give security similar to those one would find in the trust provisions of a widely drafted occupational pension scheme.

3.32 Section 116 allows the Secretary of State to pay, out of funds provided by Parliament, towards the Board's administrative expenses. This does not include expenditure payable out of the PPF or the FCF.

#### 6. Administration Levy

3.33 Under s 117, regulations will be introduced which will provide for the imposition of an 'administration levy' in respect of eligible schemes. The levy is designed to meet the costs of establishing the Board and any expenditure of the Secretary of State under s 116.

The rate and frequency of payment of the levy will be prescribed by regulations, but the Secretary of State must consult with the Board before determining the levy rate. The levy will be payable by or on behalf of the trustees or managers of an eligible scheme (or any other prescribed person), and counts as a debt due to the Secretary of State. The administration levy can be recovered either by the Secretary of State, or by the Regulator on his behalf. 3.34

Secondary legislation will set out provisions relating to the collection and recovery of amounts payable in respect of the administration levy and the circumstances in which any such amount may be waived. 3.35

### 7. Annual Reports

Under s 119, the Board is obliged to prepare an annual report for the Secretary of State. The report should cover the activities of the Board for that financial year, and must include the report prepared under s 112(5) by the committee established under that section (see para 3.27 above). 3.36

The report should be submitted to the Secretary of State as soon as practicable after the end of the financial year for which it is prepared. The Secretary of State must then lay a copy of each report before both Houses of Parliament. 3.37

### C. SUMMARY OF PPF PROCEDURE

As already noted, a significant proportion of the 2004 Act is devoted to detailed treatment of the mechanisms for the establishment and maintenance of the PPF, including extensive information gathering powers, procedures for review of its own decisions, and specific provisions dealing with fraud compensation. Nevertheless, the core role of the PPF and its Board will be in relation to the administration of the new pensions compensation regime. Detailed discussion of the requirements for entry into (and entitlement to benefit under) the PPF in this context are set out at paras 3.45 to 3.142 below, however, the key aspects can be summarized as follows: 3.38

### 1. Eligibility

Certain types of schemes will be excluded from the scope of the PPF, primarily those which provide money purchase benefits only and therefore do not offer a promise of a defined level of benefits on retirement or leaving service. In addition, schemes which commence winding up before the PPF comes into force will also not be eligible. 3.39

### 2. Qualifying Conditions

There are three situations that will trigger the possibility of the Board assuming responsibility for a scheme: 3.40

(a) The occurrence of a qualifying insolvency event;

(b) Application by the trustees of the scheme (where they believe the employer is unlikely to continue as a going concern); or

(c) Where the Regulator notifies the Board that the employer is unlikely to continue as a going concern.

3.41   Before assuming responsibility for the scheme following one of these events, the Board must be satisfied that the assets of the scheme are insufficient to meet its 'protected liabilities' and that a 'scheme rescue' is not possible. Protected liabilities are the cost of securing benefits that would be payable in respect of the scheme under the PPF, other liabilities of the scheme and the estimated cost of winding up.

### 3. Assessment Period

3.42   Following the insolvency event (or application or notification) there will be an assessment period during which the Board will determine whether it is appropriate for the PPF to cover the scheme. Various restrictions will apply to the scheme during this period so that, in particular, no new members may be admitted, no further contributions are payable (other than those already due), and benefit accrual will cease. In addition, the Board is given power to make directions to protect the position of the scheme, including in relation to investment of the scheme's assets, incurring of expenditure, and the instigation and conduct of legal proceedings.

### 4. Valuation

3.43   During the assessment period the Board will obtain a valuation of the scheme's assets and liabilities as at the date immediately before the insolvency or other triggering event in order to establish whether the scheme is able to meet the protected liabilities.

### 5. Assumption of Responsibility

3.44   The Board assumes responsibility by means of a transfer notice under which all property, rights, and liabilities of the scheme pass to the Board. The Board will then become responsible for payments of appropriate pension compensation to members. The level of compensation payable under the PPF will be restricted so that (subject to some relatively minor exceptions) benefits for those below normal pension age will be limited to 90% of a capped amount.

## D. EFFECT OF EMPLOYER'S INSOLVENCY

The occurrence of an insolvency event in relation to a scheme employer is one of the key mechanisms for entry into the PPF arrangements. In this context, the relevant insolvency practitioner is given a vital role in determining the status of the scheme and whether it will fall under the auspices of the new regime. This process is set out in some detail under Ch 2 of Pt 2 of the Act.  **3.45**

The essential features of the insolvency practitioner's role are to notify various parties that an insolvency event has occurred, and to determine whether some form of scheme rescue is possible, or whether the scheme must fall to be assessed for coverage by the PPF. Subsequently, the PPF Board may ratify or overturn the insolvency practitioner's decision and, where necessary, may also make the decision in place of the insolvency practitioner.  **3.46**

### 1. Duty to Notify Insolvency Events in Respect of Employers

Section 120 imposes a duty on the insolvency practitioner in relation to the employer to notify the Board, the Regulator, and the trustees or managers of the scheme of the employer's insolvency. Regulations are likely to impose an obligation on scheme trustees to pass this information on to scheme members. The notice must be in a prescribed form and given within a prescribed notification period, beginning either with the insolvency date or the date on which the insolvency practitioner became aware of the existence of the scheme.  **3.47**

### 2. Insolvency Event, Insolvency Date, and Insolvency Practitioner

Section 121 sets out the key definitions for the purposes of these provisions. The various forms of insolvency event in relation to individuals, companies, and partnerships are set out in detail and, in general, are widely defined. In addition, s 121(5) allows other prescribed events to be included within the scope of the section. Insolvency events in relation to a company will include administration, administrative receivership, a creditors' voluntary arrangement, and an insolvent liquidation. A members' voluntary winding up, or solvent liquidation, will not generally be caught by the legislation, save where this is converted into a creditors' voluntary winding up by a meeting of the creditors under s 95 of the Insolvency Act 1986. The 'insolvency date' is simply the date on which the insolvency event occurs.  **3.48**

Insolvency practitioner is defined by reference to the standard Insolvency Act 1986 definitions, but with provision for regulations to include certain other specified individuals within the term. One such instance may be in the context of schemes of arrangement under the Companies Act 1985 (which do not involve an insolvency practitioner).  **3.49**

## 3. Notices Confirming Status of Scheme

3.50 As soon as reasonably practicable the insolvency practitioner must determine the status of the scheme and issue a notice to that effect (s 122). This may be a 'scheme failure notice' in circumstances where he is of the view that a scheme rescue is not possible, or a 'withdrawal notice' where he believes that a scheme rescue has occurred. There is no indication as to what will constitute a scheme rescue although there is provision for regulations to prescribe set criteria which must be fulfilled. The examples given in parliamentary debate on the section included where an employer emerges successfully from insolvency proceedings with a scheme intact, and where a purchaser of a business agrees to take over a scheme and protect members' benefits.

3.51 If the insolvency proceedings in relation to the employer have been stayed or come to an end and the insolvency practitioner cannot confirm whether or not a scheme rescue is possible, he must issue a notice to that effect.

3.52 A notice under this section must be in a prescribed form and a copy must be issued to the Board, the Regulator, and the trustees or managers of the scheme.

## 4. Board Approval of Notices under Section 122 and Duties where Section 122 is not Complied with

3.53 When the insolvency practitioner has issued a notice with reference to the status of the scheme under s 122, the Board is required by s 123 to determine whether to approve that notice. It does so by means of a 'determination notice', a copy of which must be issued to the Regulator, the trustees and managers of the scheme, any insolvency practitioner in relation to the employer or, if none, the employer itself. The Board's determination is reviewable under ss 206 and 207 and Sch 9.

3.54 If the Board determines not to approve any s 122 notice issued by the insolvency practitioner, or if the insolvency practitioner has failed to issue such a notice where he should have done so, the obligations of the insolvency practitioner fall on the Board which must then issue its own s 122 notice.

## 5. Circumstances in which a Notice Becomes Binding

3.55 Any notice issued by an insolvency practitioner under s 122 is not treated as binding until:

(a) The Board has issued a determination notice approving it;

(b) The period in which the determination notice may be reviewed has expired; and

(c) Where the determination notice is reviewed, all of the various appeals procedures have been exhausted (s 125(1)).

3.56 Similarly, a s 122 notice issued by the Board will not be binding until any review period has expired and any relevant appeals procedures have been completed.

On the notice becoming binding, the Board must notify the Regulator, the trustees and managers, the relevant insolvency practitioner or, if none, the employer. 3.57

## E. ELIGIBLE SCHEMES

Eligibility for the PPF is defined in the negative by specifying those types of scheme which will fall outside its coverage. Section 126 sets out those types of occupational pension schemes which will be excluded from the protection of the PPF. Thus, an 'eligible scheme' must not be a money purchase scheme, a prescribed scheme, or a scheme of a prescribed description. 'Money purchase scheme' for these purposes is defined by reference to the PSA 1993 as 'a pension scheme under which all the benefits that may be provided are money purchase benefits' (where 'money purchase benefits' means 'benefits the rate or amount of which is calculated by reference to a payment or payments made by the member or by any other person in respect of the member and which are not average salary benefits').[5] It is understood that the additional prescribed exclusions here will largely cover those schemes which are currently exempted from the application of the Minimum Funding Requirement imposed by s 56 of the 1995 Act.[6] Examples would include death benefit only schemes, unapproved arrangements, single member schemes, and public service schemes. 3.58

In addition, a scheme will not be considered an eligible scheme if it is being wound up immediately before 6 April 2005. It appears that a scheme which has not formally commenced winding up prior to the effective date of this section may still be covered even if an insolvency event has occurred in relation to its sponsoring employer prior to that date. However, in these latter circumstances in order to qualify the employer would need to suffer a further insolvency event following the introduction of the PPF, for instance a liquidation following an administration or receivership. 3.59

## F. DUTY TO ASSUME RESPONSIBILITY FOR A SCHEME

Sections 127 and 128 set out three basic routes through which the Board can be required to assume responsibility for a scheme and hence for the scheme to benefit from the PPF. The requirements for PPF coverage will depend upon which of these routes is utilized in the particular circumstances. In essence, the scheme can benefit from the PPF if: 3.60

---

[5] PSA 1993, s 181(1).
[6] The Occupational Pension Schemes (Minimum Funding Requirement and Actuarial Valuations) Regulations (SI 1996/1536), reg 28.

### 3. The Pension Protection Fund

(a) The employer is insolvent; or

(b) The trustees or managers have applied to the Board in circumstances where the employer is unlikely to continue as a going concern; or

(c) The Regulator has notified the Board that the employer is unlikely to continue as a going concern.

**3.61** The legislation as drafted presents these three processes as alternatives which may be applied in any case. However, it was emphasized in the Committee Stage in the House of Lords that this is not the intention.[7] The bulk of schemes will enter the coverage of the PPF as a result of an employer insolvency event. The alternative routes—via a trustee or manager application or Regulator's notification—are to be reserved for those situations where the employer cannot suffer a UK insolvency event. The types of schemes which are intended to be covered here are public sector schemes without a Crown guarantee (for instance, the Arts Council and Audit Commission schemes) and schemes with a foreign employer (and which are subject to foreign insolvency proceedings). It is understood that regulations under the Act will make this distinction, and the Government's intention, clear.

#### 1. Employer Insolvency

**3.62** As noted, this is likely to be the main mechanism through which a scheme enters the PPF process. The Board will assume responsibility for a scheme where a qualifying insolvency event (as defined in s 127(3)) has occurred in relation to the employer provided that:

(a) The value of the assets of the scheme is less than the amount required to cover the PPF liabilities;

(b) A binding scheme failure notice (under s 122(2)(a)) has been issued after the relevant time; and

(c) A withdrawal event (see para 3.98 below) has not occurred.

**3.63** The scheme's assets for these purposes exclude the value of any rights in respect of money purchase benefits under the scheme. The 'relevant time' is the time immediately before the qualifying insolvency event occurs. The section is also subject to the provisions of ss 146 and 147 dealing with circumstances in which the Board must refuse to assume responsibility for a scheme.

**3.64** An insolvency event will be a 'qualifying insolvency event' in relation to the scheme if:

(a) it occurs on or after the day appointed under s 126(2) (6 April 2005); and

---

[7] *Hansard*, HL Grand Committee, cols 49–62 (19 July 04).

(b) (i) it is the first insolvency event to occur in relation to the employer on or after that day; or
    (ii) it does not occur within an assessment period (see paras 3.71 and 3.72 below) in relation to the scheme which began before the occurrence of the current event.

In other words, subsequent insolvency events will only be disregarded for these purposes if they occur within an existing assessment period.

## 2. Applications and Notifications

3.65 As discussed, these provisions are likely to have more limited application than those dealing with employer insolvency. Section 128 requires either (a) an application by the trustees and managers under s 129(1); or (b) a notice from the Board to the trustees or managers under s 129(5)(a) (following on from the Board itself receiving a notification from the Regulator).

3.66 In both cases, this will be in circumstances where the employer is unlikely to continue as a going concern. The procedure under s 128 then simply mirrors that under s 127 (following an employer insolvency event). Therefore, the Board must assume responsibility where:

(a) The assets are insufficient to meet the PPF liabilities;
(b) After the relevant time the Board has issued a binding scheme failure notice; and
(c) No withdrawal event has occurred.

3.67 The relevant time in this context is the time immediately before the s 129 application was made or the s 129 notification is received.

3.68 Section 129 sets out further requirements for applications and notifications for the purposes of s 128, and the Board's duties on receipt of such notification/application are set out under s 130. Essentially, the Board must either confirm that a scheme rescue is not possible and issue a 'scheme failure notice' to that effect, or confirm that a scheme rescue has occurred and issue a 'withdrawal notice'.

## 3. Protected Liabilities

3.69 Sections 127 and 128 both provide that a scheme will only be covered by the PPF if its assets are insufficient to cover the 'protected liabilities'. In addition to the cost of securing the capped level of benefits which the PPF itself will provide, these 'protected liabilities' are defined to include liabilities of the scheme which are not liabilities to, or in respect of, its members (presumably encompassing the likes of outstanding professional fees and administration costs) and the estimated cost of winding up the scheme.

## G. THE ASSESSMENT PERIOD

3.70 Once the Board has assumed responsibility for a scheme, that scheme will then enter a formal assessment period, during which the Board determines whether the funding position of the scheme is such that it should be covered by the PPF. During the assessment period a wide range of restrictions is placed upon the scheme and its trustees so that effectively contributions and benefits under the scheme are frozen pending the Board's completion of its consideration of the scheme. The intention here is to attempt to achieve a degree of stability in the funding of the scheme and to ensure that schemes do not receive an unintended benefit as a result of undergoing a long assessment period. In addition, the Board will assume the ability to direct and control the key functions of the trustees for this period to attempt to prevent any worsening of the position of the scheme during this time.

### 1. Duration of the Assessment Period

3.71 The commencement of the assessment period depends upon how the involvement of the Board is triggered. If the trigger is a qualifying insolvency event, the assessment period will commence with the occurrence of that event. If it is an application under s 129(1) or a notification under s 129(5)(a) it is the date the application is made or the notification received by the trustees or managers.

3.72 In either case, the assessment period will then continue until whichever of the following events occurs first:

(a) The Board ceases to be involved with the scheme under s 149;
(b) The trustees or managers receive a transfer notice under s 160; or
(c) The conditions in s 154(2) (no scheme rescue but sufficient assets to meet protected liabilities, etc) are met.

### 2. Restrictions on New Members, Contributions, and Benefits

3.73 Once the assessment period has commenced (and for the duration of that period) the scheme in question will be effectively frozen so that:

(a) No new members may be admitted to the scheme;
(b) Save in prescribed circumstances, no further contributions can be made to the scheme; and
(c) No further benefits may accrue to, or in respect of, scheme members (s 133).

3.74 Regulations may provide for contributions to nevertheless be required in certain circumstances, for instance where these became due prior to the assessment period or where a debt is owed to the scheme by the employer under s 75 of the 1995 Act.

3.75 The remainder of s 133 introduces some small practical qualifications to these broad restrictions. For instance, any indexation of benefits will be excluded from the restriction on further accrual and the money purchase element of benefits under a hybrid scheme can still benefit from investment gains during the assessment period. There are also further consequential amendments to allow the trustees to comply with the terms of a pension sharing order[8] in matrimonial proceedings by providing a divorced spouse with rights under the scheme notwithstanding that such pension sharing order arises during the assessment period.

3.76 Any action taken in contravention of these restrictions is void and trustees or managers who fail to secure compliance with s 133 can be subject to civil penalties under the terms of s 10 of the 1995 Act.

## 3. Directions

3.77 In addition to the restrictions on benefits and contributions already outlined, the Board is also given wide powers to intervene in the running of the scheme during the assessment period. The provisions of s 134 allow the Board to issue directions aimed at restricting the excess of the scheme's protected liabilities over its assets so as to limit the possibility of a claim on the PPF's own resources.

3.78 Such directions may be issued to a range of individuals including the trustees, managers or sponsoring employer and may cover:

(a) The investment of the scheme's assets (excluding any assets relating to money purchase benefits);
(b) The incurring of expenditure;
(c) The instigation and conduct of legal proceedings; and
(d) Other prescribed matters.

3.79 The Board retains power to revoke or vary its own directions and fines and penalties may again be applied to trustees, managers, and others in the absence of reasonable excuse.

## 4. Restrictions on Winding Up, etc

3.80 Section 135 effectively prevents the trustees or the employer from exercising any power they may have under the scheme rules to wind up the scheme during the assessment period. The scheme can still, however, be wound up during the period following an order of the Regulator under s 11(3A) of the 1995 Act.

3.81 No transfers or transfer payments can be made in respect of members during the assessment period and no other steps may be taken to discharge scheme

---

[8] Matrimonial Causes Act 1973, s 21A.

### 3. The Pension Protection Fund

liabilities in respect of members in relation to pensions or other benefits and other prescribed liabilities. This restriction applies even if the scheme is being wound up pursuant to an order of the Regulator. In addition, the Regulator is restricted from making a freezing order during the assessment period.

3.82 Once again, there are consequential amendments in respect of pension sharing orders, allowing such liabilities to be discharged. Action taken in contravention of the section is void unless validated by the Board under s 136 and the trustees or managers can be subject to civil penalties for breach.

3.83 The Board will only validate a contravention of s 135 if it is satisfied that this is consistent with the objective of minimizing the protected liabilities in comparison with the scheme assets and hence the likelihood of a claim on the PPF. Whether or not the Board validates a particular action, it is required to issue a notice to that effect. Copies of the notice must be provided to the Regulator, trustees or managers, any insolvency practitioner in relation to the employer or, if none, the employer itself, and any other person who appears to the Board to be directly affected by the determination. The notice must also contain a statement of the Board's reasons. The validation does not take effect until any period for review of the notice under Ch 6 has expired and, if reviewed, any review and the various appeals procedures have been exhausted.

#### 5. Board to Act as Creditor of the Employer

3.84 When any debt is owed to the trustees or managers of a scheme by the employer, s 137 allows the Board to stand in their place as creditor and to exercise any rights and powers they may have in relation to that debt, whether it is one arising under s 75 of the 1995 Act or otherwise. In the event that any amounts are paid to the Board in settlement of the debt, they must however be paid across to the trustees or managers.

#### 6. Payment of Scheme Benefits

3.85 During the assessment period benefits payable under scheme rules must be reduced to ensure they do not exceed the compensation which would be payable under the PPF. The trustees or managers also retain the power to take such steps as they consider appropriate (including adjusting future payments under the scheme rules) to recover any overpayment or pay any shortfall. Regulations may provide for certain benefits, in particular those arising on the death of a member where the member died before commencement of the assessment period, to be treated as having become payable before the commencement of the assessment period.

3.86 Where the scheme has insufficient assets to pay even the reduced level of benefits as they fall due the Board may, in response to an application by the trustees or managers, make a loan of such amounts as the Board considers necessary to pay those benefits. The loan(s) will be on such terms as the Board thinks fit and subject to a prescribed rate of interest. The amount and any interest will be repayable on:

(a) The time the Board ceases to be involved with the scheme; or
(b) If earlier—
    (i) When during the assessment period an order is made by the Regulator under s 11(3A) of the 1995 Act for the winding up of the scheme; or
    (ii) When the assessment period ends because the conditions in s 154(2) or (5) are satisfied (see para 3.109 below).

## 7. Reviewable Ill Health Pensions

Sections 140 to 142 set out specific provisions designed to prevent manipulation of the PPF in the years immediately before any insolvency event occurs. Under the PPF, ill health pensioners are granted 100% compensation with no cap on the yearly pension payable whereas other individuals who retire below normal pension age will only receive 90% compensation capped at £25,000 per annum. The perceived risk here is that company directors and trustees who are also members of the scheme may, on becoming aware of the potential failure of the business, seek to protect their own pension position by applying for retirement on the more favourable ill health terms. Consequently, these provisions aim to protect both the PPF and levy payers from such potential abuses of the system. 3.87

The main principles set out under s 140 are that during the assessment period the Board may review ill health pensions where the member is entitled to 100% compensation (under para 3 of Sch 7), he is below normal pension age on the date the assessment period begins and the pension is attributable to the member's pensionable service. The ill health pension can only, however, be reviewed if it was awarded during the three years immediately before commencement of the assessment period, or within a prescribed period, if the application was made before the assessment period began. Regulations will set out the procedure for any such review. 3.88

If there are outstanding ill health applications at the commencement of the assessment period, the trustees or managers must decide these within a prescribed period. If they fail to do so, they may be subject to civil penalties under s 10 of the 1995 Act. Awards of ill health pensions made following commencement of the assessment period cannot be backdated and will only take effect from the date the decision is made for compensation purposes. 3.89

In circumstances where the Board undertakes a review of an ill health award, it may decide that the compensation payable where it assumes responsibility for a scheme will be determined in a prescribed manner. For this power to apply, the following conditions set out within s 141(3) must be satisfied: 3.90

(a) The annual rate of compensation payable if the Board assumed responsibility for the scheme would exceed a 'notional reviewed rate of compensation';

(b) The Board is satisfied that:
 (i) the award was made in ignorance of, or was based upon a mistake as to, a material fact relevant to the decision;
 (ii) at the time the decision was made, the member knew or could reasonably have been expected to know of that fact and that it was relevant to the decision; and
 (iii) had the trustees or managers known, or not been mistaken as to, that fact, they could not reasonably have decided to make the award; and

(c) the Board is not satisfied that the criteria in the admissible rules (as defined in Sch 7) (see para 3.125 below) for entitlement to ill health pension were met after the original decision but before commencement of the assessment period.

3.91 The provision set out in (c) above allows the Board to take account of any significant deterioration in the member's health during this period.

3.92 Where compensation is reviewed by the Board under these provisions, such compensation is only payable on that basis from the date a scheme valuation becomes binding during the assessment period. Such decisions must be made within a reasonable time and cannot be made after the Board approves a scheme valuation under s 144.

### 8. Valuation of Assets and Liabilities

3.93 Clearly a key part of the assessment period process is the determination of the assets and liabilities of the scheme in question. In order to decide whether a scheme will qualify for PPF protection the Board is required (under s 143) to obtain an actuarial valuation of the scheme in a prescribed manner and form. The purpose of the valuation is to determine whether the scheme's assets are sufficient to cover the 'protected liabilities'. The valuation must be obtained as soon as reasonably practicable but its effective date must be as at the time immediately before the qualifying insolvency event occurred. Where there is no qualifying insolvency event the date will be the time immediately before the trustees' application to the Board under s 129, or before they are informed by the Board of the Regulator's notification under the same section. Regulations will deal with how such valuations are to take account of various matters in assessing the assets and liabilities including, for instance, contribution notice debts or obligations under a financial support direction. The valuation cannot be started whilst the Board may still review certain ill health pensions, as such reviews may obviously affect the result of the valuation.

3.94 When the Board is satisfied that a valuation has been obtained in accordance with s 143, it must approve that valuation and supply copies to the Regulator, the trustees or managers, and any insolvency practitioner or, if none, the employer. A valuation does not become binding until it has been approved and the period during which such approval may be reviewed has expired. Once the valuation becomes binding, notice must be given to the Regulator, trustees or managers, insolvency practitioner or employer (as above). A binding valuation is conclusive for the purposes of establishing whether the protected liabilities are met, subject to the possibility of subsequent fraud compensation payments being taken into account in certain circumstances.

## H. REFUSAL TO ASSUME RESPONSIBILITY FOR A SCHEME

As is apparent from the ill health review provisions described at paras 3.87 to 3.92 above, the new legislation has been drafted in the knowledge that unscrupulous employers and trustees may seek to take advantage of the pension protection arrangements by manipulating the benefits under their schemes or the constitution of the schemes themselves. Consequently, the Act sets out some explicit anti-avoidance provisions aimed at preventing such exploitation of the new regime. Equally, it is recognized that the occurrence of certain external events during the assessment period may mean that it is not necessary for the Board to continue to be involved with the scheme. 3.95

### 1. Anti-avoidance

Section 146 allows the Board to refuse to assume responsibility for a scheme which, although it is now classified as an eligible scheme, was not an eligible scheme during a prescribed period. An example of an abuse of the system here would be a scheme which artificially increases the number of scheme members in order to fall within the eligible scheme definition. 3.96

Section 147 allows the Board to refuse responsibility for a new scheme which has been established to replace an existing scheme of the same employer and has received a transfer from that scheme where one of the main purposes of those actions was to enable the members to benefit from the PPF pension compensation provisions. An employer might seek to make such a transfer from a scheme which has never contributed to the levy, for instance, or from a scheme which commenced winding up before the effective date of the PPF provisions. 3.97

### 2. Cessation of Involvement with a Scheme

When an assessment period has begun, there are various trigger events which lead to the cessation of the Board's involvement with the scheme, essentially in circumstances where it is no longer appropriate to be considered for pension compensation. The Board will cease to be involved with a scheme on the occurrence of the first withdrawal event occurring after the beginning of the assessment period. The possible withdrawal events (listed in s 149(2)) occur when the following notices become binding: 3.98

(a) A withdrawal notice issued by an insolvency practitioner where a scheme rescue has occurred;

(b) A withdrawal notice issued by the Board (following an application by the trustees or a notification by the Regulator) where a scheme rescue has occurred;

(c) A withdrawal notice issued by the Board where it refuses to assume responsibility for the scheme as a result of the anti-avoidance provisions under ss 146 and 147;

(d) A withdrawal notice issued by the Board (under s 148) following a notice issued by the insolvency practitioner in relation to his inability to confirm the scheme status, in circumstances where the Board concludes that no insolvency event has occurred or is likely to occur.

**3.99** To ensure that members do not suffer as a result of the assessment period process, s 150 deals with various measures which will apply following the cessation of the Board's involvement. In particular, this means that benefits payable under the scheme rules which were not paid during the assessment period by virtue of s 138 will now be payable. Regulations may provide for members in employment during the assessment period to be treated as having accrued benefits during that time. The secondary legislation may also make provision for benefits not to accrue unless contributions are paid within a prescribed period.

## I. RECONSIDERATION

**3.100** In circumstances where the assets of a scheme exceed the value of the protected liabilities, the Board cannot assume responsibility for the scheme and, normally, the scheme will proceed to be wound up. However, there may be situations where, notwithstanding the Board's valuation of the scheme, it is impossible in practice for the scheme trustees to secure the protected level of benefits with an insurer. Consequently, s 151 allows the trustees or managers to apply to the Board to reconsider its decision. An application under the section must be in a prescribed form, accompanied by (a) a protected benefits quotation (in the prescribed form) and (b) audited scheme accounts for the reassessment period.

**3.101** For these purposes, a 'protected benefits quotation' means a quotation for one or more annuities from one or more insurers to secure whichever is the lower of the PPF level of benefits or the scheme benefits. The application must be made within the 'authorized period' which will be a prescribed period which begins with whichever is the later of the date the trustees or managers receive a copy of the relevant binding scheme failure notice or the day on which they receive a copy of the binding scheme valuation.

**3.102** Where an application is made for reconsideration under s 151, the Board must assume responsibility for the scheme if it is satisfied that the value of the assets of the scheme at the reconsideration time is insufficient to meet the aggregate of:

(a) The amount quoted in the protected benefits quotation;
(b) The amount at that time of the liabilities of the scheme which are not liabilities to, or in respect of, members of the scheme; and
(c) The estimated costs of winding up the scheme.

If it is so satisfied the Board must issue a determination notice in a prescribed form but is not formally required to assume responsibility for the scheme until that notice becomes binding (which will occur once all avenues of review and appeal have been exhausted). The Board may also obtain its own valuation of the assets of the scheme at the reconsideration date to assist in this process if it wishes to do so. **3.103**

## J. CLOSED SCHEMES AND WINDING UP

In circumstances where the valuation of the scheme has shown that the protected liabilities can be covered by the scheme assets then, in the absence of a successful application by the trustees for reconsideration, the scheme must be wound up. However, the legislation does recognize that the current marketplace for bulk buy-out quotations is restricted and it is quite possible that large schemes in particular (perhaps those with assets over £500 million) may find it impossible to secure a buy-out quotation of any description. Consequently, provision is made under s 153 for such schemes to apply to the Board to be allowed to continue as closed schemes. Whilst such schemes will not be taken over by the PPF, because their level of assets exceeds that required to meet the protected liabilities, they will nevertheless be subject to a degree of supervision and monitoring by the Board ('a shadow of an assessment period', as this was termed in the House of Lords[9]) to ensure that there is no manipulation of such schemes to enable them to fall within the coverage of the PPF. **3.104**

### 1. Closed Schemes

To be considered as a closed scheme, the scheme must fall within s 151(2) or (3), where a scheme rescue is not possible but the scheme has sufficient assets to meet the protected liabilities. In addition, the trustees or managers must have taken all reasonable steps to obtain a full buy-out quotation in respect of the scheme. The trustees' application will need to be in a prescribed form containing prescribed information and must be accompanied by evidence of the reasonable steps taken by the trustees. The application must be made within the authorized period, defined for these purposes in the same manner as for s 151. **3.105**

On receipt of such an application the Board must, if it is satisfied that the **3.106**

---

[9] *Hansard*, HL Grand Committee, col 190 (7 September 04).

trustees have taken the required reasonable steps, authorize the scheme to continue as a closed scheme. The Board must then issue a determination notice and supply a copy to the trustees or managers and the Regulator. There are civil penalties for trustees who fail to make an application or fail to take reasonable steps to secure a buy-out quotation. Further supplementary provisions in relation to closed schemes are set out in ss 155 to 159 and are discussed below (see paras 3.112 to 3.117).

## 2. Winding Up

3.107 Where a scheme rescue is not possible but the scheme has sufficient assets to meet the protected liabilities, then (unless it can rely on the special provisions outlined above in relation to closed schemes) it must wind up or continue to wind up if this process has already commenced.

3.108 Section 154 provides that where an assessment period comes to an end because the conditions in s 154(2) are satisfied, the trustees or managers must wind up the scheme or, where the winding up began before the assessment period, continue the winding up of the scheme.

3.109 The conditions in s 154(2) are as follows:

(a) A scheme rescue is not possible but the scheme has sufficient assets to meet the protected liabilities (s 151(2) or (3));

(b) The trustees or managers did not make an application for the scheme to be treated as a closed scheme (s 153(2)) within the authorized period (or any such application has been withdrawn or finally determined); and

(c) The Board is not required to assume responsibility for a scheme following an application for reconsideration under s 151.

No application under condition (b) is to be treated as finally determined until the Board has issued a determination notice and the period in which the notice can be reviewed and appealed has expired. A separate set of conditions apply where a closed scheme is subject to a further assessment period under s 159 (see para 3.117 below).

3.110 Where a scheme is wound up in accordance with s 154, the winding up is treated as beginning immediately before the assessment period. During such winding up, the Board can give directions in relation to the manner of the winding up of the scheme. This power is without prejudice to the Board's general power to make directions under s 134. The Regulator may also direct specified persons to take certain steps in relation to the winding up of the scheme (under s 154(8)).

3.111 A winding up under this section is to be considered effective in law as if it had been made under powers conferred by or under the scheme, and the section is to be taken as overriding any enactment or rule of law which would otherwise prevent the winding up or require the implementation of any procedure or obtaining of consent with a view to winding up. Provision may also be made where a public service pension scheme is to be wound up for an order modifying any enactment governing that scheme.

## 3. Further Provisions Applying to Closed Schemes

3.112 Sections 155 to 159 set out various additional provisions which will apply where a scheme has been allowed by virtue of s 153 to continue as a closed scheme. These provisions are essentially designed to ensure adequate supervision of the closed scheme to prevent a manipulation of the scheme's position leading to a call on the PPF.

3.113 Under s 155, various provisions will apply in relation to a closed scheme at any time when the trustees or managers are required to wind up or continue winding up the scheme under s 154 as if that time fell within an assessment period. The relevant provisions are those dealing with:

(a) The Board acting as creditor for a debt due by virtue of a contribution notice or restoration order;

(b) The restrictions on admission of new members, payment of contributions, etc under s 133;

(c) The making of directions under s 134; and

(d) The Board acting as creditor of the employer under s 137.

A regulation making power is also introduced in order to place restrictions on the ability of closed schemes to discharge any of their liabilities. Such regulations may be used, for instance, to prevent schemes from buying out all liabilities in excess of the PPF compensation level, hence triggering a potential claim on the PPF. Equally, it is recognized that closed schemes will need the flexibility to discharge certain liabilities, for instance in relation to regular pension payments.

3.114 Closed schemes will also be subject to regular valuations at prescribed intervals. Trustees or managers will be required to obtain such valuations under s 156 in order to determine the benefits payable under the scheme rules and whether they need to make an application for a reconsideration of the scheme by the Board under s 157. A combination of regulations and guidance issued by the Board will determine how the assets and liabilities are to be assessed for these purposes and any provision of the scheme rules which limits the scheme's liabilities by reference to the amount of its assets is to be disregarded for these purposes.

3.115 If as a consequence of such periodic valuations, the trustees or managers become aware that the scheme has insufficient assets to meet the protected liabilities, they are required by s 157 to apply to the Board to assume responsibility for the scheme. Similarly, if the Regulator becomes aware that the level of assets is less than the protected liabilities, it must give a notice to that effect to the Board. Where the application is by the trustees or managers, the Board must notify the Regulator and where the notice is by the Regulator the Board must notify the trustees or managers. Notices and applications will need to be in a prescribed form and there are civil penalties for trustees and managers who fail to comply.

3.116 In the event of an application from the trustees or managers, or a notice to the trustees or managers from the Board following a notification by the Regulator under s 157, the Board must assume responsibility for the scheme if the value of the assets at the relevant time is less than the amount of the protected liabilities. In order to determine whether this is the case, the Board must, as soon as reasonably practicable, obtain an actuarial valuation as at the relevant time. For these purposes the 'relevant time' means the time immediately before the trustees' or managers' application or the notice from the Board to the trustees or managers following a notification by the Regulator.

3.117 Finally, s 159 allows for further assessment periods to apply in relation to closed schemes where the trustees or managers have made an application or the Regulator has notified the Board under s 157 as a consequence of the assets of the scheme falling below the level of the protected liabilities. In such circumstances a new assessment period will begin with the date on which the application is made or the date on which the trustees or managers are notified by the Board of the Regulator's notification. The assessment period will continue until either the trustees or managers receive a transfer notice under s 160, or the conditions within s 154(5) are satisfied (essentially where the closed scheme has sufficient assets to meet the protected liabilities).

## K. PAYMENT OF COMPENSATION

### 1. Assumption of Responsibility for a Scheme

3.118 Where the Board assumes responsibility for a scheme it must issue managers and trustees with a 'transfer notice' under s 160 of the Act. If the Board assumes responsibility for a scheme under s 127 (duty to assume responsibility for schemes following insolvency event) or s 128 (duty to assume responsibility for schemes following application or notification), a transfer notice may not be issued until a valuation of the scheme's assets and protected liabilities (under s 143) is binding. Where responsibility is assumed for a closed scheme under s 158, a transfer notice cannot be given until the valuation obtained under s 158(3) is binding.

3.119 Transfer notices may not be given where the issue of, or failure to issue, a withdrawal notice (in relation to the refusal by the Board to assume responsibility for a scheme) is still subject to review or appeal (see chapter 6 below). In any event, no transfer notices may be issued within the first twelve months of an assessment period, or whilst a fraud compensation application is pending (see chapter 4 below).

3.120 The Board must provide copies of a transfer notice to the Regulator and the insolvency practitioner in relation to the employer (or the employer itself where there is no insolvency practitioner appointed).

## 2. Effect of a Transfer Notice

3.121 Under s 161, once a transfer notice has been given to the trustees of an eligible scheme the Board then assumes responsibility for that scheme. The effect of this is that the property, rights and liabilities of the scheme are transferred automatically to the Board from the date that the trustees or managers receive the transfer notice. The definition of 'liabilities' is restricted so that only liabilities in respect of money purchase benefits and such other liabilities as may be prescribed transfer to the Board (although the Board will of course be liable to make PPF pension compensation payments). Further provisions in respect of the transfer of the property and the rights and liabilities of a scheme are set out in Sch 6 (which may also be expanded by regulations). Once the scheme assets have been transferred, the trustees or managers are discharged from their pension obligations in relation to the scheme and the Board takes on the responsibility for ensuring that compensation is paid in accordance with the relevant provisions of the Act. The scheme is to be treated as winding up immediately after this date. 'Pension obligations' in this context are defined as obligations to provide members with pensions and other benefits (including GMPs) and to administer the scheme.

3.122 Under s 161(7), regulations may be introduced authorizing the Board to modify the terms of a 'relevant contract of insurance' where any rights or liabilities under the contract have been transferred to the Board and the Board is required as a result of a term of that contract to pay an amount to or in respect of a member of the scheme. 'A relevant contract of insurance' for these purposes is a contract of insurance which is intended to secure the whole or part of a scheme's liability for any pension or other benefit payable in respect of a particular person whose entitlement to that benefit has arisen, and any benefit payable on his death. In addition, it must be a contract which may not be surrendered, or in respect of which the amount payable on surrender does not exceed the liability secured.

## 3. Pension Compensation Provisions

3.123 Section 162 and Sch 7 set out the provisions for payment of compensation in relation to a scheme for which the Board assumes responsibility. This includes provision for:

(a) Periodic compensation to be paid to or in respect of members;
(b) Lump sum compensation to be paid to members;
(c) A cap to be imposed on the periodic compensation and lump sum compensation payable; and

### 3. The Pension Protection Fund

(d) Annual increases to be made to periodic compensation.

3.124 Schedule 7 sets out in detail the terms on which compensation will be calculated. For these purposes, those over normal pension age (and certain pensioners under that age) at the assessment date are distinguished from other scheme members and are subject to more favourable treatment. The level of compensation that will be payable to members over normal pension age at the assessment date will be 100% of PPF compensation (ie 100% of the member's entitlement to benefits under the 'admissible rules' (see para 3.125 below)). This will also apply to individuals of any age who are in receipt of an ill health or survivorship pension at the assessment date. 'Normal pension age' is defined as the earliest age specified in the admissible rules at which the scheme pension becomes payable without actuarial reduction. 'Assessment date' is defined as the date on which the assessment period begins (see para 3.71 above). Any members under normal pension age at the assessment date will be entitled to 90% of PPF compensation subject to a cap on the maximum compensation payable. Non ill health early retirement will also be limited to 90% of the capped level of compensation. Surviving spouses will be entitled to a pension which will be the equivalent of 50% of the deceased beneficiary's PPF entitlement.

3.125 All compensation under the PPF will be subject to a scheme's 'admissible rules'. These are defined as the governing rules of the scheme, but excluding any recent rule changes and discretionary increases if the combined effect of these changes and increases is that the protected liabilities in relation to the scheme before the assessment period are greater than they would otherwise have been. Recent rule changes and discretionary increases are defined as those which took effect in the period of three years ending with the assessment date.

3.126 PPF compensation will be revalued from the assessment date by the percentage increase in RPI during the revaluation period determined in the prescribed manner or 5%, whichever is the lesser.

3.127 Under regulations, members will be able to commute part of their PPF compensation to a lump sum, to a maximum of 25% (this proportion may be amended by the Secretary of State by order).

3.128 Under certain circumstances (to be prescribed) a member may become entitled to PPF compensation before reaching normal pension age. In such a case, the Board will have the power to decide what actuarial reduction should be applied to take account of early receipt.

3.129 Schedule 7 also provides details of the cap on PPF compensation and when this will apply. The cap will apply to members under normal pension age, who are not in receipt of an ill health or survivorship pension at the assessment date. The cap will be £27,777.78 per annum, and the 90% rate is applied on top of this (ie the compensation cap is equal to £25,000 per annum for those who become entitled to compensation at age 65). The schedule allows for the cap to be altered by order, and sets out the basis for applying an annual increase to the cap.

3.130 There is also provision under Sch 7 for applying annual increases to PPF

## Payment of Compensation

periodic compensation, which will be the lesser of the increase in the RPI or 2.5% (in respect of amounts attributable to pensionable service on or after 6 April 1997) reflecting the more general reduction in the statutory requirement for limited price indexation (see paras 9.188 to 9.191 below). Indexation will not be applied to pensionable service before 6 April 1997.

**3.131** Section 163 of the Act sets out the adjustments to be made to any compensation payments where the Board assumes responsibility for a scheme. Any benefits (other than money purchase benefits) which were payable under the scheme to or in respect of a member from the period beginning with the assessment date and ending with the receipt of a transfer notice, and which have been paid out during this period, are to be counted towards discharging any liability of the Board to pay compensation to a particular individual. Regulations may provide that where a member of the scheme dies prior to the assessment period, but during the period beginning with the assessment date and ending with the service of a transfer notice an individual becomes entitled to a benefit of a prescribed description in respect of that member, then that benefit is to be treated as if it had become payable before the assessment date.

**3.132** If any amount is paid out during the assessment period which exceeds a member's entitlement under the pension compensation provisions, the Board is under an obligation to take appropriate steps (including adjusting future compensation payments) to recover the amount of any excess, together with interest. If, on the other hand, the amount paid out is less than the individual's entitlement under the pension compensation provisions, then the Board is under an obligation to make up any shortfall, together with interest. The figures referred to do not include amounts paid out in respect of money purchase benefits or any other amount of a prescribed description. Regulations may prescribe circumstances in which the Board is *not* required to recover any amounts paid out. In addition, the Board is not required to recover amounts which it considers to be trivial.

**3.133** Section 164 states that regulations may be introduced so that where the Board assumes liability for a scheme, it will have the power to postpone a member's entitlement to compensation for the whole or part of the assessment period where that individual continues in employment after reaching normal pension age. 'Normal pension age' is defined in para 34 of Sch 7 as the age specified in the admissible rules as being the earliest age at which a pension or lump sum becomes payable without actuarial adjustment, excluding any provisions as to early payment on the grounds of ill health. The terms and conditions of such a postponement will be set out in regulations.

**3.134** Under s 165, the Board is under a duty, where it assumes liability for a scheme, to notify the Commissioners of the Inland Revenue as soon as practicable that the trustees or managers of the scheme are discharged from their duties to provide guaranteed minimum pensions under the PSA 1993 to or in respect of members of the scheme. There is a consequential amendment to s 47 of the PSA 1993 so that an individual will be treated as being entitled to a guaranteed minimum pension, in spite of the fact that the trustees or managers of a scheme have been discharged from their responsibility to provide that pension. These notional GMP entitlements will then be taken into account in calculating members' state scheme benefits.

3.135 Under s 166, where the Board assumes responsibility for a scheme, it is under a duty to pay out any amounts which an individual had become entitled to under the scheme rules prior to the assessment date and which are still unpaid at the time the transfer notice is received by the trustees or managers of the scheme. This provision does not apply where the individual has postponed payment of the amount that he is entitled to, neither does it apply to a transfer payment, nor to any payments in respect of a refund of contributions. Under s 166(5), regulations may be introduced so that where a member of a scheme dies before the assessment period begins and an individual becomes entitled during the assessment period to a benefit (of a prescribed description) in respect of that member, then that individual's entitlement is to be treated as having arisen before the assessment date. Under s 166(6), regulations may require the Board to take steps, including making payments, in respect of members' entitlements arising immediately before the commencement of the assessment period. This provision is subject to any modifications to the pension protection provisions or to the scheme rules as may be prescribed.

3.136 Regulations may be introduced to modify the pension protection provisions contained in Ch 3 of Pt 2 of the Act where liabilities are discharged during the assessment period (s 167). This is designed to cover the situation where a member has been bought out or a partial scheme rescue has taken place, and is intended to allow the Board to amend the valuation to take account of these facts.

3.137 Section 168 states that regulations will make provision for the operation and administration of compensation payments by the Board. Compensation is defined as compensation payable under Sch 7 (or s 141(2), in relation to reviewable ill health pensions) of the Act. The regulations will include provisions for:

(a) Prescribing the method and timing of payment;
(b) Calculating the amount of compensation payable;
(c) Prescribing the circumstances in which compensation payable to a beneficiary may be paid to another person on behalf of the beneficiary;
(d) Paying compensation to people claiming entitlement on death of an individual, and for dispensing with strict proof of their title;
(e) Recovering excess payments, including interest; and
(f) Suspending payment of compensation.

These bear some obvious similarity to the powers and procedures one would expect to find within the trust documentation of an occupational pension scheme.

## 4. Discharge of the Board's Liabilities

Where the Board assumes responsibility for an eligible scheme, it can discharge a liability to pay compensation either by taking out insurance policies or annuity contracts, or by transferring the benefit of such policies or contracts. Cash payments may also be made in prescribed circumstances (s 169).   3.138

Section 170 relates to the discharge of liabilities in respect of money purchase benefits. Where the Board assumes liability for a scheme which has one or more members who are entitled to, or have, accrued rights[10] under the scheme rules to money purchase benefits, the Board must ensure that liabilities in respect of these benefits are discharged in the prescribed manner. The regulations will also prescribe the manner in which protected rights within the meaning of the PSA 1993[11] are to be dealt with.   3.139

## 5. Equal Treatment

Section 171 is designed to ensure that men and women are treated equally under the compensation provisions and that no discrimination arises as a result of provisions in the scheme rules. Where any such discrimination exists, the provision must be modified in order to remove the discriminatory effect. The provision applies to all service after 17 May 1990, except where the Board can establish that a difference in treatment is due to a genuine material factor that is not based on sex. Section 171 ensures, therefore, that the PPF is subject to similar requirements to those which already apply to occupational pension schemes under s 62 of the 1995 Act and under wider European law obligations.[12] Regulations may provide for circumstances in which the Board's payment functions will not need to be modified.   3.140

## 6. Relationship with Fraud Compensation Regime

Under s 172, the Board cannot issue a transfer notice within the first twelve months of an assessment period in relation to a scheme, in order to allow sufficient investigations to be made into the status of the scheme including the possibility of a fraud compensation payment application. Moreover, where such an application has been made under s 182, a transfer notice cannot be given until the Board has determined the application, the period for reviewing that decision has expired, and any review, reconsideration, referral or appeal of that decision has been disposed of.   3.141

If a decision is made by the Board during the assessment period to make a   3.142

---

[10] 1995 Act s 124(2)—definition of 'accrued rights'.
[11] PSA 1993, s 10—definition of 'protected rights'.
[12] Treaty of Rome, Art 141.

fraud compensation payment to the scheme, then any such payment is to be regarded as an asset of the scheme for the purposes of the Board's assessment of whether the value of the assets is less than the scheme's liabilities. This does not apply where the fraud compensation is payable in respect of a reduction in the value of money purchase assets under the scheme.

## L. THE FUND

3.143 Section 173 sets out the income and outgoings of the PPF. The PPF's assets, which will be held separately from the FCF assets, will comprise:

(a) Property and rights transferred to the Board;

(b) Contributions from the initial levy and pension protection levy;

(c) Money borrowed by the Board;

(d) Any investment income or capital gain on the assets of the fund, which the Board must credit to the fund;

(e) Any amount paid to the Board through the repayment of loans to trustees or managers and payments of interest;

(f) Any overpayments which are recovered;

(g) Any amounts paid in respect of debts due to the Board by virtue of a s 38 contribution notice;

(h) Any property transferred or money paid to the Board pursuant to a restoration order under s 52;

(i) Any amount paid to the Board by virtue of a contribution notice under s 55;

(j) Any fraud compensation transfer payments; and

(k) Any other amounts of a prescribed description.

3.144 The following items are to be paid for out of the assets of the PPF:

(a) Sums required to meet the liabilities transferred to the Board;

(b) Payments under the pension compensation provisions;

(c) The repayment of loans (and interest);

(d) Loans to trustees or managers;

(e) Sums required to make payments in respect of underpayments during the assessment period;

(f) Payments of unpaid scheme benefits;

(g) The discharge of liabilities in respect of compensation or money purchase benefits;

(h) Any sums required to meet liabilities arising from obligations imposed on the Board by a restoration order under s 52;

(i) Any property required to meet liabilities arising from obligations imposed by a restoration order under s 52;
(j) Any expenditure incurred in the transfer of property, rights and liabilities to the Board; and
(k) Sums required for prescribed purposes.

## M. THE LEVIES

3.145 The initial costs of establishing the PPF will be met by a government loan of £20 million. Thereafter, the costs of funding both in terms of compensation payable and general running costs will be covered by a variety of levies payable by pension schemes. Different levies cover different aspects of the PPF's functions and not all schemes will pay all levies, nor will they necessarily be liable for the same amount in relation to those levies which they do pay. In addition to the administration levy (outlined at paras 3.33 to 3.35 above) there will be an initial levy for the period following the introduction of the PPF. There will also be a specific pension protection levy to fund pension compensation payments for the future and a separate fraud compensation levy (see paras 4.30 to 4.33 below) to meet the obligations of the FCF. Schemes will already be familiar with the concept of levy payments since the introduction of the 1995 Act. However, the existing general levy and PCB levy are not particularly burdensome for most schemes, whereas the new pension protection levies in particular (which will take account of such factors as the funding position of the scheme, the nature of its investments and the potential for employer insolvency) seem destined to prove controversial. It remains to be seen whether the new levy system can be established on a basis which is regarded as both equitable and effective.

### 1. The Initial Levy

3.146 Section 174 of the Act makes provision for imposing the 'initial levy' on schemes for an 'initial period' of twelve months beginning on a day appointed by regulations.

3.147 Regulations will set out the factors which must be taken into account in assessing the rate of the initial levy, and the time or times during the initial period when the levy (or any instalment) will be payable. It is anticipated that the initial levy will be based on scheme factors only (see para 3.150 below for a discussion of what will be regarded as a 'scheme-based' factor).

3.148 Under s 175, for each financial year following the initial period, the Board will impose both a risk-based and scheme-based pension protection levy in respect of all eligible schemes (ie those schemes which are eligible for PPF coverage under s 126).

## 2. The 'Risk-based' Levy

3.149 Under s 175(2)(a), a risk-based pension protection levy will be assessed by reference to the difference between the value of the scheme's assets (excluding assets relating to money purchase benefits) and the amount of its protected liabilities, as well as the likelihood of an insolvency event occurring in relation to the scheme employer. Other risk-based factors which the Board may take into account include the risks associated with the nature of a scheme's investments when compared with the nature of its liabilities, and any other matters that may be prescribed by regulation.

## 3. The 'Scheme-based' Levy

3.150 Under s 175(2)(b), a scheme-based pension protection levy is a levy assessed by reference to the amount of a scheme's liabilities to or in respect of members (excluding money purchase liabilities) and, if appropriate, the number of members in the scheme, the total annual amount of pensionable earnings of active members in the scheme, and any other factors that may be prescribed.

## 4. Calculation of the Levies and the 'Levy Ceiling'

3.151 Before the beginning of each financial year, the Board will need to determine the factors which it will take into account in calculating the levies, the periods of time during which these factors will be considered, the rate of the levies, and the dates when the levies (including any instalments) will be payable. Different risk factors, scheme factors, or rates can be applied to different categories of scheme and the rate for a particular category of scheme can be nil.

3.152 The Board is under a duty to carry out an appropriate consultation process in respect of the first financial year that the levies are imposed, or in subsequent years if any of the levy factors or rates are to be varied. The Board must publish the details of its determinations under this section.

3.153 Section 177 sets out the amounts to be raised by the pension protection levies. First, the Board has to estimate the amount that will be raised by the levies it proposes to impose. This should not exceed the levy ceiling (see paras 3.156 and 3.157 below) for that financial year.

3.154 The levies imposed in any one year must result in at least 80% of the amount raised coming from the risk-based pension protection levy. This figure was increased from 50% during the Bill's passage through Parliament following representations from industry, the NAPF, and many large pension schemes to the effect that a lower risk-based levy would result in stable, well-funded schemes having to subsidize those which are poorly managed and insufficiently funded.

3.155 In the second financial year following the transitional period (see para 3.159 below) and in subsequent years, the amount which the Board estimates it will

## The Levies

raise cannot exceed the amount calculated in the previous financial year by more than 25%. (Following consultation, this percentage can be altered by the Secretary of State by order and with the approval of the Treasury).

**3.156** Section 178 sets out the mechanism for calculating the levy ceiling. Before the beginning of each financial year the Secretary of State must specify by order the levy ceiling for that year. The levy ceiling for the first financial year in which levies are imposed must be approved by the Treasury. In subsequent years, the levy ceiling should be increased in line with increases in the 'level of earnings' during the 'review period'. The 'level of earnings' is defined as the general level of earnings in the UK and the 'review period' relates to a twelve-month period ending with a prescribed date in the previous financial year.

**3.157** It is the duty of the Secretary of State to review the general level of earnings in the UK and, where the general level of earnings has increased during the review period, the Secretary of State has to specify by order the 'earnings percentage' by which they have increased. It is this percentage which is then applied to increase the levy ceiling. The Secretary of State can increase the levy ceiling by an amount exceeding the earnings percentage on the recommendation of the Board and with the approval of the Treasury, but the Board must undertake appropriate consultation before making such a recommendation.

**3.158** In order to calculate risk-based levies, regulations under s 179 will make provision requiring the trustees or managers of eligible schemes to provide the Board, or the Regulator on the Board's behalf, with an actuarial valuation of the scheme at prescribed intervals and, where necessary, to provide other information to the Board in respect of its assets and protected liabilities. Regulations may prescribe how assets and protected liabilities are to be determined, calculated, and verified, and the Board will issue guidance on this. In calculating liabilities for the purposes of a valuation, any provision in the scheme rules which limits the amount of the scheme's liabilities by reference to the value of its assets is to be disregarded. Any reference to 'assets' does not include assets representing the value of any rights in respect of money purchase benefits under the scheme rules.

**3.159** During the transitional period, regulations may modify the provisions relating to the calculation of the pension protection levies and the levy ceilings. The 'transitional period' is defined as the prescribed period beginning immediately after the initial period and will allow the Board time to implement a full risk-based levy. The Regulator, under s 180, may also provide for the levy ceiling to be set at a lower amount during the transitional period. This is designed to prevent the Board from increasing the levy beyond a set limit during these early stages, when the yearly 25% increase rule does not apply.

**3.160** Section 181 deals with the calculation, collection, and recovery of levies. Both the initial levy and subsequent levies are payable to the Board by or on behalf of the trustees or managers of the scheme or any other prescribed person.

**3.161** The Board must decide which schemes the levy is to be imposed upon, calculate the amount of the levy in respect of those schemes and notify whoever is

### 3. The Pension Protection Fund

liable to pay the levy. The Board may require the Regulator to discharge these functions on its behalf. As noted above, only schemes which are eligible for PPF protection will be required to pay the pension protection levies. Consequently, pure money purchase schemes will be exempt although they will still be obliged to meet the fraud compensation levy. If a scheme is an eligible scheme for only part of the period for which the levy is imposed, then only a proportion of the levy will be payable.

3.162 Levies payable count as debts due to the Board and may be recovered by either the Board or the Regulator on its behalf. Regulations will set out the provisions regarding the collection and recovery of amounts payable by way of a levy and the circumstances in which these amounts may be waived.

# 4
# FRAUD COMPENSATION

| A. Introduction | 4.01 |
| --- | --- |
| B. Cases where Fraud Compensation Payments can be made | 4.05 |
| C. Fraud Compensation Payments | 4.18 |
| D. Interim Payments | 4.23 |
| E. Interaction with the Pension Protection Fund | 4.25 |
| F. Fraud Compensation Fund | 4.28 |
| G. Fraud Compensation Levy | 4.30 |

## A. INTRODUCTION

**4.01** Chapter 4 of Pt 2 deals with the new Fraud Compensation Fund (FCF) established under the Act. The chapter essentially re-enacts in modified form the existing fraud compensation provisions operated by the Pensions Compensation Board (PCB), which was created in 1997 under the terms of the 1995 Act. The 1995 Act brought the PCB into existence as a new statutory body charged with compensating pension schemes for any reduction in the value of the scheme's assets arising from fraud, theft, or other offences of dishonesty in cases where the employer is insolvent and unable to make up the loss.

**4.02** The PCB currently provides compensation limited as follows:

(a) In the case of final salary schemes: up to 100% of the scheme's liabilities for pensioners and those within ten years of retirement; and 90% of the liabilities for other members calculated on the Minimum Funding Requirement basis up to the value of the assets lost; and
(b) In the case of money purchase schemes: 90% of the assets lost.

**4.03** One of the key changes proposed under the new regime is the extension of this level of compensation to 100% of the loss suffered for both types of scheme.

**4.04** The FCF will be run by the Board of the PPF and will take over the functions of the PCB which will at that point cease to exist. The Board will nevertheless retain distinct funds to represent the fraud compensation regime and the

## 4. Fraud Compensation

separate arrangements operated by the PPF in circumstances where members have lost benefits in the absence of fraud or similar wrongdoing. The bulk of the modifications to the existing PCB regime relate to the interaction of the FCF with the new and wider PPF procedural framework.

### B. CASES WHERE FRAUD COMPENSATION PAYMENTS CAN BE MADE

4.05 Section 182 sets out the conditions which must be met in order for the Board to make a payment or series of payments to an occupational pension scheme under the fraud compensation provisions. Such payments are defined throughout Pt 2 as 'fraud compensation payments' and should be distinguished from the wider non-fraud related 'pension compensation' payments also operated by the PPF Board. The criteria which must be satisfied are as follows:

(a) The scheme is not a prescribed scheme or a scheme of a prescribed description;

(b) There has been a reduction in the value of the scheme's assets since the relevant date and the Board considers that there are reasonable grounds for believing that the reduction was attributable to an act or omission constituting a prescribed offence;

(c) One of the three circumstances set out in s 182(2) to (4) applies (essentially where the employer is insolvent or unlikely to continue as a going concern);

(d) An application is made by a prescribed person in a prescribed manner; and

(e) The application is made within the authorized period.

4.06 Much of the detail of how these provisions will operate is left to regulation (in particular those terms dealing with which schemes will be excluded from the scope of the fraud compensation regime and the mechanism for making an application). In practice, however, it is to be expected that the secondary legislation will closely mirror the existing requirements for the PCB.

### 1. Eligible Schemes

4.07 Regulations made under s 182 will prescribe certain individually named schemes and classes of scheme which are not eligible for fraud compensation payments. The intention is that such schemes will also not be subject to the fraud compensation levy (see para 4.30 below). It is likely that the Government will choose to make similar exceptions to those set out in the Occupational Pension Schemes (Pensions Compensation Provisions) Regulations 1997 ('the Pensions Compensation Regulations') which currently exclude from the scope of the regime schemes such as death benefit only arrangements, unapproved schemes, small self-administered schemes, and public service schemes. Schemes subject to

Crown guarantee are also likely to be excluded. The intention is that regulations will also be made to extend coverage of the fraud compensation provisions to trust-based stakeholder pension schemes to ensure consistency with the current scope of the PCB.

## 2. Relevant Date

For the purposes of any fraud compensation claim the reduction in assets must have taken place after 6 April 1997 in the case of an occupational pension scheme established under trust. The date for other types of schemes is to be set by the Secretary of State. 4.08

## 3. Prescribed Offences

Offences covered by fraud compensation are to be set out in regulations. The existing PCB provisions (under reg 3 of the Pensions Compensation Regulations) provide that the offence must involve dishonesty (which, for the avoidance of doubt, includes an intent to defraud). There were some discussions at Committee Stage in the House of Lords as to whether culpable negligence might be encompassed by the secondary legislation, although this seems unlikely in practice. 4.09

## 4. The Circumstances Set Out in Section 182(2), (3), and (4)

The various pre-conditions set out under s 182(2), (3), and (4) are designed to link the fraud compensation provisions with the wider PPF requirements under Ch 3 of Pt 2 of the Act. Only one of these pre-conditions needs to be met in order to satisfy this element of the criteria. Which provision will apply depends upon whether an insolvency event has occurred in relation to the scheme employer (or, in the absence of such an event, it is nevertheless unlikely to continue as a going concern) and whether the scheme is of a type which would be eligible for non-fraud based pension compensation. 4.10

(a) *Section 182(2)*
Section 182(2) applies where a qualifying insolvency event (as defined below) has occurred in relation to the employer in relation to the scheme and the insolvency practitioner has subsequently issued a scheme failure notice under s 122(2)(a) confirming that a scheme rescue is not possible and that notice has become binding. Section 182(2) will not, however, apply where a 'cessation event' has occurred in the period beginning with the qualifying insolvency event and ending immediately before the issue of the scheme failure notice. 4.11

An insolvency event in relation to the employer will be treated as a 'qualifying insolvency event' if: 4.12

## 4. Fraud Compensation

(a) It occurs on or after a date to be appointed (likely to be 6 April 2005), and
(b) Either:
  (i) It is the first insolvency event to occur in relation to the employer on or after that day; or
  (ii) A cessation event has occurred in relation to the scheme in respect of a cessation notice issued during the period beginning with the occurrence of the last insolvency event which occurred before the current event and ending with the occurrence of the current event.

A cessation event occurs when a cessation notice in relation to the scheme becomes binding. A cessation notice will be one of a variety of notices issued by the insolvency practitioner or the PPF Board. Essentially, it will signal the end of the Board's involvement with the scheme following a decision about whether a scheme rescue has occurred. See chapter 3 for a discussion of when the various types of notice will be treated as binding.

(b) *Section 182(3)*

4.13 Section 182(3) applies in relation to a defined benefit scheme where no insolvency event has occurred in relation to the employer but where the employer is unlikely to continue as a going concern. In such circumstances fraud compensation may still be payable if the trustees have made an application to the Board under s 129 or have been informed by the Board that it has received a notification from the Regulator under the same section. The Board must also have issued a binding scheme failure notice under s 130(2) confirming that a scheme rescue is not possible.

(c) *Section 182(4)*

4.14 Section 182(4) deals with the specific position of schemes which are not eligible for pension compensation under Ch 3 of Pt 2 but which may be eligible for fraud compensation under Ch 4 and where there has been no UK insolvency event. An 'eligible scheme' for these purposes is defined by reference to s 126. The most obvious example of a scheme which would not qualify for pension compensation but may qualify for fraud compensation would be a money purchase scheme. However, other categories of scheme may fall within the remit of this subsection depending on the scope of the relevant regulations for the two types of compensation. To come within the scope of s 182(4) a scheme will still need to be able to establish that the scheme employer is unlikely to continue as a going concern and satisfy certain other requirements yet to be prescribed. In addition, the Board must have issued a binding notice under s 183(2) confirming that a scheme rescue is not possible.

### 5. The Application and the Authorized Period

4.15 The detail of who can make an application and how such an application may be made is left to be prescribed by regulations although these will presumably include at least the trustees, scheme administrators, members, and other beneficiaries, as under the existing PCB regime.

The application must also be made within the 'authorized period'. This is defined by s 182(6) as being within twelve months of whichever is the later of the date of the 'relevant event' or the time when the scheme auditor, actuary, or the trustees or managers of the scheme knew or ought reasonably to have known that a reduction in value attributable to an act or omission constituting a prescribed offence had occurred. The Board retains a discretion to extend this period in appropriate cases. 4.16

For the purposes of determining the authorized period, the definition of 'the relevant event' will depend upon which of s 182(2) to (4) is relied upon: 4.17

(a) Where s 182(2) applies in relation to an eligible scheme, 'the relevant event' is the occurrence of a qualifying insolvency event;

(b) Where s 182(2) applies, where the scheme is not an eligible scheme, it is the issue of a scheme failure notice under s 122(2)(a) by the insolvency practitioner;

(c) Where s 182(3) applies, it is the date of the application by the trustees or managers of the scheme under s 129 or the date the Board informs the trustees or manager that it has received a notification from the Regulator, to the effect that the Regulator considers that the employer is unlikely to continue as a going concern, under the same section; and

(d) Where s 182(4) applies, it is where the trustees or managers become aware that the employer is unlikely to continue as a going concern and certain prescribed requirements are met.

## C. FRAUD COMPENSATION PAYMENTS

Sections 185 and 186 deal with the terms on which fraud compensation may be paid under the new regime, together with the possibility of interim payments. Once again, these provisions largely mirror the existing PCB requirements, including the obligation on trustees to attempt to recover the misappropriated funds. 4.18

Prior to receiving any fraud compensation payment, the trustees or managers of the scheme in question must attempt to recover the value of the loss attributable to the offence to the extent that this is possible 'without disproportionate cost and within a reasonable time'. Fraud compensation payments cannot be made until the Board, following consultation with the trustees or managers, has fixed a settlement date after which further 'recoveries of value' are unlikely to be obtained without undue cost or delay. The application of a settlement date allows trustees to draw a line under their attempts to make recoveries whether 4.19

# 4. Fraud Compensation

through court action or otherwise and to proceed with the administration of the scheme going forward with a degree of certainty.

4.20 For the purposes of this section a 'recovery of value' means any increase in the value of the assets of the scheme as a result of a payment received (other than from the Board) by the trustees or managers in respect of the offence. The Board determines what is to be treated as a 'payment received' in this context, and the payment may be in money or money's worth for these purposes.

4.21 Once the Board is satisfied that no further recoveries are possible in a particular case, the procedure for making fraud compensation payments under s 185 can be implemented. Fraud compensation payments must be made to the trustees or managers and may be made on such terms and conditions as the Board considers appropriate. These terms could include a requirement for repayment in whole or in part.

4.22 The amount of the payment (or payments in aggregate) must not exceed the value of the reduction in the fund (taking account of any recoveries of value obtained). Regulations will determine the amount of the fraud compensation payment, and such payment must take into account any interim payments already made (see para. 4.23 below). The restrictions which currently apply to PCB applications are removed by s 277 of the Act and consequently 100% of the actual loss is likely to be able to be recovered regardless of the type of scheme or its current funding level.

## D. INTERIM PAYMENTS

4.23 In appropriate circumstances the Board can arrange for interim payments if it believes that the criteria for payment of fraud compensation under s 182 are or may be met but no settlement date has yet been fixed. Further, the trustees or managers must be unable to meet certain prescribed liabilities to qualify for such interim payments. Regulations setting out these prescribed liabilities are not yet available, but the corresponding PCB provisions essentially cover pensions in payment at the application date and those which become payable between the application date and the settlement date.

4.24 The interim amounts payable under this section cannot exceed the value of any fraud compensation payments ultimately payable. They may be recovered if the Board subsequently determines that the criteria under s 182 do not apply or if the amount was excessive.

## E. INTERACTION WITH THE PENSION PROTECTION FUND

4.25 There is obviously considerable scope for overlap between the PPF and the FCF. For instance, s 172 provides that no notice can be served for a transfer of assets to the PPF while an application for fraud compensation is pending, and any fraud compensation payment will count as a scheme asset when determining whether the scheme is underfunded for the purposes of the PPF.

Once the Board has assumed responsibility for a scheme under the PPF pension compensation arrangements, the scheme effectively ceases to exist in its own right, and the trustees of the scheme are no longer able to make a fraud compensation claim. However, if fraud is discovered subsequently, the Board itself can take advantage of the fraud compensation provisions to ensure that members are not penalized. To give effect to this, s 187 gives the Board power to make a transfer payment from the FCF to the PPF in appropriate circumstances. This is in line with the view that any funds ultimately recoverable in respect of fraud and other relevant offences should be regarded as a deferred element of the assets of the scheme. 4.26

As is the case with the trustees or managers under s 184, the Board must attempt to recover the value of the loss to the extent that this can be done without undue cost or delay. 'Recoveries of value' for these purposes mean any increase in the value of the PPF as opposed to the pension scheme. The amount of such 'fraud compensation transfer payments' will be determined in accordance with regulations but, as for normal fraud compensation, must not exceed the difference between the reduction in value and any subsequent recoveries. 4.27

## F. FRAUD COMPENSATION FUND

Although administered by the PPF Board, the FCF will be a separate entity with its own assets and liabilities. Following the dissolution of the PCB, the starting point for the FCF will be the custody of those assets which have transferred from the PCB. Section 188 sets out in more detail the FCF's assets and those items of expenditure payable from it. In addition to the property and rights transferred from the PCB under s 302, the FCF's income will consist of: 4.28

(a) Payments from schemes under the fraud compensation levy;
(b) Money borrowed by the Board (under s 115) from a financial institution that has statutory permission to take deposits;
(c) Interim payments recovered by the Board from the trustees of the scheme; and
(d) Any income or capital gain arising from the assets of the Fund.

Expenditure will fall into the following categories: 4.29

(a) Sums required to meet outstanding liabilities of the PCB following its dissolution;
(b) Fraud compensation payments made to the trustees of schemes under s 185;
(c) Interim compensation payments made to scheme trustees under s 186;
(d) Fraud compensation transfer payments under s 187; and

(e) Capital repayments and interest payments made to financial institutions where the Board has borrowed money under s 115.

## G. FRAUD COMPENSATION LEVY

4.30 As with the PPF (and the existing PCB), the FCF is to be funded by a levy on occupational pension schemes. The terms of the levy are to be set out in regulations, and will not apply to those schemes which are not eligible for fraud compensation.

4.31 The levy is payable to the Board by or on behalf of the trustees or managers of the scheme or by other persons to be prescribed. The Board will determine the rate and payment dates for the levy and, in setting the levy, is allowed to take account of past and future fraud compensation expenditure.

4.32 The amount payable by a person in respect of the fraud compensation levy is to be treated as a debt due from him to the Board, and such amounts may be recovered by the Board or by the Regulator on the Board's behalf. There is provision for regulations to determine the collection and recovery of the levy and the circumstances in which any such amount may be waived.

4.33 In practice, only two levies have been set for the PCB since its introduction in 1997 and there have only been a very small number of successful claims on the fund to date. It remains to be seen whether the extension of the coverage to 100% of the loss suffered will have any appreciable effect on the number of claims or the amount schemes are required to contribute to these arrangements.

# 5
# GATHERING INFORMATION

| | |
|---|---|
| A. Introduction | 5.01 |
| B. Requirement to Disclose Information to the Board | 5.02 |
| C. Powers of the Board to Obtain Information | 5.03 |
| D. Penalties | 5.08 |
| E. Disclosure of Information by the Board | 5.18 |

## A. INTRODUCTION

**5.01** In order to determine whether a scheme is likely to qualify for compensation, it will clearly be necessary for the Board of the PPF to carry out investigations into the status and background of the scheme. Consequently, the Board is given wide-ranging powers to gather information relevant to its functions, whether by requiring production of data by specified individuals or by physical inspection of premises (Pt 2, Ch 5 of the Act). To a large extent, these provisions are similar to those powers given to the Regulator under Pt 1 of the Act. In view of the importance of the information gathering task, there are criminal sanctions for failure to provide requested information or knowingly providing false information.

## B. REQUIREMENT TO DISCLOSE INFORMATION TO THE BOARD

**5.02** Section 190 of the Act provides that secondary legislation will require certain individuals to disclose prescribed information to the Board (or to someone authorized to gather information by the Board). This information is most likely to be required for the purposes of making a determination of entitlement to compensation under the PPF. If the information is to be provided to someone authorized by the Board, rather than the Board itself, then regulations will set out the mechanism for notifying the individual required to produce the information of the identity of the authorized person.

## 5. Gathering Information

### C. POWERS OF THE BOARD TO OBTAIN INFORMATION

#### 1. Notices Requiring Provision of Information

5.03 A written notice may be issued by the Board (or someone authorized by them) requiring the production of documents or other information specified in the notice (s 191). The documents or information requested must be relevant to the exercise of the Board's functions. The Board can require information from anyone who appears to hold relevant information but the following are specifically listed:

(a) A trustee or manager of the scheme;

(b) A professional adviser in relation to the scheme;

(c) The employer in relation to the scheme;

(d) An insolvency practitioner in relation to the scheme.

#### 2. Entry of Premises

5.04 The Board has the power to appoint someone to enter 'scheme premises' in order to gather information relevant to the functions of the PPF (s 192). This includes the power to:

(a) Make any necessary examination or inquiry;

(b) Secure the production of any relevant documents;

(c) Take copies of such documents;

(d) Take the original documents if necessary in order to preserve or prevent interference with them;

(e) Require any information which is held in electronic form to be made accessible; and

(f) Interview anyone on the premises where there are reasonable grounds for believing that he/she might hold relevant information.

5.05 It is anticipated that it will be a routine matter for the Board to arrange for an appointed person to visit scheme premises during the assessment period (normally by prior appointment). The rights of the Regulator to make an on-site inspection, by contrast, are couched in terms reflecting the unusual and serious nature of a personal visit being required—for the Regulator, inspection at premises will not be a matter of routine.

5.06 Premises count as 'scheme premises' if there are reasonable grounds to believe that:

(a) They are being used for the employer's business;

(b) An insolvency practitioner is acting there in relation to the employer;

(c) Documents relevant to the administration of the scheme or the employer are being kept there; or
(d) Work in connection with the administration of the scheme is carried out there.

These provisions do not apply to a private dwelling which is not being used for business purposes.

5.07 Anyone who is appointed by the Board must produce his certificate of appointment if requested to do so. If any documents are taken away in exercise of these powers, they can be retained for an initial period of twelve months, which can be extended for a further period of twelve months on an ongoing basis.

## D. PENALTIES

### 1. Refusal or Failure to Supply Information

5.08 Section 193 of the Act introduces criminal sanctions for any person who refuses or fails to supply a document or information when required to do so in accordance with s 191. Any person who, without reasonable excuse, intentionally delays or obstructs someone from exercising any of the powers set out in s 192 (entry of premises), or fails to provide the documents or information requested under that section, will also be guilty of an offence.

5.09 Any person who is convicted of an offence under s 193 is liable on summary conviction to a fine not exceeding level 5 on the standard scale (currently £5,000). It appears that these penalties will only be used in exceptional circumstances and they are designed to act as a deterrent and to encourage the cooperation that the Board of the PPF will need in order to carry out its role.[1]

5.10 Any person who deliberately alters, conceals, or destroys a document which has been requested under ss 191 or 192 is also guilty of an offence. On summary conviction a fine can be imposed and on indictment, the penalty may be a fine or imprisonment for up to two years.

### 2. Issue of Warrants

5.11 A Justice of the Peace can, on request, issue a warrant where information has been provided on behalf of the Board and he is satisfied that a document, duly requested under s 191 or 192, has not been supplied. Warrants will, however, only be issued where there are reasonable grounds for believing that a document might be removed from the premises, hidden, altered, or destroyed or where it appears that a misuse or misappropriation of assets of an occupational pension scheme may occur (s 194).

---

[1] Explanatory Notes to Pensions Act, para 705.

# 5. Gathering Information

5.12 In serious cases the inspector may need to use reasonable force to enter and search the premises, obtain or preserve documents, etc, and the warrant will permit this. The inspector also has the power to take copies of the document and require any person named in the warrant to provide an explanation of the document, or to provide information on its whereabouts or assist with access (s 194).

5.13 When executing a warrant an inspector can be accompanied by other people if he deems this appropriate (for example, an expert to carry out a valuation of the property, or an accountant to review relevant financial records).

5.14 A warrant is valid for one month beginning on the day that it is issued. Any documents which are retained under this section can be held for a period of twelve months, which can be extended for a further twelve-month period on an ongoing basis.

**3. Provision of False or Misleading Information**

5.15 Section 195 creates a further offence of providing false or misleading information to the Board. This offence is committed where someone knowingly or recklessly provides false or misleading information, if such information is provided in response to a request for information under ss 190 to 192. An offence is also committed where the information has not been requested under ss 190 to 192, but the person providing the information could reasonably be expected to know that it would be used for those purposes.

5.16 Anyone found guilty of an offence under s 195 is liable on summary conviction to a fine (up to the statutory maximum) and on conviction on indictment to a fine or two years' imprisonment or both.

5.17 Under s 196, any information provided to the Board under the above provisions may be used by the Board in the exercise of any of its functions.

## E. DISCLOSURE OF INFORMATION BY THE BOARD

**1. Restricted Information**

5.18 As with existing arrangements applying to statutory bodies such as OPRA and the Pensions Ombudsman, it is anticipated that the Board will in certain circumstances share information it has gathered with other organizations and individuals. Nevertheless, it is recognized that, as with the Regulator, there should be limits on this. A concept of 'restricted information' is introduced (s 197) together with limitations on the disclosure of such information.

5.19 'Restricted information' is defined as any information obtained by the Board in the exercise of its functions, unless the information was already publicly available or the information is presented in such a way that it is not possible to identify information relating to particular individuals from it. There are however broad exceptions (ss 198 to 203 and 235).

Disclosing restricted information is an offence and carries a penalty on summary conviction of a fine up to the statutory maximum, or on conviction on indictment, to a fine or imprisonment for a maximum of two years, or both. 5.20

Information supplied to the Board, pursuant to a statutory request for information which would be 'restricted information' had it been obtained by the Board itself, is to be treated as restricted information received by the Board for the purposes of ss 198 to 203. 5.21

The exceptions to restrictions on the Board as to the use and transfer of information include: 5.22

(a) Any information which is already on the public record (s 197);
(b) Information contained in a list or collection where ascertaining the information on a specific individual is not possible (s 197);
(c) The disclosure is necessary to the functions of the Board (s 198), the Regulator (s 199), the Secretary of State or other relevant 'supervisory authorities' (ss 200 and 201).

## 2. Provision of Information to Members of Schemes and Others

Under s 203, regulations will require the Board to disclose certain information to scheme trustees or managers, the employer, and certain other individuals involved in the scheme. In particular, the Board will be responsible for notifying members of their entitlement, inter alia, to compensation once their scheme has been taken on by the PPF. 5.23

Regulations will also impose a duty on trustees or managers of occupational pension schemes to provide information relating to the Board's involvement in their scheme, or relating to any notice, application, or determination made under Chs 2, 3, or 4 of the Act in respect of their scheme. For example, scheme valuation details should be made available to members so that they can appeal against the calculation of their entitlements. 5.24

Under s 203(2), the restrictions on the disclosure of information under s 197 do not apply to information which relates to an individual's entitlement to compensation under Ch 3 if the disclosure is made to that individual, or to someone authorized by him. 5.25

Similarly, under s 203(3), the Board is permitted to disclose restricted information where that information relates to the exercise of the Board's functions, the disclosure is made to all affected persons, and the Board is satisfied that it is reasonable to make such a disclosure. An 'affected person' is defined as a member of a scheme or someone nominated by them for the purposes of that subsection. The nomination must be made by the member in writing and becomes effective once it has been received by the Board. It remains in force until the Board receives a further written notice from the member withdrawing the nomination. 5.26

Pursuant to s 203(6), the Board is permitted to disclose restricted information 5.27

to trustees and managers of, and professional advisers to, occupational pension schemes where the information is relevant to the exercise of those individuals' functions in relation to the scheme and the Board considers it reasonable to do so. The Board is also permitted to disclose restricted information to an employer or insolvency practitioner in relation to an employer.

**3. Reports**

5.28 According to s 205, the Board can publish a report relating to the exercise of its functions in any particular case if it considers it appropriate to do so. Such reports might relate to matters such as individual decisions, consultation exercises, and good practice recommendations. The Board has a complete discretion as to the form and content of any such report (so, for example, internet publication would be permitted). For the purposes of the law of defamation, any publication by the Board is to be regarded as privileged, unless it can be shown that the publication was made with malice.

# 6

# REVIEWS, APPEALS, AND MALADMINISTRATION

| | |
|---|---|
| A. Introduction | 6.01 |
| B. Investigation of Complaints by the Board | 6.05 |
| C. The PPF Ombudsman | 6.19 |

## A. INTRODUCTION

Chapter 6 of Part 2 of the Act sets out the procedure for challenging the decisions of the PPF Board. Interested parties will be able to make written applications to the Board in respect of 'reviewable matters' (which include, amongst other things, the Board's refusal to assume responsibility for a scheme and a determination on entitlement to compensation). 6.01

The Board will also deal with complaints by a person who is or might be entitled to pension compensation or fraud compensation and who believes they have suffered injustice as a consequence of maladministration by the Board. 6.02

The Board will be required to review its decisions under a two-stage procedure of 'review' and 'reconsideration'. It will have the power to vary or revoke its determination or make a new determination and will have the power to award compensation in certain circumstances. 6.03

Determinations may also be referred to the PPF Ombudsman, who will have the power to make a determination or refer it back to the Board with directions on how it should proceed. As a last resort, appeals can be made to the High Court (or Court of Session in Scotland) on points of law. 6.04

## B. INVESTIGATION OF COMPLAINTS BY THE BOARD

### 1. Review of Board Determinations

Section 206 of the Act, together with Sch 9, sets out what is meant by a 'reviewable matter' (ie those of the Board's determinations which may be subject to challenge in this manner). 6.05

## 6. Reviews, Appeals, and Maladministration

6.06　Under s 206(2), where Sch 9 refers to a failure by the Board to do any act or make any determination, Regulations may provide that such a reference should be construed as a failure to do so within a prescribed period. Regulations may also provide that a reference in Sch 9 to a 'failure' is to be read as not including a failure which first occurs after a prescribed time.

6.07　Under s 206(3), secondary legislation will provide that the effect of any decision or determination by the Board should be suspended pending the outcome of any review, reconsideration or reference to the PPF Ombudsman and any appeal against any determination or direction in relation to that matter.

6.08　Under s 206(4) and (5), Sch 9 and any other related provision under Pt 2 may be amended by regulations.

6.09　Section 207 relates to the review and consideration by the Board of reviewable matters. This will be a two-stage process, involving an initial 'review' stage and a subsequent 'reconsideration' stage.

6.10　Under s 207(1), regulations will provide for the Board, following a written application by an 'interested person', to give a 'review decision' in respect of any reviewable matter. The Board must set up a committee in order to reconsider any review decisions where it receives a written application from the interested party and to provide a 'reconsideration decision'. Who will count as an 'interested person' has yet to be prescribed. Regulations may permit a review decision or a reconsideration decision to be made otherwise than by the written application process (ie giving the Board the power to review a decision of its own volition).

6.11　On completing the review or reconsideration stage, the Board will have the power to vary, revoke, or substitute a different decision, or pay such compensation as it may determine.

6.12　Regulations will also allow the Board to deal with issues arising on the review or reconsideration of a matter, as if they had arisen at the time of the original decision or determination.

6.13　Under s 207(5), regulations made under s 207(1) must set out the application process for a review or reconsideration of a decision, and in particular the time limits within which such an application must be made. They must also require a notice of any application or decision to be given to interested parties in the matter. The regulations must also specify that the same individuals who make the initial review decision should not be involved in any subsequent reconsideration of the same matter.

6.14　The regulations will set out the procedure for reaching and giving decisions, including the rights of interested parties to make representations and the times within which decisions are to be given. They will also require that a notice of a review or reconsideration decision is served on any interested parties.

### 2. Complaints of Maladministration

6.15　Section 208 sets out the procedure for investigations by the Board of complaints of maladministration. The procedure for dealing with such 'relevant complaints' will be set out in regulations. A 'relevant complaint' is defined for these purposes as a complaint made by a person who might have an entitlement to compensation under the pension compensation provisions, or who is entitled to make an application under the fraud compensation provisions set out in s 182, where the person alleges that he has suffered injustice as a result of maladministration by the Board or any person acting on its behalf.

6.16 Regulations will allow the Board to investigate and give initial decisions on such complaints, and provide for a committee of the Board to review any applications which are made following such decisions.

6.17 The regulations will also set out the process for making complaints, including the time limits during which they can be made. The regulations must ensure that persons who were involved in the matter which is the subject of the relevant complaint are not also involved in the adjudication of the complaint. Regulations will also set out the procedure for making decisions, including the rights of an individual to make representations to the Board and the time limits on this process. Written notices of a relevant decision in respect of a complaint will need to be provided. The detail of this process is to be set out in regulations.

6.18 Under s 208(5), the Board will also have the power to pay compensation to any person who has suffered injustice as a result of a matter complained of.

## C. THE PPF OMBUDSMAN

**1. Establishment**

6.19 Section 209 of the Act makes provision for a PPF Ombudsman, who will be appointed by the Secretary of State on such terms and conditions as the Secretary of State decides. Those terms will govern, amongst other things, the appointment, resignation, or removal of the PPF Ombudsman. Under s 209(4), the Secretary of State will also be able to make, by order, provision in terms of the remuneration of the PPF Ombudsman, the reimbursement of expenses incurred by him, the staff and other facilities available to him, and the delegation of the PPF Ombudsman's functions to his staff. He will also be able to make provisions authorizing the PPF Ombudsman to charge fees where appropriate and where the PPF Ombudsman has the power to charge a fee, he will also have the power to decide when that fee is due and provide that any fee owed to the PPF Ombudsman can be recovered as a debt due to him. In addition, the Secretary of State may give the Ombudsman the power to obtain the information and documents he might need in order to perform his functions properly. Any money needed to pay the PPF Ombudsman under s 209(4) must be paid out of funds provided by Parliament. Section 209(7) allows these funds to be raised through the imposition of a levy on eligible schemes.

6.20 Under s 210, the Secretary of State has the power to appoint one or more Deputy PPF Ombudsmen. Again, the Secretary of State has the power to decide

## 6. Reviews, Appeals, and Maladministration

the terms of these appointments. As with the PPF Ombudsman himself, those terms will govern the appointment, resignation and removal of a Deputy PPF Ombudsman.

6.21 Under s 210(4), a Deputy PPF Ombudsman will be able to perform the functions of the PPF Ombudsman in the event that the office of the PPF Ombudsman is vacant, or the PPF Ombudsman is unable to carry out his functions, or at any other time with the consent of the Secretary of State. This means that any reference to the PPF Ombudsman's functions should be read to include a reference to his deputies.

6.22 An order made by the Secretary of State regarding the remuneration and reimbursement of the PPF Ombudsman (see para 6.19 above) also applies to any Deputy PPF Ombudsman.

6.23 Under s 211(1) and (2), certain provisions of the House of Commons Disqualification Act 1975 and the Northern Ireland Assembly Disqualification Act 1975 are amended so that the PPF Ombudsman and any deputies are disqualified from being a member of either the House of Commons or the Northern Ireland Assembly.

6.24 Under s 211(3), the Superannuation Act 1972 is amended so that persons to or in respect of whom benefits may be provided by schemes under s 1 of that Act will include the PPF Ombudsman, his deputies, and employees. However, the PPF Ombudsman will be obliged to pay the Minister for the Civil Service for the extra cost incurred in providing these benefits.

6.25 Under s 212, the PPF Ombudsman has to prepare an annual report, which must be submitted to the Secretary of State as soon as practicable following the end of each financial year, which the Secretary of State must then have published. 'Financial year' is defined as the period beginning with the date on which the PPF Ombudsman is first established and ending on the 31 March that follows, and each successive period of twelve months thereafter.

### 2. References to the PPF Ombudsman

6.26 Under s 213, regulations will make provision for a reviewable matter to be referred to the PPF Ombudsman where a reconsideration decision has been made under s 207. The PPF Ombudsman will then investigate the matter and decide what action, if any, the Board should take, and will provide them with directions to give effect to any decision.

6.27 The regulations will also set out the procedure for referring a matter to the PPF Ombudsman, including who can make a reference, the time and manner in which references should be made, who should be notified of a reference and the result of any determination or decision.

6.28 Under s 213(3) and (4), where a reviewable matter is referred to the PPF Ombudsman, regulations will require him to either conduct an oral hearing, or deal with the matter by way of written representations. The regulations will allow the PPF Ombudsman to consider any other evidence that may not have been available in an earlier review or reconsideration. They will also make provision about the procedure for matters such as conducting investigations and making determinations. Regulations will set out who will be entitled to make representations to the PPF Ombudsman, or be heard or represented at an oral hearing. They will also cover the treatment of evidence by the PPF Ombudsman, including the production of documents, oral hearings, expert evidence, and attendance of witnesses.

6.29 Provision will be made under the regulations so that certain prescribed persons will have the right to pursue an appeal to the PPF Ombudsman, where the person who made the original reference has either died or is no longer able to act for himself. Provision will also be made regarding any costs or expenses incurred by prescribed persons.

6.30 Regulations will permit certain individuals to apply for a stay in certain legal proceedings which begin after a reference has been made and will confer a power on the relevant Court to make an order staying the proceedings, if it is satisfied that certain criteria have been fulfilled.

6.31 The regulations may also allow for provisions to ensure that any determination or direction which is made by the PPF Ombudsman is binding on certain prescribed persons.

6.32 The same regulations may give the PPF Ombudsman the power to direct the Board to pay compensation where he considers it appropriate to do so. They will give the PPF Ombudsman the power to direct the Board to treat any direction or determination that is varied as a result of a referral to the Ombudsman, as though it had been made at any time that he considers appropriate (this can be a time prior to his determination or direction). This power also applies in relation to the direction by the PPF Ombudsman to vary or substitute a notice issued by the Board.

6.33 Section 214 relates to investigations by the PPF Ombudsman into complaints of maladministration. It states that regulations will set out the procedure for the investigation and determination of relevant complaints which have been referred to the PPF Ombudsman following an earlier decision by the Board or the committee of the Board, referred to in s 208(3)(b).

6.34 The regulations will set out the categories of person who can make a reference to the PPF Ombudsman, the procedure and timing of a reference, the procedure for investigating the complaint and making determinations, including any time limits for making a determination.

6.35 Regulations will give the PPF Ombudsman the power to direct the Board to pay compensation in respect of any injustice that he believes the complainant has suffered as a result of the maladministration. He will also have the power to direct the Board to take or refrain from taking any other steps that he may specify.

6.36 Regulations will set out who will be entitled to make representations to the PPF Ombudsman, or be heard or represented at an oral hearing in relation to any matter which is referred to the PPF Ombudsman under this section.

### 6. Reviews, Appeals, and Maladministration

Regulations will also lay down the requirements for the consideration of evidence by the PPF Ombudsman, including the production of documents, oral hearings, expert evidence, and the attendance of witnesses.

6.37 Regulations will permit certain individuals to apply for a stay in certain legal proceedings which begin after a reference has been made and will confer power on the relevant court to make an order staying the proceedings if it is satisfied that certain criteria have been fulfilled.

6.38 Regulations may also allow for provisions to ensure that any determination or direction which is made by the PPF Ombudsman is binding on certain prescribed persons.

6.39 Under s 215, the PPF Ombudsman has the power to refer any question of law that arises in connection with a reviewable matter referred to him under s 213 or a complaint of maladministration referred to him under s 214 to the High Court (or the Court of Session in Scotland).

6.40 Under s 217, anyone who is bound by a determination or direction by the PPF Ombudsman will be allowed to appeal on a point of law to the High Court (or the Court of Session in Scotland). Any determination or direction of the PPF Ombudsman is enforceable in a County Court in England and Wales or a Sheriff Court in Scotland.

6.41 Under s 216, the PPF Ombudsman has the power to publish a report in relation to any of his investigations under ss 213 or 214, including the result of that investigation. For defamation purposes, the publication of any such report will be absolutely privileged.

6.42 Under s 218, it is an offence for someone to obstruct the PPF Ombudsman in the performance of his duties without lawful excuse, or where he acts during an investigation by the PPF Ombudsman in such a way that if that investigation were a proceeding in the court, it would constitute contempt of court. This offence also applies in Scotland as if contempt of court were categorized as an offence in Scottish law. The PPF Ombudsman can certify the offence to the court, which can then investigate the matter and deal with it in the same way that it could if the offence had been committed in court.

# 7

# SCHEME FUNDING

| A. Introduction | 7.01 |
| --- | --- |
| B. Statutory Funding Objective | 7.04 |
| C. Statement of Funding Principles | 7.07 |
| D. Agreement of the Employer | 7.11 |
| E. Advice to the Actuary | 7.13 |
| F. Powers for the Regulator | 7.14 |

## A. INTRODUCTION

The 2004 Act introduces significant changes to the law on pension scheme funding. In part, the provisions relate to failings in the current regime of pension funding (such as abolition of the Minimum Funding Requirement (MFR)). All arise from concerns as to the funding position of UK pension schemes generally. However, the provisions of the Act also deal with the legislation and the requirements of the EU Pensions Directive.[1] The terms of the directive must be implemented into UK law by September 2005. The abolition of the MFR comes as no surprise. It is widely recognized as having failed to achieve, by any measure, adequate funding of pension arrangements. For some years now, even whilst the MFR remained in force, trustees have been recommended by scheme actuaries not to rely on the MFR as a funding standard. Concerns also related to the 'one size fits all' approach which the MFR laid down. 7.01

In the Green Paper[2] the Government noted that the MFR had given rise to a number of concerns. It said that the MFR: 7.02

has proved to be too inflexible—it does not take account of the specific circumstances of individual schemes. It has also encouraged some schemes to focus on short-term market

---

[1] Directive 2003/41 on the activities and supervision of institutions for occupational retirement provision [2003] OJ L235/10.
[2] At Ch 4, para 31.

## 7. Scheme Funding

conditions instead of the most appropriate longer term investment strategy for meeting their specific pension commitments.[3]

7.03 Accordingly, the MFR's replacement is to be a 'scheme specific funding' standard. This is the term used in consultation and in particular in the Green Paper but, in fact, is not a term which is used in the Act itself. Indeed, it is only possible to discern a bare framework of the new approach on funding from the Act. A great deal of the detail is left for regulations to flesh out. Accordingly, from a perusal of the Act, it is difficult to discern exactly how scheme specific a funding standard schemes will be permitted to adopt.

### B. STATUTORY FUNDING OBJECTIVE

7.04 Section 221 of the Act makes it clear that the new funding objectives applied to defined benefit arrangements are not to be required for money purchase schemes. A number of prescribed schemes will also be exempt from the scheme funding provisions.

7.05 In s 222, a new statutory funding objective is proposed. This provision adopts the wording of the EU Pensions Directive by stating that 'every scheme ... must have sufficient and appropriate assets to cover its technical provisions'. The directive term 'technical provisions' is defined for the purposes of the Act as the 'amount required, on an actuarial calculation, to make provision for the scheme's liabilities'.[4] This is clearly a very broad and open ended definition, reinforcing the point that much of the detail remains to be fixed by regulations.

7.06 It is clear that the details of the methodology for determining or valuing the assets and choice of methods of calculating liabilities will be set out in regulations. The Government has stated that there will be a choice of methods for 'calculating the technical provisions'. The code of practice from the Regulator will, apparently, 'give guidance on factors trustees must consider in determining the appropriate assumptions for their scheme'.

### C. STATEMENT OF FUNDING PRINCIPLES

7.07 Under s 223 of the Act, the trustees will be required to prepare and keep under review a statement of funding principles. According to the legislation, this is the trustees' written statement of their policy for securing that the statutory funding objective is met. The trustees are required to reach agreement with the employer on the terms of the statement (s 229). This is an interesting departure from

---

[3] At Ch 4, para 31.
[4] ibid.

## Statement of Funding Principles

existing requirements to consult with the employer. The clear intention is to ensure that the trustees and employer focus attention on the statutory funding objective and how it should be met. If agreement cannot be reached on the statement of funding principles, then the trustees are likely to need to turn to the Regulator to assist them in reaching a decision on the future of the scheme, including the possibility of a winding up.

**7.08** Trustees will need to obtain an actuarial valuation every year, although this could be reduced to an obligation to produce a valuation every three years so long as an actuarial report is produced for the intervening years covering developments affecting the 'technical provisions' (ie compliance with the Statutory Funding Objective (SFO)) occurring since the last valuation. Much of the detail in relation to obtaining actuarial valuation reports is to be set out in regulations. It is clear, however, that there is an obligation for the actuary to certify compliance with the 'technical provisions'. If after attaining an actuarial valuation report it appears to the trustees that the SFO was not met at the effective date of the valuation, there is also a requirement for a recovery plan (s 226). Under the legislation this will need to be produced within a prescribed period to be set out in regulations. The recovery plan will set out the trustees' strategy for restoring the scheme to its full funding. Trustees are required to take into consideration the nature of the circumstances of the scheme and certain additional factors to be set out in the regulations. In most cases (the exceptions to be set out in regulations) the trustees will need to send a copy to the Regulator.

**7.09** The now familiar employer schedule of contributions introduced under the 1995 Act re-appears in the new legislation (s 227). As now, the schedule of contributions will need to be kept under regular review. Regulations will set out further details on the content, application, and review mechanism for the schedule of contributions. The Act, however, specifies that the schedule of contributions must be certified by the scheme actuary who must state whether in his or her opinion the schedule is consistent with the statement of funding principles and meeting the SFO. The failure to prepare a schedule of contributions must be reported to the Regulator (s 227).

**7.10** As we have seen (in chapter 2) the Regulator has wide powers to freeze benefits and contributions, to replace or add further trustees and to direct the winding up of a scheme. The failure to comply with the legislation on funding will need to be reported to the Regulator, who will monitor the situation closely with a view to applying the appropriate powers accordingly. Where there is a failure to pay contributions, however, this fact only needs to be reported to the Regulator if the trustees 'have reasonable cause to believe that the failure is likely to be of material significance in the exercise by the Regulator of any of its functions' (s 228). This is a curious requirement. It is not unexpected that there may be a requirement to inform the Regulator if there is a failure to make contributions in accordance with the duly prepared schedule of contributions. Nor is it surprising that only breaches which are of 'material significance' need to be reported to the Regulator. However, what is surprising is the requirement for the trustees to decide if the breach is likely to be of significance for the 'exercise of the Regulator's functions'. Surely this is something on which only the Regulator might be able to reach a determination? It is not altogether clear why the trustees are set this test. A test based on the reality of the failure to make payments to the detriment of the solvency and security of the scheme would have made a lot more sense.

## D. AGREEMENT OF THE EMPLOYER

7.11 Section 229 confirms those matters which must be agreed with the employer in relation to funding. These include:

(a) Methods and assumptions used in calculating the scheme's technical provisions;

(b) The content of the statement of funding principles;

(c) Any provisions of a recovery plan; and

(d) The content of the schedule of contributions.

7.12 If it appears to the trustees that employers are not going to be forthcoming, the trustees are able by resolution to modify the scheme as regards future accrual of benefits. This is presumably to allow for the possibility of reduction of the value of benefits promised to accord with the funding available (or security of funding). The modifications cannot affect existing rights of the scheme for past service. In addition, any resolution of modification must be (a) recorded in writing by the trustees; and (b) notified to the active members within one month of the modification taking affect.

## E. ADVICE TO THE ACTUARY

7.13 Under s 230, the actuary's advice is required on the following points:

(a) Any specific method or assumption which is to be used in calculating the scheme's technical provisions;

(b) Preparing or revising the statement of funding principles, a recovery plan, or the schedule of contributions; and

(c) Any modification as regards the future accrual of benefits introduced by resolution of the trustees under s 229.

## F. POWERS FOR THE REGULATOR

Where there is a breach of the requirements in relation to the funding provisions including a failure to prepare a statement of funding principles, where the actuary is unable to provide the relevant funding certificate, or where a schedule of contributions is not agreed or the employer fails to make payments under an agreed schedule, the Regulator's powers (s 231) include:

7.14

(a) Modifying the scheme as to the future accrual of benefits (but not so as to affect adversely any subsisting rights);
(b) Giving directions on how the 'technical provisions' on funding should be calculated;
(c) Determining the period over which the shortfall is to be made up; and
(d) Imposing a schedule of contributions.

# 8
# FINANCIAL PLANNING FOR RETIREMENT

| | |
|---|---|
| A. Introduction | 8.01 |
| B. Legislation | 8.04 |

## A. INTRODUCTION

As proposed in the DWP Green Paper,[1] Pt 4 of the Act provides the Government with wide powers to promote and facilitate planning by individuals for retirement and authorizes the Government to obtain and hold information which will enable individuals to do so. **8.01**

Part 4 also includes powers requiring schemes to provide combined pension forecasts of State and occupational or personal pension provision and requiring employers to provide employees with access to information and advice about pension saving. **8.02**

As some of the clauses allow or require the provision of information about individuals, they may breach the requirements of Arts 8 and/or 10 of the European Convention on Human Rights, but the Government considers that the provisions are proportionate and meet a legitimate aim. Furthermore, they are considered to protect the rights of individuals and to be in the economic interest of the country. **8.03**

## B. LEGISLATION

### 1. Retirement Planning

Section 234 of the Act enables the Secretary of State to encourage and assist individuals to plan financially for retirement by establishing an internet-based retirement planner which will enable an individual to: **8.04**

---

[1] Cm 5677.

(a) Estimate the financial resources the individual will need after retirement;

(b) Estimate the financial resources likely to be available to the individual after his retirement; and

(c) Ascertain what action could be taken to eliminate any shortfall between the financial resources available and those which are needed.

## 2. Provision of Information

**8.05** Under s 235, anyone holding information which the Secretary of State requires to enable him to carry out the functions contained in s 234 is authorized to supply that information to the Secretary of State or to an organization providing services to the Secretary of State. The Secretary of State or other recipient may only pass information relating to an individual to another person or organization other than the individual himself if the individual concerned gives his consent or where the information is to be used in connection with criminal proceedings under the 2004 Act, the PSA 1993, the 1995 Act, or any other enactment corresponding to any of those Acts (s 235(3)).

## 3. Use of Information

**8.06** Whilst some of the information required for the purposes of the retirement planner will be provided by the individual and/or his employer's pension scheme, various government departments already hold a substantial amount of personal information, but only for the purposes for which it was originally supplied. Section 236 and Sch 10 to the Act extend the purposes for which that information can be used to include the encouragement of and assistance with retirement planning.

**8.07** Paragraph 1 of Sch 10 amends s 3 of the Social Security Act 1998 so that any information already held by the Secretary of State for the purposes of social security, child support or war pensions, employment or training can now be used to encourage and assist financial planning for retirement.

**8.08** Paragraph 2 of the Schedule permits the use of information held by the Inland Revenue or Customs and Excise (or a person providing services to either of those organizations) for the same purpose. Finally, para 3 amends s 122D of the Social Security Administration Act 1992 to permit the use of information held by the Secretary of State for the purposes of administering housing benefit or council tax benefit.

## 4. Combined Pension Forecasts

**8.09** In a further attempt to persuade individuals to take an interest in their retirement planning, for some time the Government has been encouraging trustees or managers of occupational and personal pension schemes to provide individuals with a combined pension forecast of their State, occupational, and personal pension benefits. Many of the larger occupational schemes have already started issuing such statements but there has been a poor response from the smaller schemes.

8.10 One of the main reasons for this has been the absence of any power authorizing the Secretary of State to disclose details about State pensions to any individual or organization other than the trustees or managers of the relevant scheme. As many smaller schemes use a third party administrator, such organizations were unable to receive the State pension information from either the trustees or managers or directly from the Secretary of State. However, s 298 of the Act corrects this omission by introducing such a power.

8.11 The Government still hopes that such statements will be provided voluntarily by the trustees or managers but, if this should not occur, s 237 includes reserve powers by which the Secretary of State can require trustees or managers to issue such statements at such time or times as may be specified in regulations.

8.12 The regulations may require the trustees or managers to provide the following information to a member:

(a) State pension information as specified in s 42 of the Child Support, Pensions and Social Security Act 2000 which has been disclosed to the trustees or managers under that section (or is treated as having been disclosed) and is of a description specified in regulations (s 237(2)); and
(b) Information relating to the benefits which are likely to accrue to the member or are capable of being secured by him under the scheme and is of a description specified in regulations (s 237(3)).

8.13 The regulations may also specify the time or times when the information has to be supplied to members (s 237(4)).

## 5. Provision by Employers of Information and Advice to Employees

8.14 As the final piece in the jigsaw of providing employees with information to assist them in their financial planning for retirement, s 238 of the Act includes reserve powers under which the Secretary of State may issue regulations which will require employers to take action to enable employees to obtain information and advice about pensions and saving for retirement.

8.15 The regulations may:

(a) Only apply to employers and employees of a prescribed description;
(b) Make different provisions for different descriptions of employers and employees;
(c) Make provision as to the action to be taken by the employer (including the frequency and time and place at which action is to be taken);

## 8. Financial Planning for Retirement

    (d) Make provision as to the description of information and advice in relation to which requirements apply; and

    (e) Make provision about the description of persons authorized to provide any such advice.

**8.16** Further details of these requirements will not be known until Summer 2005 at the earliest. The Government intends to undertake various pilot studies to decide how to implement these requirements and the results of these studies are unlikely to be known before then.

**8.17** To add some teeth to this requirement, s 238(3) requires employers to account to the Regulator for the action they have taken. Section 238(4) makes provision for further regulations dealing with:

    (a) The information to be provided to the Regulator;

    (b) The form and manner in which the information is to be provided; and

    (c) The period within which the information is to be provided.

**8.18** Failure to provide the information to the Regulator without reasonable excuse may result in penalties under s 10 of the 1995 Act.

**8.19** For the purposes of s 238, 'employer' means any employer, whether or not resident or incorporated in any part of the UK.

# 9

# MISCELLANEOUS PROVISIONS

| A. Introduction | 9.01 |
| --- | --- |
| B. Trustee Obligations | 9.03 |
| C. Employer Obligations | 9.45 |
| D. Scheme Modification | 9.77 |
| E. Pension Disputes | 9.100 |
| F. Scheme Design and Regulatory | 9.143 |

## A. INTRODUCTION

Part 5 of the 2004 Act brings together a number of rather disparate elements within the new legislation. These are largely modifications to, and in some cases expansions upon, the existing legal requirements under the 1995 Act. In some instances these alterations constitute a relaxation of the more prescriptive elements of the existing legislation. Indeed, in promoting the new measures, the Government has made much of the likely administrative and cost savings which may ensue and hence supposedly make occupational pension provision more attractive to employers. However, these simplifications sit alongside increased prescription in other areas and it is also debatable whether the relaxations in relation to, for instance, scheme modification and internal dispute procedures will in fact have any discernable effect in practice.  **9.01**

The main provisions can be usefully divided into those dealing with new trustee and employer obligations, scheme modification, changes in relation to pension dispute handling, scheme benefit design and regulatory issues. These are considered in turn below.  **9.02**

## B. TRUSTEE OBLIGATIONS

### 1. Introduction

9.03 The main provisions of the 2004 Act could be characterized as focusing on the regulation of the employer's relationship with its pension scheme whether in terms of guaranteeing adequate funding of pension promises going forward or dealing with the consequences of employer (and hence scheme) failure. There are nevertheless new, more onerous obligations for trustees of schemes as well, both in the context of the composition of the trustee board and as a result of the imposition of new statutory standards of care to supplement existing case law and best practice.

### 2. New Trustee Duties

9.04 Sections 244 to 249 of Pt 5 set out the obligations of trustees of occupational pension schemes, namely duties in relation to investment, powers and restrictions in relation to borrowing and the requirement for trustees to have adequate knowledge and understanding for the purpose of enabling them to exercise their trustee functions. Existing standards for pension scheme trustees derive from a combination of general trust duties under both statute and case law and more nebulous best practice and governance requirements. These changes should therefore be seen not only in the light of recent developments in the area of corporate governance but also in the context of a desire to codify trustee obligations to a greater extent, reinforcing and expanding upon the specific duties in relation to investment originally imposed by the 1995 Act.

9.05 The new provisions relating to trustee duties and obligations are, in part, a result of the Myners Review of Institutional Investment in the UK in 2001 ('the Myners Review')[1] and the recommendations made therein. Amongst other matters, the Myners Review highlighted the lack of investment understanding amongst trustees. Recommendations were made that there should be a legal obligation for trustees making investment decisions to be familiar with the relevant issues.

9.06 In the Green Paper, issued in December 2002, it was concluded that action should be taken in response to the Myners Review but with the focus on trustees' investment obligations rather than any wider duties. These principles relating to investment duties have been adopted in ss 244 to 249 of the Act but widened to all areas which trustees need to be familiar with. These sections of the Act are also designed to comply with the requirements of the EU

---

[1] Myners Review of Institutional Investment in the UK, March 2001 available at www.hm-treasury.gov.uk.

Pensions Directive[2] which is due to be implemented in the UK by September 2005.

9.07 Whilst there is little in the new obligations to argue with, and few would criticize the principle that trustees should have appropriate knowledge to perform their functions, the logical consequence of these changes is likely to be the decline of the UK's admirable tradition of lay trusteeship. Increasingly ordinary scheme members are likely to be reluctant to assume what is perceived to be an increasingly onerous role, a development which, of course, sits rather uncomfortably with the requirements of the Member Nominated Trustee (MNT) provisions (see paras 9.29 to 9.44 below) and the Government's stated objective of improving member representation and involvement.

## 3. Investment Principles

9.08 Section 244 requires that the existing s 35 of the 1995 Act (investment principles) will be replaced by a new s 35. However, the new section contains largely the same provisions as the previous one, the most noticeable difference being a requirement to review the statement of investment principles at specified intervals (albeit the duration of the intervals are yet to be confirmed by regulations) rather than the previous requirement to revise the statement from time to time.

9.09 The new s 35 provides that the trustees of an occupational pension scheme must ensure that a statement of investment principles is prepared and maintained (ie a written statement of the investment principles governing decisions about investments for the purposes of the scheme). Regulations will be introduced to cover most of the new provisions relating to the statement of investment principles and will set out:

(a) How often the statement of investment principles will need to be reviewed. It is expected that regulations will specify that the statement must be reviewed at least every three years, as this will comply with the requirements of Art 12 of the EU Pensions Directive;

(b) What requirements trustees must comply with before implementing a statement of investment principles. Regulations are likely to specify that, before a statement is prepared or revised, trustees must obtain and consider written advice from an investment manager and must consult with the employer;

(c) What form the statement of investment principles should take;

(d) What the statement should cover. It is anticipated that the statement will be required to cover the following:
  (i) the kind of investments to be held;
  (ii) the balance between the different types of investments;

---

[2] Directive 2003/41 of the European Parliament and the Council on the activities and supervision of institutions for occupational retirement provision (IORPs) [2003] OJ L235/10.

(iii) risk;
(iv) expected returns on investments;
(v) the extent (if at all) to which social, environmental, or ethical considerations are taken into account in the selection, retention and realization of investments; and
(vi) if relevant, trustee policy in relation to the exercise of the rights (including voting rights) attaching to investments;
(e) schemes that will be exempt from the requirements.

9.10 Section 244 provides that trust schemes cannot, either through the statement of investment principles or otherwise, impose any restriction on the power to make investments which requires the consent of the employer (as opposed to the employer's right to be consulted).[3]

9.11 The section also covers the penalties to be imposed on trustees who fail to take all reasonable steps to secure compliance with the provisions. These are civil penalties in accordance with s 10 of the 1995 Act.

9.12 There has been no clear guidance on when the above provisions (and the other provisions of the Act dealing with trustee investment and borrowing (see paras 9.13 to 9.16 below)) will come into operation but it is unlikely that they will commence before the EU Pensions Directive implementation date of September 2005.

## 4. Power to Make Regulations Governing Investment by Trustees

9.13 Section 245 amends s 36 of the 1995 Act (choosing investments) to allow regulations to be introduced to govern choice of investment by trustees. The previous s (36)2 stated that trustees, or fund managers, should have regard to the need for diversification of investments and the suitability to the scheme of the investments. This subsection will be deleted and regulations will expand upon the current provisions to specify criteria to be applied in choosing investments. The amendment is designed to ensure compliance with Art 18(1) of the EU Pensions Directive which requires investments to be carried out in accordance with the 'prudent persons' principle which is a key concept of the directive.

9.14 It is expected that regulations will provide that the following should be taken into account when choosing investments:

(a) Investments should not adversely affect the overall quality of the investment fund;
(b) Investments should be made predominantly on regulated markets;

---

[3] Recent case law (*Pitmans Trustees v The Telecommunications Group plc* [2004] 32 PBLR) has emphasized that the employer's right to be consulted should be properly observed. In this particular case the trustees did not give the employer sufficient time to make meaningful comments on the proposed change in investment strategy.

(c) Any investments in derivatives should contribute towards a strategy of risk reduction or efficient portfolio management.

The remainder of the existing provisions of s 36 of the 1995 Act (mostly dealing with the need to obtain proper advice when exercising powers of investment) generally remain the same, although a new s 36(9) has been added to allow the above provisions to be disapplied in relation to certain schemes. These schemes will be described in regulations but it is anticipated that an exemption will be considered for small schemes where all the active members are trustees.  9.15

## 5. Borrowing by Trustees

Section 246 deals with borrowing by trustees and inserts a new s 36A into the 1995 Act. This provision has been introduced in order to comply with Art 18(2) of the EU Pensions Directive. This prohibits pension schemes generally from borrowing or acting as a guarantor on behalf of third parties. Some borrowing is permitted under the directive but only for liquidity purposes and on a temporary basis. The new provision inserted into the 1995 Act will allow borrowing only in prescribed cases to be set out in regulations. It is expected that regulations will specify that trustees may borrow subject to the restrictions set out in the EU Pensions Directive and will prohibit trustees from guaranteeing loans. It is also anticipated that regulations will provide that schemes may be exempt where they are small in nature and all active members are trustees.  9.16

## 6. Requirement for Knowledge and Understanding of Trustees

Sections 247 to 249 contain the new more specific requirements for trustees to have knowledge and understanding in relation to their pension scheme. Case law over the years has confirmed that trustees should be familiar with their scheme documents and should be judged on what they ought to know rather than what they do know.[4] Sections 247 to 249 convert this case law principle and others into statutory duties.  9.17

Section 247 is relevant to individual trustees of occupational pension schemes and provides that the trustees must be conversant with:  9.18

(a) The trust deed and rules;

(b) The statement of investment principles (if one is required);

(c) The statement of funding principles (if appropriate); and

(d) Any other documents recording policies for the time being adopted by the trustees relating to the administration of the scheme generally.

---

[4] See, for example, *Lansing Linde v Alber* [2000] OPLR 1 and *AMP (UK) v Barker* [2001] Pens LR 77.

## 9. Miscellaneous Provisions

9.19 In addition, trustees must have knowledge and understanding of the law in relation to pensions and trusts and the principles relating to the funding and investment of occupational pension schemes. Additional areas where trustees will be required to have knowledge and understanding may be introduced by regulations (although there has been no indication at present that any further areas will be introduced).

9.20 The section also provides that the degree of knowledge and understanding required will be that appropriate for the purposes of enabling the individual to exercise his functions as trustee. The Regulator will issue a code of practice which will hopefully clarify what is meant by knowledge and understanding by setting out more details of the kind of knowledge, training, experience, or qualifications regarded as necessary to fulfil the requirements of the section.

9.21 In relation to the duty to have knowledge and understanding of the law, it is expected that the level required will not be too onerous. Also, it is anticipated that trustees will not be expected to have knowledge of law which is not relevant to their scheme (for example, trustees of public sector schemes would not be expected to be as familiar with the statutory debt on employer provisions of s 75 of the 1995 Act as trustees of private sector schemes).

9.22 In relation to the duty to have knowledge and understanding of funding and investment principles, it is expected that the level required may vary amongst trustees of a scheme where there is a funding/investment sub-committee. Here, it is anticipated that trustees on the sub-committee would be expected to have sufficient understanding to review issues knowledgeably (again, hopefully the code of practice will expand on what this means) but those not on the sub-committee would only be expected to have a basic understanding.

9.23 Much has been made in the press of the need for trustees to undergo regular training in order to comply with these new requirements. It is likely that training will not be made mandatory and that the Regulator will test the duty by looking at how well schemes are operated, rather than by requesting information on how many training courses trustees have attended. However, in practice, regular training will obviously be seen as a way of helping to discharge the duties, and training bodies are already planning new trustee qualifications which, if gained, would obviously increase member confidence in trustees. It is, of course, debatable whether the new trustee standards of care actually impose a greater burden on trustees in reality or whether they are simply statutory restatements of existing pension trust principles.

9.24 Section 248 basically sets out the same provisions as s 247 but in relation to corporate trustees. Here the obligation is on the trustee company to ensure that each individual who exercises any function which the company has as a trustee of the scheme is conversant with the trust deed and rules, statements of investment and funding principles, and other relevant documentation and has the necessary level of knowledge and understanding. Knowledge and understanding in this context must be appropriate for the purpose of enabling the individual properly to exercise the function in question.

Section 249 contains supplementary provisions relating to knowledge and understanding and, in particular, states that regulations may provide for the above provisions not to apply in prescribed circumstances, or to apply with some modification. It is expected that these regulations will exempt from the duties the following: 9.25

(a) Newly appointed trustees until a reasonable period of time has elapsed;

(b) A trustee who is the sole member of the scheme; and

(c) A trustee of a trust scheme where all the members are trustees.

The section also states that the provisions will not affect any rule of law requiring a trustee to have knowledge of, or expertise in, any matter. 9.26

There is no concrete guidance at present as to how the Regulator will enforce these provisions. However, it is expected that the Regulator will have a primarily educative rather than a punitive role. As mentioned (see para 9.23 above), it is likely that the Regulator will regard well run schemes as having complied with the duty and will only become involved in assessing compliance where schemes are at risk in general. 9.27

It is anticipated that these provisions relating to trustees' knowledge and understanding will take effect by April 2006. 9.28

### 7. Requirements for Member Nominated Trustees and Directors

(a) *Background*

The original Member Nominated Trustee (MNT) provisions were regarded as one of the central planks of member protection introduced by the 1995 Act. It was felt that increased member representation on trustee boards would ensure greater monitoring of scheme procedures and prevent employer manipulation of trustee decision-making. However, the current protections have been subject to considerable criticism from a variety of quarters. From the trade unions' perspective the protection they provide to members is inadequate because only one third of the trustee board needs to be member nominated and, in fact, the employer can choose to opt-out of the MNT requirements altogether. From the employers' point of view, the regulations are overly prescriptive and unnecessarily complex. The new provisions have gone some way towards addressing the concerns of both constituencies. 9.29

Sections 241 to 243 of Pt 5 set out the new requirements for MNTs and Member Nominated Directors of Corporate Trustees (MNDs). These provisions replace the existing MNT requirements (contained in sections 16 to 21 of the 1995 Act). 9.30

In order for the requirements under the 1995 Act to be met, either: 9.31

(a) The employer had to put forward proposals to the pension scheme membership for approval (the so-called 'employer opt-out'); or

## 9. Miscellaneous Provisions

(b) The trustees had to arrange for at least one third of their number to be selected by the members (if the scheme had 100 or more members there had to be at least two MNTs. For schemes with less than 100 members there had to be at least one MNT).

**9.32** Following the introduction of the original MNT/MND provisions, in practice many schemes went down the 'employer opt-out' route. The employer opt-out was inserted in the 1995 Act following consultation because it was recognized that many schemes already operated trustee arrangements which allowed for some form of member representation without necessarily complying with the one third minimum or the rigid nomination and election procedures specified in the legislation. Nevertheless, the opt-out process itself was still quite complicated. Having notified the trustees that it wished to put forward opt-out arrangements, the employer had a maximum period of six months to obtain approval to the arrangements. The employer had to seek views on its proposals from the members, under the 'statutory consultation procedures' laid down in regulations under the 1995 Act.[5] The employer had to obtain the approval of eligible members. This meant at least active and pensioner members. The trustees could also decide that some or all of the deferred members should be included in the consultation process and, if so, had to advise the employer accordingly. The employer had to write to each eligible member giving notice of its proposals, and had to provide certain information as laid down under the statutory consultation procedures. Members had to be given at least one calendar month in which to object. The employer could choose from two methods to get the members' approval to the proposals, the objection method and the direct ballot route:

(a) Under the objection method, the employer put its proposals to the eligible members for approval. If sufficient numbers of eligible members objected (generally 10% or more), the employer could put forward revised proposals (providing there was still sufficient time to do so within the initial six months approval period) or the trustees would have to ensure the default rules were applied, ie that one third of the trustees were selected by the membership;

(b) Under the direct ballot method, the eligible members were balloted at the outset.

**9.33** Employer arrangements implemented in 1996/7 and new ones made since then (for example when a new scheme was established) were originally given approval for six years. However, regulations[6] which came into force on 6 October 2002 extended the period, for all arrangements already in place at that date, to

---

[5] The Occupational Pension Schemes (Member-Nominated Trustees and Directors) Regulations 1996 (SI 1996/1216).

[6] The Occupational Pension Schemes (Member-Nominated Trustees and Directors) Amendment Regulations 2002 (SI 2002/2327).

ten years. All new arrangements made on or after 6 October 2002 were given approval for four years, in view of the Government's proposals to review the existing MNT framework.

(b) *The new provisions*
The most noticeable change within the new provisions is the removal of the employer opt-out procedure. 9.34

Section 241 deals with the new requirement for MNTs. It provides that trustees of an occupational pension scheme must put in place arrangements, within a reasonable period of the commencement date, to ensure that at least one third of all trustees are member nominated. The provisions are expected to be in place by April 2006 and trustees will have to follow these requirements when their existing arrangements come to an end after that date. There is no longer any requirement, as there was under the 1995 Act, for a minimum of two member nominated trustees (or one in the case of a scheme with less than one hundred members). It is possible to have more MNTs than is required to meet the minimum but this must be approved by the employer. The term 'reasonable period' is used here and appears several times within the new provisions. A code of practice will be issued by the Regulator on the meaning of this phrase. 9.35

MNTs are defined as trustees of an occupational pension scheme who are: 9.36

(a) Nominated via a procedure involving at least all active members and pensioner members of the scheme or organizations which adequately represent those classes of members. The Regulator will issue a code of practice dealing with the issue of what will count as an 'adequately representative organisation' for the purposes of ss 241 and 242; and

(b) Selected through a process in which some or all members of the scheme can participate. This includes active, deferred, pensioner, and pension credit members.

The nomination and selection procedure must take place within a reasonable time of the requirement arising. Where a position is not filled because the number of nominations received is insufficient, the process must be repeated at reasonable intervals until such time as the vacancy is filled. 9.37

It is possible for a person who is not a member of the scheme to be a MNT but employer approval will be required. In addition, where the number of nominations is equal to or less than the number of vacancies, the nominees may be deemed to be selected. 9.38

As under the existing legislation, in order to remove a MNT, the agreement of all other trustees is required and it is not permitted to exclude MNTs from carrying out the same functions as the other trustees simply on the basis of being MNTs. 9.39

## 9. Miscellaneous Provisions

9.40 The requirement for a scheme to have MNTs does not apply where:

(a) Every member of the scheme is a trustee of the scheme and no other person is such a trustee;

(b) Every trustee of the scheme is a company (in which case the requirements for MNDs (s 242, see para 9.42 below) may apply) or;

(c) The scheme is of a prescribed description. Regulations will elaborate and it is expected that they will provide that the same types of scheme that are currently exempt from the MNT requirements under the 1995 Act will also be exempt under these provisions (for instance, schemes with only one member, schemes providing death benefits only, and schemes where the employer has become insolvent and an independent trustee is required to be or has been appointed).

9.41 As under the existing legislation where any trustee fails to take reasonable steps to comply with the member nominated trustee requirements, civil penalties in accordance with s 10 of the 1995 Act will apply.

9.42 Section 242 provides that similar provisions will apply where a company is a trustee of an occupational pension scheme and every other trustee is also a company (although references to MNTs are replaced with references to MNDs). Where a trustee company is the trustee of two or more occupational pension schemes the provisions have effect as if the schemes were a single scheme and the members of the two or more schemes were members of a single scheme. However, the trustee company can elect not to aggregate the schemes in this way or to only aggregate some of its schemes. Professional trustees are likely to take advantage of this particular provision for obvious reasons.

9.43 Alan Johnson, Secretary of State for Work and Pensions, announced at the Trade Union Congress in October 2004, that the then Pensions Bill would be amended to require that 50% of trustees should be member nominated. In his reasoning for this change he commented that this may help employees feel they have a say in the running of their pension scheme and, as a result, could encourage more new joiners. He also commented that more MNTs would mean more varied experience to draw upon in the trustee board. The amendment that eventually made its way into the Act is contained in s 243. It provides that the Secretary of State may amend ss 241 and 242 at some point in the future to provide that the requirements for one third of MNTs/MNDs may be altered to a requirement for one half of all trustees to be member nominated. The change to 50% representation will not be introduced immediately but it is anticipated that this may be in force by 2008. It is not clear whether professional independent trustees would be included in the 50% split. There will no doubt be concern for such trustees over how this provision may affect them where there is no insolvency of the employer. If they are not included in the 50% member nominated part of the trustee board, an employer may be reluctant to further dilute its own position by appointing a professional independent trustee. Equally, however, the increasingly onerous obligations imposed upon trustees may well lead to a shortage of willing candidates from the membership and professional trustees may be the only viable option particularly in the context of closed schemes with few or no active members.

Section 243 also provides that regulations may be introduced to modify the provisions of ss 241 and 242 in certain cases. **9.44**

## C. EMPLOYER OBLIGATIONS

### 1. Introduction

As already noted, much of the new Act is concerned with increased regulation of the employer's relationship with the pension scheme which it sponsors. The specific employer obligations highlighted in Pt 5 of the 2004 Act focus on the need to protect members in the event of a business sale and in relation to employer proposals to restructure or remove existing pension arrangements (whether in a pre or post sale context or otherwise). Both sets of changes need to be examined in the light of wider UK and European employment law obligations and recent developments in these areas. **9.45**

### 2. Pension Protection on Transfer of Employment

(a) *Introduction*

Sections 257 and 258 of Pt 5 set out the new protections for pension rights on the transfer of employment. Historically, rights under an occupational pension scheme have not automatically transferred on change of employer. The terms of the Transfer of Undertakings (Protection of Employment) Regulations 1981 (TUPE) (under which the UK implemented the EU Acquired Rights Directive ('the Acquired Rights Directive')),[7] provide that all employment related rights and liabilities are generally transferred to the new employer where there has been a transfer of the whole or part of an undertaking which is covered by the regulations.[8] However, reg 7 of TUPE excludes from the transfer any rights under an occupational pension scheme relating to 'old age, invalidity or survivors' benefits'. Rights in relation to personal pension schemes as opposed to employer sponsored occupational pension schemes do not fall within the exclusion. Consequently, the contractual right of an employee to payment of a certain level of employer contributions into his personal pension scheme will become an obligation of the receiving employer. **9.46**

In practice, however, recent case law has cast considerable doubt on the extent of this so-called 'pensions exception' in the context of occupational pension **9.47**

---

[7] Directive 1977/187 [1977] OJ L61/26.
[8] Transfer of Undertakings (Protection of Employment) Regulations 1981, reg 5.

## 9. Miscellaneous Provisions

schemes. In the case of *Beckmann v Dynamco Whicheloe Macfarlane Ltd*[9] the claimant successfully argued that exclusion of rights under an occupational pension scheme relating to 'old age, invalidity or survivors' benefits' did not encompass early retirement pensions on redundancy and consequently these rights were held to transfer under TUPE.

9.48 The European Court's subsequent decision in *Martin v South Bank University*[10] reinforced the conclusion and went on to suggest that there was no reason in principle to distinguish early retirement rights on redundancy from early retirement in other circumstances (ie a more general right to retire prior to normal retirement age might also fall outside the TUPE exception). The full scope and meaning of these decisions is still unclear.

9.49 It has long been recognized that there are difficulties with the interpretation of TUPE in a pensions context and issues in relation to whether the UK legislation accurately reflects the requirements and intention of the Acquired Rights Directive. Moreover, the pensions exception does not sit well with European law generally under which pensions have been regarded as pay and consequently have been accorded treatment consistent with other components of pay.

9.50 Amendments made to the Acquired Rights Directive in 1998 allowed Member States to take further steps to protect pension obligations on transfer of a business should they wish to do so. In light of these developments, the Government began a detailed consultation process in September 2001.[11] The original proposals and options outlined in the 2001 consultation paper were narrowed down and included within the wider proposals on pension provision generally contained within the 2002 Green Paper and further refined in the White Paper issued in 2003.

9.51 In the White Paper, the Government commented that they intended to amend the pension exclusion in TUPE to achieve a degree of fairness for transferring workers but to balance this with the need to avoid placing an excessive burden on receiving employers. Consequently, they proposed 'a flexible and worthwhile provision for a contribution to a stakeholder pension'.[12] It was envisaged that this would take the form of an obligation to match employee contributions up to 6%. This is the basis of the provisions to be found in the 2004 Act.

(b) *Individuals covered by the new protections*

9.52 Section 257 sets out the individuals who will be protected by the new provisions. Where there has been a transfer of the whole or part of an undertaking which is covered by TUPE and where, immediately before the transfer, the transferring

---

[9] Case C–164/00 [2002] ECR I–4893.
[10] Case C–4/01, not yet reported.
[11] Public Consultation Document—Transfer of Undertakings (Protection of Employment) Regulations 1981 (TUPE)—Government proposals for reform.
[12] Chapter 2, para 31 of the White Paper.

employer participated in an occupational pension scheme, then an employee will be protected by the new provisions where:

(a) The employee was an active member of the occupational pension scheme;

(b) The employee was eligible to become a member of the occupational pension scheme; or

(c) The employee was not eligible to join the occupational pension scheme but if he had been employed by the transferring employer for a longer period of time he would have been eligible.

In any of these cases, if the scheme provides money purchase benefits in order for the employee to qualify for protection the employer must either have been required to contribute to the scheme on behalf of the employee (or have contributed notwithstanding that it was not obliged to).

9.53 It is interesting that prospective members are covered here (under (c) above) but only if they would have been eligible had they been employed longer. There are other ways in which employees may become eligible to join occupational pension schemes which are not dealt with, for instance, achieving a specific age or a certain pay grade.

9.54 The section also provides that the categories of employee set out in (a) to (c) above will still be protected if the transferring employer took any action, by reason of the TUPE transfer, to withdraw the occupational pension scheme.

(c) *The new protections*

9.55 The form of protection to be offered to the relevant categories of employee is set out in s 258. It will be a condition of those individuals' contracts of employment that one of two alternatives will apply following the transfer.

9.56 The first alternative is that the receiving employer must make sure that the employee becomes a member or becomes eligible to be a member of an occupational pension scheme in which the employer participates. If the scheme is money purchase in nature the employer must make contributions on behalf of the employee at a level to be set out in regulations (see para 9.58 below) (or be required to make such contributions if the eligible employee subsequently joins the scheme). If the scheme is not money purchase, the scheme must either satisfy the statutory standard for contracted out salary related schemes ('the Reference Scheme Test')[13] or an alternative requirement prescribed in regulations. The draft regulations provide that the alternative requirement will be that the overall value of the benefits must be at least equal to benefits under the transferring employer's scheme. Therefore, if the transferring employer's scheme exceeds the requirements of the Reference Scheme Test, the receiving employer can provide, as a minimum, benefits which meet the Reference Scheme Test. However, if the transferring employer's scheme does not meet the Reference Scheme Test, the

---

[13] Pensions Schemes Act 1993, s 12A.

receiving employer will have to provide overall equivalent value benefits. If the value of the benefits in the transferring employer's scheme are reduced prior to the transfer and by reason of the transfer then the draft regulations provide that the value of the benefits will be taken to be the previous higher value. It is not clear how this will be policed. Presumably, employees affected will be able to bring claims in the employment tribunal.

9.57 The second alternative is for the receiving employer to make contributions (at a rate to be set by regulations) to a stakeholder pension scheme of which the employee is a member. If the employee is not a member of a stakeholder pension scheme the employer must offer to make such contributions to a stakeholder scheme that the employee is eligible to join and the employer must not withdraw the offer to contribute. This alternative is much less burdensome for the receiving employer and will probably be chosen in most cases, except where the receiving employer already offers some form of defined benefit arrangement and wishes to harmonize the pension terms of its employees on that more generous basis.

9.58 The draft regulations provide that the rate of contributions to be made to the receiving employer's money purchase scheme or a stakeholder pension scheme will match employee contributions up to a maximum of 6% (ie the employer must contribute 6% if the employee pays 6%). Contributions must be based on basic pay and must be calculated each time remuneration is paid to the employee. A problem in practice will be that many transferring employers will have reserved the right to vary the contribution rate but it is unclear whether this right will transfer to the receiving employer.

9.59 It is disappointing that the new provisions do not clarify the issues of interpretation highlighted in the *Beckmann*[14] and *Martin*[15] cases mentioned above. Consequently, the new provisions should be regarded as little more than a statutory minimum whilst actual pension obligations will still need to be assessed in light of potential contractual commitments, agreements with employees and unions and (in the context of public sector outsourcing) wider government policy guidelines.

9.60 Section 258 also provides that the employee and receiving employer can agree to contract out of these requirements although, presumably, this will only happen in practice if the employee is compensated in some way. There is no guidance as to how such contracting out can be achieved without breaching more general restrictions on contracting out of TUPE.

9.61 The intention is to have the pension protection provisions in place by April 2005.

---

[14] See n 9 above.
[15] See n 10 above.

## 3. Consultation by Employers

(a) *Background*

**9.62** Sections 259 to 261 of Pt 5 set out the new duties of consultation by employers in relation to pension changes. These requirements need to be viewed both in the light of wider developments in the field of employment law and in the context of an increasing number of employers seeking to reduce or remove final salary pension provision for existing employees in response to stock market falls, improved mortality, and other factors.

**9.63** There has previously been no specific legislative requirement for employers, trustees, or scheme administrators to consult on proposed changes to a pension scheme although, depending upon the nature of the change, and whether pension rights are regarded as contractual in a particular case, wider employment law requirements may have an impact.

**9.64** Existing employer obligations in respect of alterations to pension provision derive from a variety of sources, including statutory notification procedures, the terms of the scheme documentation, commitments under employment contracts or collective bargaining agreements, and the implied duty of mutual trust and confidence within the employment relationship.[16] There are, for instance, requirements under statute to notify members of changes to the scheme and to inform members and consult with recognized trade unions in the context of a decision to contract out of the state scheme.[17] It would be highly unusual for the scheme's own terms to require consultation with scheme members (as opposed to the trustees) in relation to prospective alterations, although a requirement to notify employees of forthcoming changes within a set period is much more common. A contractual entitlement to a particular type or level of pension provision is relatively rare in modern service contracts but even so the employer may well consider a process of member communication and consultation to be a necessary means of reducing the risk of industrial action or employee and trustee resistance to its proposals generally and to avoid a charge of breaching the duty of mutual trust and confidence.

**9.65** Nevertheless, whilst it is seen as good practice to consult with (as opposed to simply notify) members in relation to proposed changes, in the past it has been rare for meaningful consultation to occur. Recent years have, however, seen an increasing number of employers moving towards a greater degree of workforce involvement in pension changes with, for instance, members of an existing final salary scheme being offered the option of, say, higher contributions, reduced benefits or a later normal retirement date. The new

---

[16] This principle was formally extended to the pension scheme context by the decision in *Imperial Group Pensions Trust Limited v Imperial Tobacco* [1991] 1 WLR 589.

[17] The Occupational Pension Schemes (Disclosure of Information) Regulations 1996 (SI 1996/1655) and the Occupational Pension Schemes (Contracting out) Regulations 1996 (SI 1996/1172).

9.66 The main criticism of the new requirements from an employee and trade union perspective will undoubtedly be that, although those provisions are a step forward, they are not enough as there is no requirement for negotiation and agreement, simply consultation.

(b) *The new duty to consult*

9.67 Section 259 covers the new consultation requirement in relation to occupational pension schemes. It provides that regulations may require an employer who is proposing to make certain decisions in relation to the scheme, or who has been notified by the trustees or those responsible for the management of the scheme that they propose to make such decisions, to consult with certain individuals in a prescribed manner before such decisions are made. Likewise, regulations may require the trustees or those responsible for the management of the scheme not to make any prescribed decisions unless they have notified the employer and have been satisfied that the employer has undertaken the required steps on consultation.

9.68 The types of decisions which are expected to be covered in regulations are those changing future pension arrangements which will be classed as major or significant changes such as:

(a) Winding up a scheme;

(b) Closure to further accrual of benefits;

(c) Closure to new members;

(d) Conversion from defined benefit to defined contribution; and

(e) Significantly reducing or removing the employer contribution level to a defined contribution scheme.

9.69 It remains to be seen whether more limited alterations such as an increase in the employee contribution rate, a reduction in the future accrual rate or a change to normal retirement age will count as sufficiently significant to require consultation.

9.70 The definition of 'employer' and those employers to be exempt from the requirements will be set out in regulations.

9.71 Regulations will also elaborate on the individuals who must be consulted. It is expected that the consultation will involve prospective and active affected members only and not deferreds or pensioners.

9.72 Section 260 deals with personal pensions in a similar manner. This section provides that regulations may require an employer, who makes contributions to a personal pension scheme for or on behalf of at least one of its employees, to consult with certain individuals in the prescribed manner if it proposes to make certain decisions before those decisions can be made. Once again, the definition of employer and the individuals who must be consulted are to be set out in regulations. It is expected that the types of decisions that will require consultation are decisions resulting in the removal or substantial reduction of the employer contribution towards the arrangement.

9.73 As we have already seen, the bulk of the new provisions will be contained in regulations. Section 261 expands further upon the matters which may be covered by the secondary legislation as follows:

(a) The time permitted for consultation. Employers will presumably welcome certainty here as they will not wish to be prevented indefinitely from implementing changes which could have a cost implication;

(b) The type of information to be provided in a consultation exercise;

(c) The fact that, in certain cases, the employer will have some discretion over who needs to be consulted;

(d) Employees may be able to be consulted via representatives;

(e) The methods by which employee representatives can be selected and the requirement/authorization for holding a ballot;

(f) Employee representatives will be afforded protection against suffering any detriment or unfair dismissal by reason of carrying out their consultation duties. They also must be given adequate time and remuneration to carry out their consultation duties;

(g) The Regulator may be able to waive and relax requirements in certain cases; and

(h) The employer may be required to communicate to the trustees or those responsible for the management of the scheme any representations received.

9.74 Both ss 259 and 260 provide that if those charged with duties fail to comply with the specified steps, the decision taken will still be valid. However, s 261 states that the Regulator will have the power to monitor the situation by requiring those responsible for consultation to provide information about action they have taken to comply. It is expected that employers who fail to consult could face fines of up to £50,000. Moreover, s 259(2) provides that regulations may require the trustees or managers of a scheme not to make a prescribed decision unless they have both notified the employer of the proposed decision and they are satisfied that the employer has undertaken any required consultation. Depending on the extent of the regulations, it may therefore be the case that trustees will be prevented from, for instance, consenting to a scheme amendment proposed by the employer where inadequate consultation has taken place.

9.75 Finally, s 261 also makes it clear that the duty to consult under the above sections will not affect any duties to consult imposed by other law. This provision could be problematic as it means that these consultation requirements will run alongside the consultation obligations contained in the new Information

## 9. Miscellaneous Provisions

and Consultation of Employees Regulations 2004[18] ('the ICE Regulations') (which are required to be implemented further to the European Information and Consultation Directive agreed in March 2002). The ICE Regulations will come into force on 6 April 2005 and will give employees new rights to be informed and consulted about issues that affect their employment and the prospects of the business, including where decisions are being made which are likely to lead to substantial changes in work organization or contractual relations (which could cover pension and welfare issues). The ICE Regulations set out different duties for employers (in some cases, if appropriate consultation practices are in place, employers will be exempt from the strict standard provisions) and the penalties for failure to comply also differ. In practice, employers will have to be familiar with both pieces of legislation and adhere to whichever duties are most onerous.

9.76 The Government intends to have all consultation requirements under the 2004 Act in place from April 2006.

### D. SCHEME MODIFICATION

#### 1. Introduction

9.77 Following the Report of the Pensions Law Review Committee[19] in 1993, the Government accepted the report's recommendation that amendments which detrimentally affect the accrued rights of scheme members should not generally be permitted. This principle was enshrined in s 67 of the 1995 Act (restriction on powers to alter schemes). This section permitted occupational pension schemes to modify existing accrued rights and entitlements with retrospective effect only if members' consents to the change were obtained or the scheme actuary certified that the modification would not adversely affect any member in respect of his entitlement to accrued rights.

9.78 Since it came into effect on 6 April 1997, the legal and actuarial professions have spent a considerable amount of time determining the precise meaning and application of s 67. The strictness of the certification requirements has meant that many actuaries have been unable to provide the necessary certification where changes are proposed. Even if the number of members affected or the impact of the change is minor in comparison with the advantages to the employer and trustees in making the change, s 67 operates to prevent the change being introduced. To compound these difficulties the precise meanings of 'modification', 'members', and 'accrued rights and entitlements' have also come under close scrutiny in an attempt to determine whether or not a proposed amendment falls within the scope of s 67. In response to these practical

---

[18] SI 2004/3426.
[19] Chairman and author, Prof Roy Goode (30 September 1993).

difficulties in altering members' accrued rights and entitlements, the pensions industry called for the simplification of s 67.

## 2. New Provisions on Modification of Pension Rights

Section 262 replaces s 67 of the 1995 Act with ten new sections (67 to 67I). It sets out the scope of the 'subsisting rights' sections which are being inserted into the 1995 Act in place of the current s 67 and the requirements which must be satisfied when making a change to a scheme which would or might have a detrimental effect on any member's accrued rights. Like the original s 67, the replacement section applies to any power that a person has to modify an occupational pension scheme other than a public service scheme and extends the exemption to cover 'a prescribed scheme or a scheme of a prescribed description'. It is understood that this is intended only to enable unapproved retirement benefit schemes to be amended without reference to s 67. It remains to be seen whether lobbying from the pensions industry will result in any further exemptions when the relevant regulations are being drawn up. The revised s 67 also replaces the term 'accrued rights and entitlements' with the term 'subsisting rights'.   9.79

'Subsisting rights' are defined under the new s 67A as accrued rights to future benefits under an occupational pension scheme at the time of the modification or any other entitlement to benefits which a person has at the time of the modification under the scheme rules (including any pension credit granted as part of a pension sharing order). For so long as a member remains in pensionable service, his subsisting rights are determined as if he had opted to terminate his service immediately before the time of the modification. In relation to a survivor of a member of the scheme, the term includes any entitlement to a survivor's benefit in payment or right to any future benefits. In addition to this basic definition three types of modification are identified: a protected modification, a detrimental modification, and a regulated modification (the latter simply being defined as a modification which is either or both of the two other types of modification).   9.80

A 'protected modification' is a modification to an occupational pension scheme which would or might result in either a member's (or survivor's) subsisting rights under the scheme becoming money purchase benefits, or a reduction in the prevailing rate of pensions in payment under the scheme rules. Section 67B requires that in these circumstances the trustees must give the member a written explanation of the proposed modification and its effect on him, telling him he is entitled to make representations, and giving him a reasonable opportunity to do so. They must also obtain his written consent to the modification.   9.81

A 'detrimental modification' is one which would or might adversely affect either a member's (or survivor's) subsisting rights under the scheme. In these circumstances, the trustees can either obtain the member's (or survivor's)   9.82

consent in accordance with the terms of s 67B or comply with the actuarial equivalence requirements of ss 67C and 67D. Three elements make up the actuarial equivalence requirements: the information requirements, the actuarial value requirement, and the actuarial equivalence statement.

9.83 In order to satisfy the information requirement the trustees must, before the modification is made, inform the member that the actuarial equivalence requirements are being applied and provide a written explanation of the proposed modification and its effect on him. The member must be informed that he is entitled to make representations and given a reasonable opportunity to do so.

9.84 The actuarial value requirement places a duty on the trustees to take steps to satisfy themselves that the actuarial value of the member's (or survivor's) subsisting rights after the modification will be equal to or greater than the value of their subsisting rights immediately before it.

9.85 The third requirement is that within a reasonable period from the date the modification takes effect, the trustees must obtain a statement from the scheme actuary that the actuarial value of the member's (or survivor's) subsisting rights after the modification will be equal to or greater than the value of his subsisting rights immediately before it.

9.86 Whether a protected or a detrimental modification is being sought, s 67E requires the trustees either to confirm their willingness to exercise the amendment powers vested in them under the scheme's trust deed or, where the power is vested either jointly with or solely in some other person (such as the employer), to consent to the power being exercised. In either case, the trustees must first be satisfied that the information and (where appropriate) the actuarial equivalence requirements have been met. Where a member's consent has been obtained, the trustees are required to approve the modification within a reasonable period after the date the member first gave his consent. The trustees cannot therefore proceed with the modification where there has been an unreasonable delay.

9.87 The trustees are then required by s 67F to notify all affected members that they intend to exercise their powers to make the modification. In the case of a member who has consented to the change, this notification must be prior to the date that the modification is to take effect. If the actuarial equivalence requirements are being used, the notification requirement is relaxed slightly so that it must be given as soon as is reasonable.

9.88 Any exercise of an amendment power that does not comply with the subsisting rights provisions is voidable at the direction of the Regulator under the terms of s 67G and 67H. Where the Regulator believes that a modification will be in breach of s 67, he can make a direction, either before or after the date when the modification takes effect, that the modification powers should not be exercised at all. Alternatively, the Regulator may direct that the modification must itself be modified in some way within specified time limits, for example that only that part of the modification in respect of active members affected by the change can be applied, rather than to all the membership groups originally included within the proposed modification.

Under s 67I, the Regulator may impose a civil penalty on the trustees if he feels that they have failed to comply with the subsisting rights provisions or have failed to take all reasonable steps to comply with his direction to ensure that the modification is altered to comply with those provisions. The Regulator may also impose a fine on persons other than the trustees where they exercise the power of amendment and have done so either without the trustees' consent or without full regard to the subsisting rights provisions.

**3. Areas of Concern**

The new section has been designed to give schemes greater flexibility in amending their rules whilst retaining the safeguards for scheme members' accrued rights. The key change in the provisions is that schemes are now able to amend past service rights without members' consents, as long as the actuarial value of the accrued rights is maintained. For schemes which have merged with other schemes in the past, it is hoped that this increased flexibility will enable the trustees to rationalize the various past service benefit promises which have, up to now, had to be maintained to comply with the requirements of s 67 of the 1995 Act. Under the new section, trustees can replace one accrued right with another, provided that the overall actuarial value of each person's accrued right is not reduced. The other major difference is that the amendment is not invalid if the s 67 requirements are not met. Instead it is voidable at the order of the Regulator.

Many within the pensions industry had hoped for a simplification of s 67 with less, rather than more, prescription when amending scheme rules. The new provision extends the statutory conditions from one to ten sections and both regulations and codes of practice are to follow. Sadly, therefore, to those responsible for modifying their schemes it will seem that rather than simplifying scheme amendments one set of difficulties is simply being replaced with another.

Many of the difficulties under the old section focused upon what constituted 'accrued rights and entitlements' and to what extent a change fell within s 67. During the House of Commons' Standing Committee debate[20] it was suggested that the Regulator be given the role of deciding, prior to the making of any proposed modification, whether it did in fact fall within s 67. Such a procedure would have gone some way towards minimizing the time and expense currently spent by lawyers and actuaries in trying to assess whether s 67 should apply or not. The Government, however, rejected the suggestion believing that it should not be a decision for the Regulator, although it will be asked to issue guidance. It is hoped that this will be both clear and practical.

One attempt at clarification within the section itself has been the inclusion of a specific reference to survivor's benefits, although death in service pensions will continue to be excluded from the scope of s 67. In addition, s 67A(10) means that

---

[20] *Hansard*, HC Standing Committee B, col 751 (27 April 2004).

any changes which have the effect of extending or restricting the persons who may be eligible to receive pension on the death of a member will need to comply with s 67. Where this sort of change is proposed the only practical route open to trustees is to meet the actuarial equivalence requirements, as obtaining consents from all of a member's 'survivors' would be an almost impossible task.

9.94 A further area of concern is the information and notification requirements. Not all the requirements are new, but they do appear to represent a significant administrative cost for the scheme, particularly where the proposed change is minor in nature. Trustees are required to give advance notice of the changes and give members the opportunity to make representations about the proposals. The trustees are then expected to give their consent to the change in light of any feedback received from scheme members. Asking for representations is not the same as a requirement for consent. However, it may be difficult for the trustees to justify adopting their original proposal without some adjustment where a large number of member representations are made, notwithstanding that the actuarial equivalence requirements are met. In addition, there is a risk of some overlap between the consultation requirements of ss 259 to 261 of the Act and the new s 67 requirements because some changes could potentially affect both future and past service benefits. However, the two provisions appear to have been drafted in isolation from each other and do not contemplate this scenario. Complying with each of the relevant sections of the Act may lead to a duplication or apparent contradiction of duties.

9.95 Whilst trustees may prefer to rely upon the actuarial equivalence requirements of s 67 rather than seek members' consents to scheme changes, they need to be mindful of the requirement under s 67E to approve the scheme modification within a reasonable time after members' consents have been obtained. It is not clear for how long a delay will remain reasonable. If this issue is not clarified by a regulation or a code of practice then it will almost certainly be the subject of future Pensions Ombudsman decisions or pensions litigation.

9.96 Moreover, the actuarial equivalence requirements have been subject to criticism, in particular from the Institute and Faculty of Actuaries. Some actuaries have warned that because the term is insufficiently defined within the section they will not be in a position to sign a certificate. Section 67D(5) provides for the actuarial equivalence test to be applied in accordance with guidance prepared by a prescribed body and approved by the Secretary of State and it is to be hoped that this guidance will bring the desired clarity of meaning.

9.97 The Institute and Faculty of Actuaries have also stated that whilst the new actuarial equivalence test protects the actuarial value of a member's accrued rights, it cannot ensure that benefits remain in the same form that members have previously expected. This, they claim, will inevitably create 'losers' amongst individual scheme members. The example cited is of an unmarried member with no dependants who may object to a proposal to reduce his or her accrued pension entitlement and 'compensate' with additional spouse's pension because the compensation on offer has little personal value to that particular member.

Despite members lodging their opposition to a change, it should be borne in mind that when trustees consider whether to approve a proposed modification they have a fiduciary duty to decide what is best for the scheme as a whole, rather than trying to accommodate the wishes and preferences of some individual members. The operation of the new section has the potential to create situations where members are worse off. This would be the very situation it sought to avoid.

Whilst failure to comply with all the requirements of s 67 no longer makes an amendment automatically invalid, it appears that the powers granted to the Regulator to declare a change void can only be exercised with effect from the date of the change. There does not seem to be any flexibility for him to allow the change to continue for the future without the scheme first taking the remedial compliance steps necessary in respect of the period between the effective date and the date the Regulator issues his non-compliance order. Putting non-compliance right will therefore be a costly administrative exercise. 9.98

Finally, the revised provisions have done nothing to improve the position for employers seeking to control pension scheme costs. In particular, many had hoped that simplification might make it easier to convert the accrued final salary pension entitlements remaining in the scheme into money purchase entitlements where future accrual is already on a money purchase basis. Such changes are, however, only to be permitted under the new regime with member consent. In addition, under the revised section no change can be made without trustee approval and where it is proposed to make a change to members' accrued rights those members must be given advance notice of the change telling them exactly how they are affected and giving them the opportunity to make representations about the proposal. 9.99

## E. PENSION DISPUTES

### 1. Introduction

In the area of pension disputes, the Act introduces some welcome changes to increase flexibility for schemes in relation to establishment of their own internal procedures for resolving complaints from beneficiaries, together with some clarificatory amendments in relation to the Pensions Ombudsman's jurisdiction. Both of these sets of changes simply build upon the existing legislation (primarily the 1995 Act and the PSA 1993) and are likely to have only limited practical impact. 9.100

### 2. New Dispute Resolution Requirements

The requirement for pension schemes to have an internal dispute resolution procedure was introduced in 1997 by s 50 of the 1995 Act. The underlying 9.101

## 9. Miscellaneous Provisions

regulations are the Occupational Pension Schemes (Internal Dispute Resolution Procedures) Regulations 1996[21] ('the IDRP Regulations').

**9.102** Section 50(2) of the 1995 Act required pension schemes to have a two-stage Internal Dispute Resolution Procedure (IDRP). Under that procedure, a stage one decision is made by an appointed decision maker (to be nominated by the trustees). If the complainant remains dissatisfied, he can appeal and there is then a requirement for a stage two decision to be determined by the trustees themselves. The IDRP Regulations set out detailed requirements on how the dispute procedure must be operated including prescriptive time limits applicable to each stage of the decision-making process.

**9.103** Views had been expressed that the current process required by the 1995 Act was too complex, time consuming, and overly prescriptive. The Pensions Ombudsman expressed similar concerns in his recent reports. The changes introduced by the 2004 Act are driven by a desire for simplification and the need to allow schemes to tailor the dispute resolution process to their particular circumstances and to make that process more manageable.

**9.104** The existing provisions under the 1995 Act are to be replaced with new sections inserted by s 273 of the 2004 Act. Whilst the trustees are still required to have an internal dispute resolution arrangement in place, the new requirements differ from the existing regime in a number of important respects:

(a) There is no longer any requirement for a two-stage procedure;

(b) The list of potential complainants is expanded to include 'non-dependant beneficiaries' entitled to death benefits; and

(c) Under the current regime, there are prescribed time limits in which to respond and provide a decision to the complainant or his representative in relation to a stage one and a stage two complaint. The time limit normally requires the decision to be notified to the complainant within two months of receiving certain prescribed information. If notice of the decision is not issued within the two month deadline, an interim reply must be sent to the complainant and his representative explaining the reasons for the delay and an expected date for issuing the decision. The new regime no longer has time limits for reaching and notifying decisions but the trustees must respond within a reasonable time.

**9.105** Trustees and managers will need to review their existing procedures in the light of the new arrangements and may wish to adopt a more simple, tailored approach for their own schemes. Nevertheless, whilst the statutory relaxations under the 2004 Act are to be welcomed, the practical impact of these changes may well be limited. Schemes may, for instance, feel uncomfortable with making changes to an established procedure especially if a reduction from a two-stage to a one-stage procedure is perceived as the removal of a right of appeal. In

---

[21] SI 1996/1270.

addition, the new legislative requirements do nothing to address some of the more intractable problems with the existing IDRP regime. There is no consideration, for example, of the interaction of these provisions with separate grievance and dispute procedures under employment law. Equally the 2004 Act does not seek to alleviate the difficulties faced by many smaller schemes, in particular, where the trustee board may include individuals directly involved in making the original decision which is the subject of the complaint and where there are therefore concerns of about whether the dispute process is regarded as fair and equitable.

## 3. Requirement for Dispute Resolution

Section 273 inserts new ss 50, 50A, and 50B into the 1995 Act. These sections replace the existing s 50 and are effectively a modified restatement of much of the existing provisions, incorporating some of the detail from the IDRP Regulations and adopting slightly revised terminology. **9.106**

Section 50(1) and (2) require trustees or managers of an occupational pension scheme to secure that arrangements for the resolution of pension disputes in accordance with the terms of the section are made and implemented. Section 50(3) defines a pension dispute as being a dispute about matters relating to the scheme between the trustees or managers of a scheme and one or more persons 'with an interest in the scheme', except where the dispute is exempted under s 50(9). 'Disagreements' under the existing legislation become 'pension disputes' under the new rules but it is unclear whether there is any significance in this change. **9.107**

Section 50(4) requires that the new dispute resolution arrangements provide a mechanism for any person with an 'interest in the scheme' to apply to the trustees or managers of the scheme to make a decision on the matters in dispute, termed 'an application for the resolution of a pension dispute'. **9.108**

There are no longer detailed and prescriptive time limits for making and notifying complainants of decisions. Section 50(5) provides that where an application for the resolution of a pension dispute is referred to the trustees or managers for a decision, they must make a decision within a 'reasonable period' of receiving the application and notify the applicant of the decision within a 'reasonable period', the meaning of which will be set out in a code of practice to be issued by the Regulator. **9.109**

Whilst the new rules generally allow much greater flexibility in terms of procedures to be adopted, s 50(6) still requires that the dispute resolution arrangements must as a minimum comply with the requirements set out in the new s 50B (see paras 9.118 to 9.121 below). **9.110**

Section 50(7) provides that the new arrangements only have effect in relation to applications made on or after the commencement date of the new s 50. The new regime is expected to take effect from 23 September 2005. Any complaints received by existing schemes before the commencement of the 2004 Act **9.111** provisions will fall under the current regime (s 50(7)). Therefore, there will be an overlapping period when schemes may effectively be operating two dispute resolution regimes. As a consequence, it is perhaps questionable whether schemes with a number of existing complaints will take advantage of the new relaxations in the short term at least.

9.112   Section 50(8) provides that the provisions of the new section will not apply to schemes where every member of the scheme is a trustee and schemes with no more than one member. These exemptions mirror the existing exclusions under reg 8 of the IDRP Regulations. Additionally, the subsection provides a power for further schemes to be exempted by regulations.

9.113   Section 50(9) sets out the types of dispute to which the new procedures will not apply. Consequently, where proceedings in respect of the dispute have commenced in any court or tribunal or where the Pensions Ombudsman has commenced an investigation in respect of the dispute there will be no requirement to operate the new IDRP. Once again, these exclusions reflect the existing regime. There is also provision for further exemptions to be set out in regulations.

9.114   As under the 1995 Act provisions, there are potential civil penalties for trustees or managers who do not take 'all reasonable steps' to make or implement dispute resolution arrangements under the new s 50(10).

## 4. Persons with an Interest in the Scheme

9.115   A new s 50A to the 1995 Act is also introduced by s 273 setting out the meaning of a 'person with an interest' in the scheme for the purposes of s 50. Section 50A(1) details the categories of individual who can bring a complaint under the new regime. It reflects the definitions set out in the current regulations but also now includes a 'non-dependant beneficiary'. A person is a person with 'an interest' in an occupational pension scheme if he:

(a) Is a member of the scheme;
(b) Is a widow, widower, or surviving dependant of a deceased member of the scheme;
(c) Is a surviving non-dependant beneficiary of a deceased member of the scheme;
(d) Is a prospective member of the scheme;
(e) Has ceased to be within any of the categories (a) to (d); or
(f) Claims to be a person as is mentioned in categories (a) to (e) above and the dispute relates to whether he is such a person.

9.116   For these purposes, a 'non-dependant beneficiary' in relation to a deceased member is a person who, on the death of the member, is entitled to the payment of benefits under the scheme. This is a sensible amendment to the list of possible complainants reflecting the Inland Revenue's relaxation of its own requirements in relation to dependency.

## Pension Disputes

'Prospective member' is given the same meaning as under the current regime and means any person who, under the terms of his/her contract of employment or the rules of the scheme: **9.117**

(a) Is able, at his own option, to become a member of the scheme;
(b) Will become so able if he continues in the same employment for a sufficiently long time;
(c) Will be admitted to the scheme automatically unless he makes an election not to become a member; or
(d) May be admitted to it subject to the consent of his employer (s 50A(3)).

### 5. Minimum Requirements for the Dispute Resolution Procedure

A new s 50B is introduced setting out a list of minimum requirements for any dispute resolution procedure under the new arrangements (although the restrictions themselves are not new). Section 50B(2) reflects the current legislation and states that the dispute resolution procedure must provide that a dispute may be made or continued on behalf of a person who is a party to the dispute where: **9.118**

(a) That person dies, by his personal representatives;
(b) That person is a minor or a person otherwise incapable of acting, by a member of his family or some other suitable person; or
(c) In any other case, by a representative nominated by him.

Whilst the new regime refrains from imposing statutory time limits, s 50B(3) provides that the trustees and managers may decide to include such time limits within the procedure which they adopt. Such arrangements must, however, include a six-month time limit for making the application where the person ceases to be a member, prospective member, or other beneficiary under the scheme. **9.119**

The procedure must set out details about how the application is to be made, what information should be included in the application, and the way in which decisions are to be reached and given. **9.120**

The arrangements must also provide that the process of resolving the dispute will cease if, after the application is made, the dispute becomes one in respect of which proceedings have been commenced in any court or tribunal or one where the Pensions Ombudsman has commenced an investigation as a result of a complaint made or a dispute referred to him. **9.121**

### 6. Background to New Requirements in Relation to the Pensions Ombudsman

The office of the Pensions Ombudsman ('the Ombudsman') was established by the Social Security Act 1990 with the first Ombudsman being appointed by the **9.122**

## 9. Miscellaneous Provisions

Secretary of State in 1991. The relevant statutory provisions setting out the Ombudsman's appointment, jurisdiction, and powers are now to be found in Pt X, ss 145 to 152 of the PSA 1993 as amended by the 1995 Act and the Child Support, Pensions and Social Security Act 2000 (CSPSSA 2000). Since the role was introduced, the Ombudsman's jurisdiction has been extended in piecemeal fashion through legislation and via the courts and the 2004 Act continues this trend by direct amendment of the relevant provisions of the PSA 1993 and the CSPSSA 2000.

9.123 The 2004 Act introduces the possibility of delegation by the Ombudsman to one or more deputies and an extension of the Ombudsman's jurisdiction in relation to scheme administrators (in response to recent case law developments in this area). However, the new provisions also formally remove the Ombudsman's powers to investigate group actions. The power to do so was introduced by the CSPSSA 2000, but never brought into force. Consequently, these modifications are likely to have relatively little practical effect and may come to be seen as more significant for their failure to embrace a wider role for the Ombudsman than for those changes which they do in fact introduce.

### 7. Appointment of Deputy Pensions Ombudsmen

9.124 Section 274(1) and (2) of the Act amends the provisions of s 145 of the PSA 1993. These new subsections provide that the Ombudsman may resign or be removed from office only on the grounds set out in his terms of appointment. The remainder of the section introduces the new provisions for the appointment of one or more persons to act as a Deputy Pensions Ombudsman ('Deputy Ombudsman').

9.125 At present, s 145(4C) of the PSA 1993 enables the Ombudsman to delegate most of his functions to any of his employees, but he cannot delegate the determination of complaints and disputes that are referred to him. This means that if the Ombudsman is incapacitated or resigns from office, no determinations can be made until a new Ombudsman is appointed. Equally, where the Ombudsman has a particularly heavy workload, resolution of complaints and disputes awaiting determination will inevitably be delayed.

9.126 The new provision to allow and appoint any number of Deputy Ombudsmen on terms to be determined by the Secretary of State answers a call from the Ombudsman to help him and his office to deal with the ever increasing caseload. David Laverick's third annual report as Ombudsman revealed his frustrations at the lack of resources available to his office in relation to the large number of complaints received but also noted that 'the present legislation inevitably means that the Ombudsman acts as a bottleneck'.[22] It is to be hoped that these changes will facilitate reduced timescales for the resolution of complaints and disputes to

---

[22] *Annual Report of the Pensions Ombudsman* 2003–4, p 8.

the benefit of members, trustees, and employers alike, although the funding of these new appointments will inevitably be an issue.

9.127 Section 274(3) of the Act inserts a new s 145A into the PSA 1993, providing for the creation of one or more Deputy Ombudsmen who will have all the functions and powers of the Ombudsman. It also provides that such appointments are to be made upon such terms and conditions as the Secretary of State may think fit, mirroring the existing provisions relating to the Ombudsman.

9.128 Section 145A(3) provides that a Deputy Ombudsman may only be removed from office by the Secretary of State in accordance with the terms and conditions of appointment, and that a Deputy Ombudsman may resign by giving notice to the Secretary of State. This reflects the amendment made to the circumstances in which the Ombudsman may resign or be removed from his office (see para 9.124 above).

9.129 Section 145A(4) sets out the circumstances in which a Deputy Ombudsman may carry out the functions of the Ombudsman, which include:

(a) A situation where there is a vacancy in that office;
(b) Any time when the Ombudsman is, for any reason, unable to discharge his functions; and
(c) When the Secretary of State thinks fit (such as when the Ombudsman's workload means the assistance of a Deputy Ombudsman is required).

9.130 Section 145A(5) makes it clear that any provisions in legislation relating to the performance of the Ombudsman's functions should be interpreted as including any Deputy Ombudsman thus avoiding the need to amend all of the provisions of Pt X of the PSA 1993 (detailing the Ombudsman's functions) in the context of the role of the Deputy Ombudsman.

9.131 Section 145A(6) provides for the Secretary of State to pay to or in respect of a Deputy Ombudsman remuneration, compensation for loss of office, pension, allowances and gratuities, or other benefits as determined by the Secretary of State.

9.132 Section 274(4) and (5) provides for any Deputy Ombudsman to be added to the persons disqualified from being elected as a Member of Parliament (or, consequently, a Member of the European Parliament) or to the Northern Ireland Assembly. These provisions again mirror those applicable to the Ombudsman himself.

## 8. Jurisdiction of the Ombudsman

9.133 Section 275(1) of the Act inserts a new subsection (4A) into s 146 of the PSA 1993. Under the existing s 146(4) of the PSA 1993, regulations may be made to treat a person who is not a trustee, manager or employer, but who is concerned with the financing, administration of, or provision of benefits under a pension scheme as though he were a person responsible for the management of the scheme. The new provision will make it clear that persons responsible for carrying out single acts of administration are deemed to be concerned with the administration of the pension scheme and hence can be the subject of an Ombudsman's investigation and determination.

9.134 The new s 146(4A) will not have retrospective effect and will only apply in relation to disputes and complaints in relation to matters taking place on or after the date on which the amended provision comes into force.

9.135 Existing regulations made under the PSA 1993 give the Ombudsman power to investigate and determine complaints of maladministration 'concerning the administration of a personal or an occupational pension scheme' and arising 'in connection with an act or omission of an administrator of the scheme'.[23] For these purposes, an 'administrator' is defined to include any person concerned with the administration of the scheme, other than the trustees or managers of the scheme or the employer'.[24] The Ombudsman appears to have generally adopted the position that these provisions are widely drawn and may be interpreted to cover one off or occasional acts of actuaries, auditors, solicitors, and others who would not otherwise be regarded as dealing with the administration of the scheme. The courts have, however, taken a more conservative approach and, in particular, have sought to distinguish between doing an administrative act in connection with a pension scheme and being concerned with its administration.[25]

9.136 The new extension to s 146 of the PSA 1993 clarifies the position of the Ombudsman and confirms that persons will be treated as concerned with the administration of the scheme where they are 'responsible for carrying out an act of administration concerned with the scheme' (ie a single act will now be sufficient for those purposes).

9.137 Section 146(4) of the PSA 1993 also provided a regulation-making power to widen the scope of those regarded as involved in the management of the scheme to encompass persons concerned with the 'financing' of, or the 'provision of benefits' under, a scheme. Yet regulations have never been drafted to this effect. It is regrettable that the Government have not taken the opportunity to extend the definition to include these groups. Consequently, it is possible that actuaries, investment managers, and others may still attempt to avoid the Ombudsman's jurisdiction by arguing that the scope of their activities does not come within the definition of administrative acts.

---

[23] Regulation 2(1) of the Personal and Occupational Pension Schemes (Pensions Ombudsman) Regulations 1996 (SI 1996/2475).
[24] ibid, reg 1(2).
[25] *R v Pensions Ombudsman ex parte Britannic Asset Management Ltd* [2002] 90 PBLR.

## 9. Investigations—The Ombudsman and Group Actions

Section 276 of the Act repeals s 54 of the CSPSSA 2000, which made changes to ss 148, 149, and 151 of the PSA 1993, dealing with the extension of the Ombudsman's jurisdiction to group actions and the possibility of the appointment of representative beneficiaries in such cases. These were enabling provisions only and the necessary rules and regulations have never in fact been brought into force.  **9.138**

Part X of the PSA 1993 and regulations made under it do not make any provision for the representation of class interests. The Ombudsman (unlike the court) is unable to appoint a representative of a class of beneficiaries other than the complainant to take part in his investigation. Therefore, the Ombudsman is unable to make a determination in favour of an individual which has an effect upon the rights and/or benefits of other scheme beneficiaries. Despite attempts by the Ombudsman to extend his jurisdiction in this regard, recent case law has confirmed that the Ombudsman should not accept jurisdiction in relation to a complaint if the investigation of it would impact upon the interests, and particularly the financial interests, of those not directly involved in the case.[26] This is because such persons are not able to make representations to him and, therefore, should not be bound by his determinations in such circumstances. Following the Court of Appeal decision in *Edge v Pensions Ombudsman*,[27] s 54 of the CSPSSA 2000 set out an amendment to the PSA 1993 which would have extended the jurisdiction of the Ombudsman to enable him to investigate matters which would impact upon the interests of those not directly involved in the case and to appoint a representative in relation to a class of beneficiaries other than the complainant to take part in his investigation.  **9.139**

The amendments introduced by s 54 of the CSPSSA 2000 would have been a far-reaching extension of the Ombudsman's powers, yet a number of concerns were raised about its provisions. The main worry was that the Government would be giving an inquisitorial body powers to make representation orders and to fund the costs of any investigation from scheme assets. Practitioners in the pensions industry criticized the amendments on the basis that the Ombudsman should be channelling the efforts of his office towards individual claims and not involving himself with group or class actions, which, it was argued, the courts have dealt with effectively and efficiently over the years. There was also the added complication of inconsistent practice developing between the Ombudsman's office and the Civil Procedure Rules, with potentially inequitable results.  **9.140**

In view of these perceived problems, it was announced on 18 March 2003 that s 54 of the CSPSSA 2000 would not be brought into effect, the Government  **9.141**

---

[26] *Edge v Pensions Ombudsman* [1999] 4 All ER 546; see also *Marsh & McLennan Companies UK Ltd v Pensions Ombudsman* [2001] OPLR 221.
[27] ibid.

having concluded that 'the changes made by section 54 would not be as beneficial as originally envisaged and that they would also add a further layer of complexity to an area of legislation which needs to be simplified and not complicated further'.[28]

9.142 In practical terms, the repeal of these provisions is likely to limit the effectiveness of the Ombudsman's office and increase his reluctance to address scheme-wide issues such as equalization of guaranteed minimum pensions even though this may inadvertently reduce access to justice for the individual complainant.

## F. SCHEME DESIGN AND REGULATORY

### 1. Categories of Pension Scheme

9.143 The distinction between occupational pension schemes and personal pension schemes will be abolished when tax simplification takes effect in April 2006. It has therefore been necessary to amend the definitions of 'occupational pension scheme' and 'personal pension scheme' in s 1 of the PSA 1993 as the distinction remains relevant for pensions legislation purposes. The distinction determines to which regulatory regime (ie the new Pensions Regulator for occupational pension schemes, and the Financial Services Authority for personal pension schemes) a scheme is subject.

9.144 The amendment has been made by s 239 which provides that in order for a scheme to be an 'occupational pension scheme':

(a) It must provide benefits for people with service in employment (or self-employment) of a kind described in the scheme rules and may also provide benefits to members who are not in that kind of employment (or self-employment);

(b) It must have its main administration in the UK or outside the European Union;

(c) At least one of the people establishing it must be an employer, employee, self-employed person, or a representative of such a person;

(d) It can be established for paid office-holders by the person who pays them; and

(e) It may cater for more than one kind of employment (or self-employment).

9.145 A 'personal pension scheme' is a scheme which is not an occupational pension scheme and is established by:

---

[28] DWP press release 18 March 2003, 'Amendments to the Personal and Occupational Pension Schemes (Pensions Ombudsman) (Procedure) Rules 1995—Pension Ombudsman's Jurisdiction'.

(a) An insurance company;

(b) A unit trust scheme manager;

(c) An operator, trustee, or depository of a recognized EEA collective investment scheme;

(d) An authorized open-ended investment company;

(e) A building society;

(f) A bank; or

(g) An EEA (European Economic Area) investment portfolio manager.

This new definition ties in with the Finance Act 2004.

The definition of 'employer' in s 125 of the 1995 Act is also amended so that its scope can be altered by regulations as and when the need arises. **9.146**

## 2. Payment of Surplus to Employer

The Income and Corporation Taxes Act 1988 (ICTA 1988) imposes a tax charge to the extent a pension fund has a surplus in excess of 105% and does not apply it in improving benefits and/or in a contribution reduction or repayment to the employer. The test of 105% funding is based on assumptions laid down by the Government Actuary's Department. This provision is to fall away in line with the Finance Act 2004 changes to be implemented with effect from April 2006. Essentially the legislation makes two changes: **9.147**

(a) Removal of the ICTA 1988 requirement to release surplus in excess of 105%;

(b) Substantial revision of legislation (s 37 of the 1995 Act) which required that trustees must first be asked for consent to a return of surplus, notifying the membership and OPRA of the same, and that a first charge on a refund of surplus to the employer is the provision of Limited Price Indexation (LPI) for past and future service.

The tax charge imposed on excessive surplus is to be withdrawn as part of the Finance Act 2004 changes. The terms of s 37 of the 1995 Act are replaced with a new provision which gives trustees an overriding power of consent to repayment of surplus to the employer and a requirement that trustee approval must be obtained where this is not provided by the scheme rules. Essentially the trustees can permit a return of surplus if the following conditions are satisfied: **9.148**

(a) The trustees have obtained a valuation of the scheme's assets and liabilities in the appropriate form;

(b) The trustees have a certificate that the level of the surplus is sufficient to allow repayment—essentially a requirement that the scheme is able to meet possible buy-out costs of benefits (and any expenses of winding up): only then will any balance be subject to repayment to the employer;

(c) The trustees are satisfied that the payment is in the interests of the members;

(d) The Regulator does not object to the repayment;

(e) The members have been duly notified of the intention to repay.

9.149 Essentially this means that there is a much more onerous requirement than currently applies on the payment of surplus. In the present funding climate, schemes are much more likely to have a deficit than a surplus above the current 105% limit sufficient to allow a refund of surplus after meeting all buy-out costs.

### 3. Restrictions on Payment into Occupational Pension Schemes

(a) *UK-based scheme to be trust with effective rules*

9.150 Section 252 provides that occupational pension schemes which have their main administration in the UK must be established under irrevocable trusts, and can only accept contributions and transfer values if this requirement is satisfied. Regulations may be made to exempt certain schemes from this requirement, and it is likely that these would be used to exempt statutory schemes.

9.151 In addition, schemes must have proper written rules setting out the benefits provided before they can accept payments.

9.152 The Pensions Regulator has power to sanction trustees or managers who accept payments into a scheme which is not trust based or which does not have written rules.

(b) *Non-European scheme to be trust with UK-resident trustee*

9.153 Section 253 sets out requirements for schemes which have their main administration outside the EU, but receive contributions from:

(a) Employers based in the UK (regardless of where their employees work); or

(b) Employers based anywhere in the world in respect of their employees who are employed in the UK.

The employers must not make contributions to the scheme unless it is established under irrevocable trusts, and there is a trustee who is resident in the UK. For this purpose, in accordance with s 254, anyone appointed by the trustees to act as a representative of the overseas scheme in the UK is to be treated as a trustee under UK pensions legislation.

9.154 Failure to comply with the above requirements can render an employer liable to civil sanctions.

### 4. Activities of Occupational Pension Schemes

9.155 The EU Pensions Directive must be implemented in the UK on or before 22 September 2005. Article 7 of the Directive requires each Member State to ensure that occupational pension schemes located within its territory limit their activities to retirement benefit related operations and activities arising therefrom. The existing requirement in the tax legislation will disappear as a result of the Finance Act 2004, and it has therefore been necessary for a provision to be included in order to restore this restriction.

9.156 Section 255 places a requirement on an occupational pension scheme that has its main administration in the UK that it must limit its activities to those relating to providing retirement benefits. It cannot, for example, provide mortgages. Retirement benefits and retirement benefit activities are defined in line with the Directive, and schemes may therefore provide benefits relating to reaching retirement and may also provide supplementary benefits such as benefits on death, disability, cessation of employment, sickness, or poverty.

9.157 A power is included for certain schemes to be exempted from this limitation. This accords with Art 5 of the Directive which enables Member States to exempt schemes with less than 100 members and certain statutory schemes from these provisions.

9.158 The Pensions Regulator has power to impose a civil penalty on trustees or managers who fail to take all reasonable steps to ensure that the scheme's activities are exclusively related to retirement benefit provision.

### 5. No Indemnification for Fines or Civil Penalties

9.159 Section 256 provides that when a trustee or manager of an occupational or personal pension scheme fails to comply with a duty to protect the assets or benefits of scheme members, and the failure is such that the Pensions Regulator takes action in the form of a penalty, that person may not be indemnified from the scheme assets in respect of a failure for which they are held personally liable. This includes reimbursement for the payment of premiums in respect of an insurance policy, where the risks include the imposition of a fine or the requirement to pay such a penalty. This is in line with existing provisions within the 1995 Act which prevent fines and penalties (or premiums for insurance in respect of the same) from being met from scheme funds. The restriction does not, of course, prevent indemnification of trustees and managers by the employer itself or through an insurance policy paid for by the employer.

9.160 Where any amount is paid out of the assets in contravention of this restriction, civil penalties may be applied to any trustee or manager who fails to take all reasonable steps to ensure compliance. A trustee or manager who is *knowingly* reimbursed out of scheme assets will be guilty of an offence unless he has taken all reasonable steps to ensure that he is not so reimbursed. In these circumstances, a guilty person is liable on summary conviction to a fine and, on conviction on indictment, to a fine or imprisonment, or both.

### 6. Short Service Benefit

9.161 Section 263 amends s 71 of the PSA 1993, which provides for the basic preservation of benefits for people who leave pensionable service before normal pension age and who have at least two years' qualifying service, or have had a transfer

## 9. Miscellaneous Provisions

payment into the scheme in respect of rights under a personal pension scheme. Section 71(3) of the PSA 1993 provides that deferred short service benefits payable under scheme rules must be payable from normal pension age, or if that is earlier than 60, no later than age 60. This provision was aimed at a small number of occupations which anticipate retirement before age 60 because of the nature of their work (for example, fire-fighters).

9.162 The amendment under s 263 changes the latest age from which a deferred pension is payable in schemes with an early normal pension age. The age is increased to 65. This amendment has been made on the basis that if a person was, for example, a fire-fighter for only a few years early on in their career, there is no reason why the pension in respect of that service should have to be paid by 60 as opposed to 65.

9.163 A new provision is added to the effect that payment of short service benefit from an age other than normal pension age does not conflict with the basic principle that short service beneficiaries are not treated less favourably than long service beneficiaries.

### 7. Early Leavers

9.164 Under existing legislation, a member who leaves a scheme within two years of joining only has a statutory entitlement to a refund of his own contributions and has no right to either a deferred pension or a cash equivalent transfer value. Section 264 introduces a fifth chapter into Pt IV of the PSA 1993 consisting of new ss 101AA to 101AI. The new provisions entitle members who leave after three months' pensionable service in a scheme, but before their rights have vested in the scheme, to a cash transfer or a refund of employee contributions. It does not provide for those rights to be preserved in the scheme (ie the member will still not have a right to a deferred pension until he has completed two years' pensionable service).

9.165 The trustees are required to provide an early leaver with information on his options within 'a reasonable period' after termination of his pensionable service. The trustees must then give the member a 'reasonable period' to exercise his right to take either a cash transfer lump sum or a refund of contributions. If no response is received, the trustees may pay the refund of contributions to the member, following which they are discharged from any further obligation to that member. The Pensions Regulator will issue a code of practice setting out what is a 'reasonable period' for these purposes. Civil penalties will apply to any trustee or manager who has failed to take all reasonable steps to secure compliance with these provisions.

9.166 Those schemes which currently provide for immediate vesting of benefits would appear to have the opportunity to repay contributions in respect of early leavers who do not opt for the cash transfer sum.

9.167 The methodology for calculating the cash transfer sum is expected to be on the same lines as for calculating cash equivalent transfer values, and will be laid down in regulations. The sum must be used to acquire transfer credits under an occupational or personal pension scheme that satisfies requirements to be prescribed by regulations or for purchasing an annuity. The legislation allows reduction of the sum in certain circumstances including to reflect the state of the scheme funding.

9.168 Regulations will also prescribe how the refund of contributions is to be calculated. It is assumed that these will allow for the refund to be reduced for tax and the member's share, for contracted out schemes, of the contributions equivalent premium. In money purchase schemes, it is anticipated that these will also allow the refund to be reduced for adverse investment return.

9.169 It has been suggested that in order to circumvent the new requirements employers may, for example, introduce waiting periods, ie requiring an employee to be in service, for example, for one year before being entitled to join the scheme. Similar exclusions were permitted under the requirements for stakeholder pensions, so it is not inconceivable that this approach may be allowed.

## 8. Safeguarding Pension Rights

(a) *Paternity leave and adoption leave*

9.170 Section 265 is aimed at bringing paid paternity and adoption leave into line with the legislation on paid maternity leave, which requires employer contributions during periods of paid maternity leave to be made as if the woman were working normally.

9.171 New provisions are inserted into Sch 5 of the Social Security Act 1989 which provide that for any period of paternity leave during which an employee receives statutory paternity pay or contractual remuneration, he must be treated no less favourably in terms of employer contributions than if he were working normally. The member is only required to pay contributions based on the remuneration he actually receives. Similar provisions are included in relation to adoption leave.

9.172 The new provisions apply to 'employment-related benefit schemes', which are defined in the Social Security Act 1989 as relating to schemes which provide service related benefits. There is therefore some doubt about the application of the provisions to money purchase schemes.

(b) *Inalienability of occupational pension*

9.173 Section 266 makes provision for charges, liens, or set-offs to be exercised against a member's benefits to recover overpayments made to him from the scheme. This is achieved by the addition of a further exception to s 91(5) of the 1995 Act, and is a clarificatory amendment. It was always the intention that monies should be able to be recovered from members where an overpayment has been made in error, and this new provision gives effect to that intention. The change removes any concerns trustees may have had under the existing s 91 of the 1995 Act that such recovery would be prohibited.

## 9. Voluntary Contributions

9.174 Section 267 repeals the existing provision in s 111 of the PSA 1993 which requires schemes to allow members to pay additional voluntary contributions.

9.175 Since most voluntary contribution arrangements are on the defined contribution basis, they do not usually have a cost to employers, so it is difficult to see that this change achieves anything of great importance from the employer's point of view. It may impact upon members, however, particularly when the Pensions Commission[29] is recommending that people save more for their retirement. It should be noted that although employers will no longer be required to offer payment of voluntary contributions, those which have already been paid and the rights deriving from them will remain.

## 10. Payments by Employers

9.176 Currently, if payments of employer contributions are not made by their due dates, reports must be made to OPRA and the affected members must be told. In practice, OPRA has found the number of such notifications difficult to handle.

(a) *Payments made by employers to personal pension schemes*

9.177 Section 268 amends s 111A of the PSA 1993 so that there is no longer an automatic duty to notify the Regulator and the affected members if employer contributions to personal pension schemes are not paid by their due date. Notification need only be given if 'the failure to pay the contributions is likely to be of material significance in the exercise by the Regulatory Authority of any of their functions'. The Regulator will be issuing a code of practice on the meaning of 'material significance'.

9.178 There will no longer be any obligation on the employer to maintain a record of payments, although in practice it would still need to maintain some records as the trustees are entitled to receive payment information, and failure to comply within a reasonable period would mean that the trustees would need to notify the Regulator.

(b) *Payments made by employers and members to occupational pension schemes*

9.179 Similar provisions are also introduced for occupational pension schemes. Sections 49 and 88 of the 1995 Act are amended by s 269 so that there is no longer an automatic requirement for the Regulator to be notified if contributions deducted from members' earnings or employer contributions to money purchase schemes are not paid by their due dates.

---

[29] *Pensions: Challenges and Choices—The first Report of the Pensions Commission* (12 October 2004).

The requirement will only now arise if 'the failure to pay the contributions is likely to be of material significance in the exercise by the Authority of any of their functions'. As previously mentioned in connection with personal pension schemes above (see para 9.177 above), the Regulator will be issuing a code of practice on the meaning of 'material significance'. 9.180

Where there is a significant failure, notification must be given to the Regulator and the scheme members within a reasonable period after the due date for payment. The Regulator will be issuing a code of practice on the meaning of 'reasonable period'. 9.181

The changes here for both personal and occupational pension schemes are in line with OPRA's recent relaxation of its approach towards late payment of contributions and its revised guidelines on reporting breaches of pension legislation. 9.182

## 11. Deficiency in Assets of Certain Occupational Pension Schemes

(a) *Introduction*

Under s 75 of the 1995 Act, where a salary related scheme commences winding up and assets are insufficient to secure liabilities on the 'buy-out' basis, the shortfall (together with any expenses of winding up) becomes a debt payable by the employer to the trustees or managers of the scheme in question. There have been recent developments in legislation, in particular to increase the level of the debt payable from the MFR basis to the buy-out basis. The provisions of the new Act (ss 271 and 272) amend rather than replace, the existing s 75. These changes appear intended to coincide with the new provisions on insolvency of employers and the operation of the Pension Protection Fund. The legislation also attempts to grapple with the difficult situation where the operation of the debt on employer legislation is confused by the fact that there are a number of employers all participating in a group scheme. 9.183

(b) *Revisions of section 75 of the 1995 Act*

A difficulty under the current legislation is determining the appropriate date on which the debt should be calculated. In order to retain flexibility for schemes wound up with a solvent employer it is for the trustees to determine when the assets and liabilities are valued for the purposes of the debt due from that employer. 9.184

Where, however, the employer becomes insolvent (including a members' voluntary winding up or where an insolvency event has not yet been triggered but the board of the Pension Protection Fund has been told the scheme is unlikely to continue as a going concern), member debt is fixed immediately before the 'relevant event' by the insolvency event itself. 9.185

(c) *Scheme rescue*

The legislation recognizes that even on the occurrence of a relevant insolvency 9.186

or similar event, it may not be appropriate in every case to proceed to winding up. If a scheme rescue is possible (under s 122 or 130), then the scheme may be able to continue on whatever basis is set out under the scheme rescue arrangement. If a scheme rescue is not possible, the scheme will be treated as winding up and notice will be given as appropriate that a scheme rescue is not possible.

(d) *Multi-employer schemes*

9.187 The intention behind the new s 75A of the 1995 Act is to create more flexibility in relation to calculation of liabilities and operation of current legislation. In particular, there have been difficulties in relation to multi-employer schemes where employers have left a group in what might have been regarded as uncontroversial or routine circumstances but 'inadvertently' a s 75 debt had been triggered. In addition, the Government has announced its intention to introduce regulations which will ensure that the amount of debt in the case of a multi-employer scheme is to be calculated on the full buy-out basis not, as currently, on the MFR test. Regulations will however allow an alternative basis for calculation to the full buy-out where an agreement is reached between the employers and the trustees on a suitable alternative funding plan.

## 12. Annual Increase in Rate of Pensions

(a) *Annual Increase in Rate of Certain Occupational Pensions*

9.188 No statutory increases are currently required in respect of pensions relating to service before 6 April 1997, or in the case of money purchase schemes, contributions relating to service before 6 April 1997. The 1995 Act required that certain occupational pensions derived from benefits built up on or after 6 April 1997 be increased annually by at least the lesser of the annual percentage increase in the Retail Prices Index (RPI) or 5%.

9.189 Section 278 provides that:

(a) Pensions which relate to service after the date s 278 comes into force must increase by at least the lesser of the increase in the RPI or 2.5%;

(b) Pensions which relate to service/contributions before the new provisions come into force but on or after 6 April 1997 must increase by at least the lesser of the increase in the RPI or 5%.

9.190 Furthermore, s 278 removes completely the requirement to provide statutory increases for defined contribution schemes, where the pension comes into payment after the commencement date for this provision. Commentators believe that this will hasten the end of defined benefit provision, because it is thought that the take up of personal pensions and contract-based defined contribution funds will be encouraged by this increased flexibility.

9.191 It should be noted that if it is desired to take advantage of the lower statutory rate of increases, an amendment to a scheme's governing documentation is likely to be required, and this should be made before the pensionable service to which the reduction relates has occurred. Trustees will need to consider the merits of any proposals from an employer to reduce the level of pension increases.

(b) *Annual increase in rate of certain personal pensions*
Section 162 of the 1995 Act made similar statutory increase provisions for the element of any personal pension arrangements derived from protected rights (ie rights in relation to contracted out money purchase benefits).[30]  9.192

Section 279 amends the statutory increase requirements in a similar way to the changes set out in relation to occupational schemes, so that pensions derived from protected rights coming into payment after the provision comes into force will not be required to provide statutory increases.  9.193

(c) *Power to increase pensions giving effect to pension credits, etc*
The Welfare Reform and Pensions Act 1999 contains provisions allowing the Secretary of State to protect occupational pension benefits derived from pension sharing on divorce from inflation.  9.194

Section 280 amends the provisions to require increases of the rise in the RPI up to 2.5% where the entitlement to the pension credit arises after the section comes into effect. Increases continue to be required of the rise in the RPI up to 5% in the case of pension credit benefits where the entitlement arises before that date.  9.195

## 13. Revaluation

Section 281 amends s 84 of the PSA 1993 to enable schemes to satisfy the statutory revaluation requirements by revaluing a member's total benefits fully in line with the RPI.  9.196

This amendment restores the situation to that which existed before the provision which was originally contained in s 84 of the PSA 1993 was repealed by the 1995 Act.  9.197

## 14. Contracting out

(a) *Meaning of 'working life' in the Pension Schemes Act 1993*
'Working life' is a term used in connection with calculating an earner's Guaranteed Minimum Pension (GMP). This is currently defined as the period between the tax year in which a person reaches age 16 and the tax year before he reaches pensionable age. Pensionable age for this purpose is defined by reference  9.198

---

[30] PSA 1993, s 10.

to State Pension Age, which is currently age 65 for men and 60 for women, but is being equalized gradually at 65 between 2010 and 2020.

9.199 Despite the change in State Pension Age, pensionable age for the purposes of calculating GMPs will remain at 65 for men and 60 for women after 2010. To bring it into line with pensionable age for GMP purposes, s 282 therefore alters the definition of 'working life' so that it ends with the tax year before the person reaches age 65 if male, or 60 if female, or the tax year before the person dies if the death occurs before reaching State Pension Age.

(b) *Power to prescribe conditions by reference to Inland Revenue approval*

9.200 The PSA 1993 currently sets out a variety of requirements for schemes to satisfy in order to be certified as contracted out. Section 283 adds a new provision enabling regulations to be made to link conditions for contracting out to Inland Revenue tax approval.

(c) *Restrictions on commutation and age at which benefits may be received*

9.201 One of the Government's promised reforms in relation to contracting out was to relax some restrictions on contracted out rights forming part of the tax free lump sum permitted to be paid under Inland Revenue rules.

9.202 Section 21 of the PSA 1993 currently only allows commutation of contracted out salary related benefits on grounds of triviality. Section 284 amends this provision to remove the restrictions on commuting such rights, although there is the possibility of additional regulatory limitations. The section also provides clarification that payment of a lump sum will not affect the GMP for the member's widow or widower—the commutation is ignored for this purpose.

9.203 Certain restrictions on protected rights which build up in contracted out money purchase schemes and appropriate personal pension schemes are also removed. The restrictions on the age at which members' protected rights can be given effect are removed, except in occupational schemes where (unless the member agrees a later date) they will continue to be required to be paid by age 65.

9.204 The amendments referred to above, which are made by ss 282 to 284 are minor tidying up amendments to existing legislation and fall short of the wholesale reform of contracting out requirements originally proposed by the Green and White Papers.

### 15. Stakeholder Pensions

9.205 The new Act introduces some minor technical changes in the context of stakeholder pension schemes.

9.206 The Welfare Reform and Pensions Act 1999 limits the amount by which the value of a member's rights under a stakeholder arrangement can be reduced by administration expenses. Section 285 clarifies that the restriction applies equally to contributions made by third parties (such as the member's relatives and his employer).

Section 285 amends the Welfare Reform and Pensions Act 1999 to clarify that stakeholder pension schemes must be contracted out to satisfy a qualifying condition for registration by the Regulator. They must also accept transfer payments (including contracted out rights) in respect of members' rights in other private pension schemes in order to qualify. 9.207

# 10
# FINANCIAL ASSISTANCE SCHEME

| | |
|---|---|
| A. Introduction | 10.01 |
| B. Framework provisions for the FAS | 10.08 |
| C. Practical Issues | 10.15 |

## A. INTRODUCTION

The introduction of the Financial Assistance Scheme (FAS) was first announced on 14 May 2004 at a time when the Pensions Bill was already some considerable way through the parliamentary process. The stated aim of the FAS is to help those members of underfunded defined benefit occupational pension schemes, where the employer has become insolvent and the scheme has begun to wind up before the introduction of the PPF. The Government's view is that the PPF compensation regime should only be seen as a solution to member protection issues for the future. It would be inappropriate to make coverage by the PPF retrospective because 'it is similar to an insurance scheme in some respects' and therefore 'should not cover people against events that have already happened'.[1] The creation of the FAS represents a recognition that there are nevertheless a considerable number of scheme members who will already have suffered reduced benefits on scheme failure.   10.01

The DWP's own research on this[2] suggests that there are at least some 65,000 members facing significant losses (in excess of 20%) to their pension entitlement which will not qualify for PPF protection. Moreover, these estimates are based on fairly restrictive criteria (and do not for instance include pre-April 1997 wind ups) and should therefore be regarded as a rather conservative assessment of the scale of the problem. Whilst emphasizing that they do not have a legal liability in relation to such schemes and therefore the term 'compensation' is inappropriate,   10.02

---

[1] *Hansard*, HC, col 991 (19 May 04).
[2] *Insolvent Pension Wind-up—Report on Numbers Affected*, Final Report for House Libraries (DWP, June 2004).

the Government has, however, recognized an 'ethical duty to act through the introduction of the proposed assistance scheme.³

10.03 The basic provisions for the establishment of the FAS are set out in s 286 of the Act, but this is little more than framework legislation with the detail to be fleshed out in regulations, which will cover such matters as the level of the assistance to be provided and the administrative arrangements for running the scheme. The Government has said that it anticipates that the scheme will be in place by spring 2005, with the first payments to be made soon afterwards.

10.04 The lack of detail surrounding the implementation of the FAS has given cause for concern, with the Government itself even admitting during the committee stages of the Pensions Bill that the FAS was 'technically defective',[4] and agreeing with criticism from opposition peers that the lack of detail about the scheme was unsatisfactory.

10.05 The Government has committed £400 million, spread over twenty years, to fund the FAS, with the possibility of further contributions from industry. There has been widespread criticism that £400 million will be insufficient to provide an adequate level of cover for qualifying members and there have been comments from some quarters that the FAS does not in fact represent any new money as such, as it would have been paid to affected members through means tested benefits in any event. In addition, payments from the FAS will be subject to tax deductions, so that arguably the FAS will cost the Government even less than the £400 million it has promised.

10.06 It has been confirmed that underfunded pension schemes that started winding up between 1 January 1997 and 5 April 2005 (the day before the PPF comes into force) will potentially be eligible for help from the FAS.[5] This first date was chosen on the basis of information gathered on affected schemes and discussions with industry, which indicated that the majority of schemes that started winding up with significant funding shortfalls did so after January 1997.

10.07 To minimize bureaucracy and maximize payments to those who have lost out the most, ministers are considering including only those who would expect payments from the FAS of £10 a week or more. To ensure that the money available is distributed fairly, they are also considering a cap on annual pension payments which is expected to be set at a lower level than that for the PPF. It is accepted that the FAS will not offer the same level of protection as the PPF.

## B. FRAMEWORK PROVISIONS FOR THE FAS

10.08 Under the terms of s 286, the Secretary of State is required to provide through regulations for a financial assistance scheme to make payments to or in respect of 'qualifying members' of 'qualifying pension schemes'.

---

[3] *Hansard*, HC, col 985 (19 May 2004).
[4] *Hansard*, HL Grand Committee, col 112 (13 October 2004).
[5] *Hansard*, HC, col 1740W (21 December 2004).

Under s 286(2) a 'qualifying member' is defined as either:  10.09

(a) A member of a pension scheme whose pension liabilities are unlikely to be satisfied in full because the scheme has insufficient assets; or

(b) Someone who is no longer a member of the scheme, but whose pension liabilities were not satisfied in full before he left the scheme because the scheme had insufficient assets.

Further requirements may be prescribed in regulations.

A 'qualifying pension scheme' is defined as an occupational pension scheme (which includes a scheme that has been fully wound up), but excludes money purchase schemes and schemes of a 'prescribed description'. There are additional requirements that the scheme must have begun to wind up within a prescribed period but before the cut-off date for the qualification for the PPF (6 April 2005) and the scheme employer must also satisfy certain prescribed requirements.  10.10

A scheme is regarded as having 'insufficient assets' if the scheme has, or had, insufficient assets to satisfy the scheme's liabilities in full (which must be calculated in a prescribed manner).  10.11

As already indicated, the detailed working of the FAS will be set out in regulations. These will make provision:  10.12

(a) For the FAS to be managed by the Secretary of State, or a different body prescribed by regulations;

(b) For the manager of the FAS ('the scheme manager') to hold, manage, and apply a fund in accordance with either regulations or a deed of trust;

(c) For the transfer of scheme property to the scheme manager and the discharge from liability of the trustees or managers of the transferring scheme;

(d) For prescribing the circumstances in which payments will be made to qualifying members and method of calculating any such payment;

(e) For authorizing the Secretary of State to pay grants to the FAS;

(f) For prescribing the circumstances in which amounts can be paid into or out of the fund;

(g) For the review of or appeal against determinations, or a failure to make a determination in relation to the FAS or for investigating complaints relating to the FAS;

(h) For giving the Regulator or the Board of the PPF certain powers in relation to the FAS;

(i) For setting out any discretions which may be exercised in relation to the FAS; and

(j) For applying any provision of Pts 1 (the Pensions Regulator) or 2 (the Board of the Pension Protection Fund) to the FAS with such modifications as may be prescribed.

10.13 Under s 286(4), any amount paid out of the FAS is to be paid out of money provided by Parliament.

10.14 Section 286(5) clarifies that the FAS cannot be funded through a levy and 286(6) states that assistance under the FAS cannot be means-tested. The specific exclusion of the levy method of funding sits rather uncomfortably with the Government's apparent expectation that further funding should be forthcoming from industry at some point in the future.

## C. PRACTICAL ISSUES

10.15 The Government's announcement of the FAS has caused some uncertainty for trustees of occupational pension schemes with underfunded defined benefit liabilities, especially for those schemes already in wind up, as there was a concern that progressing or completing the wind up process might jeopardize eligibility for assistance under the FAS.

10.16 In response to these concerns, OPRA has issued updated guidance[6] to scheme trustees advising them to actively continue the wind up process where this has already begun. The DWP have also indicated[7] that scheme members will not be excluded from FAS coverage simply because trustees have completed the wind up process or have bought annuities and that where trustees consider it to be in the members' best interests they should secure benefits in an appropriate manner.

10.17 Whilst some guidance on this area from government and the current regulator is to be welcomed, the position remains a not entirely satisfactory one from the trustee's perspective. The OPRA guidance emphasizes the importance of maintaining scheme records in order to substantiate an FAS claim, the need to keep members informed about developments in relation to the FAS when updating them on progress with the winding up generally, and the need to consult annuity providers about the practicalities and costs of buying out liabilities at different times. The requirement to maintain scheme records may not be hugely onerous, however, member communication in the short term will be problematic when so few details of the new arrangements are available. In addition, trustees will understandably be concerned that a particular course of action now, albeit taken in good faith, may prejudice claims on the FAS for the future. Bland assurances to the effect that it is their duty to act in the interests of scheme beneficiaries based on all the available information are unlikely to prove of much comfort to hard-pressed trustees in such circumstances.

---

[6] OPRA Update, 'The Financial Assistance Scheme and Completing Scheme Wind-ups' (Ref: OPRA/PN/04/13).
[7] See FAS website http://www.dwp.gov.uk/lifeevent/penret/fas.asp.

# 11

# CROSS BORDER ACTIVITIES WITHIN THE EUROPEAN UNION

| A. Introduction | 11.01 |
| B. Legislation | 11.03 |
| C. Commentary | 11.29 |

## A. INTRODUCTION

Part 7 of the 2004 Act (ss 287 to 295) is concerned with the implementation of those areas of the EU Pensions Directive ('the Directive')[1] relating to cross border activity.  **11.01**

Cross border activity occurs where an occupational pension scheme administered in one EU Member State (the 'Home State') accepts contributions from employers located in another Member State (the 'Host State'). A key aim of the Directive is to put in place a framework which will permit cross border activity as this is the first step towards a single market for occupational retirement provision.  **11.02**

## B. LEGISLATION

### 1. UK Scheme, European Employer—Conditions UK Scheme Must Satisfy

Section 287 of the Act details the conditions an occupational scheme located in the UK has to satisfy before it can begin to operate as a cross border scheme. The conditions are:  **11.03**

(a) The trustees or managers of the scheme must be authorized under s 288 of the Act by the Pensions Regulator established under Pt 1 of the Act;

---

[1] Directive 2003/41 on the activities and supervision of institutions for occupational retirement provision [2003] OJ L235/10.

## 11. Cross Border Activities within the European Union

(b) The trustees or managers of the scheme must have been approved by the Regulator under s 289 of the Act in relation to the European Employer; and

(c) Either a period of two months must have passed since the Regulator notified the trustees or managers that the scheme was approved under s 289(2)(a)(ii) or, before the end of that period, the trustees or managers must have received from the Regulator details about the social and labour law of the Host State (s 290(1)) and in relation to the other matters dealt with in Art 20(5) of the Directive.

**11.04** Where trustees or managers commence cross border activity before complying with the conditions contained in s 287, the Regulator may take action to impose a civil penalty under s 10 of the 1995 Act.

### 2. UK Scheme, European Employer—General Authorization of UK Scheme

**11.05** Section 288 makes provision for the authorization process, which will be set out in regulations. The regulations will specify the form and manner in which applications for authorization have to be made. Where the Regulator is satisfied that the applicant meets the conditions to be detailed in the regulations, it must grant authorization. In any other case, it must refuse authorization.

**11.06** The Regulator will also have power to revoke an existing authorization. The criteria to be applied in reaching such a decision will be set out in regulations.

### 3. UK Scheme, European Employer—Authorization for Particular European Employer

**11.07** On receipt of general authorization by the Regulator pursuant to s 288, under s 289 the trustees or managers of an occupational scheme must apply to the Regulator for approval in relation to any European employer from whom they wish to accept contributions. Such an application must be made in a prescribed form. The information to be supplied consists of:

(a) The name of the employer(s);

(b) A statement of their intention, subject to approval under this section, to accept contributions from the named employer(s);

(c) The name of the Host State; and

(d) Such other information to be prescribed in regulations.

**11.08** Section 289(2) provides that where the Regulator is satisfied that the trustees or managers fulfil the conditions contained in regulations then, within three months of receipt of the prescribed form, the Regulator must:

(a) Notify the competent authority in the Host State of receipt of the application;

(b) Supply that competent authority with the information contained in the application; and
(c) Advise the trustees or managers that they have been approved for the purposes of s 289 in relation to the specified employer(s).

Competent authority is defined in s 295 as a national authority designated in accordance with the laws of the Member State to carry out the duties provided for in the Directive.

**11.09** Should the Regulator determine that the trustees or managers of the occupational scheme have not satisfied the prescribed conditions, the Regulator must inform the trustees or managers that they have not been approved. There is no time limit specified in the Act for such notification but should a reply not have been received from the Regulator within three months of the date on which the Regulator received the prescribed notice, under s 289(3) the trustees or managers may proceed as if approval had been received.

**11.10** The Regulator will also have power to revoke a prior approval. Section 289(4) provides for regulations which will specify the process and criteria for such revocation.

## 4. UK Scheme, European Employer—Notification by Host State of Legal Requirements

**11.11** Where:

(a) The Regulator has forwarded details of the employer(s) to the competent authority in the relevant Host States; and
(b) Within a period of two months (the maximum period permitted in accordance with Art 20(5) of the Directive) of receipt of the details about the employer(s), the Host State's competent authority has supplied the Regulator with details of the relevant social and labour law of the Host State;

the Regulator must, in accordance with s 290, forward that information as soon as practicable to the trustees or managers.

**11.12** Similarly, should the competent authority of the Host State, in accordance with Art 20(8) of the Directive, supply the Regulator with information relating to the social and labour law of the Host State which affects any information previously forwarded, the Regulator must, in accordance with s 290(2), forward that information as soon as practicable to the trustees or managers.

## 5. UK Scheme, European Employer—UK Trustees to Act in Accordance with Host State's Legal Requirements

**11.13** Section 291 places an obligation on the trustees or managers to operate the scheme, so far as it relates to members who are or have been employed by an employer located in the Host State, in accordance with the relevant social and

## 11. Cross Border Activities within the European Union

labour law of the Host State in addition to UK law. If the trustees or managers fail to take all reasonable steps to secure compliance, s 10 (Civil Penalties) of the 1995 Act will apply.

11.14 Section 291(2) provides for regulations to be made which may modify any provision of UK pensions law in its application to the employer. Pensions law for this purpose means:

(a) The PSA 1993;

(b) Part 1 of the 1995 Act (other than ss 62 to 66A (equal treatment));

(c) Part 1 or s 33 of the Welfare Reform and Pensions Act 1999; or

(d) The 2004 Act.

### 6. UK Scheme, European Employer—Ringfencing of Assets

11.15 Under s 292, where trustees or managers of a scheme are accepting contributions from an employer located in a Host State, the Regulator may, in circumstances to be prescribed in regulations, issue a notice requiring the trustees or managers to take, or refrain from taking, such steps as shall be set out in the regulations and as are specified in the notice for the purpose of ringfencing (as defined in the Directive) some or all of the assets or liabilities (or both) of the scheme. If the trustees or managers fail to take reasonable steps to comply with such a notice, s 10 of the 1995 Act will apply.

### 7. European Scheme, UK Employer—Duties of Regulator

11.16 Where a UK employer makes (or proposes to make) contributions to an occupational pension scheme based in a Home State, s 293 places certain duties on the Regulator. These duties are those which Art 20 of the Directive requires or authorizes the competent authority of the Host State to exercise.

11.17 Under s 293(2), the Regulator must, within two months of receipt of a notification pursuant to Art 20(4) of the Directive from a competent authority of a Home State, inform that authority of any relevant legal requirements applicable in the UK.

11.18 Any subsequent significant change to those legal requirements must under s 293(3) be notified to the competent authority in the Home State as soon as practicable.

11.19 The Regulator is required under s 293(4) to monitor compliance by the relevant scheme or institution in the Home State with the relevant UK legal requirements. If the Regulator becomes aware of any breach by the relevant scheme or institution of those legal requirements, it is required to inform the competent authority in that Home State of the breach.

11.20 Further, by s 293(5), the Regulator may issue a notice to the UK employer directing it:

(a) To take or refrain from taking such steps as are specified in the notice so as to remedy the breach by the scheme or institution; or

(b) Cease to make any further contributions to the relevant scheme or institution.

Regulations may make further provisions about the effect of a notice of this type, including conferring functions on the Regulator.

Section 10 of the 1995 Act applies to any UK employers who fail, without reasonable excuse, to comply with a notice under s 293(5).

11.21

Section 293(8) contains various definitions, including:

11.22

(a) 'European pensions institution' which is defined as an institution for occupational retirement provision, as defined in Art 6(a) of the Directive, that has its main administration in a Member State other than the UK;

(b) 'Relevant legal requirements' which means such requirements of UK law as may be prescribed relating to occupational pension schemes as applies in any part of the UK; and

(c) 'UK employer' which means an employer who is a body corporate incorporated under UK law or, in any other case, is resident in the UK.

## 8. European Scheme, UK Employer—Restrictions on Disposal of UK-held Assets of European Scheme

Section 294 prevents the free disposal of UK-held assets of a European occupational pension scheme that has its main administration in another Member State.

11.23

If the Regulator receives a request from the competent authority of another Member State, then the High Court or, in Scotland, the Court of Session may, on an application by the Regulator in respect of such assets, grant an injunction restraining (or, in Scotland, an interdict prohibiting) a defendant from disposing or otherwise dealing with the assets to which the application relates.

11.24

Where an injunction or interdict is granted, under s 294(3), the court may by subsequent orders make provision for such incidental and supplementary matters as it considers necessary to enable the competent authority who submitted the request to perform any of its functions in relation to the assets subject to the injunction or interdict.

11.25

Should the European occupational pension scheme not be a party to the court proceedings, by s 294(4), it has the same rights to notice of the proceedings as a defendant (or, in Scotland, a defender or a respondent) and may take part as a party in the proceedings.

11.26

Where the European occupational pension scheme takes part as a party, the court may take account of the additional expense that any other party to the proceedings has incurred and award the whole or a part of this additional

11.27

expense as costs to the party who incurred it, whatever the outcome of the Regulator's application.

**11.28** UK-held assets are defined in s 294(6) as assets held by a depositary or custodian located in the UK. Assets, depositary, custodian, and located have the same meaning as in Art 19(3) of the Directive.

## C. COMMENTARY

**11.29** The Government does not appear to expect any rapid movement in relation to these provisions as most of the details have yet to be worked out. Whilst Britain, the Netherlands, and Ireland have well developed occupational schemes and Germany has some, other Member States have very few. Representatives of the regulatory regimes of all Member States are to meet to harmonize structures and develop the detail. The meetings are taking place from late October 2004.

**11.30** Overall, there was little criticism of this Part of the Act during its passage through Parliament. Apart from some comment as to the complications involved, the sections were welcomed with the hope that progress can be made and opportunities can be opened up for those institutions operating in the UK in the appropriate markets.

# 12

# STATE PENSIONS

| A. Introduction | 12.01 |
| --- | --- |
| B. Legislation | 12.04 |
| C. Commentary | 12.34 |

## A. INTRODUCTION

State retirement pensions are paid to people who have reached pensionable age (currently age 65 for men and 60 for women—although the latter is gradually to increase to 65 for those women born between 6 April 1950 and 5 April 1955 (s 126 and Sch 4 to the 1995 Act)). To get a full basic state retirement pension, about 90% of an individual's working life (49 years for men and between 44 and 49 years for women, depending on their date of birth and pensionable age) must be made up of 'qualifying years'. A qualifying year is a tax year in which a person receives (or is treated as having received) qualifying earnings of at least 52 times the lower earnings limit for that year.  **12.01**

Part 8 of the 2004 Act contains various changes to the State pension system. In one case (s 296), it corrects an omission from existing legislation, whilst in another (s 297), it amends the current provisions for deferring the State pension as proposed in the Green Paper.  **12.02**

Part 8 also includes powers to permit the disclosure of State pension information so that employees are better able to plan for their retirement. Furthermore, it reflects the termination of the reciprocal agreement with Australia set out in Sch 1 to the Social Security (Australia) Order 1992[1] and in the Social Security (Australia) Order (Northern Ireland) 1992[2] as subsequently amended by the exchange of notes set out in Sch 3 to those orders.  **12.03**

---

[1] Social Security (Australia) Order 1992 (SI 1992/1312).
[2] Social Security (Australia) Order (Northern Ireland) 1992 (SI 1992/269).

## B. LEGISLATION

### 1. Persons Entitled to More than One Category B Pension

**12.04** Under legislation in existence before April 1992, those persons entitled to more than one category B pension (this covers married women, widows, and widowers) were able to choose the most beneficial pension for them. However, in 1992, contributory benefits legislation was consolidated into the Social Security Contributions and Benefits Act 1992 ('the 1992 Act') and, in doing so, the ability to choose was omitted by mistake.

**12.05** Section 43 of the 1992 Act enabled a person who is entitled to two State retirement pensions of a different category to choose which one is most beneficial, but it did not permit such a choice where a person was entitled to two State retirement pensions of the same category. It is the Government's policy intention that persons entitled to more than one State retirement pension (whether of the same category or not) should be allowed to notify the Secretary of State in writing which of the pensions he wishes to receive.

**12.06** The ability to choose was reinstated on an extra-statutory basis in 2001 when the Government discovered the mistake which had arisen in 1992. Section 296 of the Act amends s 43(3) of the 1992 Act to restore the choice which was available under legislation before April 1992.

### 2. Deferral of State Pensions

**12.07** For a person to receive any State retirement pension, a claim must be made. Failure to do so means that no pension is paid between pensionable age and the date of the claim. The pension payable from the date of the claim will, however, be increased to compensate for the period of deferral. The rate of increase is 1/7 of 1% of the weekly pension for each 'incremental period' (equivalent to a week) in the period of deferral. Increments of less than 1% are not awarded, so the minimum period of deferral is seven weeks. The incremental rate is currently equivalent to 7.4% for each full year of deferral.

**12.08** Deferral may be as a result of a conscious decision to defer the pension or failure to claim it when the person reached State Pension Age. It can also arise where a person has already started to receive his State pension but decides to cancel his entitlement at a later date. This option is available once only.

**12.09** The Government included proposals for amending the arrangements for those who choose to defer their State pension in the Green Paper.

**12.10** Section 297 and Sch 11 amend the current statutory provisions relating to deferral of State retirement pensions after State Pension Age (ss 55 and 55C of the 1992 Act and para 6 of Sch 4 to the 1995 Act).

**12.11** The improvement to the rate of increase where State pensions are deferred was originally contained in para 6 of Sch 4 to the 1995 Act, and was due to come into force in April 2010. After that date, the weekly rate of increase was to be 1/5 of 1% for each period of five weeks of deferral which is equivalent to 10.4% for each full year of deferral. The limit of five years on the period of deferral was to be removed. These changes are now to be introduced from April 2005.

### 3. Lump Sum Alternative

12.12 At the same time, the alternative of a lump sum instead of increments to a member's pension will be introduced. Section 297(1) and (2) of the 2004 Act introduce new ss 55 and 55C to the 1992 Act.

12.13 The new s 55 states the new option available to a person who defers taking his State pension, namely (a) an increase to their State pension calculated as described above; or (b) a taxable lump sum. The new s 55C makes corresponding provision where a shared additional pension is deferred.

12.14 Section 297(3) amends Sch 4 of the 1995 Act to bring the changes to the rate at which increments accrue to State pensions into force from 6 April 2005.

12.15 Finally, s 297(4) introduces Sch 11 which amends Schedule 5 to the 1992 Act and other related enactments and makes certain transitional provisions.

### 4. Choice of Pension Increments or Lump Sum

12.16 Paragraph 4 of Sch 11 of the 2004 Act inserts a new para A1 at the beginning of Sch 5 of the 1992 Act, which requires a person who has deferred his State pension for a minimum period of twelve months to choose between increments or a lump sum when he decides to claim his pension. However, the new para A1(4) prevents a person whose State pension includes a GMP from choosing the lump sum for that component of their State pension. The Government's intention is that only increments to such a pension will be permitted. This will avoid the need for alterations to the rules of contracted out schemes.

### 5. Pension Increments

12.17 Paragraph 5 inserts a new para 1 in Sch 5 of the 1992 Act, which provides that increments will be added to a person's State pension where the period of deferral is less than twelve months or, if longer, the person elected to receive increments. It also preserves the previous provision that the minimum increment must be at least 1%. Using the new incremental rate of 1/5 of 1% means that the minimum deferral period is now five weeks (previously it was seven weeks).

12.18 Paragraph 6 corrects an omission in existing legislation. In calculating increments, the policy intention is that additions to the pension for a dependent husband or wife under ss 83 and 84 of the 1992 Act are excluded. Paragraph 2(5)(b) of Sch 5 to that Act only excludes additions under s 83 (paid to a husband for his wife). From April 2010 both sections are replaced by s 83A

## 12. State Pensions

which equalizes the additions for dependent husbands and wives. Paragraph 6(1) substitutes a reference to s 83A for that to s 83 whilst para 6(2) provides that until s 83A comes into force in 2010, it is to be read as a reference to ss 83 and 84.

### 6. Lump Sum

12.19 Paragraph 7 deals with the calculation of an increase to a State pension where the person elected to receive a lump sum but part of the pension consists of GMP. As mentioned in para 12.16 above, lump sums are not available in lieu of increments to such pensions.

12.20 Paragraph 8(1) introduces new paras 3A and 3B into Sch 5 of the 1992 Act. Paragraph 3A provides that a person is entitled to a lump sum if he has deferred his entitlement to his State pension and either elected, or is treated as having so elected, to receive a lump sum.

12.21 Paragraph 3B sets out the formula used to calculate the lump sum. This is modelled on the same principle as an interest bearing savings account—interest is applied each week and compounded. To capture accurately the amount of State pension foregone, the 'accrual period' will match the provisions which determine what constitutes a person's benefit week. A benefit week is a period of seven days commencing on the benefit payday appropriate to that person.

12.22 In the Explanatory Notes, the Government included the following example of how the formula works.

> Assume Miss Smith would have been entitled to retirement pension of £100 per week from April 2005 had she claimed at that point, and that the prescribed interest rate at the start of the period of deferment is 6.00%. This is equivalent to a weekly increase factor of $\sqrt[52]{} = 1.001121$, where 1.06 refers to a prescribed interest rate of 6.00%.
>
> At the end of the first accrual period, the amount accrued would be:
>
> $$(£0.00 + £100) \times \sqrt[52]{} = £100.11$$
>
> (note that in the first week, there is no 'accrued amount' to bring forward from the previous week, therefore this is shown as zero).
>
> At the end of the second accrual period, the amount accrued would increase to:
>
> $$(£100.11 + £100) \times \sqrt[52]{} = £200.34$$
>
> At the end of the third accrual period, the amount accrued would increase to:
>
> $$(£200.34 + £100) \times \sqrt[52]{} = £300.67$$
>
> After 52 weeks, Miss Smith would have accrued a lump sum of £5357.49.
>
> Assume Miss Smith continues to defer and her retirement pension entitlement increases to £103 with effect from April 2006. The lump sum will

# Legislation

> continue to be calculated in the same manner as above, except that £100 changes to £103. At the end of the first accrual period using the new rate, the lump sum would be:
>
> $$(£5357.49 + £103) \times {}^{52}\sqrt{} = £5466.61$$
>
> At the end of the second accrual period using the new rate, the lump sum would be:
>
> $$(£5466.61 + £103) \times {}^{52}\sqrt{} = £5678.85$$
>
> If Miss Smith chose to defer for two years altogether, at the end of March 2007 she would be entitled to a lump sum of £11,197.15.

The prescribed interest rate will be that which is 2% higher than the Bank of England base rate or such higher rate as may be prescribed in regulations made under para 19 of the Schedule.

## 7. Options for Spouse

Paragraph 9 inserts a new para 3C into Sch 5 of the 1992 Act. This enables the spouse of a person who has deferred his pension for at least twelve months and dies before claiming it, to choose between inheriting an increased pension or a lump sum. Such choice can only be made at the same time as the spouse claims her own pension. 12.23

Paragraph 10 amends para 4 of Sch 5 of the 1992 Act to provide that a spouse will inherit increments if the deceased was receiving them on his death if the spouse so chooses or if the period of deferral was less than twelve months. 12.24

The new paras 7A and 7B inserted by para 11 replicate the provisions of paras 3A and 3B in relation to the calculation of the lump sum for a widowed person. 12.25

Paragraph 12 inserts a new para 7C which provides that: 12.26

(a) A lump sum will be rounded to the nearest penny (para 7C(1)); and

(b) When prescribing the interest rate to be used in the lump sum calculation, the Secretary of State must have regard to the national economic situation and any other matters he considers relevant (para 7C(2)).

## 8. Consequential Amendments

Paragraph 14 makes various consequential amendments to para 8 of Sch 5 of the 1992 Act to include references to the lump sum calculation. The new sub-paras (4) to (6) prevent increments being inherited by a surviving spouse in respect of a deferred pension that was either wholly or partly based on the survivor's own contributions. 12.27

A new Sch 5A is inserted in the 1992 Act by para 15. This Schedule offers a 12.28

choice between a lump sum and weekly pension increments where a person has deferred a shared additional pension. It further states how that lump sum or increase is calculated.

12.29 Paragraphs 1, 2, 4, and 5 of the new schedule replicate the provisions in paras A1, 1, 3A, and 3B of Sch 5 (as substituted by paras 4, 5, and 8(1) of Sch 11) as regards choosing between increments or a lump sum and the calculation of the lump sum.

12.30 The consequential amendments contained in Pt 2 of Sch 11 are:

(a) Paragraph 17—this amends s 62(1) of the 1992 Act so that where any entitlement to State Graduated Pension has been deferred, regulations may offer the choice between increments and a lump sum;

(b) Paragraph 18—this amends s 122(1) of the same Act to include a definition of 'Bank of England base rate' for the purpose of calculating any lump sum and extends the definitions of 'deferred' and 'period of deferment' to cover deferment of shared additional pensions;

(c) Paragraph 19—amends s 176 of the 1992 Act to provide that regulations prescribing the percentage rate to be used in the calculation of the lump sum shall be made by the affirmative procedure;

(d) Paragraphs 20 to 22—these paragraphs amend the Social Security Administration Act 1992 to allow a lump sum to be uprated where a surviving spouse has not already attained pensionable age on the death of the spouse and is not entitled to a State pension;

(e) Paragraph 24—this omits s 50(2) of the Welfare Reform and Pensions Act 1999, which increased the rate at which increments accrue and removed the time limits for accrual in shared additional pension from 2010. These amendments are now part of the new Sch 5A;

(f) Paragraph 25—this enables the modifications to the inherited State Earnings Related Pension Scheme provisions to be extended to the calculation of the lump sum for surviving spouses;

(g) Paragraph 26—this restricts a widower from inheriting a lump sum or increments if he reaches pensionable age before 6 April 2010 unless he was over pensionable age on the death of the spouse; and

(h) Paragraph 27—introduces a regulation making power in relation to cases where a period of deferment spans a period before and after 6 April 2005.

### 9. Disclosure of State Pension Information

12.31 Section 298 introduces a power enabling the Secretary of State to disclose details about State pensions to individuals or organizations who provide services to the trustees, managers, or employers of occupational and personal pension schemes in connection with the provision of combined pension forecasts. (These powers already exist in relation to the trustees, managers, and employers themselves.) These statements are considered by the Government to be an essential part of their plans to promote financial planning by individuals for retirement (see Pt 4 of the Act).

## 10. Claims for State Pensions Following Termination of Reciprocal Agreement with Australia

The final section of Pt 8 deals with claims for certain benefits following the termination of the reciprocal social security agreement with Australia. Under s 299(1) and (2), the claims concerned are for retirement pension, bereavement benefit, or widow's benefit made on or after 1 March 2001 or one for retirement pension or widow's benefit made before 1 March 2001 where the claimant only became entitled to the pension or benefit on or after that date. 12.32

For the purposes of these claims, under s 299(3) and (4), various provisions of the reciprocal agreement are treated as continuing in force and the relevant UK legislation shall be treated as if modified to the extent necessary to give effect to those provisions. These are: 12.33

(a) References to periods when a person was resident in Australia shall only include periods before 6 April 2001 which form part of a period of such residency which commenced before 1 March 2001;

(b) Entitlement by virtue of previous receipt of a pension in Australia under Arts 3(3) and 5(2) of the agreement applies only to persons who were last in Australia during a period falling within para (a) above;

(c) Any reference to the territory of the UK shall exclude Jersey, Guernsey, Alderney, Herm, or Jethou;

(d) Widow's benefit, widow's payment, widow's pension, and widowed mother's allowance shall be deemed to include, respectively, bereavement benefit, bereavement payment, bereavement allowance, and widowed parent's allowance; and

(e) For the purposes of claims by widowers, references to widows and husbands shall include widowers and wives.

### C. COMMENTARY

Little comment was made during the Act's passage through Parliament in relation to the changes enabling a person to choose to receive the most beneficial of two or more State pensions to which he was entitled. Some attempt was made to remove the requirement of a minimum of ten years' contribution before becoming entitled to any State pension but this failed to attract support. 12.34

## 12. State Pensions

**12.35** Similarly, s 297 (relating to the ability to defer retirement pensions and shared additional pensions) attracted little comment other than to request that the rate of interest used would be that applicable at the date the benefit becomes payable not that at the date of deferral.

# APPENDIX 1

# Pensions Act 2004

2004 Chapter 35

CONTENTS

PART 1
THE PENSIONS REGULATOR

*Establishment*   178

Section
1. The Pensions Regulator
2. Membership of the Regulator
3. Further provision about the Regulator

*General provisions about functions*   178

4. Regulator's functions
5. Regulator's objectives
6. Supplementary powers
7. Transfer of OPRA's functions to the Regulator

*Non-executive functions*   180

8. Non-executive functions

*The determinations panel*   181

9. The Determinations Panel
10. Functions exercisable by the Determinations Panel

*Annual report*   183

11. Annual reports to Secretary of State

*Provision of information, education and assistance*   183

12. Provision of information, education and assistance

## Pensions Act 2004

*New powers in respect of occupational and personal pension schemes*     184

13. Improvement notices
14. Third party notices
15. Injunctions and interdicts
16. Restitution
17. Power of the Regulator to recover unpaid contributions
18. Pension liberation: interpretation
19. Pension liberation: court's power to order restitution
20. Pension liberation: restraining orders
21. Pension liberation: repatriation orders

*Powers in relation to winding up of occupational pension schemes*     190

22. Powers to wind up occupational pension schemes
23. Freezing orders
24. Consequences of freezing order
25. Period of effect etc of freezing order
26. Validation of action in contravention of freezing order
27. Effect of determination to wind up scheme on freezing order
28. Effect of winding up order on freezing order
29. Effect of assessment period under Part 2 on freezing order
30. Power to give a direction where freezing order ceases to have effect
31. Notification of trustees, managers, employers and members
32. Sections 23 to 31: supplementary

*Trustees of occupational pension schemes*     198

33. Prohibition orders
34. Suspension orders
35. Appointments of trustees by the Regulator
36. Independent trustees
37. Disqualification

*Contribution notices where avoidance of employer debt*     202

38. Contribution notices where avoidance of employer debt
39. The sum specified in a section 38 contribution notice
40. Content and effect of a section 38 contribution notice
41. Section 38 contribution notice: relationship with employer debt
42. Section 38 contribution notice: clearance statements

*Financial support directions*     207

43. Financial support directions
44. Meaning of "service company" and "insufficiently resourced"
45. Meaning of "financial support"

46. Financial support directions: clearance statements
47. Contribution notices where non-compliance with financial support direction
48. The sum specified in a section 47 contribution notice
49. Content and effect of a section 47 contribution notice
50. Section 47 contribution notice: relationship with employer debt
51. Sections 43 to 50: interpretation

*Transactions at an undervalue* 214

52. Restoration orders where transactions at an undervalue
53. Restoration orders: supplementary
54. Content and effect of a restoration order
55. Contribution notice where failure to comply with restoration order
56. Content and effect of a section 55 contribution notice

*Sections 38 to 56: partnerships and limited liability partnerships* 218

57. Sections 38 to 56: partnerships and limited liability partnerships

*Applications under the insolvency act 1986* 219

58. Regulator's right to apply under section 423 of Insolvency Act 1986

*Register of schemes* 220

59. Register of occupational and personal pension schemes
60. Registrable information
61. The register: inspection, provision of information and reports etc
62. The register: duties of trustees or managers
63. Duty of the Regulator to issue scheme return notices
64. Duty of trustees or managers to provide scheme return
65. Scheme returns: supplementary

*Register of prohibited trustees* 224

66. Register of prohibited trustees
67. Accessibility of register of prohibited trustees

*Collecting information relevant to the board of the pension protection fund* 225

68. Information relevant to the Board
69. Duty to notify the Regulator of certain events

*Reporting breaches of the law* 226

70. Duty to report breaches of the law

**Pensions Act 2004**

*Reports by skilled persons*   227

71. Reports by skilled persons

*Gathering information*   228

72. Provision of information
73. Inspection of premises
74. Inspection of premises in respect of employers' obligations
75. Inspection of premises: powers of inspectors
76. Inspection of premises: supplementary
77. Penalties relating to sections 72 to 75
78. Warrants
79. Sections 72 to 78: interpretation

*Provision of false or misleading information*   234

80. Offences of providing false or misleading information

*Use of information*   235

81. Use of information

*Disclosure of information*   235

82. Restricted information
83. Information supplied to the Regulator by corresponding overseas authorities
84. Disclosure for facilitating exercise of functions by the Regulator
85. Disclosure for facilitating exercise of functions by the Board
86. Disclosure for facilitating exercise of functions by other supervisory authorities
87. Other permitted disclosures
88. Tax information

*Reports*   239

89. Publishing reports etc

*Codes of practice*   239

90. Codes of practice
91. Procedure for issue and publication of codes of practice
92. Revocation of codes of practice

*Exercise of regulatory functions*   241

93. The Regulator's procedure in relation to its regulatory functions
94. Publication of procedure in relation to regulatory functions

95. Application of standard and special procedure
96. Standard procedure
97. Special procedure: applicable cases
98. Special procedure
99. Compulsory review
100. Duty to have regard to the interests of members etc
101. Powers to vary or revoke orders, notices or directions etc

*The pensions regulator tribunal* 249

102. The Pensions Regulator Tribunal
103. References to the Tribunal
104. Appeal on a point of law
105. Redetermination etc by the Tribunal
106. Legal assistance scheme

PART 2
THE BOARD OF THE PENSION PROTECTION FUND

CHAPTER 1
THE BOARD

*Establishment* 252

107. The Board of the Pension Protection Fund
108. Membership of the Board
109. Further provision about the Board

*General provision about functions* 253

110. Board's functions
111. Supplementary powers

*Non-executive functions* 253

112. Non-executive functions

*Financial matters* 254

113. Investment of funds
114. Investment principles
115. Borrowing
116. Grants
117. Administration levy
118. Fees

*Annual reports* 256

119. Annual reports to Secretary of State

## CHAPTER 2
## INFORMATION RELATING TO EMPLOYER'S INSOLVENCY ETC

*Insolvency events* 257

120. Duty to notify insolvency events in respect of employers
121. Insolvency event, insolvency date and insolvency practitioner

*Status of scheme* 259

122. Insolvency practitioner's duty to issue notices confirming status of scheme
123. Approval of notices issued under section 122

*Board's duties* 260

124. Board's duty where there is a failure to comply with section 122
125. Binding notices confirming status of scheme

## CHAPTER 3
## PENSION PROTECTION

*Eligible schemes* 262

126. Eligible schemes

*Circumstances in which board assumes responsibility for eligible schemes* 262

127. Duty to assume responsibility for schemes following insolvency event
128. Duty to assume responsibility for schemes following application or notification
129. Applications and notifications for the purposes of section 128
130. Board's duty where application or notification received under section 129
131. Protected liabilities

*Restrictions on schemes during the assessment period* 266

132. Assessment periods
133. Admission of new members, payment of contributions etc
134. Directions
135. Restrictions on winding up, discharge of liabilities etc
136. Power to validate contraventions of section 135
137. Board to act as creditor of the employer
138. Payment of scheme benefits

139. Loans to pay scheme benefits

*Ill health pensions* 272

140. Reviewable ill health pensions
141. Effect of a review
142. Sections 140 and 141: interpretation

*Valuation of assets and liabilities* 274

143. Board's obligation to obtain valuation of assets and protected liabilities
144. Approval of valuation
145. Binding valuations

*Refusal to assume responsibility* 277

146. Schemes which become eligible schemes
147. New schemes created to replace existing schemes
148. Withdrawal following issue of section 122(4) notice

*Cessation of involvement with a scheme* 279

149. Circumstances in which Board ceases to be involved with an eligible scheme
150. Consequences of the Board ceasing to be involved with a scheme

*Reconsideration* 282

151. Application for reconsideration
152. Duty to assume responsibility following reconsideration

*Closed schemes* 285

153. Closed schemes

*Winding up* 286

154. Requirement to wind up schemes with sufficient assets to meet protected liabilities

*Provisions applying to closed schemes* 288

155. Treatment of closed schemes
156. Valuations of closed schemes

*Reconsideration of closed schemes* 289

157. Applications and notifications where closed schemes have insufficient assets

158. Duty to assume responsibility for closed schemes
159. Closed schemes: further assessment periods

*Assumption of responsibility for a scheme* 291

160. Transfer notice
161. Effect of Board assuming responsibility for a scheme
162. The pension compensation provisions
163. Adjustments to be made where the Board assumes responsibility for a scheme
164. Postponement of compensation entitlement for the assessment period
165. Guaranteed minimum pensions
166. Duty to pay scheme benefits unpaid at assessment date etc
167. Modification of Chapter where liabilities discharged during assessment period
168. Administration of compensation

*Discharge of Board's liabilities* 296

169. Discharge of liabilities in respect of compensation
170. Discharge of liabilities in respect of money purchase benefits

*Equal treatment* 297

171. Equal treatment

*Relationship with fraud compensation regime* 298

172. Relationship with fraud compensation regime

*The fund* 298

173. Pension Protection Fund

*The levies* 300

174. Initial levy
175. Pension protection levies
176. Supplementary provisions about pension protection levies
177. Amounts to be raised by the pension protection levies
178. The levy ceiling
179. Valuations to determine scheme underfunding
180. Pension protection levies during the transitional period
181. Calculation, collection and recovery of levies

## CHAPTER 4
## FRAUD COMPENSATION

*Entitlement to fraud compensation* 304

182. Cases where fraud compensation payments can be made
183. Board's duties in respect of certain applications under section 182
184. Recovery of value
185. Fraud compensation payments
186. Interim payments
187. Board's powers to make fraud compensation transfer payments

*The fund* 310

188. Fraud Compensation Fund

*The levy* 310

189. Fraud compensation levy

## CHAPTER 5
## GATHERING INFORMATION

190. Information to be provided to the Board etc
191. Notices requiring provision of information
192. Entry of premises
193. Penalties relating to sections 191 and 192
194. Warrants

*Provision of false or misleading information* 315

195. Offence of providing false or misleading information to the Board

*Use of information* 315

196. Use of information

*Disclosure of information* 316

197. Restricted information
198. Disclosure for facilitating exercise of functions by the Board
199. Disclosure for facilitating exercise of functions by the Regulator
200. Disclosure for facilitating exercise of functions by other supervisory authorities
201. Other permitted disclosures
202. Tax information

**Pensions Act 2004**

*Provision of information to members of schemes etc*   319

203. Provision of information to members of schemes etc

*Interpretation*   320

204. Sections 190 to 203: interpretation

*Reports*   320

205. Publishing reports etc

## CHAPTER 6
## REVIEWS, APPEALS AND MALADMINISTRATION

*Review etc by the Board*   321

206. Meaning of "reviewable matters"
207. Review and reconsideration by the Board of reviewable matters
208. Investigation by the Board of complaints of maladministration

*The PPF Ombudsman*   323

209. The Ombudsman for the Board of the Pension Protection Fund
210. Deputy PPF Ombudsmen
211. Status etc of the PPF Ombudsman and deputies
212. Annual reports to Secretary of State

*References to the PPF Ombudsman*   326

213. Reference of reviewable matter to the PPF Ombudsman
214. Investigation by PPF Ombudsman of complaints of maladministration
215. Referral of questions of law
216. Publishing reports etc
217. Determinations of the PPF Ombudsman
218. Obstruction etc of the PPF Ombudsman

## CHAPTER 7
## MISCELLANEOUS

*Backdating the winding up of eligible schemes*   329

219. Backdating the winding up of eligible schemes

*Pension sharing*     330

220. Pension sharing

## PART 3
## SCHEME FUNDING

*Introductory*     331

221. Pension schemes to which this Part applies

*Scheme funding*     331

222. The statutory funding objective
223. Statement of funding principles
224. Actuarial valuations and reports
225. Certification of technical provisions
226. Recovery plan
227. Schedule of contributions
228. Failure to make payments
229. Matters requiring agreement of the employer
230. Matters on which advice of actuary must be obtained
231. Powers of the Regulator

*Supplementary provisions*     337

232. Power to modify provisions of this Part
233. Construction as one with the Pensions Act 1995

## PART 4
## FINANCIAL PLANNING FOR RETIREMENT

*Retirement planning*     337

234. Promoting and facilitating financial planning for retirement
235. Supply of information for purposes of section 234
236. Use and supply of information: private pensions policy and retirement planning
237. Combined pension forecasts

*Employee information and advice*     339

238. Information and advice to employees

## PART 5
## OCCUPATIONAL AND PERSONAL PENSION SCHEMES: MISCELLANEOUS PROVISIONS

*Categories of pension scheme* 339

239. Categories of pension scheme
240. Meaning of "employer" in Part 1 of the Pensions Act 1995

*Requirements for member-nominated trustees and directors* 341

241. Requirement for member-nominated trustees
242. Requirement for member-nominated directors of corporate trustees
243. Member-nominated trustees and directors: supplementary

*Obligations of trustees of occupational pension schemes* 344

244. Investment principles
245. Power to make regulations governing investment by trustees
246. Borrowing by trustees
247. Requirement for knowledge and understanding: individual trustees
248. Requirement for knowledge and understanding: corporate trustees
249. Requirement for knowledge and understanding: supplementary

*Payment of surplus to employer* 347

250. Payment of surplus to employer
251. Payment of surplus to employer: transitional power to amend scheme

*Restrictions on payment into occupational pension schemes* 349

252. UK-based scheme to be trust with effective rules
253. Non-European scheme to be trust with UK-resident trustee
254. Representative of non-European scheme to be treated as trustee

*Activities of occupational pension schemes* 350

255. Activities of occupational pension schemes

*No indemnification for fines or civil penalties* 350

256. No indemnification for fines or civil penalties

*Pension protection on transfer of employment* 351

257. Conditions for pension protection
258. Form of protection

*Consultation by employers* — 353

259. Consultation by employers: occupational pension schemes
260. Consultation by employers: personal pension schemes
261. Further provisions about regulations relating to consultation

*Modification of pension rights* — 355

262. Modification of subsisting rights

*Short service benefit* — 363

263. Increase in age at which short service benefit must be payable

*Early leavers* — 363

264. Early leavers: cash transfer sums and contribution refunds

*Safeguarding pension rights* — 369

265. Paternity leave and adoption leave
266. Inalienability of occupational pension

*Voluntary contributions* — 372

267. Voluntary contributions

*Payments by employers* — 372

268. Payments made by employers to personal pension schemes
269. Payments made by employers and members to occupational pension schemes

*Winding up* — 373

270. Winding up

*Deficiency in assets of certain occupational pension schemes* — 379

271. Debt due from the employer when assets insufficient
272. Debt due from the employer in the case of multi-employer schemes

*Pension disputes* — 384

273. Resolution of disputes

**Pensions Act 2004**

*The pensions ombudsman*     386

274. The Pensions Ombudsman and Deputy Pensions Ombudsmen
275. Jurisdiction
276. Investigations

*Pension compensation*     388

277. Amendments relating to the Pensions Compensation Board

*Annual increases in rate of pensions*     389

278. Annual increase in rate of certain occupational pensions
279. Annual increase in rate of certain personal pensions
280. Power to increase pensions giving effect to pension credits etc

*Revaluation*     391

281. Exemption from statutory revaluation requirement

*Contracting out*     392

282. Meaning of "working life" in Pension Schemes Act 1993
283. Power to prescribe conditions by reference to Inland Revenue approval
284. Restrictions on commutation and age at which benefits may be received

*Stakeholder pensions*     393

285. Meaning of "stakeholder pension scheme"

### PART 6
### FINANCIAL ASSISTANCE SCHEME FOR MEMBERS OF CERTAIN PENSION SCHEMES

286. Financial assistance scheme for members of certain pension schemes

### PART 7
### CROSS-BORDER ACTIVITIES WITHIN EUROPEAN UNION

*UK occupational pension scheme receiving contributions from european employer*     395

287. Occupational pension scheme receiving contributions from European employer
288. General authorisation to accept contributions from European employers
289. Approval in relation to particular European employer

290. Notification of legal requirements of host member State outside United Kingdom
291. Duty of trustees or managers to act consistently with law of host member State
292. Power of Regulator to require ringfencing of assets

*European occupational pension scheme receiving contributions from UK employer* 398

293. Functions of Regulator in relation to institutions administered in other member States

*Assistance for other european regulators* 398

294. Stopping disposal of assets of institutions administered in other member States

*Interpretation* 399

295. Interpretation of Part

## PART 8
## STATE PENSIONS

*Entitlement to more than one pension* 400

296. Persons entitled to more than one Category B retirement pension

*Deferral of state pension* 400

297. Deferral of retirement pensions and shared additional pensions

*Miscellaneous* 402

298. Disclosure of state pension information
299. Claims for certain benefits following termination of reciprocal agreement with Australia

## PART 9
## MISCELLANEOUS AND SUPPLEMENTARY

*Dissolution of existing bodies* 404

300. Dissolution of OPRA
301. Transfer of employees from OPRA to the Regulator
302. Dissolution of the Pensions Compensation Board

**Pensions Act 2004**

*Service of notifications etc and electronic working*     405

303. Service of notifications and other documents
304. Notification and documents in electronic form
305. Timing and location of things done electronically

*General*     408

306. Overriding requirements
307. Modification of this Act in relation to certain categories of schemes
308. Modification of pensions legislation that refers to employers
309. Offences by bodies corporate and partnerships
310. Admissibility of statements
311. Protected items
312. Liens
313. Crown application

*Regulations and orders*     413

314. Breach of regulations
315. Subordinate legislation (general provisions)
316. Parliamentary control of subordinate legislation
317. Consultations about regulations

*Interpretation*     415

318. General interpretation

*Miscellaneous and supplementary*     417

319. Minor and consequential amendments
320. Repeals and revocations
321. Pre-consolidation amendments
322. Commencement
323. Extent
324. Northern Ireland
325. Short title

**Schedules**

| | | |
|---|---|---|
| Schedule 1 | The Pensions Regulator | 420 |
| Part 1 | Members of the Regulator | |
| Part 2 | Staff of the Regulator | |
| Part 3 | Members of the Determinations Panel | |
| Part 4 | Proceedings and delegation etc | |
| Part 5 | Funding and accounts | |
| Part 6 | Status and liability etc | |

| | | |
|---|---|---|
| Schedule 2 | The reserved regulatory functions | 430 |
| Part 1 | Functions under the Pension Schemes Act 1993 (c. 48) | |
| Part 2 | Functions under the Pensions Act 1995 (c. 26) | |
| Part 3 | Functions under the Welfare Reform and Pensions Act 1999 (c. 30) | |
| Part 4 | Functions under this Act | |
| Schedule 3 | Restricted information held by the Regulator: certain permitted disclosures to facilitate exercise of functions | 433 |
| Schedule 4 | The Pensions Regulator Tribunal | 436 |
| Part 1 | The Tribunal | |
| Part 2 | Constitution of the Tribunal | |
| Part 3 | Tribunal Procedure | |
| Part 4 | Status etc | |
| Schedule 5 | The Board of the Pension Protection Fund | 441 |
| Part 1 | Members of the Board | |
| Part 2 | Staff of the Board | |
| Part 3 | Proceedings and delegation etc | |
| Part 4 | Accounts | |
| Part 5 | Status and liability etc | |
| Schedule 6 | Transfer of property, rights and liabilities to the Board | 449 |
| Schedule 7 | Pension compensation provisions | 451 |
| Schedule 8 | Restricted information held by the Board: certain permitted disclosures to facilitate exercise of functions | 474 |
| Schedule 9 | Reviewable matters | 477 |
| Schedule 10 | Use and supply of information: private pensions policy and retirement planning | 479 |
| Schedule 11 | Deferral of retirement pensions and shared additional pensions | 481 |
| Part 1 | Principal amendments of Social Security Contributions and Benefits Act 1992 (c. 4) | |
| Part 2 | Consequential amendments | |
| Part 3 | Transitional provisions | |
| Schedule 12 | Minor and consequential amendments | 492 |
| Schedule 13 | Repeals and revocations | 507 |
| Part 1 | Repeals | |
| Part 2 | Revocations | |

PENSIONS ACT 2004

PART 1
THE PENSIONS REGULATOR

*Establishment*

**1  The pensions regulator**

There shall be a body corporate called the Pensions Regulator (in this Act referred to as "the Regulator").

**2  Membership of the regulator**

(1) The Regulator is to consist of the following members—
   (a) a chairman appointed by the Secretary of State,
   (b) the Chief Executive of the Regulator, and
   (c) at least five other persons appointed by the Secretary of State after consulting the chairman.
(2) The chairman must not be appointed from the staff of the Regulator or be the chairman of the Board of the Pension Protection Fund (see section 108).
(3) At least two of the members appointed under subsection (1)(c) must be appointed from the staff of the Regulator.
(4) In appointing persons under subsection (1)(c) the Secretary of State must secure that a majority of the members of the Regulator are non-executive members.
(5) No member of the staff of the Board of the Pension Protection Fund is eligible for appointment as a member of the Regulator.
(6) In this Part—
   (a) references to executive members of the Regulator are to—
      (i) the Chief Executive, and
      (ii) the members appointed under subsection (1)(c) from the staff of the Regulator, and
   (b) references to non-executive members of the Regulator are to members who are not executive members.

**3  Further provision about the regulator**

Schedule 1 makes further provision about the Regulator, including provision as to—
   the terms of appointment, tenure and remuneration of members,
   the appointment of the Chief Executive and other staff,
   the proceedings of the Regulator,
   its funding and accounts, and
   the status and liability of the Regulator, its members and staff.

*General provisions about functions*

**4  Regulator's functions**

(1) The Regulator has—
   (a) the functions transferred to it from the Occupational Pensions Regulatory

Authority by virtue of this Act or any provisions in force in Northern Ireland corresponding to this Act, and
  (b) any other functions conferred by, or by virtue of, this or any other enactment.
(2) As regards the exercise of the Regulator's functions—
  (a) the non-executive functions listed in subsection (4) of section 8 must, by virtue of subsection (2) of that section, be discharged by the committee established under that section,
  (b) the functions mentioned in the following provisions are exercisable only by the Determinations Panel—
    (i) section 10(1) (the power in certain circumstances to determine whether to exercise the functions listed in Schedule 2 and to exercise them), and
    (ii) section 99(10) (the functions concerning the compulsory review of certain determinations), and
  (c) the exercise of other functions of the Regulator may be delegated by the Regulator under paragraph 20 of Schedule 1.
(3) Subsection (2) is subject to any regulations made by the Secretary of State under paragraph 21 of Schedule 1 (power to limit or permit delegation of functions).

## 5 Regulator's objectives

(1) The main objectives of the Regulator in exercising its functions are—
  (a) to protect the benefits under occupational pension schemes of, or in respect of, members of such schemes,
  (b) to protect the benefits under personal pension schemes of, or in respect of, members of such schemes within subsection (2),
  (c) to reduce the risk of situations arising which may lead to compensation being payable from the Pension Protection Fund (see Part 2), and
  (d) to promote, and to improve understanding of, the good administration of work-based pension schemes.
(2) For the purposes of subsection (1)(b) the members of personal pension schemes within this subsection are—
  (a) the members who are employees in respect of whom direct payment arrangements exist, and
  (b) where the scheme is a stakeholder pension scheme, any other members.
(3) In this section—
  "stakeholder pension scheme" means a personal pension scheme which is or has been registered under section 2 of the Welfare Reform and Pensions Act 1999 (c. 30) (register of stakeholder schemes);
  "work-based pension scheme" means—
    (a) an occupational pension scheme,
    (b) a personal pension scheme where direct payment arrangements exist in respect of one or more members of the scheme who are employees, or
    (c) a stakeholder pension scheme.

## 6 Supplementary powers

The Regulator may do anything (except borrow money) which—
  (a) is calculated to facilitate the exercise of its functions, or
  (b) is incidental or conducive to their exercise.

**7 Transfer of OPRA's functions to the regulator**

(1) Subject to the provisions of this Act, the functions of the Occupational Pensions Regulatory Authority ("OPRA") conferred by or by virtue of—
   (a) the Pension Schemes Act 1993 (c. 48),
   (b) the Pensions Act 1995 (c. 26), and
   (c) the Welfare Reform and Pensions Act 1999,
   are hereby transferred to the Regulator.

(2) Accordingly—
   (a) in section 181(1) of the Pension Schemes Act 1993 (which defines "the Regulatory Authority" to mean OPRA), for the definition of "the Regulatory Authority" substitute—
       "the Regulatory Authority" means the Pensions Regulator;",
   (b) in section 124(1) of the Pensions Act 1995 (which defines "the Authority", in Part 1 of that Act, to mean OPRA), for the definition of "the Authority" substitute—
       "the Authority" means the Pensions Regulator,",
   (c) in section 8(1) of the Welfare Reform and Pensions Act 1999 (c. 30) (which defines "the Authority", in Part 1 of that Act to mean OPRA), for the definition of "the Authority" substitute—
       "the Authority" means the Pensions Regulator;", and
   (d) in section 33 of that Act (time for discharge of pension credit liability), in subsection (5) for "the Occupational Pensions Regulatory Authority" substitute "the Pensions Regulator".

*Non-executive functions*

**8 Non-executive functions**

(1) The functions listed in subsection (4) (in this Part referred to as "the non-executive functions") are functions of the Regulator.

(2) The Regulator must establish a committee to discharge the non-executive functions on its behalf.

(3) Only non-executive members of the Regulator may be members of the committee.

(4) The non-executive functions are—
   (a) the duty to keep under review the question whether the Regulator's internal financial controls secure the proper conduct of its financial affairs;
   (b) the duty to determine under paragraph 8(4)(b) of Schedule 1, subject to the approval of the Secretary of State, the terms and conditions as to remuneration of any Chief Executive appointed under paragraph 8(4)(a) of that Schedule.

(5) The committee established under this section must prepare a report on the discharge of the non-executive functions for inclusion in the Regulator's annual report to the Secretary of State under section 11.

(6) The committee's report must relate to the same period as that covered by the Regulator's report.

(7) The committee may establish sub-committees, and the members of any such sub-committee—
   (a) may include persons who are not members of the committee or of the Regulator, but

(b) must not include persons who are executive members or other staff of the Regulator.
(8) The committee may authorize any of its members or any of its sub-committees to discharge on its behalf—
   (a) any of the non-executive functions;
   (b) the duty to prepare a report under subsection (5).
(9) The committee (or any of its sub-committees) may be authorized under paragraph 20(1) of Schedule 1 to exercise further functions of the Regulator.
(10) This section is subject to any regulations made by the Secretary of State under paragraph 21 of Schedule 1 (power to limit or permit delegation of functions).

*The determinations panel*

## 9 The determinations panel

(1) The Regulator must establish and maintain a committee consisting of—
   (a) a chairman, and
   (b) at least six other persons,
   (in this Part referred to as "the Determinations Panel").
(2) The Regulator must appoint as the chairman of the Panel the person nominated in accordance with paragraph 11 of Schedule 1 (nomination by a committee established by the chairman of the Regulator).
(3) The chairman of the Panel must—
   (a) decide the number of persons to be appointed as the other members of the Panel, and
   (b) nominate a person suitable for each of those appointments.
(4) The Regulator must then appoint as the other members of the Panel the persons nominated by the chairman of the Panel.
(5) The following are ineligible for appointment as members of the Panel—
   (a) any member of the Regulator;
   (b) any member of the staff of the Regulator;
   (c) any member of the Board of the Pension Protection Fund;
   (d) any member of the staff of that Board.
(6) The Panel may establish sub-committees consisting of members of the Panel.
(7) Further provision about the Panel is made in Schedule 1, including provision as to the terms of appointment, tenure and remuneration of members and as to its procedure.

## 10 Functions exercisable by the determinations panel

(1) The Determinations Panel is to exercise on behalf of the Regulator—
   (a) the power to determine, in the circumstances described in subsection (2), whether to exercise a reserved regulatory function, and
   (b) where it so determines to exercise a reserved regulatory function, the power to exercise the function in question.
(2) Those circumstances are—
   (a) where the Regulator considers that the exercise of the reserved regulatory function may be appropriate, or
   (b) where an application is made under, or by virtue of, any of the provisions listed in subsection (6) for the Regulator to exercise the reserved regulatory function.

(3) Where subsection (1) applies, the powers mentioned in that subsection are not otherwise exercisable by or on behalf of the Regulator.
(4) For the purposes of this Part, a function of the Regulator is a "reserved regulatory function" if it is a function listed in Schedule 2.
(5) Regulations may amend Schedule 2 by—
   (a) adding any function of the Regulator conferred by, or by virtue of, this or any other enactment,
   (b) omitting any such function, or
   (c) altering the description of any such function contained in that Schedule.
(6) The provisions referred to in subsection (2)(b) are—
   (a) section 20(10) (application to permit payments out of an account that is subject to a restraining order);
   (b) section 26(2) (application for order validating action taken in contravention of freezing order);
   (c) section 41(7) (application for the issue of a revised contribution notice under section 41(9));
   (d) section 50(7) (application for the issue of a revised contribution notice under section 50(9));
   (e) section 3(3) of the Pensions Act 1995 (c. 26) (application for revocation of prohibition order);
   (f) section 4(5) of that Act (application for revocation of a suspension order);
   (g) section 7(5A) of that Act (application for appointment of a trustee under section 7(3)(a) or (c) of that Act);
   (h) section 29(5) of that Act (application for waiver of disqualification);
   (i) section 69(1) of that Act (application for order authorising modification or modifying a scheme);
   (j) section 71A(2) of that Act (application for modifying a scheme to secure winding up);
   (k) section 99(4A) of the Pension Schemes Act 1993 (c. 48) (application for extension under section 99(4) of that Act of a period for compliance);
   (l) section 101J(6)(a) of that Act (application for extension under section 101J(2) of that Act of a period for compliance).
(7) Regulations may amend subsection (6) by—
   (a) adding any provision of this or any other enactment to the list in that subsection, or
   (b) omitting or altering the description of any provision mentioned in that list.
(8) The Panel may be authorized under paragraph 20(4) or (6) of Schedule 1 to exercise further functions of the Regulator on behalf of the Regulator.
(9) The Panel may authorize any of its members or any of its sub-committees to exercise on its behalf—
   (a) any of the functions of the Regulator which are exercisable by the Panel on behalf of the Regulator, or
   (b) any of the functions of the Panel under section 93(3), section 99(11) and paragraph 18(2) of Schedule 1 (procedure).
(10) This section is subject to any regulations made by the Secretary of State under paragraph 21 of Schedule 1 (power to limit or permit delegation of functions).

*Annual report*

## 11  Annual reports to secretary of state

(1) The Regulator must prepare a report for each financial year.
(2) Each report—
    (a) must deal with the activities of the Regulator in the financial year for which it is prepared, including the matters mentioned in subsection (3), and
    (b) must include the report prepared under subsection (5) of section 8 by the committee established under that section.
(3) The matters referred to in subsection (2)(a) are—
    (a) the strategic direction of the Regulator and the manner in which it has been kept under review;
    (b) the steps taken to scrutinize the performance of the Chief Executive in securing that the Regulator's functions are exercised efficiently and effectively;
    (c) the Regulator's objectives and targets (including its main objectives as set out in section 5 or in any corresponding provision in force in Northern Ireland) and the steps taken to monitor the extent to which they are being met.
(4) The Regulator must send each report to the Secretary of State as soon as practicable after the end of the financial year for which it is prepared.
(5) The Secretary of State must lay before each House of Parliament a copy of every report received by him under this section.
(6) In this section "financial year" means—
    (a) the period beginning with the date on which the Regulator is established and ending with the next following 31st March, and
    (b) each successive period of 12 months.

*Provision of information, education and assistance*

## 12  Provision of information, education and assistance

(1) The Regulator may provide such information, education and assistance as it considers appropriate to those involved in—
    (a) the administration of work-based pension schemes, or
    (b) advising the trustees or managers in relation to such schemes as to their operation.
(2) To the extent that it is not authorized to do so under subsection (1), the Regulator may also provide such information, education and assistance as it considers appropriate to—
    (a) employers in relation to work-based pension schemes,
    (b) persons involved in advising such employers as to the operation of such schemes, or
    (c) persons upon whom duties are imposed by or by virtue of section 238 (information and advice to employees).
(3) For the purposes of subsection (2), "employers in relation to work-based pension schemes" means, in the case of stakeholder pension schemes, the persons upon whom duties are imposed by or by virtue of section 3 of the Welfare Reform and Pensions Act 1999 (c. 30) (duty of employers to facilitate access to stakeholder pension schemes).
(4) In this section—

"assistance" does not include financial assistance;
"stakeholder pension scheme" and "work-based pension scheme" have the same meaning as in section 5 (Regulator's objectives).

*New powers in respect of occupational and personal pension schemes*

## 13 Improvement notices

(1) If the Regulator is of the opinion that a person—
   (a) is contravening one or more provisions of the pensions legislation, or
   (b) has contravened one or more of those provisions in circumstances that make it likely that the contravention will continue or be repeated,
   it may issue a notice (an "improvement notice") to that person directing him to take, or refrain from taking, such steps as are specified in the notice in order to remedy or prevent a recurrence of the contravention.
(2) An improvement notice must—
   (a) state that the Regulator is of that opinion and specify the provision or provisions of the pensions legislation in question,
   (b) contain a statement of the matters which it is asserted constitute the contravention and of the evidence on which that opinion is based, and
   (c) in respect of each step specified in the notice, state the period (being a period of not less than 21 days beginning with the date of the notice) within which it must be complied with.
(3) Directions in an improvement notice—
   (a) may be framed to any extent by reference to a code of practice issued by the Regulator under section 90, and
   (b) may be framed so as to afford the person to whom the notice is issued a choice between different ways of remedying or preventing the recurrence of the contravention.
(4) Directions in an improvement notice may be expressed to be conditional on compliance by a third party with a specified direction, or specified directions, contained in a notice under section 14 (third party notices).
(5) An improvement notice may direct the person to whom it is issued to inform the Regulator, within such period as may be specified in the notice, of how he has complied, or is complying, with the notice.
(6) Where a contravention of a provision of the pensions legislation consists of a failure to take action within a time limit, for the purposes of this section the contravention continues until such time as the action is taken.
(7) In this section "pensions legislation" means any enactment contained in or made by virtue of—
   (a) the Pension Schemes Act 1993 (c. 48),
   (b) Part 1 of the Pensions Act 1995 (c. 26), other than sections 62 to 66A of that Act (equal treatment),
   (c) Part 1 or section 33 of the Welfare Reform and Pensions Act 1999 (c. 30), or
   (d) this Act.
(8) If the trustees or managers of an occupational or personal pension scheme fail to comply with an improvement notice issued to them, section 10 of the Pensions Act 1995 (civil penalties) applies to any trustee or manager who has failed to take all

reasonable steps to secure compliance.
(9) That section also applies to any other person who, without reasonable excuse, fails to comply with an improvement notice issued to him.

## 14 Third party notices

(1) Where the Regulator is of the opinion that—
- (a) a person—
  - (i) is contravening one or more provisions of the pensions legislation, or
  - (ii) has contravened one or more of those provisions in circumstances that make it likely that the contravention will continue or be repeated,
- (b) the contravention is or was, wholly or partly, a result of a failure of another person ("the third party") to do any thing, and
- (c) that failure is not itself a contravention of the pensions legislation,

the Regulator may issue a notice (a "third party notice") directing the third party to take, or refrain from taking, such steps as are specified in the notice in order to remedy or prevent a recurrence of his failure.

(2) A third party notice must—
- (a) state that the Regulator is of that opinion and specify the provision or provisions of the pensions legislation in question,
- (b) contain a statement of—
  - (i) the matters which it is asserted constitute the contravention of the provision or provisions, and
  - (ii) the matters which it is asserted constitute the failure by the third party,

and the evidence on which that opinion is based, and
- (c) in respect of each step specified in the notice, state the period (being a period of not less than 21 days beginning with the date of the notice) within which it must be complied with.

(3) Directions in a third party notice may be framed so as to afford the third party a choice between different ways of remedying or preventing the recurrence of his failure.

(4) A third party notice may direct the third party to inform the Regulator, within such period as may be specified in the notice, of how he has complied, or is complying, with the notice.

(5) Where a contravention of a provision of the pensions legislation consists of a failure to take action within a time limit, for the purposes of this section the contravention continues until such time as the action is taken.

(6) Section 10 of the Pensions Act 1995 (c. 26) (civil penalties) applies to a person who, without reasonable excuse, fails to comply with a third party notice issued to him.

(7) No duty to which a person is subject is to be regarded as contravened merely because of anything required to be done in compliance with a third party notice.
This is subject to section 311 (protected items).

(8) In this section "pensions legislation" has the same meaning as in section 13.

## 15 Injunctions and interdicts

(1) If, on the application of the Regulator, the court is satisfied that—
- (a) there is a reasonable likelihood that a particular person will do any act which constitutes a misuse or misappropriation of any of the assets of an occupational or personal pension scheme, or

(b) a particular person has done any such act and there is a reasonable likelihood that he will continue or repeat the act in question or do a similar act,

the court may grant an injunction restraining him from doing so or, in Scotland, an interdict prohibiting him from doing so.

(2) The jurisdiction conferred by this section is exercisable by the High Court or the Court of Session.

## 16 Restitution

(1) If, on the application of the Regulator, the court is satisfied that there has been a misuse or misappropriation of any of the assets of an occupational or personal pension scheme, it may order any person involved to take such steps as the court may direct for restoring the parties to the position in which they were before the misuse or misappropriation occurred.

(2) For this purpose a person is "involved" if he appears to the court to have been knowingly concerned in the misuse or misappropriation of the assets.

(3) The jurisdiction conferred by this section is exercisable by the High Court or the Court of Session.

## 17 Power of the regulator to recover unpaid contributions

(1) Where any employer contribution payable towards an occupational or personal pension scheme is not paid on or before its due date, the Regulator may, on behalf of the trustees or managers of the scheme, exercise such powers as the trustees or managers have to recover that contribution.

(2) For the purposes of subsection (1), any employer contribution payable towards a personal pension scheme which is not paid on or before its due date is, if not a debt due from the employer to the trustees or managers apart from this subsection, to be treated as if it were such a debt.

(3) In this section—

"due date"—

(a) in relation to employer contributions payable towards an occupational pension scheme in accordance with a schedule of contributions under section 227, has the same meaning as in section 228,

(b) in relation to employer contributions payable in accordance with a payment schedule under section 87 of the Pensions Act 1995 (c. 26) (schedules of payments to money purchase schemes), has the meaning given by subsection (2)(c) of that section, and

(c) in relation to employer contributions payable towards a personal pension scheme, has the same meaning as in section 111A of the Pension Schemes Act 1993 (c. 48) (monitoring of employer payments to personal pension schemes);

"employer contribution"—

(a) in relation to an occupational pension scheme, means any contribution payable by or on behalf of the employer towards the scheme in accordance with a schedule of contributions under section 227 of this Act or a payment schedule under section 87 of the Pensions Act 1995 (c. 26) (schedules of payments to money purchase schemes) whether—

(i) on the employer's own account (but in respect of one or more employees), or

(ii) on behalf of an employee out of deductions from the employee's earnings, and
    (b) in relation to a personal pension scheme, means any contribution payable towards the scheme under direct payment arrangements.

## 18 Pension liberation: interpretation

(1) In this section and sections 19 to 21—
    (a) "pension scheme" means an occupational pension scheme or a personal pension scheme,
    (b) "deposit-taker" has the meaning given by subsections (8A) and (8B) of section 49 of the Pensions Act 1995, except that, for the purposes of this definition, subsection (8A)(c) of that section has effect with the omission of the words from "or" to the end,
    (c) references to money liberated from a pension scheme are to be read in accordance with subsection (2),
    (d) "liberated member", in relation to money liberated from a pension scheme, means the member of the pension scheme who is referred to in subsection (2)(a), and
    (e) "restraining order" means a restraining order under section 20.
(2) Money is to be taken to have been liberated from a pension scheme if—
    (a) the money directly or indirectly represents an amount that, in respect of accrued rights of a member of a pension scheme, has been transferred out of the scheme in pursuance of—
        (i) a relevant statutory provision, or
        (ii) a provision of the applicable rules, other than a relevant statutory provision,
    (b) the trustees or managers of the scheme transferred the amount out of the scheme on the basis that a third party ("the liberator") would secure that the amount was used in an authorized way,
    (c) the amount has not been used in an authorized way, and
    (d) the liberator has not secured, and is not likely to secure, that the amount will be used in an authorized way.
(3) The following are "relevant statutory provisions" for the purposes of subsection (2)—
    (a) section 94(1)(a), (aa) or (b) of the Pension Schemes Act 1993 (c. 48) (right to cash equivalent under Chapter 4 of Part 4 of that Act);
    (b) section 101AB(1)(a) of that Act (right to cash transfer sum under Chapter 5 of Part 4 of that Act);
    (c) section 101F(1) of that Act (right to cash equivalent of pension credit benefit).
(4) In subsection (2) "authorized way" means—
    (a) where the amount concerned is transferred out of the scheme in pursuance of a provision mentioned in subsection (3)(a), a way specified in subsection (2) or, as the case may be, subsection (3) of section 95 of the Pension Schemes Act 1993;
    (b) where that amount is transferred out in pursuance of the provision mentioned in subsection (3)(b), a way specified in section 101AE(2) of that Act;
    (c) where that amount is transferred out in pursuance of the provision mentioned in subsection (3)(c), a way specified in subsection (2) or, as the case may be, subsection (3) of section 101F of that Act;

(d) where that amount is transferred out in pursuance of a provision of the kind mentioned in subsection (2)(a)(ii), a way that is authorized by the applicable rules for amounts transferred out in pursuance of that provision.

(5) In this section "the applicable rules" has the same meaning as, in the case of the pension scheme concerned, that expression has in section 94 of the Pension Schemes Act 1993.

**19 Pension liberation: court's power to order restitution**

(1) This section applies where money has been liberated from a pension scheme.
(2) In this section "recoverable property" means (subject to subsection (3))—
    (a) the money or any of it, or
    (b) property (of any kind and wherever situated) that, directly or indirectly, represents any of the money.
(3) Where a person acquires the beneficial interest in recoverable property in good faith, for value and without notice that the property is, or (as the case may be) represents, money liberated from a pension scheme—
    (a) the property ceases to be recoverable property, and
    (b) no property that subsequently represents it is recoverable property.
(4) The court, on the application of the Regulator, may make such order as the court thinks just and convenient for the purpose of securing that recoverable property, or money representing its value or proceeds of its sale, is transferred—
    (a) towards a pension scheme,
    (b) towards an annuity or insurance policy, or
    (c) to the liberated member.
(5) An order under subsection (4) may (in particular) direct a person who holds recoverable property, or has any degree of control over recoverable property, to take steps for the purpose mentioned in that subsection.
(6) Where the court makes an order under paragraph (a) of subsection (4), it may by order direct the trustees or managers of the scheme referred to in that paragraph—
    (a) to take steps for the purpose mentioned in that subsection;
    (b) to apply the property or money transferred, in such manner as the court may direct, for the purpose of providing benefits under that scheme to or in respect of the liberated member.
(7) Regulations may modify any of the provisions of the Pension Schemes Act 1993 (c. 48) as it applies in relation to cases where an order is made under subsection (6).
(8) The jurisdiction conferred by this section is exercisable by the High Court or the Court of Session.
(9) The generality of the jurisdiction conferred by section 16 is not to be taken to be prejudiced by this section.
(10) The generality of the jurisdiction conferred by this section is not to be taken to be prejudiced by section 21.

**20 Pension liberation: restraining orders**

(1) The Regulator may make a restraining order in relation to an account with a deposit-taker if—
    (a) it is satisfied that the account contains money which has been liberated from a pension scheme,
    (b) it is satisfied that the account is held by or on behalf of—

(i) the liberator, or
(ii) a person who has to, or in practice is likely to, ensure that the account is operated in accordance with the liberator's directions, and
(c) the order is made pending consideration being given to the making of one or more repatriation orders in relation to the account under section 21.
(2) A restraining order is an order directing that no credit or debit of any amount may be made to the account concerned ("the restrained account") during the period for which the order has effect.
(3) A restraining order must—
(a) specify the name of the deposit-taker in respect of which it is made,
(b) identify the account in respect of which it is made, and
(c) contain such other information as may be prescribed.
(4) A restraining order—
(a) takes effect when the deposit-taker concerned is notified by the Regulator of the making of the order, and
(b) (subject to subsection (7)) ceases to have effect through expiry of time at the end of the six months beginning with the day when it is made.
(5) The Regulator may, at a time when a restraining order has effect, make an order extending (or further extending) the restraining order.
(6) An order under subsection (5) (an "extension order") takes effect—
(a) when the deposit-taker concerned is notified by the Regulator of the making of the order, but
(b) only if notification under paragraph (a) occurs at a time when the restraining order concerned has effect.
(7) Where an extension order takes effect—
(a) the restraining order concerned does not cease to have effect through expiry of time until the end of the six months beginning with the time when it would have ceased to have effect through expiry of time had it not been extended, but
(b) for so long as the extension order has effect, no further extension order can take effect before that time in relation to the restraining order.
(8) A restraining order does not prevent the crediting to the restrained account of an amount representing interest payable by the deposit-taker on any amount which is, or has been, in the account.
(9) Where a restraining order has effect, the deposit-taker must return to the payer any money credited to the restrained account in breach of the order.
(10) Where a restraining order has effect, the Regulator may, on an application made by or with the consent of the person by whom the restrained account is held, by order permit a payment specified in the order to be made out of the account if the Regulator is satisfied—
(a) that the payment will be made for the purpose of enabling—
(i) any individual to meet his reasonable living expenses, or
(ii) any person to carry on a trade, business, profession or occupation,
(b) that the beneficial interest in the money out of which the payment will be made belongs—
(i) to the individual, or person, concerned, or
(ii) to a person who consents to the making of the payment, and
(c) that the money out of which the payment will be made is not money liberated from a pension scheme.

(11) Section 10 of the Pensions Act 1995 (c. 26) (civil penalties) applies to a deposit-taker who, without reasonable excuse, fails to comply with any obligation imposed by a restraining order or by this section.

**21  Pension liberation: repatriation orders**

(1) Subsections (2) and (3) apply where—
   (a) a restraining order has effect, and
   (b) the Regulator is satisfied that the restrained account contains an amount of money liberated from a pension scheme.
(2) The Regulator may by order—
   (a) direct the deposit-taker concerned to pay from the account a sum not exceeding that amount—
      (i) towards a pension scheme,
      (ii) towards an annuity or insurance policy, or
      (iii) to the liberated member, and
   (b) where it makes an order under paragraph (a)(i), direct the trustees or managers of the scheme to apply the sum, in such manner as the Regulator may direct, for the purpose of providing benefits under the scheme to or in respect of the liberated member.
(3) If it appears to the Regulator, on taking an overall view of transactions taking place before the restraining order was made, that there are two or more individuals each of whom is a person who is or may be the liberated member in relation to some of the money, the Regulator may determine the sums to be paid from the restrained account under subsection (2) on any basis that appears to the Regulator to be just and reasonable.
(4) Regulations may modify any of the provisions of the Pension Schemes Act 1993 (c. 48) as it applies in relation to cases where an order is made under subsection (2)(b).
(5) Section 10 of the Pensions Act 1995 (c. 26) (civil penalties) applies to a deposit-taker who, without reasonable excuse, fails to comply with a direction given to him under subsection (2)(a).
(6) If the trustees or managers of a pension scheme fail to comply with a direction given to them under subsection (2)(b), that section applies to any trustee or manager who has failed to take all reasonable steps to secure compliance.
(7) In this section "restrained account" has the meaning given by section 20.

*Powers in relation to winding up of occupational pension schemes*

**22  Powers to wind up occupational pension schemes**

In section 11 of the Pensions Act 1995 (powers to wind up occupational pension schemes)—
   (a) omit subsection (3),
   (b) before subsection (4) insert—

   "(3A) The Authority may, during an assessment period (within the meaning of section 132 of the Pensions Act 2004 (meaning of "assessment period" for the purposes of Part 2 of that Act)) in relation to an occupational pension scheme, by order direct the scheme to be wound up if they are satisfied that it is necessary to do so in order—

(a) to ensure that the scheme's protected liabilities do not exceed its assets, or
(b) if those liabilities do exceed its assets, to keep the excess to a minimum.
(3B) In subsection (3A)—
(a) "protected liabilities" has the meaning given by section 131 of the Pensions Act 2004, and
(b) references to the assets of the scheme are references to those assets excluding any assets representing the value of any rights in respect of money purchase benefits (within the meaning of that Act) under the scheme.",
(c) at the end of subsection (4) insert—
"This subsection is subject to sections 28, 135 and 219 of the Pensions Act 2004 (winding up order made when freezing order has effect in relation to scheme, during assessment period under Part 2 of that Act etc).", and
(d) after subsection (6) insert—
"(6A) Subsection (6) does not have effect to authorize the Authority to make an order as mentioned in paragraph (a) or (b) of that subsection, if their doing so would be unlawful as a result of section 6(1) of the Human Rights Act 1998 (unlawful for public authority to act in contravention of a Convention right)."

## 23 Freezing orders

(1) This section applies to an occupational pension scheme which is not a money purchase scheme.
(2) The Regulator may make a freezing order in relation to such a scheme if and only if—
  (a) the order is made pending consideration being given to the making of an order in relation to the scheme under section 11(1)(c) of the Pensions Act 1995 (c. 26) (power to wind up schemes where necessary to protect the generality of members), and
  (b) the Regulator is satisfied that—
    (i) there is, or is likely to be if the order is not made, an immediate risk to the interests of members under the scheme or the assets of the scheme, and
    (ii) it is necessary to make the freezing order to protect the interests of the generality of the members of the scheme.
But no freezing order may be made in relation to a scheme during an assessment period (within the meaning of section 132) in relation to the scheme (see section 135(11)).
(3) A freezing order is an order directing that during the period for which it has effect—
  (a) no benefits are to accrue under the scheme rules to, or in respect of, members of the scheme, and
  (b) winding up of the scheme may not begin.
(4) A freezing order may also contain one or more of the following directions which have effect during the period for which the order has effect—
  (a) a direction that no new members, or no specified classes of new member, are to be admitted to the scheme;
  (b) a direction that—
    (i) no further contributions or payments, or
    (ii) no further specified contributions or payments,

are to be paid towards the scheme by or on behalf of the employer, any members or any specified members of the scheme;

(c) a direction that any amount or any specified amount which—
    (i) corresponds to any contribution which would be due to be paid towards the scheme on behalf of a member but for a direction under paragraph (b), and
    (ii) has been deducted from a payment of any earnings in respect of an employment,

is to be repaid to the member in question by the employer;

(d) a direction that no benefits, or no specified benefits, are to be paid to or in respect of any members or any specified members under the scheme rules;

(e) a direction that payments of all benefits or specified benefits under the scheme rules to or in respect of all the members or specified members may only be made from the scheme if they are reduced in a specified manner or by a specified amount;

(f) a direction that—
    (i) no transfers or no specified transfers of, or no transfer payments or no specified transfer payments in respect of, any member's rights under the scheme rules are to be made from the scheme, or
    (ii) no other steps or no specified other steps are to be taken to discharge any liability of the scheme to or in respect of a member of the scheme in respect of pensions or other benefits;

(g) a direction that no statements of entitlement are to be provided to members of the scheme under section 93A of the Pension Schemes Act 1993 (c. 48) (salary related schemes: right to statement of entitlement);

(h) a direction that—
    (i) no refunds of, or no specified refunds of, or in respect of, contributions paid by or in respect of a member towards the scheme are to be made from the scheme, or
    (ii) refunds or specified refunds of, or in respect of, contributions paid by or in respect of a member towards the scheme may only be made from the scheme if they are determined in a specified manner and satisfy such other conditions as may be specified.

(5) In subsection (4)(b)—
(a) the references to contributions do not include contributions due to be paid before the order takes effect, and
(b) the references to payments towards a scheme include payments in respect of pension credits where the person entitled to the credit is a member of the scheme.

(6) A freezing order may not contain a direction under subsection (4)(d) or (e) which reduces the benefits payable to or in respect of a member, for the period during which the order has effect, below the level to which the trustees or managers of the scheme would have power to reduce them if a winding up of the scheme had begun at the time when the freezing order took effect.

(7) A direction under subsection (4)(f) may, in particular, provide that transfers or specified transfers of, or transfer payments or specified transfer payments in respect of, any member's rights under the scheme rules may not be made from the scheme unless the amounts paid out from the scheme in respect of the transfers or transfer payments are determined in a specified manner and the transfer or transfer payments satisfy such other conditions as may be specified.

(8) A freezing order may also require the trustees or managers of the scheme to obtain an actuarial valuation within a specified period.
(9) A freezing order containing such a requirement must specify—
   (a) the date by reference to which the assets and liabilities are to be valued,
   (b) the assets and liabilities which are to be taken into account,
   (c) the manner in which the valuation must be prepared,
   (d) the information and statements which it must contain, and
   (e) any other requirements that the valuation must satisfy.
(10) For the purposes of subsection (8)—
   "an actuarial valuation" means a written valuation of the scheme's assets and liabilities prepared and signed by the actuary;
   "the actuary" means—
      (a) the actuary appointed under section 47(1)(b) of the Pensions Act 1995 (c. 26) (professional advisers) in relation to the scheme, or
      (b) if no such actuary has been appointed—
         (i) a person with prescribed qualifications or experience, or
         (ii) a person approved by the Secretary of State.
(11) In this section "specified" means specified in the freezing order.

## 24 Consequences of freezing order

(1) If a freezing order is made in relation to a scheme any action taken in contravention of the order is void except to the extent that the action is validated by an order under section 26.
(2) A freezing order in relation to a scheme does not prevent any increase in a benefit which is an increase which would otherwise accrue in accordance with the scheme or any enactment during the period for which the order has effect, unless the order contains a direction to the contrary.
(3) A freezing order in relation to a scheme does not prevent the scheme being wound up in pursuance of an order under section 11 of the Pensions Act 1995 (power to wind up occupational pension schemes).
(4) If a freezing order contains a direction under section 23(4)(b) that no further contributions, or no further specified contributions, are to be paid towards a scheme during the period for which the order has effect—
   (a) any contributions which are the subject of the direction and which would otherwise be due to be paid towards the scheme during that period are to be treated as if they do not fall due, and
   (b) any obligation to pay those contributions (including any obligation under section 49(8) of the Pensions Act 1995 to pay amounts deducted corresponding to such contributions) is to be treated as if it does not arise.
(5) If a freezing order contains a direction under section 23(4)(f) (no transfers or discharge of member's rights) it does not prevent—
   (a) giving effect to a pension sharing order or provision, or
   (b) giving effect to a pension ear-marking order in a case where—
      (i) the order requires a payment to be made if a payment in respect of any benefits under the scheme becomes due to a person, and
      (ii) a direction under section 23(4)(d) or (e) does not prevent the payment becoming due.

(6) For the purposes of subsection (5)—

"pension sharing order or provision" means an order or provision falling within section 28(1) of the Welfare Reform and Pensions Act 1999 (c. 30) (activation of pension sharing);

"pension ear-marking order" means—

(a) an order under section 23 of the Matrimonial Causes Act 1973 (c. 18) (financial provision orders in connection with divorce etc) so far as it includes provision made by virtue of section 25B or 25C of that Act (powers to include provision about pensions),

(b) an order under section 12A(2) or (3) of the Family Law (Scotland) Act 1985 (c. 37) (powers in relation to pension lump sums when making a capital sum order), or

(c) an order under Article 25 of the Matrimonial Causes (Northern Ireland) Order 1978 (S.I. 1978/1045 (N.I.15)) so far as it includes provision made by virtue of Article 27B or 27C of that Order (Northern Ireland powers corresponding to those mentioned in paragraph (a)).

(7) Regulations may modify any provisions of—

(a) Chapter 4 of Part 4 of the Pension Schemes Act 1993 (c. 48) (protection for early leavers: transfer values), or

(b) Chapter 5 of that Part (protection for early leavers: cash transfer sums and contribution refunds),

in their application to an occupational pension scheme in relation to which a freezing order is made containing a direction under section 23(4)(f), (g) or (h) (no transfers etc in respect of member's rights or refunds of contributions etc from the scheme).

(8) Disregarding subsection (1), if a freezing order made in relation to a scheme is not complied with, section 10 of the Pensions Act 1995 (c. 26) (civil penalties) applies to any trustee or manager of the scheme who has failed to take all reasonable steps to secure compliance.

(9) Subsection (8) does not apply in the case of non-compliance with a direction under section 23(4)(c) (direction that certain deducted contributions are to be repaid by the employer).

(10) In such a case, section 10 of the Pensions Act 1995 (civil penalties) applies to an employer who, without reasonable excuse, fails to repay an amount as required by the direction.

## 25 Period of effect etc of freezing order

(1) A freezing order must specify the period for which it has effect.

(2) The period specified must not exceed three months.

(3) The Regulator may on one or more occasions by order extend the period for which the order has effect.

(4) But the total period for which the order has effect must not exceed six months.

(5) This section is subject to sections 27, 28 and 29 (effect of winding up and assessment period on freezing orders).

## 26 Validation of action in contravention of freezing order

(1) If a freezing order is made in relation to a scheme, the Regulator may by order validate action taken in contravention of the order.

(2) Any of the following persons may apply to the Regulator for an order under this section validating particular action—

(a) the trustees or managers of the scheme;
(b) any person directly affected by the action.

## 27 Effect of determination to wind up scheme on freezing order

(1) This section applies where—
   (a) the Regulator determines to make an order under section 11 of the Pensions Act 1995 (c. 26) (power to wind up occupational pension schemes) in relation to a scheme ("a winding up order"),
   (b) that determination is made during the period for which a freezing order has effect in relation to the scheme,
   (c) the case is not one to which the special procedure in section 98 applies (immediate exercise of powers where immediate risk to assets etc), and
   (d) the winding up order accordingly cannot be made until the expiry of the period specified in section 96(5) (no exercise during period of referral to the Tribunal etc).
(2) In such a case the freezing order is to continue to have effect until—
   (a) where the winding up order is made, it ceases to have effect under section 28 from the time when that order is made, or
   (b) the determination to make the winding up order is revoked.
(3) Subsection (2) is subject to the Regulator's power under section 101 to revoke the freezing order at any time.

## 28 Effect of winding up order on freezing order

(1) This section applies where—
   (a) an order is made under section 11 of the Pensions Act 1995 ("the 1995 Act") (power to wind up occupational pension schemes) in relation to a scheme, and
   (b) the order is made during the period for which a freezing order has effect in relation to the scheme.
(2) In such a case—
   (a) the winding up of the scheme in pursuance of the order under section 11 of the 1995 Act is to be taken as beginning at the time when the freezing order took effect, and
   (b) the freezing order ceases to have effect from the time when the order under section 11 of the 1995 Act is made.
(3) The Regulator may by order direct any specified person—
   (a) to take such specified steps as it considers are necessary as a result of the winding up of the scheme being deemed under subsection (2)(a) to have begun at the time when the freezing order took effect, and
   (b) to take those steps within a specified period.
(4) If the trustees or managers of a scheme fail to comply with a direction to them contained in an order under this section, section 10 of the 1995 Act (civil penalties) applies to any trustee or manager who has failed to take all reasonable steps to secure compliance.
(5) That section also applies to any other person who, without reasonable excuse, fails to comply with a direction to him contained in an order under this section.
(6) In this section "specified" means specified in an order under this section.

## 29 Effect of assessment period under part 2 on freezing order

Where an assessment period (within the meaning of section 132) begins in relation to a scheme, any freezing order in relation to the scheme ceases to have effect when the assessment period begins.

## 30 Power to give a direction where freezing order ceases to have effect

(1) This section applies where—
   (a) the Regulator revokes a freezing order in relation to a scheme or it otherwise ceases to have effect, and
   (b) at the time when the freezing order ceases to have effect, the Regulator has not made an order under section 11 of the Pensions Act 1995 (c. 26) ("the 1995 Act") in relation to the scheme.
(2) In such a case the Regulator may make an order under this section in relation to the scheme containing a direction that, if specified conditions are met, specified benefits are to accrue under the scheme rules to, or in respect of, specified members of the scheme in respect of specified periods of service being service in employment which but for the freezing order would have qualified the member in question for those benefits under the scheme rules.
(3) The conditions mentioned in subsection (2) may include—
   (a) a requirement that specified benefits do not accrue to, or in respect of, a member or a specified member unless a contribution of a specified amount is paid by or on behalf of the member towards the scheme within a specified period;
   (b) a requirement that a contribution of a specified amount must be paid by or on behalf of the employer within a specified period;
   (c) a requirement that such contributions as are specified under paragraph (a) or (b) are to be accepted for the period for which the freezing order had effect or any part of that period.
(4) Where the freezing order contained a direction under section 23(4)(d) or (e) and any amount of any benefit under the scheme rules was not paid as a result of the direction—
   (a) the direction does not affect any entitlement to that benefit, and
   (b) any benefit to which a member, or a person in respect of a member, remains entitled at the end of the period for which the freezing order had effect is an amount which falls due to the member or, as the case may be, the person at the end of that period.
(5) If an order made under this section in relation to a scheme is not complied with, section 10 of the 1995 Act (civil penalties) applies to a trustee or a manager of the scheme who has failed to take all reasonable steps to secure compliance.
(6) Subsection (7) applies if—
   (a) an order is made under this section in relation to a scheme,
   (b) the order contains a requirement as described in subsection (3)(b) that a contribution of a specified amount must be paid by or on behalf of the employer within a specified period, and
   (c) the contribution is not paid within that period.
(7) In such a case—
   (a) section 10 of the 1995 Act applies to the employer if he has failed, without reasonable excuse, to secure compliance,

(b) the amount which for the time being remains unpaid after the end of the specified period is to be treated as a debt due from the employer to the trustees or managers of the scheme, and
(c) except in prescribed circumstances, the trustees or managers must, within a prescribed period, give notice of the failure to pay to the Regulator and to the member.
(8) If in any case subsection (7)(c) is not complied with, section 10 of the 1995 Act applies to any trustee or manager who has failed to take all reasonable steps to secure compliance.
(9) In this section "specified" means specified in an order under this section.

**31  Notification of trustees, managers, employers and members**

(1) This section applies where—
(a) a freezing order is made in relation to a scheme,
(b) an order is made under section 26 validating action taken in contravention of a freezing order made in relation to a scheme,
(c) an order is made under section 28 directing specified steps to be taken following the winding up of a scheme, or
(d) an order is made under section 30 in relation to a scheme where a freezing order ceases to have effect.
(2) The Regulator must, as soon as reasonably practicable after the order has been made, notify—
(a) the trustees or managers of the scheme, and
(b) the employer in relation to the scheme,
of the fact that the order has been made and of its effect.
(3) The Regulator may by order direct the trustees or managers of the scheme to notify—
(a) all the members of the scheme, or
(b) the members of the scheme specified in the order,
of the fact that the order mentioned in subsection (1) has been made and of its effect.
(4) Notification is to be within the period and in the manner specified in the order under subsection (3).
(5) If the trustees or managers of a scheme fail to comply with a direction to them contained in an order made under subsection (3), section 10 of the Pensions Act 1995 (c. 26) (civil penalties) applies to any trustee or manager who has failed to take all reasonable steps to secure compliance.

**32  Sections 23 to 31: supplementary**

(1) An order may be made in relation to a scheme under any of sections 23, 25, 26, 28, 30 and 31—
(a) in spite of any enactment or rule of law, or any rule of the scheme, which would otherwise operate to prevent the order being made, and
(b) without regard to any such enactment, rule of law or rule of the scheme as would otherwise require, or might otherwise be taken to require, the implementation of any procedure or the obtaining of any consent, with a view to the making of the order.
(2) Subsection (1) does not have effect to authorize the Regulator to make an order as mentioned in that subsection if its doing so would be unlawful as a result of section

6(1) of the Human Rights Act 1998 (c. 42) (unlawful for public authority to act in contravention of a Convention right).

*Trustees of occupational pension schemes*

### 33 Prohibition orders

For section 3 of the Pensions Act 1995 (c. 26) (prohibition orders) substitute—

"**3 Prohibition orders**

(1) The Authority may by order prohibit a person from being a trustee of—
   (a) a particular trust scheme,
   (b) a particular description of trust schemes, or
   (c) trust schemes in general,
if they are satisfied that he is not a fit and proper person to be a trustee of the scheme or schemes to which the order relates.
(2) Where a prohibition order is made under subsection (1) against a person in respect of one or more schemes of which he is a trustee, the order has the effect of removing him.
(3) The Authority may, on the application of any person prohibited under this section, by order revoke the order either generally or in relation to a particular scheme or description of schemes.
(4) An application under subsection (3) may not be made—
   (a) during the period within which the determination to exercise the power to make the prohibition order may be referred to the Tribunal under section 96(3) or 99(7) of the Pensions Act 2004, and
   (b) if the determination is so referred, until the reference, and any appeal against the Tribunal's determination, has been finally disposed of.
(5) A revocation made at any time under this section cannot affect anything done before that time.
(6) The Authority must prepare and publish a statement of the policies they intend to adopt in relation to the exercise of their powers under this section.
(7) The Authority may revise any statement published under subsection (6) and must publish any revised statement.
(8) In this section "the Tribunal" means the Pensions Regulator Tribunal established under section 102 of the Pensions Act 2004."

### 34 Suspension orders

In section 4 of the Pensions Act 1995 (c. 26) (suspension orders)—
(a) after subsection (1)(a) insert—
   "(aa) pending consideration being given to the institution of proceedings against him for an offence involving dishonesty or deception,",
(b) in subsection (2)—
   (i) in paragraph (a) after "paragraph (a)" insert "or (aa)",
   (ii) after "have effect" insert "in relation to a trust scheme", and
   (iii) after "section 3(1)" insert "in relation to that scheme",
(c) after subsection (5) insert—
   "(5A) An application under subsection (5) may not be made—
      (a) during the period within which the determination to exercise the power to

make an order under subsection (1) may be referred to the Tribunal under section 96(3) or 99(7) of the Pensions Act 2004, and
    (b) if the determination is so referred, until the reference, and any appeal against the Tribunal's determination, has been finally disposed of.", and
    (d) after subsection (6) insert—
"(7) In this section "the Tribunal" means the Pensions Regulator Tribunal established under section 102 of the Pensions Act 2004."

## 35 Appointments of trustees by the regulator

(1) In section 7 of the Pensions Act 1995 (appointment of trustees)—
    (a) omit subsection (4), and
    (b) after subsection (5) insert—
"(5A) An application may be made to the Authority in relation to a trust scheme by—
    (a) the trustees of the scheme,
    (b) the employer, or
    (c) any member of the scheme,
for the appointment of a trustee of the scheme under subsection (3)(a) or (c)."
(2) In section 8 of that Act (consequences of appointment of trustees under section 7), for subsections (1) and (2) substitute—
"(1) An order under section 7 appointing a trustee may provide for any fees and expenses of trustees appointed under the order to be paid—
    (a) by the employer,
    (b) out of the resources of the scheme, or
    (c) partly by the employer and partly out of those resources.
(2) Such an order may also provide that an amount equal to the amount (if any) paid out of the resources of the scheme by virtue of subsection (1)(b) or (c) is to be treated for all purposes as a debt due from the employer to the trustees of the scheme."

## 36 Independent trustees

(1) Part 1 of the Pensions Act 1995 (c. 26) (occupational pension schemes) is amended as follows.
(2) In section 22 (circumstances in which provisions relating to independent trustees apply)—
    (a) in subsection (1)(b) omit "or" at the end of sub-paragraph (i) and after that sub-paragraph insert—
        "(ia) the interim receiver of the property of a person who is the employer in relation to the scheme, or",
    (b) in subsection (2), after "a scheme" insert "by virtue of subsection (1)",
    (c) after subsection (2) insert—
        "(2A) To the extent that it does not already apply by virtue of subsection (1), this section also applies in relation to a trust scheme—
            (a) at any time during an assessment period (within the meaning of section 132 of the Pensions Act 2004) in relation to the scheme, and
            (b) at any time, not within paragraph (a), when the scheme is authorized under section 153 of that Act (closed schemes) to continue as a closed scheme", and

(d) after subsection (2A) (inserted by paragraph (c) above) insert—
"(2B) The responsible person must, as soon as reasonably practicable, give notice of an event within subsection (2C) to—
 (a) the Authority,
 (b) the Board of the Pension Protection Fund, and
 (c) the trustees of the scheme.
(2C) The events are—
 (a) the practitioner beginning to act as mentioned in subsection (1)(a), if immediately before he does so this section does not apply in relation to the scheme;
 (b) the practitioner ceasing to so act, if immediately after he does so this section does not apply in relation to the scheme;
 (c) the official receiver beginning to act in a capacity mentioned in subsection (1)(b)(i), (ia) or (ii), if immediately before he does so this section does not apply in relation to the scheme;
 (d) the official receiver ceasing to act in such a capacity, if immediately after he does so this section does not apply in relation to the scheme.
(2D) For the purposes of subsection (2B) "the responsible person" means—
 (a) in the case of an event within subsection (2C)(a) or (b) the practitioner, and
 (b) in the case of an event within subsection (2C)(c) or (d), the official receiver.
(2E) Regulations may require prescribed persons in prescribed circumstances where this section begins or ceases to apply in relation to a trust scheme by virtue of subsection (2A) to give a notice to that effect to—
 (a) the Authority,
 (b) the Board of the Pension Protection Fund, and
 (c) the trustees of the scheme.
(2F) A notice under subsection (2B), or regulations under subsection (2E), must be in writing and contain such information as may be prescribed."
(3) For sections 23 and 24 (appointment of independent trustees) substitute—

**"23 Power to appoint independent trustees**

(1) While section 22 applies in relation to a trust scheme, the Authority may by order appoint as a trustee of the scheme a person who—
 (a) is an independent person in relation to the scheme, and
 (b) is registered in the register maintained by the Authority in accordance with regulations under subsection (4).
(2) In relation to a particular trust scheme, no more than one trustee may at any time be an independent trustee appointed under subsection (1).
(3) For the purposes of this section a person is independent in relation to a trust scheme only if—
 (a) he has no interest in the assets of the employer or of the scheme otherwise than as trustee of the scheme,
 (b) he is neither connected with, nor an associate of—
  (i) the employer,
  (ii) any person for the time being acting as an insolvency practitioner in relation to the employer, or

(iii) the official receiver acting in any of the capacities mentioned in section 22(1)(b) in relation to the employer, and
(c) he satisfies any prescribed requirements;
and any reference in this Part to an independent trustee is to be construed accordingly.
(4) Regulations must provide for the Authority to compile and maintain a register of persons who satisfy the prescribed conditions for registration.
(5) Regulations under subsection (4) may provide—
(a) for copies of the register or of extracts from it to be provided to prescribed persons in prescribed circumstances;
(b) for the inspection of the register by prescribed persons in prescribed circumstances.
(6) The circumstances which may be prescribed under subsection (5)(a) or (b) include the payment by the person to whom the copy is to be provided, or by whom the register is to be inspected, of such reasonable fee as may be determined by the Authority.
(7) This section is without prejudice to the powers conferred by section 7."
(4) In section 25 (appointment and powers of independent trustees: further provisions)—
(a) for subsection (4)(a) substitute—
"(a) he must as soon as reasonably practicable give written notice of that fact to the Authority, and",
(b) after subsection (5) insert—
"(5A) Section 10 applies to any person who, without reasonable excuse, fails to comply with subsection (4)(a).", and
(c) for subsection (6) substitute—
"(6) An order under section 23(1) may provide for any fees and expenses of the trustee appointed under the order to be paid—
(a) by the employer,
(b) out of the resources of the scheme, or
(c) partly by the employer and partly out of those resources.
(7) Such an order may also provide that an amount equal to the amount (if any) paid out of the resources of the scheme by virtue of subsection (6)(b) or (c) is to be treated for all purposes as a debt due from the employer to the trustees of the scheme.
(8) Where, by virtue of subsection (6)(b) or (c), an order makes provision for any fees or expenses of the trustee appointed under the order to be paid out of the resources of the scheme, the trustee is entitled to be so paid in priority to all other claims falling to be met out of the scheme's resources."

## 37 Disqualification

In section 30 of the Pensions Act 1995 (c. 26) (consequences of disqualification under section 29), for subsection (1) substitute—

"(1) Where a person who is a trustee of a trust scheme becomes disqualified under section 29 in relation to the scheme, his becoming so disqualified has the effect of removing him as a trustee."

*Contribution notices where avoidance of employer debt*

## 38 Contribution notices where avoidance of employer debt

(1) This section applies in relation to an occupational pension scheme other than—
   (a) a money purchase scheme, or
   (b) a prescribed scheme or a scheme of a prescribed description.
(2) The Regulator may issue a notice to a person stating that the person is under a liability to pay the sum specified in the notice (a "contribution notice")—
   (a) to the trustees or managers of the scheme, or
   (b) where the Board of the Pension Protection Fund has assumed responsibility for the scheme in accordance with Chapter 3 of Part 2 (pension protection), to the Board.
(3) The Regulator may issue a contribution notice to a person only if—
   (a) the Regulator is of the opinion that the person was a party to an act or a deliberate failure to act which falls within subsection (5),
   (b) the person was at any time in the relevant period—
      (i) the employer in relation to the scheme, or
      (ii) a person connected with, or an associate of, the employer,
   (c) the Regulator is of the opinion that the person, in being a party to the act or failure, was not acting in accordance with his functions as an insolvency practitioner in relation to another person, and
   (d) the Regulator is of the opinion that it is reasonable to impose liability on the person to pay the sum specified in the notice.
(4) But the Regulator may not issue a contribution notice, in such circumstances as may be prescribed, to a person of a prescribed description.
(5) An act or a failure to act falls within this subsection if—
   (a) the Regulator is of the opinion that the main purpose or one of the main purposes of the act or failure was—
      (i) to prevent the recovery of the whole or any part of a debt which was, or might become, due from the employer in relation to the scheme under section 75 of the Pensions Act 1995 (c. 26) (deficiencies in the scheme assets), or
      (ii) otherwise than in good faith, to prevent such a debt becoming due, to compromise or otherwise settle such a debt, or to reduce the amount of such a debt which would otherwise become due,
   (b) it is an act which occurred, or a failure to act which first occurred—
      (i) on or after 27th April 2004, and
      (ii) before any assumption of responsibility for the scheme by the Board in accordance with Chapter 3 of Part 2, and
   (c) it is either—
      (i) an act which occurred during the period of six years ending with the determination by the Regulator to exercise the power to issue the contribution notice in question, or
      (ii) a failure which first occurred during, or continued for the whole or part of, that period.
(6) For the purposes of subsection (3)—
   (a) the parties to an act or a deliberate failure include those persons who knowingly assist in the act or failure, and
   (b) "the relevant period" means the period which—

(i) begins with the time when the act falling within subsection (5) occurs or the failure to act falling within that subsection first occurs, and
(ii) ends with the determination by the Regulator to exercise the power to issue the contribution notice in question.

(7) The Regulator, when deciding for the purposes of subsection (3)(d) whether it is reasonable to impose liability on a particular person to pay the sum specified in the notice, must have regard to such matters as the Regulator considers relevant including, where relevant, the following matters—
   (a) the degree of involvement of the person in the act or failure to act which falls within subsection (5),
   (b) the relationship which the person has or has had with the employer (including, where the employer is a company within the meaning of subsection (11) of section 435 of the Insolvency Act 1986 (c. 45), whether the person has or has had control of the employer within the meaning of subsection (10) of that section),
   (c) any connection or involvement which the person has or has had with the scheme,
   (d) if the act or failure to act was a notifiable event for the purposes of section 69 (duty to notify the Regulator of certain events), any failure by the person to comply with any obligation imposed on the person by subsection (1) of that section to give the Regulator notice of the event,
   (e) all the purposes of the act or failure to act (including whether a purpose of the act or failure was to prevent or limit loss of employment),
   (f) the financial circumstances of the person, and
   (g) such other matters as may be prescribed.

(8) For the purposes of this section references to a debt due under section 75 of the Pensions Act 1995 (c. 26) include a contingent debt under that section.

(9) Accordingly, in the case of such a contingent debt, the reference in subsection (5)(a)(ii) to preventing a debt becoming due is to be read as including a reference to preventing the occurrence of any of the events specified in section 75(4C)(a) or (b) of that Act upon which the debt is contingent.

(10) For the purposes of this section—
   (a) section 249 of the Insolvency Act 1986 (connected persons) applies as it applies for the purposes of any provision of the first Group of Parts of that Act,
   (b) section 435 of that Act (associated persons) applies as it applies for the purposes of that Act, and
   (c) section 74 of the Bankruptcy (Scotland) Act 1985 (c. 66) (associated persons) applies as it applies for the purposes of that Act.

(11) For the purposes of this section "insolvency practitioner", in relation to a person, means—
   (a) a person acting as an insolvency practitioner, in relation to that person, in accordance with section 388 of the Insolvency Act 1986, or
   (b) an insolvency practitioner within the meaning of section 121(9)(b) (persons of a prescribed description).

## 39 The sum specified in a section 38 contribution notice

(1) The sum specified by the Regulator in a contribution notice under section 38 may be either the whole or a specified part of the shortfall sum in relation to the scheme.
(2) Subject to subsection (3), the shortfall sum in relation to a scheme is—
   (a) in a case where, at the relevant time, a debt was due from the employer to the

trustees or managers of the scheme under section 75 of the Pensions Act 1995 (c. 26) ("the 1995 Act") (deficiencies in the scheme assets), the amount which the Regulator estimates to be the amount of that debt at that time, and

(b) in a case where, at the relevant time, no such debt was due, the amount which the Regulator estimates to be the amount of the debt under section 75 of the 1995 Act which would become due if—
  (i) subsection (2) of that section applied, and
  (ii) the time designated by the trustees or managers of the scheme for the purposes of that subsection were the relevant time.

(3) Where the Regulator is satisfied that the act or failure to act falling within section 38(5) resulted—
  (a) in a case falling within paragraph (a) of subsection (2), in the amount of the debt which became due under section 75 of the 1995 Act being less than it would otherwise have been, or
  (b) in a case falling within paragraph (b) of subsection (2), in the amount of any such debt calculated for the purposes of that paragraph being less than it would otherwise have been,
the Regulator may increase the amounts calculated under subsection (2)(a) or (b) by such amount as the Regulator considers appropriate.

(4) For the purposes of this section "the relevant time" means—
  (a) in the case of an act falling within subsection (5) of section 38, the time of the act, or
  (b) in the case of a failure to act falling within that subsection—
    (i) the time when the failure occurred, or
    (ii) where the failure continued for a period of time, the time which the Regulator determines and which falls within that period.

(5) For the purposes of this section—
  (a) references to a debt due under section 75 of the 1995 Act include a contingent debt under that section, and
  (b) references to the amount of such a debt include the amount of such a contingent debt.

**40 Content and effect of a section 38 contribution notice**

(1) This section applies where a contribution notice is issued to a person under section 38.

(2) The contribution notice must—
  (a) contain a statement of the matters which it is asserted constitute the act or failure to act which falls within subsection (5) of section 38,
  (b) specify the sum which the person is stated to be under a liability to pay, and
  (c) identify any other persons to whom contribution notices have been or are issued as a result of the act or failure to act in question and the sums specified in each of those notices.

(3) Where the contribution notice states that the person is under a liability to pay the sum specified in the notice to the trustees or managers of the scheme, the sum is to be treated as a debt due from the person to the trustees or managers of the scheme.

(4) In such a case, the Regulator may, on behalf of the trustees or managers of the scheme, exercise such powers as the trustees or managers have to recover the debt.

(5) But during any assessment period (within the meaning of section 132) in relation to

the scheme, the rights and powers of the trustees or managers of the scheme in relation to any debt due to them by virtue of a contribution notice are exercisable by the Board of the Pension Protection Fund to the exclusion of the trustees or managers and the Regulator.

(6) Where, by virtue of subsection (5), any amount is paid to the Board in respect of a debt due by virtue of a contribution notice, the Board must pay the amount to the trustees or managers of the scheme.

(7) Where the contribution notice states that the person is under a liability to pay the sum specified in the notice to the Board, the sum is to be treated as a debt due from the person to the Board.

(8) Where the contribution notice so specifies, the person to whom the notice is issued ("P") is to be treated as jointly and severally liable for the debt with any persons specified in the notice who are persons to whom corresponding contribution notices are issued.

(9) For the purposes of subsection (8), a corresponding contribution notice is a notice which—

(a) is issued as a result of the same act or failure to act falling within subsection (5) of section 38 as the act or failure as a result of which P's contribution notice is issued,

(b) specifies the same sum as is specified in P's contribution notice, and

(c) specifies that the person to whom the contribution notice is issued is jointly and severally liable with P, or with P and other persons, for the debt in respect of that sum.

(10) A debt due by virtue of a contribution notice is not to be taken into account for the purposes of section 75(2) and (4) of the Pensions Act 1995 (c. 26) (deficiencies in the scheme assets) when ascertaining the amount or value of the assets or liabilities of a scheme.

## 41 Section 38 contribution notice: relationship with employer debt

(1) This section applies where a contribution notice is issued to a person ("P") under section 38 and condition A or B is met.

(2) Condition A is met if, at the time at which the contribution notice is issued, there is a debt due under section 75 of the Pensions Act 1995 ("the 1995 Act") (deficiencies in the scheme assets) from the employer—

(a) to the trustees or managers of the scheme, or

(b) where the Board of the Pension Protection Fund has assumed responsibility for the scheme in accordance with Chapter 3 of Part 2 (pension protection), to the Board.

(3) Condition B is met if, after the contribution notice is issued but before the whole of the debt due by virtue of the notice is recovered, a debt becomes due from the employer to the trustees or managers of the scheme under section 75 of the 1995 Act.

(4) The Regulator may issue a direction to the trustees or managers of the scheme not to take any or any further steps to recover the debt due to them under section 75 of the 1995 Act pending the recovery of all or a specified part of the debt due to them by virtue of the contribution notice.

(5) If the trustees or managers fail to comply with a direction issued to them under subsection (4), section 10 of the 1995 Act (civil penalties) applies to any trustee or manager who has failed to take all reasonable steps to secure compliance.

## s 41, Pensions Act 2004

(6) Any sums paid—
   (a) to the trustees or managers of the scheme in respect of any debt due to them by virtue of the contribution notice, or
   (b) to the Board in respect of any debt due to it by virtue of the contribution notice,
   are to be treated as reducing the amount of the debt due to the trustees or managers or, as the case may be, to the Board under section 75 of the 1995 Act.

(7) Where a sum is paid to the trustees or managers of the scheme or, as the case may be, to the Board in respect of the debt due under section 75 of the 1995 Act, P may make an application under this subsection to the Regulator for a reduction in the amount of the sum specified in P's contribution notice.

(8) An application under subsection (7) must be made as soon as reasonably practicable after the sum is paid to the trustees or managers or, as the case may be, to the Board in respect of the debt due under section 75 of the 1995 Act.

(9) Where such an application is made to the Regulator, the Regulator may, if it is of the opinion that it is appropriate to do so—
   (a) reduce the amount of the sum specified in P's contribution notice by an amount which it considers reasonable, and
   (b) issue a revised contribution notice specifying the revised sum.

(10) For the purposes of subsection (9), the Regulator must have regard to such matters as the Regulator considers relevant including, where relevant, the following matters—
   (a) the amount paid in respect of the debt due under section 75 of the 1995 Act since the contribution notice was issued,
   (b) any amounts paid in respect of the debt due by virtue of that contribution notice,
   (c) whether contribution notices have been issued to other persons as a result of the same act or failure to act falling within subsection (5) of section 38 as the act or failure as a result of which P's contribution notice was issued,
   (d) where such contribution notices have been issued, the sums specified in each of those notices and any amounts paid in respect of the debt due by virtue of those notices,
   (e) whether P's contribution notice specifies that P is jointly and severally liable for the debt with other persons, and
   (f) such other matters as may be prescribed.

(11) Where—
   (a) P's contribution notice specifies that P is jointly and severally liable for the debt with other persons, and
   (b) a revised contribution notice is issued to P under subsection (9) specifying a revised sum,
   the Regulator must also issue revised contribution notices to those other persons specifying the revised sum and their joint and several liability with P for the debt in respect of that sum.

(12) For the purposes of this section—
   (a) references to a debt due under section 75 of the 1995 Act include a contingent debt under that section, and
   (b) references to the amount of such a debt include the amount of such a contingent debt.

## 42 Section 38 contribution notice: clearance statements

(1) An application may be made to the Regulator under this section for the issue of a clearance statement within paragraph (a), (b) or (c) of subsection (2) in relation to circumstances described in the application.

(2) A clearance statement is a statement, made by the Regulator, that in its opinion in the circumstances described in the application—
   (a) the applicant would not be, for the purposes of subsection (3)(a) of section 38, a party to an act or a deliberate failure to act falling within subsection (5)(a) of that section,
   (b) it would not be reasonable to impose any liability on the applicant under a contribution notice issued under section 38, or
   (c) such requirements of that section as may be prescribed would not be satisfied in relation to the applicant.

(3) Where an application is made under this section, the Regulator—
   (a) may request further information from the applicant;
   (b) may invite the applicant to amend the application to modify the circumstances described.

(4) Where an application is made under this section, the Regulator must as soon as reasonably practicable—
   (a) determine whether to issue the clearance statement, and
   (b) where it determines to do so, issue the statement.

(5) A clearance statement issued under this section binds the Regulator in relation to the exercise of the power to issue a contribution notice under section 38 to the applicant unless—
   (a) the circumstances in relation to which the exercise of the power under that section arises are not the same as the circumstances described in the application, and
   (b) the difference in those circumstances is material to the exercise of the power.

*Financial support directions*

## 43 Financial support directions

(1) This section applies in relation to an occupational pension scheme other than—
   (a) a money purchase scheme, or
   (b) a prescribed scheme or a scheme of a prescribed description.

(2) The Regulator may issue a financial support direction under this section in relation to such a scheme if the Regulator is of the opinion that the employer in relation to the scheme—
   (a) is a service company, or
   (b) is insufficiently resourced,
   at a time determined by the Regulator which falls within subsection (9) ("the relevant time").

(3) A financial support direction in relation to a scheme is a direction which requires the person or persons to whom it is issued to secure—
   (a) that financial support for the scheme is put in place within the period specified in the direction,
   (b) that thereafter that financial support or other financial support remains in place while the scheme is in existence, and

(c) that the Regulator is notified in writing of prescribed events in respect of the financial support as soon as reasonably practicable after the event occurs.
(4) A financial support direction in relation to a scheme may be issued to one or more persons.
(5) But the Regulator may issue such a direction to a person only if—
   (a) the person is at the relevant time a person falling within subsection (6), and
   (b) the Regulator is of the opinion that it is reasonable to impose the requirements of the direction on that person.
(6) A person falls within this subsection if the person is—
   (a) the employer in relation to the scheme,
   (b) an individual who—
      (i) is an associate of an individual who is the employer, but
      (ii) is not an associate of that individual by reason only of being employed by him, or
   (c) a person, other than an individual, who is connected with or an associate of the employer.
(7) The Regulator, when deciding for the purposes of subsection (5)(b) whether it is reasonable to impose the requirements of a financial support direction on a particular person, must have regard to such matters as the Regulator considers relevant including, where relevant, the following matters—
   (a) the relationship which the person has or has had with the employer (including, where the employer is a company within the meaning of subsection (11) of section 435 of the Insolvency Act 1986 (c. 45), whether the person has or has had control of the employer within the meaning of subsection (10) of that section),
   (b) in the case of a person falling within subsection (6)(b) or (c), the value of any benefits received directly or indirectly by that person from the employer,
   (c) any connection or involvement which the person has or has had with the scheme,
   (d) the financial circumstances of the person, and
   (e) such other matters as may be prescribed.
(8) A financial support direction must identify all the persons to whom the direction is issued.
(9) A time falls within this subsection if it is a time which falls within a prescribed period which ends with the determination by the Regulator to exercise the power to issue the financial support direction in question.
(10) For the purposes of subsection (3), a scheme is in existence until it is wound up.
(11) No duty to which a person is subject is to be regarded as contravened merely because of any information or opinion contained in a notice given by virtue of subsection (3)(c).
This is subject to section 311 (protected items).

**44 Meaning of "service company" and "insufficiently resourced"**

(1) This section applies for the purposes of section 43 (financial support directions).
(2) An employer ("E") is a "service company" at the relevant time if—
   (a) E is a company within the meaning given by section 735(1) of the Companies Act 1985 (c. 6),
   (b) E is a member of a group of companies, and
   (c) E's turnover, as shown in the latest available accounts for E prepared in accordance with section 226 of that Act, is solely or principally derived from amounts

charged for the provision of the services of employees of E to other members of that group.

(3) The employer in relation to a scheme is insufficiently resourced at the relevant time if—
 (a) at that time the value of the resources of the employer is less than the amount which is a prescribed percentage of the estimated section 75 debt in relation to the scheme, and
 (b) there is at that time a person who falls within subsection (6)(b) or (c) of section 43 and the value at that time of that person's resources is not less than the amount which is the difference between—
  (i) the value of the resources of the employer, and
  (ii) the amount which is the prescribed percentage of the estimated section 75 debt.

(4) For the purposes of subsection (3)—
 (a) what constitutes the resources of a person is to be determined in accordance with regulations, and
 (b) the value of a person's resources is to be determined, calculated and verified in a prescribed manner.

(5) In this section the "estimated section 75 debt", in relation to a scheme, means the amount which the Regulator estimates to be the amount of the debt which would become due from the employer to the trustees or managers of the scheme under section 75 of the Pensions Act 1995 (c. 26) (deficiencies in the scheme assets) if—
 (a) subsection (2) of that section applied, and
 (b) the time designated by the trustees or managers of the scheme for the purposes of that subsection were the relevant time.

(6) When calculating the estimated section 75 debt in relation to a scheme under subsection (5), the amount of any debt due at the relevant time from the employer under section 75 of the Pensions Act 1995 (c. 26) is to be disregarded.

(7) In this section "the relevant time" has the same meaning as in section 43.

## 45 Meaning of "financial support"

(1) For the purposes of section 43 (financial support directions), "financial support" for a scheme means one or more of the arrangements falling within subsection (2) the details of which are approved in a notice issued by the Regulator.

(2) The arrangements falling within this subsection are—
 (a) an arrangement whereby, at any time when the employer is a member of a group of companies, all the members of the group are jointly and severally liable for the whole or part of the employer's pension liabilities in relation to the scheme;
 (b) an arrangement whereby, at any time when the employer is a member of a group of companies, a company (within the meaning given in section 736 of the Companies Act 1985 (c. 6)) which meets prescribed requirements and is the holding company of the group is liable for the whole or part of the employer's pension liabilities in relation to the scheme;
 (c) an arrangement which meets prescribed requirements and whereby additional financial resources are provided to the scheme;
 (d) such other arrangements as may be prescribed.

(3) The Regulator may not issue a notice under subsection (1) approving the details of

one or more arrangements falling within subsection (2) unless it is satisfied that the arrangement is, or the arrangements are, reasonable in the circumstances.

(4) In subsection (2), "the employer's pension liabilities" in relation to a scheme means—
 (a) the liabilities for any amounts payable by or on behalf of the employer towards the scheme (whether on his own account or otherwise) in accordance with a schedule of contributions under section 227, and
 (b) the liabilities for any debt which is or may become due to the trustees or managers of the scheme from the employer whether by virtue of section 75 of the Pensions Act 1995 (deficiencies in the scheme assets) or otherwise.

## 46 Financial support directions: clearance statements

(1) An application may be made to the Regulator under this section for the issue of a clearance statement within paragraph (a), (b) or (c) of subsection (2) in relation to circumstances described in the application and relating to an occupational pension scheme.

(2) A clearance statement is a statement, made by the Regulator, that in its opinion in the circumstances described in the application—
 (a) the employer in relation to the scheme would not be a service company for the purposes of section 43,
 (b) the employer in relation to the scheme would not be insufficiently resourced for the purposes of that section, or
 (c) it would not be reasonable to impose the requirements of a financial support direction, in relation to the scheme, on the applicant.

(3) Where an application is made under this section, the Regulator—
 (a) may request further information from the applicant;
 (b) may invite the applicant to amend the application to modify the circumstances described.

(4) Where an application is made under this section, the Regulator must as soon as reasonably practicable—
 (a) determine whether to issue the clearance statement, and
 (b) where it determines to do so, issue the statement.

(5) A clearance statement issued under this section binds the Regulator in relation to the exercise of the power to issue a financial support direction under section 43 in relation to the scheme to the applicant unless—
 (a) the circumstances in relation to which the exercise of the power under that section arises are not the same as the circumstances described in the application, and
 (b) the difference in those circumstances is material to the exercise of the power.

## 47 Contribution notices where non-compliance with financial support direction

(1) This section applies where there is non-compliance with a financial support direction issued in relation to a scheme under section 43.

(2) The Regulator may issue a notice to any one or more of the persons to whom the direction was issued stating that the person is under a liability to pay to the trustees or managers of the scheme the sum specified in the notice (a "contribution notice").

(3) The Regulator may issue a contribution notice to a person only if the Regulator is of

the opinion that it is reasonable to impose liability on the person to pay the sum specified in the notice.
(4) The Regulator, when deciding for the purposes of subsection (3) whether it is reasonable to impose liability on a particular person to pay the sum specified in the notice, must have regard to such matters as the Regulator considers relevant including, where relevant, the following matters—
   (a) whether the person has taken reasonable steps to secure compliance with the financial support direction,
   (b) the relationship which the person has or has had with the employer (including, where the employer is a company within the meaning of subsection (11) of section 435 of the Insolvency Act 1986 (c. 45), whether the person has or has had control of the employer within the meaning of subsection (10) of that section),
   (c) in the case of a person to whom the financial support direction was issued as a person falling within section 43(6)(b) or (c), the value of any benefits received directly or indirectly by that person from the employer,
   (d) the relationship which the person has or has had with the parties to any arrangements put in place in accordance with the direction (including, where any of those parties is a company within the meaning of subsection (11) of section 435 of the Insolvency Act 1986, whether the person has or has had control of that company within the meaning of subsection (10) of that section),
   (e) any connection or involvement which the person has or has had with the scheme,
   (f) the financial circumstances of the person, and
   (g) such other matters as may be prescribed.
(5) A contribution notice may not be issued under this section in respect of non-compliance with a financial support direction in relation to a scheme where the Board of the Pension Protection Fund has assumed responsibility for the scheme in accordance with Chapter 3 of Part 2 (pension protection).

## 48 The sum specified in a section 47 contribution notice

(1) The sum specified by the Regulator in a contribution notice under section 47 may be either the whole or a specified part of the shortfall sum in relation to the scheme.
(2) The shortfall sum in relation to a scheme is—
   (a) in a case where, at the time of non-compliance, a debt was due from the employer to the trustees or managers of the scheme under section 75 of the Pensions Act 1995 (c. 26) ("the 1995 Act") (deficiencies in the scheme assets), the amount which the Regulator estimates to be the amount of that debt at that time, and
   (b) in a case where, at the time of non-compliance, no such debt was due, the amount which the Regulator estimates to be the amount of the debt under section 75 of the 1995 Act which would become due if—
      (i) subsection (2) of that section applied, and
      (ii) the time designated by the trustees or managers of the scheme for the purposes of that subsection were the time of non-compliance.
(3) For the purposes of this section "the time of non-compliance" means—
   (a) in the case of non-compliance with paragraph (a) of subsection (3) of section 43 (financial support directions), the time immediately after the expiry of the period specified in the financial support direction for putting in place the financial support,

(b) in the case of non-compliance with paragraph (b) of that subsection, the time when financial support for the scheme ceased to be in place,
(c) in the case of non-compliance with paragraph (c) of that subsection, the time when the prescribed event occurred in relation to which there was the failure to notify the Regulator, or
(d) where more than one of paragraphs (a) to (c) above apply, whichever of the times specified in the applicable paragraphs the Regulator determines.

**49 Content and effect of a section 47 contribution notice**

(1) This section applies where a contribution notice is issued to a person under section 47.
(2) The contribution notice must—
(a) contain a statement of the matters which it is asserted constitute the non-compliance with the financial support direction in respect of which the notice is issued, and
(b) specify the sum which the person is stated to be under a liability to pay.
(3) The sum specified in the notice is to be treated as a debt due from the person to the trustees or managers of the scheme.
(4) The Regulator may, on behalf of the trustees or managers of the scheme, exercise such powers as the trustees or managers have to recover the debt.
(5) But during any assessment period (within the meaning of section 132) in relation to the scheme, the rights and powers of the trustees or managers of the scheme in relation to any debt due to them by virtue of a contribution notice, are exercisable by the Board of the Pension Protection Fund to the exclusion of the trustees or managers and the Regulator.
(6) Where, by virtue of subsection (5), any amount is paid to the Board in respect of a debt due by virtue of a contribution notice, the Board must pay the amount to the trustees or managers of the scheme.
(7) The contribution notice must identify any other persons to whom contribution notices have been or are issued in respect of the non-compliance in question and the sums specified in each of those notices.
(8) Where the contribution notice so specifies, the person to whom the notice is issued ("P") is to be treated as jointly and severally liable for the debt with any persons specified in the notice who are persons to whom corresponding contribution notices are issued.
(9) For the purposes of subsection (8), a corresponding contribution notice is a notice which—
(a) is issued in respect of the same non-compliance with the financial support direction as the non-compliance in respect of which P's contribution notice is issued,
(b) specifies the same sum as is specified in P's contribution notice, and
(c) specifies that the person to whom the contribution notice is issued is jointly and severally liable with P, or with P and other persons, for the debt in respect of that sum.
(10) A debt due by virtue of a contribution notice is not to be taken into account for the purposes of section 75(2) and (4) of the Pensions Act 1995 (c. 26) (deficiencies in the scheme assets) when ascertaining the amount or value of the assets or liabilities of a scheme.

**50  Section 47 contribution notice: relationship with employer debt**

(1) This section applies where a contribution notice is issued to a person ("P") under section 47 and condition A or B is met.

(2) Condition A is met if, at the time at which the contribution notice is issued, there is a debt due from the employer to the trustees or managers of the scheme under section 75 of the Pensions Act 1995 ("the 1995 Act") (deficiencies in the scheme assets).

(3) Condition B is met if, after the contribution notice is issued but before the whole of the debt due by virtue of the notice is recovered, a debt becomes due from the employer to the trustees or managers of the scheme under section 75 of the 1995 Act.

(4) The Regulator may issue a direction to the trustees or managers of the scheme not to take any or any further steps to recover the debt due to them under section 75 of the 1995 Act pending the recovery of all or a specified part of the debt due to them by virtue of the contribution notice.

(5) If the trustees or managers fail to comply with a direction issued to them under subsection (4), section 10 of the 1995 Act (civil penalties) applies to any trustee or manager who has failed to take all reasonable steps to secure compliance.

(6) Any sums paid—
   (a) to the trustees or managers of the scheme in respect of any debt due to them by virtue of the contribution notice, or
   (b) to the Board of the Pension Protection Fund in respect of any debt due to it by virtue of the contribution notice (where it has assumed responsibility for the scheme in accordance with Chapter 3 of Part 2 (pension protection)),
   are to be treated as reducing the amount of the debt due to the trustees or managers or, as the case may be, to the Board under section 75 of the 1995 Act.

(7) Where a sum is paid to the trustees or managers of the scheme or, as the case may be, to the Board in respect of the debt due under section 75 of the 1995 Act, P may make an application under this subsection to the Regulator for a reduction in the amount of the sum specified in P's contribution notice.

(8) An application under subsection (7) must be made as soon as reasonably practicable after the sum is paid to the trustees or managers or, as the case may be, to the Board in respect of the debt due under section 75 of the 1995 Act.

(9) Where such an application is made to the Regulator, the Regulator may, if it is of the opinion that it is appropriate to do so—
   (a) reduce the amount of the sum specified in P's contribution notice by an amount which it considers reasonable, and
   (b) issue a revised contribution notice specifying the revised sum.

(10) For the purposes of subsection (9), the Regulator must have regard to such matters as the Regulator considers relevant including, where relevant, the following matters—
   (a) the amount paid in respect of the debt due under section 75 of the 1995 Act since the contribution notice was issued,
   (b) any amounts paid in respect of the debt due by virtue of that contribution notice,
   (c) whether contribution notices have been issued to other persons in respect of the same non-compliance with the financial support direction in question as the non-compliance in respect of which P's contribution notice was issued,
   (d) where such contribution notices have been issued, the sums specified in each of

those notices and any amounts paid in respect of the debt due by virtue of those notices,

(e) whether P's contribution notice specifies that P is jointly and severally liable for the debt with other persons, and

(f) such other matters as may be prescribed.

(11) Where—

(a) P's contribution notice specifies that P is jointly and severally liable for the debt with other persons, and

(b) a revised contribution notice is issued to P under subsection (9) specifying a revised sum,

the Regulator must also issue revised contribution notices to those other persons specifying the revised sum and their joint and several liability with P for the debt in respect of that sum.

**51  Sections 43 to 50: interpretation**

(1) In sections 43 to 50—

"group of companies" means a holding company and its subsidiaries within the meaning given by section 736(1) of the Companies Act 1985 (c. 6) and "member" in relation to such a group is to be construed accordingly;

"holding company" has the meaning given by section 736(1) of that Act.

(2) For the purposes of those sections—

(a) references to a debt due under section 75 of the Pensions Act 1995 (c. 26) include a contingent debt under that section, and

(b) references to the amount of such a debt include the amount of such a contingent debt.

(3) For the purposes of those sections—

(a) section 249 of the Insolvency Act 1986 (c. 45) (connected persons) applies as it applies for the purposes of any provision of the first Group of Parts of that Act,

(b) section 435 of that Act (associated persons) applies as it applies for the purposes of that Act, and

(c) section 74 of the Bankruptcy (Scotland) Act 1985 (c. 66) (associated persons) applies as it applies for the purposes of that Act.

*Transactions at an undervalue*

**52  Restoration orders where transactions at an undervalue**

(1) This section applies in relation to an occupational pension scheme other than—

(a) a money purchase scheme, or

(b) a prescribed scheme or a scheme of a prescribed description.

(2) The Regulator may make a restoration order in respect of a transaction involving assets of the scheme if—

(a) a relevant event has occurred in relation to the employer in relation to the scheme, and

(b) the transaction is a transaction at an undervalue entered into with a person at a time which—

(i) is on or after 27th April 2004, but

(ii) is not more than two years before the occurrence of the relevant event in relation to the employer.
(3) A restoration order in respect of a transaction involving assets of a scheme is such an order as the Regulator thinks fit for restoring the position to what it would have been if the transaction had not been entered into.
(4) For the purposes of this section a relevant event occurs in relation to the employer in relation to a scheme if and when on or after the appointed day—
   (a) an insolvency event occurs in relation to the employer, or
   (b) the trustees or managers of the scheme make an application under subsection (1) of section 129 or receive a notice from the Board of the Pension Protection Fund under subsection (5)(a) of that section (applications and notifications prior to the Board assuming responsibility for a scheme).
(5) For the purposes of subsection (4)—
   (a) the "appointed day" means the day appointed under section 126(2) (no pension protection under Chapter 3 of Part 2 if the scheme begins winding up before the day appointed by the Secretary of State),
   (b) section 121 (meaning of "insolvency event") applies for the purposes of determining if and when an insolvency event has occurred in relation to the employer, and
   (c) the reference to an insolvency event in relation to the employer does not include an insolvency event which occurred in relation to him before he became the employer in relation to the scheme.
(6) For the purposes of this section and section 53, a transaction involving assets of a scheme is a transaction at an undervalue entered into with a person ("P") if the trustees or managers of the scheme or appropriate persons in relation to the scheme—
   (a) make a gift to P or otherwise enter into a transaction with P on terms that provide for no consideration to be provided towards the scheme, or
   (b) enter into a transaction with P for a consideration the value of which, in money or money's worth, is significantly less than the value, in money or money's worth, of the consideration provided by or on behalf of the trustees or managers of the scheme.
(7) In subsection (6) "appropriate persons" in relation to a scheme means a person who, or several persons each of whom is a person who, at the time at which the transaction in question is entered into, is—
   (a) a person of a prescribed description, and
   (b) entitled to exercise powers in relation to the scheme.
(8) For the purposes of this section and section 53—
   "assets" includes future assets;
   "transaction" includes a gift, agreement or arrangement and references to entering into a transaction are to be construed accordingly.
(9) The provisions of this section apply without prejudice to the availability of any other remedy, even in relation to a transaction where the trustees or managers of the scheme or appropriate persons in question had no power to enter into the transaction.

## 53 Restoration orders: supplementary

(1) This section applies in relation to a restoration order under section 52 in respect of a transaction involving assets of a scheme ("the transaction").

(2) The restoration order may in particular—
 (a) require any assets of the scheme (whether money or other property) which were transferred as part of the transaction to be transferred back—
  (i) to the trustees or managers of the scheme, or
  (ii) where the Board of the Pension Protection Fund has assumed responsibility for the scheme, to the Board;
 (b) require any property to be transferred to the trustees or managers of the scheme or, where the Board has assumed responsibility for the scheme, to the Board if it represents in any person's hands—
  (i) any of the assets of the scheme which were transferred as part of the transaction, or
  (ii) property derived from any such assets so transferred;
 (c) require such property as the Regulator may specify in the order, in respect of any consideration for the transaction received by the trustees or managers of the scheme, to be transferred—
  (i) by the trustees or managers of the scheme, or
  (ii) where the Board has assumed responsibility for the scheme, by the Board,
  to such persons as the Regulator may specify in the order;
 (d) require any person to pay, in respect of benefits received by him as a result of the transaction, such sums (not exceeding the value of the benefits received by him) as the Regulator may specify in the order—
  (i) to the trustees or managers of the scheme, or
  (ii) where the Board has assumed responsibility for the scheme, to the Board.

(3) A restoration order is of no effect to the extent that it prejudices any interest in property which was acquired in good faith and for value or any interest deriving from such an interest.

(4) Nothing in subsection (3) prevents a restoration order requiring a person to pay a sum of money if the person received a benefit as a result of the transaction otherwise than in good faith and for value.

(5) Where a person has acquired an interest in property from a person or has received a benefit as a result of the transaction and—
 (a) he is one of the trustees or managers or appropriate persons who entered into the transaction as mentioned in subsection (6) of section 52, or
 (b) at the time of the acquisition or receipt—
  (i) he has notice of the fact that the transaction was a transaction at an undervalue,
  (ii) he is a trustee or manager, or the employer, in relation to the scheme, or
  (iii) he is connected with, or an associate of, any of the persons mentioned in paragraph (a) or (b)(ii),
then, unless the contrary is shown, it is to be presumed for the purposes of subsections (3) and (4) that the interest was acquired or the benefit was received otherwise than in good faith.

(6) For the purposes of this section—
 (a) section 249 of the Insolvency Act 1986 (c. 45) (connected persons) applies as it

applies for the purposes of any provision of the first Group of Parts of that Act,
- (b) section 435 of that Act (associated persons) applies as it applies for the purposes of that Act, and
- (c) section 74 of the Bankruptcy (Scotland) Act 1985 (c. 66) (associated persons) applies as it applies for the purposes of that Act.

(7) For the purposes of this section "property" includes—
- (a) money, goods, things in action, land and every description of property wherever situated, and
- (b) obligations and every description of interest, whether present or future or vested or contingent, arising out of, or incidental to, property.

(8) References in this section to where the Board has assumed responsibility for a scheme are to where the Board has assumed responsibility for the scheme in accordance with Chapter 3 of Part 2 (pension protection).

## 54 Content and effect of a restoration order

(1) This section applies where a restoration order is made under section 52 in respect of a transaction involving assets of a scheme.

(2) Where the restoration order imposes an obligation on a person to do something, the order must specify the period within which the obligation must be complied with.

(3) Where the restoration order imposes an obligation on a person ("A") to transfer or pay a sum of money to a person specified in the order ("B"), the sum is to be treated as a debt due from A to B.

(4) Where the trustees or managers of the scheme are the persons to whom the debt is due, the Regulator may on their behalf, exercise such powers as the trustees or managers have to recover the debt.

(5) But during any assessment period (within the meaning of section 132) in relation to the scheme, the rights and powers of the trustees or managers of the scheme in relation to any debt due to them by virtue of a restoration order are exercisable by the Board of the Pension Protection Fund to the exclusion of the trustees or managers and the Regulator.

(6) Where, by virtue of subsection (5), any amount is transferred or paid to the Board in respect of a debt due by virtue of a restoration order, the Board must pay the amount to the trustees or managers of the scheme.

## 55 Contribution notice where failure to comply with restoration order

(1) This section applies where—
- (a) a restoration order is made under section 52 in respect of a transaction involving assets of a scheme ("the transaction"), and
- (b) a person fails to comply with an obligation imposed on him by the order which is not an obligation to transfer or pay a sum of money.

(2) The Regulator may issue a notice to the person stating that the person is under a liability to pay the sum specified in the notice (a "contribution notice")—
- (a) to the trustees or managers of the scheme, or
- (b) where the Board of the Pension Protection Fund has assumed responsibility for the scheme in accordance with Chapter 3 of Part 2 (pension protection), to the Board.

(3) The sum specified by the Regulator in a contribution notice may be either the whole or a specified part of the shortfall sum in relation to the scheme.

(4) The shortfall sum in relation to the scheme is the amount which the Regulator estimates to be the amount of the decrease in the value of the assets of the scheme as a result of the transaction having been entered into.

**56  Content and effect of a section 55 contribution notice**

(1) This section applies where a contribution notice is issued to a person under section 55.
(2) The contribution notice must—
    (a) contain a statement of the matters which it is asserted constitute the failure to comply with the restoration order under section 52 in respect of which the notice is issued, and
    (b) specify the sum which the person is stated to be under a liability to pay.
(3) Where the contribution notice states that the person is under a liability to pay the sum specified in the notice to the trustees or managers of the scheme, the sum is to be treated as a debt due from the person to the trustees or managers of the scheme.
(4) In such a case, the Regulator may, on behalf of the trustees or managers of the scheme, exercise such powers as the trustees or managers have to recover the debt.
(5) But during any assessment period (within the meaning of section 132) in relation to the scheme, the rights and powers of the trustees or managers of the scheme in relation to any debt due to them by virtue of a contribution notice, are exercisable by the Board of the Pension Protection Fund to the exclusion of the trustees or managers and the Regulator.
(6) Where, by virtue of subsection (5), any amount is paid to the Board in respect of a debt due by virtue of a contribution notice, the Board must pay the amount to the trustees or managers of the scheme.
(7) Where the contribution notice states that the person is under a liability to pay the sum specified in the notice to the Board, the sum is to be treated as a debt due from the person to the Board.

*Sections 38 to 56: partnerships and limited liability partnerships*

**57  Sections 38 to 56: partnerships and limited liability partnerships**

(1) For the purposes of any of sections 38 to 56, regulations may modify any of the definitions mentioned in subsection (2) (as applied by any of those sections) in relation to—
    (a) a partnership or a partner in a partnership;
    (b) a limited liability partnership or a member of such a partnership.
(2) The definitions mentioned in subsection (1) are—
    (a) section 249 of the Insolvency Act 1986 (c. 45) (connected persons),
    (b) section 435 of that Act (associated persons),
    (c) section 74 of the Bankruptcy (Scotland) Act 1985 (c. 66) (associated persons), and
    (d) section 736 of the Companies Act 1985 (c. 6) (meaning of "subsidiary" and "holding company" etc).
(3) Regulations may also provide that any provision of sections 38 to 51 applies with such modifications as may be prescribed in relation to—
    (a) any case where a partnership is or was—
        (i) the employer in relation to an occupational pension scheme, or

(ii) for the purposes of any of those sections, connected with or an associate of the employer;
(b) any case where a limited liability partnership is—
(i) the employer in relation to an occupational pension scheme, or
(ii) for the purposes of any of those sections, connected with or an associate of the employer.
(4) Regulations may also provide that any provision of sections 52 to 56 applies with such modifications as may be prescribed in relation to a partnership or a limited liability partnership.
(5) For the purposes of this section—
(a) "partnership" includes a firm or entity of a similar character formed under the law of a country or territory outside the United Kingdom, and
(b) references to a partner are to be construed accordingly.
(6) For the purposes of this section, "limited liability partnership" means—
(a) a limited liability partnership formed under the Limited Liability Partnerships Act 2000 (c. 12) or the Limited Liability Partnerships Act (Northern Ireland) 2002 (c. 12 (N.I.)), or
(b) an entity which is of a similar character to such a limited liability partnership and which is formed under the law of a country or territory outside the United Kingdom,
and references to a member of a limited liability partnership are to be construed accordingly.
(7) This section is without prejudice to—
(a) section 307 (power to modify this Act in relation to certain categories of scheme), and
(b) section 318(4) (power to extend the meaning of "employer").

*Applications under the Insolvency Act 1986*

**58 Regulator's right to apply under section 423 of insolvency act 1986**

(1) In this section "section 423" means section 423 of the Insolvency Act 1986 (transactions defrauding creditors).
(2) The Regulator may apply for an order under section 423 in relation to a debtor if—
(a) the debtor is the employer in relation to an occupational pension scheme, and
(b) condition A or condition B is met in relation to the scheme.
(3) Condition A is that an actuarial valuation under section 143 obtained by the Board of the Pension Protection Fund in respect of the scheme indicates that the value of the assets of the scheme at the relevant time, as defined by that section, was less than the amount of the protected liabilities, as defined by section 131, at that time.
(4) Condition B is that an actuarial valuation, as defined by section 224(2), obtained by the trustees or managers of the scheme indicates that the statutory funding objective in section 222 is not met.
(5) In a case where the debtor—
(a) has been adjudged bankrupt,
(b) is a body corporate which is being wound up or is in administration, or
(c) is a partnership which is being wound up or is in administration,
subsection (2) does not enable an application to be made under section 423 except with the permission of the court.

(6) An application made under this section is to be treated as made on behalf of every victim of the transaction who is—
  (a) a trustee or member of the scheme, or
  (b) the Board.
(7) This section does not apply where the valuation mentioned in subsection (3) or (4) is made by reference to a date that falls before the commencement of this section.
(8) Expressions which are defined by section 423 for the purposes of that section have the same meaning when used in this section.

*Register of schemes*

**59 Register of occupational and personal pension schemes**

(1) The Regulator must compile and maintain a register of occupational pension schemes and personal pension schemes which are, or have been, registrable schemes (referred to in this Act as "the register").
(2) In this section and sections 62 to 65 "registrable scheme" means an occupational pension scheme, or a personal pension scheme, of a prescribed description.
(3) In respect of each registrable scheme, the Regulator must record in the register—
  (a) the registrable information most recently provided to it in respect of the scheme, and
  (b) if the Regulator has received—
    (i) a notice under section 62(5) (scheme which is wound up or ceases to be registrable),
    (ii) a copy of a notice under section 160 (transfer notice), or
    (iii) any notice, or copy of a notice, under any provision in force in Northern Ireland corresponding to a provision mentioned in sub-paragraph (i) or (ii),
  that fact.
(4) In respect of each scheme which has been a registrable scheme, but
  (a) has been, or is treated as having been, wound up, or
  (b) has ceased to be a registrable scheme,
  the Regulator must maintain in the register the registrable information last provided to it in respect of the scheme.
(5) Information recorded in the register must be so recorded in such manner as the Regulator considers appropriate.
(6) In particular, the register may consist of more than one part.
(7) In this section references to "registrable information", in relation to a scheme to which any provision in force in Northern Ireland corresponding to section 60(2) ("the corresponding Northern Ireland provision") applies, are to information of any description within the corresponding Northern Ireland provision.

**60 Registrable information**

(1) For the purposes of sections 59 to 65 "registrable information", in relation to an occupational or personal pension scheme, means information within subsection (2).
(2) That information is—
  (a) the name of the scheme;
  (b) the address of the scheme;
  (c) the full names and addresses of each of the trustees or managers of the scheme;

(d) the status of the scheme with respect to the following matters—
    (i) whether new members may be admitted to the scheme;
    (ii) whether further benefits may accrue to, or in respect of, members under the scheme;
    (iii) whether further contributions may be paid towards the scheme;
    (iv) whether any members of the scheme are active members;
(e) the categories of benefits under the scheme;
(f) in the case of an occupational pension scheme—
    (i) the name and address of each relevant employer, and
    (ii) any other name by which any relevant employer has been known at any time on or after the relevant date;
(g) in the case of an occupational pension scheme, the number of members of the scheme on the later of—
    (i) the last day of the scheme year which ended most recently, and
    (ii) the day on which the scheme became a registrable scheme; and
(h) such other information as may be prescribed.
(3) Regulations may make provision about the interpretation of any of the descriptions in subsection (2).
(4) For the purposes of subsection (2)(f)—
    "relevant employer" means any person—
    (a) who is, or
    (b) who, at any time on or after 6th April 1975, has been,
    the employer in relation to the scheme;
    "relevant date", in relation to a relevant employer, means—
    (a) 6th April 1975, or
    (b) if later, the date on which the relevant employer first became the employer in relation to the scheme.

## 61 The register: inspection, provision of information and reports etc

(1) Regulations may provide—
    (a) for—
        (i) information recorded in the register,
        (ii) extracts from the register, or
        (iii) copies of the register or of extracts from it,
    to be provided to prescribed persons in prescribed circumstances, and
    (b) for the inspection of—
        (i) the register,
        (ii) extracts from the register, or
        (iii) copies of the register or of extracts from it,
    by prescribed persons in prescribed circumstances.
(2) Regulations under subsection (1) may, in particular—
    (a) confer functions on—
        (i) the Secretary of State, or
        (ii) a person authorized by him for the purposes of the regulations;
    (b) make provision with respect to the disclosure of information obtained by virtue of the regulations.
(3) Regulations which contain any provision made by virtue of subsection (2)(b) may, in particular, modify section 82 (restricted information).

(4) The Secretary of State may direct the Regulator to submit to him statistical and other reports concerning—
   (a) information recorded in the register, and
   (b) the operation of the Regulator's functions in relation to the register.
(5) A direction under subsection (4) may specify—
   (a) the form in which, and
   (b) the times at which,
   reports required by the direction are to be submitted.
(6) The Secretary of State may publish any report submitted to him by virtue of a direction under subsection (4) in such manner as he considers appropriate.

**62  The register: duties of trustees or managers**

(1) Subsection (2) applies where—
   (a) a registrable scheme is established, or
   (b) an occupational or personal pension scheme otherwise becomes a registrable scheme.
(2) The trustees or managers of the scheme must, before the end of the initial notification period—
   (a) notify the Regulator that the scheme is a registrable scheme, and
   (b) provide to the Regulator all the registrable information with respect to the scheme.
(3) In subsection (2), the "initial notification period" means the period of three months beginning with—
   (a) the date on which the scheme is established, or
   (b) if later, the date on which it becomes a registrable scheme.
(4) Where there is a change in any registrable information in respect of a registrable scheme, the trustees or managers of the scheme must as soon as reasonably practicable, notify the Regulator—
   (a) of that fact, and
   (b) of the new registrable information.
(5) Where a registrable scheme—
   (a) ceases to be a registrable scheme, or
   (b) is wound up (otherwise than under section 161(2) (effect of Board assuming responsibility for scheme)),
   the trustees or managers of the scheme must as soon as reasonably practicable, notify the Regulator of that fact.
(6) If subsection (2), (4) or (5) is not complied with, section 10 of the Pensions Act 1995 (c. 26) (civil penalties) applies to any trustee or manager who has failed to take all reasonable steps to secure compliance.

**63  Duty of the regulator to issue scheme return notices**

(1) The Regulator must issue scheme return notices in accordance with this section requiring scheme returns to be provided in respect of registrable schemes.
(2) In respect of each registrable scheme, the Regulator—
   (a) must issue the first scheme return notice in accordance with subsection (3), and
   (b) must issue subsequent scheme return notices in accordance with subsection (4).
(3) The return date specified in a scheme return notice issued in respect of a scheme under subsection (2)(a)—

(a) must fall within the period of three years beginning with—
  (i) the date on which the Regulator receives a notice under section 62(2)(a) in respect of the scheme, or
  (ii) if earlier, the date on which the Regulator first becomes aware that the scheme is a registrable scheme, and
(b) if the trustees or managers have complied with paragraph (b) of section 62(2), must fall after the end of the period of one year beginning with the date on which they provided the information required by that paragraph to the Regulator.

(4) The return date specified in a scheme return notice issued in respect of a scheme under subsection (2)(b) must fall—
(a) within the period of three years, but
(b) after the end of the period of one year,
beginning with the return date specified in the previous scheme return notice issued in respect of the scheme.

## 64 Duty of trustees or managers to provide scheme return

(1) The trustees or managers of a registrable scheme in respect of which a scheme return notice is issued must, on or before the return date, provide a scheme return to the Regulator.
(2) If a scheme return in respect of a scheme is not provided in compliance with subsection (1), section 10 of the Pensions Act 1995 (c. 26) (civil penalties) applies to any trustee or manager of the scheme who has failed to take all reasonable steps to secure compliance.

## 65 Scheme returns: supplementary

(1) This section has effect for the purposes of sections 63 and 64.
(2) In those sections and this section, in relation to a scheme return notice—
"return date" means the date specified under subsection (3)(b) in the scheme return notice;
"scheme return" means a document in the form (if any) specified in the scheme return notice, containing the information required by the notice.
(3) A scheme return notice must specify—
(a) the descriptions of information required by it, and
(b) the return date,
and may specify the form in which that information is to be provided.
(4) A scheme return notice in respect of a registrable scheme—
(a) must require all registrable information in relation to the scheme, and
(b) may require other information which the Regulator reasonably requires for the purposes of the exercise of its functions in relation to the scheme.
(5) The return date specified in a scheme return notice must fall after the end of the period of 28 days beginning with the date on which the notice is issued.
(6) A scheme return notice must be in writing and is treated as issued in respect of a registrable scheme when it is sent to the trustees or managers of the scheme.

*Register of prohibited trustees*

## 66 Register of prohibited trustees

(1) The Regulator must keep in such manner as it thinks fit a register of all persons who are prohibited under section 3 of the Pensions Act 1995 ("the prohibition register").

(2) Arrangements made by the Regulator for the prohibition register must secure that the contents of the register are not disclosed or otherwise made available to members of the public except in accordance with section 67.

(3) Nothing in subsection (2) requires the Regulator to exclude any matter from a report published under section 89 (reports of Regulator's consideration of cases).

## 67 Accessibility of register of prohibited trustees

(1) The Regulator must make arrangements to secure that the prohibition register is open, during its normal working hours, for inspection in person and without notice at—
   (a) the principal office used by it for the carrying out of its functions, and
   (b) such other of its offices (if any) as it considers to be places where it would be reasonable for a copy of the register to be kept open for inspection.

(2) If a request is made to the Regulator—
   (a) to state whether a particular person identified in the request is a person appearing in the prohibition register as prohibited in respect of an occupational trust scheme specified in the request,
   (b) to state whether a particular person so identified is a person appearing in that register as prohibited in respect of a particular description of occupational trust schemes so specified, or
   (c) to state whether a particular person so identified is a person appearing in that register as prohibited in respect of all occupational trust schemes,
   the Regulator must promptly comply with the request in such manner as it considers reasonable.

(3) The Regulator may, in such manner as it considers appropriate, publish a summary of the prohibition register if (subject to subsections (6) to (8)) the summary—
   (a) contains all the information described in subsection (4),
   (b) arranges that information in the manner described in subsection (5),
   (c) does not (except by identifying a person as prohibited in respect of all occupational trust schemes, in respect of a particular description of such schemes or in respect of a particular such scheme) identify any of the schemes in respect of which persons named in the summary are prohibited, and
   (d) does not disclose any other information contained in the register.

(4) That information is—
   (a) the full names and titles, so far as the Regulator has a record of them, of all the persons appearing in the register as persons who are prohibited,
   (b) the dates of birth of such of those persons as are persons whose dates of birth are matters of which the Regulator has a record, and
   (c) in the case of each person whose name is included in the published summary, whether that person appears in the register—
      (i) as prohibited in respect of only one occupational trust scheme,
      (ii) as prohibited in respect of one or more particular descriptions of such schemes, but not in respect of all such schemes, or

(iii) as prohibited in respect of all such schemes.
(5) For the purposes of paragraph (c) of subsection (4), the information in the published register must be arranged in three separate lists, one for each of the descriptions of prohibition specified in the sub-paragraphs of that paragraph.
(6) The Regulator must ensure, in the case of any published summary, that a person is not identified in the summary as a prohibited person if it appears to the Regulator that the determination by virtue of which that person appears in the register—
    (a) is the subject of any pending reference, review, appeal or legal proceedings which could result in that person's removal from the register, or
    (b) is a determination which might still become the subject of any such reference, review, appeal or proceedings.
(7) The Regulator must ensure, in the case of any published summary, that the particulars relating to a person do not appear in a particular list mentioned in subsection (5) if it appears to the Regulator that a determination by virtue of which that person's particulars would appear in that list—
    (a) is the subject of any pending reference, review, appeal or legal proceedings which could result in such a revocation or other overturning of a prohibition of that person as would require his particulars to appear in a different list, or
    (b) is a determination which might still become the subject of any such reference, review, appeal or proceedings.
(8) Where subsection (7) prevents a person's particulars from being included in a particular list in the published summary, they must be included, instead, in the list (if any) in which they would have been included if the prohibition to which the reference, review, appeal or proceedings relate or might relate had already been revoked or otherwise overturned.
(9) For the purposes of this section a determination is one which might still become the subject of a reference, review, appeal or proceedings if, and only if, in the case of that determination—
    (a) the time for the making of an application for a review or reference, or for the bringing of an appeal or other proceedings, has not expired, and
    (b) there is a reasonable likelihood that such an application might yet be made, or that such an appeal or such proceedings might yet be brought.
(10) In this section—

"name", in relation to a person any of whose names is recorded by the Regulator as an initial, means that initial;
"occupational trust scheme" means an occupational pension scheme established under a trust.

*Collecting information relevant to the board of the pension protection fund*

**68 Information relevant to the board**

The Regulator may collect any information which appears to it to be relevant to the exercise of the functions of the Board of the Pension Protection Fund.

**69 Duty to notify the regulator of certain events**

(1) Except where the Regulator otherwise directs, the appropriate person must give notice of any notifiable event to the Regulator.

(2) In subsection (1) "notifiable event" means—
   (a) a prescribed event in respect of an eligible scheme, or
   (b) a prescribed event in respect of the employer in relation to an eligible scheme.
(3) For the purposes of subsection (1)—
   (a) in the case of an event within subsection (2)(a), each of the following is "the appropriate person"—
      (i) the trustees or managers of the scheme,
      (ii) a person of a prescribed description, and
   (b) in relation to an event within subsection (2)(b), each of the following is "the appropriate person"—
      (i) the employer in relation to the scheme,
      (ii) a person of a prescribed description.
(4) A notice under subsection (1)—
   (a) must be in writing, and
   (b) subject to subsection (5), must be given as soon as reasonably practicable after the person giving it becomes aware of the notifiable event.
(5) Regulations may require a notice under subsection (1) to be given before the beginning of the prescribed period ending with the notifiable event in question.
(6) No duty to which a person is subject is to be regarded as contravened merely because of any information or opinion contained in a notice under this section.
This is subject to section 311 (protected items).
(7) Where the trustees or managers of a scheme fail to comply with an obligation imposed on them by subsection (1), section 10 of the Pensions Act 1995 (c. 26) (civil penalties) applies in relation to any trustee or manager who has failed to take all reasonable steps to secure compliance with that subsection.
(8) That section also applies to any other person who, without reasonable excuse, fails to comply with an obligation imposed on him by subsection (1).
(9) In this section—
"eligible scheme" has the meaning given by section 126;
"event" includes a failure to act.

*Reporting breaches of the law*

**70 Duty to report breaches of the law**

(1) Subsection (2) imposes a reporting requirement on the following persons—
   (a) a trustee or manager of an occupational or personal pension scheme;
   (b) a person who is otherwise involved in the administration of such a scheme;
   (c) the employer in relation to an occupational pension scheme;
   (d) a professional adviser in relation to such a scheme;
   (e) a person who is otherwise involved in advising the trustees or managers of an occupational or personal pension scheme in relation to the scheme.
(2) Where the person has reasonable cause to believe that—
   (a) a duty which is relevant to the administration of the scheme in question, and is imposed by or by virtue of an enactment or rule of law, has not been or is not being complied with, and
   (b) the failure to comply is likely to be of material significance to the Regulator in the exercise of any of its functions,

he must give a written report of the matter to the Regulator as soon as reasonably practicable.

(3) No duty to which a person is subject is to be regarded as contravened merely because of any information or opinion contained in a written report under this section.
This is subject to section 311 (protected items).

(4) Section 10 of the Pensions Act 1995 (c. 26) (civil penalties) applies to any person who, without reasonable excuse, fails to comply with an obligation imposed on him by this section.

*Reports by skilled persons*

## 71 Reports by skilled persons

(1) The Regulator may issue a notice (a "report notice") to—
　(a) the trustees or managers of a work-based pension scheme,
　(b) any employer in relation to such a scheme, or
　(c) any person who is otherwise involved in the administration of such a scheme,
requiring them or, as the case may be, him to provide the Regulator with a report on one or more specified matters which are relevant to the exercise of any of the Regulator's functions.

(2) A report notice must require the person appointed to make the report to be a person—
　(a) nominated or approved by the Regulator, and
　(b) appearing to the Regulator to have the skills necessary to make a report on the matter or matters concerned.

(3) A report notice may require the report to be provided to the Regulator—
　(a) in a specified form;
　(b) before a specified date.

(4) The costs of providing a report in accordance with a report notice must be met by the person to whom the notice is issued ("the notified person").

(5) But a report notice may require a specified person (other than the Regulator) to reimburse to the notified person the whole or any part of the costs of providing the report.

(6) Where, by virtue of subsection (5), an amount is required to be reimbursed by a specified person to the notified person, that amount is to be treated as a debt due from the specified person to the notified person.

(7) If the trustees or managers of a work-based pension scheme fail to comply with a report notice issued to them, section 10 of the Pensions Act 1995 (civil penalties) applies to any trustee or manager who has failed to take all reasonable steps to secure compliance.

(8) That section also applies to any other person who, without reasonable excuse, fails to comply with a report notice issued to him.

(9) Where a report notice is issued, any person who is providing (or who at any time has provided) services to the notified person in relation to a matter on which the report is required must give the person appointed to make the report such assistance as he may reasonably require.

(10) The duty imposed by subsection (9) is enforceable, on the application of the Regulator, by an injunction or, in Scotland, by an order for specific performance under section 45 of the Court of Session Act 1988 (c. 36).

(11) In this section—
"specified", in relation to a report notice, means specified in the notice;
"work-based pension scheme" has the same meaning as in section 5 (Regulator's objectives).

*Gathering information*

**72 Provision of information**

(1) The Regulator may, by notice in writing, require any person to whom subsection (2) applies to produce any document, or provide any other information, which is—
   (a) of a description specified in the notice, and
   (b) relevant to the exercise of the Regulator's functions.
(2) This subsection applies to—
   (a) a trustee or manager of an occupational or personal pension scheme,
   (b) a professional adviser in relation to an occupational pension scheme,
   (c) the employer in relation to—
      (i) an occupational pension scheme, or
      (ii) a personal pension scheme where direct payment arrangements exist in respect of one or more members of the scheme who are employees, and
   (d) any other person appearing to the Regulator to be a person who holds, or is likely to hold, information relevant to the exercise of the Regulator's functions.
(3) Where the production of a document, or the provision of information, is required by a notice given under subsection (1), the document must be produced, or information must be provided, in such a manner, at such a place and within such a period as may be specified in the notice.

**73 Inspection of premises**

(1) An inspector may, for the purposes of investigating whether, in the case of any occupational pension scheme, the occupational scheme provisions are being, or have been, complied with, at any reasonable time enter premises liable to inspection.
(2) In subsection (1), the "occupational scheme provisions" means provisions contained in or made by virtue of—
   (a) any of the following provisions of this Act—
      this Part;
      Part 3 (scheme funding);
      sections 241 to 243 (member-nominated trustees and directors);
      sections 247 to 249 (requirement for knowledge and understanding);
      section 252 (UK-based scheme to be trust with effective rules);
      section 253 (non-European scheme to be trust with UK-resident trustee);
      section 255 (activities of occupational pension schemes);
      section 256 (no indemnification for fines or civil penalties);
      sections 259 and 261 (consultation by employers);
      Part 7 (cross-border activities within European Union);
      Part 9 (miscellaneous and supplementary);
   (b) either of the following provisions of the Welfare Reform and Pensions Act 1999 (c. 30)—

section 33 (time for discharge of pension credit liability);
section 45 (information);
(c) any of the provisions of Part 1 of the Pensions Act 1995 (c. 26) (occupational pension schemes), other than—
  (i) sections 51 to 54 (indexation), and
  (ii) sections 62 to 65 (equal treatment);
(d) any of the following provisions of the Pension Schemes Act 1993 (c. 48)—
Chapter 4 of Part 4 (transfer values);
Chapter 5 of Part 4 (early leavers: cash transfer sums and contribution refunds);
Chapter 2 of Part 4A (pension credit transfer values);
section 113 (information);
section 175 (levy);
(e) any provisions in force in Northern Ireland corresponding to any provisions within paragraphs (a) to (d).
(3) An inspector may, for the purposes of investigating whether, in the case of a stakeholder scheme—
(a) sections 1 and 2(4) of the Welfare Reform and Pensions Act 1999 (stakeholder pension schemes: registration etc), or
(b) any corresponding provisions in force in Northern Ireland,
are being, or have been, complied with, at any reasonable time enter premises liable to inspection.
(4) An inspector may, for the purposes of investigating whether, in the case of any trust-based personal stakeholder scheme, the trust-based scheme provisions are being, or have been, complied with, at any reasonable time enter premises liable to inspection.
(5) In subsection (4)—
"trust-based personal stakeholder scheme" means a personal pension scheme which—
(a) is a stakeholder scheme, and
(b) is established under a trust;
the "trust-based scheme provisions" means any provisions contained in or made by virtue of—
(a) any provision which applies in relation to trust-based personal stakeholder schemes by virtue of paragraph 1 of Schedule 1 to the Welfare Reform and Pensions Act 1999 (c. 30), as the provision applies by virtue of that paragraph, or
(b) any corresponding provision in force in Northern Ireland.
(6) Premises are liable to inspection for the purposes of this section if the inspector has reasonable grounds to believe that—
(a) members of the scheme are employed there,
(b) documents relevant to the administration of the scheme are being kept there, or
(c) the administration of the scheme, or work connected with that administration, is being carried out there.
(7) In this section, "stakeholder scheme" means an occupational pension scheme or a personal pension scheme which is or has been registered under—
(a) section 2 of the Welfare Reform and Pensions Act 1999 (register of stakeholder schemes), or
(b) any corresponding provision in force in Northern Ireland.

**74 Inspection of premises in respect of employers' obligations**

(1) An inspector may, for the purposes of investigating whether an employer is complying, or has complied, with the requirements under—
   (a) section 3 of the Welfare Reform and Pensions Act 1999 (duty of employers to facilitate access to stakeholder pension schemes), or
   (b) any corresponding provision in force in Northern Ireland,
   at any reasonable time enter premises liable to inspection.

(2) Premises are liable to inspection for the purposes of subsection (1) if the inspector has reasonable grounds to believe that—
   (a) employees of the employer are employed there,
   (b) documents relevant to the administration of the employer's business are being kept there, or
   (c) the administration of the employer's business, or work connected with that administration, is being carried out there.

(3) In subsections (1) and (2), "employer" has the meaning given by section 3(9) of the Welfare Reform and Pensions Act 1999 (or, where subsection (1)(b) applies, by any corresponding provision in force in Northern Ireland).

(4) An inspector may, for the purposes of investigating whether, in the case of any direct payment arrangements relating to a personal pension scheme, any of the following provisions—
   (a) regulations made by virtue of sections 260 and 261 (consultation by employers),
   (b) section 111A of the Pension Schemes Act 1993 (c. 48) (monitoring of employers' payments to personal pension schemes), or
   (c) any corresponding provisions in force in Northern Ireland,
   is being, or has been, complied with, at any reasonable time enter premises liable to inspection.

(5) Premises are liable to inspection for the purposes of subsection (4) if the inspector has reasonable grounds to believe that—
   (a) employees of the employer are employed there,
   (b) documents relevant to the administration of—
       (i) the employer's business,
       (ii) the direct payment arrangements, or
       (iii) the scheme to which those arrangements relate,
   are being kept there, or
   (c) either of the following is being carried out there—
       (i) the administration of the employer's business, the arrangements or the scheme;
       (ii) work connected with that administration.

(6) In the application of subsections (4) and (5) in relation to any provision mentioned in subsection (4)(c) (a "corresponding Northern Ireland provision"), references in those subsections to—
   direct payment arrangements,
   a personal pension scheme,
   the employer, or
   employees of the employer, are to be read as having the meanings that they have for the purposes of the corresponding Northern Ireland provision.

## 75 Inspection of premises: powers of inspectors

(1) Subsection (2) applies where, for a purpose mentioned in subsection (1), (3) or (4) of section 73 or subsection (1) or (4) of section 74, an inspector enters premises which are liable to inspection for the purposes of that provision.

(2) While there, the inspector—
   (a) may make such examination and inquiry as may be necessary for the purpose for which he entered the premises,
   (b) may require any person on the premises to produce, or secure the production of, any document relevant to compliance with the regulatory provisions for his inspection,
   (c) may take copies of any such document,
   (d) may take possession of any document appearing to be a document relevant to compliance with the regulatory provisions or take in relation to any such document any other steps which appear necessary for preserving it or preventing interference with it,
   (e) may, in the case of any such document which consists of information which is stored in electronic form and is on, or accessible from, the premises, require the information to be produced in a form—
      (i) in which it can be taken away, and
      (ii) in which it is legible or from which it can readily be produced in a legible form, and
   (f) may, as to any matter relevant to compliance with the regulatory provisions, examine, or require to be examined, either alone or in the presence of another person, any person on the premises whom he has reasonable cause to believe to be able to give information relevant to that matter.

## 76 Inspection of premises: supplementary

(1) This section applies for the purposes of sections 73 to 75.

(2) Premises which are a private dwelling-house not used by, or by permission of, the occupier for the purposes of a trade or business are not liable to inspection.

(3) Any question whether—
   (a) anything is being or has been done or omitted which might by virtue of any of the regulatory provisions give rise to a liability for a civil penalty under or by virtue of section 10 of the Pensions Act 1995 (c. 26) or section 168(4) of the Pension Schemes Act 1993 (c. 48) (or under or by virtue of any provision in force in Northern Ireland corresponding to either of them), or
   (b) an offence is being or has been committed under any of the regulatory provisions,
   is to be treated as a question whether the regulatory provision is being, or has been, complied with.

(4) An inspector applying for admission to any premises for the purposes of section 73 or 74 must, if so required, produce his certificate of appointment.

(5) When exercising a power under section 73, 74 or 75 an inspector may be accompanied by such persons as he considers appropriate.

(6) Any document of which possession is taken under section 75 may be retained—
   (a) if the document is relevant to proceedings against any person for any offence which are commenced before the end of the retention period, until the conclusion of those proceedings, and

(b) otherwise, until the end of the retention period.
(7) In subsection (6), "the retention period" means the period comprising—
    (a) the period of 12 months beginning with the date on which possession was taken of the document, and
    (b) any extension of that period under subsection (8).
(8) The Regulator may, by a direction made before the end of the retention period (including any extension of it under this subsection), extend it by such period not exceeding 12 months as the Regulator considers appropriate.
(9) "The regulatory provisions", in relation to an inspection under subsection (1), (3) or (4) of section 73 or subsection (1) or (4) of section 74, means the provision or provisions referred to in that subsection.

### 77 Penalties relating to sections 72 to 75

(1) A person who, without reasonable excuse, neglects or refuses to provide information or produce a document when required to do so under section 72 is guilty of an offence.
(2) A person who without reasonable excuse—
    (a) intentionally delays or obstructs an inspector exercising any power under section 73, 74 or 75,
    (b) neglects or refuses to produce, or secure the production of, any document when required to do so under section 75, or
    (c) neglects or refuses to answer a question or to provide information when so required,
    is guilty of an offence.
(3) A person guilty of an offence under subsection (1) or (2) is liable on summary conviction to a fine not exceeding level 5 on the standard scale.
(4) An offence under subsection (1) or (2)(b) or (c) may be charged by reference to any day or longer period of time; and a person may be convicted of a second or subsequent offence by reference to any period of time following the preceding conviction of the offence.
(5) Any person who intentionally and without reasonable excuse alters, suppresses, conceals or destroys any document which he is or is liable to be required to produce under section 72 or 75 is guilty of an offence.
(6) Any person guilty of an offence under subsection (5) is liable—
    (a) on summary conviction, to a fine not exceeding the statutory maximum;
    (b) on conviction on indictment, to a fine or imprisonment for a term not exceeding two years, or both.

### 78 Warrants

(1) A justice of the peace may issue a warrant under this section if satisfied on information on oath given by or on behalf of the Regulator that there are reasonable grounds for believing—
    (a) that there is on, or accessible from, any premises any document—
        (i) whose production has been required under section 72 or 75, or any corresponding provision in force in Northern Ireland, and
        (ii) which has not been produced in compliance with that requirement,
    (b) that there is on, or accessible from, any premises any document whose production could be so required and, if its production were so required, the document—

(i) would not be produced, but
(ii) would be removed, or made inaccessible, from the premises, hidden, tampered with or destroyed, or

(c) that—
(i) an offence has been committed,
(ii) a person will do any act which constitutes a misuse or misappropriation of the assets of an occupational pension scheme or a personal pension scheme,
(iii) a person is liable to pay a penalty under or by virtue of section 10 of the Pensions Act 1995 (c. 26) (civil penalties) or section 168(4) of the Pension Schemes Act 1993 (c. 48) (civil penalties for breach of regulations), or under or by virtue of any provision in force in Northern Ireland corresponding to either of them, or
(iv) a person is liable to be prohibited from being a trustee of an occupational or personal pension scheme under section 3 of the Pensions Act 1995 (prohibition orders), including that section as it applies by virtue of paragraph 1 of Schedule 1 to the Welfare Reform and Pensions Act 1999 (c. 30) (stakeholder schemes), or under or by virtue of any corresponding provisions in force in Northern Ireland,

and that there is on, or accessible from, any premises any document which relates to whether the offence has been committed, whether the act will be done or whether the person is so liable, and whose production could be required under section 72 or 75 or any corresponding provision in force in Northern Ireland.

(2) A warrant under this section shall authorize an inspector—
   (a) to enter the premises specified in the information, using such force as is reasonably necessary for the purpose,
   (b) to search the premises and—
      (i) take possession of any document appearing to be such a document as is mentioned in subsection (1), or
      (ii) take in relation to such a document any other steps which appear necessary for preserving it or preventing interference with it,
   (c) to take copies of any such document,
   (d) to require any person named in the warrant to provide an explanation of any such document or to state where it may be found or how access to it may be obtained, and
   (e) in the case of any such document which consists of information which is stored in electronic form and is on, or accessible from, the premises, to require the information to be produced in a form—
      (i) in which it can be taken away, and
      (ii) in which it is legible or from which it can readily be produced in a legible form.

(3) In subsection (1), any reference in paragraph (a) or (b) to a document does not include any document which is relevant to whether a person has complied with—
   (a) subsection (3) of section 238 (information and advice to employees) or regulations under subsection (4) of that section, or
   (b) any provision in force in Northern Ireland which corresponds to that subsection (3) or is made under provision corresponding to that subsection (4),
   and is not relevant to the exercise of the Regulator's functions for any other reason.

(4) For the purposes of subsection (1)(c)(iii), any liability to pay a penalty under—

(a) section 10 of the Pensions Act 1995 (c. 26), or

(b) any corresponding provision in force in Northern Ireland,

which might arise out of a failure to comply with any provision within subsection (3)(a) or (b) is to be disregarded.

(5) References in subsection (2) to such a document as is mentioned in subsection (1) are to be read in accordance with subsections (3) and (4).

(6) When executing a warrant under this section, an inspector may be accompanied by such persons as he considers appropriate.

(7) A warrant under this section continues in force until the end of the period of one month beginning with the day on which it is issued.

(8) Any document of which possession is taken under this section may be retained—

(a) if the document is relevant to proceedings against any person for any offence which are commenced before the end of the retention period, until the conclusion of those proceedings, and

(b) otherwise, until the end of the retention period.

(9) In subsection (8), "the retention period" means the period comprising—

(a) the period of 12 months beginning with the date on which possession was taken of the document, and

(b) any extension of that period under subsection (10).

(10) The Regulator may, by a direction made before the end of the retention period (including any extension of it under this subsection), extend it by such period not exceeding 12 months as the Regulator considers appropriate.

(11) In the application of this section in Scotland—

(a) the reference to a justice of the peace is to be read as a reference to the sheriff, and

(b) the references in subsections (1) and (2)(a) to information are to be read as references to evidence.

**79 Sections 72 to 78: interpretation**

(1) This section applies for the purposes of sections 72 to 78.

(2) "Document" includes information recorded in any form, and any reference to production of a document, in relation to information recorded otherwise than in a legible form, is to producing a copy of the information—

(a) in a legible form, or

(b) in a form from which it can readily be produced in a legible form.

(3) "Inspector" means a person appointed by the Regulator as an inspector.

*Provision of false or misleading information*

**80 Offences of providing false or misleading information**

(1) Any person who knowingly or recklessly provides the Regulator with information which is false or misleading in a material particular is guilty of an offence if the information—

(a) is provided in purported compliance with a requirement under—

(i) section 62 (the register: duties of trustees or managers),

(ii) section 64 (duty of trustees or managers to provide scheme return),

(iii) section 72 (provision of information), or

(iv) section 75 (inspection of premises: powers of inspectors),

(b) is provided in applying for registration of a pension scheme under section 2 of the Welfare Reform and Pensions Act 1999 (c. 30) (registration of stakeholder pension schemes), or

(c) is provided otherwise than as mentioned in paragraph (a) or (b) but in circumstances in which the person providing the information intends, or could reasonably be expected to know, that it would be used by the Regulator for the purpose of exercising its functions under this Act or the Pensions Act 1995 (c. 26).

(2) Any person guilty of an offence under subsection (1) is liable—

(a) on summary conviction, to a fine not exceeding the statutory maximum;

(b) on conviction on indictment, to a fine or imprisonment for a term not exceeding two years, or both.

*Use of information*

## 81 Use of information

Information—

(a) contained in the register, or

(b) otherwise held by the Regulator in the exercise of any of its functions,

may be used by the Regulator for the purposes of, or for any purpose connected with or incidental to, the exercise of its functions.

*Disclosure of information*

## 82 Restricted information

(1) Restricted information must not be disclosed—

(a) by the Regulator, or

(b) by any person who receives the information directly or indirectly from the Regulator.

(2) Subsection (1) is subject to—

(a) subsection (3), and

(b) sections 71(9), 83 to 88 and 235.

(3) Subject to section 88(4), restricted information may be disclosed with the consent of the person to whom it relates and (if different) the person from whom the Regulator obtained it.

(4) For the purposes of this section and sections 83 to 87, "restricted information" means any information obtained by the Regulator in the exercise of its functions which relates to the business or other affairs of any person, except for information—

(a) which at the time of the disclosure is or has already been made available to the public from other sources, or

(b) which is in the form of a summary or collection of information so framed as not to enable information relating to any particular person to be ascertained from it.

(5) Any person who discloses information in contravention of this section is guilty of an offence and liable—

(a) on summary conviction, to a fine not exceeding the statutory maximum;

(b) on conviction on indictment, to a fine or imprisonment for a term not exceeding two years, or both.

## 83 Information supplied to the regulator by corresponding overseas authorities

(1) Subject to subsection (2), for the purposes of section 82, "restricted information" includes information which has been supplied to the Regulator, for the purposes of its functions, by an authority which exercises functions corresponding to the functions of the Regulator in a country or territory outside the United Kingdom.

(2) Sections 84 to 87 do not apply to such information as is mentioned in subsection (1), and such information must not be disclosed except—
   (a) as provided in section 82(3),
   (b) for the purpose of enabling or assisting the Regulator to discharge its functions, or
   (c) by or on behalf of—
      (i) the Regulator, or
      (ii) any public authority (within the meaning of section 6 of the Human Rights Act 1998 (c. 42)) which receives the information directly or indirectly from the Regulator,
   for any of the purposes specified in section 17(2)(a) to (d) of the Anti-terrorism, Crime and Security Act 2001 (c. 24) (criminal proceedings and investigations).

(3) Section 18 of the Anti-terrorism, Crime and Security Act 2001 (restriction on disclosure of information for overseas purposes) has effect in relation to a disclosure authorized by subsection (2) as it has effect in relation to a disclosure authorized by any of the provisions to which section 17 of that Act applies.

## 84 Disclosure for facilitating exercise of functions by the regulator

(1) Section 82 does not preclude the disclosure of restricted information in any case in which disclosure is for the purpose of enabling or assisting the Regulator to exercise its functions.

(2) Subsection (3) applies where, in order to enable or assist the Regulator properly to exercise any of its functions, the Regulator considers it necessary to seek advice from any qualified person on any matter of law, accountancy, valuation or other matter requiring the exercise of professional skill.

(3) Section 82 does not preclude the disclosure by the Regulator to a person qualified to provide that advice of such information as appears to the Regulator to be necessary to ensure that he is properly informed with respect to the matters on which his advice is sought.

## 85 Disclosure for facilitating exercise of functions by the board

Section 82 does not preclude the disclosure of restricted information in any case in which disclosure is for the purpose of enabling or assisting the Board of the Pension Protection Fund to exercise its functions.

## 86 Disclosure for facilitating exercise of functions by other supervisory authorities

(1) Section 82 does not preclude the disclosure by the Regulator of restricted information to any person specified in the first column of Schedule 3 if the Regulator considers that the disclosure would enable or assist that person to exercise the functions specified in relation to him in the second column of that Schedule.

(2) The Secretary of State may after consultation with the Regulator—
   (a) by order amend Schedule 3 by—

(i) adding any person exercising regulatory functions and specifying functions in relation to that person,
(ii) removing any person for the time being specified in the Schedule, or
(iii) altering the functions for the time being specified in the Schedule in relation to any person, or

(b) by order restrict the circumstances in which, or impose conditions subject to which, disclosure may be made to any person for the time being specified in the Schedule.

## 87 Other permitted disclosures

(1) Section 82 does not preclude the disclosure by the Regulator of restricted information to—
(a) the Secretary of State,
(b) the Commissioners of Inland Revenue or their officers, or
(c) the Department for Social Development in Northern Ireland,
if the disclosure appears to the Regulator to be desirable or expedient in the interests of members of occupational pension schemes or personal pension schemes or in the public interest.

(2) Section 82 does not preclude the disclosure of restricted information—
(a) by or on behalf of—
(i) the Regulator, or
(ii) any public authority (within the meaning of section 6 of the Human Rights Act 1998 (c. 42)) which receives the information directly or indirectly from the Regulator,
for any of the purposes specified in section 17(2)(a) to (d) of the Anti-terrorism, Crime and Security Act 2001 (c. 24) (criminal proceedings and investigations),
(b) in connection with any proceedings arising out of—
(i) this Act,
(ii) the Welfare Reform and Pensions Act 1999 (c. 30),
(iii) the Pensions Act 1995 (c. 26), or
(iv) the Pension Schemes Act 1993 (c. 48),
or any corresponding enactment in force in Northern Ireland, or any proceedings for breach of trust in relation to an occupational pension scheme,
(c) with a view to the institution of, or otherwise for the purposes of, proceedings under—
(i) section 7 or 8 of the Company Directors Disqualification Act 1986 (c. 46), or
(ii) Article 10 or 11 of the Companies (Northern Ireland) Order 1989 (S.I. 1989/2404 (N.I. 18)) or of the Company Directors Disqualification (Northern Ireland) Order 2002 (S.I. 2002/3150 (N.I. 4)),
(d) in connection with any proceedings under—
(i) the Insolvency Act 1986 (c. 45), or
(ii) the Insolvency (Northern Ireland) Order 1989 (S.I. 1989/2405 (N.I. 19)),
which the Regulator has instituted or in which it has a right to be heard,
(e) with a view to the institution of, or otherwise for the purposes of, any disciplinary proceedings relating to the exercise of his professional duties by a solicitor, an actuary, an accountant or an insolvency practitioner,
(f) with a view to the institution of, or otherwise for the purposes of, any disciplinary proceedings relating to the exercise by a public servant of his functions,

(g) for the purpose of enabling or assisting an authority in a country outside the United Kingdom to exercise functions corresponding to those of the Regulator under this Act, the Welfare Reform and Pensions Act 1999 (c. 30), the Pensions Act 1995 (c. 26) or the Pension Schemes Act 1993 (c. 48), or

(h) in pursuance of a Community obligation.

(3) In subsection (2)(f), "public servant" means an officer or servant of the Crown or of any prescribed authority.

(4) Section 82 does not preclude the disclosure by the Regulator of restricted information to—
   (a) the Director of Public Prosecutions,
   (b) the Director of Public Prosecutions for Northern Ireland,
   (c) the Lord Advocate,
   (d) a procurator fiscal, or
   (e) a constable.

(5) Section 82 does not preclude the disclosure of restricted information in any case where the disclosure is required by or by virtue of an enactment.

(6) Section 82 does not preclude the disclosure of restricted information in any case where the disclosure is to a Regulator-appointed trustee of an occupational pension scheme for the purpose of enabling or assisting him to exercise his functions in relation to the scheme.

(7) In subsection (6), "Regulator-appointed trustee" means a trustee appointed by the Regulator under section 7 or 23(1) of the Pensions Act 1995 or any corresponding provision in force in Northern Ireland.

(8) Section 82 does not preclude the disclosure by any person mentioned in subsection (1) or (4) of restricted information obtained by the person by virtue of that subsection, if the disclosure is made with the consent of the Regulator.

(9) Section 82 does not preclude the disclosure by any person specified in the first column of Schedule 3 of restricted information obtained by the person by virtue of section 86(1), if the disclosure is made—
   (a) with the consent of the Regulator, and
   (b) for the purpose of enabling or assisting the person to exercise any functions specified in relation to him in the second column of the Schedule.

(10) Before deciding whether to give its consent to such a disclosure as is mentioned in subsection (8) or (9), the Regulator must take account of any representations made to it, by the person seeking to make the disclosure, as to the desirability of the disclosure or the necessity for it.

(11) Section 18 of the Anti-terrorism, Crime and Security Act 001 (c. 24) (restriction on disclosure of information for overseas purposes) has effect in relation to a disclosure authorized by subsection (2) as it has effect in relation to a disclosure authorized by any of the provisions to which section 17 of that Act applies.

## 88  Tax information

(1) This section applies to information held by any person in the exercise of tax functions about any matter which is relevant, for the purposes of those functions, to tax or duty in the case of an identifiable person (in this section referred to as "tax information").

(2) No obligation as to secrecy imposed by section 182 of the Finance Act 1989 (c. 26)

or otherwise shall prevent the disclosure of tax information to the Regulator for the purpose of enabling or assisting the Regulator to discharge its functions.
(3) Where tax information is disclosed to the Regulator by virtue of subsection (2) above or section 19 of the Anti-terrorism, Crime and Security Act 2001 (disclosure of information held by revenue departments), it must, subject to subsection (4), be treated for the purposes of section 82 as restricted information.
(4) Sections 82(3), 83 to 87 and 235 do not apply to tax information which is disclosed to the Regulator as mentioned in subsection (3), and such information may not be disclosed by the Regulator or any person who receives the information directly or indirectly from the Regulator except—
  (a) to, or in accordance with authority given by, the Commissioners of Inland Revenue or the Commissioners of Customs and Excise, or
  (b) with a view to the institution of, or otherwise for the purposes of, any criminal proceedings.
(5) In this section "tax functions" has the same meaning as in section 182 of the Finance Act 1989.

*Reports*

## 89 Publishing reports etc

(1) The Regulator may, if it considers it appropriate to do so in any particular case, publish a report of the consideration given by it to the exercise of its functions in relation to that case and the results of that consideration.
(2) The publication of a report under subsection (1) may be in such form and manner as the Regulator considers appropriate.
(3) For the purposes of the law of defamation, the publication of any matter by the Regulator is privileged unless the publication is shown to be made with malice.

*Codes of practice*

## 90 Codes of practice

(1) The Regulator may issue codes of practice—
  (a) containing practical guidance in relation to the exercise of functions under the pensions legislation, and
  (b) regarding the standards of conduct and practice expected from those who exercise such functions.
(2) The Regulator must issue one or more such codes of practice relating to the following matters—
  (a) what constitutes a "reasonable" period for the purposes of any provision of the pensions legislation (other than any enactment contained in or made by virtue of Part 2) which requires any action to be taken within such a period;
  (b) the discharge of the duty imposed by section 69 (duty to notify Regulator of certain events);
  (c) the discharge of the duty imposed by section 70 (duty to report breaches of the law);
  (d) the discharge of duties imposed on trustees or managers of occupational pension schemes by, or by virtue of, Part 3 (scheme funding);

(e) the discharge of the duties imposed by sections 241 and 242 (member-nominated trustees and directors);
(f) the obligations imposed by sections 247 and 248 (requirements for knowledge and understanding: individual and corporate trustees);
(g) the discharge of the duty imposed by section 49(9)(b) of the Pensions Act 1995 (c. 26) (duty of trustees or managers of occupational pension schemes to report material failures by employers to pay contributions deducted from employee's earnings timeously);
(h) the discharge of the duties imposed by sections 67 to 67I of that Act (the subsisting rights provisions);
(i) the discharge of the duty imposed by section 88(1) of that Act (duties of trustees and managers of money purchase schemes to report failures to pay employer contributions etc timeously);
(j) the discharge of the duty imposed by section 111A(7A) of the Pension Schemes Act 1993 (c. 48) (duty of trustees or managers of personal pension schemes to report material failures to pay employer contributions timeously);
(k) such other matters as are prescribed for the purposes of this section.

(3) The Regulator may from time to time revise the whole or any part of a code of practice issued under this section and issue that revised code.

(4) A failure on the part of any person to observe any provision of a code of practice does not of itself render that person liable to any legal proceedings.

This is subject to section 13(3)(a) and (8) (power for improvement notice to direct that person complies with code of practice and civil penalties for failure to comply).

(5) A code of practice issued under this section is admissible in evidence in any legal proceedings and, if any provision of such a code appears to the court or Tribunal concerned to be relevant to any question arising in the proceedings, it must be taken into account in determining that question.

(6) In this section—

"legal proceedings" includes proceedings of the Pensions Ombudsman, proceedings of the Ombudsman for the Board of the Pension Protection Fund and proceedings of the Board of the Pension Protection Fund under section 207 or 208; and

"the pensions legislation" means any enactment contained in or made by virtue of—
(a) the Pension Schemes Act 1993 (c. 48),
(b) Part 1 of the Pensions Act 1995 (c. 26), other than sections 62 to 66A of that Act (equal treatment),
(c) Part 1 or section 33 of the Welfare Reform and Pensions Act 1999 (c. 30), or
(d) this Act.

(7) Sections 91 and 92 make provision about the procedure to be followed when a code of practice is issued or revoked.

## 91 Procedure for issue and publication of codes of practice

(1) Where the Regulator proposes to issue a code of practice it must prepare and publish a draft of the code.

(2) Where the Regulator publishes a draft under subsection (1), it must consult—
(a) such persons as it considers appropriate, and
(b) any other persons the Secretary of State requires it to consult.

(3) Having considered any representations made on the draft, the Regulator must make such modifications to it as it considers appropriate.
(4) Subsections (2) and (3) do not apply—
   (a) to a code made for the purpose only of consolidating other codes issued under section 90, or
   (b) to a code if the Secretary of State considers consultation inexpedient by reason of urgency.
(5) If the Regulator determines to proceed with a draft, it must send it to the Secretary of State who—
   (a) if he approves of it, must lay it before Parliament, and
   (b) if he does not approve of it, must publish details of his reasons for withholding approval.
(6) Where a draft is laid before Parliament under subsection (5)(a)—
   (a) if within the period mentioned in subsection (7) either House so resolves, no further proceedings may be taken on the draft code;
   (b) if no such resolution is passed, the Regulator must issue the code in the form of the draft.
(7) The period referred to in subsection (6)(a) is the period of 40 days—
   (a) beginning with the day on which the draft is laid before Parliament (or, if it is laid before the two Houses on different days, with the later of the two days), and
   (b) ignoring any period during which Parliament is dissolved or prorogued or during which both Houses are adjourned for more than four days.
(8) The fact that no further proceedings may be taken on a draft code in accordance with subsection (6)(a) does not prevent the laying of a new draft.
(9) A code issued in accordance with subsection (6)(b) shall come into effect on such day as the Secretary of State may by order appoint.
Without prejudice to section 315, such an order may contain such transitional provisions or savings as appear to the Secretary of State to be necessary or expedient in connection with the code of practice brought into operation.
(10) The Regulator must arrange for any code issued by it under section 90 to be published in the way appearing to it to be appropriate.
(11) The Regulator may charge a reasonable fee for providing a person with a copy of a code published under this section.
(12) This section applies to a revised code as it applies to the first issue of a code.

## 92 Revocation of codes of practice

(1) A code of practice may be revoked by the Secretary of State by order.
(2) An order under this section may be made only with the consent of the Regulator.
(3) Without prejudice to section 315, an order under this section may contain such savings as appear to the Secretary of State to be necessary or expedient in connection with the revocation of the code.

*Exercise of regulatory functions*

## 93 The regulator's procedure in relation to its regulatory functions

(1) The Regulator must determine the procedure that it proposes to follow in relation to the exercise of its regulatory functions.
(2) For the purposes of this Part the "regulatory functions" of the Regulator are—

(a) the power to issue an improvement notice under section 13,
(b) the power to issue a third party notice under section 14,
(c) the reserved regulatory functions (see Schedule 2),
(d) the power to issue a clearance statement under section 42,
(e) the power to issue a notice under section 45(1) approving the details of arrangements,
(f) the power to issue a clearance statement under section 46,
(g) the power to vary or revoke under section 101 (to the extent that it does not fall within paragraph (c)),
(h) the power to make an order under section 154(8),
(i) the power to make an order under section 219(4),
(j) the power to grant or revoke authorisation under section 288,
(k) the power to grant or revoke approval under section 289,
(l) the power to issue a notice under section 293(5),
(m) the power by direction under section 2(3)(a) of the Welfare Reform and Pensions Act 1999 (c. 30) to refuse to register a scheme under section 2 of that Act,
(n) the power to make an order under section 7 of the Pensions Act 1995 (c. 26) appointing a trustee (to the extent that it does not fall within paragraph (c)),
(o) the power to make an order under section 23 of that Act appointing an independent trustee,
(p) the power to give directions under section 72B of that Act (directions facilitating winding up), and
(q) such other functions of the Regulator as may be prescribed.

(3) The Determinations Panel must determine the procedure to be followed by it in relation to any exercise by it on behalf of the Regulator of—
(a) the power to determine whether to exercise a regulatory function, and
(b) where the Panel so determines to exercise a regulatory function, the power to exercise the function in question.

(4) The procedure determined under this section—
(a) must provide for the procedure required under—
 (i) section 96 (standard procedure), and
 (ii) section 98 (special procedure), and
(b) may include such other procedural requirements as the Regulator or, as the case may be, the Panel considers appropriate.

(5) This section is subject to—
(a) sections 99 to 104 (the remaining provisions concerning the procedure in relation to the regulatory functions), and
(b) any regulations made by the Secretary of State under paragraph 19 of Schedule 1.

**94 Publication of procedure in relation to regulatory functions**

(1) The Regulator must issue a statement of the procedure determined under section 93.
(2) The Regulator must arrange for the statement to be published in the way appearing to it to be appropriate.
(3) The Regulator may charge a reasonable fee for providing a person with a copy of the statement.
(4) If the procedure determined under section 93 is changed in a material way, the Regulator must publish a revised statement.

(5) The Regulator must, without delay, give the Secretary of State a copy of any statement which it issues under this section.

**95 Application of standard and special procedure**

(1) The Regulator must comply with the standard procedure (see section 96) or, where section 97 applies, the special procedure (see section 98) in a case where—
 (a) the Regulator considers that the exercise of one or more of the regulatory functions may be appropriate, or
 (b) an application is made under or by virtue of—
  (i) any of the provisions listed in section 10(6), or
  (ii) any prescribed provision of this or any other enactment,
 for the Regulator to exercise a regulatory function.
(2) For the purposes of section 96, references to the regulatory action under consideration in a particular case are—
 (a) in a case falling within subsection (1)(a), references to the exercise of the one or more regulatory functions which the Regulator considers that it may be appropriate to exercise, and
 (b) in a case falling within subsection (1)(b), references to the exercise of the regulatory function which is the subject-matter of the application.
(3) Neither section 96 (standard procedure) nor section 98 (special procedure) apply in relation to a determination whether to exercise a regulatory function on a review under section 99 (compulsory review of regulatory action).

**96 Standard procedure**

(1) The procedure determined under section 93 must make provision for the standard procedure.
(2) The "standard procedure" is a procedure which provides for—
 (a) the giving of notice to such persons as it appears to the Regulator would be directly affected by the regulatory action under consideration (a "warning notice"),
 (b) those persons to have an opportunity to make representations,
 (c) the consideration of any such representations and the determination whether to take the regulatory action under consideration,
 (d) the giving of notice of the determination to such persons as appear to the Regulator to be directly affected by it (a "determination notice"),
 (e) the determination notice to contain details of the right of referral to the Tribunal under subsection (3),
 (f) the form and further content of warning notices and determination notices and the manner in which they are to be given, and
 (g) the time limits to be applied at any stage of the procedure.
(3) Where the standard procedure applies, the determination which is the subject-matter of the determination notice may be referred to the Tribunal (see section 102) by—
 (a) any person to whom the determination notice is given as required under subsection (2)(d), and
 (b) any other person who appears to the Tribunal to be directly affected by the determination.
(4) Subsection (3) does not apply where the determination which is the subject-matter of

the determination notice is a determination to issue a clearance statement under section 42 or 46.

(5) Where the determination which is the subject-matter of the determination notice is a determination to exercise a regulatory function and subsection (3) applies, the Regulator must not exercise the function—
   (a) during the period within which the determination may be referred to the Tribunal (see section 103(1)), and
   (b) if the determination is so referred, until the reference, and any appeal against the Tribunal's determination, has been finally disposed of.

(6) Subsection (5) does not apply where the determination is a determination to exercise any of the following functions—
   (a) the power to make a direction under section 76(8) extending the retention period for documents taken into possession under section 75;
   (b) the power to make a direction under section 78(10) extending the retention period for documents taken into possession under that section;
   (c) the power to make an order under section 154(8);
   (d) the power to make an order under section 219(4);
   (e) the power to grant or revoke authorisation under section 288;
   (f) the power to grant or revoke approval under section 289;
   (g) the power to issue a notice under section 293(5);
   (h) the power to make an order under section 3(1) of the Pensions Act 1995 (c. 26) prohibiting a person from being a trustee;
   (i) the power to make an order under section 3(3) of that Act revoking such an order;
   (j) the power to make an order under section 4(1) of that Act suspending a trustee;
   (k) the power to make an order under section 4(2) of that Act extending the period for which an order under section 4(1) of that Act has effect;
   (l) the power to make an order under section 4(5) of that Act revoking an order under section 4(1) of that Act suspending a trustee;
   (m) the power to make an order under section 7 of that Act appointing a trustee;
   (n) the power under section 9 of that Act to exercise by order the same jurisdiction and powers as the High Court or the Court of Session for vesting property in, or transferring property to, trustees in consequence of the appointment or removal of a trustee;
   (o) the power to make an order under section 23 of that Act appointing an independent trustee;
   (p) the power under section 29(5) of that Act to give a notice waiving a disqualification under section 29 of that Act;
   (q) the power under section 30(2) of that Act to exercise by order the same jurisdiction and powers as the High Court or the Court of Session for vesting property in, or transferring property to, the trustees where a trustee becomes disqualified under section 29 of that Act;
   (r) the power to give directions under section 72B of that Act facilitating a winding up;
   (s) the power by direction under section 99(4) of the Pension Schemes Act 1993 (c. 48) to grant an extension of the period within which the trustees or managers of a scheme are to carry out certain duties;

(t) the power by direction under section 101J(2) of that Act to extend the period for compliance with a transfer notice;
(u) such other regulatory functions as may be prescribed;
(v) the power under section 101(1)(b) to vary or revoke in relation to the exercise of any of the regulatory functions mentioned in paragraphs (a) to (u) other than those mentioned in paragraph (i) or (l).

**97 Special procedure: applicable cases**

(1) The special procedure in section 98 (and not the standard procedure) applies to—
    (a) a case falling within subsection (2),
    (b) a case falling within subsection (3), and
    (c) a case falling within subsection (4).
(2) A case falls within this subsection if—
    (a) the Regulator considers that it may be necessary to exercise a regulatory function listed in subsection (5) immediately because there is, or the Regulator considers it likely that if a warning notice were to be given there would be, an immediate risk to—
        (i) the interests of members under an occupational or personal pension scheme, or
        (ii) the assets of such a scheme,
    (b) the Regulator accordingly dispenses with the giving of a warning notice and an opportunity to make representations as described in section 96(2)(a) and (b), and
    (c) the Regulator determines to exercise the function immediately on the basis that it is necessary to do so because there is, or the Regulator considers it likely that if the function were not exercised immediately there would be, an immediate risk to—
        (i) the interests of members under an occupational or personal pension scheme, or
        (ii) the assets of such a scheme.
(3) A case falls within this subsection if—
    (a) the Regulator gives a warning notice as described in section 96(2)(a) in relation to a determination whether to exercise a regulatory function listed in subsection (5), and
    (b) before it has considered the representations of those persons to whom the warning notice is given, the Regulator determines to exercise the function immediately on the basis that it is necessary to do so because there is, or the Regulator considers it likely that if the function were not exercised immediately there would be, an immediate risk to—
        (i) the interests of members under an occupational or personal pension scheme, or
        (ii) the assets of such a scheme.
(4) A case falls within this subsection if the Regulator—
    (a) gives a warning notice as described in section 96(2)(a) in relation to a determination whether to exercise a regulatory function which—
        (i) is listed in subsection (5), and
        (ii) is not a function listed in section 96(6) (functions which may be exercised immediately under the standard procedure),

(b) considers the representations of those persons to whom the warning notice is given, and
(c) determines to exercise the function immediately on the basis that it is necessary to do so because there is, or the Regulator considers it likely that if the function were not exercised immediately there would be, an immediate risk to—
   (i) the interests of members under an occupational or personal pension scheme, or
   (ii) the assets of such a scheme.

(5) The regulatory functions referred to in subsections (2), (3) and (4) are—
   (a) the power to make or extend a restraining order under section 20;
   (b) the power to make a freezing order under section 23;
   (c) the power to make an order under section 25(3) extending the period for which a freezing order has effect;
   (d) the power to make an order under section 26 validating action taken in contravention of a freezing order;
   (e) the power to make an order under section 28 directing that specified steps are taken;
   (f) the power to make an order under section 30 giving a direction where a freezing order ceases to have effect;
   (g) the power to make an order under section 31(3) directing the notification of members;
   (h) the power to make an order under section 231 modifying a scheme, giving directions or imposing a schedule of contributions;
   (i) the power to make an order under section 3(1) of the Pensions Act 1995 (c. 26) prohibiting a person from being a trustee;
   (j) the power to make an order under section 3(3) of that Act revoking such an order;
   (k) the power to make an order under section 4(1) of that Act suspending a trustee;
   (l) the power to make an order under section 4(5) of that Act revoking such an order;
   (m) the power to make an order under section 7 of that Act appointing a trustee;
   (n) the power under section 9 of that Act to exercise by order the same jurisdiction and powers as the High Court or the Court of Session for vesting property in, or transferring property to, trustees in consequence of the appointment or removal of a trustee;
   (o) the power to make an order under section 11 of that Act directing or authorising an occupational pension scheme to be wound up;
   (p) the power to make an order under section 23 of that Act appointing an independent trustee;
   (q) the power under section 29(5) of that Act to give a notice waiving a disqualification under section 29 of that Act;
   (r) the power under section 30(2) of that Act to exercise by order the same jurisdiction and powers as the High Court or the Court of Session for vesting property in, or transferring property to, the trustees where a trustee becomes disqualified under section 29 of that Act;
   (s) the power to make an order under section 67G(2) of that Act by virtue of which any modification of, or grant of rights under, an occupational pension scheme is void to any extent;

(t) the power to make an order under section 67H(2) of that Act prohibiting, or specifying steps to be taken in relation to, the exercise of a power to modify an occupational pension scheme;
(u) such other regulatory functions as may be prescribed;
(v) the power under section 101(1)(b) to vary or revoke in relation to the exercise of any of the regulatory functions mentioned in paragraphs (a) to (u) other than those mentioned in paragraph (j) or (l).

**98 Special procedure**

(1) The procedure determined under section 93 must make provision for the special procedure.
(2) The "special procedure" is a procedure which provides for—
    (a) the giving of notice of the determination to exercise the regulatory function to such persons as appear to the Regulator to be directly affected by it (a "determination notice"),
    (b) the determination notice to contain details of the requirement for the Regulator to review the determination under section 99(1) and of any subsequent right of referral to the Tribunal under section 99(7),
    (c) the persons to whom the determination notice was given (as required under paragraph (a)) to have an opportunity to make representations in relation to the determination before it is reviewed under section 99(1),
    (d) the consideration of any such representations before the determination on the review,
    (e) the giving of a notice in accordance with section 99(4) of the determination on the review (a "final notice"),
    (f) the final notice to contain details of the right of referral to the Tribunal under section 99(7),
    (g) the form and further content of determination notices and final notices and the manner in which they are to be given, and
    (h) the time limits to be applied at any stage of the procedure.

**99 Compulsory review**

(1) In a case where the special procedure applies, the Regulator must review the determination to exercise the regulatory function.
(2) The review must be determined as soon as reasonably practicable.
(3) The Regulator's powers on a review under this section include power to—
    (a) confirm, vary or revoke the determination,
    (b) confirm, vary or revoke any order, notice or direction made, issued or given as a result of the determination,
    (c) substitute a different determination, order, notice or direction,
    (d) deal with the matters arising on the review as if they had arisen on the original determination, and
    (e) make savings and transitional provision.
(4) When the Regulator has completed a review under this section a notice of its determination on the review must be given to such persons as appear to it to be directly affected by its determination on the review.
(5) If the final notice contains a determination to exercise a different regulatory function to the function which was the subject-matter of the determination notice, then the final notice may not be given unless—

**s 99, Pensions Act 2004**

    (a) such persons as appear to the Regulator to be directly affected by the exercise of the regulatory function have been given an opportunity to make representations, and

    (b) the Regulator has considered any such representations before it makes its determination on the review.

(6) Subsection (5) does not apply if the regulatory function is listed in section 97(5) and the Regulator determines to exercise it immediately on the basis that it is necessary to do so because there is, or the Regulator considers it likely that if the function were not exercised immediately there would be, an immediate risk to—

    (a) the interests of members under an occupational or personal pension scheme, or

    (b) the assets of such a scheme.

(7) The determination which is the subject-matter of a final notice may be referred to the Tribunal (see section 102) by—

    (a) any person to whom the final notice is given as required under subsection (4), and

    (b) any other person who appears to the Tribunal to be directly affected by the determination.

(8) Where that determination is a determination to exercise a different regulatory function to the function which was the subject-matter of the determination notice, the Regulator must not exercise the regulatory function—

    (a) during the period within which the determination may be referred to the Tribunal (see section 103(1)), and

    (b) if the determination is so referred, until the reference, and any appeal against the Tribunal's determination, has been finally disposed of.

(9) Subsection (8) does not apply where—

    (a) the regulatory function in question is a function listed in section 96(6) (functions which may be exercised immediately under the standard procedure), or

    (b) the regulatory function in question is a function listed in section 97(5) (functions which may be exercised immediately under the special procedure) and the Regulator determines to exercise it immediately on the basis described in subsection (6).

(10) The functions of the Regulator under this section are exercisable on behalf of the Regulator by the Determinations Panel (and are not otherwise exercisable by or on behalf of the Regulator).

(11) The Panel must determine the procedure that it proposes to follow in relation to the exercise of those functions.

(12) Section 94 (publication of Regulator's procedure) applies in relation to the procedure determined under subsection (11) as it applies to the procedure determined under section 93 (procedure in relation to the regulatory functions).

**100 Duty to have regard to the interests of members etc**

(1) The Regulator must have regard to the matters mentioned in subsection (2)—

    (a) when determining whether to exercise a regulatory function—

        (i) in a case where the requirements of the standard or special procedure apply, or

        (ii) on a review under section 99, and

    (b) when exercising the regulatory function in question.

(2) Those matters are—

(a) the interests of the generality of the members of the scheme to which the exercise of the function relates, and
(b) the interests of such persons as appear to the Regulator to be directly affected by the exercise.

**101  Powers to vary or revoke orders, notices or directions etc**

(1) The Regulator may vary or revoke—
 (a) any determination by the Regulator whether to exercise a regulatory function, or
 (b) any order, notice or direction made, issued or given by the Regulator in the exercise of a regulatory function.
(2) Subsection (1)(b) does not apply to—
 (a) an order under section 3(3) of the Pensions Act 1995 (c. 26) revoking a prohibition order under that section,
 (b) an order under section 4(5) of that Act revoking a suspension order under that section,
 (c) a direction under section 2(3) of the Welfare Reform and Pensions Act 1999 (c. 30) refusing to register a scheme under section 2 of that Act or removing a scheme from the register of stakeholder pension schemes, or
 (d) such other orders, notices or directions made, issued or given by the Regulator, in the exercise of a regulatory function, as may be prescribed.
(3) A variation or revocation of an order, a notice or a direction must be made by an order, a notice or a direction (as the case may be).
(4) A variation or revocation made under this section must take effect from a specified time which must not be a time earlier than the time when the variation or revocation is made.
(5) The power to vary or revoke under this section—
 (a) is not to be treated for the purposes of subsection (1) as a regulatory function, and
 (b) is in addition to any such power which is conferred on the Regulator by, or by virtue of, this or any other enactment.

*The pensions regulator tribunal*

**102  The pensions regulator tribunal**

(1) There shall be a Tribunal to be known as the Pensions Regulator Tribunal (in this Act referred to as "the Tribunal").
(2) The Tribunal is to have the functions conferred on it by this Act or any provisions in force in Northern Ireland corresponding to this Act.
(3) The Lord Chancellor may by rules make such provision as appears to him to be necessary or expedient in respect of the conduct of proceedings before the Tribunal.
(4) Schedule 4 (which makes provision as respects the Tribunal and its proceedings) has effect.
(5) But that Schedule does not limit the Lord Chancellor's powers under this section.

**103  References to the tribunal**

(1) A reference to the Tribunal under this Act must be made—
 (a) in the case of a reference under section 96(3) (referral following determination under standard procedure), during the period of 28 days beginning with the day on which the determination notice in question is given,

(b) in the case of a reference under section 99(7) (referral following determination under special procedure), during the period of 28 days beginning with the day on which the final notice in question is given, or

(c) in either case, during such other period as may be specified in rules made under section 102.

(2) Subject to rules made under section 102, the Tribunal may allow a reference to be made after the end of the relevant period specified in or under subsection (1).

(3) On a reference, the Tribunal may consider any evidence relating to the subject-matter of the reference, whether or not it was available to the Regulator at the material time.

(4) On a reference, the Tribunal must determine what (if any) is the appropriate action for the Regulator to take in relation to the matter referred to the Tribunal.

(5) On determining a reference, the Tribunal must remit the matter to the Regulator with such directions (if any) as the Tribunal considers appropriate for giving effect to its determination.

(6) Those directions may include directions to the Regulator—
   (a) confirming the Regulator's determination and any order, notice or direction made, issued or given as a result of it;
   (b) to vary or revoke the Regulator's determination, and any order, notice or direction made, issued or given as a result of it;
   (c) to substitute a different determination, order, notice or direction;
   (d) to make such savings and transitional provision as the Tribunal considers appropriate.

(7) The Regulator must act in accordance with the determination of, and any direction given by, the Tribunal (and accordingly sections 96 to 99 (standard and special procedure) do not apply).

(8) The Tribunal may, on determining a reference, make recommendations as to the procedure followed by the Regulator or the Determinations Panel.

(9) An order of the Tribunal may be enforced—
   (a) as if it were an order of a county court, or
   (b) in Scotland, as if it were an order of the Court of Session.

**104 Appeal on a point of law**

(1) A party to a reference to the Tribunal may with permission appeal—
   (a) to the Court of Appeal, or
   (b) in Scotland, to the Court of Session,
on a point of law arising from a decision of the Tribunal disposing of the reference.

(2) "Permission" means permission given by—
   (a) the Tribunal, or
   (b) if it is refused by the Tribunal, by the Court of Appeal or, in Scotland, the Court of Session.

(3) If, on an appeal under subsection (1), the court considers that the decision of the Tribunal was wrong in law, it may—
   (a) remit the matter to the Tribunal for rehearing and determination by it under section 103, or
   (b) itself make a determination.

(4) An appeal may not be brought from a decision of the Court of Appeal under subsection (3) except with the leave of—
   (a) the Court of Appeal, or

(b) the House of Lords.
(5) An appeal lies, with the leave of the Court of Session or the House of Lords, from any decision of the Court of Session under this section, and such leave may be given on such terms as to costs, expenses or otherwise as the Court of Session or the House of Lords may determine.
(6) Rules made under section 102 may make provision for regulating or prescribing any matters incidental to or consequential on an appeal under this section.

## 105 Redetermination etc by the tribunal

(1) This section applies where an application is made to the Tribunal for permission under section 104(2)(a) to appeal from a decision of the Tribunal disposing of a reference.
(2) If the person who constitutes, or is the chairman of, the Tribunal for the purposes of dealing with that application considers that the decision of the Tribunal disposing of the reference was wrong in law, he may set aside the decision and refer the matter—
   (a) for rehearing and redetermination by the Tribunal under section 103, or
   (b) for rehearing and determination under that section by a differently constituted Tribunal.

## 106 Legal assistance scheme

(1) The Lord Chancellor may by regulations establish a scheme governing the provision of legal assistance in connection with proceedings before the Tribunal.
(2) The legal assistance scheme may, in particular, make provision as to—
   (a) the kinds of legal assistance that may be provided;
   (b) the persons by whom legal assistance may be provided;
   (c) the manner in which applications for legal assistance are to be made;
   (d) the criteria on which eligibility for legal assistance is to be determined;
   (e) the persons or bodies by whom applications are to be determined;
   (f) appeals against refusals of applications;
   (g) the revocation or variation of decisions;
   (h) its administration and the enforcement of its provisions.
(3) Legal assistance under the scheme may be provided subject to conditions or restrictions.
(4) Those conditions may include conditions as to the making of contributions by the person to whom the assistance is provided.
(5) The Lord Chancellor must fund, out of money provided by Parliament, the costs of the scheme including the costs of legal assistance provided under it.
(6) In this Part "the legal assistance scheme" means any scheme in force by virtue of subsection (1).

## PART 2
## THE BOARD OF THE PENSION PROTECTION FUND

### CHAPTER 1
### THE BOARD

*Establishment*

**107 The Board of the Pension Protection Fund**

There shall be a body corporate called the Board of the Pension Protection Fund (in this Act referred to as "the Board").

**108 Membership of the board**

(1) The Board is to consist of the following members—
  (a) a chairman,
  (b) the Chief Executive of the Board, and
  (c) at least five other persons ("ordinary members").
(2) The chairman must not be appointed from the staff of the Board or be the chairman of the Regulator.
(3) The number of ordinary members must not exceed any maximum number which may be prescribed.
(4) At least two ordinary members must be appointed from the staff of the Board.
(5) No member of the Determinations Panel established by the Regulator under section 9, or member of the staff of the Regulator, is eligible for appointment as a member of the Board.
(6) Any power to appoint ordinary members must be exercised so as to secure that a majority of the members of the Board are non-executive members.
(7) In this Part—
  (a) references to executive members of the Board are to—
    (i) the Chief Executive, and
    (ii) the ordinary members appointed from the staff of the Board, and
  (b) references to non-executive members of the Board are to members who are not executive members.

**109 Further provision about the Board**

Schedule 5 makes further provision about the Board, including provision as to—

the appointment of members,
the terms of appointment, tenure and remuneration of members,
the appointment of the Chief Executive and other staff,
the proceedings of the Board,
its accounts, and
the status and liability of the Board, its members and staff.

*General provision about functions*

### 110 Board's functions

(1) The Board must hold, manage and apply, in accordance with this Part and any provision in force in Northern Ireland corresponding to it—
 (a) a fund to be known as the Pension Protection Fund, and
 (b) a fund to be known as the Fraud Compensation Fund.
(2) Sections 175 and 189 make provision for contributions to those funds to be levied by the Board.
(3) The Board also has such other functions as are conferred on it by, or by virtue of, this or any other enactment.

### 111 Supplementary powers

The Board may do anything which—
 (a) is calculated to facilitate the exercise of its functions, or
 (b) is incidental or conducive to their exercise.

*Non-executive functions*

### 112 Non-executive functions

(1) The functions listed in subsection (4) (in this Part referred to as "the non-executive functions") are functions of the Board.
(2) The Board must establish a committee to discharge the non-executive functions on its behalf.
(3) Only non-executive members of the Board may be members of that committee.
(4) The non-executive functions are—
 (a) the duty to keep under review the question whether the Board's internal financial controls secure the proper conduct of its financial affairs;
 (b) the duty to determine under sub-paragraph (5)(a) of paragraph 12 of Schedule 5, subject to the approval of the Secretary of State, the terms and conditions as to remuneration of any Chief Executive appointed under sub-paragraph (4) of that paragraph;
 (c) the duty to determine under paragraph 13(3)(a) of that Schedule, subject to the approval of the Secretary of State, the terms and conditions as to remuneration of any member of the staff who is also to be an executive member of the Board;
 (d) the duty to determine under paragraph 13(3)(b) of that Schedule, the terms and conditions as to remuneration of any member of the staff of a description prescribed for the purposes of that provision.
(5) The committee established under this section must prepare a report on the discharge of the non-executive functions for inclusion in the Board's annual report to the Secretary of State under section 119.
(6) The committee's report must relate to the same period as that covered by the Board's report.
(7) The members of any sub-committee of the committee (established by virtue of paragraph 15(2) of Schedule 5)—
 (a) may include persons who are not members of the committee, but
 (b) must not include persons who are executive members or other staff of the Board.
(8) The committee may authorize any of its sub-committees to discharge on its behalf—

(a) any of the non-executive functions;
(b) the duty to prepare a report under subsection (5).

*Financial matters*

**113 Investment of funds**

(1) The Board may invest for the purposes of the prudent management of its financial affairs.
(2) When exercising the power conferred by subsection (1) in relation to the Pension Protection Fund, the Board must have regard to—
   (a) the interests of persons who are or may become entitled to compensation under the pension compensation provisions (see section 162) or any corresponding provisions in force in Northern Ireland, and
   (b) the effect of the exercise of the power on the rate of any levy which may be imposed under section 174 or 175 or any corresponding provision in force in Northern Ireland and the interests which persons have in the rate of any such levy.
(3) When exercising the power conferred by subsection (1) in relation to the Fraud Compensation Fund, the Board must have regard to—
   (a) the interests of members of occupational pension schemes in relation to which section 189(1), or any corresponding provision in force in Northern Ireland, applies, and
   (b) the effect of the exercise of the power on the level of any levy which may be imposed under section 189 or any corresponding provision in force in Northern Ireland and the interests which persons have in the rate of any such levy.
(4) For the purposes of subsection (1) there must be at least two fund managers.
(5) For this purpose "fund manager" means an individual who or firm which is appointed by the Board to manage the fund maintained under section 173 (the Pension Protection Fund).
(6) The Board must not appoint an individual or firm as a fund manager unless it is satisfied—
   (a) in the case of an individual, that the individual has the appropriate knowledge and experience for managing the investments of the Pension Protection Fund, or
   (b) in the case of a firm, that arrangements are in place to secure that any individual who will exercise functions which the firm has as fund manager will, at the time he exercises those functions, have the appropriate knowledge and experience for managing the investments of that Fund.

**114 Investment principles**

(1) The Board must secure—
   (a) that a statement of investment principles is prepared and maintained, and
   (b) that the statement is reviewed at such intervals, and on such occasions, as may be prescribed and, if necessary, revised.
(2) In this section "statement of investment principles" means a written statement of the investment principles governing determinations about investments made by or on behalf of the Board.
(3) Before preparing or revising a statement of investment principles, the Board must comply with any prescribed requirements.

(4) A statement of investment principles must be in the prescribed form and cover, amongst other things, the prescribed matters.

**115 Borrowing**

(1) The Board may—
    (a) borrow from a deposit-taker such sums as it may from time to time require for exercising any of its functions;
    (b) give security for any money borrowed by it.
(2) The Board may not borrow if the effect would be—
    (a) to take the aggregate amount outstanding in respect of the principal of sums borrowed by it over its borrowing limit, or
    (b) to increase the amount by which the aggregate amount so outstanding exceeds that limit.
(3) In this section—
    "borrowing limit" means such limit as the Secretary of State may specify by order;
    "deposit-taker" means—
    (a) a person who has permission under Part 4 of the Financial Services and Markets Act 2000 (c. 8) to accept deposits, or
    (b) an EEA firm of the kind mentioned in paragraph 5(b) of Schedule 3 to that Act which has permission under paragraph 15 of that Schedule (as a result of qualifying for authorisation under paragraph 12 of that Schedule) to accept deposits.
(4) The definition of "deposit-taker" in subsection (3) must be read with—
    (a) section 22 of the Financial Services and Markets Act 2000,
    (b) any relevant order under that section, and
    (c) Schedule 2 to that Act.

**116 Grants**

The Secretary of State may pay the Board out of money provided by Parliament such sums as he may determine towards any of its expenses, other than expenditure which by virtue of section 173(3) or 188(3) is payable out of—
    (a) the Pension Protection Fund, or
    (b) the Fraud Compensation Fund.

**117 Administration levy**

(1) Regulations may provide for the imposition of a levy ("administration levy") in respect of eligible schemes (see section 126) for the purpose of meeting—
    (a) expenditure of the Secretary of State relating to the establishment of the Board;
    (b) any expenditure of the Secretary of State under section 116.
(2) An administration levy is payable to the Secretary of State by or on behalf of—
    (a) the trustees or managers of an eligible scheme, or
    (b) any other prescribed person.
(3) An administration levy is payable at the prescribed rate and at prescribed times.
(4) Before prescribing a rate under subsection (3), the Secretary of State must consult the Board.
(5) An amount payable by a person on account of an administration levy is a debt due from him to the Secretary of State.

(6) An amount so payable is recoverable by the Secretary of State or, if he so determines, by the Regulator on his behalf.
(7) Without prejudice to the generality of subsections (1), (5) and (6), regulations under this section may include provision relating to—
    (a) the collection and recovery of amounts payable by way of levy under this section;
    (b) the circumstances in which any such amount may be waived.

**118 Fees**

(1) Regulations may authorize the Board—
    (a) to charge prescribed fees;
    (b) to charge fees sufficient to meet prescribed costs.
(2) Regulations under subsection (1) may prescribe, or authorize the Board to determine, the time at which any fee is due.
(3) Any fee which is owed to the Board by virtue of regulations under this section may be recovered as a debt due to the Board.

*Annual reports*

**119 Annual reports to Secretary of State**

(1) The Board must prepare a report for each financial year.
(2) Each report—
    (a) must deal with the activities of the Board in the financial year for which it is prepared, including the matters mentioned in subsection (3), and
    (b) must include the report prepared under subsection (5) of section 112 by the committee established under that section.
(3) The matters referred to in subsection (2)(a) are—
    (a) the strategic direction of the Board and the manner in which it has been kept under review;
    (b) the steps taken to scrutinize the performance of the Chief Executive in securing that the Board's functions are exercised efficiently and effectively;
    (c) the Board's objectives and targets and the steps taken to monitor the extent to which they are being met.
(4) The Board must send each report to the Secretary of State as soon as practicable after the end of the financial year for which it is prepared.
(5) The Secretary of State must lay before each House of Parliament a copy of every report received by him under this section.
(6) In this section "financial year" means—
    (a) the period beginning with the date on which the Board is established and ending with the next following 31st March, and
    (b) each successive period of 12 months.

## CHAPTER 2
## INFORMATION RELATING TO EMPLOYER'S INSOLVENCY ETC

*Insolvency events*

**120 Duty to notify insolvency events in respect of employers**

(1) This section applies where, in the case of an occupational pension scheme, an insolvency event occurs in relation to the employer.

(2) The insolvency practitioner in relation to the employer must give a notice to that effect within the notification period to—
 (a) the Board,
 (b) the Regulator, and
 (c) the trustees or managers of the scheme.

(3) For the purposes of subsection (2) the "notification period" is the prescribed period beginning with the later of—
 (a) the insolvency date, and
 (b) the date the insolvency practitioner becomes aware of the existence of the scheme.

(4) A notice under this section must be in such form and contain such information as may be prescribed.

**121 Insolvency event, insolvency date and insolvency practitioner**

(1) In this Part each of the following expressions has the meaning given to it by this section—
 "insolvency event"
 "insolvency date"
 "insolvency practitioner".

(2) An insolvency event occurs in relation to an individual where—
 (a) he is adjudged bankrupt or sequestration of his estate has been awarded;
 (b) the nominee in relation to a proposal for a voluntary arrangement under Part 8 of the Insolvency Act 1986 (c. 45) submits a report to the court under section 256(1) or 256A(3) of that Act which states that in his opinion a meeting of the individual's creditors should be summoned to consider the debtor's proposal;
 (c) a deed of arrangement made by or in respect of the affairs of the individual is registered in accordance with the Deeds of Arrangement Act 1914 (c. 47);
 (d) he executes a trust deed for his creditors or enters into a composition contract;
 (e) he has died and—
  (i) an insolvency administration order is made in respect of his estate in accordance with an order under section 421 of the Insolvency Act 1986, or
  (ii) a judicial factor appointed under section 11A of the Judicial Factors (Scotland) Act 1889 (c. 39) is required by that section to divide the individual's estate among his creditors.

(3) An insolvency event occurs in relation to a company where—
 (a) the nominee in relation to a proposal for a voluntary arrangement under Part 1 of the Insolvency Act 1986 submits a report to the court under section 2 of that Act (procedure where nominee is not the liquidator or administrator) which states that in his opinion meetings of the company and its creditors should be summoned to consider the proposal;

(b) the directors of the company file (or in Scotland lodge) with the court documents and statements in accordance with paragraph 7(1) of Schedule A1 to that Act (moratorium where directors propose voluntary arrangement);
(c) an administrative receiver within the meaning of section 251 of that Act is appointed in relation to the company;
(d) the company enters administration within the meaning of paragraph 1(2)(b) of Schedule B1 to that Act;
(e) a resolution is passed for a voluntary winding up of the company without a declaration of solvency under section 89 of that Act;
(f) a meeting of creditors is held in relation to the company under section 95 of that Act (creditors' meeting which has the effect of converting a members' voluntary winding up into a creditors' voluntary winding up);
(g) an order for the winding up of the company is made by the court under Part 4 or 5 of that Act.

(4) An insolvency event occurs in relation to a partnership where—
(a) an order for the winding up of the partnership is made by the court under any provision of the Insolvency Act 1986 (c. 45) (as applied by an order under section 420 of that Act (insolvent partnerships));
(b) sequestration is awarded on the estate of the partnership under section 12 of the Bankruptcy (Scotland) Act 1985 (c. 66) or the partnership grants a trust deed for its creditors;
(c) the nominee in relation to a proposal for a voluntary arrangement under Part 1 of the Insolvency Act 1986 (as applied by an order under section 420 of that Act) submits a report to the court under section 2 of that Act (procedure where nominee is not the liquidator or administrator) which states that in his opinion meetings of the members of the partnership and the partnership's creditors should be summoned to consider the proposal;
(d) the members of the partnership file with the court documents and statements in accordance with paragraph 7(1) of Schedule A1 to that Act (moratorium where directors propose voluntary arrangement) (as applied by an order under section 420 of that Act);
(e) an administration order under Part 2 of that Act (as applied by section 420 of that Act) is made in relation to the partnership.

(5) An insolvency event also occurs in relation to a person where an event occurs which is a prescribed event in relation to such a person.

(6) Except as provided by subsections (2) to (5), for the purposes of this Part an event is not to be regarded as an insolvency event in relation to a person.

(7) The Secretary of State may by order amend subsection (4)(e) to make provision consequential upon any order under section 420 of the Insolvency Act 1986 (insolvent partnerships) applying the provisions of Part 2 of that Act (administration) as amended by the Enterprise Act 2002 (c. 40).

(8) "Insolvency date", in relation to an insolvency event, means the date on which the event occurs.

(9) "Insolvency practitioner", in relation to a person, means—
(a) a person acting as an insolvency practitioner, in relation to that person, in accordance with section 388 of the Insolvency Act 1986;
(b) in such circumstances as may be prescribed, a person of a prescribed description.

(10) In this section—

"company" means a company within the meaning given by section 735(1) of the Companies Act 1985 (c. 6) or a company which may be wound up under Part 5 of the Insolvency Act 1986 (c. 45) (unregistered companies);

"person acting as an insolvency practitioner", in relation to a person, includes the official receiver acting as receiver or manager of any property of that person.

(11) In applying section 388 of the Insolvency Act 1986 under subsection (9) above—
  (a) the reference in section 388(2)(a) to a permanent or interim trustee in sequestration must be taken to include a reference to a trustee in sequestration, and
  (b) section 388(5) (which includes provision that nothing in the section applies to anything done by the official receiver or the Accountant in Bankruptcy) must be ignored.

*Status of scheme*

## 122 Insolvency practitioner's duty to issue notices confirming status of scheme

(1) This section applies where an insolvency event has occurred in relation to the employer in relation to an occupational pension scheme.

(2) An insolvency practitioner in relation to the employer must—
  (a) if he is able to confirm that a scheme rescue is not possible, issue a notice to that effect (a "scheme failure notice"), or
  (b) if he is able to confirm that a scheme rescue has occurred, issue a notice to that effect (a "withdrawal notice").

(3) Subsection (4) applies where—
  (a) in prescribed circumstances, insolvency proceedings in relation to the employer are stayed or come to an end, or
  (b) a prescribed event occurs.

(4) If a person who was acting as an insolvency practitioner in relation to the employer immediately before this subsection applies has not been able to confirm in relation to the scheme—
  (a) that a scheme rescue is not possible, or
  (b) that a scheme rescue has occurred,
  he must issue a notice to that effect.

(5) For the purposes of this section—
  (a) a person is able to confirm that a scheme rescue has occurred in relation to an occupational pension scheme if, and only if, he is able to confirm such matters as are prescribed for the purposes of this paragraph, and
  (b) a person is able to confirm that a scheme rescue is not possible, in relation to such a scheme if, and only if, he is able to confirm such matters as are prescribed for the purposes of this paragraph.

(6) Where an insolvency practitioner or former insolvency practitioner in relation to the employer issues a notice under this section, he must give a copy of that notice to—
  (a) the Board,
  (b) the Regulator, and
  (c) the trustees or managers of the scheme.

(7) A person must comply with an obligation imposed on him by subsection (2), (4) or (6) as soon as reasonably practicable.

(8) Regulations may require notices issued under this section—
   (a) to be in a prescribed form;
   (b) to contain prescribed information.

**123 Approval of notices issued under section 122**

(1) This section applies where the Board receives a notice under section 122(6) ("the section 122 notice").
(2) The Board must determine whether to approve the section 122 notice.
(3) The Board must approve the section 122 notice if, and only if, it is satisfied—
   (a) that the insolvency practitioner or former insolvency practitioner who issued the notice was required to issue it under that section, and
   (b) that the notice complies with any requirements imposed by virtue of subsection (8) of that section.
(4) Where the Board makes a determination for the purposes of subsection (2), it must issue a determination notice and give a copy of that notice to—
   (a) the Regulator,
   (b) the trustees or managers of the scheme,
   (c) the insolvency practitioner or the former insolvency practitioner who issued the section 122 notice,
   (d) any insolvency practitioner in relation to the employer (who does not fall within paragraph (c)), and
   (e) if there is no insolvency practitioner in relation to the employer, the employer.
(5) In subsection (4) "determination notice" means a notice which is in the prescribed form and contains such information about the determination as may be prescribed.

*Board's duties*

**124 Board's duty where there is a failure to comply with section 122**

(1) This section applies where in relation to an occupational pension scheme—
   (a) the Board determines under section 123 not to approve a notice issued under section 122 by an insolvency practitioner or former insolvency practitioner in relation to the employer, or
   (b) an insolvency practitioner or former insolvency practitioner in relation to the employer fails to issue a notice under section 122 and the Board is satisfied that such a notice ought to have been issued under that section.
(2) The obligations on the insolvency practitioner or former insolvency practitioner imposed by subsections (2) and (4) of section 122 are to be treated as obligations imposed on the Board and the Board must accordingly issue a notice as required under that section.
(3) Subject to subsections (4) and (5), where a notice is issued under section 122 by the Board by virtue of this section, it has effect as if it were a notice issued under section 122 by an insolvency practitioner or, as the case may be, former insolvency practitioner in relation to the employer.
(4) Where a notice is issued under section 122 by virtue of this section, section 122(6) does not apply and the Board must, as soon as reasonably practicable, give a copy of the notice to—
   (a) the Regulator,

(b) the trustees or managers of the scheme,
(c) the insolvency practitioner or former insolvency practitioner mentioned in subsection (1),
(d) any insolvency practitioner in relation to the employer (who does not fall within paragraph (c)), and
(e) if there is no insolvency practitioner in relation to the employer, the employer.

(5) Where the Board—
(a) is required to issue a notice under section 122 by virtue of this section, and
(b) is satisfied that the notice ought to have been issued at an earlier time,
it must specify that time in the notice and the notice is to have effect as if it had been issued at that time.

**125 Binding notices confirming status of scheme**

(1) Subject to subsection (2), for the purposes of this Part, a notice issued under section 122 is not binding until—
(a) the Board issues a determination notice under section 123 approving the notice,
(b) the period within which the issue of the determination notice under that section may be reviewed by virtue of Chapter 6 has expired, and
(c) if the issue of the determination notice is so reviewed—
  (i) the review and any reconsideration,
  (ii) any reference to the PPF Ombudsman in respect of the issue of the notice, and
  (iii) any appeal against his determination or directions,
has been finally disposed of and the determination notice has not been revoked, varied or substituted.

(2) Where a notice is issued under section 122 by the Board by virtue of section 124, the notice is not binding until—
(a) the period within which the issue of the notice may be reviewed by virtue of Chapter 6 has expired, and
(b) if the issue of the notice is so reviewed—
  (i) the review and any reconsideration,
  (ii) any reference to the PPF Ombudsman in respect of the issue of the notice, and
  (iii) any appeal against his determination or directions,
has been finally disposed of and the notice has not been revoked, varied or substituted.

(3) Where a notice issued under section 122 becomes binding, the Board must as soon as reasonably practicable give a notice to that effect together with a copy of the binding notice to—
(a) the Regulator,
(b) the trustees or managers of the scheme,
(c) the insolvency practitioner or former insolvency practitioner who issued the notice under section 122 or, where that notice was issued by the Board by virtue of section 124, the insolvency practitioner or former insolvency practitioner mentioned in subsection (1) of that section,
(d) any insolvency practitioner in relation to the employer (who does not fall within paragraph (c)), and
(e) if there is no insolvency practitioner in relation to the employer, the employer.

(4) A notice under subsection (3)—
   (a) must be in the prescribed form and contain such information as may be prescribed, and
   (b) where it is given in relation to a withdrawal notice issued under section 122(2)(b) which has become binding, must state the time from which the Board ceases to be involved with the scheme (see section 149).

## CHAPTER 3
## PENSION PROTECTION

*Eligible schemes*

**126  Eligible schemes**

(1) Subject to the following provisions of this section, in this Part references to an "eligible scheme" are to an occupational pension scheme which—
   (a) is not a money purchase scheme, and
   (b) is not a prescribed scheme or a scheme of a prescribed description.
(2) A scheme is not an eligible scheme if it is being wound up immediately before the day appointed by the Secretary of State by order for the purposes of this subsection.
(3) Regulations may provide that where—
   (a) an assessment period begins in relation to an eligible scheme (see section 132), and
   (b) after the beginning of that period, the scheme ceases to be an eligible scheme,
   the scheme is, in such circumstances as may be prescribed, to be treated as remaining an eligible scheme for the purposes of such of the provisions mentioned in subsection (4) as may be prescribed.
(4) Those provisions are—
   (a) any provision of this Part, and
   (b) any other provision of this Act in which "eligible scheme" has the meaning given by this section.
(5) Regulations may also provide that a scheme which would be an eligible scheme in the absence of this subsection is not an eligible scheme in such circumstances as may be prescribed.

*Circumstances in which Board assumes responsibility for eligible schemes*

**127  Duty to assume responsibility for schemes following insolvency event**

(1) This section applies where a qualifying insolvency event has occurred in relation to the employer in relation to an eligible scheme.
(2) The Board must assume responsibility for the scheme in accordance with this Chapter if—
   (a) the value of the assets of the scheme at the relevant time was less than the amount of the protected liabilities at that time (see sections 131 and 143),
   (b) after the relevant time a scheme failure notice is issued under section 122(2)(a) in relation to the scheme and that notice becomes binding, and
   (c) a withdrawal event has not occurred in relation to the scheme in respect of a withdrawal notice which has been issued during the period—

(i) beginning with the occurrence of the qualifying insolvency event, and
(ii) ending immediately before the issuing of the scheme failure notice under section 122(2)(a),
and the occurrence of such a withdrawal event in respect of a withdrawal notice issued during that period is not a possibility (see section 149).
(3) For the purposes of this section, in relation to an eligible scheme an insolvency event ("the current event") in relation to the employer is a qualifying insolvency event if—
   (a) it occurs on or after the day appointed under section 126(2), and
   (b) it—
      (i) is the first insolvency event to occur in relation to the employer on or after that day, or
      (ii) does not occur within an assessment period (see section 132) in relation to the scheme which began before the occurrence of the current event.
(4) For the purposes of this section—
   (a) the reference in subsection (2)(a) to the assets of the scheme is a reference to those assets excluding any assets representing the value of any rights in respect of money purchase benefits under the scheme rules, and
   (b) "the relevant time" means the time immediately before the qualifying insolvency event occurs.
(5) This section is subject to sections 146 and 147 (cases where Board must refuse to assume responsibility for a scheme).

**128 Duty to assume responsibility for schemes following application or notification**

(1) This section applies where, in relation to an eligible scheme, the trustees or managers of the scheme—
   (a) make an application under subsection (1) of section 129 (a "section 129 application"), or
   (b) receive a notice from the Board under subsection (5)(a) of that section (a "section 129 notification").
(2) The Board must assume responsibility for the scheme in accordance with this Chapter if—
   (a) the value of the assets of the scheme at the relevant time was less than the amount of the protected liabilities at that time (see sections 131 and 143),
   (b) after the relevant time the Board issues a scheme failure notice under section 130(2) in relation to the scheme and that notice becomes binding, and
   (c) a withdrawal event has not occurred in relation to the scheme in respect of a withdrawal notice which has been issued during the period—
      (i) beginning with the making of the section 129 application or, as the case may be, the receipt of the section 129 notification, and
      (ii) ending immediately before the issuing of the scheme failure notice under section 130(2),
   and the occurrence of such a withdrawal event in respect of a withdrawal notice issued during that period is not a possibility (see section 149).
(3) In subsection (2)—
   (a) the reference in paragraph (a) to the assets of the scheme is a reference to those assets excluding any assets representing the value of any rights in respect of money purchase benefits under the scheme rules, and

(b) "the relevant time" means the time immediately before the section 129 application was made or, as the case may be, the section 129 notification was received.
(4) An application under section 129(1) or notification under section 129(5)(a) is to be disregarded for the purposes of subsection (1) if it is made or given during an assessment period (see section 132) in relation to the scheme which began before the application was made or notification was given.
(5) This section is subject to sections 146 and 147 (cases where Board must refuse to assume responsibility for a scheme).

**129  Applications and notifications for the purposes of section 128**

(1) Where the trustees or managers of an eligible scheme become aware that—
   (a) the employer in relation to the scheme is unlikely to continue as a going concern, and
   (b) the prescribed requirements are met in relation to the employer,
   they must make an application to the Board for it to assume responsibility for the scheme under section 128.
(2) Where the Board receives an application under subsection (1), it must give a copy of the application to—
   (a) the Regulator, and
   (b) the employer.
(3) An application under subsection (1) must—
   (a) be in the prescribed form and contain the prescribed information, and
   (b) be made within the prescribed period.
(4) Where the Regulator becomes aware that—
   (a) the employer in relation to an eligible scheme is unlikely to continue as a going concern, and
   (b) the requirements mentioned in subsection (1)(b) are met in relation to the employer,
   it must give the Board a notice to that effect.
(5) Where the Board receives a notice under subsection (4), it must—
   (a) give the trustees or managers of the scheme a notice to that effect, and
   (b) give the employer a copy of that notice.
(6) The duty imposed by subsection (1) does not apply where the trustees or managers of an eligible scheme become aware as mentioned in that subsection by reason of a notice given to them under subsection (5).
(7) The duty imposed by subsection (4) does not apply where the Regulator becomes aware as mentioned in that subsection by reason of a copy of an application made by the trustees or managers of the eligible scheme in question given to the Regulator under subsection (2).
(8) Regulations may require notices under this section to be in the prescribed form and contain the prescribed information.

**130  Board's duty where application or notification received under section 129**

(1) This section applies where the Board—
   (a) receives an application under subsection (1) of section 129 and is satisfied that paragraphs (a) and (b) of that subsection are satisfied in relation to the application, or
   (b) is notified by the Regulator under section 129(4).

(2) If the Board is able to confirm that a scheme rescue is not possible, it must as soon as reasonably practicable issue a notice to that effect (a "scheme failure notice").
(3) If the Board is able to confirm that a scheme rescue has occurred, it must as soon as reasonably practicable issue a notice to that effect (a "withdrawal notice").
(4) The Board must, as soon as reasonably practicable, give a copy of any notice issued under subsection (2) or (3) to—
   (a) the Regulator,
   (b) the trustees or managers of the scheme, and
   (c) the employer.
(5) For the purposes of this section—
   (a) the Board is able to confirm that a scheme rescue has occurred in relation to an occupational pension scheme if, and only if, it is able to confirm such matters as are prescribed for the purposes of this paragraph, and
   (b) the Board is able to confirm that a scheme rescue is not possible in relation to such a scheme if, and only if, it is able to confirm such matters as are prescribed for the purposes of this paragraph.
(6) For the purposes of this Part a notice issued under subsection (2) or (3) is not binding until—
   (a) the period within which the issue of the notice may be reviewed by virtue of Chapter 6 has expired, and
   (b) if the issue of the notice is so reviewed—
      (i) the review and any reconsideration,
      (ii) any reference to the PPF Ombudsman in respect of the issue of the notice, and
      (iii) any appeal against his determination or directions,
      has been finally disposed of and the notice has not been revoked, varied or substituted.
(7) Where a notice issued under subsection (2) or (3) becomes binding, the Board must as soon as reasonably practicable give a notice to that effect together with a copy of the binding notice to—
   (a) the Regulator,
   (b) the trustees or managers of the scheme, and
   (c) the employer.
(8) Notices under this section must be in the prescribed form and contain such information as may be prescribed.
(9) A notice given under subsection (7) in relation to a withdrawal notice under subsection (3) which has become binding must state the time from which the Board ceases to be involved with the scheme (see section 149).

## 131 Protected liabilities

(1) For the purposes of this Chapter the protected liabilities, in relation to an eligible scheme, at a particular time ("the relevant time") are—
   (a) the cost of securing benefits for and in respect of members of the scheme which correspond to the compensation which would be payable, in relation to the scheme, in accordance with the pension compensation provisions (see section 162) if the Board assumed responsibility for the scheme in accordance with this Chapter,

(b) liabilities of the scheme which are not liabilities to, or in respect of, its members, and
(c) the estimated cost of winding up the scheme.

(2) For the purposes of determining the cost of securing benefits within subsection (1)(a), references in sections 140 to 142 and Schedule 7 (pension compensation provisions) to the assessment date are to be read as references to the date on which the time immediately after the relevant time falls.

*Restrictions on schemes during the assessment period*

**132 Assessment periods**

(1) In this Part references to an assessment period are to be construed in accordance with this section.
(2) Where, in relation to an eligible scheme, a qualifying insolvency event occurs in relation to the employer, an assessment period—
   (a) begins with the occurrence of that event, and
   (b) ends when—
      (i) the Board ceases to be involved with the scheme (see section 149),
      (ii) the trustees or managers of the scheme receive a transfer notice under section 160, or
      (iii) the conditions in section 154(2) (no scheme rescue but sufficient assets to meet protected liabilities etc) are satisfied in relation to the scheme,
      whichever first occurs.
(3) In subsection (2) "qualifying insolvency event" has the meaning given by section 127(3).
(4) Where, in relation to an eligible scheme, an application is made under section 129(1) or a notification is received under section 129(5)(a), an assessment period—
   (a) begins when the application is made or the notification is received, and
   (b) ends when—
      (i) the Board ceases to be involved with the scheme (see section 149),
      (ii) the trustees or managers of the scheme receive a transfer notice under section 160, or
      (iii) the conditions in section 154(2) (no scheme rescue but sufficient assets to meet protected liabilities etc) are satisfied in relation to the scheme,
      whichever first occurs.
(5) For the purposes of subsection (4) an application under section 129(1) or notification under section 129(5)(a) is to be disregarded if it is made or given during an assessment period in relation to the scheme which began before the application was made or notification was given.
(6) This section is subject to section 159 (which provides for further assessment periods to begin in certain circumstances where schemes are required to wind up or continue winding up under section 154).

**133 Admission of new members, payment of contributions etc**

(1) This section applies where there is an assessment period in relation to an eligible scheme.
(2) No new members of any class may be admitted to the scheme during the assessment period.

(3) Except in prescribed circumstances and subject to prescribed conditions, no further contributions (other than those due to be paid before the beginning of the assessment period) may be paid towards the scheme during the assessment period.
(4) Any obligation to pay contributions towards the scheme during the assessment period (including any obligation under section 49(8) of the Pensions Act 1995 (c. 26) to pay amounts deducted corresponding to such contributions) is to be read subject to subsection (3) and section 150 (obligation to pay contributions when assessment period ends).
(5) No benefits may accrue under the scheme rules to, or in respect of, members of the scheme during the assessment period.
(6) Subsection (5) does not prevent any increase, in a benefit, which would otherwise accrue in accordance with the scheme or any enactment.
This subsection is subject to section 138 (which limits the scheme benefits payable during an assessment period).
(7) Subsection (5) does not prevent the accrual of money purchase benefits to the extent that they are derived from income or capital gains arising from the investment of payments which are made by, or in respect of, a member of the scheme.
(8) Where a person is entitled to a pension credit derived from another person's shareable rights under the scheme, nothing in this section prevents the trustees or managers of the scheme discharging their liability in respect of the credit under Chapter 1 of Part 4 of the Welfare Reform and Pensions Act 1999 (c. 30) (sharing of rights under pension arrangements) by conferring appropriate rights under the scheme on that person.
(9) In subsection (8)—
"appropriate rights" has the same meaning as in paragraph 5 of Schedule 5 to that Act (pension credits: mode of discharge);
"shareable rights" has the same meaning as in Chapter 1 of Part 4 of that Act (sharing of rights under pension arrangements).
(10) Any action taken in contravention of this section is void.
(11) Disregarding subsection (10), section 10 of the Pensions Act 1995 (civil penalties) applies to any trustee or manager of a scheme who fails to take all reasonable steps to secure compliance with this section.

## 134 Directions

(1) This section applies where there is an assessment period in relation to an eligible scheme.
(2) With a view to ensuring that the scheme's protected liabilities do not exceed its assets or, if they do exceed its assets, that the excess is kept to a minimum, the Board may give a relevant person in relation to the scheme directions regarding the exercise during that period of his powers in respect of—
   (a) the investment of the scheme's assets,
   (b) the incurring of expenditure,
   (c) the instigation or conduct of legal proceedings, and
   (d) such other matters as may be prescribed.
(3) In subsection (2)—
   (a) "relevant person" in relation to a scheme means—
      (i) the trustees or managers of the scheme,

(ii) the employer in relation to the scheme, or

(iii) such other persons as may be prescribed, and

(b) the reference to the assets of the scheme is a reference to those assets excluding any assets representing the value of any rights in respect of money purchase benefits under the scheme rules.

(4) The Board may revoke or vary any direction under this section.

(5) Where a direction under this section given to the trustees or managers of a scheme is not complied with, section 10 of the Pensions Act 1995 (c. 26) (civil penalties) applies to any such trustee or manager who has failed to take all reasonable steps to secure compliance with the direction.

(6) That section also applies to any other person who, without reasonable excuse, fails to comply with a direction given to him under this section.

**135  Restrictions on winding up, discharge of liabilities etc**

(1) This section applies where there is an assessment period in relation to an eligible scheme.

(2) Subject to subsection (3), the winding up of the scheme must not begin during the assessment period.

(3) Subsection (2) does not apply to the winding up of the scheme in pursuance of an order by the Regulator under section 11(3A) of the Pensions Act 1995 (Regulator's powers to wind up occupational pension schemes to protect Pension Protection Fund) directing the scheme to be wound up (and section 219 makes provision for the backdating of the winding up).

(4) During the assessment period, except in prescribed circumstances and subject to prescribed conditions—

(a) no transfers of, or transfer payments in respect of, any member's rights under the scheme rules are to be made from the scheme, and

(b) no other steps may be taken to discharge any liability of the scheme to or in respect of a member of the scheme in respect of—

(i) pensions or other benefits, or

(ii) such other liabilities as may be prescribed.

(5) Subsection (4)—

(a) is subject to section 138, and

(b) applies whether or not the scheme was being wound up immediately before the assessment period or began winding up by virtue of subsection (3).

(6) Subsection (7) applies where, on the commencement of the assessment period—

(a) a member's pensionable service terminates, and

(b) he becomes a person to whom Chapter 5 of Part 4 of the Pension Schemes Act 1993 (c. 48) (early leavers: cash transfer sums and contribution refunds) applies.

Section 150(5) (retrospective accrual of benefits in certain circumstances) is to be disregarded for the purposes of determining whether a member falls within paragraph (a) or (b).

(7) Where this subsection applies, during the assessment period—

(a) no right or power conferred by that Chapter may be exercised, and

(b) no duty imposed by that Chapter may be discharged.

(8) Where a person is entitled to a pension credit derived from another person's shareable rights (within the meaning of Chapter 1 of Part 4 under of the Welfare Reform and Pensions Act 1999 (c. 30) (sharing of rights under pension arrangements)) under

the scheme, nothing in subsection (4) prevents the trustees or managers of the scheme discharging their liability in respect of the credit in accordance with that Chapter.

(9) Any action taken in contravention of this section is void, except to the extent that the Board validates the action (see section 136).

(10) Disregarding subsection (9), where there is a contravention of this section, section 10 of the Pensions Act 1995 (c. 26) (civil penalties) applies to any trustee or manager who has failed to take all reasonable steps to secure compliance with this section.

(11) The Regulator may not make a freezing order (see section 23) in relation to the scheme during the assessment period.

**136  Power to validate contraventions of section 135**

(1) The Board may validate an action for the purposes of section 135(9) only if it is satisfied that to do so is consistent with the objective of ensuring that the scheme's protected liabilities do not exceed its assets or, if they do exceed its assets, that the excess is kept to a minimum.

(2) Where the Board determines to validate, or not to validate, any action of the trustees or managers for those purposes, it must issue a notice to that effect and give a copy of that notice to—
 (a) the Regulator,
 (b) the trustees or managers of the scheme,
 (c) any insolvency practitioner in relation to the employer or, if there is no such insolvency practitioner, the employer, and
 (d) any other person who appears to the Board to be directly affected by the determination.

(3) A notice under subsection (2) must contain a statement of the Board's reasons for the determination.

(4) The validation of an action does not take effect—
 (a) until—
  (i) the Board has issued a notice under subsection (2) relating to the determination, and
  (ii) the period within which the issue of that notice may be reviewed by virtue of Chapter 6 has expired, and
 (b) if the issue of the notice is so reviewed, until—
  (i) the review and any reconsideration,
  (ii) any reference to the PPF Ombudsman in respect of the issue of the notice, and
  (iii) any appeal against his determination or directions,
  has been finally disposed of.

(5) In subsection (1) the reference to the assets of the scheme is a reference to those assets excluding any assets representing the value of any rights in respect of money purchase benefits under the scheme rules.

**137  Board to act as creditor of the employer**

(1) Subsection (2) applies where there is an assessment period in relation to an eligible scheme.

(2) During the assessment period, the rights and powers of the trustees or managers of the scheme in relation to any debt (including any contingent debt) due to them by the

**s 137, Pensions Act 2004**

employer, whether by virtue of section 75 of the Pensions Act 1995 (c. 26) (deficiencies in the scheme assets) or otherwise, are exercisable by the Board to the exclusion of the trustees or managers.

(3) Where, by virtue of subsection (2), any amount is paid to the Board in respect of such a debt, the Board must pay that amount to the trustees or managers of the scheme.

**138 Payment of scheme benefits**

(1) Subsections (2) and (3) apply where there is an assessment period in relation to an eligible scheme.

(2) The benefits payable to or in respect of any member under the scheme rules during the assessment period must be reduced to the extent necessary to ensure that they do not exceed the compensation which would be payable to or in respect of the member in accordance with this Chapter if—
   (a) the Board assumed responsibility for the scheme in accordance with this Chapter, and
   (b) the assessment date referred to in Schedule 7 were the date on which the assessment period began.

(3) But where, on the commencement of the assessment period—
   (a) a member's pensionable service terminates, and
   (b) he becomes a person to whom Chapter 5 of Part 4 of the Pension Schemes Act 1993 (c. 48) (early leavers: cash transfer sums and contribution refunds) applies,
no benefits are payable to or in respect of him under the scheme during the assessment period.

(4) Section 150(5) (retrospective accrual of benefits in certain circumstances) is to be disregarded for the purposes of determining whether a member falls within paragraph (a) or (b) of subsection (3).

(5) Nothing in subsection (3) prevents the payment of benefits attributable (directly or indirectly) to a pension credit, during the assessment period, in accordance with subsection (2).

(6) Where at any time during the assessment period the scheme is being wound up, subject to any reduction required under subsection (2) and to subsection (3), the benefits payable to or in respect of any member under the scheme rules during that period are the benefits that would have been so payable in the absence of the winding up of the scheme.

(7) Subsections (2), (3) and (6) are subject to sections 150(1) to (3) and 154(13) (which provide for the adjustment of amounts paid during an assessment period when that period ends other than as a result of the Board assuming responsibility for the scheme).

(8) For the purposes of subsections (2) and (3) the trustees or managers of the scheme may take such steps as they consider appropriate (including steps adjusting future payments under the scheme rules) to recover any overpayment or pay any shortfall.

(9) Section 10 of the Pensions Act 1995 (c. 26) (civil penalties) applies to a trustee or manager of a scheme who fails to take all reasonable steps to secure compliance with subsections (2) and (3).

(10) Regulations may provide that, where there is an assessment period in relation to an eligible scheme—

(a) in such circumstances as may be prescribed subsection (2) does not operate to require the reduction of benefits payable to or in respect of any member;

(b) the commencement of a member's pension or payment of a member's lump sum or other benefits is, in such circumstances and on such terms and conditions as may be prescribed, to be postponed for the whole or any part of the assessment period for which he continues in employment after attaining normal pension age.

(11) For the purposes of subsection (10)—

(a) "normal pension age", in relation to an eligible scheme and any pension or other benefit under it, means the age specified in the scheme rules as the earliest age at which the pension or other benefit becomes payable without actuarial adjustment (disregarding any scheme rule making special provision as to early payment on the grounds of ill health), and

(b) where different ages are so specified in relation to different parts of a pension or other benefit—

(i) subsection (10) has effect as if those parts were separate pensions or, as the case may be, benefits, and

(ii) in relation to a part of a pension or other benefit, the reference in that subsection to normal pension age is to be read as a reference to the age specified in the scheme rules as the earliest age at which that part becomes so payable.

(12) Regulations may provide that, in prescribed circumstances, where—

(a) a member of the scheme died before the commencement of the assessment period, and

(b) during the assessment period, a person becomes entitled under the scheme rules to a benefit of a prescribed description in respect of the member,

the benefit, or any part of it, is, for the purposes of subsection (2), to be treated as having become payable before the commencement of the assessment period.

(13) Nothing in subsection (2) or (3) applies to money purchase benefits.

## 139  Loans to pay scheme benefits

(1) Subsection (2) applies where section 138(2) applies in relation to an eligible scheme.

(2) Where the Board is satisfied that the trustees or managers of the scheme are not able to pay benefits under the scheme rules (reduced in accordance with section 138(2)) as they fall due, it may, on an application by the trustees or managers, lend to them such amounts as the Board considers appropriate for the purpose of enabling them to pay those benefits.

(3) Where an amount lent to the trustees or managers of a scheme under subsection (2) is outstanding at—

(a) the time the Board ceases to be involved with the scheme, or

(b) if earlier—

(i) the time during the assessment period when an order is made under section 11(3A) of the Pensions Act 1995 (c. 26) directing the winding up of the scheme, or

(ii) where no such order is made during that period, the time when the assessment period ends because the conditions in section 154(2) or (5) are satisfied,

that amount, together with the appropriate interest on it, falls to be repaid by the trustees or managers of the scheme to the Board at that time.

(4) No loan may be made under subsection (2) after the time mentioned in subsection (3)(b)(i).

(5) In subsection (2) the reference to "benefits" does not include money purchase benefits.

(6) In subsection (3) "the appropriate interest" on an amount lent under subsection (2) means interest at the prescribed rate from the time the amount was so lent until repayment.

(7) Subject to this section, the Board may make a loan under subsection (2) on such terms as it thinks fit.

*Ill health pensions*

**140 Reviewable ill health pensions**

(1) This section applies where there is an assessment period in relation to an eligible scheme.

(2) The Board may review a reviewable ill health pension in respect of a member if—
   (a) disregarding section 141, the member would be entitled to compensation under paragraph 3 of Schedule 7 in respect of the pension if the Board assumed responsibility for the scheme,
   (b) the member did not attain normal pension age in respect of the pension before the assessment date, and
   (c) the pension is attributable to the member's pensionable service.

(3) An ill health pension in respect of a member is reviewable for the purposes of subsection (2) if the member is entitled to the pension by reason of an award under the scheme rules ("the award") which was made—
   (a) in the period of three years ending immediately before the assessment date, or
   (b) before the end of the prescribed period beginning with the assessment date, in response to an application made before that date.

(4) Where—
   (a) before the assessment date, an application was made under the scheme for the award of a pension before normal pension age by virtue of any provision of the scheme rules making special provision as to early payment of pension on grounds of ill health, and
   (b) the trustees or managers of the scheme failed to decide the application before the end of the period mentioned in subsection (3)(b),

section 10 of the Pensions Act 1995 (c. 26) (civil penalties) applies to any trustee or manager who has failed to take all reasonable steps to secure that the application was decided before the end of that period.

(5) Where—
   (a) the award was made in response to an application which—
      (i) was made on or after the assessment date, or
      (ii) was made before that date but not decided by the trustees or managers of the scheme before the end of the period mentioned in subsection (3)(b), and
   (b) in the absence of this subsection, the award would take effect before the assessment date,

the award is, for the purposes of determining the compensation payable under this Chapter in a case where the Board assumes responsibility for the scheme, to be treated as taking effect after the date on which the decision to make the award was made.

(6) Regulations must prescribe the procedure to be followed in relation to the review of a pension under this section and any subsequent decision under section 141.

**141 Effect of A review**

(1) This section applies where, during an assessment period in relation to an eligible scheme, the Board reviews an ill health pension by virtue of section 140.
(2) Where the conditions of subsection (3) are satisfied, the Board may determine that the compensation payable in respect of the pension, in a case where the Board assumes responsibility for the scheme, is to be determined in the prescribed manner on and after the relevant date.
(3) The conditions are—
   (a) that the annual rate of compensation which would be payable under this Part in respect of the pension at the assessment date, if the Board assumed responsibility for the scheme, exceeds the notional reviewed rate of compensation in respect of the pension,
   (b) that the Board is satisfied—
      (i) that the decision to make the award was made in ignorance of, or was based upon a mistake as to, a material fact relevant to the decision,
      (ii) that, at the time that decision was made, the member knew or could reasonably have been expected to know of that fact and that it was relevant to the decision, and
      (iii) that, had the trustees or managers known about, or not been mistaken as to, that fact, they could not reasonably have decided to make the award, and
   (c) that the Board is not satisfied that the criteria in the admissible rules governing entitlement to early payment of pension on grounds of ill health were satisfied in respect of the member at any time after that decision but before the assessment date.
(4) For the purposes of subsection (2) "the relevant date" means the date during the assessment period on which a scheme valuation in relation to the scheme becomes binding.
(5) The power to make a decision in respect of the pension under subsection (2) may only be exercised at a time which falls—
   (a) during the assessment period but before the time the Board first approves a scheme valuation under section 144 in relation to the scheme, and
   (b) within a reasonable period beginning with the assessment date or, where the decision to make the award was made at a later date, that date.
(6) Regulations made for the purposes of subsection (2) may, in particular, include provision applying any provision of Schedule 7 with such modifications as may be prescribed.

**142 Sections 140 and 141: interpretation**

(1) For the purposes of sections 140 and 141—
   "admissible rules" is to be construed in accordance with Schedule 7;
   "assessment date" means the date on which the assessment period begins;
   "ill health pension", in relation to a scheme, means a pension which, immediately before the assessment date, is a pension to which a person is entitled under the admissible rules in circumstances where that entitlement arose before normal

pension age by virtue of any provision of the admissible rules making special provision as to early payment of pension on grounds of ill health;

"normal pension age", in relation to a scheme and any pension under it, means the age specified in the admissible rules as the earliest age at which the pension becomes payable without actuarial adjustment (disregarding any admissible rule making special provision as to early payment on the grounds of ill health) and sub-paragraphs (2) and (3) of paragraph 34 of Schedule 7 apply in relation to this section as they apply in relation to that Schedule;

"notional reviewed rate of compensation", in respect of an ill health pension, means—

(a) the annual rate of compensation which would be payable in respect of the pension at the assessment date, if the Board assumed responsibility for the scheme and the compensation so payable at that date was determined in accordance with regulations under section 141(2), or

(b) if no such compensation would have been so payable at that date, nil;

"pensionable service" is to be construed in accordance with Schedule 7;

"scheme valuation", in relation to a scheme, means a valuation under section 143 of the assets and protected liabilities of the scheme as at the time immediately before the assessment period begins.

(2) For the purposes of section 140(4)—
 (a) the definition of "normal pension age" in subsection (1), and
 (b) sub-paragraphs (2) and (3) of paragraph 34 of Schedule 7 as they apply by virtue of that definition,
have effect as if the references in those provisions to the admissible rules were references to the scheme rules.

(3) Paragraph 37(4) of Schedule 7 (references to "ill health" to be construed in accordance with regulations) applies in relation to sections 140 and 141 and this section as if, in that provision, the reference to that Schedule included a reference to those sections and this section.

(4) In those sections references to the Board assuming responsibility for the scheme are to the Board assuming responsibility for the scheme in accordance with this Chapter at the time the assessment period in question comes to an end.

*Valuation of assets and liabilities*

**143 Board's obligation to obtain valuation of assets and protected liabilities**

(1) This section applies in a case within subsection (1) of section 127 or 128.

(2) For the purposes of determining whether the condition in subsection (2)(a) of the section in question is satisfied, the Board must, as soon as reasonably practicable, obtain an actuarial valuation of the scheme as at the relevant time.

(3) For those purposes, regulations may provide that any of the following are to be regarded as assets or protected liabilities of the scheme at the relevant time if prescribed requirements are met—
 (a) a debt due to the trustees or managers of the scheme by virtue of a contribution notice issued under section 38, 47 or 55 during the pre-approval period;
 (b) an obligation arising under financial support for the scheme (within the meaning of section 45) put in place during the pre-approval period in accordance with a financial support direction issued under section 43;

(c) an obligation imposed by a restoration order made under section 52 during the pre-approval period in respect of a transaction involving assets of the scheme.
(4) For the purposes of this section, regulations may prescribe how—
   (a) the assets and the protected liabilities of eligible schemes, and
   (b) their amount or value,
   are to be determined, calculated and verified.
(5) Regulations under subsection (4) may provide, in particular, that when calculating the amount or value of assets or protected liabilities of an eligible scheme at the relevant time which consist of any of the following—
   (a) a debt (including any contingent debt) due to the trustees or managers of the scheme from the employer under section 75 of the Pensions Act 1995 (c. 26) (deficiencies in the scheme assets),
   (b) a debt due to the trustees or managers of the scheme by virtue of a contribution notice issued under section 38, 47 or 55,
   (c) an obligation arising under financial support for the scheme (within the meaning of section 45) put in place in accordance with a financial support direction issued under section 43, or
   (d) an obligation imposed by a restoration order made under section 52 in respect of a transaction involving assets of the scheme,
   account must be taken in the prescribed manner of prescribed events which occur during the pre-approval period.
(6) Subject to any provision made under subsection (4), the matters mentioned in paragraphs (a) and (b) of that subsection are to be determined, calculated and verified in accordance with guidance issued by the Board.
(7) In calculating the amount of any liabilities for the purposes of this section, a provision of the scheme rules which limits the amount of the scheme's liabilities by reference to the value of its assets is to be disregarded.
(8) The duty imposed by subsection (2) ceases to apply if and when the Board ceases to be involved with the scheme.
(9) Nothing in subsection (2) requires the actuarial valuation to be obtained during any period when the Board considers that an event may occur which, by virtue of regulations under subsection (3) or (4), may affect the value of the assets or the amount of the protected liabilities of the scheme for the purposes of the valuation.
(10) In a case where there are one or more reviewable ill health pensions (within the meaning of section 140), nothing in subsection (2) requires the actuarial valuation to be obtained during the period mentioned in section 141(5)(b) (period during which Board may exercise its power to make a decision following a review) relating to any such pension.
(11) For the purposes of this section—
   (a) "actuarial valuation", in relation to the scheme, means a written valuation of the assets and protected liabilities of the scheme which—
      (i) is in the prescribed form and contains the prescribed information, and
      (ii) is prepared and signed by—
         (a) a person with prescribed qualifications or experience, or
         (b) a person approved by the Secretary of State,
   (b) "the pre-approval period", in relation to the scheme, means the period which—
      (i) begins immediately after the relevant time, and

(ii) ends immediately before the time the Board first approves a valuation of the scheme under section 144 after the relevant time,
(c) "the relevant time"—
   (i) in a case within subsection (1) of section 127, has the meaning given in subsection (4)(b) of that section, and
   (ii) in a case within subsection (1) of section 128, has the meaning given in subsection (3)(b) of that section, and
(d) references to "assets" do not include assets representing the value of any rights in respect of money purchase benefits under the scheme rules.

**144 Approval of valuation**

(1) This section applies where the Board obtains a valuation in respect of a scheme under section 143.
(2) Where the Board is satisfied that the valuation has been prepared in accordance with that section, it must—
   (a) approve the valuation, and
   (b) give a copy of the valuation to—
      (i) the Regulator,
      (ii) the trustees or managers of the scheme, and
      (iii) any insolvency practitioner in relation to the employer or, if there is no such insolvency practitioner, the employer.
(3) Where the Board is not so satisfied, it must obtain another valuation under that section.

**145 Binding valuations**

(1) For the purposes of this Chapter a valuation obtained under section 143 is not binding until—
   (a) it is approved under section 144,
   (b) the period within which the approval may be reviewed by virtue of Chapter 6 has expired, and
   (c) if the approval is so reviewed—
      (i) the review and any reconsideration,
      (ii) any reference to the PPF Ombudsman in respect of the approval, and
      (iii) any appeal against his determination or directions,
   has been finally disposed of.
(2) For the purposes of determining whether or not the condition in section 127(2)(a) or, as the case may be, section 128(2)(a) (condition that scheme assets are less than protected liabilities) is satisfied in relation to a scheme, a binding valuation is conclusive.

   This subsection is subject to section 172(3) and (4) (treatment of fraud compensation payments).
(3) Where a valuation becomes binding under this section the Board must as soon as reasonably practicable give a notice to that effect together with a copy of the binding valuation to—
   (a) the Regulator,
   (b) the trustees or managers of the scheme, and
   (c) any insolvency practitioner in relation to the employer or, if there is no such insolvency practitioner, the employer.

(4) A notice under subsection (3) must be in the prescribed form and contain the prescribed information.

*Refusal to assume responsibility*

**146 Schemes which become eligible schemes**

(1) Regulations may provide that where the Board is satisfied that an eligible scheme was not such a scheme throughout such period as may be prescribed, the Board must refuse to assume responsibility for the scheme under this Chapter.

(2) Where, by virtue of subsection (1), the Board is required to refuse to assume responsibility for a scheme, it—
   (a) must issue a notice to that effect (a "withdrawal notice"), and
   (b) give a copy of that notice to—
      (i) the Regulator,
      (ii) the trustees or managers of the scheme, and
      (iii) any insolvency practitioner in relation to the employer or, if there is no such insolvency practitioner, the employer.

(3) For the purposes of this Part a withdrawal notice issued by virtue of this section is not binding until—
   (a) the period within which the issue of the notice may be reviewed by virtue of Chapter 6 has expired, and
   (b) if the issue of the notice is so reviewed—
      (i) the review and any reconsideration,
      (ii) any reference to the PPF Ombudsman in respect of the issue of the notice, and
      (iii) any appeal against his determination or directions,
      has been finally disposed of and the notice has not been revoked, varied or substituted.

(4) Where a withdrawal notice issued by virtue of this section becomes binding, the Board must as soon as reasonably practicable give a notice to that effect together with a copy of the binding notice to—
   (a) the Regulator,
   (b) the trustees or managers of the scheme, and
   (c) any insolvency practitioner in relation to the employer or, if there is no such insolvency practitioner, the employer.

(5) Notices under this section must be in the prescribed form and contain such information as may be prescribed.

(6) A notice given under subsection (4) must state the time from which the Board ceases to be involved with the scheme (see section 149).

**147 New schemes created to replace existing schemes**

(1) The Board must refuse to assume responsibility for a scheme ("the new scheme") under this Chapter where it is satisfied that—
   (a) the new scheme was established during such period as may be prescribed,
   (b) the employer in relation to the new scheme was, at the date of establishment of that scheme, also the employer in relation to a scheme established before the new scheme (the "old scheme"),
   (c) a transfer or transfers of, or a transfer payment or transfer payments in respect

of, any rights of members under the old scheme has or have been made to the new scheme, and

(d) the main purpose or one of the main purposes of establishing the new scheme and making the transfer or transfers, or transfer payment or transfer payments, was to enable those members to receive compensation under the pension compensation provisions in respect of their rights under the new scheme in circumstances where, in the absence of the transfer or transfers, regulations under section 146 would have operated to prevent such payments in respect of their rights under the old scheme.

(2) Where, under subsection (1), the Board is required to refuse to assume responsibility for a scheme, it—
- (a) must issue a notice to that effect (a "withdrawal notice"), and
- (b) give a copy of that notice to—
  - (i) the Regulator,
  - (ii) the trustees or managers of the scheme, and
  - (iii) any insolvency practitioner in relation to the employer or, if there is no such insolvency practitioner, the employer.

(3) For the purposes of this Part a withdrawal notice issued under this section is not binding until—
- (a) the period within which the issue of the notice may be reviewed by virtue of Chapter 6 has expired, and
- (b) if the issue of the notice is so reviewed—
  - (i) the review and any reconsideration,
  - (ii) any reference to the PPF Ombudsman in respect of the issue of the notice, and
  - (iii) any appeal against his determination or directions,

  has been finally disposed of and the notice has not been revoked, varied or substituted.

(4) Where a withdrawal notice issued under this section becomes binding, the Board must as soon as reasonably practicable give a notice to that effect together with a copy of the binding notice to—
- (a) the Regulator,
- (b) the trustees or managers of the scheme, and
- (c) any insolvency practitioner in relation to the employer or, if there is no such insolvency practitioner, the employer.

(5) Notices under this section must be in the prescribed form and contain such information as may be prescribed.

(6) A notice given under subsection (4) must state the time from which the Board ceases to be involved with the scheme (see section 149).

## 148 Withdrawal following issue of section 122(4) notice

(1) This section applies where—
- (a) a notice under section 122(4) (inability to confirm status of scheme) is issued in relation to an eligible scheme and becomes binding, and
- (b) a withdrawal event has not occurred in relation to the scheme in respect of a withdrawal notice which has been issued during the period—
  - (i) beginning with the occurrence of the last insolvency event in relation to the employer, and

(ii) ending immediately before the notice under section 122(4) becomes binding, and the occurrence of such a withdrawal event in respect of a withdrawal notice issued during that period is not a possibility (see section 149).
(2) The Board must determine whether any insolvency event—
   (a) has occurred in relation to the employer since the issue of the notice under section 122(4), or
   (b) is likely to so occur before the end of the period of six months beginning with the date on which this section applies.
(3) If the Board determines under subsection (2) that no insolvency event has occurred or is likely to occur as mentioned in that subsection, it must issue a notice to that effect (a "withdrawal notice").
(4) Where—
   (a) no withdrawal notice is issued under subsection (3) before the end of the period mentioned in subsection (2)(b), and
   (b) no further insolvency event occurs in relation to the employer during that period, the Board must issue a notice to that effect (a "withdrawal notice").
(5) Where the Board is required to issue a withdrawal notice under this section, it must give a copy of the notice to—
   (a) the Regulator,
   (b) the trustees or managers of the scheme, and
   (c) the employer.
(6) For the purposes of this Part, a withdrawal notice issued under this section is not binding until—
   (a) the period within which the issue of the notice may be reviewed by virtue of Chapter 6 has expired, and
   (b) if the issue of the notice is so reviewed—
      (i) the review and any reconsideration,
      (ii) any reference to the PPF Ombudsman in respect of the issue of the notice, and
      (iii) any appeal against his determination or directions,
      has been finally disposed of and the notice has not been revoked, varied or substituted.
(7) Where a withdrawal notice issued under this section becomes binding, the Board must as soon as reasonably practicable give a notice to that effect together with a copy of the binding notice to—
   (a) the Regulator,
   (b) the trustees or managers of the scheme, and
   (c) the employer.
(8) Notices under this section must be in the prescribed form and contain such information as may be prescribed.
(9) A notice given under subsection (7) must state the time from which the Board ceases to be involved with the scheme (see section 149).

*Cessation of involvement with a scheme*

## 149 Circumstances in which Board ceases to be involved with an eligible scheme

(1) Where an assessment period begins in relation to an eligible scheme, the Board ceases to be involved with the scheme, for the purposes of this Part, on the occurrence of the first withdrawal event after the beginning of that period.

(2) For this purpose the following are withdrawal events in relation to a scheme—
- (a) a withdrawal notice issued under section 122(2)(b) (scheme rescue has occurred) becoming binding;
- (b) a withdrawal notice issued under section 130(3) (scheme rescue has occurred) becoming binding;
- (c) a withdrawal notice issued under or by virtue of section 146 or 147 (refusal to assume responsibility) becoming binding;
- (d) a withdrawal notice issued under section 148 (no insolvency event has occurred or is likely to occur) becoming binding;

and references in this Chapter to a "withdrawal event" are to be construed accordingly.

(3) Subsection (4) applies where a withdrawal notice mentioned in subsection (2) is issued in relation to a scheme and becomes binding and—
- (a) an insolvency event in relation to the employer occurs during the interim period and, if subsection (4) did not apply, the event would not be a qualifying insolvency event within the meaning given by subsection (3) of section 127 solely because the condition in sub-paragraph (ii) of paragraph (b) of that subsection would not be satisfied, or
- (b) an application under section 129(1) is made, or a notification under section 129(5)(a) is given, in relation to the scheme during the interim period and, if subsection (4) did not apply, the application or notification would be disregarded for the purposes of—
  - (i) subsection (1) of section 128 by virtue of subsection (4) of that section, and
  - (ii) subsection (4) of section 132 by virtue of subsection (5) of that section.

(4) In such a case, the withdrawal notice is to be treated for the purposes of subsections (1) and (2), as if the time when it became binding was the time immediately before—
- (a) in a case falling within subsection (3)(a), the occurrence of the insolvency event, and
- (b) in a case falling within subsection (3)(b), the making of the application under section 129(1) or, as the case may be, the giving of the notification under section 129(5)(a).

(5) For the purposes of subsection (3), the "interim period" in relation to a scheme means the period beginning with the issuing of the withdrawal notice in relation to the scheme and ending with that notice becoming binding.

(6) For the purposes of this Chapter—
- (a) the occurrence of a withdrawal event in relation to a scheme in respect of a withdrawal notice issued during a particular period ("the specified period") is a possibility until each of the following are no longer reviewable—
  - (i) any withdrawal notice which has been issued in relation to the scheme during the specified period,
  - (ii) any failure to issue such a withdrawal notice during the specified period,
  - (iii) any notice which has been issued by the Board under Chapter 2 or this Chapter which is relevant to the issue of a withdrawal notice in relation to the scheme during the specified period or to such a withdrawal notice which has been issued during that period becoming binding,
  - (iv) any failure to issue such a notice as is mentioned in sub-paragraph (iii), and
- (b) the issue of, or failure to issue, a notice is to be regarded as reviewable—

(i) during the period within which it may be reviewed by virtue of Chapter 6, and
(ii) if the matter is so reviewed, until—
(a) the review and any reconsideration,
(b) any reference to the PPF Ombudsman in respect of the matter, and
(c) any appeal against his determination or directions,
has been finally disposed of.

**150 Consequences of the Board ceasing to be involved with a scheme**

(1) Where—
  (a) an assessment period comes to an end by virtue of the Board ceasing to be involved with an eligible scheme, and
  (b) during the assessment period any amount of any benefit payable to a member, or to a person in respect of a member, under the scheme rules was not paid by reason of section 138 (requirement to pay benefits in accordance with the pension compensation provisions),
  that amount falls due to the member, or as the case may be, person at the end of that period.

(2) Where the winding up of the scheme began before the end of the assessment period (whether by virtue of section 219 (backdating the winding up of eligible schemes) or otherwise), the reference in subsection (1)(b) to the amount of any benefit payable to a member, or to a person in respect of a member, under the scheme rules is a reference to the amount so payable taking account of any reduction required by virtue of sections 73 to 73B of the Pensions Act 1995 (c. 26) (provisions relating to the winding up of certain schemes).

(3) Where—
  (a) an assessment period comes to an end by virtue of the Board ceasing to be involved with an eligible scheme, and
  (b) during the assessment period the amount of benefit paid to a member, or to a person in respect of a member, under the scheme rules exceeded the amount that would have been payable in the absence of section 138(6) (requirement to disregard winding up when paying benefits during assessment period),
  the trustees or managers of the scheme must, at the end of that period, take such steps as they consider appropriate (including steps to adjust future payments under the scheme rules) to recover an amount equal to the excess from the person to whom it was paid.

(4) Subsections (1) to (3) are without prejudice to section 73A(2)(b) of the Pensions Act 1995 (c. 26) (requirement to adjust benefits paid to reflect liabilities which can be met on winding up).

(5) Regulations may provide that, in cases within paragraph (a) of subsection (1), benefits are to accrue under the scheme rules, in such circumstances as may be prescribed, to or in respect of members of the scheme in respect of any specified period of service being service in employment which, but for section 133(5), would have qualified the member in question for those benefits under the scheme rules.

(6) Regulations under subsection (5) may in particular make provision—
  (a) for benefits not to accrue to, or in respect of, a member unless contributions are paid by or on behalf of the member towards the scheme within a prescribed period;

(b) for contributions towards the scheme which, but for section 133, would have been payable by or on behalf of the employer (otherwise than on behalf of an employee) during the assessment period, to fall due;

(c) requiring that such contributions as are mentioned in paragraph (a) or (b) are accepted for the assessment period or any part of that period;

(d) modifying section 31 of the Welfare Reform and Pensions Act 1999 (c. 30) (reduction of benefit where a person's shareable rights are subject to a pension debit), in its application in relation to cases where benefits accrue under the scheme by virtue of regulations under subsection (5).

(7) In this section "contributions" means, in relation to an eligible scheme, contributions payable towards the scheme by or on behalf of the employer or the active members of the scheme in accordance with the schedule of contributions maintained under section 227 in respect of the scheme.

*Reconsideration*

**151 Application for reconsideration**

(1) Where subsection (2) or (3) applies in relation to an eligible scheme, the trustees or managers of the scheme may make an application to the Board under this section for it to assume responsibility for the scheme in accordance with this Chapter.

(2) This subsection applies where—
   (a) a scheme failure notice has been issued under section 122(2)(a) in relation to the scheme, that notice has become binding and the trustees or managers have received a copy of the binding notice under section 125(3),
   (b) the valuation obtained by the Board under section 143 in respect of the scheme has become binding, and
   (c) the Board would have been required to assume responsibility for the scheme under section 127 but for the fact that the condition in subsection (2)(a) of that section was not satisfied.

(3) This subsection applies where—
   (a) the Board has issued a scheme failure notice under subsection (2) of section 130 in relation to the scheme, that notice has become binding and the trustees or managers have received a copy of the binding notice under subsection (7) of that section,
   (b) the valuation obtained by the Board under section 143 in respect of the scheme has become binding, and
   (c) the Board would have been required to assume responsibility for the scheme under section 128 but for the fact that the condition in subsection (2)(a) of that section was not satisfied.

(4) An application under this section must be in the prescribed form, contain the prescribed information and be accompanied by—
   (a) a protected benefits quotation in the prescribed form, and
   (b) audited scheme accounts for a period which—
      (i) begins with such date as may be determined in accordance with regulations, and
      (ii) ends with a date which falls within the prescribed period ending with the day on which the application is made.

(5) An application under this section must be made within the authorized period.

(6) In this section "the authorized period" means the prescribed period which begins—
 (a) where subsection (2) applies, with the later of—
  (i) the day on which the trustees or managers received the copy of the binding notice mentioned in paragraph (a) of that subsection, and
  (ii) the day on which they received a copy of the binding valuation mentioned in paragraph (b) of that section, and
 (b) where subsection (3) applies, with the later of—
  (i) the day on which the trustees or managers received the copy of the binding notice mentioned in paragraph (a) of that subsection, and
  (ii) the day on which they received a copy of the binding valuation mentioned in paragraph (b) of that subsection.
(7) Where the Board receives an application under subsection (1), it must give a copy of the application to the Regulator.
(8) For the purposes of this section—
 "audited scheme accounts", in relation to a scheme, means—
  (a) accounts obtained by the trustees or managers of the scheme ("the scheme accounts") which are prepared in accordance with subsections (9) to (11) and audited by the auditor in relation to the scheme, and
  (b) a report by the auditor, in the prescribed form, as to whether or not such requirements as may be prescribed are satisfied in relation to the scheme accounts;
 "auditor", in relation to a scheme, has the meaning given by section 47 of the Pensions Act 1995 (c. 26);
 "protected benefits quotation", in relation to a scheme, means a quotation for one or more annuities from one or more insurers, being companies willing to accept payment in respect of the members from the trustees or managers of the scheme, which would provide in respect of each member of the scheme from the reconsideration time—
  (a) benefits for or in respect of the member corresponding to the compensation which would be payable to or in respect of the member in accordance with the pension compensation provisions if the Board assumed responsibility for the scheme by virtue of this section, or
  (b) benefits in accordance with the member's entitlement or accrued rights (including pension credit rights within the meaning of section 124(1) of the Pensions Act 1995 (c. 26)) under the scheme rules (other than his entitlement or rights in respect of money purchase benefits),
 whichever benefits can, in the case of that member, be secured at the lower cost;
 "the reconsideration time", in relation to an application under this section, means the time immediately before the end of the period to which the audited scheme accounts mentioned in subsection (4)(b) relate.
(9) The scheme accounts are prepared in accordance with this subsection if, subject to subsections (10) and (11), they—
 (a) include a statement of the assets of the scheme (excluding any assets representing the value of any rights in respect of money purchase benefits under the scheme rules) as at the reconsideration time, and
 (b) are prepared in accordance with such other requirements as may be prescribed.
(10) Subject to subsection (11), regulations under subsection (4) of section 143 (other than regulations made by virtue of subsection (5) of that section), and guidance

under subsection (6) of that section, apply to the scheme accounts as they apply for the purposes of a valuation under that section.

(11) Regulations may provide that, where an asset of a prescribed description has been acquired during the assessment period, the value assigned to the asset as at the reconsideration time is to be determined, for the purposes of the scheme accounts, in the prescribed manner.

(12) For the purposes of this section—
  (a) regulations may prescribe how the cost of securing the benefits mentioned in paragraph (a) of the definition of "protected benefits quotation" in subsection (8) is to be determined, calculated and verified, and
  (b) subject to any provision made under paragraph (a), that cost is to be determined, calculated and verified in accordance with guidance issued by the Board.

(13) Where the scheme is being wound up, for the purposes of determining the benefits which fall within paragraph (b) of the definition of "protected benefits quotation" in subsection (8) no account is to be taken of the winding up of the scheme.

**152 Duty to assume responsibility following reconsideration**

(1) This section applies where an application is made in respect of a scheme in accordance with section 151.

(2) The Board must assume responsibility for the scheme in accordance with this Chapter if it is satisfied that the value of the assets of the scheme at the reconsideration time is less than the aggregate of—
  (a) the amount quoted in the protected benefits quotation accompanying the application,
  (b) the amount at that time of the liabilities of the scheme which are not liabilities to, or in respect of, members of the scheme, and
  (c) the estimated costs of winding up the scheme at that time.

(3) Where the Board makes a determination for the purposes of subsection (2), it must issue a determination notice and give a copy of that notice to—
  (a) the trustees or managers of the scheme, and
  (b) the Regulator.

(4) In subsection (3) "determination notice" means a notice which is in the prescribed form and contains such information about the determination as may be prescribed.

(5) But where the Board is satisfied of the matters mentioned in subsection (2), it is not required to assume responsibility for the scheme under subsection (2) until the determination notice issued under subsection (3) becomes binding.

(6) For the purposes of subsection (5) a determination notice is not binding until—
  (a) the period within which the issue of the notice may be reviewed by virtue of Chapter 6 has expired, and
  (b) if the issue of the notice is so reviewed—
    (i) the review and any reconsideration,
    (ii) any reference to the PPF Ombudsman in respect of the issue of the notice, and
    (iii) any appeal against his determination or directions,
    has been finally disposed of and the notice has not been revoked, varied or substituted.

(7) Where a determination notice issued under subsection (3) becomes binding, the

Board must as soon as reasonably practicable give a notice to that effect together with a copy of the binding notice to—
   (a) the trustees or managers of the scheme, and
   (b) the Regulator.
(8) A notice under subsection (7) must be in the prescribed form and contain such information as may be prescribed.
(9) The Board may—
   (a) for the purposes of subsection (2), obtain its own valuation of the assets of the scheme as at the reconsideration time (within the meaning of section 151), and
   (b) for the purposes of subsection (2)(b), obtain its own valuation of the liabilities of the scheme as at that time;
   and where it does so, subsections (9)(b), (10) and (11) of section 151 apply in relation to the valuation as they apply in relation to the scheme accounts (within the meaning of that section).
(10) Regulations under subsection (4) of section 143, and guidance under subsection (6) of that section, apply for the purposes of this section in relation to the estimated costs within subsection (2)(c) as they apply for the purposes of section 143 in relation to protected liabilities within section 131(1)(c).
(11) In this section references to the assets of the scheme do not include assets representing the value of any rights in respect of money purchase benefits under the scheme rules.
(12) This section is subject to sections 146 and 147 (refusal to assume responsibility for a scheme).

*Closed schemes*

### 153  Closed schemes

(1) This section applies where section 151(2) or (3) (scheme rescue not possible but scheme has sufficient assets to meet the protected liabilities) applies in relation to an eligible scheme.
(2) If the trustees or managers of the scheme are unable to obtain a full buy-out quotation, they must, within the authorized period, apply to the Board for authority to continue as a closed scheme.
(3) For the purposes of determining whether they must make an application under subsection (2), the trustees or managers of the scheme must take all reasonable steps to obtain a full buy-out quotation in respect of the scheme.
(4) An application under subsection (2) must—
   (a) be in the prescribed form and contain the prescribed information, and
   (b) be accompanied by evidence in the prescribed form which shows that the trustees or managers of the scheme have complied with the obligation under subsection (3) but were unable to obtain a full buy-out quotation.
(5) Where the Board receives an application under subsection (2), if it is satisfied that the trustees or managers have complied with the obligation under subsection (3) but were unable to obtain a full buy-out quotation, it must authorize the scheme to continue as a closed scheme.
(6) Where the Board determines an application in respect of a scheme under this section, it must issue a determination notice and give a copy of that notice to—

(a) the trustees or managers of the scheme, and
(b) the Regulator.
(7) In this section—
"authorized period" has the same meaning as in section 151;
"determination notice" means a notice which is in the prescribed form and contains such information about the determination as may be prescribed;
"full buy-out quotation", in relation to a scheme, means a quotation for one or more annuities from one or more insurers (being companies willing to accept payment in respect of the members from the trustees or managers of the scheme) which would provide in respect of each member of the scheme, from a relevant date, benefits in accordance with the member's entitlement or accrued rights, including pension credit rights, under the scheme rules (other than his entitlement or rights in respect of money purchase benefits);
"pension credit rights" has the meaning given by section 124(1) of the Pensions Act 1995 (c. 26);
"relevant date" means a date within the authorized period.
(8) If the trustees or managers of the scheme fail to comply with subsection (2) or (3), section 10 of the Pensions Act 1995 (civil penalties) applies to any trustee or manager who has failed to take all reasonable steps to secure compliance.

*Winding up*

**154 Requirement to wind up schemes with sufficient assets to meet protected liabilities**

(1) Where, in relation to an eligible scheme, an assessment period within section 132(2) or (4) comes to an end because the conditions in subsection (2) of this section are satisfied, the trustees or managers of the scheme must—
(a) wind up the scheme, or
(b) where the winding up of the scheme began before the assessment period (whether by virtue of section 219 or otherwise), continue the winding up of the scheme.
(2) The conditions are—
(a) that subsection (2) or (3) of section 151 (scheme rescue not possible but scheme has sufficient assets to meet the protected liabilities) applies in relation to the scheme,
(b) that—
(i) the trustees or managers did not make an application under that section or section 153(2) within the authorized period (within the meaning of section 151(6)) (or any such application has been withdrawn), or
(ii) if such an application was made, it has been finally determined, and
(c) that, if an application was made under section 151, the Board is not required to assume responsibility for the scheme by virtue of section 152(2).
(3) For the purposes of subsection (2)(b)(ii) an application is not finally determined until—
(a) the Board has issued a determination notice in respect of the application under section 152 or, as the case may be, section 153,
(b) the period within which the issue of the notice may be reviewed by virtue of Chapter 6 has expired, and

(c) if the issue of the notice is so reviewed—
  (i) the review and any reconsideration,
  (ii) any reference to the PPF Ombudsman in respect of the issue of the notice, and
  (iii) any appeal against his determination or directions,
  has been finally disposed of.
(4) Where, in relation to an eligible scheme, an assessment period within section 159(3) comes to an end because the conditions in subsection (5) of this section are satisfied, the trustees or managers of the scheme must continue the winding up of the scheme begun (whether in accordance with this section or otherwise) before that assessment period.
(5) The conditions are—
  (a) that an application is made by, or notice is given to, the trustees or managers of the scheme under section 157 (applications and notifications where closed schemes have insufficient assets),
  (b) that the valuation obtained by the Board in respect of the scheme under section 158(3) has become binding, and
  (c) that the Board is not required to assume responsibility for the scheme by virtue of section 158(1) (duty to assume responsibility for closed scheme).
(6) Where a scheme is wound up in accordance with subsection (1)(a), the winding up is to be taken as beginning immediately before the assessment period.
(7) Without prejudice to the power to give directions under section 134, but subject to any order made under subsection (8), the Board may give the trustees or managers of the scheme directions relating to the manner of the winding up of the scheme under this section (and may vary or revoke any such direction given by it).
(8) The Regulator may by order direct any person specified in the order—
  (a) to take such steps as are so specified as it considers are necessary as a result of—
    (i) the winding up of the scheme beginning, by virtue of subsection (6), immediately before the assessment period, or
    (ii) the winding up of the scheme being continued under subsection (1)(b), and
  (b) to take those steps within a period specified in the order.
(9) If the trustees or managers of a scheme fail to comply with a direction to them under subsection (7), or contained in an order under subsection (8), section 10 of the Pensions Act 1995 (c. 26) (civil penalties) applies to any trustee or manager who has failed to take all reasonable steps to secure compliance.
(10) That section also applies to any other person who, without reasonable excuse, fails to comply with a direction to him contained in an order under subsection (8).
(11) The winding up of a scheme under this section is as effective in law as if it had been made under powers conferred by or under the scheme.
(12) This section must be complied with in relation to a scheme—
  (a) in spite of any enactment or rule of law, or any rule of the scheme, which would otherwise operate to prevent the winding up, and
  (b) without regard to any such enactment, rule of law or rule of the scheme as would otherwise require or might otherwise be taken to require the implementation of any procedure or the obtaining of any consent with a view to the winding up.
(13) Where an assessment period in relation to an eligible scheme comes to an end by virtue of the conditions in subsection (2) or (5) being satisfied, subsections (1) to (4)

of section 150 apply as they apply where an assessment period comes to an end by virtue of the Board ceasing to be involved with the scheme, except that in subsection (2) of that section the reference to section 219 is to be read as a reference to subsection (6) of this section.
(14) Where a public service pension scheme is required to be wound up under this section, the appropriate authority may by order make provision modifying any enactment in which the scheme is contained or under which it is made.
(15) In subsection (14) "the appropriate authority", in relation to a scheme, means such Minister of the Crown or government department as may be designated by the Treasury as having responsibility for the particular scheme.

*Provisions applying to closed schemes*

### 155 Treatment of closed schemes

(1) In this section "closed scheme" means an eligible scheme which is authorized under section 153 to continue as a closed scheme.
(2) The provisions mentioned in subsection (3) apply in relation to a closed scheme at any time when the trustees or managers of the scheme are required to wind up or continue winding up the scheme under section 154 as if that time fell within an assessment period in relation to the scheme.
(3) The provisions are—
　(a) section 40(5) and (6) (Board to act as creditor for debt due by virtue of a contribution notice under section 38);
　(b) section 49(5) and (6) (Board to act as creditor for debt due by virtue of a contribution notice under section 47);
　(c) section 54(5) and (6) (Board to act as creditor for debt due by virtue of a restoration order under section 52);
　(d) section 56(5) and (6) (Board to act as creditor for debt due by virtue of a contribution notice under section 55);
　(e) section 133 (admission of new members, payment of contributions etc);
　(f) section 134 (directions);
　(g) section 137 (Board to act as creditor of the employer).
(4) Regulations may require the trustees or managers of a closed scheme in relation to which the provisions mentioned in subsection (3) apply to comply with such requirements as may be prescribed when providing for the discharge of any liability to, or in respect of, a member of the scheme for pensions or other benefits.

### 156 Valuations of closed schemes

(1) Regulations may make provision requiring the trustees or managers of closed schemes to obtain actuarial valuations of the scheme at such intervals as may be prescribed for the purposes of enabling them to determine—
　(a) the benefits payable under the scheme rules;
　(b) whether to make an application under section 157.
(2) Regulations under this section may prescribe how—
　(a) the assets, the full scheme liabilities and the protected liabilities in relation to closed schemes, and
　(b) their amount or value,
are to be determined, calculated and verified.

(3) Subject to any provision made under subsection (2), those matters are to be determined, calculated and verified in accordance with guidance issued by the Board.

(4) In calculating the amount of any liabilities for the purposes of a valuation required by virtue of this section, a provision of the scheme rules which limits the amount of the scheme's liabilities by reference to the value of its assets is to be disregarded.

(5) Nothing in regulations under this section may require the trustees or managers of a closed scheme to obtain an actuarial valuation of the scheme until—
   (a) the period within which the issue of the determination notice, under section 153(6), in respect of the Board's determination to authorize the scheme to continue as a closed scheme, may be reviewed by virtue of Chapter 6 has expired, and
   (b) if the issue of the notice is so reviewed—
      (i) the review and any reconsideration,
      (ii) any reference to the PPF Ombudsman in respect of the issue of the notice, and
      (iii) any appeal against his determination or directions,
      has been finally disposed of and the notice has not been revoked, varied or substituted.

(6) In this section, in relation to a scheme—
   "actuarial valuation" means a written valuation of—
      (a) the scheme's assets,
      (b) the full scheme liabilities, and
      (c) the protected liabilities in relation to the scheme,
      prepared and signed by the actuary;
   "the actuary" means—
      (a) the actuary appointed under section 47(1)(b) of the Pensions Act 1995 (c. 26) (professional advisers) in relation to the scheme, or
      (b) if no such actuary has been appointed—
         (i) a person with prescribed qualifications or experience, or
         (ii) a person approved by the Secretary of State;
   "assets" do not include assets representing the value of any rights in respect of money purchase benefits under the scheme rules;
   "closed scheme" has the same meaning as in section 155;
   "full scheme liabilities" means—
      (a) the liabilities under the scheme rules to or in respect of members of the scheme,
      (b) other liabilities of the scheme, and
      (c) the estimated cost of winding up the scheme;
   "liabilities" does not include liabilities in respect of money purchase benefits under the scheme rules.

*Reconsideration of closed schemes*

**157 Applications and notifications where closed schemes have insufficient assets**

(1) If at any time the trustees or managers of a closed scheme become aware that the value of the assets of the scheme is less than the amount of the protected liabilities in

relation to the scheme, they must, before the end of the prescribed period beginning with that time, make an application to the Board for it to assume responsibility for the scheme.

(2) Where the Board receives an application under subsection (1), it must give a copy of the application to the Regulator.

(3) If at any time the Regulator becomes aware that the value of the assets of the scheme is less than the amount of the protected liabilities in relation to the scheme, it must give the Board a notice to that effect.

(4) Where the Board receives a notice under subsection (3), it must give the trustees or managers of the scheme a notice to that effect.

(5) The duty imposed by subsection (1) does not apply where the trustees or managers of a closed scheme become aware as mentioned in that subsection by reason of a notice given to them under subsection (4).

(6) The duty imposed by subsection (3) does not apply where the Regulator becomes aware as mentioned in that subsection by reason of a copy of an application made by the trustees or managers of the closed scheme being given to it under subsection (2).

(7) Regulations may require notices and applications under this section to be in the prescribed form and contain the prescribed information.

(8) If the trustees or managers of a closed scheme fail to comply with subsection (1), section 10 of the Pensions Act 1995 (c. 26) (civil penalties) applies to any trustee or manager who has failed to take all reasonable steps to secure compliance.

(9) In this section—
"assets", in relation to a scheme, do not include assets representing the value of any rights in respect of money purchase benefits under the scheme rules;
"closed scheme" has the same meaning as in section 155.

## 158 Duty to assume responsibility for closed schemes

(1) Where the trustees or managers of a closed scheme—
(a) make an application under subsection (1) of section 157, or
(b) receive a notice from the Board under subsection (4) of that section,
the Board must assume responsibility for the scheme in accordance with this Chapter if the value of the assets of the scheme at the relevant time was less than the amount of the protected liabilities at that time.

(2) In subsection (1) the reference to the assets of the scheme is a reference to those assets excluding any assets representing the value of any rights in respect of money purchase benefits under the scheme rules.

(3) For the purposes of determining whether the condition in subsection (1) is satisfied, the Board must, as soon as reasonably practicable, obtain an actuarial valuation (within the meaning of section 143) of the scheme as at the relevant time.

(4) Subject to subsection (6), subsection (3) of section 143 applies for those purposes as it applies for the purposes mentioned in subsection (2) of that section (and the definitions contained in paragraphs (b) and (d) of subsection (11) of that section apply accordingly).

(5) Subject to subsection (6), the following provisions apply in relation to a valuation obtained under subsection (3) as they apply in relation to a valuation obtained under section 143—
(a) subsections (4) to (7) and (11)(b) and (d) of that section;

(b) section 144 (approval of valuation), other than subsection (2)(b)(iii) (duty to give copy of approved valuation to employer's insolvency practitioner);
(c) section 145 (binding valuations), other than subsection (3)(c) (duty to give copy of binding valuation to employer's insolvency practitioner).

(6) In the application of sections 143 and 145 by virtue of subsection (4) or (5)—
   (a) subsections (3), (5) and (11)(b) and (d) of section 143 apply as if the references to "the relevant time" were references to that term as defined in subsection (8) below, and
   (b) subsection (2) of section 145 applies as if the reference to section 128(2)(a) included a reference to subsection (1) of this section.

(7) An application under subsection (1) of section 157, or notification under subsection (4) of that section, is to be disregarded for the purposes of subsection (1) if it is made or given during an assessment period (see sections 132 and 159) in relation to the scheme which began before the application was made or notification was given.

(8) In this section—
"closed scheme" has the same meaning as in section 155;
"the relevant time" means the time immediately before the application mentioned in subsection (1)(a) was made, or (as the case may be) the notice mentioned in subsection (1)(b) was received, by the trustees or managers of the scheme.

## 159  Closed schemes: further assessment periods

(1) Subsection (3) applies where—
   (a) an application is made under subsection (1) of section 157 in relation to a closed scheme, or
   (b) the trustees or managers of the scheme receive a notice under subsection (4) of that section.

(2) For the purposes of subsection (1) an application under subsection (1) of section 157, or notification under subsection (4) of that section, is to be disregarded if it is made or given during an assessment period (see section 132 and this section) in relation to the scheme which began before the application was made or notification was given.

(3) An assessment period—
   (a) begins when the application is made or the notice is received by the trustees or managers of the scheme, and
   (b) ends when—
      (i) the trustees or managers receive a transfer notice under section 160, or
      (ii) the conditions in section 154(5) (closed scheme with sufficient assets to meet protected liabilities etc) are satisfied in relation to the scheme,
      whichever first occurs.

(4) In this section "closed scheme" has the same meaning as in section 155.

*Assumption of responsibility for a scheme*

## 160  Transfer notice

(1) This section applies where the Board is required to assume responsibility for a scheme under section 127, 128, 152 or 158.
(2) The Board must give the trustees or managers a notice (a "transfer notice").

## s 160, Pensions Act 2004

(3) In a case to which section 127 or 128 applies, a transfer notice may not be given until the valuation obtained under section 143 is binding.

(4) In a case to which section 158 applies, a transfer notice may not be given until the valuation obtained under subsection (3) of that section is binding.

(5) A transfer notice may not be given in relation to a scheme during any period when the issue of, or failure to issue, a withdrawal notice under or by virtue of section 146 or 147 (refusal to assume responsibility) is reviewable (see section 149(6)(b)).

(6) The Board must give a copy of any notice given under subsection (2) to—
 (a) the Regulator, and
 (b) any insolvency practitioner in relation to the employer or, if there is no such insolvency practitioner, the employer.

(7) This section is subject to section 172(1) and (2) (no transfer notice within first 12 months of assessment period or when fraud compensation application is pending).

**161 Effect of Board assuming responsibility for a scheme**

(1) Where a transfer notice is given to the trustees or managers of an eligible scheme, the Board assumes responsibility for the scheme in accordance with this Chapter.

(2) The effect of the Board assuming responsibility for a scheme is that—
 (a) the property, rights and liabilities of the scheme are transferred to the Board, without further assurance, with effect from the time the trustees or managers receive the transfer notice,
 (b) the trustees or managers of the scheme are discharged from their pension obligations from that time, and
 (c) from that time the Board is responsible for securing that compensation is (and has been) paid in accordance with the pension compensation provisions,
and, accordingly, the scheme is to be treated as having been wound up immediately after that time.

(3) In subsection (2)(a) the reference to liabilities of the scheme does not include any liability to, or in respect of, any member of the scheme, other than—
 (a) liabilities in respect of money purchase benefits, and
 (b) such other liabilities as may be prescribed.

(4) In subsection (2)(b) "pension obligations" in relation to the trustees or managers of the scheme means—
 (a) their obligations to provide pensions or other benefits to or in respect of persons (including any obligation to provide guaranteed minimum pensions within the meaning of the Pension Schemes Act 1993 (c. 48)), and
 (b) their obligations to administer the scheme in accordance with the scheme rules and this or any other enactment.

(5) Schedule 6 makes provision in respect of the transfer of the property, rights and liabilities of a scheme under subsection (2)(a).

(6) Regulations may make further provision regarding such transfers.

(7) Without prejudice to the generality of subsection (6), regulations may authorize the Board to modify a term of a relevant contract of insurance if—
 (a) any rights or liabilities under the contract are transferred to the Board by virtue of subsection (2)(a), and
 (b) as a result of the transfer, the Board is required, by reason of that term, to pay a specified amount or specified amounts to a specified person who, immediately

before the time mentioned in subsection (2)(a), was a member of the scheme or a person entitled to benefits in respect of such a member.

(8) In subsection (7)—
"relevant contract of insurance" means a contract of insurance which—
   (a) is entered with a view to securing the whole or part of the scheme's liability for—
      (i) any pension or other benefit payable to or in respect of one particular person whose entitlement to payment of a pension or other benefit has arisen, and
      (ii) any benefit which will be payable in respect of that person on his death, and
   (b) is a contract—
      (i) which may not be surrendered, or
      (ii) in respect of which the amount payable on surrender does not exceed the liability secured;
"specified" means specified in, or determined in accordance with, the contract of insurance.

## 162 The pension compensation provisions

(1) Schedule 7 makes provision for compensation to be paid in relation to a scheme for which the Board assumes responsibility in accordance with this Chapter, including provision for—
   (a) periodic compensation to be paid to or in respect of members,
   (b) lump sum compensation to be paid to members,
   (c) a cap to be imposed on the periodic compensation and lump sum compensation payable, and
   (d) annual increases to be made to periodic compensation.

(2) In this Part references to the pension compensation provisions are to the provisions of, and the provisions made by virtue of, this section, sections 140 to 142, 161(2)(c), 164 and 168 and Schedule 7.
(Those references do not include any provision of, or made by virtue of, section 170 (discharge of liabilities in respect of money purchase benefits).)

## 163 Adjustments to be made where the Board assumes responsibility for a scheme

(1) This section applies where the Board assumes responsibility for an eligible scheme in accordance with this Chapter.

(2) Any benefits (other than money purchase benefits) which—
   (a) were payable under the scheme rules to any member, or to any person in respect of any member, during the period beginning with the assessment date and ending with the receipt by the trustees or managers of the transfer notice, and
   (b) have been paid before the trustees or managers receive the transfer notice,
are to be regarded as going towards discharging any liability of the Board to pay compensation to the member or, as the case may be, person in accordance with the pension compensation provisions.

(3) Regulations may provide that, in prescribed circumstances, where—
   (a) a member of the scheme died before the commencement of the assessment period, and

(b) during the period mentioned in subsection (2)(a), a person became entitled under the scheme rules to a benefit of a prescribed description in respect of the member,

the benefit, or any part of it, is, for the purposes of subsection (2), to be treated as having become payable before the assessment date.

(4) The Board must—
   (a) if any amount paid, during the period mentioned in subsection (2)(a), by the trustees or managers of the scheme to a member, or to a person in respect of a member, exceeded the entitlement of that member or person under the pension compensation provisions, take such steps as it considers appropriate (including adjusting future compensation payments made in accordance with those provisions) to recover an amount equal to the aggregate of—
      (i) the amount of the excess, and
      (ii) interest on that amount, at the prescribed rate, for the period which begins when the excess was paid by the trustees or managers and ends with the recovery of the excess, and
   (b) if any amount so paid was less than that entitlement (or no amount was paid in respect of that entitlement), pay an amount to the member or person concerned equal to the aggregate of—
      (i) the amount of the shortfall, and
      (ii) interest on that amount, at the prescribed rate, for the period which begins when the shortfall ought to have been paid by the trustees or managers and ends with the payment of the shortfall by the Board.
(5) In subsection (4) references to an amount paid do not include—
   (a) an amount paid in respect of any money purchase benefit, or
   (b) any other amount of a prescribed description.
(6) Nothing in subsection (4) requires the Board—
   (a) to recover any amount from a person in such circumstances as may be prescribed, or
   (b) to recover from any person any amount which it considers to be trivial.
(7) In this section "assessment date" is to be construed in accordance with Schedule 7.

### 164  Postponement of compensation entitlement for the assessment period

(1) Regulations may provide that, where the Board assumes responsibility for an eligible scheme, the entitlement of any member of the scheme to compensation under this Chapter is, in such circumstances as may be prescribed, postponed for the whole or any part of the assessment period for which he continued in employment after attaining normal pension age.
(2) Regulations under subsection (1) may provide that the postponement is on such terms and conditions (including those relating to increments) as may be prescribed.
(3) In subsection (1) the reference to "normal pension age" is to normal pension age, within the meaning of paragraph 34 of Schedule 7, in relation to the pension or lump sum in respect of which the entitlement to compensation arises.

### 165  Guaranteed minimum pensions

(1) The Board must notify the Commissioners of Inland Revenue where, by reason of it assuming responsibility for an eligible scheme in accordance with this Chapter, the trustees or managers of the scheme are discharged from their liability to provide a

guaranteed minimum pension (within the meaning of the Pension Schemes Act 1993 (c. 48)) to or in respect of a member of the scheme.
(2) Notification under subsection (1) must be given as soon as reasonably practicable.
(3) In section 47 of the Pension Schemes Act 1993 (further provision concerning entitlement to a guaranteed minimum pension for the purposes of section 46), after subsection (7) insert—

"(8) For the purposes of section 46, a person shall be treated as entitled to a guaranteed minimum pension to which he would have been entitled but for the fact that the trustees or managers were discharged from their liability to provide that pension on the Board of the Pension Protection Fund assuming responsibility for the scheme."

**166 Duty to pay scheme benefits unpaid at assessment date etc**

(1) This section applies where the Board assumes responsibility for a scheme in accordance with this Chapter.
(2) Subject to subsection (4), the Board must pay any amount by way of pensions or other benefits which a person had become entitled to payment of under the scheme rules before the assessment date but which remained unpaid at the time the transfer notice was received by the trustees or managers of the scheme.
(3) If, immediately before the assessment date, the person is entitled to the amount but has postponed payment of it, subsection (2) does not apply.
(4) Subsection (2) does not apply in relation to the amount of—
    (a) any transfer payment, or
    (b) any payment in respect of a refund of contributions.
(5) Regulations may provide that, in prescribed circumstances, where—
    (a) a member of the scheme died before the commencement of the assessment period, and
    (b) during the period beginning with the assessment date and ending with the receipt by the trustees or managers of the transfer notice, a person became entitled under the scheme rules to a benefit of a prescribed description in respect of the member,
    that person's entitlement to the benefit, or to any part of it, is, for the purposes of subsection (2), to be treated as having arisen before the assessment date.
(6) Regulations may make provision requiring the Board, in such circumstances as may be prescribed, to take such steps (including making payments) as may be prescribed in respect of rights of prescribed descriptions to which members of the scheme were entitled immediately before the commencement of the assessment period.
(7) For the purposes of regulations made under subsection (6)—
    (a) this Chapter (other than this subsection), and
    (b) the scheme rules (including any relevant legislative provision within the meaning of section 318(3)),
    are to have effect subject to such modifications as may be prescribed.
(8) In this section "assessment date" is to be construed in accordance with Schedule 7.

**167 Modification of Chapter where liabilities discharged during assessment period**

(1) Regulations may modify any of the provisions of this Chapter as it applies to cases—
    (a) where any liability to provide pensions or other benefits to or in respect of any

member or members under a scheme is discharged during an assessment period in relation to the scheme by virtue of—
    (i) regulations under section 135(4), or
    (ii) the Board validating any action mentioned in section 135(9), or
    (b) where, in prescribed circumstances, any such liability of a prescribed description is discharged on the assessment date but before the commencement of the assessment period.
(2) In this section "assessment date" is to be construed in accordance with Schedule 7.

**168 Administration of compensation**

(1) Regulations may make further provision regarding the operation and administration of this Chapter.
(2) Regulations under subsection (1) may, in particular, make provision—
    (a) prescribing the manner in which and time when compensation is to be paid (including provision requiring periodic compensation to be paid by instalments);
    (b) for calculating the amounts of compensation according to a prescribed scale or otherwise adjusting them to avoid fractional amounts or facilitate computation;
    (c) prescribing the circumstances and manner in which compensation to which a person ("the beneficiary") is entitled may be made to another person on behalf of the beneficiary for any purpose (including the discharge in whole or in part of an obligation of the beneficiary or any other person);
    (d) for the payment or distribution of compensation to or among persons claiming to be entitled on the death of any person and for dispensing with strict proof of their title;
    (e) for the recovery of amounts of compensation paid by the Board in excess of entitlement (together with interest on such amounts for the period from payment until recovery);
    (f) specifying the circumstances in which payment of compensation can be suspended.
(3) In this section "compensation" means compensation payable under Schedule 7 or under section 141(2).

*Discharge of Board's liabilities*

**169 Discharge of liabilities in respect of compensation**

(1) This section applies where the Board assumes responsibility for an eligible scheme in accordance with this Chapter.
(2) The Board may provide for the discharge of any liability imposed by this Chapter to provide compensation—
    (a) by the taking out of a policy of insurance or a number of such policies;
    (b) by the entry into an annuity contract or a number of such contracts;
    (c) by the transfer of the benefit of such a policy or policies or such a contract or contracts;
    (d) in prescribed circumstances, by the payment of a cash sum calculated in the prescribed manner.

**170 Discharge of liabilities in respect of money purchase benefits**

(1) This subsection applies where—

(a) the Board assumes responsibility for an eligible scheme in accordance with this Chapter, and
(b) one or more members are entitled, or have accrued rights, under the scheme rules to money purchase benefits.
(2) Regulations must make provision in respect of cases to which subsection (1) applies requiring the Board to secure that liabilities in respect of such benefits transferred to the Board under section 161 are discharged by it in the prescribed manner.
(3) The provision made under subsection (2) must include provision prescribing the manner in which protected rights are to be given effect to.
(4) In this section—
"accrued rights", under the scheme rules of a scheme, include pension credit rights within the meaning of section 124(1) of the Pensions Act 1995 (c. 26);
"protected rights" has the meaning given by section 10 of the Pension Schemes Act 1993 (c. 48) (protected rights and money purchase benefits).

*Equal treatment*

**171 Equal treatment**

(1) This section applies where—
   (a) a woman has been employed on like work with a man in the same employment,
   (b) a woman has been employed on work rated as equivalent with that of a man in the same employment, or
   (c) a woman has been employed on work which, not being work in relation to which paragraph (a) or (b) applies, was, in terms of the demands made on her (for instance under such headings as effort, skill and decision), of equal value to that of a man in the same employment,
   and service in that employment was pensionable service under an occupational pension scheme.
(2) If, apart from this subsection, any of the payment functions so far as it relates (directly or indirectly) to that pensionable service—
   (a) is or becomes less favourable to the woman than it is to the man, or
   (b) is or becomes less favourable to the man than it is to the woman,
   that function has effect with such modifications as are necessary to ensure that the provision is not less favourable.
(3) Subsection (2) does not operate in relation to any difference as between a woman and a man in the operation of any of the payment functions if the Board proves that the difference is genuinely due to a material factor which—
   (a) is not the difference of sex, but
   (b) is a material difference between the woman's case and the man's case.
(4) Subsection (2) does not apply in such circumstances as may be prescribed.
(5) This section has effect in relation to the exercise of any payment function in so far as it relates (directly or indirectly) to any pensionable service on or after 17th May 1990.
(6) In this section—
"payment function" means any function conferred on the Board by or by virtue of this Chapter which relates to a person's entitlement to or the payment of any amount under or by virtue of—
   (a) the pension compensation provisions,

(b) section 166 (duty to pay scheme benefits unpaid at assessment date etc),
(c) section 169 (discharge of liabilities in respect of compensation), or
(d) section 170 (discharge of liabilities in respect of money purchase benefits);
"pensionable service" has the meaning given by section 124(1) of the Pensions Act 1995 (c. 26).

*Relationship with fraud compensation regime*

**172 Relationship with fraud compensation regime**

(1) No transfer notice may be given in respect of a scheme within the first 12 months of an assessment period in relation to the scheme.
(2) Where an application has been made under section 182 (application for fraud compensation payment), no transfer notice may be given until—
    (a) the Board has determined the application,
    (b) the period within which the Board's determination may be reviewed by virtue of Chapter 6 has expired, and
    (c) if the determination is so reviewed—
        (i) the review and any reconsideration,
        (ii) any reference to the PPF Ombudsman in respect of the determination, and
        (iii) any appeal against his determination or directions,
    has been finally disposed of.
(3) Subsection (4) applies where during an assessment period in relation to a scheme the Board determines to make one or more fraud compensation payments ("the fraud compensation") to the trustees or managers of the scheme under Chapter 4 of this Part.
(4) For the purposes of determining whether the condition in section 127(2)(a), 128(2)(a), 152(2) or 158(1) is satisfied, any fraud compensation payment which becomes payable after the relevant time is, to the extent that it relates to a loss incurred by the scheme before that time, to be regarded as an asset of the scheme at that time.
(5) For the purposes of subsection (4) "the relevant time"—
    (a) in the case of section 127(2)(a), has the same meaning as in that provision,
    (b) in the case of section 128(2)(a), has the same meaning as in that provision,
    (c) in the case of section 152(2) means the reconsideration time (within the meaning of section 151), and
    (d) in the case of section 158(1), has the same meaning as in that provision.
(6) Subsection (4) does not apply to the extent that the fraud compensation is payable in respect of a reduction in the value of money purchase assets of the scheme.
    For this purpose "money purchase assets" means assets representing the value of any rights in respect of money purchase benefits under the scheme rules.

*The fund*

**173 Pension Protection Fund**

(1) The Pension Protection Fund shall consist of—
    (a) property and rights transferred to the Board under section 161(2)(a),
    (b) contributions levied under section 174 or 175 (initial and pension protection levies),

(c) money borrowed by the Board under section 115 for the purposes of this Chapter,

(d) any income or capital gain credited under subsection (2),

(e) any amount paid to the Board by virtue of section 139 (repayment of loans to trustees or managers and payment of interest),

(f) amounts recovered under section 163(4)(a) or by virtue of section 168(2)(e) (overpayments),

(g) any amount paid to the Board in respect of a debt due to the Board under section 40(7) by virtue of a contribution notice under section 38,

(h) any property transferred or amounts paid to the Board as required by a restoration order under section 52,

(i) any amount paid to the Board in respect of a debt due to the Board under section 56(7) by virtue of a contribution notice under section 55,

(j) amounts transferred from the Fraud Compensation Fund under section 187 (fraud compensation transfer payments), and

(k) amounts of a prescribed description (other than amounts paid, directly or indirectly, to the Board by the Crown).

(2) The Board must credit to the Pension Protection Fund any income or capital gain arising from the assets in the Fund.

(3) The following are to be paid or transferred out of the Pension Protection Fund—

(a) any sums required to meet liabilities transferred to the Board under section 161(2)(a),

(b) any sums required to make payments in accordance with the pension compensation provisions,

(c) any sums required for the repayment of, and the payment of interest on, money within subsection (1)(c),

(d) any sums required to make loans under section 139 (loans to trustees or managers),

(e) any sums required to make payments under section 163(4)(b) (underpayments during the assessment period),

(f) any sums required to make payments under section 166 (payment of unpaid scheme benefits etc),

(g) any sums required to discharge liabilities under section 169 or 170 (discharge of liabilities in respect of compensation or money purchase benefits),

(h) any sums required to meet any liabilities arising from obligations imposed on the Board by a restoration order under section 52,

(i) any property (other than sums) required to meet any liabilities—

(i) transferred to the Board as mentioned in paragraph (a) and arising from obligations imposed by a restoration order under section 52, or

(ii) arising from obligations imposed on the Board by such an order,

(j) any sums required to meet expenditure incurred by virtue of section 161(5) and paragraph 7 of Schedule 6 (expenditure associated with transfer of property, rights and liabilities to the Board), and

(k) sums required for prescribed purposes.

(4) No other amounts are to be paid or transferred out of the Pension Protection Fund.

(5) In subsection (1) (other than paragraph (d)) and subsection (3) (other than paragraph (c)) any reference to a provision of this Act is to be read as including a reference to any provision in force in Northern Ireland corresponding to that provision.

*The levies*

## 174 Initial levy

(1) Regulations must make provision for imposing a levy ("the initial levy") in respect of eligible schemes for the period ("the initial period") which—
   (a) begins with the day appointed for this purpose by the regulations, and
   (b) ends on the following 31st March or, if the regulations so provide, 12 months after the day referred to in paragraph (a).
(2) The regulations must prescribe—
   (a) the factors by reference to which the initial levy is to be assessed,
   (b) the rate of the levy, and
   (c) the time or times during the initial period when the levy, or any instalment of the levy, becomes payable.
(3) Regulations under this section may only be made with the approval of the Treasury.

## 175 Pension protection levies

(1) For each financial year falling after the initial period, the Board must impose both of the following—
   (a) a risk-based pension protection levy in respect of all eligible schemes;
   (b) a scheme-based pension protection levy in respect of eligible schemes.
   In this Chapter "pension protection levy" means a levy imposed in accordance with this section.
(2) For the purposes of this section—
   (a) a risk-based pension protection levy is a levy assessed by reference to—
      (i) the difference between the value of a scheme's assets (disregarding any assets representing the value of any rights in respect of money purchase benefits under the scheme rules) and the amount of its protected liabilities,
      (ii) except in relation to any prescribed scheme or scheme of a prescribed description, the likelihood of an insolvency event occurring in relation to the employer in relation to a scheme, and
      (iii) if the Board considers it appropriate, one or more other risk factors mentioned in subsection (3), and
   (b) a scheme-based pension protection levy is a levy assessed by reference to—
      (i) the amount of a scheme's liabilities to or in respect of members (other than liabilities in respect of money purchase benefits), and
      (ii) if the Board considers it appropriate, one or more other scheme factors mentioned in subsection (4).
(3) The other risk factors referred to in subsection (2)(a)(iii) are factors which the Board considers indicate one or more of the following—
   (a) the risks associated with the nature of a scheme's investments when compared with the nature of its liabilities;
   (b) such other matters as may be prescribed.
(4) The other scheme factors referred to in subsection (2)(b)(ii) are—
   (a) the number of persons who are members, or fall within any description of member, of a scheme;
   (b) the total annual amount of pensionable earnings of active members of a scheme;
   (c) such other factors as may be prescribed.
(5) The Board must, before the beginning of each financial year, determine in respect of that year—

(a) the factors by reference to which the pension protection levies are to be assessed,
(b) the time or times by reference to which those factors are to be assessed,
(c) the rate of the levies, and
(d) the time or times during the year when the levies, or any instalment of levy, becomes payable.

(6) Different risk factors, scheme factors or rates may be determined in respect of different descriptions of scheme.

(7) The rate determined in respect of a description of scheme may be nil.

(8) In this section—
"initial period" is to be construed in accordance with section 174;
"pensionable earnings", in relation to an active member under a scheme, means the earnings by reference to which a member's entitlement to benefits would be calculated under the scheme rules if he ceased to be an active member at the time by reference to which the factor within subsection (4)(b) is to be assessed.

(9) In this section and sections 176 to 181 "financial year" means a period of 12 months ending with 31st March.

(10) The Board's duty to impose pension protection levies in respect of any financial year is subject to—
(a) section 177 (amounts to be raised by the pension protection levies), and
(b) section 180 (transitional provision).

## 176 Supplementary provisions about pension protection levies

(1) The Board must consult such persons as it considers appropriate in the prescribed manner before making a determination under section 175(5) in respect of a financial year if—
(a) that year is the first financial year for which the Board is required to impose levies under section 175,
(b) any of the proposed levy factors or levy rates is different, or applies to a different description of scheme, from the levy factors and levy rates in respect of the pension protection levies imposed in the previous financial year, or
(c) no consultation has been required under this subsection in relation to the pension protection levies imposed for either of the previous two financial years.

(2) The Board must publish details of any determination under section 175(5) in the prescribed manner.

## 177 Amounts to be raised by the pension protection levies

(1) Before determining the pension protection levies to be imposed for a financial year, the Board must estimate the amount which will be raised by the levies it proposes to impose.

(2) The Board must impose levies for a financial year in a form which it estimates will raise an amount not exceeding the levy ceiling for the financial year.

(3) The pension protection levies imposed for a financial year must be in a form which the Board estimates will result in at least 80% of the amount raised by the levies for that year being raised by the risk-based pension protection levy.

(4) For the first financial year after the transitional period, regulations may modify subsection (2) so as to provide that the reference to the levy ceiling for the financial year is to be read as a reference to such lower amount as is prescribed.

(5) For the second financial year after the transitional period and for any subsequent

financial year, the Board must impose pension protection levies in a form which it estimates will raise an amount which does not exceed by more than 25% the amount estimated under subsection (1) in respect of the pension protection levies imposed for the previous financial year.

(6) The Secretary of State may by order substitute a different percentage for the percentage for the time being specified in subsection (5).

(7) Before making an order under subsection (6), the Secretary of State must consult such persons as he considers appropriate.

(8) Regulations under subsection (4), or an order under subsection (6), may be made only with the approval of the Treasury.

(9) In this section—
   (a) "risk-based pension protection levy" and "scheme-based pension protection levy" are to be construed in accordance with section 175, and
   (b) "transitional period" has the meaning given by section 180(3).

**178 The levy ceiling**

(1) The Secretary of State must, before the beginning of each financial year for which levies are required to be imposed under section 175, specify by order the amount which is to be the levy ceiling for that year for the purposes of section 177.

(2) An order under subsection (1) in respect of the first financial year for which levies are imposed under section 175 may be made only with the approval of the Treasury.

(3) Subject to subsection (8), the amount specified under subsection (1) for a financial year ("the current year") after the first year for which levies are imposed under section 175 must be—
   (a) where it appears to the Secretary of State that the level of earnings in the review period has increased, the amount specified under subsection (1) for the previous financial year increased by the earnings percentage for that review period specified under subsection (6), and
   (b) in any other case, the amount specified under subsection (1) for the previous financial year.

(4) In subsection (3)—
"level of earnings" means the general level of earnings obtaining in Great Britain;
"review period" in relation to the current year means the period of 12 months ending with the prescribed date in the previous financial year.

(5) For the purposes of subsection (3), the Secretary of State must, in respect of each review period, review the general level of earnings obtaining in Great Britain and any changes in that level; and for the purposes of such a review the Secretary of State may estimate the general level of earnings in such manner as he thinks appropriate.

(6) Where it appears to the Secretary of State that the general level of earnings has increased during the review period, he must by order specify the percentage by which that level has so increased ("the earnings percentage").

(7) The Secretary of State must discharge the duties imposed by subsections (5) and (6) in respect of a review period before the beginning of the prescribed period which ends at the time the first financial year after the review period begins.

(8) The Secretary of State may, on the recommendation of the Board and with the approval of the Treasury, make an order under subsection (1) in respect of a financial

year which specifies an amount exceeding the amount required to be specified under subsection (3).

(9) Before making a recommendation for the purposes of subsection (8), the Board must consult such persons as it considers appropriate in the prescribed manner.

## 179 Valuations to determine scheme underfunding

(1) For the purposes of enabling risk-based pension protection levies (within the meaning of section 175) to be calculated in respect of eligible schemes, regulations may make provision requiring the trustees or managers of each such scheme to provide the Board or the Regulator on the Board's behalf—
   (a) with an actuarial valuation of the scheme at such intervals as may be prescribed, and
   (b) with such other information as the Board may require in respect of the assets and protected liabilities of the scheme at such times as may be prescribed.

(2) For the purposes of this section, in relation to a scheme—
   "an actuarial valuation" means a written valuation of the scheme's assets and protected liabilities prepared and signed by the actuary;
   "the actuary" means—
   (a) the actuary appointed under section 47(1)(b) of the Pensions Act 1995 (c. 26) (professional advisers) in relation to the scheme, or
   (b) if no such actuary has been appointed—
      (i) a person with prescribed qualifications or experience, or
      (ii) a person approved by the Secretary of State.

(3) Regulations under this section may prescribe how—
   (a) the assets and the protected liabilities of schemes, and
   (b) their amount or value,
are to be determined, calculated and verified.

(4) Subject to any provision made under subsection (3), those matters are to be determined, calculated and verified in accordance with guidance issued by the Board.

(5) In calculating the amount of any liabilities for the purposes of a valuation required by virtue of this section, a provision of the scheme rules which limits the amount of the scheme's liabilities by reference to the value of its assets is to be disregarded.

(6) In this section references to "assets" do not include assets representing the value of any rights in respect of money purchase benefits under the scheme rules.

## 180 Pension protection levies during the transitional period

(1) Regulations may provide that in respect of any financial year during the transitional period—
   (a) sections 175 and 177(3) are to apply with such modifications as may be prescribed;
   (b) section 177(2) is to apply as if the reference to the levy ceiling for the financial year were a reference to such lower amount as is specified in the regulations.

(2) Regulations which contain provision made by virtue of subsection (1)(b) may only be made with the approval of the Treasury.

(3) For the purposes of this section "the transitional period" means the prescribed period beginning immediately after the initial period (within the meaning of section 174).

(4) If the transitional period begins with a date other than 1st April, regulations may provide that any provision of this section or of sections 175 to 179 applies, with such modifications as may be prescribed, in relation to—
   (a) the period beginning at the same time as the transitional period and ending with the following 31st March, and
   (b) the financial year which begins immediately after that period.

**181 Calculation, collection and recovery of levies**

(1) This section applies in relation to—
   (a) the initial levy imposed under section 174 in respect of a scheme, and
   (b) any pension protection levy imposed under section 175 in respect of a scheme.
(2) The levy is payable to the Board by or on behalf of—
   (a) the trustees or managers of the scheme, or
   (b) any other prescribed person.
(3) The Board must in respect of the levy—
   (a) determine the schemes in respect of which it is imposed,
   (b) calculate the amount of the levy in respect of each of those schemes, and
   (c) notify any person liable to pay the levy in respect of the scheme of the amount of the levy in respect of the scheme and the date or dates on which it becomes payable.
(4) The Board may require the Regulator to discharge, on the Board's behalf, its functions under subsection (3) in respect of the levy.
(5) Where a scheme is an eligible scheme for only part of the period for which the levy is imposed, except in prescribed circumstances, the amount of the levy payable in respect of the scheme for that period is such proportion of the full amount as that part bears to that period.
(6) An amount payable by a person on account of the levy is a debt due from him to the Board.
(7) An amount so payable may be recovered—
   (a) by the Board, or
   (b) if the Board so determines, by the Regulator on its behalf.
(8) Regulations may make provision relating to—
   (a) the collection and recovery of amounts payable by way of any levy in relation to which this section applies;
   (b) the circumstances in which any such amount may be waived.

## CHAPTER 4
## FRAUD COMPENSATION

*Entitlement to fraud compensation*

**182 Cases where fraud compensation payments can be made**

(1) The Board shall, in accordance with this section, make one or more payments (in this Part referred to as "fraud compensation payments") in respect of an occupational pension scheme if—
   (a) the scheme is not a prescribed scheme or a scheme of a prescribed description,
   (b) the value of the assets of the scheme has been reduced since the relevant date and the Board considers that there are reasonable grounds for believing that the

reduction was attributable to an act or omission constituting a prescribed offence,
  (c) subsection (2), (3) or (4) applies,
  (d) an application is made which meets the requirements of subsection (5), and
  (e) the application is made within the authorized period.
(2) This subsection applies where—
  (a) a qualifying insolvency event has occurred in relation to the employer in relation to the scheme,
  (b) after that event, a scheme failure notice has been issued under section 122(2)(a) in relation to the scheme and that notice has become binding, and
  (c) a cessation event has not occurred in relation to the scheme in respect of a cessation notice which has been issued during the period—
    (i) beginning with the occurrence of the insolvency event, and
    (ii) ending immediately before the issuing of the scheme failure notice under section 122(2)(a),
   and the occurrence of such a cessation event in respect of a cessation notice issued during that period is not a possibility.
(3) This subsection applies where—
  (a) in relation to the scheme, an application has been made under subsection (1), or a notification has been given under subsection (5)(a), of section 129, and
  (b) in response to that application, or the notice given by the Regulator under subsection (4) of that section, the Board has issued a scheme failure notice under section 130(2) in relation to the scheme and that notice has become binding.
(4) This subsection applies where—
  (a) the scheme is not an eligible scheme,
  (b) the employer in relation to the scheme is unlikely to continue as a going concern,
  (c) the prescribed requirements are met in relation to the employer,
  (d) the application under this section states that the case is one in relation to which paragraphs (b) and (c) apply, and
  (e) in response to that application the Board has issued a notice under section 183(2) confirming that a scheme rescue is not possible in relation to the scheme and that notice has become binding.
(5) An application meets the requirements of this subsection if—
  (a) it is made by a prescribed person, and
  (b) it is made in the prescribed manner and contains the prescribed information.
(6) Subject to subsection (7), an application is made within the authorized period if it is made within the period of 12 months beginning with the later of—
  (a) the time of the relevant event, or
  (b) the time when the auditor or actuary of the scheme, or the trustees or managers, knew or ought reasonably to have known that a reduction of value falling within subsection (1)(b) had occurred,
   or within such longer period as the Board may determine in any case.
(7) No application for fraud compensation may be made under this section in respect of a scheme once a transfer notice is given in relation to the scheme under section 160.
(8) For the purposes of this section, an insolvency event ("the current event") in relation to the employer is a qualifying insolvency event if—
  (a) it occurs on or after the day appointed under section 126(2), and
  (b) either—

(i) it is the first insolvency event to occur in relation to the employer on or after that day, or
(ii) a cessation event has occurred in relation to the scheme in respect of a cessation notice issued during the period—
(a) beginning with the occurrence of the last insolvency event which occurred before the current event, and
(b) ending with the occurrence of the current event.
(9) For the purposes of this section—
(a) a cessation event in relation to a scheme occurs when a cessation notice in relation to the scheme becomes binding,
(b) a "cessation notice" means—
(i) a withdrawal notice issued in relation to the scheme under section 122(2)(b) (scheme rescue has occurred),
(ii) a withdrawal notice issued in relation to the scheme under section 130(3) (scheme rescue has occurred),
(iii) a withdrawal notice issued in relation to the scheme under section 148 (no insolvency event has occurred or is likely to occur),
(iv) a notice issued in relation to the scheme under section 183(2)(b) (scheme rescue has occurred), or
(v) a notice issued under section 122(4) (inability to confirm status of scheme) in a case where the notice has become binding and section 148 does not apply,
(c) the occurrence of a cessation event in relation to a scheme in respect of a cessation notice issued during a particular period ("the specified period") is a possibility until each of the following are no longer reviewable—
(i) any cessation notice which has been issued in relation to the scheme during the specified period,
(ii) any failure to issue such a cessation notice during the specified period,
(iii) any notice which has been issued by the Board under Chapter 2 or 3 which is relevant to the issue of a cessation notice in relation to the scheme during the specified period or to such a cessation notice which has been issued during that period becoming binding,
(iv) any failure to issue such a notice as is mentioned in sub-paragraph (iii), and
(d) the issue of, or failure to issue, a notice is to be regarded as reviewable—
(i) during the period within which it may be reviewed by virtue of Chapter 6, and
(ii) if the matter is so reviewed, until—
(a) the review and any reconsideration,
(b) any reference to the PPF Ombudsman in respect of the matter, and
(c) any appeal against his determination or directions,
has been finally disposed of.
(10) In this section—
"auditor" and "actuary", in relation to an occupational pension scheme, have the meaning given by section 47 of the Pensions Act 1995 (c. 26);
"the relevant event" means—
(a) in a case where subsection (2) applies in relation to an eligible scheme, the event within paragraph (a) of that subsection,
(b) in any other case where subsection (2) applies, the issue of the scheme

failure notice under section 122(2)(a) mentioned in paragraph (b) of that subsection,
  (c) in a case where subsection (3) applies, the event within paragraph (a) of that subsection, and
  (d) in a case where subsection (4) applies, the trustees or managers becoming aware that paragraphs (b) and (c) of that subsection apply in relation to the scheme;
  "the relevant date" means—
  (a) in the case of an occupational pension scheme established under a trust, 6th April 1997, and
  (b) in any other case, the day appointed by the Secretary of State by order for the purposes of this section.
(11) This section is subject to section 184(2) (no fraud compensation payments to be made until settlement date determined).

## 183 Board's duties in respect of certain applications under section 182

(1) This section applies where, in a case to which paragraphs (a) to (c) of subsection (4) of section 182 apply (employer not likely to continue as going concern etc), the Board receives an application within paragraph (d) of that subsection.
(2) If the Board is able to confirm—
  (a) that a scheme rescue is not possible, or
  (b) that a scheme rescue has occurred,
  it must, as soon as reasonably practicable, issue a notice to that effect.
(3) Where the Board issues a notice under subsection (2), it must, as soon as reasonably practicable, give a copy of the notice to—
  (a) the Regulator,
  (b) the trustees or managers of the scheme,
  (c) if the trustees or managers did not make the application mentioned in subsection (1), the person who made that application, and
  (d) any insolvency practitioner in relation to the employer or, if there is no such insolvency practitioner, the employer.
(4) For the purposes of this Chapter a notice issued under subsection (2) is not binding until—
  (a) the period within which the issue of the notice may be reviewed by virtue of Chapter 6 has expired, and
  (b) if the issue of the notice is so reviewed—
    (i) the review and any reconsideration,
    (ii) any reference to the PPF Ombudsman in respect of the issue of the notice, and
    (iii) any appeal against his determination or directions,
  has been finally disposed of and the notice has not been revoked, varied or substituted.
(5) Where a notice issued under subsection (2) becomes binding, the Board must as soon as reasonably practicable give a notice to that effect together with a copy of the binding notice to the persons to whom it is required to give a copy notice under subsection (3).
(6) A notice under subsection (5) must be in the prescribed form and contain such information as may be prescribed.

(7) Section 130(5) (circumstances in which scheme rescue can or cannot be confirmed) applies for the purposes of this section.

**184 Recovery of value**

(1) Where an application for a fraud compensation payment is made, the trustees or managers must obtain any recoveries of value, to the extent that they may do so without disproportionate cost and within a reasonable time.
(2) No fraud compensation payment may be made until the date ("the settlement date") determined by the Board, after consulting the trustees or managers of the scheme in question, as the date after which further recoveries of value are unlikely to be obtained without disproportionate cost or within a reasonable time.
(3) In this section "recovery of value" means any increase in the value of the assets of the scheme, being an increase attributable to any payment received (otherwise than from the Board) by the trustees or managers of the scheme in respect of any act or omission—
    (a) which there are reasonable grounds for believing constituted an offence prescribed for the purposes of paragraph (b) of section 182(1), and
    (b) to which any reduction in value falling within that paragraph was attributable.
(4) It is for the Board to determine whether anything received by the trustees or managers of the scheme is to be treated as a payment received in respect of any such act or omission.
For this purpose "payment" includes any money or money's worth.

**185 Fraud compensation payments**

(1) Where the Board determines to make one or more fraud compensation payments, it must make the payment or payments to the trustees or managers of the scheme in accordance with this section.
(2) A fraud compensation payment may be made on such terms (including terms requiring repayment in whole or in part) and on such conditions as the Board considers appropriate.
(3) The amount of the payment (or, if there is more than one, the aggregate) must not exceed the difference between—
    (a) the amount of the reduction (or, if more than one, the aggregate amount of the reductions) within section 182(1)(b), and
    (b) the amount of any recoveries of value obtained before the settlement date (within the meaning of section 184(2)).
(4) Subject to subsection (3), the Board—
    (a) must determine the amount of any fraud compensation payment in accordance with regulations made for the purposes of this subsection, and
    (b) must take account of any interim payment already made under section 186.
(5) The Board must give written notice of its determination under subsection (4) to—
    (a) the Regulator,
    (b) the trustees or managers of the scheme,
    (c) if the trustees or managers did not make the application under section 182 (fraud compensation payments), the person who made that application, and
    (d) any insolvency practitioner in relation to the employer or, if there is no such insolvency practitioner, the employer.

## 186 Interim payments

(1) The Board may, on an application under section 182, make a payment or payments to the trustees or managers of an occupational pension scheme if—
  (a) it is of the opinion that—
    (i) the case is one to which subsection (1) of that section applies or may apply, and
    (ii) the trustees or managers would not otherwise be able to meet liabilities of a prescribed description, but
  (b) it has not determined the settlement date under section 184.
(2) Amounts payable under this section must not exceed the amounts determined in accordance with regulations.
(3) The Board may, except in prescribed circumstances, recover so much of any payment made under subsection (1) as it considers appropriate if, after the payment is made, it determines—
  (a) that the case is not one to which section 182(1) applies, or
  (b) that the amount of the payment was excessive.
(4) Subject to that, a payment under subsection (1) may be made on such terms (including terms requiring repayment in whole or in part) and on such conditions as the Board considers appropriate.

## 187 Board's powers to make fraud compensation transfer payments

(1) This section applies where—
  (a) the Board assumes responsibility for a scheme in accordance with Chapter 3,
  (b) the value of the assets of the scheme was reduced after the relevant date but before the transfer notice (within the meaning of section 160) was received by the trustees or managers of the scheme and there are reasonable grounds for believing that the reduction was attributable to an act or omission constituting an offence prescribed for the purposes of section 182(1)(b), and
  (c) no application was made under section 182 in respect of that reduction (or any such application was withdrawn before it was determined).
(2) The Board may transfer an amount from the Fraud Compensation Fund to the Pension Protection Fund ("fraud compensation transfer payment") in respect of the reduction in value, subject to the provisions of this section.
(3) The Board must obtain any recoveries of value, to the extent that it may do so without disproportionate cost and within a reasonable time.
(4) No fraud compensation transfer payment may be made until the date determined by the Board as the date after which further recoveries of value are unlikely to be obtained without disproportionate cost and within a reasonable time.
(5) In this section "recovery of value" means any increase in the value of the Pension Protection Fund, being an increase attributable to any payment received (otherwise than under this section) by the Board in respect of any act or omission—
  (a) which there are reasonable grounds for believing constituted an offence prescribed for the purposes of section 182(1)(b), and
  (b) to which any reduction in value falling within subsection (1)(b) above was attributable.
(6) It is for the Board to determine whether anything received by it is to be treated as a payment received in respect of any such act or omission.
  For this purpose "payment" includes any money or money's worth.

(7) The amount of any fraud compensation transfer payment (or, if there is more than one, the aggregate) must not exceed the difference between—
   (a) the amount of the reduction (or, if more than one, the aggregate amount of the reductions) within subsection (1)(b), and
   (b) the amount of any recoveries of value obtained by the Board before the date determined by the Board under subsection (4).
(8) Subject to subsection (7), the Board must determine the amount of any fraud compensation transfer payment in accordance with regulations made for the purposes of this subsection.
(9) In this section "the relevant date" has the meaning given by section 182(10).

*The fund*

**188 Fraud Compensation Fund**

(1) The Fraud Compensation Fund shall consist of—
   (a) any property and rights transferred under section 302 (dissolution of the Pensions Compensation Board) which the Board designates as assets of the Fund,
   (b) contributions levied under section 189 (fraud compensation levy),
   (c) money borrowed by the Board under section 115 for the purposes of this Chapter,
   (d) amounts recovered under section 186 (recovery of interim payments), and
   (e) any income or capital gain credited under subsection (2).
(2) The Board must credit to the Fraud Compensation Fund any income or capital gain arising from the assets in the Fund.
(3) The following are payable out of the Fraud Compensation Fund—
   (a) sums required to meet liabilities transferred to the Board under section 302 (dissolution of the Pensions Compensation Board), which the Board designates as liabilities of the Fund,
   (b) payments under section 185 (fraud compensation payments),
   (c) payments under section 186(1) (interim payments),
   (d) amounts required to be transferred to the Pension Protection Fund under section 187 (fraud compensation transfer payments),
   (e) money required for the repayment of, and the payment of interest on, money within subsection (1)(c).
(4) No other amounts are payable out of the Fraud Compensation Fund.
(5) In subsection (1) (other than paragraphs (a) and (e)) and subsection (3) (other than paragraphs (a) and (e)) any reference to a provision of this Act is to be read as including a reference to any provision in force in Northern Ireland corresponding to that provision.

*The levy*

**189 Fraud compensation levy**

(1) For the purposes of meeting expenditure payable out of the Fraud Compensation Fund, regulations may provide for the imposition of a levy ("fraud compensation levy") in respect of occupational pension schemes.

(2) Subsection (1) does not apply in relation to any scheme which is prescribed or of a description prescribed under section 182(1)(a) (schemes not eligible for fraud compensation).
(3) A fraud compensation levy imposed in respect of a scheme is payable to the Board by or on behalf of—
   (a) the trustees or managers of the scheme, or
   (b) any other prescribed person.
(4) A fraud compensation levy is so payable at prescribed times and at a rate, not exceeding the prescribed rate, determined by the Board.
(5) In determining the amount of expenditure in respect of which a fraud compensation levy is to be imposed, the Board may take one year with another (and, in doing so, must have regard to expenditure estimated to be incurred in current or future periods and to actual expenditure incurred in previous periods).
(6) Notice of the rates determined by the Board under subsection (4) must be given to prescribed persons in the prescribed manner.
(7) The Board must in respect of any fraud compensation levy imposed under this section—
   (a) determine the schemes in respect of which it is imposed,
   (b) calculate the amount of the levy in respect of each of those schemes, and
   (c) notify any person liable to pay the levy in respect of the scheme of the amount of the levy in respect of the scheme and the date or dates on which it becomes payable.
(8) The Board may require the Regulator to discharge, on the Board's behalf, its functions under subsection (7) in respect of the levy.
(9) An amount payable by a person on account of a fraud compensation levy is a debt due from him to the Board.
(10) An amount so payable may be recovered—
   (a) by the Board, or
   (b) if the Board so determines, by the Regulator on its behalf.
(11) Without prejudice to the generality of subsection (1), (9) or (10), regulations under this section may include provision relating to—
   (a) the collection and recovery of amounts payable by way of levy under this section;
   (b) the circumstances in which any such amount may be waived.

## CHAPTER 5
## GATHERING INFORMATION

### 190 Information to be provided to the Board etc

(1) Regulations may require such persons as may be prescribed to provide—
   (a) to the Board, or
   (b) to a person—
      (i) with whom the Board has made arrangements under paragraph 18 of Schedule 5, and
      (ii) who is authorised by the Board for the purposes of the regulations,
   information of a prescribed description at such times, or in such circumstances, as may be prescribed.

(2) Regulations under subsection (1) may in particular make provision for requiring such persons as may be prescribed to provide any information or evidence needed for a determination of entitlement to compensation under Chapter 3 of this Part.

(3) Regulations made by virtue of paragraph (b) of that subsection must make provision regarding the manner in which the persons required to provide information are to be notified of the identity of the person authorized as mentioned in sub-paragraph (ii) of that paragraph.

**191 Notices requiring provision of information**

(1) Any person to whom subsection (3) applies may be required by a notice in writing to produce any document, or provide any other information, which is—
   (a) of a description specified in the notice, and
   (b) relevant to the exercise of the Board's functions in relation to an occupational pension scheme.

(2) A notice under subsection (1) may be given by—
   (a) the Board, or
   (b) a person authorized by the Board for the purposes of this section in relation to the scheme.

(3) This subsection applies to—
   (a) a trustee or manager of the scheme,
   (b) a professional adviser in relation to the scheme,
   (c) the employer in relation to the scheme,
   (d) an insolvency practitioner in relation to the employer, and
   (e) any other person appearing to the Board, or person giving the notice, to be a person who holds, or is likely to hold, information relevant to the discharge of the Board's functions in relation to the scheme.

(4) Where the production of a document, or the provision of information, is required by a notice given under subsection (1), the document must be produced, or information must be provided, in such a manner, at such a place and within such a period as may be specified in the notice.

**192 Entry of premises**

(1) An appointed person may, for the purpose of enabling or facilitating the performance of any function of the Board in relation to an occupational pension scheme, at any reasonable time enter scheme premises and, while there—
   (a) may make such examination and inquiry as may be necessary for such purpose,
   (b) may require any person on the premises to produce, or secure the production of, any document relevant to that purpose for inspection by the appointed person,
   (c) may take copies of any such document,
   (d) may take possession of any document appearing to be such a document or take in relation to any such document any other steps which appear necessary for preserving it or preventing interference with it,
   (e) may, in the case of any such document which consists of information which is stored in electronic form and is on, or accessible from, the premises, require the information to be produced in a form—
      (i) in which it can be taken away, and
      (ii) in which it is legible or from which it can readily be produced in a legible form, and

(f) may, as to any matter relevant to the exercise of the Board's functions in relation to the scheme, examine, or require to be examined, either alone or in the presence of another person, any person on the premises whom he has reasonable cause to believe to be able to give information relevant to that matter.

(2) Premises are scheme premises for the purposes of subsection (1) if the appointed person has reasonable grounds to believe that—
   (a) they are being used for the business of the employer,
   (b) an insolvency practitioner in relation to the employer is acting there in that capacity,
   (c) documents relevant to—
      (i) the administration of the scheme, or
      (ii) the employer,
      are being kept there, or
   (d) the administration of the scheme, or work connected with the administration of the scheme, is being carried out there,
   unless the premises are a private dwelling-house not used by, or by permission of, the occupier for the purposes of a trade or business.

(3) An appointed person applying for admission to any premises for the purposes of this section must, if so required, produce his certificate of appointment.

(4) When exercising a power under this section an appointed person may be accompanied by such persons as he considers appropriate.

(5) Any document of which possession is taken under this section may be retained until the end of the period comprising—
   (a) the period of 12 months beginning with the date on which possession was taken of the document, and
   (b) any extension of that period under subsection (6).

(6) The Board may before the end of the period mentioned in subsection (5) (including any extension of it under this subsection) extend it by such period not exceeding 12 months as the Board considers appropriate.

(7) In this section "appointed person" means a person appointed by the Board for the purposes of this section in relation to the scheme.

## 193 Penalties relating to sections 191 and 192

(1) A person who, without reasonable excuse, neglects or refuses to provide information or produce a document when required to do so under section 191 is guilty of an offence.

(2) A person who without reasonable excuse—
   (a) intentionally delays or obstructs an appointed person exercising any power under section 192,
   (b) neglects or refuses to produce, or secure the production of, any document when required to do so under that section, or
   (c) neglects or refuses to answer a question or to provide information when so required,
   is guilty of an offence.

(3) In subsection (2)(a) "appointed person" has the same meaning as it has in section 192.

(4) A person guilty of an offence under subsection (1) or (2) is liable on summary conviction to a fine not exceeding level 5 on the standard scale.

(5) An offence under subsection (1) or (2)(b) or (c) may be charged by reference to any day or longer period of time; and a person may be convicted of a second or subsequent offence by reference to any period of time following the preceding conviction of the offence.

(6) Any person who intentionally and without reasonable excuse alters, suppresses, conceals or destroys any document which he is or is liable to be required to produce under section 191 or 192 is guilty of an offence.

(7) Any person guilty of an offence under subsection (6) is liable—
- (a) on summary conviction, to a fine not exceeding the statutory maximum;
- (b) on conviction on indictment, to a fine or imprisonment for a term not exceeding two years, or both.

### 194 Warrants

(1) A justice of the peace may issue a warrant under this section if satisfied on information on oath given by or on behalf of the Board that there are reasonable grounds for believing—
- (a) that there is on, or accessible from, any premises any document—
  - (i) whose production has been required under section 191 or 192, or any corresponding provision in force in Northern Ireland, and
  - (ii) which has not been produced in compliance with that requirement,
- (b) that there is on, or accessible from, any premises any document relevant to the exercise of the Board's functions in relation to an occupational pension scheme whose production could be so required and, if its production were so required, the document—
  - (i) would not be produced, but
  - (ii) would be removed, or made inaccessible, from the premises, hidden, tampered with or destroyed, or
- (c) that a person will do any act which constitutes a misuse or misappropriation of the assets of an occupational pension scheme and that there is on, or accessible from, any premises any document—
  - (i) which relates to whether the act will be done, and
  - (ii) whose production could be required under section 191 or 192, or any corresponding provision in force in Northern Ireland.

(2) A warrant under this section shall authorize an inspector—
- (a) to enter the premises specified in the information, using such force as is reasonably necessary for the purpose,
- (b) to search the premises and—
  - (i) take possession of any document appearing to be such a document as is mentioned in subsection (1), or
  - (ii) take in relation to such a document any other steps which appear necessary for preserving it or preventing interference with it,
- (c) to take copies of any such document,
- (d) to require any person named in the warrant to provide an explanation of any such document or to state where it may be found or how access to it may be obtained, and
- (e) in the case of any such document which consists of information which is stored in electronic form and is on, or accessible from, the premises, to require the information to be produced in a form—

        (i) in which it can be taken away, and
        (ii) in which it is legible or from which it can readily be produced in a legible form.
(3) When executing a warrant under this section, an inspector may be accompanied by such persons as he considers appropriate.
(4) A warrant under this section continues in force until the end of the period of one month beginning with the day on which it is issued.
(5) Any document of which possession is taken under this section may be retained until the end of the period comprising—
    (a) the period of 12 months beginning with the date on which possession was taken of the document, and
    (b) any extension of that period under subsection (6).
(6) The Board may before the end of the period mentioned in subsection (5) (including any extension of it under this subsection) extend it by such period not exceeding 12 months as the Board considers appropriate.
(7) In this section "inspector" means a person appointed by the Board as an inspector.
(8) In the application of this section in Scotland—
    (a) the reference to a justice of the peace is to be read as a reference to the sheriff, and
    (b) the references in subsections (1) and (2)(a) to information are to be read as references to evidence.

*Provision of false or misleading information*

## 195 Offence of providing false or misleading information to the Board

(1) Any person who knowingly or recklessly provides information which is false or misleading in a material particular is guilty of an offence if the information—
    (a) is provided in purported compliance with a requirement under—
        (i) section 190 (information to be provided to the Board etc),
        (ii) section 191 (notices requiring provision of information), or
        (iii) section 192 (entry of premises), or
    (b) is provided otherwise than as mentioned in paragraph (a) but in circumstances in which the person providing the information intends, or could reasonably be expected to know, that it would be used by the Board for the purposes of exercising its functions under this Act.
(2) Any person guilty of an offence under subsection (1) is liable—
    (a) on summary conviction, to a fine not exceeding the statutory maximum;
    (b) on conviction on indictment, to a fine or imprisonment for a term not exceeding two years, or both.

*Use of information*

## 196 Use of information

Information held by the Board in the exercise of any of its functions may be used by the Board for the purposes of, or for any purpose connected with or incidental to, the exercise of its functions.

*Disclosure of information*

## 197 Restricted information

(1) Restricted information must not be disclosed—
  (a) by the Board, or
  (b) by any person who receives the information directly or indirectly from the Board.
(2) Subsection (1) is subject to—
  (a) subsection (3), and
  (b) sections 198 to 203 and 235.
(3) Subject to section 202(4), restricted information may be disclosed with the consent of the person to whom it relates and (if different) the person from whom the Board obtained it.
(4) For the purposes of this section and sections 198 to 203, "restricted information" means any information obtained by the Board in the exercise of its functions which relates to the business or other affairs of any person, except for information—
  (a) which at the time of the disclosure is or has already been made available to the public from other sources, or
  (b) which is in the form of a summary or collection of information so framed as not to enable information relating to any particular person to be ascertained from it.
(5) Any person who discloses information in contravention of this section is guilty of an offence and liable—
  (a) on summary conviction, to a fine not exceeding the statutory maximum;
  (b) on conviction on indictment, to a fine or imprisonment for a term not exceeding two years, or both.
(6) Information which—
  (a) is obtained under section 191 by a person authorized under subsection (2)(b) of that section, but
  (b) if obtained by the Board, would be restricted information,
  is treated for the purposes of subsections (1) and (3) and sections 198 to 203 as restricted information which the person has received from the Board.

## 198 Disclosure for facilitating exercise of functions by the board

(1) Section 197 does not preclude the disclosure of restricted information in any case in which disclosure is for the purpose of enabling or assisting the Board to exercise its functions.
(2) Subsection (3) applies where, in order to enable or assist the Board properly to exercise any of its functions, the Board considers it necessary to seek advice from any qualified person on any matter of law, accountancy, valuation or other matter requiring the exercise of professional skill.
(3) Section 197 does not preclude the disclosure by the Board to a person qualified to provide that advice of such information as appears to the Board to be necessary to ensure that he is properly informed with respect to the matters on which his advice is sought.

## 199 Disclosure for facilitating exercise of functions by the Regulator

Section 197 does not preclude the disclosure of restricted information in any case in which disclosure is for the purpose of enabling or assisting the Regulator to exercise its functions.

## 200 Disclosure for facilitating exercise of functions by other supervisory authorities

(1) Section 197 does not preclude the disclosure by the Board of restricted information to any person specified in the first column of Schedule 8 if the Board considers that the disclosure would enable or assist that person to exercise the functions specified in relation to him in the second column of that Schedule.

(2) The Secretary of State may after consultation with the Board—
  (a) by order amend Schedule 8 by—
    (i) adding any person exercising regulatory functions and specifying functions in relation to that person,
    (ii) removing any person for the time being specified in the Schedule, or
    (iii) altering the functions for the time being specified in the Schedule in relation to any person, or
  (b) by order restrict the circumstances in which, or impose conditions subject to which, disclosure may be made to any person for the time being specified in the Schedule.

## 201 Other permitted disclosures

(1) Section 197 does not preclude the disclosure by the Board of restricted information to—
  (a) the Secretary of State,
  (b) the Commissioners of Inland Revenue or their officers, or
  (c) the Department for Social Development in Northern Ireland,
  if the disclosure appears to the Board to be desirable or expedient in the interests of members of occupational pension schemes or in the public interest.

(2) Section 197 does not preclude the disclosure of restricted information—
  (a) by or on behalf of—
    (i) the Board, or
    (ii) any public authority (within the meaning of section 6 of the Human Rights Act 1998 (c. 42)) which receives the information directly or indirectly from the Board,
    for any of the purposes specified in section 17(2)(a) to (d) of the Anti-terrorism, Crime and Security Act 2001 (c. 24) (criminal proceedings and investigations),
  (b) in connection with any proceedings arising out of—
    (i) this Act,
    (ii) the Welfare Reform and Pensions Act 1999 (c. 30),
    (iii) the Pensions Act 1995 (c. 26), or
    (iv) the Pension Schemes Act 1993 (c. 48),
    or any corresponding enactment in force in Northern Ireland, or any proceedings for breach of trust in relation to an occupational pension scheme,
  (c) with a view to the institution of, or otherwise for the purposes of, proceedings under—
    (i) section 7 or 8 of the Company Directors Disqualification Act 1986 (c. 46), or
    (ii) Article 10 or 11 of the Companies (Northern Ireland) Order 1989 (S.I. 1989/2404 (N.I. 18)) or of the Company Directors Disqualification (Northern Ireland) Order 2002 (S.I. 2002/3150 (N.I. 4)),
  (d) in connection with any proceedings under—

(i) the Insolvency Act 1986 (c. 45), or
   (ii) the Insolvency (Northern Ireland) Order 1989 (S.I. 1989/2405 (N.I. 19)),
   which the Board has instituted or in which it has a right to be heard,
  (e) with a view to the institution of, or otherwise for the purposes of, any disciplinary proceedings relating to the exercise of his professional duties by a solicitor, an actuary, an accountant or an insolvency practitioner,
  (f) with a view to the institution of, or otherwise for the purpose of, any disciplinary proceedings relating to the exercise by a public servant of his functions, or
  (g) in pursuance of a Community obligation.
(3) In subsection (2)(f), "public servant" means an officer or servant of the Crown or of any prescribed authority.
(4) Section 197 does not preclude the disclosure by the Board of restricted information to—
  (a) the Director of Public Prosecutions,
  (b) the Director of Public Prosecutions for Northern Ireland,
  (c) the Lord Advocate,
  (d) a procurator fiscal, or
  (e) a constable.
(5) Section 197 does not preclude the disclosure of restricted information in any case where the disclosure is required by or by virtue of an enactment.
(6) Section 197 does not preclude the disclosure of restricted information in any case where the disclosure is to a Regulator-appointed trustee of an occupational pension scheme for the purpose of enabling or assisting him to exercise his functions in relation to the scheme.
(7) In subsection (6), "Regulator-appointed trustee" means a trustee appointed by the Regulator under section 7 or 23(1) of the Pensions Act 1995 (c. 26) or any corresponding provision in force in Northern Ireland.
(8) Section 197 does not preclude the disclosure by any person mentioned in subsection (1) or (4) of restricted information obtained by the person by virtue of that subsection, if the disclosure is made with the consent of the Board.
(9) Section 197 does not preclude the disclosure by any person specified in the first column of Schedule 8 of restricted information obtained by the person by virtue of section 200(1), if the disclosure is made—
  (a) with the consent of the Board, and
  (b) for the purpose of enabling or assisting the person to exercise any functions specified in relation to him in the second column of the Schedule.
(10) Before deciding whether to give its consent to such a disclosure as is mentioned in subsection (8) or (9), the Board must take account of any representations made to it, by the person seeking to make the disclosure, as to the desirability of the disclosure or the necessity for it.
(11) Section 18 of the Anti-terrorism, Crime and Security Act 2001 (c. 24) (restriction on disclosure of information for overseas purposes) has effect in relation to a disclosure authorized by subsection (2) as it has effect in relation to a disclosure authorized by any of the provisions to which section 17 of that Act applies.

**202  Tax information**

(1) This section applies to information held by any person in the exercise of tax functions about any matter which is relevant, for the purposes of those functions, to tax

or duty in the case of an identifiable person (in this section referred to as "tax information").
(2) No obligation as to secrecy imposed by section 182 of the Finance Act 1989 (c. 26) or otherwise shall prevent the disclosure of tax information to the Board for the purpose of enabling or assisting the Board to discharge its functions.
(3) Where tax information is disclosed to the Board by virtue of subsection (2) above or section 19 of the Anti-terrorism, Crime and Security Act 2001 (disclosure of information held by revenue departments), it must, subject to subsection (4), be treated for the purposes of section 197 as restricted information.
(4) Sections 197(3), 198 to 201, 203 and 235 do not apply to tax information which is disclosed to the Board as mentioned in subsection (3), and such information may not be disclosed by the Board or any person who receives the information directly or indirectly from the Board except—
   (a) to, or in accordance with authority given by, the Commissioners of Inland Revenue or the Commissioners of Customs and Excise, or
   (b) with a view to the institution of, or otherwise for the purposes of, any criminal proceedings.
(5) In this section "tax functions" has the same meaning as in section 182 of the Finance Act 1989 (c. 26).

*Provision of information to members of schemes etc*

### 203 Provision of information to members of schemes etc

(1) Regulations may—
   (a) require the Board to provide information of prescribed descriptions to such persons as may be prescribed at prescribed times, or
   (b) require trustees or managers of occupational pension schemes to provide such information—
      (i) relating to the exercise of the Board's functions in relation to any scheme of which they are trustees or managers,
      (ii) relating to any notice issued or application or determination made under Chapter 2, 3 or 4 which relates to any such scheme, or
      (iii) otherwise relating to the Board's involvement with any such scheme,
   as may be prescribed to prescribed persons at prescribed times or in prescribed circumstances.
(2) Section 197 does not preclude the disclosure of restricted information by the Board which relates to the entitlement of a particular individual to compensation under Chapter 3 if the disclosure is made to that individual or to a person authorized by him.
(3) Section 197 does not preclude the disclosure of restricted information by the Board if—
   (a) the information relates to the exercise of the Board's functions in relation to an occupational pension scheme,
   (b) the disclosure is made to—
      (i) all affected persons, or
      (ii) all affected persons of a particular description, and
   (c) the Board is satisfied that, in all the circumstances, it is reasonable to make the disclosure.

(4) In subsection (3) "affected person", in relation to an occupational pension scheme, means a person—
   (a) who is a member of the scheme, or
   (b) who is for the time being nominated by a member of the scheme for the purposes of that subsection.
(5) A nomination by a member of the scheme under subsection (4)(b)—
   (a) may be made by notice in writing given by the member,
   (b) becomes effective when the notice is received by the Board, and
   (c) ceases to be effective when the Board receives a further notice from the member withdrawing the nomination.
(6) In the case of an occupational pension scheme, section 197 does not preclude the disclosure of restricted information by the Board if—
   (a) the disclosure is made to any of the following in relation to the scheme—
      (i) a trustee or manager,
      (ii) any professional adviser,
      (iii) the employer,
      (iv) the insolvency practitioner in relation to the employer,
   (b) the information is relevant to the exercise of that person's functions in relation to the scheme, and
   (c) the Board considers that it is reasonable in all the circumstances to make the disclosure for the purpose of facilitating the exercise of those functions.

*Interpretation*

**204 Sections 190 to 203: interpretation**

(1) This section applies for the purposes of sections 190 to 203.
(2) "Document" includes information recorded in any form, and any reference to production of a document, in relation to information recorded otherwise than in a legible form, is to producing a copy of the information—
   (a) in a legible form, or
   (b) in a form from which it can readily be produced in a legible form.
(3) Where the Board has assumed responsibility for a scheme—
   (a) any reference to the Board's functions in relation to the scheme includes a reference to the functions which it has by virtue of having assumed responsibility for the scheme, and
   (b) any reference to a trustee, manager, professional adviser or employer in relation to the scheme is to be read as a reference to a person who held that position in relation to the scheme before the Board assumed responsibility for it.

*Reports*

**205 Publishing reports etc**

(1) The Board may, if it considers it appropriate to do so in any particular case, publish a report of the exercise of, or any matter arising out of or connected with the exercise of, any of its functions in that case.
(2) The publication of a report under subsection (1) may be in such form and manner as the Board considers appropriate.
(3) For the purposes of the law of defamation, the publication of any matter by the Board is privileged unless the publication is shown to be made with malice.

## CHAPTER 6
## REVIEWS, APPEALS AND MALADMINISTRATION

*Review etc by the Board*

**206 Meaning of "Reviewable matters"**

(1) For the purposes of this Chapter, "reviewable matter" means a matter mentioned in Schedule 9.
(2) Regulations may provide, in relation to any reference in that Schedule to a failure by the Board to do any act or make any determination, that—
  (a) the reference is to be construed as a reference to a failure by the Board to do the act or make the determination within a prescribed period, and
  (b) the reference is to be construed as not including a failure to do the act or make the determination which first occurs after a prescribed time.
(3) Regulations may make provision suspending the effect of any determination, direction or other act of the Board, or any notice given or issued by it, which relates to a reviewable matter until—
  (a) the period within which the matter may be reviewed by virtue of this Chapter has expired, and
  (b) if the matter is so reviewed—
    (i) the review and any reconsideration,
    (ii) any reference to the PPF Ombudsman in respect of the matter, and
    (iii) any appeal against his determination or directions,
  has been finally disposed of.
(4) Regulations may amend Schedule 9 by—
  (a) adding to it any other description of determination, act or failure of, or matter determined or for determination by, the Board, or
  (b) removing from it any such determination, act, failure or matter for the time being mentioned in it.
(5) Regulations under subsection (4) may also modify any provision of this Part in consequence of provision made by virtue of paragraph (a) or (b) of that subsection.

**207 Review and reconsideration by the Board of reviewable matters**

(1) Regulations must—
  (a) provide for the Board, on the written application of an interested person, to give a decision ("a review decision") on any reviewable matter, and
  (b) require a committee of the Board constituted for the purposes of this section (the "Reconsideration Committee"), on the written application of an interested person following a review decision, to reconsider the reviewable matter and give a decision ("a reconsideration decision").
(2) In subsection (1), "interested person" in relation to a reviewable matter, means a person of a description prescribed in relation to reviewable matters of that description.
(3) Regulations under subsection (1) may—
  (a) permit a review decision in respect of a reviewable matter of a prescribed description to be made otherwise than on an application, and

(b) permit a reconsideration decision in respect of such a matter to be made otherwise than on an application.
(4) Regulations under subsection (1) must provide for the Board's powers on making a review decision or reconsideration decision to include power—
　　　(a) to vary or revoke the determination, direction or other decision already made by the Board in respect of the reviewable matter,
　　　(b) to substitute a different determination, direction or decision,
　　　(c) to provide for such variations, revocations or substitutions, or any determinations, directions or other decisions made as a result of the review decision or reconsideration decision, to be treated as if they were made at such time (which may be a time prior to the making of the review decision or reconsideration decision) as the Board considers appropriate,
　　　(d) to provide for any notice varied, substituted, issued or given by the Board as a result of the review decision or reconsideration decision, to be treated as if it were issued or given at such time (which may be a time prior to the making of the review decision or reconsideration decision) as the Board considers appropriate,
　　　(e) generally to deal with the matters arising on the review decision or reconsideration decision as if they had arisen on the original determination, direction or decision,
　　　(f) to pay such compensation as the Board considers appropriate to such persons as it may determine, and
　　　(g) to make savings and transitional provision.
(5) Regulations under subsection (1) must include provision—
　　　(a) about applications under the regulations for a review decision or reconsideration decision in respect of a reviewable matter, including the times by which they are to be made,
　　　(b) requiring notice—
　　　　　(i) of such applications, or
　　　　　(ii) of a decision of the Board or the Reconsideration Committee by virtue of subsection (3) to give a review decision or reconsider a reviewable matter otherwise than on such an application,
　　　to be given to interested persons in relation to the matter,
　　　(c) with a view to securing that individuals concerned in giving a reconsideration decision were not concerned in the reviewable matter in respect of which the decision is to be made,
　　　(d) as to the procedure for reaching and giving decisions under the regulations, including—
　　　　　(i) rights of interested persons to make representations to the Reconsideration Committee on a reconsideration under regulations made under subsection (1)(b), and
　　　　　(ii) the times by which decisions are to be given, and
　　　(e) requiring notice of the review decision or the reconsideration decision in respect of a reviewable matter to be given to interested persons in relation to the matter.
(6) Provision required by subsection (5)(c) may modify paragraphs 15 and 16 of Schedule 5 (membership and procedure of committees of the Board).

## 208 Investigation by the Board of complaints of maladministration

(1) Regulations must make provision for dealing with relevant complaints.
(2) For the purposes of this Chapter, "relevant complaint" means a complaint—
    (a) by a person who is or might become entitled to compensation under the pension compensation provisions, or
    (b) by a person who has or may make an application under section 182 (fraud compensation),
    alleging that he has sustained injustice in consequence of maladministration in connection with any act or omission by the Board or any person exercising functions on its behalf.
(3) Regulations under subsection (1) must—
    (a) provide for the Board to investigate and give decisions on matters complained of in relevant complaints, and
    (b) provide for a committee of the Board, on applications following such decisions, to investigate matters complained of and give decisions on them.
(4) Such regulations may, in particular, make provision—
    (a) about the making of relevant complaints and applications under the regulations, including the times by which they are to be made,
    (b) with a view to securing that individuals concerned in giving a decision were not concerned in the matter which is the subject of the relevant complaint in question,
    (c) as to the procedure for reaching and giving decisions under the regulations, including—
        (i) rights of prescribed persons to make representations to the Board, on an investigation under regulations made under subsection (3)(b), and
        (ii) the times by which decisions are to be given, and
    (d) requiring notice—
        (i) of a relevant complaint under the regulations, or
        (ii) of a decision under the regulations in respect of the complaint,
        to be given to prescribed persons in relation to the matter.
(5) Regulations under subsection (1) may confer power on the Board to pay such compensation as it considers appropriate to such persons as it considers have sustained injustice in consequence of the matters complained of.
(6) The power conferred by subsection (4)(b) includes power to modify paragraphs 15 and 16 of Schedule 5 (membership and procedure of committees of the Board).

*The PPF Ombudsman*

## 209 The Ombudsman for the Board of the Pension Protection Fund

(1) There is to be a commissioner to be known as the Ombudsman for the Board of the Pension Protection Fund (in this Act referred to as "the PPF Ombudsman").
(2) The PPF Ombudsman is to be appointed by the Secretary of State on such terms and conditions as are determined by the Secretary of State.
(3) The PPF Ombudsman—
    (a) is to hold and vacate office in accordance with the terms and conditions of his appointment, and
    (b) may resign or be removed from office in accordance with those terms and conditions.

(4) The Secretary of State may by order make provision—
- (a) about the payment, or provision for payment, of remuneration, compensation for loss of office, pension, allowances or gratuities to or in respect of the PPF Ombudsman;
- (b) about the reimbursement of the PPF Ombudsman in respect of any expenses incurred by him in the performance of his functions;
- (c) about the staff of the PPF Ombudsman and the provision of facilities (including additional staff) to him;
- (d) about the delegation of the functions of the PPF Ombudsman to his staff or to any such additional staff;
- (e) authorising the PPF Ombudsman—
  - (i) to charge such fees as are specified in the order;
  - (ii) to charge fees sufficient to meet such costs as are specified in the order;
- (f) conferring powers to enable the PPF Ombudsman to obtain such information and documents as he may require for the performance of his functions;
- (g) about restrictions on the disclosure of information held by him.

(5) An order under subsection (4)(e)—
- (a) may prescribe, or authorize the PPF Ombudsman to determine, the time at which any fee is due, and
- (b) provide that any fee which is owed to the PPF Ombudsman by virtue of an order under subsection (4)(e) may be recovered as a debt due to the PPF Ombudsman.

(6) The Secretary of State must pay to the PPF Ombudsman out of money provided by Parliament such sums as may be required to be paid by the Secretary of State to or in respect of the PPF Ombudsman by virtue of an order under subsection (4).

(7) Regulations may provide for the imposition of a levy in respect of eligible schemes for the purpose of meeting expenditure of the Secretary of State under subsection (6).

(8) Where regulations make such provision, subsections (2), (3), (5), (6) and (7) of section 117 (administration levy) apply in relation to the levy as they apply in relation to an administration levy (within the meaning of that section), except that in subsection (7) the reference to subsection (1) of that section is to be read as a reference to subsection (7) of this section.

**210 Deputy PPF Ombudsmen**

(1) The Secretary of State may appoint one or more persons to act as a deputy to the PPF Ombudsman (in this Chapter referred to as "a Deputy PPF Ombudsman").

(2) Any such appointment is to be on such terms and conditions as the Secretary of State determines.

(3) A Deputy PPF Ombudsman—
- (a) is to hold and vacate office in accordance with the terms and conditions of his appointment, and
- (b) may resign or be removed from office in accordance with those terms and conditions.

(4) A Deputy PPF Ombudsman may perform the functions of the PPF Ombudsman—
- (a) during any vacancy in that office,
- (b) at any time when the PPF Ombudsman is for any reason unable to discharge his functions, or
- (c) at any other time, with the consent of the Secretary of State.

(5) References to the PPF Ombudsman in relation to the performance of his functions are accordingly to be construed as including references to a Deputy PPF Ombudsman in relation to the performance of those functions.

(6) An order by the Secretary of State under section 209(4) may make provision—
   (a) about the payment, or provision for payment, of remuneration, compensation for loss of office, pension, allowances or gratuities to or in respect of a Deputy PPF Ombudsman;
   (b) about the reimbursement of any expenses incurred by a Deputy PPF Ombudsman in the performance of any of the PPF Ombudsman's functions.

## 211  Status etc of the PPF Ombudsman and deputies

(1) In Part 3 of Schedule 1 to the House of Commons Disqualification Act 1975 (c. 24) (other disqualifying offices), at the appropriate place insert—
   "Ombudsman for the Board of the Pension Protection Fund and any deputy to that Ombudsman appointed under section 210 of the Pensions Act 2004."

(2) In Part 3 of Schedule 1 to the Northern Ireland Assembly Disqualification Act 1975 (c. 25) (other disqualifying offices), at the appropriate place insert—
   "Ombudsman for the Board of the Pension Protection Fund and any deputy to that Ombudsman appointed under section 210 of the Pensions Act 2004."

(3) The persons to whom section 1 of the Superannuation Act 1972 (c. 11) (persons to or in respect of whom benefits may be provided by schemes under that section) applies are to include—
   the PPF Ombudsman
   a Deputy PPF Ombudsman
   the employees of the PPF Ombudsman.

(4) The PPF Ombudsman must pay to the Minister for the Civil Service, at such times as he may direct, such sums as he may determine in respect of the increase attributable to subsection (3) in the sums payable out of money provided by Parliament under that Act.

(5) In Schedule 4 to the Parliamentary Commissioner Act 1967 (c. 13) (relevant tribunals for the purposes of section 5(7) of that Act), at the appropriate place insert—
   "The Ombudsman for the Board of the Pension Protection Fund established under section 209 of the Pensions Act 2004."

## 212  Annual reports to Secretary of State

(1) The PPF Ombudsman must prepare a report on the discharge of his functions for each financial year.

(2) The PPF Ombudsman must send each report to the Secretary of State as soon as practicable after the end of the financial year for which it is prepared.

(3) The Secretary of State must arrange for the publication of each report sent to him under subsection (2).

(4) In this section "financial year" means—
   (a) the period beginning with the date on which the PPF Ombudsman is established and ending with the next following 31st March, and
   (b) each successive period of 12 months.

*References to the PPF Ombudsman*

**213 Reference of reviewable matter to the PPF Ombudsman**

(1) Regulations must make provision—
   (a) for a reviewable matter to be referred to the PPF Ombudsman following a reconsideration decision under regulations made under subsection (1)(b) or by virtue of subsection (3)(b) of section 207 in respect of the matter, and
   (b) for the PPF Ombudsman—
      (i) to investigate and determine what (if any) is the appropriate action for the Board to take in relation to the matter, and
      (ii) to remit the matter to the Board with directions for the purpose of giving effect to his determination.
(2) Regulations under subsection (1) must make provision about the making of references to the PPF Ombudsman, including provision—
   (a) about the descriptions of persons who may make them,
   (b) about the manner of making such references, including the times by which they are to be made, and
   (c) for prescribed persons to be notified of—
      (i) references made under the regulations, and
      (ii) determinations and directions given under the regulations.
(3) Regulations under subsection (1) must—
   (a) require the PPF Ombudsman to conduct an oral hearing in relation to any reviewable matter referred to him under the regulations or to dispose of the matter on the basis of written representations,
   (b) enable the PPF Ombudsman to consider evidence relating to the matter which was not available to the Board or the Reconsideration Committee, and
   (c) make other provision about the procedure for conducting investigations, and reaching and giving determinations, under the regulations, including the times by which determinations are to be given.
(4) The provision that may be made by virtue of subsection (3)(c) includes provision—
   (a) conferring rights on prescribed persons—
      (i) to make representations to the PPF Ombudsman in relation to a reviewable matter referred to him by virtue of this section,
      (ii) to be heard or represented at any oral hearing by the PPF Ombudsman in relation to such a matter,
   (b) about the consideration of evidence by the PPF Ombudsman, including—
      (i) production of documents,
      (ii) oral hearings,
      (iii) expert evidence,
      (iv) attendance of witnesses,
   (c) conferring rights on prescribed persons to continue a reference made by a person who has died or is otherwise unable to act for himself,
   (d) as to the costs or expenses of prescribed persons,
   (e) conferring rights on prescribed persons to apply for a stay (or in Scotland, for a sist) in relation to prescribed legal proceedings which begin after the reference is made and conferring power on the relevant court to make an order staying (or sisting) the proceedings if it is satisfied of prescribed matters, and

(f) for securing that any determination or direction of the PPF Ombudsman under the regulations is binding on prescribed persons.
(5) Regulations under subsection (1) may include provision—
  (a) conferring power on the PPF Ombudsman to direct the Board to pay such compensation as he considers appropriate to such persons as he may direct,
  (b) conferring power on the Board to make such payments,
  (c) conferring power on the PPF Ombudsman to direct that—
    (i) any determinations, directions or other decisions which are made by the Board in accordance with any determination or direction given by him, or
    (ii) any variations, revocations or substitutions of its determinations, directions or other decisions which are made by the Board in accordance with any determination or direction given by him,
   are to be treated as if they were made at such time (which may be a time prior to his determination or direction) as he considers appropriate,
  (d) conferring power on the PPF Ombudsman to direct that any notice varied, substituted, issued or given by the Board in accordance with any determination or direction given by him is to be treated—
    (i) as if it were issued or given at such time (which may be a time prior to his determination or direction) as he considers appropriate;
    (ii) as if it became binding for the purposes of this Part at the time at which he gives his determination or direction or at such later time as he considers appropriate,
  (e) prescribing the circumstances in which any determination or other act of the Board in accordance with any determination or direction given by the PPF Ombudsman, is not to be treated as being a reviewable matter for the purposes of this Chapter, and
  (f) conferring such other powers on the Board as may be required when a matter is remitted to it (including such powers as the Board may have on making a review decision or a reconsideration decision under regulations made under section 207(1)).

## 214 Investigation by PPF Ombudsman of complaints of maladministration

(1) Regulations must provide for the investigation and determination by the PPF Ombudsman of such matters as may be prescribed following decisions on relevant complaints given by the Board or the committee of the Board referred to in section 208(3)(b) under regulations made under that section.
(2) Regulations under this section must make provision—
  (a) prescribing the descriptions of person who may refer matters to the PPF Ombudsman under the regulations,
  (b) about the manner in which such references may be made, including the times by which they are to be made,
  (c) about the procedure for conducting investigations, and reaching and giving determinations, on such references, including the times by which the determinations are to be given,
  (d) about the powers of the PPF Ombudsman on making such determinations, including—
    (i) the power to direct the Board to pay such compensation as he considers

appropriate to such persons as he considers have sustained injustice in consequence of the matters complained of, and

　　　(ii) the power to direct the Board to take or refrain from taking such other steps as he may specify,

　(e) conferring such powers on the Board as are necessary to comply with such requirements,

　(f) for prescribed persons to be notified of—
　　　(i) references to the PPF Ombudsman under the regulations, and
　　　(ii) determinations and directions by the PPF Ombudsman under the regulations,

　(g) conferring rights on prescribed persons—
　　　(i) to make representations to the PPF Ombudsman in relation to a matter referred to him by virtue of this section,
　　　(ii) to be heard or represented at any oral hearing by the PPF Ombudsman in relation to such a matter,

　(h) about the consideration of evidence by the PPF Ombudsman, including—
　　　(i) production of documents,
　　　(ii) oral hearings,
　　　(iii) expert evidence,
　　　(iv) attendance of witnesses,

　(i) conferring rights on prescribed persons to continue a reference made by a person who has died or is otherwise unable to act for himself,

　(j) as to the costs or expenses of prescribed persons,

　(k) conferring rights on prescribed persons to apply for a stay (or in Scotland, for a sist) in relation to prescribed legal proceedings which begin after the reference is made and conferring power on the relevant court to make an order staying (or sisting) the proceedings if it is satisfied of prescribed matters, and

　(l) for securing that any determination or direction of the PPF Ombudsman under the regulations is binding on prescribed persons.

## 215　Referral of questions of law

The PPF Ombudsman may refer any question of law arising for determination in connection with—

　(a) a reviewable matter referred to him by virtue of regulations under section 213, or
　(b) a matter referred to him by virtue of regulations under section 214,

to, in England and Wales, the High Court or, in Scotland, the Court of Session.

## 216　Publishing reports etc

(1) If the PPF Ombudsman considers it appropriate to do so in any particular case, he may publish in such form and manner as he considers appropriate a report of any investigation carried out by virtue of regulations under section 213 or 214 and of the result of that investigation.

(2) For the purposes of the law of defamation, the publication of any matter by the PPF Ombudsman under or by virtue of any provision of this Chapter shall be absolutely privileged.

## 217　Determinations of the PPF Ombudsman

(1) A person bound by a determination or direction by the PPF Ombudsman by virtue

of regulations made under section 213 or 214 may appeal on a point of law arising from the determination or direction—
   (a) in England and Wales, to the High Court, or
   (b) in Scotland, to the Court of Session.
(2) Any determination or direction of the PPF Ombudsman is enforceable—
   (a) in England and Wales, in a county court as if it were a judgment or order of that court, and
   (b) in Scotland, in like manner as an extract registered decree arbitral bearing warrant for execution issued by the sheriff court of any sheriffdom in Scotland.

## 218 Obstruction etc of the PPF Ombudsman

(1) This section applies if any person—
   (a) without lawful excuse obstructs the PPF Ombudsman in the performance of his functions, or
   (b) is guilty of any act or omission in relation to an investigation by the PPF Ombudsman under regulations made under section 213 or 214, which, if that investigation were a proceeding in the court, would constitute contempt of court.
(2) The PPF Ombudsman may certify the offence to the court.
(3) Where an offence is certified under subsection (2), the court may—
   (a) inquire into the matter,
   (b) hear any witnesses who may be produced against or on behalf of the person charged with the offence and any statement that may be offered in defence, and
   (c) deal with him in any manner in which the court could deal with him if he had committed the like offence in relation to the court.
(4) This section is to be construed, in its application to Scotland, as if contempt of court were categorized as an offence in Scots law.
(5) In this section "the court" means—
   (a) in England and Wales, a county court;
   (b) in Scotland, the sheriff.

## CHAPTER 7
## MISCELLANEOUS

*Backdating the winding up of eligible schemes*

## 219 Backdating the winding up of eligible schemes

(1) Subsection (3) applies where—
   (a) a qualifying insolvency event occurs in relation to the employer in relation to an eligible scheme, and
   (b) the winding up of the scheme begins at or after the time of that event but not later than the first of the following events in relation to the scheme—
      (i) a scheme failure notice or a withdrawal notice issued under section 122(2) in relation to the scheme becoming binding,
      (ii) a withdrawal notice issued under section 148 in relation to the scheme becoming binding, or
      (iii) a notice issued under section 122(4) becoming binding in a case where section 148 does not apply.
(2) Subsection (3) also applies where—

    (a) the trustees or managers of an eligible scheme—
        (i) make an application to the Board under subsection (1) of section 129, or
        (ii) receive a notice from the Board under subsection (5)(a) of that section, and
    (b) the winding up of the scheme begins—
        (i) at or after the time the application is made or notice is received, but
        (ii) not later than a scheme failure notice or a withdrawal notice issued under section 130(2) or (3) in relation to the scheme becoming binding.
(3) The winding up of the scheme is to be taken as beginning immediately before the event within subsection (1)(a) or, as the case may be, subsection (2)(a) if—
    (a) the winding up is in pursuance of an order of the Regulator under section 11 of the Pensions Act 1995 (c. 26) directing the winding up of the scheme, or
    (b) in any other case, the trustees or managers of the scheme so determine.
(4) In a case where subsection (3) applies, the Regulator may by order direct any person specified in the order—
    (a) to take such steps as are so specified as it considers are necessary as a result of the winding up of the scheme beginning in accordance with that subsection, and
    (b) to take those steps within a period specified in the order.
(5) If the trustees or managers of a scheme fail to comply with a direction to them contained in an order under subsection (4), section 10 of the Pensions Act 1995 (civil penalties) applies to any trustee or manager who has failed to take all reasonable steps to secure compliance.
(6) That section also applies to any other person who, without reasonable excuse, fails to comply with a direction to him contained in an order under subsection (4).
(7) For the purposes of this section "qualifying insolvency event" has the same meaning as in section 127.
(8) Subsection (4) of section 128 applies for the purposes of subsection (2) of this section as it applies for the purposes of subsection (1) of that section.
(9) This section is to be read subject to section 135 (which restricts the winding up of an eligible scheme during an assessment period).

*Pension sharing*

**220 Pension sharing**

(1) Regulations may modify any of the provisions of this Part as it applies in relation to—
    (a) cases where a person's shareable rights under an eligible scheme have (at any time) become subject to a pension debit;
    (b) cases where—
        (i) a pension sharing order or provision in respect of such rights is made before the time a transfer notice under section 160 is received by the trustees or managers of the eligible scheme, and
        (ii) that order or provision takes effect on or after the receipt by them of the notice.
(2) Regulations may also modify any of the provisions of Chapter 1 of Part 4 of the Welfare Reform and Pensions Act 1999 (c. 30) (pension sharing) as it applies in relation to—
    (a) cases within subsection (1)(a) where any liability of the trustees or managers of the eligible scheme in respect of a pension credit was not discharged before the

time a transfer notice under section 160 was received by the trustees or managers of the eligible scheme;
      (b) cases within subsection (1)(b).
(3) In this section—
      "pension debit" and "shareable rights" have the same meaning as in Chapter 1 of Part 4 of the Welfare Reform and Pensions Act 1999 (c. 30) (pension sharing);
      "pension sharing order or provision" means an order or provision falling within section 28(1) of that Act (activation of pension sharing).

PART 3
SCHEME FUNDING

*Introductory*

### 221 Pension schemes to which this Part applies

(1) The provisions of this Part apply to every occupational pension scheme other than—
      (a) a money purchase scheme, or
      (b) a prescribed scheme or a scheme of a prescribed description.
(2) Regulations under subsection (1)(b) may provide for exemptions from all or any of the provisions of this Part.

*Scheme funding*

### 222 The statutory funding objective

(1) Every scheme is subject to a requirement ("the statutory funding objective") that it must have sufficient and appropriate assets to cover its technical provisions.
(2) A scheme's "technical provisions" means the amount required, on an actuarial calculation, to make provision for the scheme's liabilities.
(3) For the purposes of this Part—
      (a) the assets to be taken into account and their value shall be determined, calculated and verified in a prescribed manner, and
      (b) the liabilities to be taken into account shall be determined in a prescribed manner and the scheme's technical provisions shall be calculated in accordance with any prescribed methods and assumptions.
(4) Regulations may—
      (a) provide for alternative prescribed methods and assumptions,
      (b) provide that it is for the trustees or managers to determine which methods and assumptions are to be used in calculating a scheme's technical provisions, and
      (c) require the trustees or managers, in making their determination, to take into account prescribed matters and follow prescribed principles.
(5) Any provision of the scheme rules that limits the amount of the scheme's liabilities by reference to the value of its assets shall be disregarded.

### 223 Statement of funding principles

(1) The trustees or managers must prepare, and from time to time review and if necessary revise, a written statement of—
      (a) their policy for securing that the statutory funding objective is met, and

(b) such other matters as may be prescribed.

This is referred to in this Part as a "statement of funding principles".

(2) The statement must, in particular, record any decisions by the trustees or managers as to—
- (a) the methods and assumptions to be used in calculating the scheme's technical provisions, and
- (b) the period within which, and manner in which, any failure to meet the statutory funding objective is to be remedied.

(3) Provision may be made by regulations—
- (a) as to the period within which a statement of funding principles must be prepared, and
- (b) requiring it to be reviewed, and if necessary revised, at such intervals, and on such occasions, as may be prescribed.

(4) Where any requirement of this section is not complied with, section 10 of the Pensions Act 1995 (c. 26) (civil penalties) applies to a trustee or manager who has failed to take all reasonable steps to secure compliance.

## 224 Actuarial valuations and reports

(1) The trustees or managers must obtain actuarial valuations—
- (a) at intervals of not more than one year or, if they obtain actuarial reports for the intervening years, at intervals of not more than three years, and
- (b) in such circumstances and on such other occasions as may be prescribed.

(2) In this Part—
- (a) an "actuarial valuation" means a written report, prepared and signed by the actuary, valuing the scheme's assets and calculating its technical provisions,
- (b) the effective date of an actuarial valuation is the date by reference to which the assets are valued and the technical provisions calculated,
- (c) an "actuarial report" means a written report, prepared and signed by the actuary, on developments affecting the scheme's technical provisions since the last actuarial valuation was prepared, and
- (d) the effective date of an actuarial report is the date by reference to which the information in the report is stated.

(3) The intervals referred to in subsection (1)(a) are between effective dates of the valuations, and—
- (a) the effective date of the first actuarial valuation must be not more than one year after the establishment of the scheme, and
- (b) the effective date of any actuarial report must be not more than one year after the effective date of the last actuarial valuation, or, if more recent, the last actuarial report.

(4) The trustees or managers must ensure that a valuation or report obtained by them is received by them within the prescribed period after its effective date.

(5) Nothing in this section affects any power or duty of the trustees or managers to obtain actuarial valuations or reports at more frequent intervals or in other circumstances or on other occasions.

(6) An actuarial valuation or report (whether obtained under this section or in pursuance of any other power or duty) must be prepared in such a manner, give such information, contain such statements and satisfy such other requirements as may be prescribed.

(7) The trustees or managers must secure that any actuarial valuation or report obtained by them (whether obtained under this section or in pursuance of any other power or duty) is made available to the employer within seven days of their receiving it.

(8) Where subsection (1), (4) or (7) is not complied with, section 10 of the Pensions Act 1995 (c. 26) (civil penalties) applies to a trustee or manager who has failed to take all reasonable steps to secure compliance.

## 225 Certification of technical provisions

(1) When an actuarial valuation is carried out, the calculation of the technical provisions must be certified by the actuary.

(2) The certificate must state that in the opinion of the actuary the calculation is made in accordance with regulations under section 222.

(3) If the actuary cannot give the certificate required by subsection (2) he must report the matter in writing to the Regulator within a reasonable period after the end of the period within which the valuation must be received by the trustees or managers.
Section 10 of the Pensions Act 1995 (civil penalties) applies to the actuary if he fails without reasonable excuse to comply with this subsection.

## 226 Recovery plan

(1) If having obtained an actuarial valuation it appears to the trustees or managers of a scheme that the statutory funding objective was not met on the effective date of the valuation, they must, within the prescribed time—
   (a) if there is no existing recovery plan in force, prepare a recovery plan;
   (b) if there is an existing recovery plan in force, review and if necessary revise it.

(2) A recovery plan must set out—
   (a) the steps to be taken to meet the statutory funding objective, and
   (b) the period within which that is to be achieved.

(3) A recovery plan must comply with any prescribed requirements and must be appropriate having regard to the nature and circumstances of the scheme.

(4) In preparing or revising a recovery plan the trustees or managers must take account of prescribed matters.

(5) Provision may be made by regulations as to other circumstances in which a recovery plan may or must be reviewed and if necessary revised.

(6) The trustees or managers must, except in prescribed circumstances, send a copy of any recovery plan to the Regulator within a reasonable period after it is prepared or, as the case may be, revised.
The copy of any recovery plan sent to the Regulator must be accompanied by the prescribed information.

(7) Where any requirement of this section is not complied with, section 10 of the Pensions Act 1995 (c. 26) (civil penalties) applies to a trustee or manager who has failed to take all reasonable steps to secure compliance.

## 227 Schedule of contributions

(1) The trustees or managers must prepare, and from time to time review and if necessary revise, a schedule of contributions.

(2) A "schedule of contributions" means a statement showing—
   (a) the rates of contributions payable towards the scheme by or on behalf of the employer and the active members of the scheme, and
   (b) the dates on or before which such contributions are to be paid.

(3) Provision may be made by regulations—
   (a) as to the period within which, after the establishment of a scheme, a schedule of contributions must be prepared,
   (b) requiring the schedule of contributions to be reviewed, and if necessary revised, at such intervals, and on such occasions, as may be prescribed, and
   (c) as to the period for which a schedule of contributions is to be in force.
(4) The schedule of contributions must satisfy prescribed requirements.
(5) The schedule of contributions must be certified by the actuary and—
   (a) the duty to prepare or revise the schedule is not fulfilled, and
   (b) the schedule shall not come into force,
   until it has been so certified.
(6) The certificate must state that, in the opinion of the actuary—
   (a) the schedule of contributions is consistent with the statement of funding principles, and
   (b) the rates shown in the schedule are such that—
      (i) where the statutory funding objective was not met on the effective date of the last actuarial valuation, the statutory funding objective can be expected to be met by the end of the period specified in the recovery plan, or
      (ii) where the statutory funding objective was met on the effective date of the last actuarial valuation, the statutory funding objective can be expected to continue to be met for the period for which the schedule is to be in force.
(7) Where the statutory funding objective was not met on the effective date of the last actuarial valuation, the trustees or managers must send a copy of the schedule of contributions to the Regulator within a reasonable period after it is prepared or, as the case may be, revised.
(8) Where any requirement of the preceding provisions of this section is not complied with, section 10 of the Pensions Act 1995 (civil penalties) applies to a trustee or manager who has failed to take all reasonable steps to secure compliance.
(9) If the actuary is unable to give the certificate required by subsection (6), he must report the matter in writing to the Regulator within a reasonable period after the end of the period within which the schedule is required to be prepared or, as the case may be, revised.

   Section 10 of the Pensions Act 1995 (c. 26) (civil penalties) applies to the actuary if he fails without reasonable excuse to comply with this subsection.
(10) The provisions of subsections (1), (3) and (5) to (9) above do not apply in relation to a schedule of contributions imposed by the Regulator under section 231 or, as the case may be, where such a schedule of contributions is in force.

**228 Failure to make payments**

(1) This section applies where an amount payable in accordance with the schedule of contributions by or on behalf of the employer or an active member of a scheme is not paid on or before the due date.
(2) If the trustees or managers have reasonable cause to believe that the failure is likely to be of material significance in the exercise by the Regulator of any of its functions, they must, except in prescribed circumstances, give notice of the failure to the Regulator and to the members within a reasonable period.
(3) The amount unpaid (whether payable by the employer or not), if not a debt due from

the employer to the trustees or managers apart from this subsection, shall be treated as such a debt.
(4) Section 10 of the Pensions Act 1995 (civil penalties) applies—
   (a) where subsection (2) above is not complied with, to a trustee or manager who has failed to take all reasonable steps to secure compliance with that subsection;
   (b) to the employer if he fails without reasonable excuse to make a payment required of him—
      (i) in accordance with the schedule of contributions, or
      (ii) by virtue of subsection (3) above.
(5) This section applies in relation to a schedule of contributions imposed by the Regulator under section 231 as in relation to one agreed between the trustees or managers and the employer.

## 229 Matters requiring agreement of the employer

(1) The trustees or managers must obtain the agreement of the employer to—
   (a) any decision as to the methods and assumptions to be used in calculating the scheme's technical provisions (see section 222(4));
   (b) any matter to be included in the statement of funding principles (see section 223);
   (c) any provisions of a recovery plan (see section 226);
   (d) any matter to be included in the schedule of contributions (see section 227).
(2) If it appears to the trustees or managers that it is not otherwise possible to obtain the employer's agreement within the prescribed time to any such matter, they may (if the employer agrees) by resolution modify the scheme as regards the future accrual of benefits.
(3) No modification may be made under subsection (2) that on taking effect would or might adversely affect any subsisting right of—
   (a) any member of the scheme, or
   (b) any survivor of a member of the scheme.
   For this purpose "subsisting right" and "survivor" have the meanings given by section 67A of the Pensions Act 1995 (c. 26).
(4) Any such modification must be—
   (a) recorded in writing by the trustees or managers, and
   (b) notified to the active members within one month of the modification taking effect.
(5) If the trustees or managers are unable to reach agreement with the employer within the prescribed time on any such matter as is mentioned in subsection (1), they must report the failure in writing to the Regulator within a reasonable period.
(6) Where subsection (1), (4) or (5) is not complied with, section 10 of the Pensions Act 1995 (civil penalties) applies to a trustee or manager who has failed to take all reasonable steps to secure compliance.

## 230 Matters on which advice of actuary must be obtained

(1) The trustees or managers must obtain the advice of the actuary before doing any of the following—
   (a) making any decision as to the methods and assumptions to be used in calculating the scheme's technical provisions (see section 222(4));

(b) preparing or revising the statement of funding principles (see section 223);
(c) preparing or revising a recovery plan (see section 226);
(d) preparing or revising the schedule of contributions (see section 227);
(e) modifying the scheme as regards the future accrual of benefits under section 229(2).

(2) Regulations may require the actuary to comply with any prescribed requirements when advising the trustees or managers of a scheme on any such matter.

(3) The regulations may require the actuary to have regard to prescribed guidance.
"Prescribed guidance" means guidance that is prepared and from time to time revised by a prescribed body and, if the regulations so provide, is approved by the Secretary of State.

(4) Where subsection (1) is not complied with, section 10 of the Pensions Act 1995 (civil penalties) applies to a trustee or manager who has failed to take all reasonable steps to secure compliance.

**231 Powers of the regulator**

(1) The powers conferred by this section are exercisable where it appears to the Regulator with respect to a scheme (as a result of a report made to it or otherwise)—
   (a) that the trustees or managers have failed to comply with the requirements of section 223 with respect to the preparation or revision of a statement of funding principles;
   (b) that the trustees or managers have failed to obtain an actuarial valuation as required by section 224(1);
   (c) that the actuary is unable, on an actuarial valuation required by section 224(1), to certify the calculation of the scheme's technical provisions;
   (d) that the trustees or managers have failed to comply with the requirements of section 226 with respect to the preparation or revision of a recovery plan;
   (e) that the trustees or managers have failed to comply with the requirements of section 227 with respect to the preparation or revision of a schedule of contributions;
   (f) that the actuary is unable to certify a schedule of contributions (see section 227(6));
   (g) that the employer has failed to make payments in accordance with the schedule of contributions, or that are required of him by virtue of section 228(3), and the failure is of material significance;
   (h) that the trustees or managers have been unable to reach agreement with the employer within the prescribed time as to a matter in relation to which such agreement is required (see section 229(5)).

(2) In any of those circumstances the Regulator may by order exercise all or any of the following powers—
   (a) it may modify the scheme as regards the future accrual of benefits;
   (b) it may give directions as to—
      (i) the manner in which the scheme's technical provisions are to be calculated, including the methods and assumptions to be used in calculating the scheme's technical provisions, or
      (ii) the period within which, and manner in which, any failure to meet the statutory funding objective is to be remedied;
   (c) it may impose a schedule of contributions specifying—

(i) the rates of contributions payable towards the scheme by or on behalf of the employer and the active members of the scheme, and
(ii) the dates on or before which such contributions are to be paid.
(3) No modification may be made under subsection (2)(a) that on taking effect would or might adversely affect any subsisting right of—
(a) any member of the scheme, or
(b) any survivor of a member of the scheme.
For this purpose "subsisting right" and "survivor" have the meanings given by section 67A of the Pensions Act 1995.
(4) In exercising any of the powers conferred by this section the Regulator must comply with any prescribed requirements.
(5) The powers conferred by this section are in addition to any other powers exercisable by the Regulator under this Act or the Pensions Act 1995 (c. 26).

*Supplementary provisions*

### 232 Power to modify provisions of this Part

Regulations may modify the provisions of this Part as they apply in prescribed circumstances.

### 233 Construction as one with the Pensions Act 1995

This Part shall be construed as one with Part 1 of the Pensions Act 1995 (c. 26).

## PART 4
## FINANCIAL PLANNING FOR RETIREMENT

*Retirement planning*

### 234 Promoting and facilitating financial planning for retirement

(1) The Secretary of State and the Northern Ireland Department may take action for the purpose of promoting or facilitating financial planning for retirement.
(2) The action may in particular include the provision of facilities for the purpose of enabling or assisting an individual or a person authorized by him—
(a) to estimate the financial resources the individual is likely to need after his retirement;
(b) to estimate the financial resources that are likely to be available to the individual after his retirement, from pensions and other sources;
(c) to ascertain what action might be taken with a view to increasing the financial resources available to the individual after his retirement.
(3) This section does not authorize the Secretary of State or the Northern Ireland Department to take action which the Secretary of State or the Northern Ireland Department would otherwise be prohibited from taking under section 21 of the Financial Services and Markets Act 2000 (c. 8) (restrictions on financial promotion).
(4) In this section "the Northern Ireland Department" means the Department for Social Development in Northern Ireland.

### 235 Supply of information for purposes of section 234

(1) This section applies to—
   (a) information which is relevant for determining the pensions and other benefits that may become payable to or in respect of an individual;
   (b) information which relates to the financial resources of, or available to, an individual;
   (c) information which relates to action taken in connection with—
      (i) providing facilities for saving (for retirement or otherwise) by individuals, or
      (ii) promoting or facilitating saving (for retirement or otherwise) by individuals.
(2) A person who holds information to which this section applies may supply it to—
   (a) the Secretary of State or the Northern Ireland Department, or
   (b) a person providing services to the Secretary of State or the Northern Ireland Department,
   for use for the purposes of functions under section 234(1).
(3) Information supplied under subsection (2) must not be supplied by the recipient except—
   (a) if the information relates to an individual—
      (i) to the individual or a person authorized by him;
      (ii) to another person, with the consent of the individual;
   (b) in any case—
      (i) to a person to whom it could be supplied under subsection (2);
      (ii) to any person with a view to the institution of relevant criminal proceedings or otherwise for the purposes of relevant criminal proceedings.
(4) In subsection (3) "relevant criminal proceedings" means criminal proceedings under—
   (a) the Pension Schemes Act 1993 (c. 48);
   (b) the Pensions Act 1995 (c. 26);
   (c) this Act;
   (d) any enactment in force in Northern Ireland corresponding to an Act mentioned in any of paragraphs (a) to (c).
(5) In this section "the Northern Ireland Department" means the Department for Social Development in Northern Ireland.
(6) This section is subject to sections 88 and 202 (tax information disclosed to the Regulator or the Board).

### 236 Use and supply of information: private pensions policy and retirement planning

Schedule 10 (which makes provision about the use and supply of information for purposes relating to private pensions policy and retirement planning) has effect.

### 237 Combined pension forecasts

(1) Regulations may require the trustees or managers of an occupational or personal pension scheme to provide any member of the scheme with—
   (a) the information specified in subsection (2), together with
   (b) the information specified in subsection (3).
(2) The information referred to in subsection (1)(a) is information relating to the member which—
   (a) is State pension information for the purposes of section 42 of the Child Support, Pensions and Social Security Act 2000 (c. 19),

(b) has been disclosed to the trustees or managers under that section (or, by virtue of that section, is treated as having been so disclosed), and
(c) is of a description specified in the regulations.
(3) The information referred to in subsection (1)(b) is information which—
(a) relates to the pensions and other benefits likely to accrue to the member, or capable of being secured by him, under the scheme, and
(b) is of a description specified in the regulations.
(4) Regulations under subsection (1) may require information referred to in that subsection to be provided at a time or times specified in the regulations.

*Employee information and advice*

### 238  Information and advice to employees

(1) Regulations may require employers to take action for the purpose of enabling employees to obtain information and advice about pensions and saving for retirement.
(2) Regulations under subsection (1) may in particular—
(a) provide that they are to apply in relation to employers of a prescribed description and employees of a prescribed description;
(b) make different provision for different descriptions of employers and employees;
(c) make provision as to the action to be taken by employers (including the frequency at which, and the time and place at which, action is to be taken);
(d) make provision as to the description of information and advice in relation to which requirements apply;
(e) make provision about the description of person authorized to provide any such information and advice.
(3) Employers to whom regulations under subsection (1) apply must provide information to the Regulator about the action taken by them for the purpose of complying with the regulations.
(4) Regulations may make provision as to—
(a) the information to be provided under subsection (3);
(b) the form and manner in which the information is to be provided;
(c) the period within which the information is to be provided.
(5) Section 10 of the Pensions Act 1995 (c. 26) (civil penalties) applies to any person who, without reasonable excuse, fails to comply with subsection (3).
(6) In this section "employer" means any employer, whether or not resident or incorporated in any part of the United Kingdom.

### PART 5
### OCCUPATIONAL AND PERSONAL PENSION SCHEMES: MISCELLANEOUS PROVISIONS

*Categories of pension scheme*

### 239  Categories of pension scheme

(1) Section 1 of the Pension Schemes Act 1993 (c. 48) (categories of pension scheme) is amended as follows.
(2) The provisions of the section shall become subsection (1) of the section.

(3) In that subsection, for the definitions of "occupational pension scheme" and "personal pension scheme" substitute—
"'occupational pension scheme' means a pension scheme—
(a) that—
(i) for the purpose of providing benefits to, or in respect of, people with service in employments of a description, or
(ii) for that purpose and also for the purpose of providing benefits to, or in respect of, other people,
is established by, or by persons who include, a person to whom subsection (2) applies when the scheme is established or (as the case may be) to whom that subsection would have applied when the scheme was established had that subsection then been in force, and
(b) that has its main administration in the United Kingdom or outside the member States,
or a pension scheme that is prescribed or is of a prescribed description;
'personal pension scheme' means a pension scheme that—
(a) is not an occupational pension scheme, and
(b) is established by a person within any of the paragraphs of section 154(1) of the Finance Act 2004;".
(4) After that subsection insert—
"(2) This subsection applies—
(a) where people in employments of the description concerned are employed by someone, to a person who employs such people,
(b) to a person in an employment of that description, and
(c) to a person representing interests of a description framed so as to include—
(i) interests of persons who employ people in employments of the description mentioned in paragraph (a), or
(ii) interests of people in employments of that description.
(3) For the purposes of subsection (2), if a person is in an employment of the description concerned by reason of holding an office (including an elective office) and is entitled to remuneration for holding it, the person responsible for paying the remuneration shall be taken to employ the office-holder.
(4) In the definition in subsection (1) of 'occupational pension scheme', the reference to a description includes a description framed by reference to an employment being of any of two or more kinds.
(5) In subsection (1) 'pension scheme' (except in the phrases 'occupational pension scheme', 'personal pension scheme' and 'public service pension scheme') means a scheme or other arrangements, comprised in one or more instruments or agreements, having or capable of having effect so as to provide benefits to or in respect of people—
(a) on retirement,
(b) on having reached a particular age, or
(c) on termination of service in an employment.
(6) The power of the Treasury under section 154(4) of the Finance Act 2004 (power to amend sections 154 and 155) includes power consequentially to amend—
(a) paragraph (a) of the definition in subsection (1) of 'personal pension scheme', and
(b) any provision in force in Northern Ireland corresponding to that paragraph."

**240 Meaning of "employer" in Part 1 of the Pensions Act 1995**

(1) In section 125 of the Pensions Act 1995 (c. 26) (supplementary provision relating to interpretation), in subsection (3) (extension of meaning of "employer")—
 (a) after "include" insert "—
   (a)", and
 (b) after "scheme" insert ";
   (b) such other persons as may be prescribed".
(2) In section 175 of that Act (parliamentary control of orders and regulations), in subsection (2) (instruments subject to affirmative resolution procedure), omit "or" at end of paragraph (c) and after that paragraph insert—
  "(ca) section 125(3)(b), or".

*Requirements for member-nominated trustees and directors*

**241 Requirement for member-nominated trustees**

(1) The trustees of an occupational trust scheme must secure—
 (a) that, within a reasonable period of the commencement date, arrangements are in place which provide for at least one-third of the total number of trustees to be member-nominated trustees, and
 (b) that those arrangements are implemented.
(2) "Member-nominated trustees" are trustees of an occupational trust scheme who—
 (a) are nominated as the result of a process in which at least the following are eligible to participate—
   (i) all the active members of the scheme or an organisation which adequately represents the active members, and
   (ii) all the pensioner members of the scheme or an organisation which adequately represents the pensioner members, and
 (b) are selected as a result of a process which involves some or all of the members of the scheme.
(3) The "commencement date", in relation to a scheme, is—
 (a) the date upon which this section first applies in relation to the scheme, or
 (b) in the case of a scheme to which this section has ceased to apply and then reapplies, the date on which the section reapplies to it.
(4) The arrangements may provide for a greater number of member-nominated trustees than that required to satisfy the one-third minimum mentioned in subsection (1)(a) only if the employer has approved the greater number.
(5) The arrangements—
 (a) must provide for the nomination and selection process to take place within a reasonable period of any requirement arising under the arrangements to appoint a member-nominated trustee,
 (b) must provide, where a vacancy is not filled because insufficient nominations are received, for the nomination and selection process to be repeated at reasonable intervals until the vacancy is filled,
 (c) must provide that where the employer so requires, a person who is not a member of the scheme must have the employer's approval to qualify for selection as a member-nominated trustee, and
 (d) subject to paragraph (c), may provide that, where the number of nominations

**s 241, Pensions Act 2004**

received is equal to or less than the number of appointments required, the nominees are deemed to be selected.
(6) The arrangements must provide that the removal of a member-nominated trustee requires the agreement of all the other trustees.
(7) Nothing in the arrangements or in the provisions of the scheme may exclude member-nominated trustees from the exercise of functions exercisable by other trustees by reason only of the fact that they are member-nominated trustees.
(8) This section does not apply in relation to an occupational trust scheme if—
   (a) every member of the scheme is a trustee of the scheme and no other person is such a trustee,
   (b) every trustee of the scheme is a company, or
   (c) the scheme is of a prescribed description.
(9) If, in the case of an occupational trust scheme, the arrangements required by subsection (1)—
   (a) are not in place as required by subsection (1)(a), or
   (b) are not being implemented,
   section 10 of the Pensions Act 1995 (c. 26) (civil penalties) applies to any trustee who has failed to take all reasonable steps to secure compliance.

## 242 Requirement for member-nominated directors of corporate trustees

(1) Where a company is a trustee of an occupational trust scheme and every trustee of the scheme is a company, the company must secure—
   (a) that, within a reasonable period of the commencement date, arrangements are in place which provide for at least one-third of the total number of directors of the company to be member-nominated directors, and
   (b) that those arrangements are implemented.
(2) "Member-nominated directors" are directors of the company in question who—
   (a) are nominated as the result of a process in which at least the following are eligible to participate—
      (i) all the active members of the occupational trust scheme or an organisation which adequately represents the active members, and
      (ii) all the pensioner members of the occupational trust scheme or an organisation which adequately represents the pensioner members, and
   (b) are selected as a result of a process which involves some or all of the members of that scheme.
(3) The "commencement date", in relation to a company, is—
   (a) the date upon which this section first applies in relation to the company, or
   (b) in the case of a company to which this section has ceased to apply and then reapplies, the date on which the section reapplies to it.
(4) The arrangements may provide for a greater number of member-nominated directors than that required to satisfy the one-third minimum mentioned in subsection (1)(a) only if the employer has approved the greater number.
(5) The arrangements—
   (a) must provide for the nomination and selection process to take place within a reasonable period of any requirement arising under the arrangements to appoint a member-nominated director,
   (b) must provide, where a vacancy is not filled because insufficient nominations are

received, for the nomination and selection process to be repeated at reasonable intervals until the vacancy is filled,
- (c) must provide that where the employer so requires, a person who is not a member of the scheme must have the employer's approval to qualify for selection as a member-nominated director, and
- (d) subject to paragraph (c), may provide that, where the number of nominations received is equal to or less than the number of appointments required, the nominees are deemed to be selected.

(6) The arrangements must provide that the removal of a member-nominated director requires the agreement of all the other directors.

(7) Nothing in the arrangements may exclude member-nominated directors from the exercise of functions exercisable by other directors by reason only of the fact that they are member-nominated directors.

(8) Where the same company is a trustee of two or more occupational trust schemes by reference to each of which this section applies to the company, then, subject to subsection (9), the preceding provisions of this section have effect as if—
- (a) the schemes were a single scheme,
- (b) the members of each of the schemes were members of that single scheme, and
- (c) the references to "the employer" were references to all the employers in relation to the schemes.

(9) Where, apart from this subsection, subsection (8) would apply in relation to a company, the company may elect that subsection (8)—
- (a) is not to apply as mentioned in that subsection, or
- (b) is to apply but only in relation to some of the schemes to which it would otherwise apply.

(10) This section does not apply in relation to an occupational trust scheme if the scheme is of a prescribed description.

(11) If, in the case of a company which is a trustee of an occupational trust scheme, the arrangements required by subsection (1)—
- (a) are not in place as required by subsection (1)(a), or
- (b) are not being implemented,

section 10 of the Pensions Act 1995 (c. 26) (civil penalties) applies to the company.

**243 Member-nominated trustees and directors: supplementary**

(1) The Secretary of State may, by order, amend sections 241(1)(a) and (4) and 242(1)(a) and (4) by substituting, in each of those provisions, "one-half" for "one-third".

(2) Regulations may modify sections 241 and 242 (including any of the provisions mentioned in subsection (1)) in their application to prescribed cases.

(3) In sections 241 and 242—

"company" means a company within the meaning given by section 735(1) of the Companies Act 1985 (c. 6) or a company which may be wound up under Part 5 of the Insolvency Act 1986 (c. 45) (unregistered companies);

"occupational trust scheme" means an occupational pension scheme established under a trust.

*Obligations of trustees of occupational pension schemes*

## 244 Investment principles

For section 35 of the Pensions Act 1995 (investment principles) substitute—

### "35 Investment principles

(1) The trustees of a trust scheme must secure—
   (a) that a statement of investment principles is prepared and maintained for the scheme, and
   (b) that the statement is reviewed at such intervals, and on such occasions, as may be prescribed and, if necessary, revised.
(2) In this section 'statement of investment principles', in relation to a trust scheme, means a written statement of the investment principles governing decisions about investments for the purposes of the scheme.
(3) Before preparing or revising a statement of investment principles, the trustees of a trust scheme must comply with any prescribed requirements.
(4) A statement of investment principles must be in the prescribed form and cover, amongst other things, the prescribed matters.
(5) Neither a trust scheme nor a statement of investment principles may impose restrictions (however expressed) on any power to make investments by reference to the consent of the employer.
(6) If in the case of a trust scheme—
   (a) a statement of investment principles has not been prepared, is not being maintained or has not been reviewed or revised, as required by this section, or
   (b) the trustees have not complied with the obligation imposed on them by subsection (3),
section 10 applies to any trustee who has failed to take all reasonable steps to secure compliance.
(7) Regulations may provide that this section is not to apply to any scheme which is of a prescribed description."

## 245 Power to make regulations governing investment by trustees

(1) Section 36 of the Pensions Act 1995 (c. 26) (choosing investments) is amended as follows.
(2) For subsection (1) substitute—

   "(1) The trustees of a trust scheme must exercise their powers of investment in accordance with regulations and in accordance with subsections (3) and (4), and any fund manager to whom any discretion has been delegated under section 34 must exercise the discretion in accordance with regulations.
   (1A) Regulations under subsection (1) may, in particular—
       (a) specify criteria to be applied in choosing investments, and
       (b) require diversification of investments."
(3) Omit subsection (2).
(4) In subsection (3) for "the matters mentioned in subsection (2) and" substitute "the requirements of regulations under subsection (1), so far as relating to the suitability of investments, and to".
(5) For subsection (8) substitute—
   "(8) If the trustees of a trust scheme—

(a) fail to comply with regulations under subsection (1), or
(b) do not obtain and consider advice in accordance with this section,
section 10 applies to any trustee who has failed to take all reasonable steps to secure compliance."

(6) After subsection (8) insert—
"(9) Regulations may exclude the application of any of the preceding provisions of this section to any scheme which is of a prescribed description."

## 246 Borrowing by trustees

After section 36 of the Pensions Act 1995 insert—

**"36A Restriction on borrowing by trustees**

Regulations may prohibit the trustees of a trust scheme, or the fund manager to whom any discretion has been delegated under section 34, from borrowing money or acting as a guarantor, except in prescribed cases."

## 247 Requirement for knowledge and understanding: individual trustees

(1) This section applies to every individual who is a trustee of an occupational pension scheme.
(2) In this section, "relevant scheme", in relation to an individual, means any occupational pension scheme of which he is a trustee.
(3) An individual to whom this section applies must, in relation to each relevant scheme, be conversant with—
   (a) the trust deed and rules of the scheme,
   (b) any statement of investment principles for the time being maintained under section 35 of the Pensions Act 1995 (c. 26),
   (c) in the case of a relevant scheme to which Part 3 (scheme funding) applies, the statement of funding principles most recently prepared or revised under section 223, and
   (d) any other document recording policy for the time being adopted by the trustees relating to the administration of the scheme generally.
(4) An individual to whom this section applies must have knowledge and understanding of—
   (a) the law relating to pensions and trusts,
   (b) the principles relating to—
      (i) the funding of occupational pension schemes, and
      (ii) investment of the assets of such schemes, and
   (c) such other matters as may be prescribed.
(5) The degree of knowledge and understanding required by subsection (4) is that appropriate for the purposes of enabling the individual properly to exercise his functions as trustee of any relevant scheme.

## 248 Requirement for knowledge and understanding: corporate trustees

(1) This section applies to any company which is a trustee of an occupational pension scheme.
(2) In this section, "relevant scheme", in relation to a company, means any occupational pension scheme of which it is a trustee.
(3) A company to which this section applies must, in relation to each relevant scheme,

secure that each individual who exercises any function which the company has as trustee of the scheme is conversant with each of the documents mentioned in subsection (4) so far as it is relevant to the exercise of the function.

(4) Those documents are—
  (a) the trust deed and rules of the scheme,
  (b) any statement of investment principles for the time being maintained under section 35 of the Pensions Act 1995,
  (c) in the case of a relevant scheme to which Part 3 (scheme funding) applies, the statement of funding principles most recently prepared or revised under section 223, and
  (d) any other document recording policy for the time being adopted by the trustees relating to the administration of the scheme generally.

(5) A company to which this section applies must secure that any individual who exercises any function which the company has as trustee of any relevant scheme has knowledge and understanding of—
  (a) the law relating to pensions and trusts,
  (b) the principles relating to—
    (i) the funding of occupational pension schemes, and
    (ii) investment of the assets of such schemes, and
  (c) such other matters as may be prescribed.

(6) The degree of knowledge and understanding required by subsection (5) is that appropriate for the purposes of enabling the individual properly to exercise the function in question.

(7) References in this section to the exercise by an individual of any function of a company are to anything done by the individual on behalf of the company which constitutes the exercise of the function by the company.

(8) In this section "company" means a company within the meaning given by section 735(1) of the Companies Act 1985 (c. 6) or a company which may be wound up under Part 5 of the Insolvency Act 1986 (c. 45) (unregistered companies).

## 249 Requirement for knowledge and understanding: supplementary

(1) For the purposes of sections 247 and 248, a person's functions as trustee of a relevant scheme are any functions which he has by virtue of being such a trustee and include, in particular—
  (a) any functions which he has as one of the trustees authorized under section 34(5)(a) of the Pensions Act 1995 (c. 26) (delegation of investment discretions) in the case of the scheme, and
  (b) any functions which he otherwise has as a member of a committee of the trustees of the scheme.

(2) Regulations may provide for any provision in section 247 or 248—
  (a) not to apply, or
  (b) to apply with modifications,
  to a trustee in prescribed circumstances.

(3) Nothing in either of those sections affects any rule of law requiring a trustee to have knowledge of, or expertise in, any matter.

*Payment of surplus to employer*

## 250 Payment of surplus to employer

For section 37 of the Pensions Act 1995 (payment of surplus to employer) substitute—

**"37 Payment of surplus to employer**

(1) This section applies to a trust scheme if—
   (a) apart from this section power is conferred on the employer or any other person to make payments to the employer out of funds held for the purposes of the scheme, and
   (b) the scheme is not being wound up.
(2) Where the power referred to in subsection (1)(a) is conferred by the scheme on a person other than the trustees—
   (a) it cannot be exercised by that person but may instead be exercised by the trustees, and
   (b) any restriction imposed by the scheme on the exercise of the power shall, so far as capable of doing so, apply to its exercise by the trustees.
(3) The power referred to in subsection (1)(a) may only be exercised if—
   (a) the trustees have obtained a written valuation of the scheme's assets and liabilities prepared and signed by a prescribed person;
   (b) there is a certificate in force—
      (i) stating that in the opinion of that person the prescribed requirements are met as at the date by reference to which the assets are valued and the liabilities are calculated, and
      (ii) specifying what in the opinion of that person is the maximum amount of payment that may be made to the employer;
   (c) the payment does not exceed the maximum amount specified in the certificate;
   (d) the trustees are satisfied that it is in the interests of the members that the power is exercised in the manner proposed;
   (e) where the power is conferred by the scheme on the employer, the employer has asked for the power to be exercised, or consented to its being exercised, in the manner proposed;
   (f) there is no freezing order in force in relation to the scheme under section 23 of the Pensions Act 2004; and
   (g) notice of the proposal to exercise the power has been given, in accordance with prescribed requirements, to the members of the scheme.
(4) Provision may be made by regulations as to—
   (a) the requirements (which may be alternative requirements) that must be met, in relation to any proposed payment to the employer out of funds held for the purposes of a scheme, with respect to the value of the scheme's assets and the amount of its liabilities;
   (b) the assets and liabilities to be taken into account for that purpose and the manner in which their value or amount is to be determined, calculated and verified;
   (c) the maximum amount of the payment that may be made to the employer, having regard to the value of the scheme's assets and the amount of its liabilities;
   (d) the giving of a certificate as to the matters mentioned in paragraphs (a) and (c); and
   (e) the period for which such a certificate is to be in force.

(5) The trustees must also comply with any other prescribed requirements in connection with the making of a payment under this section.

(6) If the trustees—
   (a) purport to exercise the power referred to in subsection (1)(a) without complying with the requirements of this section, or
   (b) fail to comply with any requirement of regulations under subsection (5),
   section 10 applies to any of them who has failed to take all reasonable steps to secure compliance.

(7) If a person other than the trustees purports to exercise the power referred to in subsection (1)(a), section 10 applies to him.

(8) Regulations may provide that in prescribed circumstances this section does not apply, or applies with prescribed modifications, to schemes of a prescribed description."

**251 Payment of surplus to employer: transitional power to amend scheme**

(1) This section applies to a scheme which immediately before the commencement of section 250 was one to which section 37 of the Pensions Act 1995 (c. 26) applied (see subsection (1) of that section, as it then had effect).

(2) No payment to the employer may be made out of funds held for the purposes of the scheme except by virtue of a resolution of the trustees under this section.

This applies even if the payment is one proposed to be made in fulfilment of an agreement or arrangement entered into before the commencement of this section.

(3) Where the scheme was so expressed as (apart from section 37, as it then applied) to confer power to make payments to the employer out of funds held for the purposes of the scheme otherwise than in pursuance of proposals approved under paragraph 6(1) of Schedule 22 to the Income and Corporation Taxes Act 1988 (c. 1), the trustees may resolve that the power—
   (a) shall become exercisable according to its terms, or
   (b) shall become so exercisable, but only in such circumstances and subject to such conditions as may be specified in the resolution.

(4) Where the scheme was so expressed as to confer power to make payments to the employer out of funds held for the purposes of the scheme only in pursuance of proposals approved under paragraph 6(1) of Schedule 22 to the Income and Corporation Taxes Act 1988, the trustees may resolve that the power shall instead be exercisable in such circumstances and subject to such conditions as may be specified in the resolution.

(5) In either case the trustees must be satisfied that it is in the interests of the members of the scheme that the power is exercised in the manner proposed.

(6) The power conferred by subsection (3) or (4)—
   (a) may not be exercised unless notice of the proposal to exercise it has been given, in accordance with prescribed requirements, to the employer and to the members of the scheme,
   (b) may only be exercised once, and
   (c) ceases to be exercisable five years after the commencement of this section.

(7) The exercise of any power to make payments to the employer by virtue of a resolution under this section is subject to section 37 of the Pensions Act 1995 (c. 26) as substituted by section 250.

*Restrictions on payment into occupational pension schemes*

## 252 UK-Based scheme to be trust with effective rules

(1) Subsections (2) and (3) apply to an occupational pension scheme that has its main administration in the United Kingdom.
(2) If the scheme is not established under irrevocable trusts, the trustees or managers of the scheme must secure that no funding payment is accepted.
(3) If the rules stipulating—
    (a) the benefits under the scheme, and
    (b) any conditions subject to which benefits under the scheme accrue,
    are not in force, or if those rules are not set out in writing, the trustees or managers of the scheme must secure that no funding payment is accepted.
(4) Subsection (2) or (3) does not apply to an occupational pension scheme if it is a prescribed scheme or a scheme of a prescribed description.
(5) Section 10 of the Pensions Act 1995 (civil penalties) applies to a trustee or manager of an occupational pension scheme that has its main administration in the United Kingdom if—
    (a) subsection (2) or (3) requires the trustees or managers of the scheme to secure that no funding payment is accepted,
    (b) a funding payment is accepted, and
    (c) the trustee or manager has failed to take all reasonable steps to secure that no funding payment is accepted.
(6) In this section "funding payment", in relation to a scheme, means a payment made to the scheme to fund benefits for, or in respect of, any or all of the members.

## 253 Non-European scheme to be trust with UK-resident trustee

(1) Subsections (2) and (3) apply to an occupational pension scheme that has its main administration outside the member States.
(2) An employer based in any part of the United Kingdom may cause a contribution to be paid to the scheme in respect of an employee (whether or not employed in the United Kingdom) only if the conditions in subsection (4) are satisfied at the time of payment.
(3) An employer based outside the United Kingdom may cause a contribution to be paid to the scheme in respect of an employee employed in the United Kingdom only if the conditions in subsection (4) are satisfied at the time of payment.
(4) Those conditions are—
    (a) that the scheme is established under irrevocable trusts, and
    (b) that a trustee of the scheme is resident in the United Kingdom.
(5) Subsection (2) or (3) does not apply to an occupational pension scheme if it is a prescribed scheme or a scheme of a prescribed description.
(6) Section 10 of the Pensions Act 1995 (c. 26) (civil penalties) applies to an employer who causes a contribution to be paid to an occupational pension scheme that has its main administration outside the member States if—
    (a) subsection (2) or (3) applies in relation to the payment of the contribution,
    (b) the conditions in subsection (4) are not satisfied at the time of payment, and
    (c) the employer does not have a reasonable excuse for causing payment to occur at a time when those conditions are not satisfied.
(7) In this section "based"—

(a) in relation to an employer who is a body corporate, means incorporated, and
(b) in relation to any other employer, means resident.

**254 Representative of non-European scheme to be treated as trustee**

(1) In the case of an occupational pension scheme that has its main administration outside the member States, a reference in pensions legislation to the trustees, or a trustee, of the scheme includes a person who is for the time being appointed by the trustees of the scheme to be a representative of the scheme for the purposes of this section.

(2) Subsection (1) does not apply to a prescribed reference.

(3) In subsection (1) "pensions legislation" means any enactment contained in or made by virtue of—
   (a) the Pension Schemes Act 1993 (c. 48),
   (b) the Pensions Act 1995,
   (c) Parts 1 to 4 of the Welfare Reform and Pensions Act 1999 (c. 30), or
   (d) this Act.

*Activities of occupational pension schemes*

**255 Activities of occupational pension schemes**

(1) If an occupational pension scheme has its main administration in the United Kingdom, the trustees or managers of the scheme must secure that the activities of the scheme are limited to retirement-benefit activities.

(2) Subsection (1) does not apply to a scheme if it is a prescribed scheme or a scheme of a prescribed description.

(3) Section 10 of the Pensions Act 1995 (civil penalties) applies to a trustee or manager of a scheme to which subsection (1) applies if—
   (a) the scheme has activities that are not retirement-benefit activities, and
   (b) the trustee or manager has failed to take all reasonable steps to secure that the activities of the scheme are limited to retirement-benefit activities.

(4) In this section "retirement-benefit activities" means—
   (a) operations related to retirement benefits, and
   (b) activities arising from operations related to retirement benefits.

(5) In subsection (4) "retirement benefits" means—
   (a) benefits paid by reference to reaching, or expecting to reach, retirement, and
   (b) benefits that are supplementary to benefits within paragraph (a) and that are provided on an ancillary basis—
      (i) in the form of payments on death, disability or termination of employment, or
      (ii) in the form of support payments or services in the case of sickness, poverty or need, or death.

*No indemnification for fines or civil penalties*

**256 No indemnification for fines or civil penalties**

(1) No amount may be paid out of the assets of an occupational or personal pension scheme for the purpose of reimbursing, or providing for the reimbursement of, any trustee or manager of the scheme in respect of—

(a) a fine imposed by way of penalty for an offence of which he is convicted, or
(b) a penalty which he is required to pay under or by virtue of section 10 of the Pensions Act 1995 (c. 26) or section 168(4) of the Pension Schemes Act 1993 (c. 48) (civil penalties).

(2) For the purposes of subsection (1), providing for the reimbursement of a trustee or manager in respect of a fine or penalty includes (among other things) providing for the payment of premiums in respect of a policy of insurance where the risk is or includes the imposition of such a fine or the requirement to pay such a penalty.

(3) Where any amount is paid out of the assets of an occupational or personal pension scheme in contravention of this section, section 10 of the Pensions Act 1995 (civil penalties) applies to any trustee or manager who fails to take all reasonable steps to secure compliance.

(4) Where a trustee or manager of an occupational or personal pension scheme—
(a) is reimbursed, out of the assets of the scheme or in consequence of provision for his reimbursement made out of those assets, in respect of any of the matters mentioned in subsection (1)(a) or (b), and
(b) knows, or has reasonable grounds to believe, that he has been reimbursed as mentioned in paragraph (a),

then, unless he has taken all reasonable steps to secure that he is not so reimbursed, he is guilty of an offence.

(5) A person guilty of an offence under subsection (4) is liable—
(a) on summary conviction, to a fine not exceeding the statutory maximum, and
(b) on conviction on indictment, to imprisonment for a term not exceeding two years, or a fine, or both.

*Pension protection on transfer of employment*

**257 Conditions for pension protection**

(1) This section applies in relation to a person ("the employee") where—
(a) there is a transfer of an undertaking, or part of an undertaking, to which the TUPE Regulations apply,
(b) by virtue of the transfer the employee ceases to be employed by the transferor and becomes employed by the transferee, and
(c) at the time immediately before the employee becomes employed by the transferee—
(i) there is an occupational pension scheme ("the scheme") in relation to which the transferor is the employer, and
(ii) one of subsections (2), (3) and (4) applies.

(2) This subsection applies where—
(a) the employee is an active member of the scheme, and
(b) if any of the benefits that may be provided under the scheme are money purchase benefits—
(i) the transferor is required to make contributions to the scheme in respect of the employee, or
(ii) the transferor is not so required but has made one or more such contributions.

(3) This subsection applies where—

(a) the employee is not an active member of the scheme but is eligible to be such a member, and
(b) if any of the benefits that may be provided under the scheme are money purchase benefits, the transferor would have been required to make contributions to the scheme in respect of the employee if the employee had been an active member of it.
(4) This subsection applies where—
(a) the employee is not an active member of the scheme, nor eligible to be such a member, but would have been an active member of the scheme or eligible to be such a member if, after the date on which he became employed by the transferor, he had been employed by the transferor for a longer period, and
(b) if any of the benefits that may be provided under the scheme are money purchase benefits, the transferor would have been required to make contributions to the scheme in respect of the employee if the employee had been an active member of it.
(5) For the purposes of this section, the condition in subsection (1)(c) is to be regarded as satisfied in any case where it would have been satisfied but for any action taken by the transferor by reason of the transfer.
(6) In subsection (1)(a), the reference to an undertaking, or part of an undertaking, has the same meaning as in the TUPE Regulations.
(7) In the case of a scheme which is contracted-out by virtue of section 9 of the Pension Schemes Act 1993 (c. 48), the references in subsections (2)(b), (3)(b) and (4)(b) to contributions mean contributions other than minimum payments (within the meaning of that Act).
(8) In this section—
the "TUPE Regulations" means the Transfer of Undertakings (Protection of Employment) Regulations 1981 (S.I. 1981/1794);
references to the transferor include any associate of the transferor, and section 435 of the Insolvency Act 1986 (c. 45) applies for the purposes of this section as it applies for the purposes of that Act.

**258 Form of protection**

(1) In a case where section 257 applies, it is a condition of the employee's contract of employment with the transferee that the requirements in subsection (2) or the requirement in subsection (3) are complied with.
(2) The requirements in this subsection are that—
(a) the transferee secures that, as from the relevant time, the employee is, or is eligible to be, an active member of an occupational pension scheme in relation to which the transferee is the employer, and
(b) in a case where the scheme is a money purchase scheme, as from the relevant time—
(i) the transferee makes relevant contributions to the scheme in respect of the employee, or
(ii) if the employee is not an active member of the scheme but is eligible to be such a member, the transferee would be required to make such contributions if the employee were an active member, and
(c) in a case where the scheme is not a money purchase scheme, as from the relevant time the scheme—

(i) satisfies the statutory standard referred to in section 12A of the Pension Schemes Act 1993 (c. 48), or
  (ii) if regulations so provide, complies with such other requirements as may be prescribed.
(3) The requirement in this subsection is that, as from the relevant time, the transferee makes relevant contributions to a stakeholder pension scheme of which the employee is a member.
(4) The requirement in subsection (3) is for the purposes of this section to be regarded as complied with by the transferee during any period in relation to which the condition in subsection (5) is satisfied.
(5) The condition in this subsection is that the transferee has offered to make relevant contributions to a stakeholder pension scheme of which the employee is eligible to be a member (and the transferee has not withdrawn the offer).
(6) Subsection (1) does not apply in relation to a contract if or to the extent that the employee and the transferee so agree at any time after the time when the employee becomes employed by the transferee.
(7) In this section—
  "the relevant time" means—
  (a) in a case where section 257 applies by virtue of the application of subsection (2) or (3) of that section, the time when the employee becomes employed by the transferee;
  (b) in a case where that section applies by virtue of the application of subsection (4) of that section, the time at which the employee would have been a member of the scheme referred to in subsection (1)(c)(i) of that section or (if earlier) would have been eligible to be such a member;
  "relevant contributions" means such contributions in respect of such period or periods as may be prescribed;
  "stakeholder pension scheme" means a pension scheme which is registered under section 2 of the Welfare Reform and Pensions Act 1999 (c. 30).

*Consultation by employers*

## 259 Consultation by employers: occupational pension schemes

(1) Regulations may require any prescribed person who is the employer in relation to an occupational pension scheme and who—
  (a) proposes to make a prescribed decision in relation to the scheme, or
  (b) has been notified by the trustees or managers of the scheme that they propose to make a prescribed decision in relation to the scheme,
  to consult prescribed persons in the prescribed manner before the decision is made.
(2) Regulations may require the trustees or managers of an occupational pension scheme not to make a prescribed decision in relation to the scheme unless—
  (a) they have notified the employer of the proposed decision, and
  (b) they are satisfied that the employer has undertaken any consultation required by virtue of subsection (1).
(3) The validity of any decision made in relation to an occupational pension scheme is not affected by any failure to comply with regulations under this section.
(4) Section 261 contains further provisions about regulations under this section.

**260 Consultation by employers: personal pension schemes**

(1) Regulations may require any prescribed person who—
   (a) is the employer in relation to a personal pension scheme where direct payment arrangements exist in respect of one or more members of the scheme who are his employees, and
   (b) proposes to make a prescribed decision affecting the application of the direct payment arrangements in relation to those employees,
   to consult prescribed persons in the prescribed manner before he makes the decision.
(2) The validity of any decision prescribed for the purposes of subsection (1)(b) is not affected by any failure to comply with regulations under this section.
(3) Section 261 contains further provisions about regulations under this section.

**261 Further provisions about regulations relating to consultation**

(1) In this section "consultation regulations" means regulations under section 259 or 260.
(2) Consultation regulations may—
   (a) make provision about the time to be allowed for consultation;
   (b) prescribe the information which must be provided to the persons who are required to be consulted;
   (c) confer a discretion on the employer in prescribed cases as to the persons who are to be consulted;
   (d) make provision about the representatives the employees may have for the purposes of the regulations and the methods by which those representatives are to be selected;
   (e) require or authorize the holding of ballots;
   (f) amend, apply with or without modifications, or make provision similar to, any provision of the Employment Rights Act 1996 (c. 18) (including, in particular, Parts 5, 10 and 13), the Employment Tribunals Act 1996 (c. 17) or the Trade Union and Labour Relations (Consolidation) Act 1992 (c. 52);
   (g) enable any requirement for consultation imposed by the regulations to be waived or relaxed by order of the Regulator;
   (h) require the employer to communicate to the trustees and managers of the scheme any representations received by the employer in response to any consultation required by the regulations.
(3) Persons on whom obligations are imposed by consultation regulations, either as employers or as the trustees or managers of occupational pension schemes, must, if so required by the Regulator, provide information to the Regulator about the action taken by them for the purpose of complying with the regulations.
(4) Consultation regulations may make provision as to—
   (a) the information to be provided under subsection (3);
   (b) the form and manner in which the information is to be provided;
   (c) the period within which the information is to be provided.
(5) Nothing in consultation regulations is to be regarded as affecting any duty to consult arising otherwise than under the regulations.

*Modification of pension rights*

## 262 Modification of subsisting rights

For section 67 of the Pensions Act 1995 (c. 26) substitute—

**"67 The subsisting rights provisions**

(1) The subsisting rights provisions apply to any power conferred on any person by an occupational pension scheme to modify the scheme, other than a power conferred by—
   (a) a public service pension scheme, or
   (b) a prescribed scheme or a scheme of a prescribed description.
(2) Any exercise of such a power to make a regulated modification is voidable in accordance with section 67G unless the following are satisfied in respect of the modification—
   (a) in the case of each affected member—
      (i) if the modification is a protected modification, the consent requirements (see section 67B),
      (ii) if it is not, either the consent requirements or the actuarial equivalence requirements (see section 67C),
   (b) the trustee approval requirement (see section 67E), and
   (c) the reporting requirement (see section 67F).
(3) The subsisting rights provisions do not apply in relation to the exercise of a power—
   (a) for a purpose connected with debits under section 29(1) of the Welfare Reform and Pensions Act 1999, or
   (b) in a prescribed manner.
(4) References in this section and sections 67A to 67I to "the subsisting rights provisions" are to this section and those sections.
(5) Subsection (6) applies in relation to the exercise of a power to which the subsisting rights provisions apply to make a regulated modification where a member of the scheme dies before the requirements mentioned in subsection (2), so far as they apply in his case, have been complied with in respect of the modification if—
   (a) before he died he had given his consent to the modification in accordance with section 67B(4)(b), or
   (b) before he died, or before the trustees of the scheme had become aware that he had died, the trustees had complied with section 67C(4)(a), (b) and (d) in respect of the modification in his case.
(6) Any of the requirements mentioned in subsection (2), as it applies in respect of the modification—
   (a) which is satisfied in the case of the member, or
   (b) which would have been satisfied in his case had he not died before it was satisfied, is to be taken to be satisfied in the case of any survivor of the member in respect of the modification.

**67A The subsisting rights provisions: interpretation**

(1) In the subsisting rights provisions, each of the following expressions has the meaning given to it by the following provisions of this section—
"regulated modification"
"protected modification"
"detrimental modification"

"affected member"
"subsisting right"
"scheme rules".
(2) "Regulated modification" means a modification which is—
(a) a protected modification, or
(b) a detrimental modification,
or is both.
(3) "Protected modification" means a modification of an occupational pension scheme which—
(a) on taking effect would or might result in any subsisting right of—
(i) a member of the scheme, or
(ii) a survivor of a member of the scheme,
which is not a right or entitlement to money purchase benefits becoming, or being replaced with, a right or entitlement to money purchase benefits under the scheme rules,
(b) would or might result in a reduction in the prevailing rate of any pension in payment under the scheme rules, or
(c) is of a prescribed description.
For the purposes of paragraph (a), the reference in the definition of "money purchase benefits" in section 181(1) of the Pension Schemes Act 1993 to the widow or widower of a member of an occupational pension scheme is to be read as including any other survivor of the member.
(4) "Detrimental modification" means a modification of an occupational pension scheme which on taking effect would or might adversely affect any subsisting right of—
(a) any member of the scheme, or
(b) any survivor of a member of the scheme.
(5) A person is an "affected member"—
(a) in relation to a protected modification within paragraph (a) or (b) of subsection (3), if, at the time the modification takes effect, he is—
(i) a member of the scheme, or
(ii) a survivor of a member of the scheme,
and, on taking effect, the modification would or might affect any of his subsisting rights as mentioned in that paragraph,
(b) in relation to a protected modification within paragraph (c) of that subsection, if he is of a prescribed description, and
(c) in relation to a detrimental modification which is not a protected modification if, at the time the modification takes effect, he is—
(i) a member of the scheme, or
(ii) a survivor of a member of the scheme,
and, on taking effect, the modification would or might adversely affect any of his subsisting rights.
(6) "Subsisting right" means—
(a) in relation to a member of an occupational pension scheme, at any time—
(i) any right which at that time has accrued to or in respect of him to future benefits under the scheme rules, or
(ii) any entitlement to the present payment of a pension or other benefit which he has at that time, under the scheme rules, and

(b) in relation to the survivor of a member of an occupational pension scheme, at any time, any entitlement to benefits, or right to future benefits, which he has at that time under the scheme rules in respect of the member.

For this purpose, "right" includes a pension credit right.

(7) At any time when the pensionable service of a member of an occupational pension scheme is continuing, his subsisting rights are to be determined as if he had opted, immediately before that time, to terminate that service.

(8) "Scheme rules", in relation to a scheme, means—
   (a) the rules of the scheme, except so far as overridden by a relevant legislative provision,
   (b) the relevant legislative provisions, to the extent that they have effect in relation to the scheme and are not reflected in the rules of the scheme, and
   (c) any provision which the rules of the scheme do not contain but which the scheme must contain if it is to conform with the requirements of Chapter 1 of Part 4 of the Pension Schemes Act 1993 (preservation of benefit under occupational pension schemes).

(9) For the purposes of subsection (8)—
   (a) "relevant legislative provision" means any provision contained in any of the following provisions—
      (i) Schedule 5 to the Social Security Act 1989 (equal treatment for men and women);
      (ii) Chapters 2 to 5 of Part 4 of the Pension Schemes Act 1993 (certain protection for early leavers) or regulations made under any of those Chapters;
      (iii) Part 4A of that Act (requirements relating to pension credit benefit) or regulations made under that Part;
      (iv) section 110(1) of that Act (requirement as to resources for annual increase of guaranteed minimum pensions);
      (v) this Part of this Act (occupational pensions) or subordinate legislation made or having effect as if made under this Part;
      (vi) section 31 of the Welfare Reform and Pensions Act 1999 (pension debits: reduction of benefit);
      (vii) any provision mentioned in section 306(2) of the Pensions Act 2004;
   (b) a relevant legislative provision is to be taken to override any of the provisions of the scheme if, and only if, it does so by virtue of any of the following provisions—
      (i) paragraph 3 of Schedule 5 to the Social Security Act 1989;
      (ii) section 129(1) of the Pension Schemes Act 1993;
      (iii) section 117(1) of this Act;
      (iv) section 31(4) of the Welfare Reform and Pensions Act 1999;
      (v) section 306(1) of the Pensions Act 2004.

(10) For the purposes of this section—
   (a) "survivor", in relation to a member of an occupational pension scheme, means a person who—
      (i) is the widow or widower of the member, or
      (ii) has survived the member and has any entitlement to benefit, or right to future benefits, under the scheme rules in respect of the member, and
   (b) a modification would or might adversely affect a person's subsisting right if it would alter the nature or extent of the entitlement or right so that the benefits, or

future benefits, to which the entitlement or right relates would or might be less generous.
(11) In the subsisting rights provisions, in relation to—
(a) the exercise of a power to modify an occupational pension scheme to which the subsisting rights provisions apply, or
(b) a modification made, or to be made, in exercise of such a power,
references to "the scheme" are to be read as references to the scheme mentioned in paragraph (a).

**67B The consent requirements**

(1) References in the subsisting rights provisions to the consent requirements, in respect of a regulated modification, are to be read in accordance with this section.
(2) The consent requirements apply in the case of an affected member—
(a) if the modification is a protected modification;
(b) if it is not a protected modification, unless the actuarial equivalence requirements apply in his case.
(3) The consent requirements consist of—
(a) the informed consent requirement (see subsection (4)), and
(b) the timing requirement (see subsection (6)).
(4) The informed consent requirement is satisfied in the case of an affected member if before the modification is made—
(a) the trustees have—
(i) given him information in writing adequate to explain the nature of the modification and its effect on him,
(ii) notified him in writing that he may make representations to the trustees about the modification,
(iii) afforded him a reasonable opportunity to make such representations, and
(iv) notified him in writing that the consent requirements apply in his case in respect of the modification, and
(b) after the trustees have complied with paragraph (a)(i), (ii) and (iv), the affected member has given his consent in writing to the modification.
(5) If—
(a) the modification is not a protected modification, and
(b) before the modification is made the trustees notify an affected member in writing that—
(i) if he gives his consent to the modification for the purposes of the consent requirements, those requirements apply in his case in respect of the modification, but
(ii) otherwise, the actuarial equivalence requirements apply in his case in respect of the modification,
the trustees are to be taken to have complied with subsection (4)(a)(iv) in respect of him.
(6) The timing requirement is satisfied in the case of an affected member if the modification takes effect within a reasonable period after the member has given his consent to the modification in accordance with subsection (4)(b).

**67C  The actuarial equivalence requirements**

(1) References in the subsisting rights provisions to the actuarial equivalence requirements, in respect of a detrimental modification which is not a protected modification, are to be read in accordance with this section and section 67D.

(2) The actuarial equivalence requirements apply in the case of an affected member only if—
 (a) the modification is not a protected modification, and
 (b) the trustees of the scheme determine that they are to apply in his case.

(3) The actuarial equivalence requirements consist of—
 (a) the information requirement (see subsection (4)),
 (b) the actuarial value requirement (see subsection (5)), and
 (c) the actuarial equivalence statement requirement (see subsection (6)).

(4) The information requirement is satisfied in the case of an affected member if before the modification is made the trustees have taken all reasonable steps to—
 (a) give him information in writing adequate to explain the nature of the modification and its effect on him,
 (b) notify him in writing that he may make representations to the trustees about the modification,
 (c) afford him a reasonable opportunity to make such representations, and
 (d) notify him in writing that the actuarial equivalence requirements apply in his case in respect of the modification.

(5) The actuarial value requirement is satisfied in the case of an affected member if before the modification is made the trustees have made such arrangements, or taken such steps, as are adequate to secure that actuarial value will be maintained.

(6) The actuarial equivalence statement requirement is satisfied in the case of an affected member if the trustees have, within a reasonable period beginning with the date on which the modification takes effect, obtained an actuarial equivalence statement relating to the affected member in respect of the modification.

(7) For the purposes of subsection (6) "actuarial equivalence statement" means a statement in writing which—
 (a) is given by—
  (i) the actuary appointed in relation to the scheme under section 47(1)(b), or
  (ii) a person with prescribed qualifications or experience or who is approved by the Secretary of State, and
 (b) certifies that actuarial value has been maintained.

(8) For the purposes of subsections (5) and (7) as they apply in relation to an affected member, actuarial value is maintained if the actuarial value, immediately after the time at which the modification takes effect, of the affected member's subsisting rights is equal to or greater than the actuarial value of his subsisting rights immediately before that time.

**67D  The actuarial equivalence requirements: further provisions**

(1) This section applies for the purposes of section 67C.

(2) Where—
 (a) the information requirement has been satisfied in the case of an affected member in respect of a proposed modification ("the original modification"),
 (b) before the trustees have made a determination, or given their consent, for the

purposes of section 67E(1) in relation to the original modification, the original modification has been revised, and

(c) the modification as so revised ('the revised modification') does not differ from the original modification in any material respect,

the information requirement is to be taken to have been satisfied in relation to the revised modification.

(3) The trustees are to be regarded as having taken all reasonable steps to notify an affected member as mentioned in section 67C(4)(d) in respect of a modification if they have taken all reasonable steps to notify him in writing that—

(a) if he gives his consent to the modification for the purposes of the consent requirements, those requirements apply in his case in respect of the modification, but

(b) otherwise, the actuarial equivalence requirements apply in his case in respect of the modification.

(4) Any calculation for the purposes of section 67C of the actuarial value of an affected member's subsisting rights at any time must conform with such requirements as may be prescribed.

(5) Requirements prescribed by regulations under subsection (4) may include requirements for any such calculation to be made in accordance with guidance that—

(a) is prepared and from time to time revised by a prescribed body, and

(b) if the regulations so provide, is approved by the Secretary of State.

(6) Nothing in subsections (6) and (7) of section 67C precludes actuarial equivalence statements relating to—

(a) two or more affected members, or

(b) affected members of any particular description,

in respect of a modification being given in a single document.

## 67E  The trustee approval requirement

(1) For the purposes of section 67(2)(b), the trustee approval requirement is satisfied in relation to the exercise of a power to make a regulated modification if—

(a) the trustees of the scheme have determined to exercise the power to make the modification, or

(b) if the power is exercised by another person, the trustees have consented to the exercise of the power to make the modification,

and the making of the determination, or giving of consent, complies with subsections (2) and (3).

(2) The trustees must not make a determination, or give their consent, for the purposes of subsection (1) unless, in the case of each affected member—

(a) if the modification is a protected modification, the informed consent requirement is satisfied (within the meaning of section 67B), or

(b) if it is not a protected modification—

(i) the informed consent requirement is satisfied, or

(ii) the information and actuarial value requirements are satisfied (within the meaning of section 67C),

in respect of the modification.

(3) The trustees must not make a determination, or give their consent, for the purposes of subsection (1) more than a reasonable period after the first consent given by an affected member under section 67B(4)(b) in respect of the modification was given.

## 67F The reporting requirement

(1) For the purposes of section 67(2)(c), the reporting requirement is satisfied in relation to the exercise of a power to which the subsisting rights provisions apply to make a regulated modification if the trustees have, in accordance with subsection (2)—
   (a) notified each affected member in whose case the consent requirements apply in respect of the modification, and
   (b) taken all reasonable steps to notify each affected member in whose case the actuarial equivalence requirements apply in respect of the modification,
   that they have made a determination, or given their consent, for the purposes of section 67E(1) in relation to the exercise of the power to make the modification.
(2) The trustees must give (or, where the actuarial equivalence requirements apply, take all reasonable steps to give) the notification—
   (a) within a reasonable period beginning with the date of the determination or giving of consent mentioned in subsection (1), and
   (b) before the date on which the modification takes effect.

## 67G Powers of the authority: voidable modifications

(1) Subsection (2) applies in relation to a regulated modification made in exercise of a power to which the subsisting rights provisions apply which is voidable by virtue of—
   (a) section 67(2), or
   (b) section 67H(3).
(2) The Authority may make an order declaring that subsection (6) applies in relation to the regulated modification.
(3) An order under subsection (2) relating to a regulated modification may also declare that subsection (6) applies in relation to—
   (a) any other modification of the scheme made by the exercise of the power mentioned in subsection (1), or
   (b) the grant of any rights under the scheme (whether by virtue of the attribution of notional periods as pensionable service or otherwise) in connection with the regulated modification.
(4) An order under subsection (2) relating to a regulated modification must specify the affected member or affected members or description of affected members in respect of whom subsection (6) applies ('the specified persons').
(5) An order under subsection (2) relating to a regulated modification may also—
   (a) require the trustees to take, within the time specified in the order, such steps as are so specified for the purpose of giving effect to the order;
   (b) declare that subsection (7) applies in relation to anything done by the trustees after the time at which the modification would, disregarding the order, have taken effect which—
      (i) would not have contravened any provision of the scheme rules if the modification had taken effect at that time, but
      (ii) as a result of the modification being void to any extent by virtue of the order, would (but for that subsection) contravene such a provision.
   This is without prejudice to section 174(3).
(6) Where the Authority make an order declaring that this subsection applies in relation to a modification of a scheme, or the grant of any rights under the scheme, the modification or grant is void to the extent specified in the order, and in respect of the

specified persons, as from the time when it would, disregarding the order, have taken effect.
(7) Where, by virtue of subsection (5)(b), the Authority make an order under subsection (2) declaring that this subsection applies in relation to anything done by the trustees, that thing is to be taken, for such purposes as are specified in the order, not to have contravened any provision of the trust deed or scheme rules.
(8) An order under subsection (2) relating to a regulated modification, or other modification, of a scheme or the grant of any rights under the scheme may be made before or after the time at which the modification or grant would, disregarding the order, have taken effect.

**67H  Powers of the authority to intervene**

(1) Subsection (2) applies where the Authority have reasonable grounds to believe that a power to which the subsisting rights provisions apply—
    (a) will be exercised, or
    (b) has been exercised,
    to make a regulated modification in circumstances where the modification will be voidable by virtue of section 67(2).
(2) The Authority may by order—
    (a) in a case within subsection (1)(a), direct the person on whom the power is conferred not to exercise the power to make the regulated modification;
    (b) require the trustees to take, within the time specified in the order, such steps as are so specified for the purpose of securing that any of the requirements mentioned in section 67(2) is satisfied.
(3) A regulated modification made in exercise of a power to which the subsisting rights provisions apply is voidable in accordance with section 67G if—
    (a) the exercise of the power contravened an order under paragraph (a) of subsection (2), or
    (b) the trustees fail to comply with a requirement imposed by an order under paragraph (b) of that subsection relating to any exercise of the power to make the modification.

**67I  Subsisting rights provisions: civil penalties**

(1) Subsections (2) and (3) apply where a regulated modification is voidable by virtue of section 67(2).
(2) Where the modification was made by the exercise of a power—
    (a) by the trustees of the scheme, or
    (b) by any other person in circumstances which do not fall within subsection (3),
    section 10 applies to any trustee who has failed to take all reasonable steps to secure that the modification is not so voidable.
(3) Section 10 applies to any person other than the trustees of the scheme who, without reasonable excuse, exercises a power to make the modification if—
    (a) the trustees have not given their consent, for the purposes of section 67E(1), to the exercise of the power to make the modification, or
    (b) in the case of any affected member, the timing requirement is not satisfied (within the meaning of section 67B) in respect of the modification.
(4) Where the trustees fail to comply with any requirement imposed, by virtue of subsection (5)(a) of section 67G, by an order under subsection (2) of that section, section

10 applies to any trustee who has failed to take all reasonable steps to secure such compliance.

(5) Where a regulated modification is made by the exercise of a power in contravention of an order under section 67H(2)(a)—
   (a) if the power is exercised by the trustees, section 10 applies to any trustee who has failed to take all reasonable steps to secure that the order was not contravened;
   (b) section 10 applies to any other person who without reasonable excuse exercises the power in contravention of the order.

(6) Where the trustees fail to comply with any requirement specified in an order under section 67H(2)(b), section 10 applies to any trustee who has failed to take all reasonable steps to secure such compliance."

*Short service benefit*

### 263 Increase in age at which short service benefit must be payable

(1) In section 71 of the Pension Schemes Act 1993 (c. 48) (basic principle as to short service benefit), for subsection (3) substitute—

"(3) Subject to subsection (4), short service benefit must be made payable as from an age which is no greater than—
   (a) the age of 65, or
   (b) if in the member's case normal pension age is greater than 65, normal pension age."

(2) In section 72 of that Act (no discrimination between short service and long service beneficiaries), at the end add—

"(4) This section is subject to subsections (3) and (6) of section 71 (age at which short service benefit is to be payable)."

*Early leavers*

### 264 Early leavers: cash transfer sums and contribution refunds

After section 101 of the Pension Schemes Act 1993 insert—

"CHAPTER 5
EARLY LEAVERS: CASH TRANSFER SUMS AND
CONTRIBUTION REFUNDS

**101AA Scope of Chapter 5**

(1) This Chapter applies to any member of an occupational pension scheme to which Chapter 1 applies (see section 69(3)) if—
   (a) his pensionable service terminates before he attains normal pension age, and
   (b) on the date on which his pensionable service terminates—
      (i) the three month condition is satisfied, but
      (ii) he does not have relevant accrued rights to benefit under the scheme.

(2) For the purposes of subsection (1), the three month condition is that the period of the member's pensionable service under the scheme, taken together with—
   (a) any previous period of his pensionable service under the scheme, and

(b) any period throughout which he was employed in linked qualifying service under another scheme,

amounts to at least three months.

(3) A period counts for the purposes of paragraph (a) or (b) of subsection (2) only so far as it counts towards qualification for long service benefit within the meaning of Chapter 1.

(4) For the purposes of subsection (1), "relevant accrued rights to benefit under the scheme", in relation to a member of a scheme, means rights which—
  (a) have accrued to or in respect of him under the scheme, and
  (b) entitle him to the relevant benefits which would have accrued to or in respect of him under the applicable rules if paragraphs (a) and (b) of section 71(1) (and the word "and" immediately preceding them) did not have effect.

(5) References in the following provisions of this Chapter to a member, in relation to an occupational pension scheme, are to a member of the scheme to whom this Chapter applies.

**101AB  Right to cash transfer sum and contribution refund**

(1) On the termination of his pensionable service, a member of an occupational pension scheme acquires a right to whichever one he elects of the following options—
  (a) a cash transfer sum;
  (b) a contribution refund.

(2) Subsection (1) is subject to the following provisions of this Chapter.

(3) In this Chapter "cash transfer sum" means, in relation to a member of an occupational pension scheme, the cash equivalent, at the date on which his pensionable service terminates, of the benefits mentioned in section 101AA(4)(b).

(4) In this Chapter, "contribution refund" means, in relation to a member of an occupational pension scheme, a sum representing the aggregate of—
  (a) the member's employee contributions to the scheme, and
  (b) where transfer credits have been allowed to the member under the scheme by virtue of a payment ("the transfer payment") made by the trustees or managers of another occupational pension scheme, the member's employee contributions to that other scheme, so far as they—
    (i) relate to the transfer payment, and
    (ii) do not, in aggregate, exceed the amount of the transfer payment.

(5) In subsection (4), "employee contributions" means, in relation to a member of an occupational pension scheme, contributions made to the scheme by or on behalf of the member on his own account, but does not include—
  (a) a transfer payment by virtue of which transfer credits have been allowed to the member under the scheme, or
  (b) any pension credit or amount paid to the scheme which is attributable (directly or indirectly) to a pension credit.

**101AC  Notification of right to cash transfer sum or contribution refund**

(1) This section applies where the pensionable service of a member of an occupational pension scheme has terminated.

(2) The trustees or managers of the scheme must—
  (a) within a reasonable period after the termination give the member a statement in writing containing information adequate to explain—

(i) the nature of the right acquired by him under section 101AB, and
(ii) how he may exercise the right,
and such other information as may be prescribed, and
  (b) afford the member a reasonable period after giving him that statement within which to exercise the right.
(3) The statement given under subsection (2)(a) must specify, in particular—
  (a) in relation to the cash transfer sum to which the member acquires a right under section 101AB, its amount and the permitted ways in which the member can use it,
  (b) the amount of the contribution refund to which the member so acquires a right, and
  (c) the last day on which the member may, disregarding section 101AI(2), exercise the right ('the reply date').
(4) Information which may be prescribed under subsection (2)(a) includes, in particular—
  (a) information about any tax liability in respect of, or deduction required or permitted to be made from, the cash transfer sum or contribution refund, and
  (b) information about the effect on other rights of the member (whether under the applicable rules or otherwise) of exercising the right.
(5) The trustees or managers may notify the member that, if he does not exercise the right mentioned in subsection (2)(a)(i) on or before the reply date, the trustees or managers will be entitled to pay the contribution refund to him.
(6) Where the trustees or managers of the scheme fail to comply with subsection (2), section 10 of the Pensions Act 1995 (civil penalties) applies to any trustee or manager who has failed to take all reasonable steps to secure compliance.

**101AD  Exercise of right under section 101AB**

(1) This section applies where a member of an occupational pension scheme acquires a right under section 101AB.
(2) The member may exercise the right by giving a notice in writing to that effect to the trustees or managers stating—
  (a) which of the options under section 101AB(1) he elects, and
  (b) if he elects for the cash transfer sum, the permitted way in which he requires that sum to be used.
(3) The notice under subsection (2) must be given on or before—
  (a) the reply date, or
  (b) such later date as the trustees or managers may allow in his case under section 101AI(2).

**101AE  Permitted ways of using cash transfer sum**

(1) This section applies in relation to a cash transfer sum to which a member of an occupational pension scheme acquires a right under section 101AB.
(2) The ways in which the cash transfer sum may be used are—
  (a) for acquiring transfer credits allowed under the rules of another occupational pension scheme—
    (i) whose trustees or managers are able and willing to accept the cash transfer sum, and
    (ii) which satisfies prescribed requirements,

(b) for acquiring rights allowed under the rules of a personal pension scheme—
  (i) whose trustees or managers are able and willing to accept the cash transfer sum, and
  (ii) which satisfies prescribed requirements,
(c) for purchasing one or more appropriate annuities,
(d) in such circumstances as may be prescribed, for subscribing to other pension arrangements which satisfy prescribed requirements.
(3) For the purposes of subsection (2), "appropriate annuity" means an annuity which satisfies prescribed requirements and is purchased from an insurer who—
  (a) falls within section 19(4)(a),
  (b) is chosen by the member, and
  (c) is willing to accept payment on account of the member from the trustees or managers of the scheme.

**101AF   Calculation of cash transfer sum and contribution refund**

(1) Cash transfer sums are to be calculated and verified in the prescribed manner.
(2) Any calculation of a contribution refund must conform with such requirements as may be prescribed.
(3) Regulations may provide—
  (a) for amounts to be deducted in respect of administrative costs in calculating cash transfer sums;
  (b) for a cash transfer sum or contribution refund to be increased or reduced in prescribed circumstances.
(4) The circumstances that may be prescribed under subsection (3)(b) include in particular—
  (a) a failure by the trustees or managers of the scheme to comply with section 101AG(2) or (4) in relation to the cash transfer sum or contribution refund, and
  (b) the state of funding of the scheme.
(5) Regulations under subsection (3)(b) may provide—
  (a) for a cash transfer sum to be reduced so that the member has no right to have any amount paid by way of cash transfer sum in respect of him;
  (b) for a contribution refund to be reduced so that the member has no right to receive any amount by way of contribution refund under this Chapter.

**101AG   Duties of trustees or managers following exercise of right**

(1) This section applies where a member of an occupational pension scheme has exercised a right under section 101AB in accordance with section 101AD.
(2) Where the member has elected for the cash transfer sum, the trustees or managers of the scheme must, within a reasonable period beginning with the date on which the right was exercised, do what is needed to carry out the requirement specified in the member's notice under section 101AD(2)(b).
(3) When the trustees or managers have done what is needed to carry out that requirement, they are discharged from any obligation—
  (a) in respect of any rights (including conditional rights) of, or in respect of, the member to relevant benefits under the applicable rules, and
  (b) to make any other payment by way of refund to or in respect of the member of, or in respect of—
    (i) the contributions, or any payment, mentioned in section 101AB(4), or

(ii) any other contributions made to the scheme, or any other scheme, in respect of the member (other than any pension credit or amount attributable (directly or indirectly) to a pension credit).
(4) Where the member has elected for the contribution refund, the trustees or managers of the scheme must, within a reasonable period beginning with the date on which the right was exercised, do what is needed to secure that the amount of the contribution refund is paid to the member or as he directs.
(5) When the trustees or managers have done what is needed to secure the payment of the contribution refund as mentioned in subsection (4)—
   (a) they are discharged from any obligation in respect of any rights (including conditional rights) of, or in respect of, the member to relevant benefits under the applicable rules, and
   (b) if they are required under the applicable rules, or determine in accordance with those rules, to make any payment ("the refund payment") by way of refund to or in respect of the member of, or in respect of—
      (i) the contributions, or any payment, mentioned in section 101AB(4), or
      (ii) any other contributions made to the scheme, or any other scheme, in respect of the member (other than any pension credit or amount attributable (directly or indirectly) to a pension credit),
   the amount of the contribution refund may be set off against the refund payment.
(6) Where the trustees or managers fail to comply with subsection (2) or (4), section 10 of the Pensions Act 1995 (civil penalties) applies to any trustee or manager who has failed to take all reasonable steps to secure compliance.

**101AH  Powers of trustees or managers where right not exercised**

(1) This section applies where—
   (a) a member of an occupational pension scheme does not exercise a right acquired by him under section 101AB on or before the reply date or such later date as the trustees or managers of the scheme allow in his case under section 101AI(2), and
   (b) the trustees or managers of the scheme have notified the member as mentioned in section 101AC(5).
(2) The trustees or managers may within a reasonable period beginning with—
   (a) the reply date, or
   (b) if a later date has been allowed as mentioned in subsection (1), that later date,
   pay the contribution refund to the member.
(3) When the trustees or managers have paid the contribution refund to the member—
   (a) they are discharged from any obligation in respect of any rights (including conditional rights) of, or in respect of, the member to relevant benefits under the applicable rules, and
   (b) if they are required under the applicable rules, or determine in accordance with those rules, to make any payment ("the refund payment") by way of refund to or in respect of the member of, or in respect of—
      (i) the contributions, or any payment, mentioned in section 101AB(4), or
      (ii) any other contributions made to the scheme, or any other scheme, in respect of the member (other than any pension credit or amount attributable (directly or indirectly) to a pension credit),
   the amount of the contribution refund may be set off against the refund payment.

**101AI Rights under section 101AB: further provisions**

(1) A member of an occupational pension scheme loses any right acquired by him under section 101AB—
   (a) if the scheme is wound up, or
   (b) subject to subsection (2), if he fails to exercise the right on or before the reply date.
(2) If the member has failed to exercise any such right on or before the reply date, the trustees or managers of the scheme may allow him to exercise it on or before such later date as they may determine on the application of the member.
(3) Where the trustees or managers determine a later date under subsection (2)—
   (a) they must give a notice in writing to that effect to the member, and
   (b) subsection (1)(b) applies in relation to the member as if the reference to the reply date were a reference to the later date.
(4) For the purposes of subsection (3) and sections 101AC(2) and 101AD(2), a document or notice may be given to a person—
   (a) by delivering it to him,
   (b) by leaving it at his proper address, or
   (c) by sending it by post to him at that address.
(5) For the purposes of subsection (4), and section 7 of the Interpretation Act 1978 (service of documents by post) in its application to that subsection, the proper address of a person is—
   (a) in the case of a body corporate, the address of the registered or principal office of the body, and
   (b) in any other case, the last known address of the person.
(6) This Chapter is subject to any provision made by or under section 61 (deduction of contributions equivalent premium from refund of scheme contributions)—
   (a) permitting any amount to be deducted from any payment of a contribution refund, or
   (b) requiring the payment of a contribution refund to be delayed.
(7) In this Chapter, except where the context otherwise requires, the following expressions have the following meanings—
   "the applicable rules" means—
   (a) the rules of the scheme, except so far as overridden by a relevant legislative provision,
   (b) the relevant legislative provisions, to the extent that they have effect in relation to the scheme and are not reflected in the rules of the scheme, and
   (c) any provision which the rules of the scheme do not contain but which the scheme must contain if it is to conform with the requirements of Chapter 1 of this Part;
   "member" has the meaning given in section 101AA(5);
   "permitted way", in relation to a cash transfer sum, means any of the ways specified in section 101AE(2) in which the sum may be used;
   "relevant benefits" means benefits which are not attributable (directly or indirectly) to a pension credit;
   "reply date", in relation to a member whose pensionable service has terminated, has the meaning given in section 101AC(3)(c).

## Pensions Act 2004, s 265

(8) For the purposes of subsection (7)—
  (a) "relevant legislative provision" means any provision contained in any of the following provisions—
     (i) Schedule 5 to the Social Security Act 1989 (equal treatment for men and women);
     (ii) this Chapter or Chapter 2, 3 or 4 of this Part of this Act or regulations made under this Chapter or any of those Chapters;
     (iii) Part 4A of this Act or regulations made under that Part;
     (iv) section 110(1) of this Act;
     (v) Part 1 of the Pensions Act 1995 (occupational pensions) or subordinate legislation made or having effect as if made under that Part;
     (vi) section 31 of the Welfare Reform and Pensions Act 1999 (pension debits: reduction of benefit);
     (vii) any provision mentioned in section 306(2) of the Pensions Act 2004;
  (b) a relevant legislative provision is to be taken to override any of the provisions of the scheme if, and only if, it does so by virtue of any of the following provisions—
     (i) paragraph 3 of Schedule 5 to the Social Security Act 1989;
     (ii) section 129(1) of this Act;
     (iii) section 117(1) of the Pensions Act 1995;
     (iv) section 31(4) of the Welfare Reform and Pensions Act 1999;
     (v) section 306(1) of the Pensions Act 2004."

*Safeguarding pension rights*

**265 Paternity leave and adoption leave**

(1) In Schedule 5 to the Social Security Act 1989 (c. 24) (employment-related schemes for pensions or other benefits: equal treatment), after paragraph 5 insert—

"5A

*Unfair paternity leave provisions*

(1) Where an employment-related benefit scheme includes any unfair paternity leave provisions (irrespective of any differences on the basis of sex in the treatment accorded to members under those provisions), then—
  (a) the scheme shall be regarded to that extent as not complying with the principle of equal treatment; and
  (b) subject to sub-paragraph (3), this Schedule shall apply accordingly.

(2) In this paragraph "unfair paternity leave provisions", in relation to an employment-related benefit scheme, means any provision—
  (a) which relates to continuing membership of, or the accrual of rights under, the scheme during any period of paid paternity leave in the case of any member who is (or who, immediately before the commencement of such a period, was) an employed earner and which treats such a member otherwise than in accordance with the normal employment requirement; or
  (b) which requires the amount of any benefit payable under the scheme to or in respect of any such member, to the extent that it falls to be determined by

reference to earnings during a period which included a period of paid paternity leave, to be determined otherwise than in accordance with the normal employment requirement.

(3) In the case of any unfair paternity leave provision—
   (a) the more favourable treatment required by paragraph 3(1) is treatment no less favourable than would be accorded to the member in accordance with the normal employment requirement; and
   (b) paragraph 3(2) does not authorize the making of any such election as is there mentioned;

but, in respect of any period of paid paternity leave, a member shall only be required to pay contributions on the amount of contractual remuneration or statutory paternity pay actually paid to or for him in respect of that period.

(4) In this paragraph—
"period of paid paternity leave", in the case of a member, means a period—
   (a) throughout which the member is absent from work in circumstances where sub-paragraph (5), (6) or (7) applies, and
   (b) for which the employer (or if he is no longer in his employment, his former employer) pays him any contractual remuneration or statutory paternity pay; and

"the normal employment requirement" is the requirement that any period of paid paternity leave shall be treated as if it were a period throughout which the member in question works normally and receives the remuneration likely to be paid for doing so.

(5) This sub-paragraph applies if—
   (a) the member's absence from work is due to the birth or expected birth of a child, and
   (b) the member satisfies the conditions prescribed under section 171ZA(2)(a)(i) and (ii) of the Social Security Contributions and Benefits Act 1992 in relation to that child.

(6) This sub-paragraph applies if—
   (a) the member's absence from work is due to the placement or expected placement of a child for adoption under the law of any part of the United Kingdom, and
   (b) the member satisfies the conditions prescribed under section 171ZB(2)(a)(i) and (ii) of that Act in relation to that child.

(7) This sub-paragraph applies if—
   (a) the member's absence from work is due to the adoption or expected adoption of a child who has entered the United Kingdom in connection with or for the purposes of adoption which does not involve the placement of the child for adoption under the law of any part of the United Kingdom, and
   (b) the member satisfies the conditions prescribed under section 171ZB(2)(a)(i) and (ii) of that Act (as applied by virtue of section 171ZK of that Act (adoption cases not involving placement under the law of the United Kingdom)) in relation to that child.

5B

*Unfair adoption leave provisions*

(1) Where an employment-related benefit scheme includes any unfair adoption leave provisions (irrespective of any differences on the basis of sex in the treatment accorded to members under those provisions), then—
   (a) the scheme shall be regarded to that extent as not complying with the principle of equal treatment; and
   (b) subject to sub-paragraph (3), this Schedule shall apply accordingly.
(2) In this paragraph "unfair adoption leave provisions", in relation to an employment-related benefit scheme, means any provision—
   (a) which relates to continuing membership of, or the accrual of rights under, the scheme during any period of paid adoption leave in the case of any member who is (or who, immediately before the commencement of such a period, was) an employed earner and which treats such a member otherwise than in accordance with the normal employment requirement; or
   (b) which requires the amount of any benefit payable under the scheme to or in respect of any such member, to the extent that it falls to be determined by reference to earnings during a period which included a period of paid adoption leave, to be determined otherwise than in accordance with the normal employment requirement.
(3) In the case of any unfair adoption leave provision—
   (a) the more favourable treatment required by paragraph 3(1) is treatment no less favourable than would be accorded to the member in accordance with the normal employment requirement; and
   (b) paragraph 3(2) does not authorize the making of any such election as is there mentioned;

but, in respect of any period of paid adoption leave, a member shall only be required to pay contributions on the amount of contractual remuneration or statutory adoption pay actually paid to or for him in respect of that period.

(4) In this paragraph—
"period of paid adoption leave", in the case of a member, means a period—
   (a) throughout which the member is absent from work in circumstances where sub-paragraph (5) or (6) applies, and
   (b) for which the employer (or, if he is no longer in his employment, his former employer) pays him any contractual remuneration or statutory adoption pay; and

"the normal employment requirement" is the requirement that any period of paid adoption leave shall be treated as if it were a period throughout which the member in question works normally and receives the remuneration likely to be paid for doing so.

(5) This sub-paragraph applies if—
   (a) the member's absence from work is due to the placement, or expected placement, of a child for adoption under the law of any part of the United Kingdom, and
   (b) the member is a person with whom the child is, or is expected to be, placed for such adoption.
(6) This sub-paragraph applies if—

(a) the member's absence from work is due to the adoption or expected adoption of a child who has entered the United Kingdom in connection with or for the purposes of adoption which does not involve the placement of the child for adoption under the law of any part of the United Kingdom, and

(b) the member is a person by whom the child has been or is expected to be adopted."

(2) The provision that may be made under section 142(1) of the Adoption and Children Act 2002 (c. 38) (power to make consequential etc provision to give full effect to any provision of that Act) includes provision modifying paragraph 5A or 5B of Schedule 5 to the Social Security Act 1989 (c. 24) (as inserted by subsection (1) above).

## 266  Inalienability of occupational pension

(1) Section 91 of the Pensions Act 1995 (c. 26) (inalienability of occupational pension) is amended as follows.

(2) In subsection (5) (exceptions to the rule of inalienability) at the end insert—

"(f) subject to subsection (6), a charge or lien on, or set-off against, the person in question's entitlement, or right, for the purpose of discharging some monetary obligation due from the person in question to the scheme arising out of a payment made in error in respect of the pension."

(3) In subsection (6) (limits on the charge, lien or set-off under subsection (5)(d) or (e)) for "or (e)" substitute ", (e) or (f)".

*Voluntary contributions*

## 267  Voluntary contributions

(1) Omit section 111 of the Pension Schemes Act 1993 (c. 48) (requirements for schemes to provide facilities for members to pay voluntary contributions, and relating to any such contributions).

(2) In section 132 of that Act (duty to bring schemes into conformity with indirectly-applying requirements) omit from "or the voluntary" to third "requirements".

(3) In section 181(1) of that Act (general interpretation) omit the definition of "voluntary contributions requirements".

*Payments by employers*

## 268  Payments made by employers to personal pension schemes

(1) Section 111A of the Pension Schemes Act 1993 (c. 48) (monitoring of employers' payments to personal pension schemes) is amended as follows.

(2) For subsections (3) to (7) substitute—

"(3) The trustees or managers of the scheme must monitor the payment of contributions by or on behalf of the employer under the direct payment arrangements.

(4) The trustees or managers may request the employer to provide them, (or arrange for them to be provided) with the payment information specified in the request.

(5) For the purposes of subsection (4) "payment information" is information required by the trustees or managers to enable them to discharge the duty imposed by subsection (3).

(6) The employer must comply with a request under subsection (4) within a reasonable period.

(7) Where, as a result of the employer's failure to so comply, the trustees or managers are unable to discharge the duty imposed by subsection (3), they must give notice to that effect to the Regulatory Authority within a reasonable period.

(7A) Where—
- (a) a contribution payable under the direct payment arrangements has not been paid on or before its due date, and
- (b) the trustees or managers have reasonable cause to believe that the failure to pay the contribution is likely to be of material significance in the exercise by the Regulatory Authority of any of their functions,

they must give notice to that effect to the Regulatory Authority and the employee within a reasonable period after the due date."

(3) In subsection (8) (employer's liability for civil penalties) for "subsection (3) or (5)" substitute "subsection (6) and as a result the trustees or managers of the scheme are unable to discharge the duty imposed by subsection (3)".

(4) In subsection (9) (liability of trustees or managers for civil penalties) for "subsection (6) or (7)" substitute "subsection (7) or (7A)".

## 269 Payments made by employers and members to occupational pension schemes

(1) In section 49 of the Pensions Act 1995 (c. 26) (other responsibilities of trustees, employers, etc), in subsection (9) (duty of trustee etc to report a failure by employer to pay contributions deducted from earnings on time) for paragraph (b) substitute—

"(b) if the trustees or managers have reasonable cause to believe that the failure is likely to be of material significance in the exercise by the Authority of any of their functions, they must, except in prescribed circumstances, give notice of the failure to the Authority and the member within a reasonable period after the end of the prescribed period under subsection (8)."

(2) In section 88 of that Act (schedules of payments to money purchase schemes), for subsection (1) (duty of trustees or managers to report a failure to pay amounts on time) substitute—

"(1) Where, in the case of an occupational pension scheme to which section 87 applies—
- (a) there is a failure to pay on or before the due date any amounts payable in accordance with the payment schedule, and
- (b) the trustees or managers have reasonable cause to believe that the failure is likely to be of material significance in the exercise by the Authority of any of their functions,

they must, except in prescribed circumstances, give notice of the failure to the Authority and to the members of the scheme within a reasonable period after the due date."

*Winding up*

## 270 Winding up

(1) For section 73 of the Pensions Act 1995 (c. 26) (preferential liabilities on winding up) substitute—

"**73 Preferential liabilities on winding up**

(1) This section applies where an occupational pension scheme to which this section applies is being wound up to determine the order in which the assets of the scheme are to be applied towards satisfying the liabilities of the scheme in respect of pensions and other benefits.

(2) This section applies to an occupational pension scheme other than a scheme which is—

(a) a money purchase scheme, or

(b) a prescribed scheme or a scheme of a prescribed description.

(3) The assets of the scheme must be applied first towards satisfying the amounts of the liabilities mentioned in subsection (4) and, if the assets are insufficient to satisfy those amounts in full, then—

(a) the assets must be applied first towards satisfying the amounts of the liabilities mentioned in earlier paragraphs of subsection (4) before the amounts of the liabilities mentioned in later paragraphs, and

(b) where the amounts of the liabilities mentioned in one of those paragraphs cannot be satisfied in full, those amounts must be satisfied in the same proportions.

(4) The liabilities referred to in subsection (3) are—

(a) where—

(i) the trustees or managers of the scheme are entitled to benefits under a relevant pre-1997 contract of insurance entered into in relation to the scheme, and

(ii) either that contract may not be surrendered or the amount payable on surrender does not exceed the liability secured by the contract,

the liability so secured;

(b) any liability for pensions or other benefits to the extent that the amount of the liability does not exceed the corresponding PPF liability, other than a liability within paragraph (a);

(c) any liability for pensions or other benefits which, in the opinion of the trustees or managers, are derived from the payment by any member of voluntary contributions, other than a liability within paragraph (a) or (b);

(d) any other liability in respect of pensions or other benefits.

(5) For the purposes of subsection (4)—

"corresponding PPF liability" in relation to any liability for pensions or other benefits means—

(a) where the liability is to a member of the scheme, the cost of securing benefits for or in respect of the member corresponding to the compensation which would be payable to or in respect of the member in accordance with the pension compensation provisions if the Board of the Pension Protection Fund assumed responsibility for the scheme in accordance with Chapter 3 of Part 2 of the Pensions Act 2004 (pension protection), and

(b) where the liability is to another person in respect of a member of the scheme, the cost of securing benefits for that person corresponding to the compensation which would be payable to that person in respect of the member in accordance with the pension compensation provisions if the Board assumed responsibility for the scheme in accordance with that Chapter;

"relevant pre-1997 contract of insurance" means a contract of insurance which was entered into before 6th April 1997 with a view to securing the whole or part of the scheme's liability for—

(a) any pension or other benefit payable to or in respect of one particular person whose entitlement to payment of a pension or other benefit has arisen, and

(b) any benefit which will be payable in respect of that person on his death.

(6) For the purposes of this section, when determining the corresponding PPF liability in relation to any liability of a scheme to, or in respect of, a member for pensions or other benefits, the pension compensation provisions apply with such modifications as may be prescribed.

(7) Regulations may modify subsection (4).

(8) For the purposes of that subsection—

(a) regulations may prescribe how it is to be determined whether a liability for pensions or other benefits which, in the opinion of the trustees or managers of the scheme, are derived from the payment by any member of voluntary contributions falls within paragraph (a) or (b) of that subsection;

(b) no pension or other benefit which is attributable (directly or indirectly) to a pension credit is to be regarded for the purposes of paragraph (c) of that subsection as derived from the payment of voluntary contributions.

(9) Where, on the commencement of the winding up period, a member becomes a person to whom Chapter 5 of Part 4 of the Pension Schemes Act 1993 (early leavers: cash transfer sums and contribution refunds) applies, that Chapter applies in relation to him with such modifications as may be prescribed.

(10) For the purposes of this section—

"assets" of a scheme to which this section applies do not include any assets representing the value of any rights in respect of money purchase benefits under the scheme rules;

"liabilities" of such a scheme do not include any liabilities in respect of money purchase benefits under the scheme rules;

"the pension compensation provisions" has the same meaning as in Part 2 of the Pensions Act 2004 (see section 162 of that Act);

"scheme rules" has the same meaning as in the Pensions Act 2004 (see section 318 of that Act);

"winding up period", in relation to an occupational pension scheme to which this section applies, means the period which—

(a) begins with the day on which the time immediately after the beginning of the winding up of the scheme falls, and

(b) ends when the winding up of the scheme is completed.

### 73A  Operation of scheme during winding up period

(1) This section applies where an occupational pension scheme to which section 73 applies is being wound up.

(2) During the winding up period, the trustees or managers of the scheme—

(a) must secure that any pensions or other benefits (other than money purchase benefits) paid to or in respect of a member are reduced, so far as necessary, to reflect the liabilities of the scheme to or in respect of the member which will be satisfied in accordance with section 73, and

    (b) may, for the purposes of paragraph (a), take such steps as they consider appropriate (including steps adjusting future payments) to recover any overpayment or pay any shortfall.

(3) During the winding up period—
    (a) no benefits may accrue under the scheme rules to, or in respect of, members of the scheme, and
    (b) no new members of any class may be admitted to the scheme.

(4) Subsection (3) does not prevent any increase, in a benefit, which would otherwise accrue in accordance with the scheme or any enactment.

(5) Subsection (3) does not prevent the accrual of money purchase benefits to the extent that they are derived from income or capital gains arising from the investment of payments which are made by, or in respect of, a member of the scheme.

(6) Where a person is entitled to a pension credit derived from another person's shareable rights under the scheme, subsection (3) does not prevent the trustees or managers of the scheme discharging their liability in respect of the credit under Chapter 1 of Part 4 of the Welfare Reform and Pensions Act 1999 (sharing of rights under pension arrangements) by conferring appropriate rights under the scheme on that person.

(7) Regulations may require the trustees or managers of the scheme, in prescribed circumstances—
    (a) to adjust the entitlement of a person to a pension or other benefit under the scheme rules where the entitlement arises as a result of a discretionary award which takes effect during the winding up period;
    (b) to adjust the entitlement of a person ("the survivor") to a pension or other benefit under the scheme rules where—
        (i) a member of the scheme, or a person who was (or might have become) entitled to a pension or other benefit in respect of a member, dies during the winding up period, and
        (ii) the survivor's entitlement is to a pension or other benefit in respect of the member (whether arising on the date of that death or subsequently).

(8) Regulations under subsection (7) may, in particular—
    (a) prescribe how the required adjustments to entitlement are to be determined and the manner in which they are to be made;
    (b) in a case where the commencement of the winding up of the scheme is backdated (whether in accordance with section 154 of the Pensions Act 2004 (requirement to wind up schemes with sufficient assets to meet protected liabilities) or otherwise), require any adjustment to a person's entitlement to be made with effect from the time the award takes effect;
    (c) without prejudice to sections 10(3) to (9), 73B(2) and 116, make provision about the consequences of breaching the requirements of the regulations.

(9) If the scheme confers power on any person other than the trustees or managers of the scheme to apply the assets of the scheme in respect of pensions or other benefits (including increases in pensions or benefits), it cannot be exercised by that person but may, subject to the provisions made by or by virtue of this

section and sections 73 and 73B, be exercised instead by the trustees or managers.

(10) For the purposes of this section—

"appropriate rights" has the same meaning as in paragraph 5 of Schedule 5 to the Welfare Reform and Pensions Act 1999 (pension credits: mode of discharge);

"discretionary award" means an award of a prescribed description;

"shareable rights" has the same meaning as in Chapter 1 of Part 4 of the Welfare Reform and Pensions Act 1999 (sharing of rights under pension arrangements);

and subsection (10) of section 73 applies as it applies for the purposes of that section.

## 73B  Sections 73 and 73A: supplementary

(1) Any action taken in contravention of section 73A(3) is void.
(2) If any provision made by or by virtue of the winding up provisions is not complied with in relation to a scheme to which section 73 applies, section 10 applies to any trustee or manager of the scheme who has failed to take all reasonable steps to secure compliance.
(3) For the purposes of subsection (2), when determining whether section 73A(3) has been complied with subsection (1) of this section is to be disregarded.
(4) Regulations may—
    (a) prescribe how, for the purposes of the winding up provisions—
        (i) the assets and liabilities of a scheme to which section 73 applies, and
        (ii) their value or amount,
        are to be determined, calculated and verified;
    (b) modify any of the winding up provisions as it applies—
        (i) to prescribed schemes or prescribed descriptions of schemes;
        (ii) in relation to a scheme where only part of the scheme is being wound up;
        (iii) in relation to a case where any liability of the scheme in respect of a member has been discharged by virtue of regulations under section 135(4) of the Pensions Act 2004 (power to make regulations permitting discharge of scheme's liabilities during an assessment period).
(5) Without prejudice to the generality of subsection (4), regulations under paragraph (b)(i) of that subsection may, in particular, modify any of the winding up provisions as it applies in relation to a scheme in relation to which there is more than one employer.
(6) The winding up provisions do not apply—
    (a) in relation to any liability for an amount by way of pensions or other benefits which a person became entitled to payment of, under the scheme rules, before commencement of the winding up period,
    (b) in prescribed circumstances, in relation to any liability in respect of rights of a prescribed description to which a member of the scheme became entitled under the scheme rules by reason of his pensionable service under the scheme terminating before the commencement of the winding up period,
    (c) in relation to any liability in respect of rights of prescribed descriptions to which a member of the scheme had become entitled under the scheme rules before the commencement of the winding up period, or

(d) in relation to any liability the discharge of which is validated under section 136 of the Pensions Act 2004 (power to validate actions taken during an assessment period to discharge liabilities of a scheme).

(7) But nothing in subsection (6) prevents the winding up provisions applying in relation to a liability under Chapter 4 of Part 4 of the Pension Schemes Act 1993 (transfer values) which—
 (a) arose before the commencement of the winding up of the scheme, and
 (b) was not discharged before the commencement of the winding up period.

(8) Regulations may provide that, in prescribed circumstances, where—
 (a) an occupational pension scheme to which section 73 applies is being wound up,
 (b) a member of the scheme died before the winding up began, and
 (c) during the winding up period a person becomes entitled under the scheme rules to a benefit of a prescribed description in respect of the member,
 his entitlement to payment of all or part of the benefit is, for the purposes of subsection (6), to be treated as having arisen immediately before the commencement of the winding up period.

(9) If, immediately before the winding up period in relation to an occupational pension scheme to which section 73 applies, a person is entitled to an amount but has postponed payment of it, he is not, for the purposes of subsection (6), to be regarded as having become entitled to payment of the amount before that period.

(10) For the purposes of this section—
 (a) "winding up provisions" means this section and sections 73, 73A and 74, and
 (b) subsection (10) of section 73 applies as it applies for the purposes of that section."

(2) In section 74 of the Pensions Act 1995 (c. 26) (discharge of liabilities by insurance, etc on winding up)—
 (a) for subsection (1) substitute—
  "(1) This section applies where an occupational pension scheme to which section 73 applies is being wound up.",
 (b) in subsection (2) omit "(including increases in pensions)",
 (c) in subsection (3), after paragraph (d) insert—
  "(e) by the payment of a cash sum in circumstances where prescribed requirements are met.",
 (d) in subsection (4)—
  (i) for "rules of the scheme" substitute "scheme rules", and
  (ii) omit "(including increases in pensions)",
 (e) omit subsection (5)(b) and the word "or" immediately preceding it, and
 (f) after subsection (5) insert—
  "(6) For the purposes of this section—
   (a) references to assets of the scheme do not include any assets representing the value of any rights in respect of money purchase benefits under the scheme rules, and
   (b) references to liabilities of the scheme do not include any liabilities in respect of money purchase benefits under the scheme rules;
  and "scheme rules" has the same meaning as in the Pensions Act 2004 (see section 318 of that Act)."

*Deficiency in assets of certain occupational pension schemes*

**271 Debt due from the employer when assets insufficient**

(1) Section 75 of the Pensions Act 1995 (c. 26) (deficiencies in the assets) is amended as follows.

(2) For subsections (1) to (4) substitute—

"(1) This section applies in relation to an occupational pension scheme other than a scheme which is—
   (a) a money purchase scheme, or
   (b) a prescribed scheme or a scheme of a prescribed description.

(2) If—
   (a) at any time which falls—
      (i) when a scheme is being wound up, but
      (ii) before any relevant event in relation to the employer which occurs while the scheme is being wound up,
      the value of the assets of the scheme is less than the amount at that time of the liabilities of the scheme, and
   (b) the trustees or managers of the scheme designate that time for the purposes of this subsection (before the occurrence of an event within paragraph (a)(ii)),
   an amount equal to the difference shall be treated as a debt due from the employer to the trustees or managers of the scheme.
   This is subject to subsection (3).

(3) Subsection (2) applies only if—
   (a) either—
      (i) no relevant event within subsection (6A)(a) or (b) occurred in relation to the employer during the period beginning with the appointed day and ending with the commencement of the winding up of the scheme, or
      (ii) during the period—
         (a) beginning with the occurrence of the last such relevant event which occurred during the period mentioned in sub-paragraph (i), and
         (b) ending with the commencement of the winding up of the scheme,
      a cessation notice was issued in relation to the scheme and became binding, and
   (b) no relevant event within subsection (6A)(c) has occurred in relation to the employer during the period mentioned in paragraph (a)(i).

(4) Where—
   (a) immediately before a relevant event ('the current event') occurs in relation to the employer the value of the assets of the scheme is less than the amount at that time of the liabilities of the scheme,
   (b) the current event—
      (i) occurred on or after the appointed day, and
      (ii) did not occur in prescribed circumstances,
   (c) if the scheme was being wound up immediately before that event, subsection (2) has not applied in relation to the scheme to treat an amount as a debt due from the employer to the trustees or managers of the scheme,

(d) if the current event is within subsection (6A)(a) or (b), either—
  (i) no relevant event within subsection (6A)(a) or (b) occurred in relation to the employer during the period beginning with the appointed day and ending immediately before the current event, or
  (ii) a cessation event has occurred in relation to the scheme in respect of a cessation notice issued during the period—
    (a) beginning with the occurrence of the last such relevant event which occurred during the period mentioned in sub-paragraph (i), and
    (b) ending immediately before the current event, and
(e) no relevant event within subsection (6A)(c) has occurred in relation to the employer during the period mentioned in paragraph (d)(i),
an amount equal to the difference shall be treated as a debt due from the employer to the trustees or managers of the scheme.
(4A) Where the current event is within subsection (6A)(a) or (b), the debt under subsection (4) is to be taken, for the purposes of the law relating to insolvency as it applies to the employer, to arise immediately before the occurrence of the current event.
(4B) Subsection (4C) applies if, in a case within subsection (4)—
  (a) the current event is within subsection (6A)(a) or (b), and
  (b) the scheme was not being wound up immediately before that event.
(4C) Where this subsection applies, the debt due from the employer under subsection (4) is contingent upon—
  (a) a scheme failure notice being issued in relation to the scheme after the current event and the following conditions being satisfied—
    (i) the scheme failure notice is binding,
    (ii) no relevant event within subsection (6A)(c) has occurred in relation to the employer before the scheme failure notice became binding, and
    (iii) a cessation event has not occurred in relation to the scheme in respect of a cessation notice issued during the period—
      (a) beginning with the occurrence of the current event, and
      (b) ending immediately before the issuing of the scheme failure notice,
    and the occurrence of such a cessation event in respect of a cessation notice issued during that period is not a possibility, or
  (b) the commencement of the winding up of the scheme before—
    (i) any scheme failure notice or cessation notice issued in relation to the scheme becomes binding, or
    (ii) any relevant event within subsection (6A)(c) occurs in relation to the employer."
(3) In subsection (5) for "subsection (1)" substitute "subsections (2) and (4)".
(4) In subsection (6)—
  (a) after "scheme" insert "rules", and
  (b) at the end insert—
  "In this subsection 'scheme rules' has the same meaning as in the Pensions Act 2004 ('the 2004 Act') (see section 318 of that Act)."
(5) After subsection (6) insert—
  "(6A) For the purposes of this section, a relevant event occurs in relation to the employer in relation to an occupational pension scheme if and when—
  (a) an insolvency event occurs in relation to the employer,

(b) the trustees or managers of the scheme make an application under subsection (1) of section 129 of the 2004 Act or receive a notice from the Board of the Pension Protection Fund under subsection (5)(a) of that section, or

(c) a resolution is passed for a voluntary winding up of the employer in a case where a declaration of solvency has been made under section 89 of the Insolvency Act 1986 (members' voluntary winding up).

(6B) For the purposes of this section—

(a) a "cessation notice", in the case of a relevant event within subsection (6A)(a), means—
  (i) a withdrawal notice issued under section 122(2)(b) of the 2004 Act (scheme rescue has occurred),
  (ii) a withdrawal notice issued under section 148 of that Act (no insolvency event has occurred or is likely to occur),
  (iii) a notice issued under section 122(4) of that Act (inability to confirm status of scheme) in a case where the notice has become binding and section 148 of that Act does not apply,

(b) a "cessation notice" in the case of a relevant event within subsection (6A)(b), means a withdrawal notice issued under section 130(3) of the 2004 Act (scheme rescue has occurred),

(c) a cessation event occurs in relation to a scheme when a cessation notice in relation to the scheme becomes binding,

(d) the occurrence of a cessation event in relation to a scheme in respect of a cessation notice issued during a particular period ('the specified period') is a possibility until each of the following are no longer reviewable—
  (i) any cessation notice which has been issued in relation to the scheme during the specified period,
  (ii) any failure to issue such a cessation notice during the specified period,
  (iii) any notice which has been issued by the Board under Chapter 2 or 3 of Part 2 of the 2004 Act which is relevant to the issue of a cessation notice in relation to the scheme during the specified period or to such a cessation notice which has been issued during that period becoming binding,
  (iv) any failure to issue such a notice as is mentioned in sub-paragraph (iii),

(e) the issue or failure to issue a notice is to be regarded as reviewable—
  (i) during the period within which it may be reviewed by virtue of Chapter 6 of Part 2 of the 2004 Act, and
  (ii) if the matter is so reviewed, until—
    (a) the review and any reconsideration,
    (b) any reference to the Ombudsman for the Board of the Pension Protection Fund in respect of the matter, and
    (c) any appeal against his determination or directions,
    has been finally disposed of, and

(f) a "scheme failure notice" means a scheme failure notice issued under section 122(2)(a) or 130(2) of the 2004 Act (scheme rescue not possible).

(6C) For the purposes of this section—

(a) section 121 of the 2004 Act applies for the purposes of determining if and when an insolvency event has occurred in relation to the employer,

(b) "appointed day" means the day appointed under section 126(2) of the 2004

**s 271, Pensions Act 2004**

Act (no pension protection under Chapter 3 of Part 2 of that Act if the scheme begins winding up before the day appointed by the Secretary of State),

(c) references to a relevant event in relation to an employer do not include a relevant event which occurred in relation to him before he became the employer in relation to the scheme,

(d) references to a cessation notice becoming binding are to the notice in question mentioned in subsection (6B)(a) or (b) and issued under Part 2 of the 2004 Act becoming binding within the meaning given by that Part of that Act, and

(e) references to a scheme failure notice becoming binding are to the notice in question mentioned in subsection (6B)(f) and issued under Part 2 of the 2004 Act becoming binding within the meaning given by that Part of that Act.

(6D) Where—

(a) a resolution is passed for a voluntary winding up of the employer in a case where a declaration of solvency has been made under section 89 of the Insolvency Act 1986 (members' voluntary winding up), and

(b) either—

   (i) the voluntary winding up of the employer is stayed other than in prescribed circumstances, or

   (ii) a meeting of creditors is held in relation to the employer under section 95 of that Act (creditors' meeting which has the effect of converting a members' voluntary winding up into a creditors' voluntary winding up),

this section has effect as if that resolution had never been passed and any debt which arose under this section by virtue of the passing of that resolution shall be treated as if it had never arisen."

(6) Omit subsection (9).

### 272 Debt due from the employer in the case of multi-employer schemes

After section 75 of the Pensions Act 1995 (c. 26) (deficiencies in the assets) insert—

**"75A Deficiencies in the assets: multi-employer schemes**

(1) Regulations may modify section 75 (deficiencies in the assets) as it applies in relation to multi-employer schemes.

(2) The regulations may in particular provide for the circumstances in which a debt is to be treated as due under section 75 from an employer in relation to a multi-employer scheme (a 'multi-employer debt').

(3) Those circumstances may include circumstances other than those in which the scheme is being wound up or a relevant event occurs (within the meaning of section 75).

(4) For the purposes of regulations under this section, regulations under section 75(5) may prescribe alternative manners for determining, calculating and verifying—

(a) the liabilities and assets of the scheme to be taken into account, and

(b) their amount or value.

(5) The regulations under this section may in particular—

(a) provide for the application of each of the prescribed alternative manners under section 75(5) to depend upon whether prescribed requirements are met;
(b) provide that, where in a particular case a prescribed alternative manner under section 75(5) is applied, the Authority may in prescribed circumstances issue a direction—
  (i) that any resulting multi-employer debt is to be unenforceable for such a period as the Authority may specify, and
  (ii) that the amount of the debt is to be re-calculated applying a different prescribed manner under section 75(5) if prescribed requirements are met within that period.
(6) The prescribed requirements mentioned in subsection (5) may include a requirement that a prescribed arrangement, the details of which are approved in a notice issued by the Authority, is in place.
(7) The regulations may provide that the Authority may not approve the details of such an arrangement unless prescribed conditions are met.
(8) Those prescribed conditions may include a requirement that—
  (a) the arrangement identifies one or more persons to whom the Authority may issue a contribution notice under the regulations, and
  (b) the Authority are satisfied of prescribed matters in respect of each of those persons.
(9) For the purposes of subsection (8) a "contribution notice" is a notice stating that the person to whom it is issued is under a liability to pay the sum specified in the notice—
  (a) to the trustees of the multi-employer scheme in question, or
  (b) where the Board of the Pension Protection Fund has assumed responsibility for the scheme in accordance with Chapter 3 of Part 2 of the Pensions Act 2004 (pension protection), to the Board.
(10) The regulations may provide for the Authority to have power to issue a contribution notice to a person identified in an arrangement as mentioned in subsection (8) if—
  (a) the arrangement ceases to be in place or the Authority consider that the arrangement is no longer appropriate, and
  (b) the Authority are of the opinion that it is reasonable to impose liability on the person to pay the sum specified in the notice.
(11) Where a contribution notice is issued to a person under the regulations as mentioned in subsection (8), the sum specified in the notice is to be treated as a debt due from that person to the person to whom it is to be paid as specified in the notice.
(12) Where the regulations provide for the issuing of a contribution notice by the Authority as mentioned in subsection (8)—
  (a) the regulations must—
    (i) provide for how the sum specified by the Authority in a contribution notice is to be determined,
    (ii) provide for the circumstances (if any) in which a person to whom a contribution notice is issued is jointly and severally liable for the debt,
    (iii) provide for the matters which the notice must contain, and
    (iv) provide for who may exercise the powers to recover the debt due by virtue of the contribution notice, and
  (b) the regulations may apply with or without modifications some or all of the provisions of sections 47 to 51 of the Pensions Act 2004 (contribution notices

where non-compliance with financial support direction) in relation to contribution notices issued under the regulations.

(13) In this section "multi-employer scheme" means a trust scheme which applies to earners in employments under different employers.

(14) This section is without prejudice to the powers conferred by—

section 75(5) (power to prescribe the manner of determining, calculating and verifying assets and liabilities etc),

section 75(10) (power to modify section 75 as it applies in prescribed circumstances),

section 118(1)(a) (power to modify any provisions of this Part in their application to multi-employer trust schemes), and

section 125(3) (power to extend for the purposes of this Part the meaning of "employer")."

*Pension disputes*

**273 Resolution of disputes**

For section 50 of the Pensions Act 1995 (c. 26) (resolution of disputes) substitute—

**"50 Requirement for dispute resolution arrangements**

(1) The trustees or managers of an occupational pension scheme must secure that dispute resolution arrangements are made and implemented.

(2) Dispute resolution arrangements are such arrangements as are required by this section for the resolution of pension disputes.

(3) For this purpose a pension dispute is a dispute which—
   (a) is between—
      (i) the trustees or managers of a scheme, and
      (ii) one or more persons with an interest in the scheme (see section 50A),
   (b) is about matters relating to the scheme, and
   (c) is not an exempted dispute (see subsection (9)).

(4) The dispute resolution arrangements must provide a procedure—
   (a) for any of the parties to the dispute mentioned in subsection (3)(a)(ii) to make an application for a decision to be taken on the matters in dispute ("an application for the resolution of a pension dispute"), and
   (b) for the trustees or managers to take that decision.

(5) Where an application for the resolution of a pension dispute is made in accordance with the dispute resolution arrangements, the trustees or managers must—
   (a) take the decision required on the matters in dispute within a reasonable period of the receipt of the application by them, and
   (b) notify the applicant of the decision within a reasonable period of it having been taken.

(6) The procedure provided for by the dispute resolution arrangements must include the provision required by section 50B.

(7) Dispute resolution arrangements under subsection (1) must, in the case of existing schemes, have effect on and after the date of commencement of this section in relation to applications made on or after that date.

(8) This section does not apply in relation to an occupational pension scheme if—
   (a) every member of the scheme is a trustee of the scheme,

(b) the scheme has no more than one member, or
(c) the scheme is of a prescribed description.
(9) For the purposes of this section a dispute is an exempted dispute if—
    (a) proceedings in respect of it have been commenced in any court or Tribunal,
    (b) the Pensions Ombudsman has commenced an investigation in respect of it as a result of a complaint made or a dispute referred to him, or
    (c) it is of a prescribed description.
(10) If, in the case of an occupational pension scheme, the dispute resolution arrangements required by this section to be made—
    (a) have not been made, or
    (b) are not being implemented,
    section 10 applies to any of the trustees or managers who have failed to take all reasonable steps to secure that such arrangements are made or implemented.

**50A Meaning of "person with an interest in the scheme"**

(1) For the purposes of section 50 a person is a person with an interest in an occupational pension scheme if—
    (a) is a member of the scheme,
    (b) he is a widow, widower or surviving dependant of a deceased member of the scheme,
    (c) he is a surviving non-dependant beneficiary of a deceased member of the scheme,
    (d) he is a prospective member of the scheme,
    (e) he has ceased to be within any of the categories of persons referred to in paragraphs (a) to (d), or
    (f) he claims to be such a person as is mentioned in paragraphs (a) to (e) and the dispute relates to whether he is such a person.
(2) In subsection (1)(c) a "non-dependant beneficiary", in relation to a deceased member of an occupational pension scheme, means a person who, on the death of the member, is entitled to the payment of benefits under the scheme.
(3) In subsection (1)(d) a "prospective member" means any person who, under the terms of his contract of service or the rules of the scheme—
    (a) is able, at his own option, to become a member of the scheme,
    (b) will become so able if he continues in the same employment for a sufficiently long period,
    (c) will be admitted to the scheme automatically unless he makes an election not to become a member, or
    (d) may be admitted to it subject to the consent of his employer.

**50B The dispute resolution procedure**

(1) The procedure provided for by the dispute resolution arrangements under section 50 must include the following provision.
(2) The procedure must provide that an application for the resolution of a pension dispute under section 50(4) may be made or continued on behalf of a person who is a party to the dispute mentioned in section 50(3)(a)(ii)—
    (a) where the person dies, by his personal representative,
    (b) where the person is a minor or is otherwise incapable of acting for himself, by a member of his family or some other person suitable to represent him, and
    (c) in any other case, by a representative nominated by him.

**s 273, Pensions Act 2004**

(3) The procedure may include provision about the time limits for making an application for the resolution of a pension dispute but it must require that—

    (a) in the case of a person with an interest in a scheme as mentioned in section 50A(1)(e), the time limit for making an application is the end of the period of six months beginning immediately after the date upon which he ceased to be a person with an interest as mentioned in section 50A(1)(a), (b), (c) or (d), and

    (b) in the case of a person with an interest in a scheme as mentioned in section 50A(1)(f) who is claiming to be such a person as is mentioned in section 50A(1)(e), the time limit for making an application is the end of the period of six months beginning immediately after the date upon which he claims that he ceased to be a person with an interest as mentioned in section 50A(1)(a), (b), (c) or (d).

(4) The procedure must include provision about—

    (a) the manner in which an application for the resolution of a pension dispute is to be made,

    (b) the particulars which must be included in such an application, and

    (c) the manner in which any decisions required are to be reached and given.

(5) The procedure must provide that if, after an application for the resolution of a pension dispute has been made, the dispute becomes an exempted dispute within the meaning of section 50(9)(a) or (b), the resolution of the dispute under the procedure ceases."

*The Pensions Ombudsman*

**274 The Pensions Ombudsman and Deputy Pensions Ombudsmen**

(1) In subsection (2) of section 145 of the Pension Schemes Act 1993 (c. 48) (the Pensions Ombudsman) after "hold" insert "and vacate".

(2) For subsection (3) of that section substitute—

"(3) The Pensions Ombudsman may resign or be removed from office in accordance with those terms and conditions."

(3) After that section insert—

**"145A Deputy Pensions Ombudsmen**

(1) The Secretary of State may appoint one or more persons to act as a deputy to the Pensions Ombudsman ("a Deputy Pensions Ombudsman").

(2) Any such appointment is to be upon such terms and conditions as the Secretary of State thinks fit.

(3) A Deputy Pensions Ombudsman—

    (a) is to hold and vacate office in accordance with the terms and conditions of his appointment, and

    (b) may resign or be removed from office in accordance with those terms and conditions.

(4) A Deputy Pensions Ombudsman may perform the functions of the Pensions Ombudsman—

    (a) during any vacancy in that office,

    (b) at any time when the Pensions Ombudsman is for any reason unable to discharge his functions, or

    (c) at any other time, with the consent of the Secretary of State.

(5) References to the Pensions Ombudsman in relation to the performance of his functions are accordingly to be construed as including references to a Deputy Pensions Ombudsman in relation to the performance of those functions.

(6) The Secretary of State may—

  (a) pay to or in respect of a Deputy Pensions Ombudsman such amounts—

    (i) by way of remuneration, compensation for loss of office, pension, allowances and gratuities, or

    (ii) by way of provision for any such benefits,

    as the Secretary of State may determine, and

  (b) reimburse the Pensions Ombudsman in respect of any expenses incurred by a Deputy Pensions Ombudsman in the performance of any of the Pensions Ombudsman's functions."

(4) In Part 3 of Schedule 1 to the House of Commons Disqualification Act 1975 (c. 24) (other disqualifying offices), after "Pensions Ombudsman" insert "and any deputy to that Ombudsman appointed under section 145A of the Pension Schemes Act 1993".

(5) In Part 3 of Schedule 1 to the Northern Ireland Assembly Disqualification Act 1975 (c. 25)(other disqualifying offices), at the appropriate place insert—

"Pensions Ombudsman and any deputy to that Ombudsman appointed under section 145A of the Pension Schemes Act 1993."

(6) The persons to whom section 1 of the Superannuation Act 1972 (c. 11) (persons to or in respect of whom benefits may be provided by schemes under that section) applies are to include a deputy to the Pensions Ombudsman.

(7) The Pensions Ombudsman must pay to the Minister for the Civil Service, at such times as he may direct, such sums as he may determine in respect of the increase attributable to subsection (6) in the sums payable out of money provided by Parliament under that Act.

(8) The Pensions Ombudsman must also pay to the Minister for the Civil Service, at such times as he may direct, such sums as he may determine in respect of the amount payable out of money provided by Parliament under that Act which is attributable to the following persons being persons to whom section 1 of that Act applies—

(a) the Pensions Ombudsman;

(b) the employees of the Pensions Ombudsman.

## 275 Jurisdiction

(1) After section 146(4) of the Pension Schemes Act 1993 (c. 48) (power to apply Part 10 of that Act to those concerned with the administration of a scheme) insert—

"(4A) For the purposes of subsection (4) a person or body of persons is concerned with the administration of an occupational or personal pension scheme where the person or body is responsible for carrying out an act of administration concerned with the scheme."

(2) The amendment made by this section has effect in relation to the making of any provision under section 146(4) of the Pension Schemes Act 1993 applying Part 10 of that Act in relation to a complaint or a dispute in so far as it relates to a matter which arises on or after the day on which this section comes into force.

(3) For the purposes of subsection (2), a question falling within section 146(1)(g) of the Pension Schemes Act 1993 is to be treated as a dispute.

**276 Investigations**

(1) Omit section 54 of the Child Support, Pensions and Social Security Act 2000 (c. 19) ("the 2000 Act") (which amends sections 148, 149 and 151 of the Pension Schemes Act 1993 and which has not been brought into force except for the purpose of making regulations and rules).

(2) Omit the following provisions of the Pension Schemes Act 1993—
 (a) section 148(5)(ba) and (bb) as inserted by section 54(2) of the 2000 Act,
 (b) section 149(1), (1A) and (1B) as substituted by section 54(3) of the 2000 Act,
 (c) section 149(3)(ba) as substituted by section 54(4) of the 2000 Act,
 (d) section 149(3)(d) and the word "and" immediately preceding it as inserted by section 54(5) of the 2000 Act,
 (e) section 149(8) as inserted by section 54(6) of the 2000 Act,
 (f) section 151(1)(c) and the word "and" immediately preceding it as inserted by section 54(7) of the 2000 Act,
 (g) section 151(3)(ba) and (bb) as substituted by section 54(8) of the 2000 Act, and
 (h) in section 151(3)(c) the words "any of paragraphs (a) to (bb)" as inserted by section 54(8) of the 2000 Act,

to the extent that those amendments made by section 54 of the 2000 Act have been brought into force for the purpose of making regulations and rules.

*Pension compensation*

**277 Amendments relating to the Pensions Compensation Board**

(1) The Pensions Act 1995 (c. 26) is amended as follows.
(2) In section 80 (review of decisions of the Pensions Compensation Board)—
 (a) after subsection (2) insert—
  "(2A) The Compensation Board may also review such a determination without an application being made.", and
 (b) for subsections (4) and (5) substitute—
  "(4) Regulations may make provision—
   (a) with respect to reviews under this section (or any corresponding provision in force in Northern Ireland);
   (b) with respect to applications under subsection (2) (or any corresponding provision in force in Northern Ireland) and the procedure to be adopted on any such application."
(3) In section 81 (cases where compensation provisions apply), omit subsections (1)(d), (2A) and (7).
(4) In section 83 (amount of compensation) for subsections (3) and (4) substitute—
 "(3) The amount of the payment, or (if there is more than one) the aggregate, must not exceed the aggregate of—
  (a) the amount (if any) by which the shortfall at the application date exceeds the recoveries of value made between the application date and the settlement date, and
  (b) interest at the prescribed rate for the prescribed period on the amount of that excess (if any)."

*Annual increases in rate of pensions*

**278  Annual increase in rate of certain occupational pensions**

(1) Section 51 of the Pensions Act 1995 (annual increase in rate of certain occupational pensions) is amended in accordance with subsections (2) to (6).

(2) In subsection (1)—
- (a) omit "and" at the end of sub-paragraph (i) of paragraph (a),
- (b) at the end of sub-paragraph (ii) of that paragraph insert—
  "(iii) in the case where the pension becomes a pension in payment on or after the commencement day, is not a money purchase scheme, and", and
- (c) for paragraph (b) substitute—
  "(b) the whole, or any part of, the pension is attributable—
    (i) to pensionable service on or after the appointed day, or
    (ii) in the case of money purchase benefits where the pension is in payment before the commencement day, to payments in respect of employment carried on on or after the appointed day, and
  (c) apart from this section—
    (i) the annual rate of the pension, or
    (ii) if only part of the pension is attributable as described in paragraph (b), so much of the annual rate as is attributable to that part,
  would not be increased each year by at least the appropriate percentage of that rate."

(3) In subsection (2) after "money purchase benefits" insert "where the pension is in payment before the commencement day".

(4) In subsection (4)(b) for "5 per cent per annum" substitute"—
- (i) in the case of a category X pension, 5% per annum, and
- (ii) in the case of a category Y pension, 2.5% per annum."

(5) After subsection (4) insert—
"(4A) For the purposes of this section, a pension is a category X pension if it is—
- (a) a pension which became a pension in payment before the commencement day, or
- (b) a pension—
  (i) which becomes a pension in payment on or after the commencement day, and
  (ii) the whole of which is attributable to pensionable service before that day.

(4B) For the purposes of this section, a pension is a category Y pension if it is a pension—
- (a) which becomes a pension in payment on or after the commencement day, and
- (b) the whole of which is attributable to pensionable service on or after the commencement day.

(4C) For the purposes of applying this section in the case of a pension—
- (a) which becomes a pension in payment on or after the commencement day,
- (b) part of which is attributable to pensionable service before the commencement day, and
- (c) part of which is attributable to pensionable service on or after that day,

each of those parts of the pension is to be treated as if it were a separate pension."

(6) In subsection (5)—
   (a) for "the provisions of subsections (2) and (3)" substitute "any of the provisions of this section", and
   (b) in paragraph (a), after "appointed day" insert "or the commencement day".
(7) After that section insert—

   "**51ZA  Meaning of 'The appropriate percentage'**

   (1) For the purposes of section 51(1)(c) and (2), "the appropriate percentage" in relation to an increase in the whole or part of the annual rate of a pension—
      (a) in the case of a category X pension, means the revaluation percentage for the latest revaluation period specified in the order under paragraph 2 of Schedule 3 to the Pension Schemes Act 1993 (revaluation of accrued pension benefits) which is in force at the time of the increase, and
      (b) in the case of a category Y pension, means whichever is the lesser of—
         (i) the revaluation percentage for the latest revaluation period specified in the order under paragraph 2 of Schedule 3 to the Pension Schemes Act 1993 which is in force at the time of the increase, and
         (ii) 2.5%.
   (2) In this section 'the revaluation percentage' and 'the revaluation period' have the same meaning as in paragraph 2 of Schedule 3 to the Pension Schemes Act 1993."
(8) In section 54(3) of that Act (sections 51 to 53: supplementary), at the appropriate place insert—
   " 'the commencement day' means the day appointed for the coming into force of section 278 of the Pensions Act 2004 (amendments to section 51),".

## 279 Annual increase in rate of certain personal pensions

(1) Section 162 of the Pensions Act 1995 (c. 26) (annual increase in rate of certain personal pensions) is amended in accordance with subsection (2).
(2) In subsection (1) omit "and" at the end of paragraph (a) and for paragraph (b) substitute—
   "(b) the pension became a pension in payment before the commencement day,
   (c) the whole, or any part of, the pension is attributable to contributions in respect of employment carried on on or after the appointed day, and
   (d) apart from this section—
      (i) the annual rate of the pension, or
      (ii) if only part of the pension is attributable as described in paragraph (c), so much of the annual rate as is attributable to that part,
      would not be increased each year by at least the appropriate percentage of that rate."
(3) In section 163(3) of that Act (section 162: supplementary)—
   (a) in the definition of "appropriate percentage", for the words from "revaluation period" to the end substitute "latest revaluation period specified in the order under paragraph 2 of Schedule 3 to the Pension Schemes Act 1993 (revaluation of accrued pension benefits) which is in force at the time of the increase (expressions used in this definition having the same meaning as in that paragraph of that Schedule)", and

(b) at the appropriate place insert—
"'the commencement day' means the day appointed for the coming into force of section 279 of the Pensions Act 2004 (amendments to section 162),".

## 280 Power to increase pensions giving effect to pension credits etc

(1) Section 40 of the Welfare Reform and Pensions Act 1999 (c. 30) (power of the Secretary of State to increase pensions provided to give effect to certain rights) is amended as follows.
(2) In subsection (1), for "5%" substitute "the maximum percentage".
(3) In subsection (2), for "This" substitute "Subject to subsection (2A), this".
(4) After subsection (2) insert—
"(2A) Subsection (2) does not apply to pensions which—
(a) are money purchase benefits, and
(b) become pensions in payment on or after the commencement day.
(2B) For the purposes of subsection (1) the 'maximum percentage' means—
(a) 5% in a case where—
(i) the pension is in payment before the commencement day, or
(ii) the pension is not in payment before the commencement day but the entitlement to the relevant pension credit arose before that day, and
(b) 2.5% in a case where the entitlement to the relevant pension credit arises on or after the commencement day."
(5) In subsection (3), at the appropriate places insert—
" "commencement day" means the day appointed for the coming into force of section 280 of the Pensions Act 2004 (amendments to section 40);"
" "money purchase benefit" has the meaning given by section 181(1) of the Pension Schemes Act 1993;"
" "relevant pension credit" means the pension credit to which the eligible pension credit rights or, as the case may be, the safeguarded rights are (directly or indirectly) attributable;".

*Revaluation*

## 281 Exemption from statutory revaluation requirement

(1) Section 84 of the Pension Schemes Act 1993 (c. 48) (basis of revaluation) is amended as follows.
(2) In subsection (5), after paragraph (a) insert "or
(b) under any arrangement which maintains the value of the pension or other benefit by reference to the rise in the retail prices index during that period,".
(3) After that subsection add—
"(6) In subsection (5)(b), "retail prices index" means—
(a) the general index of retail prices (for all items) published by the Office for National Statistics, or
(b) where that index is not published for a month, any substituted index or figures published by that Office."

*Contracting out*

**282 Meaning of "Working life" in pension schemes act 1993**

In section 181 of the Pension Schemes Act 1993 (c. 48) (general interpretation), in subsection (1) for the definition of "working life" substitute—

" "working life", in relation to a person, means the period beginning with the tax year in which the person attains the age of 16 and ending with—
> (a) the tax year before the one in which the person attains the age of 65 in the case of a man or 60 in the case of a woman, or
> (b) if earlier, the tax year before the one in which the person dies."

**283 Power to prescribe conditions by reference to Inland Revenue approval**

In section 9 of the Pension Schemes Act 1993 (requirements for certification of schemes: general), after subsection (5) insert—
> "(5A) Regulations about pension schemes made under this Chapter may contain provisions framed by reference to whether or not a scheme—
>> (a) is approved under Chapter 1 (retirement benefit schemes) of Part 14 of the Income and Corporation Taxes Act 1988, or is a relevant statutory scheme within the meaning of that Chapter, or
>> (b) is approved under Chapter 4 (personal pension schemes) of that Part."

**284 Restrictions on commutation and age at which benefits may be received**

(1) For section 21(1) of the Pension Schemes Act 1993 (commutation of guaranteed minimum pensions) substitute—
> "(1) A scheme may, in such circumstances and subject to such restrictions and conditions as may be prescribed, provide for the payment of a lump sum instead of a pension required to be provided by the scheme in accordance with section 13 or 17."

(2) In section 17 of that Act (minimum pensions for widows and widowers), at the end insert—
> "(8) Where—
>> (a) a lump sum is paid to an earner under provisions included in a scheme by virtue of section 21(1), and
>> (b) those provisions are of a prescribed description,
>
> the earner shall be treated for the purposes of this section as having any guaranteed minimum under section 14 that he would have had but for that payment."

(3) In section 28 of that Act (ways of giving effect to protected rights), in subsection (4) (provision of a lump sum)—
> (a) after "provision of a lump sum" insert ", subject to such restrictions as may be prescribed,",
> (b) omit paragraphs (a) and (b), and
> (c) at the end insert "; and
>> (e) such other conditions as may be prescribed are satisfied."

(4) Omit subsections (4A) and (4B) of that section.

(5) In subsections (3) and (5) of that section, for ", (4) or (4A)" substitute "or (4)".

(6) In subsection (8) of that section, in the definition of "the starting date" omit ", which must not be earlier than the member's 60th birthday,".

(7) In section 29(1) of that Act (how a pension may comply with "the pension requirements" for the purposes of section 28)—
  (a) in paragraph (a), for the words from "date" to "or on" substitute "date that is not later than the member's 65th birthday, or on", and
  (b) in paragraph (aa)(ii) omit the words from "and is not" to "75th birthday,".

*Stakeholder pensions*

### 285 Meaning of "Stakeholder pension scheme"

(1) Section 1 of the Welfare Reform and Pensions Act 1999 (c. 30) (meaning of "stakeholder pension scheme") is amended in accordance with subsections (2) to (4).
(2) In subsection (1) (requirements to be met by stakeholder pension schemes), in paragraph (a) for "to (9)" substitute "to (10)".
(3) In subsection (5) (prescribed requirements relating to administrative expenses of scheme), in paragraph (a) for "by or on behalf of" substitute "by, or on behalf or in respect of,".
(4) After subsection (9) insert—
  "(10) The ninth condition is that—
    (a) if the scheme is an occupational pension scheme, it is specified in a contracting out certificate in relation to all categories of employment to which the scheme relates, and
    (b) if the scheme is a personal pension scheme, it is an appropriate scheme within the meaning of section 7(4) of the 1993 Act."
(5) In section 2 of that Act (registration of stakeholder pension), in subsection (2)(b)(i) for "to (9)" substitute "to (10)".

## PART 6
## FINANCIAL ASSISTANCE SCHEME FOR MEMBERS OF CERTAIN PENSION SCHEMES

### 286 Financial assistance scheme for members of certain pension schemes

(1) The Secretary of State must make provision, by regulations, for a scheme for making payments to, or in respect of, qualifying members of qualifying pension schemes ("the financial assistance scheme").
(2) For the purposes of this section—
  "qualifying member", in relation to a qualifying pension scheme, means a person—
    (a) who, at such time as may be prescribed, is a member of the scheme in respect of whom the scheme's pension liabilities are unlikely to be satisfied in full because the scheme has insufficient assets, or
    (b) who, at such time as may be prescribed, had ceased to be a member of the scheme and in respect of whom the scheme's pension liabilities were not satisfied in full, before he ceased to be such a member, because the scheme had insufficient assets,
  and in respect of whom prescribed conditions are satisfied at such time as may be prescribed;
  "qualifying pension scheme" means an occupational pension scheme (including such a scheme which has been fully wound up)—

(a) which, at such time as may be prescribed, is not—
  (i) a money purchase scheme, or
  (ii) a scheme of a prescribed description,
(b) the winding up of which began during the prescribed period ending immediately before the day appointed under section 126(2),
(c) the employer in relation to which satisfies such conditions as may be prescribed at such time as may be prescribed, and
(d) prescribed details of which have been notified to such person as may be prescribed by a person of a prescribed description—
  (i) in the prescribed form and manner, and
  (ii) before the prescribed date;

"scheme's pension liabilities", in respect of a member of a qualifying pension scheme, means the liabilities of the scheme to, or in respect of, the member in respect of pensions or other benefits (including increases in pensions);

and a qualifying pension scheme has, or had, insufficient assets if the assets of the scheme are, or were, insufficient to satisfy in full the liabilities of the scheme calculated in the prescribed manner.

(3) Regulations under subsection (1) may, in particular, make provision—
  (a) for the financial assistance scheme to be managed by the Secretary of State, a body established by or for the purposes of the regulations or such other person as may be prescribed;
  (b) for the person who manages the financial assistance scheme ("the scheme manager") to hold (whether on trust or otherwise), manage and apply a fund in accordance with the regulations or, where the fund is held on trust, the deed of trust;
  (c) for the property, rights and liabilities of qualifying pension schemes to be transferred to the scheme manager in prescribed circumstances and for the trustees or managers of a qualifying pension scheme in respect of which such a transfer has occurred to be discharged from prescribed liabilities;
  (d) prescribing the circumstances in which payments are to be made by the scheme manager to, or in respect of, qualifying members of qualifying pension schemes and the manner in which the amount of any payment is to be determined, and, where the fund is held by the fund manager on trust, the circumstances and manner may be prescribed by reference to the deed of trust;
  (e) authorising the Secretary of State—
    (i) where he is not the scheme manager, to pay grants to the scheme manager;
    (ii) where he is the scheme manager, to pay amounts into the fund held by him in accordance with the regulations;
    (iii) to pay grants to other prescribed persons in connection with the financial assistance scheme;
  (f) prescribing the circumstances in which amounts are to be paid into or out of the fund held by the scheme manager;
  (g) for or in connection with—
    (i) the review of, or appeals against, any determination, or failure to make a determination, in connection with the financial assistance scheme, or
    (ii) the investigation of complaints relating to the financial assistance scheme, and for the establishment of a body or the appointment of a person or persons to hear such appeals or conduct such investigations;

- (h) conferring functions in relation to the financial assistance scheme on the Pensions Regulator or the Board of the Pension Protection Fund;
- (i) providing for a person to exercise a discretion in dealing with any matter in relation to the financial assistance scheme;
- (j) applying any provision of Part 1 or 2 with such modifications as may be prescribed;

and such regulations may make different provision for different cases or descriptions of case and include such incidental, supplementary, consequential or transitional provision as appears to the Secretary of State to be expedient.

(4) Any amount which, by virtue of subsection (3)(e), the Secretary of State pays under regulations under subsection (1) is to be to paid out of money provided by Parliament.

(5) Regulations under subsection (1) may not make provision for the imposition of a levy or charge on any person for the purpose of funding, directly or indirectly, the financial assistance scheme.

(6) Regulations under subsection (1) may not require any income or capital of a qualifying member of a qualifying pension scheme (other than income or capital which derives, directly or indirectly, from that scheme) to be taken into account when determining whether the member is entitled to a payment under the financial assistance scheme or the amount of any payment to which the member is entitled.

(7) For the purposes of subsection (6), regulations may prescribe the circumstances in which a qualifying member of a qualifying pension scheme is to be regarded as having income or capital which derives, directly or indirectly, from that scheme.

(8) A time or period prescribed under subsection (2) may fall (or, in the case of a period, wholly or partly fall) at a time before the passing of this Act.

(9) Nothing in this section prejudices the operation of section 315 (subordinate legislation (general provisions)).

PART 7

CROSS-BORDER ACTIVITIES WITHIN EUROPEAN UNION

*UK occupational pension scheme receiving contributions from European employer*

**287 Occupational pension scheme receiving contributions from European employer**

(1) The trustees or managers of an occupational pension scheme must not accept any contribution to the scheme from a European employer unless all the following conditions are met.

(2) Condition A is that the trustees or managers of the scheme are authorized by the Regulator under section 288.

(3) Condition B is that the trustees or managers of the scheme are approved by the Regulator under section 289 in relation to the European employer.

(4) Condition C is that either—
- (a) the period of two months beginning with the date on which the Regulator notified the trustees or managers of the scheme under section 289(2)(a)(ii) has expired, or
- (b) before the end of that period, the trustees or managers have received information forwarded to them by the Regulator in accordance with section 290(1).

(5) If the trustees or managers of a scheme fail to comply with subsection (1), section 10 of the Pensions Act 1995 (c. 26) (civil penalties) applies to any trustee or manager who has failed to take all reasonable steps to secure compliance.

(6) In this Part—
"European employer" has the prescribed meaning;
"host member State", in relation to a European employer, means a member State determined in accordance with regulations.

## 288 General authorisation to accept contributions from European employers

(1) An application by the trustees or managers of an occupational pension scheme for authorisation under this section must be made to the Regulator in the prescribed form and in the prescribed manner.

(2) On receipt of the application, the Regulator must—
   (a) where the Regulator is satisfied that the applicant meets prescribed conditions, grant the authorisation, and
   (b) in any other case, refuse the authorisation.

(3) Regulations may make provision as to—
   (a) the revocation by the Regulator of authorisation under this section, and
   (b) the criteria to be applied by the Regulator in reaching any decision relating to the revocation of authorisation.

## 289 Approval in relation to particular European employer

(1) An application by the trustees or managers of an occupational pension scheme for approval under this section in relation to a European employer is made by the trustees or managers of the scheme giving the Regulator in the prescribed manner a notice ("the notice of intention") in the prescribed form which—
   (a) specifies the European employer ("the specified employer"),
   (b) states their intention, subject to approval under this section, to accept contributions from the specified employer,
   (c) specifies the host member State, and
   (d) contains other prescribed information.

(2) On receipt of the notice of intention, the Regulator must within three months—
   (a) where the Regulator is satisfied that the persons giving the notice of intention meet prescribed conditions—
      (i) notify the competent authority of the host member State of the receipt by the Regulator of the notice of intention and of the contents of the notice, and
      (ii) notify the persons who gave the notice of intention that they are approved for the purposes of this section in relation to the specified employer, or
   (b) in any other case, notify the persons who gave the notification that they are not so approved.

(3) If the Regulator does not act under subsection (2)(a) or (b) within the period of three months beginning with the day on which the notice of intention was received, the persons who gave the notice of intention are to be taken to have been approved for the purposes of this section in relation to the specified employer at the end of the period.

(4) Regulations may make provision as to—
   (a) the revocation by the Regulator of approval under this section, and
   (b) the criteria to be applied by the Regulator in reaching any decision relating to the revocation of approval.

## 290 Notification of legal requirements of host member State outside United Kingdom

(1) Where—
   (a) the Regulator has notified the competent authority of the host member State under subsection (2)(a)(i) of section 289, and
   (b) in pursuance of Article 20(5) of the Directive, the Regulator receives information from the competent authority as to requirements of the social and labour law of the host member State and as to the other matters referred to in Article 20(5),
   the Regulator must as soon as reasonably practicable forward that information to the person who gave the notice of intention under section 289.

(2) Where—
   (a) the trustees or managers of an occupational pension scheme are approved under section 289 in relation to a European employer, and
   (b) in pursuance of Article 20(8) of the Directive the Regulator receives information ("the new information") from the competent authority of the host member State as to changes affecting any information previously forwarded under subsection (1),
   the Regulator must as soon as reasonably practicable forward the new information to the trustees or managers.

## 291 Duty of trustees or managers to act consistently with law of host member State

(1) Where the trustees or managers of an occupational pension scheme receive contributions to the scheme from a European employer, the trustees or managers must ensure that the scheme, so far as it relates to members who are or have been employed by the employer, is operated in a way which is consistent with the requirements of the social and labour law of the host member State.

(2) Regulations may modify any provision of pensions legislation in its application to members of an occupational pension scheme in respect of which the employer is a European employer.

(3) If the trustees or managers of a scheme fail to comply with subsection (1), section 10 of the Pensions Act 1995 (c. 26) (civil penalties) applies to any trustee or manager who has failed to take all reasonable steps to secure compliance.

(4) In this section "pensions legislation" means—
   (a) the Pension Schemes Act 1993 (c. 48),
   (b) Part 1 of the Pensions Act 1995, other than sections 62 to 66A of that Act (equal treatment),
   (c) Part 1 or section 33 of the Welfare Reform and Pensions Act 1999 (c. 30), or
   (d) this Act.

## 292 Power of regulator to require ring-Fencing of assets

(1) Where the trustees or managers of an occupational pension scheme receive contributions to the scheme from a European employer, the Regulator may in prescribed circumstances issue a notice ("a ringfencing notice") to the trustees or managers of the scheme directing them to take, or refrain from taking, such steps of a prescribed description as are specified in the notice for the purpose of ringfencing some or all of the assets or liabilities (or both) of the scheme.

(2) In subsection (1), "ringfencing" has the same meaning as in the Directive.

(3) If the trustees or managers of an occupational pension scheme fail to comply with a ringfencing notice given to them, section 10 of the Pensions Act 1995 (civil penalties) applies to any trustee or manager who has failed to take all reasonable steps to secure compliance.

*European occupational pension scheme receiving contributions from UK employer*

**293 Functions of Regulator in relation to institutions administered in other member States**

(1) Where a UK employer makes (or proposes to make) contributions to a European pensions institution, any function which Article 20 of the Directive requires or authorizes to be exercised by the competent authorities of the host member State is exercisable by the Regulator.

(2) If the Regulator receives a notification in pursuance of Article 20(4) of the Directive from the competent authority in another member State, the Regulator must within two months inform that authority of any relevant legal requirements.

(3) Where there is a significant change in any relevant legal requirements, the Regulator must as soon as reasonably practicable inform any competent authority in relation to which it has provided information under subsection (2) of that change.

(4) Where a UK employer makes contributions to a European pensions institution, the Regulator must—

(a) monitor the compliance of that institution with the relevant legal requirements, and

(b) if the Regulator becomes aware of any contravention by the institution of any relevant legal requirements, inform the competent authority of the member State in which the institution has its main administration of the failure.

(5) If the Regulator is satisfied that a European pensions institution which receives contributions from a UK employer is contravening any relevant legal requirements, the Regulator may issue a notice to the UK employer directing him—

(a) to take or refrain from taking such steps as are specified in the notice in order to remedy the failure by the institution, or

(b) to cease to make further contributions to the institution.

(6) Regulations may make further provision about the effect of a notice under subsection (5)(b), including provision conferring functions on the Regulator.

(7) Section 10 of the Pensions Act 1995 (civil penalties) applies to any UK employer who, without reasonable excuse, fails to comply with a notice under subsection (5).

(8) In this section—

"European pensions institution" means an institution for occupational retirement provision, as defined by Article 6(a) of the Directive, that has its main administration in a member State other than the United Kingdom;

"relevant legal requirements" means such requirements of the law relating to occupational pension schemes, as it applies in any part of the United Kingdom, as may be prescribed;

"UK employer" means an employer who—

(a) in the case of a body corporate, is incorporated under the law of the United Kingdom or any part of the United Kingdom, or

(b) in any other case, is resident in the United Kingdom.

*Assistance for other European Regulators*

**294 Stopping disposal of assets of institutions administered in other member States**

(1) This section applies if the Regulator receives a request from the competent authority of a member State for assistance in prohibiting the free disposal of UK-held assets

of a European pensions institution that has its main administration in that member State.

(2) The court may on an application made by the Regulator with respect to UK-held assets of the institution grant—
  (a) an injunction restraining a defendant, or
  (b) in Scotland, an interdict prohibiting a defender (or, in proceedings by petition, a respondent),
from disposing of, or otherwise dealing with, assets to which the application relates.

(3) If the court grants an injunction or interdict under subsection (2), it may by subsequent orders make provision for such incidental, consequential and supplementary matters as it considers necessary to enable the competent authority that sent the request to perform any of its functions in relation to assets subject to the injunction or interdict.

(4) If the institution is not a party to proceedings under subsection (2) or (3), the institution—
  (a) has the same rights to notice of the proceedings as a defendant (or, in Scotland, as a defender or, as the case may be, as a respondent), and
  (b) may take part as a party in the proceedings.

(5) In deciding any question as to costs or expenses, a court before which any proceedings take place—
  (a) may take account of any additional expense which it considers that any party to the proceedings has incurred as a result of the participation of the institution in pursuance of subsection (4)(b), and
  (b) may award the whole or part of the additional expense as costs or (as the case may be) expenses to the party who incurred it (whatever the outcome of the Regulator's application).

(6) For the purposes of this section—
"European pensions institution" has the meaning given by section 293;
"UK-held assets" of a European pensions institution are assets of the institution held by a depositary or custodian located in the United Kingdom, and here "assets", "depositary", "custodian" and "located" have the same meaning as in Article 19(3) of the Directive.

(7) The jurisdiction conferred by subsections (2) and (3) is exercisable by the High Court or the Court of Session.

*Interpretation*

## 295 Interpretation of Part

In this Part—

"competent authority", in relation to a member State other than the United Kingdom, means a national authority designated in accordance with the law of that State to carry out the duties provided for in the Directive;

"the Directive" means Directive 2003/41/EC of the European Parliament and of the Council on the activities and supervision of institutions for occupational retirement provision;

"European employer" has the meaning given by section 287(6);

"host member State", in relation to a European employer, has the meaning given by section 287(6);

"social and labour law", in relation to a member State other than the United Kingdom, means the social and labour law (within the meaning of Article 20 of the Directive) of that State relevant to occupational pension schemes (within the meaning of that Article).

## PART 8
## STATE PENSIONS

*Entitlement to more than one pension*

**296  Persons entitled to more than one Category B retirement pension**

In section 43(3) of the Social Security Contributions and Benefits Act 1992 (c. 4) (persons entitled to more than one retirement pension)—
- (a) for paragraph (a) substitute—
    "(a) to both a Category A retirement pension and one or more Category B retirement pensions under this Part for the same period,
    (aa) to more than one Category B retirement pension (but not a Category A retirement pension) under this Part for the same period, or", and
- (b) for the words from "paragraph (a)" to "above" substitute "paragraph (a), (aa) or (b) (as the case may be)".

*Deferral of state pension*

**297  Deferral of retirement pensions and shared additional pensions**

(1) For section 55 of the Social Security Contributions and Benefits Act 1992 (increase of retirement pension where entitlement is deferred) substitute—

**"55  Pension increase or lump sum where entitlement to retirement pension is deferred**

(1) Where a person's entitlement to a Category A or Category B retirement pension is deferred, Schedule 5 to this Act has effect.

(2) In that Schedule—
paragraph A1 makes provision enabling an election to be made where the pensioner's entitlement is deferred
paragraphs 1 to 3 make provision about increasing pension where the pensioner's entitlement is deferred
paragraphs 3A and 3B make provision about lump sum payments where the pensioner's entitlement is deferred
paragraph 3C makes provision enabling an election to be made where the pensioner's deceased spouse has deferred entitlement
paragraphs 4 to 7 make provision about increasing pension where the pensioner's deceased spouse has deferred entitlement
paragraphs 7A and 7B make provision about lump sum payments where the pensioner's deceased spouse has deferred entitlement
paragraphs 7C to 9 make supplementary provision.

(3) For the purposes of this Act a person's entitlement to a Category A or Category B retirement pension is deferred if and so long as that person—
    (a) does not become entitled to that pension by reason only—

- (i) of not satisfying the conditions of section 1 of the Administration Act (entitlement to benefit dependent on claim), or
- (ii) in the case of a Category B retirement pension payable by virtue of a spouse's contributions, of the spouse not satisfying those conditions with respect to his Category A retirement pension, or
- (b) in consequence of an election under section 54(1), falls to be treated as not having become entitled to that pension,

and, in relation to any such pension, "period of deferment" shall be construed accordingly."

(2) For section 55C of that Act (increase of shared additional pension where entitlement is deferred) substitute—

**"55C Pension increase or lump sum where entitlement to shared additional pension is deferred**

(1) Where a person's entitlement to a shared additional pension is deferred, Schedule 5A to this Act has effect.

(2) In that Schedule—

paragraph 1 makes provision enabling an election to be made where the person's entitlement is deferred

paragraphs 2 and 3 make provision about increasing pension where the person's entitlement is deferred

paragraphs 4 and 5 make provision about lump sum payments where the person's entitlement is deferred.

(3) For the purposes of this Act, a person's entitlement to a shared additional pension is deferred—
- (a) where he would be entitled to a Category A or Category B retirement pension but for the fact that his entitlement is deferred, if and so long as his entitlement to such a pension is deferred, and
- (b) otherwise, if and so long as he does not become entitled to the shared additional pension by reason only of not satisfying the conditions of section 1 of the Administration Act (entitlement to benefit dependent on claim),

and, in relation to a shared additional pension, "period of deferment" shall be construed accordingly."

(3) In paragraph 6 of Schedule 4 to the Pensions Act 1995 (c. 26) (which, with effect from 6th April 2010, amends the existing law regarding the deferment of pensions), for sub-paragraph (5) (commencement) substitute—

"(5) The preceding sub-paragraphs shall come into force as follows—
- (a) sub-paragraphs (1) and (4) shall come into force on 6th April 2005;
- (b) sub-paragraphs (2) and (3) shall have effect in relation to incremental periods (within the meaning of Schedule 5 to the Social Security Contributions and Benefits Act 1992 (c. 4)) beginning on or after that date."

(4) Schedule 11 (which contains further amendments relating to the deferral of retirement pensions and shared additional pensions) has effect.

*Miscellaneous*

## 298  Disclosure of state pension information

(1) Section 42 of the Child Support, Pensions and Social Security Act 2000 (c. 19) (disclosure of State pension information) is amended as follows.

(2) In subsection (2), for the words from the beginning to "information", substitute, "The Secretary of State may, in the prescribed manner, disclose or authorize the disclosure of any information".

(3) After subsection (3) insert—

"(3A) For the purposes of this section and of any regulations made under it, anything done by or in relation to a person who—

(a) provides, or proposes to provide, relevant services to a person falling within subsection (3) ("the qualifying person"), and

(b) is authorized in writing by the qualifying person to act for the purposes of this section,

is treated as done by or in relation to the qualifying person.

In paragraph (a) "relevant services" means services that may involve the giving of advice or forecasts to which information to which this section applies may be relevant."

(4) In subsection (7)—

(a) omit the "and" at the end of paragraph (c), and

(b) after paragraph (d) insert— ", and

(e) a projection of the amount of any lump sum to which that individual is likely to become entitled, or might become entitled in particular circumstances."

(5) In subsection (11)—

(a) for the definitions of "basic retirement pension" and "additional retirement pension", substitute—

" "additional retirement pension" means any additional pension or shared additional pension under the Social Security Contributions and Benefits Act 1992, or any graduated retirement benefit under sections 36 and 37 of the National Insurance Act 1965;

"basic retirement pension" means any basic pension under the Social Security Contributions and Benefits Act 1992;",

(b) after the definition of "employer", insert—

" "lump sum" means a lump sum under Schedule 5 or 5A to the Social Security Contributions and Benefits Act 1992;", and

(c) for the definitions of "trustee" and "manager", substitute—

" "trustee or manager", in relation to an occupational or personal pension scheme, means—

(a) in the case of a scheme established under a trust, the trustee or trustees of the scheme, and

(b) in any other case, the person or persons responsible for the management of the scheme."

## 299  Claims for certain benefits following termination of reciprocal agreement with Australia

(1) This section applies to claims for—

(a) retirement pension,

(b) bereavement benefit, or
(c) widow's benefit,

made on or after 1st March 2001 (the date from which the termination of the reciprocal agreement with Australia had effect).

(2) This section also applies to claims for retirement pension or widow's benefit made before 1st March 2001 if the claimant only became entitled to the pension or benefit on or after that date.

(3) For the purposes of such claims—
   (a) the relevant provisions of the reciprocal agreement with Australia shall be treated as continuing in force as provided by this section; and
   (b) the relevant UK legislation shall have effect as if modified to the extent required to give effect to those provisions (as they continue in force by virtue of this section).

(4) The relevant provisions of that agreement are treated as continuing in force as follows—
   (a) references to periods during which a person was resident in Australia are only to periods spent in Australia before 6th April 2001 and forming part of a period of residence in Australia which began before 1st March 2001;
   (b) Articles 3(3) and 5(2) (entitlement by virtue of previous receipt of pension in Australia) apply only to persons who were last in Australia during a period falling within paragraph (a) above;
   (c) references to the territory of the United Kingdom do not include the islands of Jersey, Guernsey, Alderney, Herm or Jethou;
   (d) references to widow's benefit, widow's payment, widow's pension and widowed mother's allowance include, respectively, bereavement benefit, bereavement payment, bereavement allowance and widowed parent's allowance;
   (e) for the purposes of claims by a widower—
      (i) for retirement pension by virtue of his wife's insurance, or
      (ii) for bereavement benefit,
      references to widows and husbands include, respectively, widowers and wives.

(5) An order made under—
   (a) section 179 of the Social Security Administration Act 1992 (c. 5), or
   (b) section 155 of the Social Security Administration (Northern Ireland) Act 1992 (c. 8),

   may, in consequence of a change in the law of Great Britain or, as the case may be, Northern Ireland, modify the relevant provisions of the reciprocal agreement with Australia as they are treated as continuing in force for the purposes of claims to which this section applies.

(6) For the purposes of this section—
   (a) "the reciprocal agreement with Australia" means the agreement set out in Schedule 1 to the Social Security (Australia) Order 1992 (S.I. 1992/1312) and the Social Security (Australia) Order (Northern Ireland) 1992 (S.R. 1992 No. 269) (as amended by the exchange of notes set out in Schedule 3 to those Orders);
   (b) "the relevant provisions" of that agreement are the provisions of Articles 1, 3, 5, 8, 18, 20 and 24, so far as they relate to the United Kingdom;
   (c) "the relevant UK legislation" is—
      (i) the Social Security Contributions and Benefits Act 1992 (c. 4);
      (ii) the Social Security Administration Act 1992;

(iii) the Social Security Contributions and Benefits (Northern Ireland) Act 1992 (c. 7); and
(iv) the Social Security Administration (Northern Ireland) Act 1992;

and, for the purposes of subsection (5), a change in the law of Great Britain or Northern Ireland includes any change made after the date of the reciprocal agreement with Australia.

(7) In this section—

"retirement pension" has the meaning given by the reciprocal agreement with Australia;

"bereavement benefit" means bereavement payment, widowed parent's allowance or bereavement allowance payable under the Social Security Contributions and Benefits Act 1992 or the Social Security Contributions and Benefits (Northern Ireland) Act 1992;

"widow's benefit" means widow's payment, widowed mother's allowance or widow's pension payable under either of those Acts.

(8) This section shall be deemed to have had effect at all times on and after 1st March 2001.

(9) Nothing in this section affects Article 2(2) of the Social Security (Australia) Order 2000 (S.I. 2000/3255) or Article 2(2) of the Social Security (Australia) Order (Northern Ireland) 2000 (S.R. 2000 No. 407) (which provide for cases where a person was in receipt of benefit on 28th February 2001 or had claimed a benefit to which he was entitled on or before that date).

## PART 9
## MISCELLANEOUS AND SUPPLEMENTARY

*Dissolution of existing bodies*

### 300 Dissolution of OPRA

(1) The Occupational Pensions Regulatory Authority ("OPRA") is hereby dissolved.

(2) An order under section 322 which appoints the day on which subsection (1) comes into force may provide—
 (a) for all property, rights and liabilities to which OPRA is entitled or subject immediately before that day to become the property, rights and liabilities of the Regulator or the Secretary of State, and
 (b) for any function of OPRA falling to be exercised on or after that day, or which fell to be exercised before that day but has not been exercised, to be exercised by the Regulator, the Secretary of State or the Department for Social Development in Northern Ireland.

(3) Subject to subsection (4), information obtained by the Regulator by virtue of subsection (2) is to be treated for the purposes of sections 82 to 87 (disclosure of information) as having been obtained by the Regulator in the exercise of its functions from the person from whom OPRA obtained it.

(4) Information obtained by the Regulator by virtue of subsection (2) which was supplied to OPRA for the purposes of its functions by an authority exercising functions corresponding to the functions of OPRA in a country or territory outside the United Kingdom (the "overseas authority") is to be treated for the purposes

mentioned in subsection (3) as having been supplied to the Regulator for the purposes of its functions by the overseas authority.

(5) Where tax information disclosed to OPRA is obtained by the Regulator by virtue of subsection (2), subsection (3) does not apply and subsections (3) and (4) of section 88 apply as if that information had been disclosed to the Regulator by virtue of subsection (2) of that section.

For this purpose "tax information" has the same meaning as in that section.

### 301 Transfer of employees from OPRA to the Regulator

(1) For the purposes of the Transfer of Undertakings (Protection of Employment) Regulations 1981 (S.I. 1981/1794) ("TUPE"), the transfer of functions from OPRA to the Regulator ("the transfer") is to be treated as a transfer of an undertaking.

(2) The provisions of Regulation 7 of TUPE (exclusion of occupational pension schemes) shall not apply in relation to the transfer.

### 302 Dissolution of the Pensions Compensation Board

(1) The Pensions Compensation Board is hereby dissolved.

(2) An order under section 322 appointing the day on which subsection (1) is to come into force may provide—
   (a) for all property, rights and liabilities to which the Pensions Compensation Board is entitled or subject immediately before that day to become property, rights and liabilities of the Board, and
   (b) for any function of the Pensions Compensation Board falling to be exercised on or after that day, or which fell to be exercised before that day but has not been exercised, to be exercised by the Board.

(3) Information obtained by the Board by virtue of subsection (2) is to be treated for the purposes of sections 197 to 201 and 203 (disclosure of information) as having been obtained by the Board in the exercise of its functions from the person from whom the Pensions Compensation Board obtained it.

(4) Where tax information disclosed to the Pensions Compensation Board is obtained by the Board by virtue of subsection (2), subsection (3) does not apply, and subsections (3) and (4) of section 202 apply as if that information had been disclosed to the Board by virtue of subsection (2) of that section.

For this purpose "tax information" has the same meaning as in that section.

(5) Where the Pensions Compensation Board's disclosure under section 114(3) of the Pensions Act 1995 (c. 26) of information to which subsection (3) applies was subject to any express restriction, the Board's powers of disclosure under sections 198 to 201 and 203, in relation to that information, are subject to the same restriction.

*Service of notifications etc and electronic working*

### 303 Service of notifications and other documents

(1) This section applies where provision made (in whatever terms) by or under this Act authorizes or requires—
   (a) a notification to be given to a person, or
   (b) a document of any other description (including a copy of a document) to be sent to a person.

(2) The notification or document may be given to the person in question—

(a) by delivering it to him,
(b) by leaving it at his proper address, or
(c) by sending it by post to him at that address.

(3) The notification or document may be given or sent to a body corporate by being given or sent to the secretary or clerk of that body.

(4) The notification or document may be given or sent to a firm by being given or sent to—
(a) a partner in the firm, or
(b) a person having the control or management of the partnership business.

(5) The notification or document may be given or sent to an unincorporated body or association by being given or sent to a member of the governing body of the body or association.

(6) For the purposes of this section and section 7 of the Interpretation Act 1978 (c. 30) (service of documents by post) in its application to this section, the proper address of a person is—
(a) in the case of a body corporate, the address of the registered or principal office of the body,
(b) in the case of a firm, or an unincorporated body or association, the address of the principal office of the firm, body or association,
(c) in the case of any person to whom the notification or other document is given or sent in reliance on any of subsections (3) to (5), the proper address of the body corporate, firm or (as the case may be) other body or association in question, and
(d) in any other case, the last known address of the person in question.

(7) In the case of—
(a) a company registered outside the United Kingdom,
(b) a firm carrying on business outside the United Kingdom, or
(c) an unincorporated body or association with offices outside the United Kingdom, the references in subsection (6) to its principal office include references to its principal office within the United Kingdom (if any).

(8) In this section "notification" includes notice; and references in this section to sending a document to a person include references to making an application to him.

(9) This section has effect subject to section 304.

**304 Notification and documents in electronic form**

(1) This section applies where—
(a) section 303 authorizes the giving or sending of a notification or other document by its delivery to a particular person ("the recipient"), and
(b) the notification or other document is transmitted to the recipient—
(i) by means of an electronic communications network, or
(ii) by other means but in a form that nevertheless requires the use of apparatus by the recipient to render it intelligible.

(2) The transmission has effect for the purposes of this Act as a delivery of the notification or other document to the recipient, but only if the requirements imposed by or under this section are complied with.

(3) Where the recipient is a relevant authority—
(a) it must have indicated its willingness to receive the notification or other document in a manner mentioned in subsection (1)(b),

(b) the transmission must be made in such manner, and satisfy such other conditions, as it may require, and
(c) the notification or other document must take such form as it may require.
(4) Where the person making the transmission is a relevant authority, it may (subject to subsection (5)) determine—
(a) the manner in which the transmission is made, and
(b) the form in which the notification or other document is transmitted.
(5) Where the recipient is a person other than a relevant authority—
(a) the recipient, or
(b) the person on whose behalf the recipient receives the notification or other document,
must have indicated to the person making the transmission the recipient's willingness to receive notifications or documents transmitted in the form and manner used.
(6) An indication given to any person for the purposes of subsection (5)—
(a) must be given to that person in such manner as he may require,
(b) may be a general indication or one that is limited to notifications or documents of a particular description,
(c) must state the address to be used and must be accompanied by such other information as that person requires for the making of the transmission, and
(d) may be modified or withdrawn at any time by a notice given to that person in such manner as he may require.
(7) An indication, requirement or determination given, imposed or made by a relevant authority for the purposes of this section is to be given, imposed or made by being published in such manner as it considers appropriate for bringing it to the attention of the persons who, in its opinion, are likely to be affected by it.
(8) Where both the recipient and the person making the transmission are relevant authorities—
(a) subsections (3) and (4) do not apply, and
(b) the recipient must have indicated to the person making the transmission the recipient's willingness to receive notifications or documents transmitted in the form and manner used.
(9) Subsection (8) of section 303 applies for the purposes of this section as it applies for the purposes of that section.
(10) In this section, "relevant authority" means the Regulator, the Board or the Secretary of State and in the application of this section to Northern Ireland by virtue of section 323(2)(g)(ii) also includes the Department for Social Development in Northern Ireland.
(11) In this section and section 305, "electronic communications network" has the same meaning as in the Communications Act 2003 (c. 21).

## 305  Timing and location of things done electronically

(1) The Secretary of State may by order make provision specifying, for the purposes of any enactment contained in, or made under, this Act, the manner of determining—
(a) the times at which things done under that enactment by means of electronic communications networks are done, and

(b) the places at which such things are so done, and at which things transmitted by means of such networks are received.

(2) The provision made under subsection (1) may include provision as to the country or territory in which an electronic address is to be treated as located.

(3) An order made by the Secretary of State may also make provision about the manner of proving in any legal proceedings—
   (a) that something done by means of an electronic communications network satisfies the requirements of an enactment contained in, or made under, this Act for the doing of that thing, and
   (b) the matters mentioned in subsection (1)(a) and (b).

(4) An order under this section may provide for such presumptions to apply (whether conclusive or not) as the Secretary of State considers appropriate.

*General*

**306 Overriding requirements**

(1) Where any provision mentioned in subsection (2) conflicts with the provisions of an occupational or personal pension scheme—
   (a) the provision mentioned in subsection (2), to the extent that it conflicts, overrides the provisions of the scheme, and
   (b) the scheme has effect with such modifications as may be required in consequence of paragraph (a).

(2) The provisions referred to in subsection (1) are those of—
   (a) any order made by the Regulator under Part 1;
   (b) any regulations made under section 19(7);
   (c) any regulations made under section 21(4);
   (d) any regulations made under section 24(7);
   (e) any direction issued by the Regulator under section 41(4);
   (f) any direction issued by the Regulator under section 50(4);
   (g) Part 2 (other than Chapter 1), any subordinate legislation made under that Part and any direction given under section 134 or 154;
   (h) Part 3 and any subordinate legislation made under that Part;
   (i) any regulations under section 237;
   (j) sections 241 and 242, any regulations made under sections 241 to 243 and any arrangements under sections 241 and 242;
   (k) sections 247 and 248 and any regulations under sections 247 to 249;
   (l) sections 256 and 258;
   (m) any ringfencing notice issued by the Regulator under section 292;
   (n) any regulations under section 286, 307, 308, 315(6) or 318(4) or (5) and any order under section 322(5).

(3) Subsection (1) is without prejudice to section 32(1) (overriding effect of freezing orders made by the Regulator) and section 154(12) (overriding effect of requirement to wind up pension scheme under Part 2).

(4) In the case of a company to which section 242 (requirement for member-nominated directors of corporate trustees) applies, where any provision mentioned in subsection (5) conflicts with the provisions of the company's memorandum or articles of association—

(a) the provision mentioned in subsection (5), to the extent that it conflicts, overrides the provisions of the memorandum or articles, and
(b) the memorandum or articles have effect with such modifications as may be required in consequence of paragraph (a).
(5) The provisions referred to in subsection (4) are those of—
(a) section 242;
(b) any regulations made under section 242 or 243;
(c) any arrangements under section 242.

**307 Modification of this Act in relation to certain categories of schemes**

(1) Regulations may modify any of the provisions mentioned in subsection (2) as it applies in relation to—
(a) hybrid schemes;
(b) multi-employer schemes;
(c) any case where a partnership is the employer, or one of the employers, in relation to an occupational pension scheme.
(2) The provisions referred to in subsection (1) are those of—
(a) Part 1 (the Pensions Regulator),
(b) Part 2 (the Board of the Pension Protection Fund), other than Chapter 1,
(c) sections 257 and 258 (pension protection),
(d) sections 259 and 261 (consultation by employers),
(e) section 286 (financial assistance scheme for members of certain pension schemes), and
(f) Part 7 (cross-border activities within European Union).
(3) Regulations may also modify any of the provisions of Part 2 as it applies in relation to an eligible scheme in respect of which a relevant public authority has—
(a) given a guarantee in relation to any part of the scheme, any benefits payable under the scheme rules or any member of the scheme, or
(b) made any other arrangements for the purposes of securing that the assets of the scheme are sufficient to meet any part of its liabilities.
(4) In this section—
"eligible scheme" has the meaning given by section 126;
"hybrid scheme" means an occupational pension scheme—
(a) which is not a money purchase scheme, but
(b) where some of the benefits that may be provided are—
(i) money purchase benefits attributable to voluntary contributions of the members, or
(ii) other money purchase benefits;
"multi-employer scheme" means an occupational pension scheme in relation to which there is more than one employer;
"relevant public authority" means—
(a) a Minister of the Crown (within the meaning of the Ministers of the Crown Act 1975 (c. 26)),
(b) a government department (including any body or authority exercising statutory functions on behalf of the Crown), or
(c) the Scottish Ministers.

**308 Modification of pensions legislation that refers to employers**

(1) Regulations may modify any provision of pensions legislation for the purpose of ensuring that it, or another provision of pensions legislation, does not purport to refer to the employer of a self-employed person.

(2) Where a provision of pensions legislation contains a reference to an employer in connection with an occupational pension scheme, regulations may modify the provision, or another provision of pensions legislation, for the purpose of excluding from the reference an employer who is a person—
  (a) who does not participate in the scheme as regards people employed by him, or
  (b) who, as regards people employed by him, participates in the scheme only to a limited extent.

(3) For the purposes of this section—
  (a) "pensions legislation" means any enactment contained in or made by virtue of—
    (i) the Pension Schemes Act 1993 (c. 48),
    (ii) Part 1 of the Pensions Act 1995 (c. 26), other than sections 62 to 66A of that Act (equal treatment),
    (iii) Part 1 of the Welfare Reform and Pensions Act 1999 (c. 30), or
    (iv) this Act;
  (b) a person is "self-employed" if he is in an employment but is not employed in it by someone else;
  (c) a person who holds an office (including an elective office), and is entitled to remuneration for holding it, shall be taken to be employed by the person responsible for paying the remuneration.

(4) In subsection (3)(b) "employment" includes any trade, business, profession, office or vocation.

**309 Offences by bodies corporate and partnerships**

(1) Where an offence under this Act committed by a body corporate is proved to have been committed with the consent or connivance of, or to be attributable to any neglect on the part of, a director, manager, secretary or other similar officer of the body, or a person purporting to act in any such capacity, he as well as the body corporate is guilty of the offence and liable to be proceeded against and punished accordingly.

(2) Where the affairs of a body corporate are managed by its members, subsection (1) applies in relation to the acts and defaults of a member in connection with his functions of management as to a director of a body corporate.

(3) Where an offence under this Act committed by a Scottish partnership is proved to have been committed with the consent or connivance of, or to be attributable to any neglect on the part of, a partner, he as well as the partnership is guilty of the offence and liable to be proceeded against and punished accordingly.

(4) In this section "Scottish partnership" means a partnership constituted under the law of Scotland.

**310 Admissibility of statements**

(1) A statement made by a person in compliance with an information requirement is admissible in evidence in any proceedings, so long as it also complies with any requirements governing the admissibility of evidence in the circumstances in question.

(2) But in proceedings to which this subsection applies—
   (a) no evidence relating to the statement may be adduced, and
   (b) no question relating to it may be asked,
   by or on behalf of the prosecution or (as the case may be) the Regulator, unless evidence relating to it is adduced, or a question relating to it is asked, in the proceedings by or on behalf of that person.
(3) Subsection (2) applies to—
   (a) criminal proceedings in which that person is charged with a relevant offence, or
   (b) proceedings as a result of which that person may be required to pay a financial penalty under or by virtue of—
      (i) section 168 of the Pension Schemes Act 1993 (c. 48) (breach of regulations) or section 10 of the Pensions Act 1995 (c. 26) (civil penalties), or
      (ii) any provision in force in Northern Ireland corresponding to a provision mentioned in sub-paragraph (i).
(4) In this section—
   "information requirement" means any statement made in compliance with any duty imposed by or by virtue of—
      (a) section 64 (duties of trustees or managers to provide scheme return);
      (b) section 70 (duty to report breaches of the law);
      (c) section 72 (requirement to provide information to the Regulator);
      (d) section 75 (inspection of premises: powers of inspectors to examine etc);
      (e) section 78(2)(d) (power of inspector entering under warrant to require a person to provide an explanation of a document);
      (f) section 190 (information to be provided to the Board);
      (g) section 191 (notices requiring provision of information to the Board etc);
      (h) section 192 (entry of premises: powers of appointed persons to examine etc);
      (i) section 194(2)(d) (power of inspector entering under warrant to require a person to provide an explanation of a document);
      (j) section 209 (power to make order enabling PPF Ombudsman to obtain information, documents etc);
      (k) section 213 or 214 (disclosure of information on references made to PPF Ombudsman);
      (l) section 228 (failure to make payments in accordance with schedule of contributions);
      (m) paragraph 19 of Schedule 1 (power to make regulations enabling Regulator to summon persons to give evidence before it);
      (n) paragraph 11 of Schedule 4 (the Pensions Regulator Tribunal: evidence);
   "relevant offence" means any offence other than one under—
      (a) section 77 (neglect or refusal to provide information etc to the Regulator);
      (b) section 80 (providing false or misleading information to the Regulator);
      (c) section 193 (neglect or refusal to provide information etc to the Board);
      (d) section 195 (providing false or misleading information to the Board);
      (e) any provision in force in Northern Ireland corresponding to a provision mentioned in paragraphs (a) to (d);
      (f) section 5 of the Perjury Act 1911 (c. 6) (false statements made otherwise than on oath);

(g) section 44(2) of the Criminal Law (Consolidation) (Scotland) Act 1995 (c. 39) (false statements made otherwise than on oath);
(h) Article 10 of the Perjury (Northern Ireland) Order 1979 (S.I. 1979/1714 (N.I. 19)).

## 311 Protected items

(1) A person may not be required under or by virtue of this Act to produce, disclose or permit the inspection of protected items.
(2) For this purpose "protected items" means—
   (a) communications between a professional legal adviser and his client or any person representing his client which fall within subsection (3);
   (b) communications between a professional legal adviser, his client or any person representing his client and any other person which fall within subsection (3) (as a result of paragraph (b) of that subsection);
   (c) items which—
      (i) are enclosed with, or referred to in, such communications,
      (ii) fall within subsection (3), and
      (iii) are in the possession of a person entitled to possession of them.
(3) A communication or item falls within this subsection if it is made—
   (a) in connection with the giving of legal advice to the client, or
   (b) in connection with, or in contemplation of, legal proceedings and for the purpose of those proceedings.
(4) A communication or item is not a protected item if it is held with the intention of furthering a criminal purpose.

## 312 Liens

If a person claims a lien on a document, its production under any provision made by or by virtue of this Act does not affect the lien.

## 313 Crown application

(1) In this section "the relevant provisions" means—
   (a) Parts 1 to 5,
   (b) sections 306, 307, 310, 311, 312, 314, 315, 318(4) and (5) and 322(5).
(2) The relevant provisions apply to a pension scheme managed by or on behalf of the Crown as they apply to other pension schemes; and, accordingly, references in those provisions to a person in his capacity as a trustee or manager of, or person prescribed in relation to, a pension scheme include the Crown, or a person acting on behalf of the Crown, in that capacity.
(3) The relevant provisions apply to persons employed by or under the Crown in like manner as if such persons were employed by a private person; and references in those provisions to a person in his capacity as an employer include the Crown, or a person acting on behalf of the Crown in that capacity.
(4) This section does not apply to any of the relevant provisions under or by virtue of which a person may be prosecuted for an offence; but such a provision applies to persons in the public service of the Crown as it applies to other persons.
(5) Nothing in the relevant provisions applies to Her Majesty in Her private capacity (within the meaning of the Crown Proceedings Act 1947 (c. 44)).

*Regulations and orders*

## 314 Breach of regulations

The following provisions of the Pensions Act 1995 (c. 26) apply to regulations under this Act as if they were regulations made by virtue of Part 1 of that Act—
- (a) section 10(3) to (9) (power to impose civil penalties for contravention of regulations under Part 1 of that Act);
- (b) section 116 (power to provide for contravention of regulations under that Part to be criminal offence).

## 315 Subordinate legislation (General provisions)

(1) Any power conferred by this Act to make subordinate legislation is exercisable by statutory instrument, except any order-making power conferred on the Regulator.

(2) Any power conferred by this Act to make subordinate legislation may be exercised—
- (a) either in relation to all cases to which the power extends, or in relation to those cases subject to specified exceptions, or in relation to any specified cases or descriptions of case;
- (b) so as to make, as respects the cases in relation to which it is exercised—
  - (i) the full provision to which the power extends or any lesser provision (whether by way of exceptions or otherwise),
  - (ii) the same provision for all cases in relation to which the power is exercised, or different provision for different cases or different descriptions of case or different provision as respects the same case or description of case for different purposes of this Act, or
  - (iii) any such provision either unconditionally or subject to any specified condition.

(3) Any power conferred by this Act to make subordinate legislation—
- (a) if it is expressed to be exercisable for alternative purposes, may be exercised in relation to the same case for any or all of those purposes, and
- (b) if it is conferred for the purposes of any one provision of this Act, is without prejudice to any power to make subordinate legislation for the purposes of any other provision.

(4) A power conferred by this Act to make subordinate legislation includes power to provide for a person to exercise a discretion in dealing with any matter.

(5) Any power conferred by this Act to make subordinate legislation also includes power to make such incidental, supplementary, consequential or transitional provision as appears to the authority making the subordinate legislation to be expedient.

(6) Regulations may, for the purposes of or in connection with the coming into force of any provisions of this Act, make any such provision as could be made by virtue of section 322(5) by an order bringing those provisions into force.

## 316 Parliamentary control of subordinate legislation

(1) Subject to subsections (2) and (3), a statutory instrument containing regulations or an order or rules under this Act is subject to annulment in pursuance of a resolution of either House of Parliament.

(2) A statutory instrument which contains—
- (a) regulations under section 117(1) or (3) (administration levy in respect of expenditure relating to the Board of the Pension Protection Fund);

(b) regulations under section 167 (modification of Chapter 3 of Part 2 where liabilities discharged during the assessment period);
(c) regulations under section 174 (the initial levy);
(d) regulations under section 175 (pension protection levies);
(e) an order under section 177(6) (orders relating to amounts to be raised by pension protection levies);
(f) an order under section 178(1) (the levy ceiling);
(g) an order or regulations under section 209 (the PPF Ombudsman);
(h) regulations under section 213 (reference of reviewable matter to the PPF Ombudsman);
(i) regulations under section 214 (investigation by PPF Ombudsman of complaints of maladministration);
(j) regulations under section 237 (combined pension forecasts);
(k) regulations under section 238 (information and advice to employees);
(l) an order under section 243(1) (power to provide for minimum fraction of member-nominated trustees or directors to be one-half);
(m) regulations which make provision by virtue of section 261(2)(f) (power to make amendments etc to certain Acts);
(n) regulations under section 286 (financial assistance scheme for members of certain pension schemes);
(o) regulations which make provision by virtue of section 314(b) (power to provide for contravention of regulations to be criminal offence);
(p) regulations under section 318(4)(b) (power to extend meaning of employer);
(q) an order under section 319(2)(a) (power to make consequential amendments to Acts);
(r) an order under paragraph 24(8) of Schedule 7 (power to vary percentage of periodic compensation that can be commuted);
(s) an order under paragraph 26(7) of that Schedule (orders specifying the compensation cap in respect of payments from the Pension Protection Fund); or
(t) an order under paragraph 30(1) of that Schedule (power to vary percentage paid as compensation from the Pension Protection Fund);

must not be made unless a draft of the instrument has been laid before and approved by a resolution of each House of Parliament.

(3) Subsection (1) does not apply to—
 (a) an order under section 91(9) (commencement of code of practice);
 (b) an order under section 126(2) (schemes winding up before day appointed by order not eligible schemes for purposes of Part 2);
 (c) an order under section 182(10) (order appointing day after which losses of non-trust schemes are relevant for fraud compensation purposes);
 (d) an order under section 322 (commencement).

### 317 Consultations about regulations

(1) Before the Secretary of State makes any regulations by virtue of this Act (other than Part 8), he must consult such persons as he considers appropriate.
(2) Subsection (1) does not apply—
 (a) to regulations contained in a statutory instrument made for the purpose only of consolidating other instruments revoked by it,

(b) in a case where it appears to the Secretary of State that by reason of urgency consultation is inexpedient,

(c) to regulations contained in a statutory instrument made before the end of the period of six months beginning with the coming into force of the provision of this Act by virtue of which the regulations are made, or

(d) to regulations contained in a statutory instrument which—
  (i) states that it contains only regulations which are consequential upon a specified enactment, and
  (ii) is made before the end of the period of six months beginning with the coming into force of that enactment.

*Interpretation*

### 318  General interpretation

(1) In this Act, unless the context otherwise requires—

"active member" has the meaning given by section 124(1) of the Pensions Act 1995 (c. 26);

"the Board" has the meaning given by section 107;

"contravention" includes failure to comply;

"direct payment arrangements", in relation to a personal pension scheme, has the same meaning as in section 111A of the Pension Schemes Act 1993 (c. 48);

"earnings" has the meaning given by section 181(1) of the Pension Schemes Act 1993;

"employee" has the meaning given by section 181(1) of the Pension Schemes Act 1993;

"employer"—
  (a) in relation to an occupational pension scheme, means the employer of persons in the description of employment to which the scheme in question relates (but see subsection (4)), and
  (b) in relation to a personal pension scheme, where direct payment arrangements exist in respect of one or more members of the scheme who are employees, means an employer with whom those arrangements exist;

"enactment" includes an enactment comprised in subordinate legislation (within the meaning of the Interpretation Act 1978 (c. 30));

"managers", in relation to an occupational or personal pension scheme (other than a scheme established under a trust), means the persons responsible for the management of the scheme;

"member", in relation to an occupational pension scheme, means any active, deferred, pensioner or pension credit member within the meaning of section 124(1) of the Pensions Act 1995 (c. 26) (but see subsection (5));

"modifications" includes additions, omissions and amendments, and related expressions are to be construed accordingly;

"money purchase benefit" has the meaning given by section 181(1) of the Pension Schemes Act 1993 (c. 48);

"money purchase scheme" has the meaning given by section 181(1) of the Pension Schemes Act 1993;

"occupational pension scheme" has the meaning given by section 1 of the Pension Schemes Act 1993;

"pension credit" has the meaning given by section 124(1) of the Pensions Act 1995;
"personal pension scheme" has the meaning given by section 1 of the Pension Schemes Act 1993;
"the PPF Ombudsman" has the meaning given by section 209(1);
"prescribed" means prescribed by regulations;
"professional adviser", in relation to an occupational pension scheme, has the meaning given by section 47 of the Pensions Act 1995;
"the register" has the meaning given by section 59(1);
"regulations" means regulations made by the Secretary of State;
"the Regulator" has the meaning given by section 1;
"the Tribunal" has the meaning given by section 102(1).

(2) In this Act, unless the context otherwise requires, references to the scheme rules, in relation to an occupational pension scheme, are references to—
   (a) the rules of the scheme, except so far as overridden by a relevant legislative provision,
   (b) the relevant legislative provisions, to the extent that they have effect in relation to the scheme and are not reflected in the rules of the scheme, and
   (c) any provision which the rules of the scheme do not contain but which the scheme must contain if it is to conform with the requirements of Chapter 1 of Part 4 of the Pension Schemes Act 1993 (preservation of benefit under occupational pension schemes).

(3) For the purposes of subsection (2)—
   (a) "relevant legislative provision" means any provision contained in any of the following provisions—
      (i) Schedule 5 to the Social Security Act 1989 (c. 24) (equal treatment for men and women);
      (ii) Chapters 2 to 5 of Part 4 of the Pension Schemes Act 1993 (c. 48) (certain protection for early leavers) or regulations made under any of those Chapters;
      (iii) Part 4A of that Act (requirements relating to pension credit benefit) or regulations made under that Part;
      (iv) section 110(1) of that Act (requirement as to resources for annual increase of guaranteed minimum pensions);
      (v) Part 1 of the Pensions Act 1995 (c. 26) (occupational pensions) or subordinate legislation made or having effect as if made under that Part;
      (vi) section 31 of the Welfare Reform and Pensions Act 1999 (c. 30) (pension debits: reduction of benefit);
      (vii) any provision mentioned in section 306(2) of this Act;
   (b) a relevant legislative provision is to be taken to override any of the provisions of the scheme if, and only if, it does so by virtue of any of the following provisions—
      (i) paragraph 3 of Schedule 5 to the Social Security Act 1989 (c. 24);
      (ii) section 129(1) of the Pension Schemes Act 1993;
      (iii) section 117(1) of the Pensions Act 1995;
      (iv) section 31(4) of the Welfare Reform and Pensions Act 1999;
      (v) section 306(1) of this Act.

(4) Regulations may, in relation to occupational pension schemes, extend for the purposes of Parts 1, 2 and 4 to 7 and this Part the meaning of "employer" to include—
   (a) persons who have been the employer in relation to the scheme;
   (b) such other persons as may be prescribed.
(5) Regulations may for any purpose of any provision of this Act—
   (a) prescribe the persons who are to be regarded as members or prospective members of an occupational or personal pension scheme, and
   (b) make provision as to the times at which and circumstances in which a person is to be treated as becoming, or as ceasing to be, such a member or prospective member.

*Miscellaneous and supplementary*

### 319 Minor and consequential amendments

(1) Schedule 12 (which makes minor and consequential amendments) has effect.
(2) The Secretary of State may by order make provision consequential on this Act amending, repealing or revoking (with or without savings) any provision of—
   (a) an Act passed before or in the same session as this Act, or
   (b) an instrument made under an Act before the passing of this Act.

### 320 Repeals and revocations

The enactments mentioned in Schedule 13 are repealed or revoked to the extent specified.

### 321 Pre-Consolidation amendments

(1) The Secretary of State may by order make such modifications of—
   (a) this Act,
   (b) the Pension Schemes Act 1993 (c. 48),
   (c) the Pensions Act 1995 (c. 26),
   (d) Parts 1 to 4 of the Welfare Reform and Pensions Act 1999 (c. 30), and
   (e) Chapter 2 of Part 2 of the Child Support, Pensions and Social Security Act 2000 (c. 19),
   as in his opinion facilitate, or are otherwise desirable in connection with, the consolidation of those enactments or any of them.
(2) No order is to be made under this section unless a Bill for repealing and re-enacting—
   (a) the enactments modified by the order, or
   (b) enactments relating to matters connected with the matters to which enactments modified by the order relate,
   has been presented to either House of Parliament.
(3) An order under this section is not to come into force until immediately before the commencement of the Act resulting from that Bill.

### 322 Commencement

(1) Subject to subsections (2) to (4), the provisions of this Act come into force in accordance with provision made by the Secretary of State by order.
(2) The following provisions come into force on the day this Act is passed—
   (a) in Part 4, sections 234, 235 and 236 and Schedule 10 (provisions relating to retirement planning);

(b) in Part 5, section 281 (exemption from statutory revaluation requirement);
(c) in Part 8—
  (i) section 296 (entitlement to more than one State pension),
  (ii) section 297(3) (commencement of amendments of State pension deferment provisions made by Pensions Act 1995),
  (iii) section 298 (disclosure of State pension information), except subsections (4) and (5)(b), and
  (iv) section 299 (claims for certain benefits following termination of reciprocal agreement with Australia);
(d) in this Part (miscellaneous and general)—
  (i) sections 303 to 305 (service of notifications etc and electronic working), and
  (ii) this section and sections 313, 315 (other than subsection (6)), 316, 317, 318 (other than subsections (4) and (5)) and 323 to 325;
(e) the repeal by this Act of section 50(2) of the Welfare Reform and Pensions Act 1999.
(3) Section 297 (and Schedule 11) (deferral of retirement pensions and shared additional pensions), other than the provisions coming into force in accordance with subsection (2)—
  (a) come into force on the day this Act is passed so far as is necessary for enabling the making of any regulations for which they provide, and
  (b) otherwise, come into force on 6th April 2005.
(4) The repeals by this Act of section 134(3) of, and paragraph 21(14) of Schedule 4 to, the Pensions Act 1995 (c. 26) come into force on 6th April 2005.
(5) Without prejudice to section 315(5), the power to make an order under this section includes power—
  (a) to make transitional adaptations or modifications—
    (i) of the provisions brought into force by the order, or
    (ii) in connection with those provisions, of any provisions of Parts 1 to 7 of this Act or of the Pension Schemes Act 1993 (c. 48), the Pensions Act 1995, Parts 1, 2 or 4 of the Welfare Reform and Pensions Act 1999 (c. 30) or Chapter 2 of Part 2 of the Child Support, Pensions and Social Security Act 2000 (c. 19), or
  (b) to save the effect of any of the repealed provisions of those Acts, or those provisions as adapted or modified by the order,
as it appears to the Secretary of State expedient, including different adaptations or modifications for different periods.

**323 Extent**

(1) Subject to the following provisions, this Act extends to England, Wales and Scotland.
(2) The following provisions of this Act also extend to Northern Ireland—
  (a) in Part 1 (the Regulator)—
    (i) sections 1, 2, 4 (other than subsection (2)(b)), 8, 9, 11, 59, 102 and 106,
    (ii) in Schedule 1, paragraphs 1 to 19, 20(1) to (3) and (7), 21 (other than paragraph (b)), 22 to 25 and 27 to 35, and section 3 so far as it relates to those provisions, and
    (iii) Schedule 4,
  (b) in Part 2 (the Board)—

(i) sections 107, 108, 109, 110(1) and (3), 112, 113, 114, 115, 118, 119, 161(2)(a), (3) and (5) to (8), 173, 188, 209 (other than paragraphs (b) to (d), (f) and (g) of subsection (4), subsection (6) so far as relating to any of those paragraphs and subsections (7) and (8)), 210, 211(3) and (4), 212 and 220,

(ii) section 111 so far as that provision has effect in relation to functions of the Board conferred by any provision of, or made under, this Act which extends to Northern Ireland,

(iii) Schedule 5 (other than paragraph 18), and

(iv) Schedule 6 (other than paragraph 7),

(c) in Part 4 (retirement planning), sections 234 and 235 and paragraph 2 of Schedule 10 (and section 236 so far as it relates to that paragraph),

(d) in Part 5 (personal and occupational pension schemes: miscellaneous provisions), sections 274 and 277(2)(b),

(e) Part 6 (financial assistance scheme for members of certain pension schemes),

(f) in Part 8 (State pensions), section 299, and

(g) in this Part—
(i) sections 300(1) and (2), 301, 302(1) and (2), 307, 308 and 310,
(ii) sections 303 to 306, 309, 313, 315, 316 and 318 so far as those provisions have effect for the purposes of provisions which themselves extend to Northern Ireland, and
(iii) this section and sections 319(2), 321, 322, 324 and 325.

(3) Section 106 (legal assistance scheme) does not extend to Scotland.

(4) An amendment or repeal contained in this Act has the same extent as the enactment to which it relates and sections 236 (except so far as it relates to paragraph 2 of Schedule 10), 319(1) and 320 have effect accordingly.

## 324 Northern ireland

(1) An Order in Council under paragraph 1(1) of the Schedule to the Northern Ireland Act 2000 (c. 1) (legislation for Northern Ireland during suspension of devolved government) which contains a statement that it is made only for purposes corresponding to those of this Act—

(a) is not subject to paragraph 2 of that Schedule (affirmative resolution of both Houses of Parliament), but

(b) is subject to annulment in pursuance of a resolution of either House of Parliament.

(2) Where an Order in Council to which subsection (1) applies makes provision ("the NI provisions") which corresponds to the GB transfer provisions, regulations may make provision to secure that any transfer of property, rights and liabilities, or modification of a term of a contract of insurance, by virtue of the NI provisions is recognized for the purposes of the law of England and Wales and the law of Scotland.

(3) In subsection (2) "the GB transfer provisions" means section 161(1), (2)(a), (3) and (5) to (8) and Schedule 6 (other than paragraph 7).

## 325 Short title

This Act may be cited as the Pensions Act 2004.

## SCHEDULES

## SCHEDULE 1

Section 3

## THE PENSIONS REGULATOR

### PART 1
### MEMBERS OF THE REGULATOR

*Terms of appointment and tenure of members*

1  (1) The members of the Regulator appointed by the Secretary of State under section 2(1)(a) or (c) are to be appointed on such terms and conditions as are determined by the Secretary of State.
   (2) Subject to sub-paragraph (3), such a member—
       (a) is to hold and vacate office in accordance with the terms and conditions of his appointment, and
       (b) may resign or be removed from office in accordance with those terms and conditions.
   (3) A person must cease to be a member of the Regulator where—
       (a) in the case of the chairman, he ceases to hold that office or becomes a member of the staff of the Regulator;
       (b) in the case of any other non-executive member, he becomes a member of the staff of the Regulator;
       (c) in the case of an executive member appointed under section 2(1)(c), he ceases to be a member of the staff of the Regulator.
2  Where a person ceases to be employed as Chief Executive, he ceases to be a member of the Regulator.
3  No person is to be prevented from being a member of the Regulator (whether as chairman or otherwise) merely because he has previously been such a member.

*Remuneration etc of members*

4  The Regulator may pay, or make provision for paying, its non-executive members such remuneration as the Secretary of State may determine.
5  The Regulator may—
   (a) pay to or in respect of any person who is or has been a non-executive member such pension, allowances or gratuities as the Secretary of State may determine, or
   (b) make such payments as the Secretary of State may determine towards provision for the payment of a pension, allowance or gratuity to or in respect of such a person.
6  Where—
   (a) a non-executive member ceases to be a member otherwise than on the expiry of his term of office, and

(b) it appears to the Secretary of State that there are circumstances which make it right for that person to receive compensation,

the Regulator may make a payment to that person of such amount as the Secretary of State may determine.

## PART 2
## STAFF OF THE REGULATOR

### *The staff*

7 (1) The staff of the Regulator consists of—
   (a) the Chief Executive of the Regulator appointed under paragraph 8,
   (b) the other employees of the Regulator appointed under paragraph 9, and
   (c) any additional staff made available by the Secretary of State under paragraph 10.
   (2) No member of the Board of the Pension Protection Fund is eligible for appointment as a member of the staff of the Regulator.

### *The Chief Executive*

8 (1) The Regulator is to employ a person as its Chief Executive.
   (2) The Chief Executive's main function is to be responsible for securing that the functions of the Regulator are exercised efficiently and effectively.
   (3) The first appointment of a Chief Executive—
       (a) is to be made by the Secretary of State, and
       (b) is to be on such terms and conditions as to remuneration and other matters as are determined by the Secretary of State.
   (4) Subsequent appointments of a Chief Executive—
       (a) are to be made by the Regulator with the approval of the Secretary of State, and
       (b) are to be on such terms and conditions as to remuneration and other matters as are determined by the Regulator with the approval of the Secretary of State.
   (5) By virtue of subsection (2) of section 8 (non-executive functions), the function conferred on the Regulator by sub-paragraph (4)(b), so far as it relates to the terms and conditions as to remuneration, is exercisable on its behalf by the committee established under that section.

### *Other employees*

9 (1) Other employees of the Regulator may be appointed by the Regulator with the approval of the Secretary of State as to numbers.
   (2) Any such appointments are to be on such terms and conditions as to remuneration and other matters as are determined by the Regulator with the approval of the Secretary of State.

### *Additional staff etc*

10 (1) The Secretary of State may make available to the Regulator such additional staff and such other facilities as he considers appropriate.

## PART 3
## MEMBERS OF THE DETERMINATIONS PANEL

*Nomination of the chairman of the Panel*

11 (1) On each occasion when the Regulator is required to appoint a person as chairman of the Determinations Panel, the chairman of the Regulator must establish a committee (in this Schedule referred to as "the appointments committee").

(2) The appointments committee must consist of—
 (a) a chairman appointed by the chairman of the Regulator from the non-executive members of the Regulator, and
 (b) one or more persons appointed by the chairman of the Regulator.

(3) At least one of the persons appointed under sub-paragraph (2)(b) must be a person who is not a member of the Regulator.

(4) But a person appointed under sub-paragraph (2)(b) must not be a person who is a member of the staff of the Regulator.

(5) The committee must nominate a person suitable for appointment as chairman of the Panel.

*Terms of appointment and tenure of members of the Panel*

12 (1) The members of the Determinations Panel are to be appointed on such terms and conditions as are determined by the Regulator with the approval of the Secretary of State.

(2) Subject to sub-paragraph (3) such a member—
 (a) is to hold and vacate office in accordance with the terms and conditions of his appointment, and
 (b) may resign or be removed from office in accordance with those terms and conditions.

(3) A person must cease to be a member of the Panel where—
 (a) in the case of the chairman, he ceases to hold that office, or
 (b) in the case of any member, he becomes a member of the Regulator or a member of the staff of the Regulator.

13 No person is to be prevented from being a member of the Panel (whether as chairman or otherwise) merely because he has previously been a member of the Panel.

*Remuneration etc of members of the Panel*

14 The Regulator may pay, or make provision for paying, the members of the Determinations Panel such remuneration as the Secretary of State may determine.

15 The Regulator may—
 (a) pay to or in respect of any person who is or has been a member of the Panel such pension, allowances or gratuities as the Secretary of State may determine, or
 (b) make such payments as the Secretary of State may determine towards provision for the payment of a pension, allowance or gratuity to or in respect of such a person.

16  Where—
   (a) a member of the Panel ceases to be a member otherwise than on the expiry of his term of office, and
   (b) it appears to the Secretary of State that there are circumstances which make it right for that person to receive compensation,
   the Regulator may make a payment to that person of such amount as the Secretary of State may determine.

## PART 4
## PROCEEDINGS AND DELEGATION ETC

*Committees*

17  (1) The Regulator may establish committees for any purpose.
   (2) Any committee so established may establish sub-committees.
   (3) The members of such committees or sub-committees may include persons who are not members of the Regulator.
   (4) The members of such sub-committees may include persons who are not members of the committee.
   (5) But the majority of the members of a committee or a sub-committee must consist of persons who are members of the Regulator or members of the staff of the Regulator.
   (6) Sub-paragraphs (2) to (5) do not apply to—
      (a) the committee established under section 8 or any of its sub-committees, or
      (b) the Determinations Panel or any of its sub-committees (see section 9).
   (7) Subject to that, references in this Schedule to the committees of the Regulator are to—
      (a) the committee established under section 8 and any of its sub-committees,
      (b) the Determinations Panel and any of its sub-committees,
      (c) the appointments committee, and
      (d) any committees or sub-committees established under this paragraph.

*Procedure*

18  (1) The Regulator may determine—
      (a) its own procedure (including quorum), and
      (b) the procedure (including quorum) of any of its committees (other than the Determinations Panel and any of that Panel's sub-committees).
   (2) The Determinations Panel may determine—
      (a) its own procedure (including quorum), and
      (b) the procedure (including quorum) of any of its sub-committees.
   (3) This paragraph is subject to—
      (a) sections 93 to 104 (procedure in relation to the regulatory functions) and any corresponding provisions in force in Northern Ireland, and
      (b) any regulations made by the Secretary of State under paragraph 19.

19  (1) The Secretary of State may make regulations—
      (a) as to the procedure (including quorum) to be followed by the Regulator or any of its committees;
      (b) as to the manner in which the functions of the Regulator are to be exercised.

(2) Such regulations may in particular—
  (a) make provision as to the hearing of parties, the taking of evidence and the circumstances (if any) in which a document of any prescribed description is to be treated for the purposes of any proceedings before the Regulator, as evidence, or conclusive evidence, of any prescribed matter;
  (b) make provision as to the manner in which parties to any proceedings before the Regulator may or are to be represented for the purposes of the proceedings;
  (c) provide for enabling the Regulator to summon persons—
    (i) to attend proceedings before the Regulator and give evidence (including evidence on oath) for any purposes of proceedings in connection with a determination whether to exercise, or the exercise of, a regulatory function (or any corresponding function under any provisions in force in Northern Ireland corresponding to this Act), or
    (ii) to produce any documents required by the Regulator for those purposes.
(3) In this paragraph references to proceedings before the Regulator include references to proceedings before the Determinations Panel and any of the Panel's sub-committees.

*Delegation*

20 (1) The Regulator may authorize—
  (a) any executive member of the Regulator,
  (b) any other member of the staff of the Regulator, or
  (c) any of its committees (other than the appointments committee, the Determinations Panel and any of that Panel's sub-committees),
to exercise, on behalf of the Regulator, such of its functions, in such circumstances, as the Regulator may determine.
(2) But sub-paragraph (1) does not apply to—
  (a) the non-executive functions of the Regulator listed in subsection (4) of section 8 (which, by virtue of subsection (2) of that section, must be discharged by the committee established under that section),
  (b) the duty of the Regulator to appoint the chairman and other members of the Determinations Panel under section 9,
  (c) the duty of the Regulator to determine the terms and conditions of their appointments under paragraph 12(1), and
  (d) the functions of the Regulator which are exercisable only by the Panel by virtue of—
    (i) section 10(1) (the power in certain circumstances to determine whether to exercise the functions listed in Schedule 2 and to exercise them) or any corresponding provision in force in Northern Ireland, or
    (ii) section 99(10) (the functions concerning the compulsory review of certain determinations) or any corresponding provision in force in Northern Ireland.
(3) The Regulator may authorize the appointments committee to exercise the power under paragraph 18 to determine the committee's own procedure (including quorum).
(4) The Regulator may authorize the Determinations Panel, in such circumstances as the Regulator may determine, to exercise on behalf of the Regulator—

(a) the power to determine whether to exercise one or more of the regulatory functions listed in sub-paragraph (5), and
(b) where the Panel so determines to exercise the regulatory function in question, the power to exercise it.

(5) The regulatory functions mentioned in sub-paragraph (4) are—
  (a) the power to issue an improvement notice under section 13;
  (b) the power to issue a third party notice under section 14;
  (c) the power to issue a clearance statement under section 42;
  (d) the power to issue a notice under section 45(1) approving the details of arrangements;
  (e) the power to issue a clearance statement under section 46;
  (f) the power to make an order under section 154(8);
  (g) the power to make an order under section 219(4);
  (h) the power to grant or revoke authorisation under section 288;
  (i) the power to grant or revoke approval under section 289;
  (j) the power to issue a notice under section 293(5);
  (k) the power by direction under section 2(3)(a) of the Welfare Reform and Pensions Act 1999 (c. 30) to refuse to register a scheme under section 2 of that Act;
  (l) the power to appoint a trustee under any of the following provisions of section 7 of the Pensions Act 1995 (c. 26)—
    (i) subsection (1) where a trustee is removed by reason of his disqualification;
    (ii) subsection (3)(b);
  (m) the power to appoint an independent trustee under section 23 of that Act;
  (n) the power to give directions under section 72B of that Act facilitating a winding up.

(6) The Regulator may also authorize the Determinations Panel, in such circumstances as the Regulator may determine, to exercise on behalf of the Regulator such functions (other than those mentioned in sub-paragraph (2)(a) to (c)) as the Regulator considers necessary for the effective exercise by the Panel of—
  (a) a function of the Regulator which it is authorized to exercise by virtue of sub-paragraph (4),
  (b) a function of the Regulator mentioned in sub-paragraph (2)(d) (functions exercisable only by the Panel), or
  (c) a function of the Panel under section 93(3), section 99(11) or paragraph 18(2) of this Schedule (procedure).

(7) This paragraph is subject to any regulations made by the Secretary of State under paragraph 21.

21  The Secretary of State may make regulations—
  (a) limiting the extent to which any of the functions mentioned in subsection (8) of section 8 may be delegated by the committee established under that section to any of its members or any of its sub-committees under that subsection;
  (b) limiting the extent to which any of the functions mentioned in subsection (9) of section 10 may be delegated by the Determinations Panel to any of its members or any of its sub-committees under that subsection;
  (c) limiting the extent to which functions of the Regulator may be delegated under paragraph 20;

(d) limiting the delegation under paragraph 20 of any power to delegate contained in that paragraph;
(e) permitting the Regulator in prescribed circumstances to delegate to prescribed persons prescribed functions of the Regulator.

*Application of seal and proof of instruments*

22 (1) The fixing of the common seal of the Regulator must be authenticated by the signature of a person authorized for that purpose by the Regulator (whether generally or specifically).
(2) Sub-paragraph (1) does not apply in relation to any document which is or is to be signed in accordance with the law of Scotland.

23 A document purporting to be duly executed under the seal of the Regulator or purporting to be signed on its behalf—
(a) is to be received in evidence, and
(b) is to be taken to be so executed or signed unless the contrary is proved.

## PART 5
## FUNDING AND ACCOUNTS

*Funding*

24 The Secretary of State may pay the Regulator out of money provided by Parliament such sums as he may determine towards its expenses.

25 (1) The Secretary of State may make regulations authorising the Regulator to charge fees to meet the costs incurred by the Regulator in connection with applications made for—
(a) the modification of an occupational pension scheme under section 69 of the Pensions Act 1995 (c. 26) or under any corresponding provision in force in Northern Ireland, or
(b) the issuing of a clearance statement under section 42 or 46 or under any corresponding provision in force in Northern Ireland.
(2) Regulations under sub-paragraph (1) may prescribe, or authorize the Regulator to determine, the time at which any fee is due.
(3) Any fee which is owed to the Regulator by virtue of regulations under this paragraph may be recovered as a debt due to the Regulator.

26 (1) Section 175 of the Pension Schemes Act 1993 (c. 48) (levies towards certain expenditure) is amended as follows.
(2) In subsection (1) omit "or" at the end of paragraph (b) and for paragraph (c) substitute—
"(c) of the Regulatory Authority (including the establishment of the Authority under the Pensions Act 2004), or
(d) of the Lord Chancellor in meeting the costs of the legal assistance scheme established by virtue of section 106 of the Pensions Act 2004 (legal assistance in connection with proceedings before the Pensions Regulator Tribunal),".
(3) In subsection (3), in paragraph (a), for the words from "any amounts paid" to the end of the paragraph substitute"—

(i) any amounts paid to the Secretary of State under section 168(4) of this Act or section 10 of the Pensions Act 1995 (civil penalties), and
(ii) any fees paid to the Authority under paragraph 25 of Schedule 1 to the Pensions Act 2004 (fees for certain applications), and".

*Accounts*

27 (1) The Regulator must—
(a) keep proper accounts and proper records in relation to the accounts, and
(b) prepare in respect of each financial year a statement of accounts.
(2) Each statement of accounts must comply with any directions given by the Secretary of State with the approval of the Treasury as to—
(a) the information to be contained in it and the manner in which it is to be presented;
(b) the methods and principles according to which the statement is to be prepared;
(c) the additional information (if any) which is to be provided for the information of Parliament.
(3) The Regulator must send a copy of each statement of accounts—
(a) to the Secretary of State, and
(b) to the Comptroller and Auditor-General,
before the end of the month of August next following the financial year to which the statement relates.
(4) The Comptroller and Auditor-General must—
(a) examine, certify and report on each statement of accounts which he receives under sub-paragraph (3), and
(b) lay a copy of each statement and of his report before each House of Parliament.
(5) In this paragraph "financial year" means—
(a) the period beginning with the date on which the Regulator is established and ending with the next following 31st March, and
(b) each successive period of 12 months.

*Other expenses*

28 (1) The Regulator may—
(a) pay, or make provision for paying, persons attending proceedings before the Regulator at its request such travelling and other allowances (including compensation for loss of remunerative time) as the Secretary of State may determine, and
(b) pay, or make provision for paying, persons from whom the Regulator may decide to seek advice, as being persons considered by the Regulator to be specially qualified to advise it on particular matters, such fees as the Regulator may determine.
(2) In this paragraph references to proceedings before the Regulator include references to proceedings before any committee of the Regulator.

PART 6

STATUS AND LIABILITY ETC

*Status*

29 (1) The Regulator is not to be regarded—
(a) as the servant or agent of the Crown, or
(b) as enjoying any status, privilege or immunity of the Crown.
(2) Accordingly, the Regulator's property is not to be regarded as property of, or held on behalf of, the Crown.

*Validity*

30 The validity of any proceedings of the Regulator (including any proceedings of any of its committees) is not to be affected by—
(a) any vacancy among the members of the Regulator or of any of its committees,
(b) any defect in the appointment of any member of the Regulator or of any of its committees, or
(c) any defect in the appointment of the Chief Executive.

*Disqualification*

31 Schedule 1 to the House of Commons Disqualification Act 1975 (c. 24) is amended as follows—
(a) in Part 2 (bodies whose members are disqualified) at the appropriate place insert—
"The Pensions Regulator.", and
(b) in Part 3 (other disqualifying offices) at the appropriate place insert—
"Member of the Determinations Panel established by the Pensions Regulator under section 9 of the Pensions Act 2004."

32 Schedule 1 to the Northern Ireland Assembly Disqualification Act 1975 (c. 25) is amended as follows—
(a) in Part 2 (bodies whose members are disqualified) at the appropriate place insert—
"The Pensions Regulator.", and
(b) in Part 3 (other disqualifying offices) at the appropriate place insert—
"Member of the Determinations Panel established by the Pensions Regulator under section 9 of the Pensions Act 2004."

*The Parliamentary Commissioner for Administration*

33 In Schedule 2 to the Parliamentary Commissioner Act 1967 (c. 13)(departments and authorities subject to investigation), at the appropriate place insert—
"The Pensions Regulator."

*The Superannuation Act 1972*

34 (1) The persons to whom section 1 of the Superannuation Act 1972 (c. 11) (persons to or in respect of whom benefits may be provided by schemes under that section) applies are to include—

the chairman of the Regulator

the employees of the Regulator.

(2) The Regulator must pay to the Minister for the Civil Service, at such times as he may direct, such sums as he may determine in respect of the increase attributable to sub-paragraph (1) in the sums payable out of money provided by Parliament under that Act.

*Exemption from liability in damages*

35 (1) Neither the Regulator nor any person who is a member of the Regulator, a member of any of its committees, or a member of its staff is to be liable in damages for anything done or omitted in the exercise or purported exercise of the functions of the Regulator conferred by, or by virtue of, this or any other enactment.

(2) Any person who is—
   (a) the chairman of the Regulator,
   (b) the Chief Executive of the Regulator, or
   (c) the chairman of the Determinations Panel,

is not to be liable in damages for anything done or omitted in the exercise or purported exercise of any function conferred on the office in question by, or by virtue of, this Act or any provisions in force in Northern Ireland corresponding to this Act.

(3) Any person who is a member of the committee established under section 8 or of any of its sub-committees is not to be liable in damages for anything done or omitted in the discharge or purported discharge of the duty to prepare a report under subsection (5) of that section on the discharge of the non-executive functions.

(4) Any person who is a member of the Determinations Panel is not to be liable in damages for anything done or omitted in the exercise or purported exercise of the functions of the Panel under—
   (a) section 93(3) (procedure in relation to regulatory functions) or any corresponding provision in force in Northern Ireland,
   (b) section 99(11) (procedure in relation to exercise of functions on a compulsory review) or any corresponding provision in force in Northern Ireland, or
   (c) paragraph 18(2) of this Schedule (general procedure).

(5) But sub-paragraphs (1) to (4) do not apply—
   (a) if it is shown that the act or omission was in bad faith, or
   (b) so as to prevent an award of damages made in respect of an act or omission on the ground that the act or omission was unlawful as a result of section 6(1) of the Human Rights Act 1998 (c. 42).

## SCHEDULE 2

Section 10

## THE RESERVED REGULATORY FUNCTIONS

### PART 1
### FUNCTIONS UNDER THE PENSION SCHEMES ACT 1993 (C. 48)

1  The power by direction under section 99(4) to grant an extension of the period within which the trustees or managers of a scheme are to carry out certain duties.
2  The power by direction under section 101J(2) to extend the period for compliance with a transfer notice.
3  The power under regulations made by virtue of section 168(4) to require a person to pay a penalty.

### PART 2
### FUNCTIONS UNDER THE PENSIONS ACT 1995 (C. 26)

4  The power to make an order under section 3(1) prohibiting a person from being a trustee.
5  The power to make an order under section 3(3) revoking such an order.
6  The power to make an order under section 4(1) suspending a trustee.
7  The power to make an order under section 4(2) extending the period for which an order under section 4(1) of that Act has effect.
8  The power to make an order under section 4(5) revoking an order under section 4(1) of that Act suspending a trustee.
9  The power to make an order appointing a trustee under any of the following provisions of section 7—
   (a) subsection (1) where a trustee is removed by an order under section 3 (prohibition orders);
   (b) subsection (3)(a) or (c).
10  The power under section 9 to exercise by order the same jurisdiction and powers as the High Court or the Court of Session for vesting property in, or transferring property to, trustees in consequence of the appointment or removal of a trustee.
11  The power to require a person to pay a penalty under section 10 (including under regulations made by virtue of subsection (3) of that section).
12  The power to make an order under section 11 directing or authorising an occupational pension scheme to be wound up.
13  The power to give directions to trustees under section 15.
14  The power under section 29(5) to give a notice waiving a disqualification under section 29 of that Act.
15  The power under section 30(2) to exercise by order the same jurisdiction and powers as the High Court or the Court of Session for vesting property in, or transferring property to, the trustees where a trustee becomes disqualified under section 29 of that Act.

16. The power to make an order under section 67G(2) by virtue of which any modification of, or grant of rights under, an occupational pension scheme is void to any extent.
17. The power to make an order under section 67H(2) prohibiting, or specifying steps to be taken in relation to, the exercise of a power to modify an occupational pension scheme.
18. The power to make an order under section 69 authorising the modification of an occupational pension scheme or modifying the scheme.
19. The power to make an order under section 71A modifying an occupational pension scheme with a view to ensuring that it is properly wound up.

### PART 3
### FUNCTIONS UNDER THE WELFARE REFORM AND PENSIONS ACT 1999 (C. 30)

20. The power by direction under section 2(3)(b) to remove a scheme from the register of stakeholder pension schemes.

### PART 4
### FUNCTIONS UNDER THIS ACT

21. The power to make or extend a restraining order under section 20.
22. The power to make an order under section 20(10) permitting payments out of an account that is subject to a restraining order.
23. The power to make a repatriation order under section 21.
24. The power to make a freezing order under section 23.
25. The power to make an order under section 25(3) extending the period for which a freezing order has effect.
26. The power to make an order under section 26 validating action taken in contravention of a freezing order.
27. The power to make an order under section 28 directing that specified steps are taken.
28. The power to make an order under section 30 giving a direction where a freezing order ceases to have effect.
29. The power to make an order under section 31(3) directing the notification of members.
30. The power to issue a contribution notice under section 38.
31. The power to issue a direction under section 41(4) to the trustees or managers of an occupational pension scheme.
32. The power to issue a revised contribution notice under section 41(9).
33. The power to issue a financial support direction under section 43.
34. The power to issue a contribution notice under section 47.
35. The power to issue a direction under section 50(4) to the trustees or managers of an occupational pension scheme.
36. The power to issue a revised contribution notice under section 50(9).
37. The power to make a restoration order under section 52.
38. The power to issue a contribution notice under section 55.
39. The power to issue a notice under section 71 requiring a report to be provided to the Regulator.

40 The power to make a direction under section 76(8) extending the retention period for documents taken into possession under section 75.
41 The power to make a direction under section 78(10) extending the retention period for documents taken into possession under that section.
42 The power to make an order under section 231 modifying a scheme, giving directions or imposing a schedule of contributions.
43 The power to issue a ringfencing notice under section 292.
44 The power to vary or revoke under section 101—
    (a) a determination made by the Determinations Panel whether to exercise one of the other functions listed in this Schedule, or
    (b) an order, notice or direction made, issued or given in the exercise of one of those functions—
        (i) by the Panel, or
        (ii) by the Regulator in compliance with a direction of the Tribunal under section 103.

## SCHEDULE 3

Section 86

## RESTRICTED INFORMATION HELD BY THE REGULATOR: CERTAIN PERMITTED DISCLOSURES TO FACILITATE EXERCISE OF FUNCTIONS

| *Persons* | *Functions* |
|---|---|
| The Secretary of State. | Functions under—<br>(a) Part 14 of the Companies Act 1985 (c. 6),<br>(b) the Insolvency Act 1986 (c. 45),<br>(c) Part 3 of the Companies Act 1989 (c. 40),<br>(d) Part 1 of the Export and Investment Guarantees Act 1991 (c. 67) (apart from sections 5 and 6),<br>(e) Part 3 of the Pension Schemes Act 1993 (c. 48),<br>(f) Part 5 of the Police Act 1997 (c. 50),<br>(g) the Financial Services and Markets Act 2000 (c. 8), or<br>(h) this Act,<br>and functions of co-operating with overseas government authorities and bodies in relation to criminal matters. |
| The Bank of England. | Any of its functions. |
| The Financial Services Authority. | Functions under—<br>(a) the legislation relating to friendly societies,<br>(b) the Building Societies Act 1986 (c. 53), or<br>(c) the Financial Services and Markets Act 2000 (c. 8). |
| The Charity Commissioners. | Functions under the Charities Act 1993 (c. 10). |
| The Pensions Regulator Tribunal. | Any of its functions. |
| The Pensions Ombudsman. | Functions under—<br>(a) the Pension Schemes Act 1993 (c. 48), or<br>(b) the Pension Schemes (Northern Ireland) Act 1993 (c. 49). |
| The Ombudsman for the Board of the Pension Protection Fund. | Any of his functions. |
| The Comptroller and Auditor-General. | Any of his functions. |
| The Auditor-General for Wales. | Any of his functions. |
| The Auditor-General for Scotland. | Any of his functions. |
| The Comptroller and Auditor-General for Northern Ireland. | Any of his functions. |
| The Commissioners of Inland Revenue or their officers. | Functions under—<br>(a) the Income and Corporation Taxes Act 1988 (c. 1),<br>(b) the Taxation of Chargeable Gains Act 1992 (c. 12),<br>(c) Part 3 of the Pension Schemes Act 1993,<br>(d) Part 3 of the Pension Schemes (Northern Ireland) Act 1993, or<br>(e) the Income Tax (Earnings and Pensions) Act 2003 (c. 1). |

**sch 3, Pensions Act 2004**

| Persons | Functions |
|---|---|
| The Commissioners of Customs and Excise. | Functions under any enactment. |
| The Official Receiver or, in Northern Ireland, the Official Receiver for Northern Ireland. | Functions under the enactments relating to insolvency. |
| An inspector appointed by the Secretary of State. | Functions under Part 14 of the Companies Act 1985 (c. 6). |
| A person authorized to exercise powers under—<br>(a) section 447 of the Companies Act 1985,<br>(b) Article 440 of the Companies (Northern Ireland) Order 1986 (S.I. 1986/1032 (N.I. 6)), or<br>(c) section 84 of the Companies Act 1989 (c. 40). | Functions under those sections or that Article. |
| A person appointed under—<br>(a) section 167 of the Financial Services and Markets Act 2000 (c. 8),<br>(b) subsection (3) or (5) of section 168 of that Act, or<br>(c) section 284 of that Act,<br>to conduct an investigation. | Functions in relation to that investigation. |
| A body designated under section 326(1) of that Act. | Functions in its capacity as a body designated under that section. |
| A recognized investment exchange or a recognized clearing house (as defined by section 285 of that Act). | Functions in its capacity as an exchange or clearing house recognized under that Act. |
| A body corporate established in accordance with section 212(1) of that Act. | Functions under the Financial Services Compensation Scheme, established in accordance with section 213 of that Act. |
| The Panel on Takeovers and Mergers. | Functions under the City Code on Takeovers and Mergers and the Rules Governing Substantial Acquisitions of Shares for the time being issued by the Panel. |
| The General Insurance Standards Council. | Functions of regulating sales and advisory and service standards in relation to insurance. |
| A recognized professional body (within the meaning of section 391 of the Insolvency Act 1986 (c. 45)). | Functions in its capacity as such a body under that Act. |
| A person on whom functions are conferred by or under Part 2, 3 or 4 of the Proceeds of Crime Act 2002 (c. 29). | The functions so conferred. |
| The Counter Fraud and Security Management Service established under the Counter Fraud and Security Management Service (Establishment and Constitution) Order 2002 (S.I. 2002/3039). | Any of its functions. |

| *Persons* | *Functions* |
| --- | --- |
| The Department of Enterprise, Trade and Investment in Northern Ireland. | Functions under—<br>(a) Part 15 of the Companies (Northern Ireland) Order 1986 (S.I. 1986/1032 (N.I. 6)),<br>(b) the Insolvency (Northern Ireland) Order 1989 (S.I. 1989/2405 (N.I. 19)), or<br>(c) Part 2 of the Companies (No. 2) (Northern Ireland) Order 1990 (S.I. 1990/1504 (N.I. 10)). |
| The Department for Social Development in Northern Ireland. | Functions under Part 3 of the Pension Schemes (Northern Ireland) Act 1993 (c. 49). |
| An Inspector appointed by the Department of Enterprise, Trade and Investment in Northern Ireland. | Functions under Part 15 of the Companies (Northern Ireland) Order 1986. |
| A recognized professional body within the meaning of Article 350 of the Insolvency (Northern Ireland) Order 1989. | Functions in its capacity as such a body under that Order. |
| The Gaming Board for Great Britain. | Functions under—<br>(a) the Gaming Act 1968 (c. 65), or<br>(b) the Lotteries and Amusements Act 1976 (c. 32). |

## SCHEDULE 4

Section 102

### THE PENSIONS REGULATOR TRIBUNAL

### PART 1
### THE TRIBUNAL

*The Panels*

1  (1) The Lord Chancellor must appoint a panel of persons for the purpose of serving as chairmen of the Tribunal ("the panel of chairmen").
   (2) A person is qualified for membership of the panel of chairmen if—
       (a) he has a 7 year general qualification within the meaning of section 71 of the Courts and Legal Services Act 1990 (c. 41),
       (b) he is an advocate or solicitor in Scotland of at least 7 years' standing,
       (c) he is a member of the Bar of Northern Ireland of at least 7 years' standing, or
       (d) he is a solicitor of the Supreme Court of Northern Ireland of at least 7 years' standing.
   (3) The panel of chairmen must include at least one member who is a person of the kind mentioned in sub-paragraph (2)(b).
   (4) The Lord Chancellor must also appoint a panel of persons who appear to him to be qualified by experience or otherwise to deal with matters of the kind that may be referred to the Tribunal ("the lay panel").

*The President*

2  (1) The Lord Chancellor must appoint one of the members of the panel of chairmen to preside over the exercise of the Tribunal's functions.
   (2) The member so appointed is to be known as the President of the Pensions Regulator Tribunal (in this Schedule referred to as "the President").
   (3) The Lord Chancellor may appoint one of the members of the panel of chairmen to be the Deputy President.
   (4) The Deputy President is to have such functions in relation to the Tribunal as the President may assign to him.
   (5) The Lord Chancellor may not appoint a person to be the President or Deputy President unless that person—
       (a) has a 10 year general qualification within the meaning of section 71 of the Courts and Legal Services Act 1990,
       (b) is an advocate or solicitor in Scotland of at least 10 years' standing,
       (c) is a member of the Bar of Northern Ireland of at least 10 years' standing, or
       (d) is a solicitor of the Supreme Court of Northern Ireland of at least 10 years' standing.
   (6) If the President ceases to be a member of the panel of chairmen, he also ceases to be the President.

Pensions Act 2004, sch 4

(7) If the Deputy President ceases to be a member of the panel of chairmen, he also ceases to be the Deputy President.
(8) If the President is absent or otherwise unable to act, his functions may be exercised—
    (a) by the Deputy President, or
    (b) if there is no Deputy President or he too is absent or otherwise unable to act, by a person appointed for that purpose from the panel of chairmen by the Lord Chancellor.

*Terms of office etc*

3  (1) Subject to the provisions of this Schedule, each member of the panel of chairmen and the lay panel—
    (a) is to hold and vacate office in accordance with the terms and conditions of his appointment, and
    (b) may resign or be removed from office in accordance with those terms and conditions.
   (2) A member of either panel is eligible for re-appointment if he ceases to hold office.

*Remuneration and allowances*

4  The Lord Chancellor may pay, or make provision for paying, out of money provided by Parliament, any person in respect of his service—
    (a) as a member of the Tribunal (including service as the President or Deputy President), or
    (b) as a person appointed under paragraph 7(4) (appointment of experts),
   such remuneration and allowances as the Lord Chancellor may determine.

*Staff*

5  (1) The Lord Chancellor may appoint such staff for the Tribunal as he may determine.
   (2) The remuneration of the Tribunal's staff is to be paid by the Lord Chancellor out of money provided by Parliament.

*Expenses*

6  The Lord Chancellor may pay, out of money provided by Parliament, such expenses of the Tribunal as the Lord Chancellor may determine.

PART 2
CONSTITUTION OF THE TRIBUNAL

7  (1) On a reference to the Tribunal, the persons to act as members of the Tribunal for the purposes of the reference are to be selected from the panel of chairmen or the lay panel in accordance with arrangements made by the President for the purposes of this paragraph ("the standing arrangements").
   (2) The standing arrangements must provide for at least one member to be selected from the panel of chairmen.

(3) If, while a reference is being dealt with, a person serving as a member of the Tribunal in respect of the reference becomes unable to act, the reference may be dealt with—
   (a) by the other members selected in respect of the reference, or
   (b) if it is being dealt with by a single member, by such other member of the panel of chairmen as may be selected in accordance with the standing arrangements for the purposes of the reference.
(4) If it appears to the Tribunal that a matter before it involves a question of fact of special difficulty, it may appoint one or more experts to provide assistance.
(5) For the purposes of this Schedule, a "reference to the Tribunal" means a reference to the Tribunal under this Act or any provisions in force in Northern Ireland corresponding to this Act.

## PART 3
## TRIBUNAL PROCEDURE

### *General*

8   For the purpose of dealing with references, or any matter preliminary or incidental to a reference, the Tribunal must sit at such times and in such place or places as the Lord Chancellor may direct.

9   Rules made by the Lord Chancellor under section 102 may, in particular, include provision—
   (a) as to the manner in which references are to be instituted;
   (b) for the holding of hearings in private in such circumstances as may be specified in the rules;
   (c) as to the persons who may appear on behalf of the parties;
   (d) for a member of the panel of chairmen to hear and determine interim matters arising on a reference;
   (e) for the Tribunal to deal with urgent cases expeditiously;
   (f) as to the withdrawal of references;
   (g) as to the registration, publication and proof of decisions and orders.

### *Practice directions*

10   The President may give directions as to the practice and procedure to be followed by the Tribunal in relation to references to it.

### *Evidence*

11   (1) The Tribunal may by summons require any person to attend, at such time and place as is specified in the summons, to give evidence or to produce any document in his custody or under his control which the Tribunal considers it necessary to examine.
   (2) The Tribunal may—
   (a) take evidence on oath and for that purpose administer oaths, or
   (b) instead of administering an oath, require the person examined to make and subscribe a declaration of the truth of the matters in respect of which he is examined.

(3) A person who without reasonable excuse refuses or fails—
  (a) to attend following the issue of a summons by the Tribunal, or
  (b) to give evidence,
is guilty of an offence.
(4) A person guilty of an offence under sub-paragraph (3) is liable on summary conviction to a fine not exceeding level 5 on the standard scale.
(5) A person who without reasonable excuse—
  (a) alters, suppresses, conceals or destroys a document which he is or is liable to be required to produce for the purposes of proceedings before the Tribunal, or
  (b) refuses to produce a document when so required,
is guilty of an offence.
(6) A person guilty of an offence under sub-paragraph (5) is liable—
  (a) on summary conviction, to a fine not exceeding the statutory maximum;
  (b) on conviction on indictment, to imprisonment for a term not exceeding two years or a fine or both.
(7) In this paragraph "document" includes information recorded in any form and, in relation to information recorded otherwise than in a legible form, references to its production include references to producing a copy of the information—
  (a) in a legible form, or
  (b) in a form from which it can readily be produced in a legible form.

*Decisions of the Tribunal*

12 (1) A decision of the Tribunal may be taken by a majority.
(2) The decision must state whether it was unanimous or taken by a majority.
(3) The decision must be recorded in a document which—
  (a) contains a statement of the reasons for the decision, and
  (b) is signed and dated by the member of the panel of chairmen dealing with the reference.
(4) The Tribunal must inform each party to the reference of its decision.
(5) The Tribunal must as soon as reasonably practicable send a copy of the document mentioned in sub-paragraph (3)—
  (a) to each of the parties to the reference, and
  (b) to such other persons as appear to the Tribunal to be directly affected by the decision.
(6) The Tribunal must send the Secretary of State and the Department for Social Development in Northern Ireland a copy of its decision.
(7) In this paragraph "document" includes information recorded in any form.

*Costs*

13 (1) If the Tribunal considers that a party to any proceedings on a reference has acted vexatiously, frivolously or unreasonably it may order that party to pay to another party to the proceedings the whole or part of the costs or expenses incurred by the other party in connection with the proceedings.
(2) If, in any proceedings on a reference, the Tribunal considers that a determination of the Regulator which is the subject of the reference was unreasonable it may order the Regulator to pay to another party to the proceedings the whole or part of the costs or expenses incurred by the other party in connection with the proceedings.

PART 4
STATUS ETC

*Disqualification*

14  In Part 3 of Schedule 1 to the House of Commons Disqualification Act 1975 (c. 24) (other disqualifying offices), at the appropriate place insert—
"Any member, in receipt of remuneration, of a panel of persons who may be selected to act as members of the Pensions Regulator Tribunal."

15  In Part 3 of Schedule 1 to the Northern Ireland Assembly Disqualification Act 1975 (c. 25) (other disqualifying offices), at the appropriate place insert—
"Any member, in receipt of remuneration, of a panel of persons who may be selected to act as members of the Pensions Regulator Tribunal."

*The Parliamentary Commissioner for Administration*

16  In Schedule 4 to the Parliamentary Commissioner Act 1967 (c. 13) (relevant tribunals for the purposes of section 5(7) of that Act), at the appropriate place insert—
"The Pensions Regulator Tribunal constituted under section 102 of the Pensions Act 2004."

*Judicial Pensions and Retirement Act 1993*

17  (1) The Judicial Pensions and Retirement Act 1993 (c. 8) is amended as follows.
    (2) In Schedule 1 (offices which may be qualifying offices), in Part 2, at the appropriate place insert—
    "President or Deputy President of the Pensions Regulator Tribunal."
    (3) In Schedule 5 (relevant offices in relation to retirement provisions), at the appropriate place insert—
    "Member of the Pensions Regulator Tribunal."

*Disclosure of information*

18  In section 449(1) of the Companies Act 1985 (c. 6) (exceptions from restrictions on publication and disclosure), after paragraph (m) insert—
"(n) for the purposes of proceedings before the Pensions Regulator Tribunal."

19  In Schedule 15D to that Act (permitted disclosures of information) (as inserted by Schedule 2 to the Companies (Audit, Investigations and Community Enterprise) Act 2004), after paragraph 44 insert—
"44A A disclosure for the purposes of proceedings before the Pensions Regulator Tribunal."

20  In section 87(2) of the Companies Act 1989 (c. 40) (exceptions from restrictions on disclosure), after paragraph (c) insert—
"(d) proceedings before the Pensions Regulator Tribunal."

21  In section 50(2) of the Courts and Legal Services Act 1990 (c. 41) (exceptions from restrictions on disclosure), after paragraph (s) insert—
"(t) the Pensions Regulator Tribunal to discharge any of its functions."

## SCHEDULE 5

Section 109

### THE BOARD OF THE PENSION PROTECTION FUND

### PART 1
### MEMBERS OF THE BOARD

*Appointment of chairman*

1 The chairman of the Board is to be appointed by the Secretary of State.

*Appointment of ordinary members*

2 (1) The appointments of the first five ordinary members are to be made by the Secretary of State.
 (2) Subsequent appointments of ordinary members are to be made by the Board, subject to sub-paragraph (4).
 (3) In making any appointment by virtue of sub-paragraph (2) the Board must act in accordance with any procedure for making such appointments that may be prescribed.
 (4) If, at any time, there are less than five ordinary members, the Secretary of State must appoint such number of ordinary members as is required to bring the number of ordinary members to five.

*Terms of appointment*

3 (1) The chairman and the ordinary members appointed by the Secretary of State are to be appointed on such terms and conditions as are determined by the Secretary of State.
 (2) The ordinary members appointed by the Board are to be appointed on such terms and conditions as are determined—
  (a) in the case of a non-executive member, by the chairman with the approval of the Secretary of State, and
  (b) in the case of an executive member, by the Chief Executive.
 (3) This paragraph is subject to paragraph 7 (remuneration of members).

*Tenure of members*

4 (1) Subject to the following provisions, the chairman and any ordinary member—
  (a) is to hold and vacate office in accordance with the terms and conditions of his appointment, and
  (b) may resign or be removed from office in accordance with those terms and conditions.
 (2) A person must cease to be a member of the Board where—
  (a) in the case of the chairman, he ceases to hold that office or becomes a member of the staff of the Board;

(b) in the case of any other non-executive member, he becomes a member of the staff of the Board;
(c) in the case of an ordinary member who is an executive member, he ceases to be a member of the staff of the Board.

5 Where a person ceases to be employed as Chief Executive, he ceases to be a member of the Board.

6 No person is to be prevented from being a member of the Board (whether as chairman or otherwise) merely because he has previously been such a member.

*Remuneration etc of members*

7 The Board may pay, or make provision for paying, its non-executive members such remuneration as the Secretary of State may determine.

8 The Board may—
(a) pay to or in respect of any person who is or has been a non-executive member such pension, allowances or gratuities as the Secretary of State may determine, or
(b) make such payments as the Secretary of State may determine towards provision for the payment of a pension, allowance or gratuity to or in respect of such a person.

9 Where—
(a) a non-executive member ceases to be a member otherwise than on the expiry of his term of office, and
(b) it appears to the Secretary of State that there are circumstances which make it right for that person to receive compensation,
the Board may make a payment to that person of such amount as the Secretary of State may determine.

*Interpretation of Part 1*

10 In this Part "ordinary member" has the same meaning as in section 108.

## PART 2
## STAFF OF THE BOARD

*The staff*

11 (1) The staff of the Board consists of—
(a) the Chief Executive of the Board appointed under paragraph 12,
(b) the other employees of the Board appointed under paragraph 13, and
(c) any additional staff made available by the Secretary of State under paragraph 14.

(2) No member of the Regulator, or of the Determinations Panel established by the Regulator under section 9, is eligible for appointment as a member of the staff of the Board.

*The Chief Executive*

12 (1) The Board is to employ a person as its Chief Executive.
   (2) The Chief Executive's main function is to be responsible for securing that the functions of the Board are exercised efficiently and effectively.
   (3) The first appointment of a Chief Executive—
       (a) is to be made by the Secretary of State, and
       (b) is to be on such terms and conditions as to remuneration and other matters as are determined by the Secretary of State.
   (4) Subsequent appointments of a Chief Executive are to be made by the Board with the approval of the Secretary of State.
   (5) Appointments under sub-paragraph (4) are to be—
       (a) on such terms and conditions as to remuneration as may be determined by the Board with the approval of the Secretary of State, and
       (b) on such other terms and conditions as may be determined by the Secretary of State.
   (6) By virtue of subsection (2) of section 112 (non-executive functions), the function conferred on the Board by sub-paragraph (5)(a) is exercisable on its behalf by the committee established under that section.

*Other employees*

13 (1) Other employees of the Board may be appointed by the Board with the approval of the Secretary of State as to numbers.
   (2) Subject to sub-paragraph (3), an appointment under sub-paragraph (1) is to be on such terms and conditions as may be determined by the Chief Executive.
   (3) The terms and conditions relating to remuneration are—
       (a) in the case of an appointment of an employee who is also to be an executive member of the Board, to be determined by the Board with the approval of the Secretary of State,
       (b) in the case of an appointment of an employee of a prescribed description, to be determined by the Board.
   (4) By virtue of subsection (2) of section 112 (non-executive functions), the functions conferred on the Board by sub-paragraph (3)(a) and (b) are exercisable on its behalf by the committee established under that section.

*Additional staff etc*

14 (1) The Secretary of State may make available to the Board such additional staff and such other facilities as he considers appropriate.
   (2) The availability of such staff and facilities may be on such terms as to payment by the Board as the Secretary of State may determine.

## PART 3
## PROCEEDINGS AND DELEGATION ETC

*Committees*

15 (1) The Board may establish committees for any purpose.
 (2) Any committee established by the Board may establish sub-committees.
 (3) The members of such committees or sub-committees may include persons who are not members of the Board.
 (4) The members of a sub-committee may include persons who are not members of the committee.
 (5) Sub-paragraphs (3) and (4) do not apply to the committee established under section 112 or any of its sub-committees.

*Procedure*

16 The Board may determine—
 (a) its own procedure (including quorum), and
 (b) the procedure (including quorum) of any of its committees or sub-committees.

*Delegation*

17 (1) The Board may authorize—
 (a) any executive member of the Board,
 (b) any other member of its staff, or
 (c) any of its committees or sub-committees (other than the committee established under section 112 or any of its sub-committees),
 to exercise on behalf of the Board, such of its functions, in such circumstances, as the Board may determine.
 (2) But sub-paragraph (1) does not apply to the non-executive functions of the Board (which must, by virtue of subsection (2) of section 112, be discharged by the committee established under that section).

18 (1) The Board may make arrangements for any of its functions mentioned in sub-paragraph (2) to be exercised, in accordance with those arrangements, by a person on behalf of the Board.
 (2) The functions are those conferred by or by virtue of—
 (a) the pension compensation provisions (see section 162);
 (b) section 163 (adjustments to be made where Board assumes responsibility for a scheme);
 (c) section 165 (duty to notify Inland Revenue in relation to guaranteed minimum pensions);
 (d) section 166 (duty to pay scheme benefits unpaid at assessment date);
 (e) sections 169 and 170 (discharge of liabilities in respect of compensation or money purchase benefits);
 (f) section 191 (notices requiring provision of information);
 (g) section 203(1)(a) (provision of information to members of schemes etc);
 (h) section 111 (supplementary powers), so far as that section relates to any function conferred by or by virtue of any provision mentioned in paragraphs (a) to (g).

(3) Where arrangements are made under this paragraph for any functions of the Board to be exercised by another person on its behalf—
   (a) section 195(1)(b) (offence of providing false or misleading information to the Board) and section 196 (use of information) apply in relation to that person and any functions of the Board exercised by him as they apply in relation to the Board and its functions;
   (b) subject to paragraph (c), sections 197 to 202 and 203(2) to (6) (disclosure of information) apply in relation to that person and any information obtained by him in the exercise of the Board's function as they apply in relation to the Board and information obtained by it in the exercise of its functions;
   (c) nothing in paragraph (b) authorizes any person to determine on behalf of the Board under section 201(1) whether the disclosure of any restricted information is desirable or expedient in the interests of members of occupational pension schemes or in the public interest.

19 (1) Where the Board makes arrangements under paragraph 18(1) for any of its functions to be exercised by a person on its behalf, those arrangements may also provide for that person to exercise on behalf of the Board any delegable review function.
   (2) Where the Regulator is required to or may exercise any function on behalf of the Board by virtue of—
      (a) section 181(4) or 189(8) (administrative functions relating to levies),
      (b) section 181(7)(b) or 189(10)(b) (recovery of levies), or
      (c) regulations under section 181(8) or 189(11) (collection, recovery and waiver of levies),
   the Board may also require the Regulator to exercise on behalf of the Board any delegable review function.
   (3) In this paragraph, "delegable review function", in relation to a delegated function, means—
      (a) any function, by virtue of section 207(1)(a) or (3)(a), to give a review decision in respect of any reviewable matter arising from the exercise of the delegated function;
      (b) in relation to any function exercisable by virtue of paragraph (a) above, any other function under regulations under section 207(1) in connection with the giving of a review decision;
      (c) any function conferred by section 111 (supplementary powers), so far as that section relates to any function mentioned in paragraph (a) or (b).
   (4) In sub-paragraph (3)—
      "delegated function" means a function which is exercisable on behalf of the Board as mentioned in sub-paragraph (1) or (2);
      "review decision" has the meaning given by section 207(1).

*Application of seal and proof of instruments*

20 (1) The fixing of the common seal of the Board must be authenticated by the signature of a person authorized for that purpose by the Board (whether generally or specifically).
   (2) Sub-paragraph (1) does not apply in relation to any document which is or is to be signed in accordance with the law of Scotland.

21  A document purporting to be duly executed under the seal of the Board or purporting to be signed on its behalf—
(a) is to be received in evidence, and
(b) is to be taken to be so executed or signed unless the contrary is proved.

## PART 4
## ACCOUNTS

*Accounts*

22  (1) The Board must—
(a) keep proper accounts and proper records in relation to the accounts, and
(b) prepare in respect of each financial year a statement of accounts.
(2) Each statement of accounts must—
(a) contain an actuarial valuation of the Pension Protection Fund, and
(b) comply with any accounting directions given by the Secretary of State with the approval of the Treasury.
(3) For the purposes of sub-paragraph (2)—
"actuarial valuation", with respect to the Fund, means a valuation, prepared and signed by the appointed actuary, of the assets and liabilities of the Fund;
"accounting direction" means a direction regarding—
(a) the information to be contained in a statement of accounts and the manner in which it is to be presented;
(b) the methods and principles according to which the statement is to be prepared;
(c) the additional information (if any) which is to be provided for the information of Parliament.
(4) In sub-paragraph (3)—
(a) "the appointed actuary" means a person with prescribed qualifications or experience, or a person approved by the Secretary of State, who is appointed by the Board for the purposes of this paragraph, and
(b) the liabilities and assets to be taken into account in preparing the actuarial valuation, and their amount or value, are to be determined, calculated and verified by the appointed actuary in the prescribed manner.
(5) The Board must send a copy of each statement of accounts—
(a) to the Secretary of State, and
(b) to the Comptroller and Auditor-General,
before the end of the month of August next following the financial year to which the statement relates.
(6) The Comptroller and Auditor-General must—
(a) examine, certify and report on each statement of accounts which he receives under sub-paragraph (5), and
(b) lay a copy of each statement and of his report before each House of Parliament.
(7) In this paragraph "financial year" means—
(a) the period beginning with the date on which the Board is established and ending with the next following 31st March, and
(b) each successive period of 12 months.

*Other expenses*

23 The Board may—
   (a) pay, or make provision for paying, persons attending proceedings of the Board at its request such travelling and other allowances (including compensation for loss of remunerative time) as the Board may determine, and
   (b) pay, or make provision for paying, persons from whom the Board may decide to seek advice, as being persons considered by the Board to be specially qualified to advise it on particular matters, such fees as the Board may determine.

## PART 5
## STATUS AND LIABILITY ETC

*Status*

24 (1) The Board is not to be regarded—
   (a) as the servant or agent of the Crown, or
   (b) as enjoying any status, privilege or immunity of the Crown.
   (2) Accordingly, the Board's property is not to be regarded as property of, or held on behalf of, the Crown.

*Validity*

25 The validity of any proceedings of the Board (including any proceedings of any of its committees or sub-committees) is not to be affected by—
   (a) any vacancy among the members of the Board or of any of its committees or sub-committees,
   (b) any defect in the appointment of any member of the Board or of any of its committees or sub-committees, or
   (c) any defect in the appointment of the Chief Executive.

*Disqualification*

26 In Schedule 1 to the House of Commons Disqualification Act 1975 (c. 24), in Part 2 (bodies whose members are disqualified), at the appropriate place insert—
   "The Board of the Pension Protection Fund."
27 In Schedule 1 to the Northern Ireland Assembly Disqualification Act 1975 (c. 25), in Part 2 (bodies whose members are disqualified), at the appropriate place insert—
   "The Board of the Pension Protection Fund."

*The Superannuation Act 1972*

28 (1) The persons to whom section 1 of the Superannuation Act 1972 (c. 11) (persons to or in respect of whom benefits may be provided by schemes under that section) applies are to include—
   the chairman of the Board
   the employees of the Board.

(2) The Board must pay to the Minister for the Civil Service, at such times as he may direct, such sums as he may determine in respect of the increase attributable to sub-paragraph (1) in the sums payable out of money provided by Parliament under that Act.

*Exemption from liability in damages*

29 (1) Neither the Board nor any person who is a member of the Board, a member of any of its committees or sub-committees, or a member of its staff is to be liable in damages for anything done or omitted in the exercise or purported exercise of the functions of the Board conferred by, or by virtue of, this or any other enactment.

(2) Any person who is the Chief Executive of the Board is not to be liable in damages for anything done or omitted in the exercise or purported exercise of any function conferred on the Chief Executive by, or by virtue of, this Act or any provisions in force in Northern Ireland corresponding to this Act.

(3) Any person who is a member of the committee established under section 112 or of any of its sub-committees is not to be liable in damages for anything done or omitted in the discharge or purported discharge of the duty to prepare a report under subsection (5) of that section on the discharge of the non-executive functions.

(4) Sub-paragraphs (1) to (3) do not apply—
   (a) if it is shown that the action or omission was in bad faith, or
   (b) so as to prevent an award of damages made in respect of an act or omission on the ground that the act or omission was unlawful as a result of section 6(1) of the Human Rights Act 1998 (c. 42).

(5) This paragraph does not prevent the Board being required to pay compensation on a direction of the PPF Ombudsman by virtue of regulations under section 213(1) or 214 or any provision in force in Northern Ireland corresponding to either of those provisions.

## SCHEDULE 6

Section 161

### TRANSFER OF PROPERTY, RIGHTS AND LIABILITIES TO THE BOARD

1. This Schedule applies where the property, rights and liabilities of an occupational pension scheme are transferred to the Board in accordance with section 161.
2. (1) Subject to sub-paragraph (2), the property, rights and liabilities so transferred include—
    - (a) property, rights and liabilities that would not otherwise be capable of being transferred or assigned,
    - (b) property situated anywhere in the United Kingdom or elsewhere, and
    - (c) rights and liabilities under the law of any part of the United Kingdom or of any country or territory outside the United Kingdom.

    (2) Where, but for this sub-paragraph, any rights or liabilities under a contract of employment between the trustees or managers of the scheme and an individual would be transferred to the Board under section 161, this sub-paragraph operates to terminate the contract of employment on the day preceding the day on which the transfer notice is received by the trustees or managers of the scheme.
3. (1) Without prejudice to the generality of section 161 and subject to sub-paragraph (2), any legal proceedings or applications to any authority pending immediately before the transfer by or against any of the trustees or managers of the scheme in their capacity as trustees or managers shall be continued by or against the Board.

    (2) The liabilities transferred by section 161 do not include any liabilities in respect of an existing or future cause of action against the trustees or managers of the scheme if, disregarding the transfer, the trustees or managers would have been personally liable to meet the claim and would not have been indemnified from the assets of the scheme.
4. The transfer is binding on all persons, even if, apart from this paragraph, it would have required the consent or concurrence of any person.
5. No person shall have any power, in consequence of the transfer, to terminate or modify any interest or right which was vested in the trustees or managers of the scheme.
6. Any reference in any agreement, document or instrument of any description to the trustees or managers of the scheme shall have effect so far as necessary for the purposes of giving effect to the transfer as a reference to the Board.
7. (1) The Board must take all such steps as may be required to secure that the vesting in the Board, by virtue of section 161, of any foreign property, right or liability is effective under the relevant foreign law.

    (2) Until the vesting of any foreign property, right or liability in the Board is effective under the relevant foreign law, the persons who were the trustees or managers of the scheme immediately before the transfer effected by section 161 must hold that property or right for the benefit of, or discharge that liability on behalf of, the Board.

(3) Nothing in this paragraph prejudices the effect under the law of England and Wales or of Scotland of the vesting in the Board, in accordance with section 161, of any foreign property, right or liability.

(4) In this paragraph references to any foreign property, right or liability are references to any property, right or liability as respects which any issue arising in any proceedings would have to be determined (in accordance with the rules of private international law) by reference to the law of a country or territory outside the United Kingdom.

## SCHEDULE 7

Section 162

### PENSION COMPENSATION PROVISIONS

*Introductory*

1 This Schedule applies for the purposes of determining the compensation payable where the Board assumes responsibility for an eligible scheme ("the scheme") in accordance with this Chapter.

2 In this Schedule references to "the assessment date" are to the date on which the assessment period in relation to the scheme, or (where there has been more than one such assessment period) the last one, began.

*Pensions in payment at assessment date*

3 (1) Compensation is payable in accordance with this paragraph where, immediately before the assessment date, a person is entitled to present payment of a pension under the admissible rules of the scheme.

(2) That person ("the pensioner") is entitled to periodic compensation in respect of that pension ("the pension") commencing at the assessment date and continuing for life or, in a case to which sub-paragraph (8) applies, until such time as entitlement to the pension would have ceased under the admissible rules.

(3) The annual rate of the periodic compensation is the appropriate percentage of the aggregate of—
  (a) the protected pension rate, and
  (b) any increases under paragraph 28 (annual increases in periodic compensation).

(4) In sub-paragraph (3) "the appropriate percentage" means—
  (a) in a case to which sub-paragraph (7) applies, 90%;, and
  (b) in any other case, 100%;.

(5) In sub-paragraph (3) "the protected pension rate" means the annual rate of the pension, under the admissible rules, immediately before the assessment date.

(6) In determining for the purposes of sub-paragraph (5) the annual rate of the pension immediately before the assessment date, any recent discretionary increase is to be disregarded if paragraph 35(3) applies.

(7) This sub-paragraph applies where the pensioner has not attained normal pension age in respect of the pension before the assessment date and his entitlement to the pension—
  (a) is attributable to his pensionable service, and
  (b) did not arise by virtue of any provision of the admissible rules of the scheme making special provision as to early payment of pension on grounds of ill health.

(8) This sub-paragraph applies where the pension was not attributable—
  (a) to the pensioner's pensionable service, or
  (b) (directly or indirectly) to a pension credit to which the pensioner became

entitled under section 29(1)(b) of the Welfare Reform and Pensions Act 1999 (c. 30).

(9) This paragraph does not apply if compensation is payable in respect of the pension in accordance with paragraph 5 (pension benefits postponed at assessment date).

(10) This paragraph is subject to—

paragraph 26 (compensation cap), and

paragraph 30 (power of Secretary of State to change percentage rates by order).

4 (1) This paragraph applies where—
  (a) the pensioner dies on or after the assessment date, and
  (b) the pension was attributable—
    (i) to the pensioner's pensionable service, or
    (ii) (directly or indirectly) to a pension credit to which the pensioner became entitled under section 29(1)(b) of the Welfare Reform and Pensions Act 1999.

(2) Subject to sub-paragraph (4), the pensioner's widow or widower is entitled to periodic compensation commencing on the day following the pensioner's death and continuing for life.

(3) The annual rate of the periodic compensation at any time is half of the annual rate of the periodic compensation (including any increases under paragraph 28) to which the pensioner would at that time have been entitled under paragraph 3 in respect of the pension had the pensioner not died.

(4) The pensioner's widow or widower is not entitled to periodic compensation under this paragraph in such circumstances as may be prescribed.

(5) In this paragraph "the pension" and "the pensioner" are to be construed in accordance with paragraph 3.

*Pension benefits postponed at assessment date*

5 (1) Compensation is payable in accordance with this paragraph where immediately before the assessment date—
  (a) a person is entitled to present payment of a pension under the admissible rules of the scheme,
  (b) payment of that pension is postponed, and
  (c) he has attained normal pension age in relation to the pension.

(2) That person ("the postponed pensioner") is entitled to periodic compensation in respect of that pension ("the pension") commencing at the assessment date and continuing for life or, in a case to which sub-paragraph (7) applies, until such time as entitlement to the pension would have ceased under the admissible rules.

(3) The annual rate of the periodic compensation is 100% of the aggregate of—
  (a) the protected pension rate, and
  (b) any increases under paragraph 28 (annual increases in periodic compensation).

(4) In sub-paragraph (3) "the protected pension rate" means what would have been the annual rate of the pension, under the admissible rules, if the postponement of payment had ceased immediately before the assessment date.

(5) In determining for the purposes of sub-paragraph (4) the annual rate of the pension immediately before the assessment date, any recent discretionary increase is to be disregarded if paragraph 35(3) applies.

(6) Where the pension is attributable (directly or indirectly) to a pension credit, the reference in sub-paragraph (1)(c) to "normal pension age" is to be read as a reference to "normal benefit age".

(7) This sub-paragraph applies where the pension was not attributable—
   (a) to the postponed pensioner's pensionable service, or
   (b) (directly or indirectly) to a pension credit to which the postponed pensioner became entitled under section 29(1)(b) of the Welfare Reform and Pensions Act 1999 (c. 30).

(8) This paragraph is subject to—
paragraph 24 (commutation), and
paragraph 30 (power of Secretary of State to change percentage rates by order).

6 (1) This paragraph applies where the postponed pensioner—
   (a) dies on or after the assessment date, and
   (b) the pension was attributable—
      (i) to the postponed pensioner's pensionable service, or
      (ii) (directly or indirectly) to a pension credit to which the postponed pensioner became entitled under section 29(1)(b) of the Welfare Reform and Pensions Act 1999.

(2) Subject to sub-paragraph (4), the postponed pensioner's widow or widower is entitled to periodic compensation commencing on the day following the postponed pensioner's death and continuing for life.

(3) The annual rate of the periodic compensation at any time is half of the annual rate of the periodic compensation (including any increases under paragraph 28) to which the postponed pensioner would at that time have been entitled under paragraph 5 in respect of the pension had the postponed pensioner not died.

(4) The postponed pensioner's widow or widower is not entitled to periodic compensation under this paragraph in such circumstances as may be prescribed.

(5) In this paragraph "the postponed pensioner" and "the pension" are to be construed in accordance with paragraph 5.

7 (1) Compensation is payable in accordance with this paragraph where immediately before the assessment date—
   (a) a person is entitled to present payment of a lump sum under the admissible rules of the scheme ("the scheme lump sum"),
   (b) payment of that lump sum is postponed, and
   (c) he has attained normal pension age in relation to the lump sum.

(2) That person is entitled to compensation in the form of a lump sum of an amount equal to 100%; of the amount of the scheme lump sum which would have been payable had the postponement ceased immediately before the assessment date.

(3) The compensation is payable at the assessment date.

(4) Where the scheme lump sum is attributable (directly or indirectly) to a pension credit, the reference in sub-paragraph (1)(c) to "normal pension age" is to be read as a reference to "normal benefit age".

(5) This paragraph does not apply in relation to a lump sum to which a person is entitled by reason of commuting any part of a pension under the scheme.

(6) This paragraph is subject to paragraph 30 (power of Secretary of State to change percentage rates by order).

*Active members over normal pension age at assessment date*

8  (1) Compensation is payable in accordance with this paragraph where a person who, under the admissible rules, is (immediately before the assessment date) an active member of the scheme has, before that date, attained normal pension age in respect of his rights under the admissible rules of the scheme to a pension.

   (2) The active member is entitled to periodic compensation in respect of that pension ("the pension") commencing at the assessment date and continuing for life.

   (3) The annual rate of the periodic compensation is 100% of the aggregate of—
       (a) the protected notional pension, and
       (b) any increases under paragraph 28 (annual increases in periodic compensation).

   (4) In sub-paragraph (3) "the protected notional pension" means the aggregate of—
       (a) the accrued amount, and
       (b) any increases in the pension to which the active member would have been entitled under the admissible rules (by virtue of the fact that the pension did not come into payment at normal pension age) if he had ceased to be an active member of the scheme immediately before the assessment date.

   (5) Subject to sub-paragraphs (6) and (7), the accrued amount is—

$$AR \times PE \times PS$$

   where—
   AR is the active member's annual accrual rate in respect of the pension under the admissible rules,
   PE is the active member's annual pensionable earnings in respect of the pension under the admissible rules, and
   PS is the active member's pensionable service in respect of the pension under the admissible rules in years (including any fraction of a year).

   (6) If the accrual rates or pensionable earnings differ in respect of different parts of the active member's pensionable service relating to the pension, an amount is calculated in accordance with the formula in sub-paragraph (5) in respect of each of those parts and the accrued amount is the aggregate of those amounts.

   For this purpose the references in that sub-paragraph to the active member's pensionable service, accrual rate and pensionable earnings are to be read as references to the part of his pensionable service in question and to his accrual rate and pensionable earnings in respect of that part.

   (7) In any case where the Board is satisfied that it is not possible to identify one or more of the elements of the formula in sub-paragraph (5), the Board may, having regard to the admissible rules, determine how the accrued amount is to be calculated.

   (8) This paragraph is subject to—
   paragraph 20 (compensation in respect of scheme right to transfer payment or contribution refund),
   paragraph 24 (commutation), and
   paragraph 30 (power of Secretary of State to change percentage rates by order).

9  (1) This paragraph applies where the active member dies on or after the assessment date.

   (2) Subject to sub-paragraph (4), the active member's widow or widower is entitled

to periodic compensation commencing on the day following the member's death and continuing for life.

(3) The annual rate of the periodic compensation at any time is half of the annual rate of the periodic compensation (including any increases under paragraph 28) to which the active member would at that time have been entitled under paragraph 8 in respect of the pension had the member not died.

(4) The active member's widow or widower is not entitled to periodic compensation under this paragraph in such circumstances as may be prescribed.

(5) In this paragraph "the pension" and "the active member" are to be construed in accordance with paragraph 8.

10 (1) Compensation is payable in accordance with this paragraph where an active member of the scheme has, before the assessment date, attained normal pension age in respect of his rights under the admissible rules of the scheme to a lump sum ("the scheme lump sum").

(2) The active member is entitled to compensation of an amount equal to 100%; of the aggregate of—
   (a) the accrued amount, and
   (b) any increases to which the active member would have been entitled under the admissible rules (by virtue of the fact that the lump sum was not paid at normal pension age) had the active member ceased to be an active member immediately before the assessment date.

(3) The compensation is payable at the assessment date.

(4) Subject to sub-paragraphs (5) and (6), the accrued amount is—

$$AR \times PE \times PS$$

where—

AR is the active member's annual accrual rate in respect of the scheme lump sum under the admissible rules,

PE is the active member's annual pensionable earnings in respect of the scheme lump sum under the admissible rules, and

PS is the active member's pensionable service in respect of the scheme lump sum, under the admissible rules, in years (including any fraction of a year).

(5) If the accrual rates or pensionable earnings differ in respect of different parts of the active member's pensionable service relating to the scheme lump sum, an amount is calculated in accordance with the formula in sub-paragraph (4) in respect of each of those parts and the accrued amount is the aggregate of those amounts.

For this purpose the references in that sub-paragraph to the active member's pensionable service, accrual rate and pensionable earnings are to be read as references to the part of his pensionable service in question and to his accrual rate and pensionable earnings in respect of that part.

(6) In any case where the Board is satisfied that it is not possible to identify one or more of the elements of the formula in sub-paragraph (4), the ay, having regard to the admissible rules, determine how the accrued amount is to be calculated.

(7) This paragraph does not apply in relation to a lump sum to which a person is entitled by reason of commuting any part of a pension under the scheme.

(8) This paragraph is subject to—
paragraph 20 (compensation in respect of scheme right to transfer payment or contribution refund), and
paragraph 30 (power of Secretary of State to change percentage rates by order).

*Active members who have not attained normal pension age at assessment date*

11 (1) Compensation is payable in accordance with this paragraph where a person who, under the admissible rules, is (immediately before the assessment date) an active member of the scheme has not, before that date, attained normal pension age in respect of his rights under the admissible rules of the scheme to a pension.

(2) If the active member survives to attain normal pension age in respect of that pension ("the pension"), he is entitled to periodic compensation in respect of the pension commencing at that age and continuing for life.

(3) The annual rate of the periodic compensation is 90%; of the aggregate of—
(a) the protected notional pension, and
(b) any increases under paragraph 28 (annual increases in periodic compensation).

(4) In sub-paragraph (3) "the protected notional pension" means the aggregate of—
(a) the accrued amount, and
(b) the revaluation amount for the revaluation period (see paragraph 12).

(5) Subject to sub-paragraphs (6) and (7), the accrued amount is—

$$AR \times PE \times PS$$

where—
AR is the active member's annual accrual rate in respect of the pension under the admissible rules,
PE is the active member's annual pensionable earnings in respect of the pension under the admissible rules, and
PS is the active member's pensionable service in respect of the pension under the admissible rules in years (including any fraction of a year).

(6) If the accrual rates or pensionable earnings differ in respect of different parts of the active member's pensionable service relating to the pension, an amount is calculated in accordance with the formula in sub-paragraph (5) in respect of each of those parts and the accrued amount is the aggregate of those amounts.

For this purpose the references in sub-paragraph (5) to the active member's pensionable service, accrual rate and pensionable earnings are to be read as references to the part of his pensionable service in question and to his accrual rate and pensionable earnings in respect of that part.

(7) In any case where the Board is satisfied that it is not possible to identify one or more of the elements of the formula in sub-paragraph (5), the Board may, having regard to the admissible rules, determine how the accrued amount is to be calculated.

(8) This paragraph is subject to—
paragraph 20 (compensation in respect of scheme right to transfer payment or contribution refund),
paragraph 24 (commutation),
paragraph 26 (compensation cap), and
paragraph 30 (power of Secretary of State to change percentage rates by order).

12 (1) This paragraph applies for the purposes of paragraph 11(4)(b).
   (2) The revaluation period is the period which—
      (a) begins with the assessment date, and
      (b) ends with the day before the day on which the active member attains normal pension age in respect of the pension.
   (3) The revaluation amount for the revaluation period is—
      (a) in a case where the revaluation period is less than one month, nil, and
      (b) in any other case, the revaluation percentage of the accrued amount.
   (4) In sub-paragraph (3) "the revaluation percentage" means the lesser of—
      (a) the percentage increase in the general level of prices in Great Britain during the revaluation period determined in the prescribed manner, and
      (b) the maximum revaluation rate.
   (5) For the purposes of sub-paragraph (4)(b) "the maximum revaluation rate" in relation to the revaluation period is—
      (a) if that period is a period of 12 months, 5%, and
      (b) in any other case, the percentage that would be the percentage mentioned in sub-paragraph (4)(a) had the general level of prices in Great Britain increased at the rate of 5%; compound per annum during that period.
      This is subject to paragraph 29 (power of Board to determine maximum revaluation rate etc).
   (6) In this paragraph "the active member", "the accrued amount" and "the pension" are to be construed in accordance with paragraph 11.
13 (1) This paragraph applies where the active member dies on or after the assessment date.
   (2) Subject to sub-paragraph (4), the widow or widower of the active member is entitled to periodic compensation commencing on the day following the active member's death and continuing for life.
   (3) The annual rate of the periodic compensation at any time is—
      (a) where the active member died after attaining normal pension age, half of the annual rate of the periodic compensation (including any increases under paragraph 28) to which the member would at that time have been entitled under paragraph 11 in respect of the pension had the member not died, and
      (b) where the active member died before attaining normal pension age, half of the annual rate of the periodic compensation (including any increases under paragraph 28) to which the member would have been entitled at normal pension age under paragraph 11 if—
         (i) normal pension age had been the member's actual age immediately before the date of the member's death, and
         (ii) the member had not died.
   (4) The active member's widow or widower is not entitled to periodic compensation under this paragraph in such circumstances as may be prescribed.
   (5) In this paragraph "the pension" and "the active member" are to be construed in accordance with paragraph 11.
14 (1) Compensation is payable in accordance with this paragraph where immediately before the assessment date, under the admissible rules of the scheme, an active member of the scheme has not attained normal pension age in respect of his rights to a lump sum ("the scheme lump sum").
   (2) If the active member survives to attain normal pension age in respect of the

scheme lump sum, he is entitled to compensation in respect of the scheme lump sum when he attains that age.

(3) The compensation is a lump sum equal to 90% of the protected amount.

(4) In sub-paragraph (3) "the protected amount" means the aggregate of—
   (a) the accrued amount, and
   (b) the revaluation amount for the revaluation period.

(5) Subject to sub-paragraphs (6) and (7), the accrued amount is—

$$AR \times PE \times PS$$

where—

AR is the active member's annual accrual rate in respect of the scheme lump sum under the admissible rules,

PE is the active member's annual pensionable earnings in respect of the scheme lump sum under the admissible rules, and

PS is the active member's pensionable service in respect of the scheme lump sum, under the admissible rules, in years (including any fraction of a year).

(6) If the accrual rates or pensionable earnings differ in respect of different parts of the active member's pensionable service relating to the scheme lump sum, an amount is calculated in accordance with the formula in sub-paragraph (5) in respect of each of those parts and the accrued amount is the aggregate of those amounts.

For this purpose the references in that sub-paragraph to the active member's pensionable service, accrual rate and pensionable earnings are to be read as references to the part of his pensionable service in question and to his accrual rate and pensionable earnings in respect of that part.

(7) In any case where the Board is satisfied that it is not possible to identify one or more of the elements of the formula in sub-paragraph (5), the Board may, having regard to the admissible rules, determine how the accrued amount is to be calculated.

(8) Paragraph 12 applies for the purpose of determining the revaluation amount except that—
   (a) in that paragraph the references to the pension are to be read as references to the scheme lump sum, and
   (b) in sub-paragraph (6) of that paragraph the reference to paragraph 11 is to be read as a reference to this paragraph.

(9) This paragraph is subject to—

paragraph 20 (compensation in respect of scheme right to transfer payment or contribution refund),

paragraph 26 (compensation cap), and

paragraph 30 (power of Secretary of State to change percentage rates by order).

*Deferred members who have not attained normal pension age at assessment date*

15 (1) Compensation is payable in accordance with this paragraph where, under the admissible rules of the scheme, a person who is a deferred member immediately before the assessment date has not attained normal pension age, in respect of his rights to a pension under the scheme, before that date.

(2) If that person ("the deferred member") survives to attain normal pension

age in respect of that pension ("the pension"), he is entitled to periodic compensation in respect of the pension commencing at that age and continuing for life.

(3) The annual rate of the periodic compensation is 90%; of the aggregate of—
  (a) the protected pension rate, and
  (b) any increases under paragraph 28 (annual increases in periodic compensation).

(4) In sub-paragraph (3) "the protected pension rate" means the aggregate of—
  (a) the accrued amount,
  (b) the revaluation amount for the first revaluation period (see paragraph 16), and
  (c) the revaluation amount for the second revaluation period (see paragraph 17).

(5) In sub-paragraph (4) "the accrued amount" means an amount equal to the initial annual rate of the pension to which the deferred member would have been entitled in accordance with the admissible rules had he attained normal pension age when the pensionable service relating to the pension ended.

(6) This paragraph is subject to—
paragraph 24 (commutation),
paragraph 26 (compensation cap), and
paragraph 30 (power of Secretary of State to change percentage rates by order).

16 (1) This paragraph applies for the purposes of paragraph 15(4)(b).
  (2) The first revaluation period is the period which—
    (a) begins with the day after the day on which the deferred member's pensionable service in respect of the pension ended, and
    (b) ends with the day before the assessment date.
  (3) The revaluation amount for the first revaluation period is—
    (a) where that period is less than one month, nil, and
    (b) in any other case, the amount determined in the prescribed manner.
  (4) In this paragraph "the deferred member" and "the pension" are to be construed in accordance with paragraph 15.

17 (1) This paragraph applies for the purposes of paragraph 15(4)(c).
  (2) The second revaluation period is the period which—
    (a) begins with the assessment date, and
    (b) ends with the day before the day on which the deferred member attains normal pension age in respect of the pension.
  (3) The revaluation amount for the second revaluation period is—
    (a) where that period is less than one month, nil, and
    (b) in any other case the revaluation percentage of the aggregate of—
      (i) the accrued amount, and
      (ii) the revaluation amount for the first revaluation period (see paragraph 16).
  (4) In sub-paragraph (3) "the revaluation percentage" means the lesser of—
    (a) the percentage increase in the general level of prices in Great Britain during the second revaluation period determined in the prescribed manner, and
    (b) the maximum revaluation rate.
  (5) For the purposes of sub-paragraph (4)(b) "the maximum revaluation rate", in relation to the second revaluation period, is—
    (a) if that period is a period of 12 months, 5%;, and
    (b) in any other case, the percentage that would be the percentage mentioned in

sub-paragraph (4)(a) had the general level of prices in Great Britain increased at the rate of 5%; compound per annum during that period.

This is subject to paragraph 29 (power of Board to determine maximum revaluation rate).

(6) In this paragraph "the deferred member", "the accrued amount" and "the pension" are to be construed in accordance with paragraph 15.

18 (1) This paragraph applies where—
   (a) the deferred member dies on or after the assessment date, and
   (b) the pension was attributable to the deferred member's pensionable service.

(2) Subject to sub-paragraph (4), the widow or widower of the deferred member is entitled to periodic compensation commencing on the day following the deferred member's death and continuing for life.

(3) The annual rate of the periodic compensation at any time is—
   (a) where the deferred member died after attaining normal pension age, half of the annual rate of the periodic compensation (including any increases under paragraph 28) to which the deferred member would at that time have been entitled under paragraph 15 in respect of the pension had the member not died,
   (b) where the deferred member died before attaining normal pension age, half of the annual rate of the periodic compensation (including any increases under paragraph 28) to which the deferred member would have been entitled at that time under paragraph 15 if—
      (i) normal pension age had been the deferred member's actual age immediately before the date of the deferred member's death, and
      (ii) the deferred member had not died.

(4) The deferred member's widow or widower is not entitled to periodic compensation under this paragraph in such circumstances as may be prescribed.

(5) In this paragraph "the deferred member" and "the pension" are to be construed in accordance with paragraph 15.

19 (1) Compensation is payable in accordance with this paragraph where, under the admissible rules of the scheme, a deferred member has not attained normal pension age in respect of his rights to a lump sum under the scheme ("the scheme lump sum") before the assessment date.

(2) If the deferred member survives to attain normal pension age in respect of the scheme lump sum, he is entitled to compensation under this paragraph on attaining that age.

(3) The compensation is a lump sum equal to 90%; of the protected amount.

(4) In sub-paragraph (3) "the protected amount" means the aggregate of—
   (a) the accrued amount,
   (b) the revaluation amount for the first revaluation period, and
   (c) the revaluation amount for the second revaluation period.

(5) In sub-paragraph (4) "the accrued amount" means an amount equal to the amount of the scheme lump sum to which the deferred member would have been entitled in accordance with the admissible rules had normal pension age been the actual age attained by the deferred member when the pensionable service relating to the lump sum ended.

(6) Paragraphs 16 and 17 apply in relation to this paragraph as if in those paragraphs—

(a) references to the pension were to the scheme lump sum, and
(b) "the deferred member" and "the accrued amount" had the same meaning as in this paragraph.

(7) This paragraph does not apply in relation to a lump sum to which a person is entitled by reason of commuting any part of a pension under the scheme.

(8) This paragraph is subject to—
paragraph 26 (compensation cap), and
paragraph 30 (power of Secretary of State to change percentage rates by order).

*Compensation in respect of scheme right to transfer payment or contribution refund*

20 (1) Compensation is payable in accordance with this paragraph where—
   (a) a person's pensionable service terminates on the commencement of the assessment period,
   (b) as a result, he has rights, under the admissible rules, to—
      (i) a transfer payment calculated by reference to the value of benefits which have accrued to him under the scheme ("the protected transfer payment"), or
      (ii) a cash payment calculated by reference to the amount of contributions made by him or on his behalf to the scheme ("the protected contribution repayment"),
   (c) Chapter 5 of Part 4 of the Pension Schemes Act 1993 (c. 48) (early leavers: cash transfer sums and contribution refunds) does not apply to him, and
   (d) he does not have relevant accrued rights to benefit (within the meaning of section 101AA(4) of that Act).

(2) That person is entitled to compensation in the form of a lump sum in respect of the protected transfer payment or protected contribution repayment.

(3) The amount of the compensation is 90%; of the amount of the protected transfer payment or protected contribution repayment (whichever is the greater).

(4) For the purposes of sub-paragraph (3), the amount of the protected transfer payment or protected contribution repayment is to be calculated in accordance with the admissible rules, which are to be applied for this purpose subject to any prescribed modifications.

(5) The compensation is payable immediately after the transfer notice given under section 160 is received by the trustees or managers of the scheme.

(6) This paragraph is subject to paragraph 30 (power of Secretary of State to change percentage rates by order).

(7) Regulations may modify any provision of paragraph 8, 10, 11 or 14 (compensation for persons who were active members immediately before assessment date) as it applies in the case of a person who is entitled to compensation under this paragraph.

(8) Regulations may modify any provision of sub-paragraphs (1) to (6) as it applies in the case of a person who is entitled to compensation under paragraph 8, 10, 11 or 14.

*Pension credit members who have not attained normal benefit age at assessment date*

21 (1) Paragraphs 15, 18 and 19 apply in relation to a pension credit member of the scheme who has not attained normal benefit age at the assessment date as they

apply to a deferred member who has not attained normal pension age at that date, subject to the modifications in sub-paragraph (2).

(2) The modifications are as follows—
- (a) in paragraph 15(1) and (2) the references to normal pension age are to be read as references to normal benefit age,
- (b) in paragraph 15(4) for the words from "the aggregate of" to the end substitute "the accrued amount",
- (c) for paragraph 15(5) substitute—

  "(5) In sub-paragraph (4) 'the accrued amount' means an amount equal to the initial annual rate of the pension which, under the admissible rules, the deferred member is entitled to receive at normal benefit age by virtue of his pension credit rights.",

- (d) for paragraph 18(1)(b) substitute—

  "(b) the pension was attributable (directly or indirectly) to a pension credit to which the deferred pensioner became entitled under section 29(1)(b) of the Welfare Reform and Pensions Act 1999 (c. 30).",

- (e) in paragraph 19(1) and (2) the references to normal pension age are to be read as references to normal benefit age,
- (f) in paragraph 19(4) for the words from "the aggregate of" to the end substitute "the accrued amount",
- (g) for paragraph 19(5) substitute—

  "(5) In sub-paragraph (4) 'the accrued amount' means an amount equal to the amount of the scheme lump sum which, under the admissible rules, the deferred member is entitled to receive at normal benefit age by virtue of his pension credit rights.", and

- (h) paragraph 19(6) does not apply.

*Survivors who do not meet conditions for scheme benefits at assessment date*

22 (1) Compensation is payable in accordance with this paragraph where—
- (a) a member of the scheme has died before the assessment date,
- (b) as a result of that death, a pension, which is attributable to the member's pensionable service, is payable to that person's widow or widower or any other person ("the survivor") if conditions specified in the scheme rules are met, and
- (c) the survivor first satisfies those conditions on or after that date.

(2) The survivor is entitled to periodic compensation in respect of that pension ("the pension")—
- (a) commencing if, and when, the pension would have become payable under the admissible rules, and
- (b) continuing until such time as entitlement to the pension would have ceased under the admissible rules.

(3) The annual rate of the periodic compensation is 100% of the aggregate of—
- (a) the initial rate of the pension which would have been payable in accordance with the admissible rules had the conditions mentioned in sub-paragraph (1)(c) been satisfied, immediately before the assessment date, and
- (b) any increases under paragraph 28 (annual increases in periodic compensation).

(4) This paragraph is subject to paragraph 30 (power of Secretary of State to change percentage rates by order).

*Compensation in form of dependants' benefits*

23 (1) Regulations may provide for compensation to be payable, in such circumstances as may be prescribed, to or in respect of—
   (a) partners of prescribed descriptions of persons of prescribed descriptions who were members of the scheme immediately before the assessment date;
   (b) dependants of prescribed descriptions of persons of prescribed descriptions who—
      (i) were members of the scheme, or had rights to benefits payable under the scheme rules in respect of a member, immediately before the assessment date,
      (ii) became entitled to benefits under the scheme rules in respect of a member on or after the assessment date but before the time the trustees or managers of the scheme received a transfer notice under section 160, or
      (iii) have become entitled to compensation under paragraph 22 (survivors who do not meet conditions for scheme benefits at assessment date), in relation to the scheme.
(2) Regulations may in particular—
   (a) provide for compensation in the form of periodic or lump sum payments;
   (b) provide for periodic compensation to be payable for a prescribed period;
   (c) apply paragraphs 28 and 29(2) (annual increases in respect of periodic compensation) in respect of compensation in the form of periodic payments (with or without modifications).

*Commutation of periodic compensation*

24 (1) In prescribed circumstances, a person entitled to periodic compensation under paragraph 5, 8, 11 or 15 may opt to commute for a lump sum a portion of the periodic compensation with effect from the time it becomes payable.
(2) Except in such circumstances as may be prescribed, the portion commuted under sub-paragraph (1) must not exceed 25%;.
(3) Any reduction required to be made under paragraph 26 (compensation cap) must be made before determining the amount of a person's periodic compensation which may be commuted under this paragraph.
(4) Where a person opts to commute any part of his periodic compensation under this paragraph, the lump sum payable under sub-paragraph (1) is the actuarial equivalent of the commuted portion of the periodic compensation calculated from tables designated for this purpose by the Board.
(5) The Board must publish in such manner as it considers appropriate the tables designated by it for the purposes of sub-paragraph (4).
(6) Regulations may prescribe the manner in which an option to commute periodic compensation under this paragraph may be exercised.
(7) This paragraph does not apply where—
   (a) before the assessment date, the person concerned has received benefits under the scheme rules which were in the form of a lump sum (otherwise than as a result of the commutation of any part of a pension) and were attributable to his own service under the scheme, or
   (b) immediately before the assessment date, the person concerned has rights to a lump sum under the admissible rules (otherwise than by commutation of any part of a pension) and those rights are attributable to such service.

**sch 7, Pensions Act 2004**

(8) The Secretary of State may, by order, amend sub-paragraph (2) to substitute a different percentage for the percentage for the time being specified in that sub-paragraph.

*Early payment of compensation*

25 (1) Regulations may prescribe circumstances in which, and conditions subject to which, a person may become entitled to—
   (a) periodic compensation under paragraph 11 or 15, or
   (b) lump sum compensation under paragraph 14 or 19,
   before he attains normal pension age (or, in a case to which paragraph 21 applies, normal benefit age).
(2) The Board must determine the amount of the actuarial reduction to be applied to compensation where a person becomes so entitled by virtue of regulations under this paragraph.
(3) Where, by virtue of this paragraph, periodic compensation is payable to a person under paragraph 11 or 15 before that person attains normal pension age—
   (a) paragraph 12(2) applies as if the reference to the date on which the active member attains normal pension age were a reference to the date on which the compensation is payable by virtue of this paragraph, and
   (b) paragraph 17(2)(b) applies as if the reference to the date on which the deferred member attains normal pension age were a reference to the date on which the compensation is payable by virtue of this paragraph.

*Compensation cap*

26 (1) Where—
   (a) a person becomes entitled to relevant compensation in respect of a benefit ("benefit A") under the scheme, and
   (b) sub-paragraph (2)(a) or (b) applies,
   the amount of the compensation must be restricted in accordance with sub-paragraph (3).
(2) For the purposes of sub-paragraph (1)—
   (a) this paragraph applies if—
      (i) the annual value of benefit A exceeds the compensation cap, and
      (ii) paragraph (b)(i) does not apply, and
   (b) this paragraph applies if—
      (i) at the same time as the person becomes entitled to relevant compensation in respect of benefit A he also becomes entitled to relevant compensation in respect of one or more other benefits under the scheme or a connected occupational pension scheme ("benefit or benefits B"), and
      (ii) the aggregate of the annual values of benefit A and benefit or benefits B exceeds the compensation cap.
(3) Where the relevant compensation in respect of benefit A is required to be restricted in accordance with this sub-paragraph—
   (a) if that compensation is within sub-paragraph (4)(a), the protected pension rate for the purposes of paragraph 3(3)(a) is the cap fraction of the rate determined in accordance with paragraph 3(5);
   (b) if that compensation is within sub-paragraph (4)(b), the protected notional

pension for the purposes of paragraph 11(3)(a) is the cap fraction of the rate determined in accordance with paragraph 11(4);

(c) if that compensation is within sub-paragraph (4)(c), the protected amount for the purposes of paragraph 14(3) is the cap fraction of the amount determined in accordance with paragraph 14(4);

(d) if that compensation is within sub-paragraph (4)(d), the protected pension rate for the purposes of paragraph 15(3)(a) is the cap fraction of the rate determined in accordance with paragraph 15(4);

(e) if that compensation is within sub-paragraph (4)(e), the protected amount for the purposes of paragraph 19(3) is the cap fraction of the amount determined in accordance with paragraph 19(4).

(4) For the purposes of this paragraph "relevant compensation" means—
  (a) periodic compensation under paragraph 3 (in a case to which sub-paragraph (7) of that paragraph applies),
  (b) periodic compensation under paragraph 11,
  (c) compensation under paragraph 14,
  (d) periodic compensation under paragraph 15, or
  (e) compensation under paragraph 19.

(5) For the purposes of this paragraph, "the cap fraction" means—

$$\frac{C}{V}$$

Where—

C is the compensation cap, and

V is the annual value of benefit A or, in a case to which sub-paragraph (2)(b) applies, the aggregate of the annual values of benefit A and benefit or benefits B.

(6) For the purposes of this paragraph the "annual value" of a benefit in respect of which a person has become entitled to relevant compensation means—
  (a) if the relevant compensation is within sub-paragraph (4)(a) and neither paragraph (b) nor (c) below applies, the amount of the protected pension rate for the purposes of paragraph 3(3)(a);
  (b) if the relevant compensation is within sub-paragraph (4)(a) and is in respect of a pension of which a portion has been commuted for a lump sum, the amount which would have been the protected pension rate for those purposes had that portion not been commuted;
  (c) if the relevant compensation is within sub-paragraph (4)(a) and the person became entitled to a relevant lump sum under the scheme at the same time as he became entitled to the pension to which that compensation relates, an amount equal to the aggregate of—
    (i) the protected pension rate for the purposes of paragraph 3(3)(a), and
    (ii) the annualized value of the relevant lump sum;
  (d) if the relevant compensation is within sub-paragraph (4)(b), the amount of the protected notional pension for the purposes of paragraph 11(3)(a);
  (e) if the relevant compensation is within sub-paragraph (4)(c), the annualized value of the protected amount for the purposes of paragraph 14(3);
  (f) if the relevant compensation is within sub-paragraph (4)(d), the amount of the protected pension rate for the purposes of paragraph 15(3)(a);

(g) if the relevant compensation is within sub-paragraph (4)(e), the annualized value of the protected amount for the purposes of paragraph 19(3);

and for the purposes of determining the annual value of a benefit any reduction required to be made by this paragraph is to be disregarded.

(7) In this paragraph—

"annualized value" of a lump sum or amount means the annualized actuarially equivalent amount of that sum or amount determined in accordance with actuarial factors published by the Board;

"the compensation cap", in relation to the person who becomes entitled to relevant compensation in respect of benefit A, means—
(a) the amount specified by the Secretary of State by order, or
(b) where the person—
  (i) has not attained the age of 65, or
  (ii) has attained the age of 66,
  at the time he first becomes entitled to that compensation, that amount as adjusted by the Board in accordance with actuarial adjustment factors published by it;

and for the purposes of this paragraph, except in prescribed circumstances, the scheme is connected with another occupational pension scheme if the same person is or was an employer in relation to both schemes.

(8) For the purposes of sub-paragraph (6)(c) a lump sum under the scheme is a relevant lump sum if the person's entitlement to the lump sum—
(a) is attributable to his pensionable service, and
(b) did not arise by virtue of any provision of the admissible rules of the scheme making special provision as to early payment of pension on grounds of ill health.

(9) Regulations may provide for this paragraph to apply with prescribed modifications where a person becomes entitled to relevant compensation in respect of a benefit and he has previously—
(a) become entitled to relevant compensation in respect of a benefit or benefits under the scheme or a connected occupational pension scheme, or
(b) become entitled to one or more lump sums under the scheme or a connected occupational pension scheme.

(10) Regulations may prescribe sums which are to disregarded for the purposes of this paragraph.

*Increasing the compensation cap in line with earnings*

27 (1) This paragraph applies where, on a review under subsection (2) of section 148 of the Social Security Administration Act 1992 (c. 5) (review of general level of earnings obtaining in Great Britain) in a tax year, the Secretary of State concludes that the general level of earnings obtaining in Great Britain ("the new level") exceeds the general level at the end of the period mentioned in paragraph (a) or, as the case may be, the date determined under paragraph (b) of that subsection ("the old level").

(2) The Secretary of State must make an order under sub-paragraph (7) of paragraph 26 which has the effect of increasing the amount specified for the purposes of that sub-paragraph by the percentage by which the new level is greater than the old level.

(3) The order must provide for the increase to have effect on and after the 1st April next following the end of the tax year to which the review relates.

*Annual increase in periodic compensation*

28  (1) This paragraph provides for the increases mentioned in sub-paragraph (3)(b) of paragraphs 3, 5, 8, 11, 15 and 22.
(2) Where a person is entitled to periodic compensation under any of those paragraphs, he is entitled, on the indexation date, to an increase under this paragraph of—
   (a) the appropriate percentage of the amount of the underlying rate immediately before that date, or
   (b) where the person first became entitled to the periodic compensation during the period of 12 months ending immediately before that date, 1/12th of that amount for each full month for which he was so entitled.
(3) In sub-paragraph (2)—
"appropriate percentage" means the lesser of—
   (a) the percentage increase in the retail prices index for the period of 12 months ending with the 31st May last falling before the indexation date, and
   (b) 2.5%;
"indexation date" means—
   (a) the 1st January next falling after a person first becomes entitled to the periodic compensation, and
   (b) each subsequent 1st January during his lifetime;
"underlying rate" means, in the case of periodic compensation under any of the paragraphs mentioned in sub-paragraph (1), the aggregate of—
   (a) so much of the amount mentioned in sub-paragraph (3)(a) of the paragraph in question as is attributable to post-1997 service, and
   (b) the amount within sub-paragraph (3)(b) of that paragraph immediately before the indexation date.
(4) Where paragraph 26(3) (compensation cap) applies to restrict the amount of periodic compensation under one of the paragraphs mentioned in sub-paragraph (1), the amount mentioned in sub-paragraph (3)(a) of the paragraph in question is attributable to post-1997 service and pre-1997 service in the same proportions as the amount so mentioned would have been so attributable had paragraph 26(3) not applied.
(5) Where a portion of periodic compensation under one of the paragraphs mentioned in sub-paragraph (1) has been commuted under paragraph 24—
   (a) for the purposes of sub-paragraph (2), the definition of "underlying rate" in sub-paragraph (3) applies as if the reference in paragraph (a) of the definition to the amount mentioned in sub-paragraph (3)(a) of the paragraph in question was a reference to that amount reduced by the commutation percentage, and
   (b) that amount (as so reduced) is attributable to post-1997 service and pre-1997 service in the same proportions as that amount would have been so attributable had no part of the periodic compensation been commuted.
(6) In this paragraph—
"post-1997 service" means—

(a) pensionable service which is within paragraph 36(4)(a) and occurs on or after 6th April 1997, or
(b) pensionable service which is within paragraph 36(4)(b) and meets such requirements as may be prescribed;

"pre-997 service" means—
(a) pensionable service which is within paragraph 36(4)(a) and occurred before 6th April 1997, or
(b) pensionable service which is within paragraph 36(4)(b) and meets such requirements as may be prescribed;

"the commutation percentage", in relation to periodic compensation, means the percentage of that compensation commuted under paragraph 24.

(7) But in this paragraph, in relation to any relevant pension credit amount, "post-1997 service" and "pre-1997 service" have such meanings as may be prescribed.

(8) In sub-paragraph (7), "relevant pension credit amount" means an amount mentioned in sub-paragraph (3)(a) of—
(a) paragraph 3,
(b) paragraph 5, or
(c) paragraph 15 as it applies by virtue of paragraph 21,
which is attributable (directly or indirectly) to a pension credit.

(9) This paragraph is subject to paragraph 29 (Board's power to alter rates of revaluation and indexation).

*Board's powers to alter rates of revaluation and indexation*

29 (1) The Board may determine the percentage that is to be the maximum revaluation rate for the purposes of paragraphs 12(4) and 17(4), and where it does so paragraphs 12(5) and 17(5) do not apply.

(2) The Board may also determine the percentage that is to be the appropriate percentage for the purposes of paragraph 28 (and where it does so the definition of "appropriate percentage" in paragraph 28(3) does not apply).

(3) Before making a determination under this paragraph the Board must—
(a) consult such persons as it considers appropriate, and
(b) publish details of the proposed determination in such manner as it considers appropriate and consider any representations made in respect of it.

(4) The rate determined under this paragraph may be nil.

(5) A determination under this paragraph may be expressed so as to have effect for a limited period.

(6) A determination under sub-paragraph (2)—
(a) has effect in relation to future increases under paragraph 28 only, and
(b) may be expressed to have effect—
(i) in all cases (whether the entitlement to the periodic compensation first arose before or after the date the determination is made), or
(ii) only in cases where entitlement to the periodic compensation first arose on or after a date determined by the Board.

(7) Notice of any determination under this paragraph must be published in such manner as the Board considers appropriate.

*Secretary of State's powers to vary percentage paid as compensation*

30 (1) The Secretary of State may, on the recommendation of the Board, by order provide that any of the provisions mentioned in sub-paragraph (2) is to have effect as if a different percentage were substituted for the percentage specified in the provision on the passing of this Act ("the original percentage").

(2) The provisions are paragraphs 3(4)(a) and (b), 5(3), 7(2), 8(3), 10(2), 11(3), 14(3), 15(3), 19(3), 20(3) and 22(3) of this Schedule (percentage used to calculate periodic or lump sum compensation entitlement).

(3) Subject to sub-paragraph (4), an order under sub-paragraph (1) has effect only in respect of any period for which the Board has, under paragraph 29—

  (a) reduced the maximum revaluation rate for the purposes of paragraphs 12(4) and 17(4) to nil, and

  (b) reduced the appropriate percentage for the purposes of paragraph 28 to nil in all cases.

(4) Sub-paragraph (3) does not prevent an order under sub-paragraph (1) having effect to the extent that it provides for paragraph 3(4)(a), 11(3), 14(3), 15(3), 19(3) or 20(3) (provisions where the original percentage is 90%) to have effect as if for the original percentage there were substituted a higher percentage.

(5) Before making a recommendation for the purposes of sub-paragraph (1) the Board must—

  (a) consult such persons as it considers appropriate, and

  (b) publish details of the proposed recommendation in such manner as it considers appropriate and consider any representations made in respect of it.

(6) Subject to sub-paragraph (3), an order under this paragraph may have effect—

  (a) for a limited period specified in the order;

  (b) in relation—

    (i) to all payments of compensation which fall to be made after such date as may be specified in the order (whether the entitlement to the periodic compensation first arose before or after that date), or

    (ii) only to payments of compensation to which a person first becomes entitled after such a date.

(7) The date specified under sub-paragraph (6)(b)(i) or (ii) must not be earlier than the date of the order.

*Special provision in relation to certain pensions in payment before the assessment date*

31 (1) The powers conferred by this paragraph are exercisable in relation to cases where—

  (a) immediately before the assessment date, a person ("the pensioner") is entitled to present payment of a pension under the scheme rules ("the pre-assessment date pension"), but

  (b) the effect of disregarding rules within paragraphs (a) and (b) of paragraph 35(2) is that the pensioner is not entitled to compensation under paragraph 3(2) by reason of the pension or a part of the pension.

(2) Regulations may provide—

  (a) for the pensioner to be treated, for the purposes of the pension compensa-

tion provisions, as entitled, immediately before the assessment date, to present payment of a pension under the admissible rules, and
(b) for the compensation payable under paragraph 3 in respect of that pension to be determined in the prescribed manner and, for this purpose, for any provision of this Schedule to be applied with such modifications as may be prescribed.
(3) Regulations may also provide, in cases where—
(a) the pensioner is not treated as entitled to present payment of a pension by virtue of regulations under sub-paragraph (2), but
(b) he is or may become entitled to compensation in respect of the pre-assessment date pension otherwise than under paragraph 3,
for any provision of this Schedule to apply with such modifications as may be prescribed.

*Short periods of service which terminate on commencement of assessment period*

32 (1) This paragraph applies to a member of the scheme if—
(a) his pensionable service terminates on the commencement of the assessment period, and
(b) as a result, he has rights, in relation to the scheme, under Chapter 5 of Part 4 of the Pension Schemes Act 1993 (c. 48) (early leavers: cash transfer sums and contribution refunds).
(2) Where this paragraph applies, for the purposes of this Schedule the member is to be treated as if, immediately before the assessment date, he—
(a) had relevant accrued rights to benefits under the scheme (within the meaning of section 101AA(4) of that Act), and
(b) did not have any other rights to benefits (other than benefits attributable (directly or indirectly) to a pension credit) under the scheme.

*Power to modify schedule in its application to certain schemes*

33 Where the scheme is a prescribed scheme or a scheme of a prescribed description, this Schedule applies with such modifications as may be prescribed.

*Normal pension age*

34 (1) In this Schedule "normal pension age", in relation to the scheme and any pension or lump sum under it, means the age specified in the admissible rules as the earliest age at which the pension or lump sum becomes payable without actuarial adjustment (disregarding any admissible rule making special provision as to early payment on the grounds of ill health).
(2) Where different ages are specified in relation to different parts of a pension or lump sum—
(a) this Schedule has effect as if those parts were separate pensions or, as the case may be, lump sums, and
(b) references in relation to a part of the pension or lump sum to the normal pension age are to be read as references to the age specified in the admissible rules as the earliest age at which that part becomes payable under the scheme without actuarial adjustment (disregarding any special provision as to early payment on grounds of ill health or otherwise).

(3) In any case where the Board is satisfied that it is not possible to identify the normal pension age from the admissible rules of the scheme, it may, having regard to those rules, determine how the normal pension age is to be determined.

*Scheme rules, admissible rules etc*

35 (1) In this Schedule, in relation to the scheme, the following expressions have the meaning given by this paragraph—
"admissible rules";
"recent rule changes";
"recent discretionary increase".
(2) The "admissible rules" means the scheme rules disregarding—
   (a) in a case where sub-paragraph (3) applies, the recent rule changes, and
   (b) in any case, any scheme rule which comes into operation on, or operates by reference, to the winding up of the scheme or any associated event.
(3) This sub-paragraph applies if the combined effect of the recent rule changes and recent discretionary increases is such that, if account were taken of those changes and increases in calculating the protected liabilities in relation to the scheme at the relevant time, those protected liabilities would be greater than they would be if all those changes and increases were disregarded.
(4) In sub-paragraph (3) "the relevant time" means the time immediately before the assessment period which begins on the assessment date.
(5) Subject to sub-paragraph (6), "recent rule changes" means—
   (a) changes to the scheme rules which took effect in the period of three years ending with the assessment date, or were made in that period and took effect by reference to an earlier time, and
   (b) any scheme rules which come into operation on, or operate by reference to—
      (i) an insolvency event in relation to the employer or any associated event, or
      (ii) any prescribed event relating to the future of the employer as a going concern.
(6) "Recent rule changes" does not include—
   (a) any scheme rules or changes attributable to paragraph 3 of Schedule 5 to the Social Security Act 1989 (c. 24), section 129 of the Pension Schemes Act 1993 (c. 48), section 117 of the Pensions Act 1995 (c. 26), section 31(4) of the Welfare Reform and Pensions Act 1999 (c. 30) or section 306 of this Act (overriding requirements),
   (b) any enactment, or any scheme rules or changes which are required or reasonably necessary to comply with an enactment,
   (c) any scheme rules or changes that come into operation on, or operate by reference to, the winding up of the scheme or any associated event, and
   (d) any scheme rules or changes of a prescribed description.
(7) "Recent discretionary increase" means an increase in the rate of any pension in payment or postponed pension under the scheme rules which took effect in the period mentioned in sub-paragraph (5)(a).
(8) For the purposes of sub-paragraph (7) an increase ("the relevant increase") in the rate of a pension in payment or postponed pension is to be disregarded to the extent that it does not exceed—
   (a) the amount by which the pension in question is required to be increased by virtue of—

(i) the admissible rules, or
(ii) sections 13(1) and 109 of the Pension Schemes Act 1993 (requirement to index and pay guaranteed minimum pensions), or

(b) if greater, the appropriate percentage of the rate of that pension.

(9) For the purposes of sub-paragraph (8)(a), no increase in the rate of a pension which is made at the discretion of the trustees or managers of the scheme, the employer or any other person is to be regarded as an increase required by virtue of the admissible rules.

(10) For the purposes of sub-paragraph (8)(b), "the appropriate percentage" is the percentage increase in the general level of prices in Great Britain during the period—
(a) beginning when the rate of the pension was last increased or, if there has been no previous increase, the date the pension first became payable (or would have been payable but for its being postponed), and
(b) ending with the time the relevant increase was made.

*Accrual rate, pensionable service and pensionable earnings*

36 (1) In this Schedule, in relation to a member's entitlement to benefits under the scheme, each of the following expressions has the meaning given by this paragraph—
"accrual rate";
"pensionable earnings";
"pensionable service".

(2) "Accrual rate" means the rate at which under the admissible rules rights to the benefits accrue over time by reference to periods of pensionable service.

(3) "Pensionable earnings" means the earnings by reference to which the benefits are calculated under the admissible rules.

(4) Subject to sub-paragraph (5), "pensionable service" means—
(a) actual service in any description of employment to which the scheme applies which qualifies the member for benefits under the scheme, and
(b) any notional service allowed in respect of the member under the admissible rules which qualifies the member for such benefits.

(5) The service within sub-paragraph (4)(b) does not include—
(a) service attributable (directly or indirectly) to a pension credit, or
(b) service of a prescribed description.

*Other definitions*

37 (1) In this Schedule—
"deferred member", in relation to the scheme, means a person who, under the admissible rules, has accrued rights other than—
(a) an active member, or
(b) a person who in respect of his pensionable service is entitled to the present payment of pension or other benefits;
"normal benefit age", in relation to the scheme and a person with rights to a pension or lump sum under it attributable (directly or indirectly) to a pension credit, means the age specified in the admissible rules as the earliest age at which that pension or lump sum becomes payable without actuarial

adjustment (disregarding any scheme rule making special provision as to early payment on grounds of ill health or otherwise);

"pension credit member", in relation to the scheme, means a person who has rights under the scheme which are attributable (directly or indirectly) to a pension credit;

"pension credit rights", in relation to the scheme, means rights to future benefits under the scheme which are attributable (directly or indirectly) to a pension credit;

"retail prices index" means—
(a) the general index of retail prices (for all items) published by the Office for National Statistics, or
(b) where that index is not published for a month, any substituted index or figures published by that Office;

"the scheme" is to be construed in accordance with paragraph 1.

(2) For the purposes of this Schedule the accrued rights of a member of the scheme at any time are the rights (other than rights attributable (directly or indirectly) to a pension credit) which, in accordance with the admissible rules, have accrued to or in respect of him at that time to future benefits.

(3) In this Schedule references to a pension or lump sum under the admissible rules of the scheme, or a right to such a pension or lump sum, do not include a pension or lump sum, or right to a pension or lump sum, which is a money purchase benefit.

(4) In this Schedule references to "ill health" are to be construed in accordance with regulations under this sub-paragraph.

## SCHEDULE 8

Section 200

## RESTRICTED INFORMATION HELD BY THE BOARD: CERTAIN PERMITTED DISCLOSURES TO FACILITATE EXERCISE OF FUNCTIONS

| *Persons* | *Functions* |
| --- | --- |
| The Secretary of State. | Functions under—<br>(a) Part 14 of the Companies Act 1985 (c. 6),<br>(b) the Insolvency Act 1986 (c. 45),<br>(c) Part 3 of the Companies Act 1989 (c. 40),<br>(d) Part 1 of the Export and Investment Guarantees Act 1991 (c. 67) (apart from sections 5 and 6),<br>(e) Part 3 of the Pension Schemes Act 1993 (c. 48),<br>(f) Part 5 of the Police Act 1997 (c. 50),<br>(g) the Financial Services and Markets Act 2000 (c. 8), or<br>(h) this Act,<br>and functions of co-operating with overseas government authorities and bodies in relation to criminal matters. |
| The Bank of England. | Any of its functions. |
| The Financial Services Authority. | Functions under—<br>(a) the legislation relating to friendly societies,<br>(b) the Building Societies Act 1986 (c. 53), or<br>(c) the Financial Services and Markets Act 2000. |
| The Charity Commissioners. | Functions under the Charities Act 1993 (c. 10). |
| The Pensions Regulator Tribunal. | Any of its functions. |
| The Pensions Ombudsman. | Functions under—<br>(a) the Pension Schemes Act 1993, or<br>(b) the Pension Schemes (Northern Ireland) Act 1993 (c. 49). |
| The Ombudsman for the Board of the Pension Protection Fund. | Any of his functions. |
| The Comptroller and Auditor-General. | Any of his functions. |
| The Auditor-General for Wales. | Any of his functions. |
| The Auditor-General for Scotland. | Any of his functions. |
| The Comptroller and Auditor-General for Northern Ireland. | Any of his functions. |
| The Commissioners of Inland Revenue or their officers. | Functions under—<br>(a) the Income and Corporation Taxes Act 1988 (c. 1),<br>(b) the Taxation of Chargeable Gains Act 1992 (c. 12),<br>(c) Part 3 of the Pension Schemes Act 1993 (c. 48),<br>(d) Part 3 of the Pension Schemes (Northern Ireland) Act 1993 (c. 49), or<br>(e) the Income Tax (Earnings and Pensions) Act 2003 (c. 1). |

**Pensions Act 2004, sch 8**

| *Persons* | *Functions* |
|---|---|
| The Commissioners of Customs and Excise. | Functions under any enactment. |
| The Official Receiver or, in Northern Ireland, the Official Receiver for Northern Ireland. | Functions under the enactments relating to insolvency. |
| An inspector appointed by the Secretary of State. | Functions under Part 14 of the Companies Act 1985 (c. 6). |
| A person authorized to exercise powers under—<br>(a) section 447 of the Companies Act 1985,<br>(b) Article 440 of the Companies (Northern Ireland) Order 1986 (S.I. 1986/1032 (N.I. 6)), or<br>(c) section 84 of the Companies Act 1989 (c. 40). | Functions under those sections or that Article. |
| A person appointed under—<br>(a) section 167 of the Financial Services and Markets Act 2000 (c. 8),<br>(b) subsection (3) or (5) of section 168 of that Act, or<br>(c) section 284 of that Act,<br>to conduct an investigation. | Functions in relation to that investigation. |
| A body designated under section 326(1) of that Act. | Functions in its capacity as a body designated under that section. |
| A recognized investment exchange or a recognized clearing house (as defined by section 285 of that Act). | Functions in its capacity as an exchange or clearing house recognized under that Act. |
| A body corporate established in accordance with section 212(1) of that Act. | Functions under the Financial Services Compensation Scheme, established in accordance with section 213 of that Act. |
| The Panel on Takeovers and Mergers. | Functions under the City Code on Takeovers and Mergers and the Rules Governing Substantial Acquisitions of Shares for the time being issued by the Panel. |
| The General Insurance Standards Council. | Functions of regulating sales and advisory and service standards in relation to insurance. |
| A recognized professional body (within the meaning of section 391 of the Insolvency Act 1986 (c. 45)). | Functions in its capacity as such a body under that Act. |
| A person on whom functions are conferred by or under Part 2, 3 or 4 of the Proceeds of Crime Act 2002 (c. 29). | The functions so conferred. |
| The Counter Fraud and Security Management Service established under the Counter Fraud and Security Management Service (Establishment and Constitution) Order 2002 (S.I. 2002/3039). | Any of its functions. |

**sch 8, Pensions Act 2004**

| Persons | Functions |
|---|---|
| The Department of Enterprise, Trade and Investment in Northern Ireland. | Functions under—<br>(a) Part 15 of the Companies (Northern Ireland) Order 1986 (S.I. 1986/1032 (N.I. 6)),<br>(b) the Insolvency (Northern Ireland) Order 1989 (S.I. 1989/2405 (N.I. 19)), or<br>(c) Part 2 of the Companies (No. 2) (Northern Ireland) Order 1990 (S.I. 1990/1504 (N.I. 10)). |
| The Department for Social Development in Northern Ireland. | Functions under Part 3 of the Pension Schemes (Northern Ireland) Act 1993 (c. 49). |
| An Inspector appointed by the Department of Enterprise, Trade and Investment in Northern Ireland. | Functions under Part 15 of the Companies (Northern Ireland) Order 1986. |
| A recognized professional body within the meaning of Article 350 of the Insolvency (Northern Ireland) Order 1989. | Functions in its capacity as such a body under that Order. |
| The Gaming Board for Great Britain. | Functions under—<br>(a) the Gaming Act 1968 (c. 65), or<br>(b) the Lotteries and Amusements Act 1976 (c. 32). |

## SCHEDULE 9

Section 206

### REVIEWABLE MATTERS

1. The issue of a determination notice under section 123 approving a notice issued under section 122.
2. The failure to issue a determination notice under section 123.
3. The issue of, or failure to issue, a notice under section 122 by the Board by virtue of section 124 (Board's duty where failure to comply with section 122).
4. The issue of, or failure to issue—
   (a) a scheme failure notice under subsection (2) of section 130 (scheme rescue not possible), or
   (b) a withdrawal notice under subsection (3) of that section (scheme rescue has occurred).
5. Any direction given under subsection (2) of section 134 (directions during an assessment period) or any variation or revocation of such a direction under subsection (4) of that section.
6. The issue of a notice under section 136(2) (power to validate contraventions of section 135).
7. The making of a loan under section 139(2) (loans to pay scheme benefits), the amount of any such loan or the failure to make such a loan.
8. The failure by the Board to obtain an actuarial valuation of a scheme under section 143(2).
9. The approval of, or failure to approve, a valuation in respect of an eligible scheme under section 144(2).
10. The issue of, or failure to issue, a withdrawal notice under or by virtue of—
    (a) section 146 (schemes which become eligible schemes), or
    (b) section 147 (new schemes created to replace existing schemes).
11. The issue of, or failure to issue, a withdrawal notice under section 148 (no insolvency event has occurred or is likely to occur).
12. The issue of, or failure to issue, a determination notice under section 152(3) (whether value of scheme assets less than aggregate of liabilities etc).
13. The issue of, or failure to issue, a determination notice under section 153(6) (authorisation to continue as closed scheme).
14. Any direction given under section 154(7) (directions about winding up of scheme with sufficient assets to meet protected liabilities) and any variation or revocation of such a direction.
15. The failure by the Board to give a transfer notice under section 160.
16. Any determination by the Board of a person's entitlement to compensation under the pension compensation provisions or the failure in any case to make such a determination.
17. Any failure by the Board to make a payment required by section 163(4)(b) (adjustments to be made where Board assumes responsibility for a scheme).
18. Any determination by the Board under section 181(3)(a) (the eligible schemes in respect of which the initial levy or the pension protection levy is imposed) or the failure to make such a determination.

19  The amount of the initial levy or any pension protection levy payable in respect of an eligible scheme determined by the Board under section 181(3)(b).
20  The making of a fraud compensation payment under section 182(1), the amount of any such payment or the failure to make such a payment.
21  The issue of, or failure to issue, a notice under section 183(2) (scheme rescue not possible or having occurred in case of scheme which is not eligible etc).
22  Any settlement date determined by the Board under section 184(2) (recovery of value) or the failure to determine a settlement date under that provision.
23  Any determination by the Board under section 184(4) (recovery of value: whether amount received in respect of particular act or omission) or the failure to make such a determination.
24  The making of a payment under section 186(1) (interim payments), the amount of any such payment or the failure to make such a payment.
25  Any term or condition imposed by the Board—
    (a) under section 185(2) on the making of a fraud compensation payment, or
    (b) under subsection (4) of section 186 (interim payments) on the making of a payment under subsection (1) of that section.
26  Any determination by the Board under section 186(3)(b) (interim payments) that the amount of a payment was excessive.
27  Any date determined by the Board under section 187(4) (earliest date for making a fraud compensation transfer payment).
28  Any determination by the Board under section 187(6) (fraud compensation transfer payments: whether payment is received in respect of particular act or omission).
29  Any determination by the Board under section 189(7)(a) (occupational pension schemes in respect of which any fraud compensation levy is imposed) or the failure to make such a determination.
30  The amount of any fraud compensation levy payable in respect of an occupational pension scheme determined by the Board under section 189(7)(b).

## SCHEDULE 10

Section 236

### USE AND SUPPLY OF INFORMATION: PRIVATE PENSIONS POLICY AND RETIREMENT PLANNING

*Use of information held by Secretary of State etc*

1  (1) Section 3 of the Social Security Act 1998 (c. 14) (use of information) is amended as follows.
   (2) In subsection (1), for the words from "social security" to "training" substitute "any of the matters specified in subsection (1A) below".
   (3) After subsection (1) insert—
   "(1A) The matters are—
   (a) social security, child support or war pensions;
   (b) employment or training;
   (c) private pensions policy;
   (d) retirement planning."
   (4) In subsection (2)(a), for the words from "social security" to "training" substitute "any of the matters specified in subsection (1A) above".
   (5) After subsection (4) insert—
   "(5) In this section—
   "private pensions policy" means policy relating to occupational pension schemes or personal pension schemes (within the meaning given by section 1 of the Pension Schemes Act 1993);
   "retirement planning" means promoting financial planning for retirement."

*Supply of information held by tax authorities*

2  (1) This paragraph applies to information which is held—
   (a) by the Commissioners of Inland Revenue;
   (b) by a person providing services to the Commissioners of Inland Revenue, in connection with the provision of those services;
   (c) by the Commissioners of Customs and Excise;
   (d) by a person providing services to the Commissioners of Customs and Excise, in connection with the provision of those services.
   (2) Information to which this paragraph applies may be supplied—
   (a) to the Secretary of State or the Northern Ireland Department, or
   (b) to a person providing services to the Secretary of State or the Northern Ireland Department,
   for use for the purposes of functions relating to private pensions policy or retirement planning.
   (3) In this paragraph—
   "private pensions policy" means policy relating to occupational pension schemes or personal pension schemes;

"retirement planning" means promoting financial planning for retirement;
"the Northern Ireland Department" means the Department for Social Development in Northern Ireland.

*Supply of housing benefit and council tax benefit information*

3 (1) Section 122D of the Social Security Administration Act 1992 (c. 5) (supply of information by authorities administering housing benefit or council tax benefit) is amended as follows.

(2) In subsection (1) for "or employment or training" substitute "employment or training, private pensions policy or retirement planning".

(3) After subsection (2) insert—

"(2A) Information supplied under subsection (2) may be used for any purpose relating to private pensions policy or retirement planning."

(4) After subsection (5) insert—

"(6) In this section—

"private pensions policy" means policy relating to occupational pension schemes or personal pension schemes (within the meaning given by section 1 of the Pension Schemes Act 1993);

"retirement planning" means promoting financial planning for retirement."

## SCHEDULE 11

Section 297

### DEFERRAL OF RETIREMENT PENSIONS AND SHARED ADDITIONAL PENSIONS

### PART 1
### PRINCIPAL AMENDMENTS OF SOCIAL SECURITY CONTRIBUTIONS AND BENEFITS ACT 1992 (C. 4)

1   In this Part of this Schedule "the principal Act" means the Social Security Contributions and Benefits Act 1992.

2   Schedule 5 to the principal Act (increase of pension where entitlement is deferred) is amended as follows.

3   For the heading, substitute "PENSION INCREASE OR LUMP SUM WHERE ENTITLEMENT TO RETIREMENT PENSION IS DEFERRED".

4   Before paragraph 1 insert—

*"Choice between increase of pension and lump sum where pensioner's entitlement is deferred*

A1 (1) Where a person's entitlement to a Category A or Category B retirement pension is deferred and the period of deferment is at least 12 months, the person shall, on claiming his pension or within a prescribed period after claiming it, elect in the prescribed manner either—
 (a) that paragraph 1 (entitlement to increase of pension) is to apply in relation to the period of deferment, or
 (b) that paragraph 3A (entitlement to lump sum) is to apply in relation to the period of deferment.

(2) If no election under sub-paragraph (1) is made within the period prescribed under that sub-paragraph, the person is to be treated as having made an election under sub-paragraph (1)(b).

(3) Regulations—
 (a) may enable a person who has made an election under sub-paragraph (1) (including one that the person is treated by sub-paragraph (2) as having made) to change the election within a prescribed period and in a prescribed manner, if prescribed conditions are satisfied, and
 (b) if they enable a person to make an election under sub-paragraph (1)(b) in respect of a period of deferment after receiving any increase of pension under paragraph 1 by reference to that period, may for the purpose of avoiding duplication of payment—
  (i) enable an amount determined in accordance with the regulations to be recovered from the person in a prescribed manner and within a prescribed period, or
  (ii) provide for an amount determined in accordance with the regulations to be treated as having been paid on account of the amount to which the person is entitled under paragraph 3A.

(4) Where the Category A or Category B retirement pension includes any increase under paragraphs 5 to 6, no election under sub-paragraph (1) applies to so much of the pension as consists of that increase (an entitlement to an increase of pension in respect of such an increase after a period of deferment being conferred either by paragraphs 1 and 2 or by paragraph 2A)."

5  For paragraph 1 (increase of pension where pensioner's entitlement is deferred) substitute—

"1 (1) This paragraph applies where a person's entitlement to a Category A or Category B retirement pension is deferred and one of the following conditions is met—
(a) the period of deferment is less than 12 months, or
(b) the person has made an election under paragraph A1(1)(a) in relation to the period of deferment.

(2) The rate of the person's Category A or Category B retirement pension shall be increased by an amount equal to the aggregate of the increments to which he is entitled under paragraph 2, but only if that amount is enough to increase the rate of the pension by at least 1 per cent."

6  (1) In paragraph 2 (calculation of increment), in sub-paragraph (5)(b), for "83 or" substitute "83A or".

(2) In relation to any incremental period (within the meaning of Schedule 5 to the principal Act) beginning before 6th April 2010, the reference in paragraph 2(5)(b) of that Schedule to section 83A of that Act is to be read as a reference to section 83 or 84 of that Act.

7  After paragraph 2 insert—

"2A (1) This paragraph applies where—
(a) a person's entitlement to a Category A or Category B retirement pension is deferred,
(b) the pension includes an increase under paragraphs 5 to 6, and
(c) the person has made (or is treated as having made) an election under paragraph A1(1)(b) in relation to the period of deferment.

(2) The rate of the person's Category A or Category B retirement pension shall be increased by an amount equal to the aggregate of the increments to which he is entitled under sub-paragraph (3).

(3) For each complete incremental period in the person's period of deferment, the amount of the increment shall be 1/5th per cent. of the weekly rate of the increase to which the person would have been entitled under paragraphs 5 to 6 for the period if his entitlement to the Category A or Category B retirement pension had not been deferred."

8  (1) After paragraph 3 insert—

*"Lump sum where pensioner's entitlement is deferred*

3A (1) This paragraph applies where—
(a) a person's entitlement to a Category A or Category B retirement pension is deferred, and
(b) the person has made (or is treated as having made) an election under paragraph A1(1)(b) in relation to the period of deferment.

(2) The person is entitled to an amount calculated in accordance with paragraph 3B (a "lump sum").

*Calculation of lump sum*

3B (1) The lump sum is the accrued amount for the last accrual period beginning during the period of deferment.

(2) In this paragraph—

"accrued amount" means the amount calculated in accordance with sub-paragraph (3);

"accrual period" means any period of seven days beginning with a prescribed day of the week, where that day falls within the period of deferment.

(3) The accrued amount for an accrual period for a person is—

$$(A + P) \times 52 \bigg/ \left(1 + \frac{R}{100}\right)$$

where—

A is the accrued amount for the previous accrual period (or, in the case of the first accrual period beginning during the period of deferment, zero);

P is the amount of the Category A or Category B retirement pension to which the person would have been entitled for the accrual period if his entitlement had not been deferred;

R is—

(a) a percentage rate two per cent. higher than the Bank of England base rate, or

(b) if regulations so provide, such higher rate as may be prescribed.

(4) For the purposes of sub-paragraph (3), any change in the Bank of England base rate is to be treated as taking effect—

(a) at the beginning of the accrual period immediately following the accrual period during which the change took effect, or

(b) if regulations so provide, at such other time as may be prescribed.

(5) For the purposes of the calculation of the lump sum, the amount of Category A or Category B retirement pension to which the person would have been entitled for an accrual period—

(a) includes any increase under section 47(1) and any increase under paragraph 4 of this Schedule, but

(b) does not include—

(i) any increase under section 83A or 85 or paragraphs 5 to 6 of this Schedule,

(ii) any graduated retirement benefit, or

(iii) in prescribed circumstances, such other amount of Category A or Category B retirement pension as may be prescribed.

(6) The reference in sub-paragraph (5)(a) to any increase under subsection (1) of section 47 shall be taken as a reference to any increase that would take place under that subsection if subsection (2) of that section and section 46(5) of the Pensions Act were disregarded."

(2) In relation to any accrual period (within the meaning of Schedule 5 to the principal Act as amended by this paragraph) ending before 6th April 2010 the reference in paragraph 3B(5)(b) of that Schedule to section 83A of that Act is to be read as a reference to section 83 or 84 of that Act.

9 After paragraph 3B (inserted by paragraph 8 of this Schedule) insert—

*"Choice between increase of pension and lump sum where pensioner's deceased spouse has deferred entitlement*

3C (1) Subject to paragraph 8, this paragraph applies where—
   (a) a widow or widower ("W") is entitled to a Category A or Category B retirement pension,
   (b) W was married to the other party to the marriage ("S") when S died,
   (c) S's entitlement to a Category A or Category B retirement pension was deferred when S died, and
   (d) S's entitlement had been deferred throughout the period of 12 months ending with the day before S's death.
(2) W shall within the prescribed period elect in the prescribed manner either—
   (a) that paragraph 4 (entitlement to increase of pension) is to apply in relation to S's period of deferment, or
   (b) that paragraph 7A (entitlement to lump sum) is to apply in relation to S's period of deferment.
(3) If no election under sub-paragraph (2) is made within the period prescribed under that sub-paragraph, W is to be treated as having made an election under sub-paragraph (2)(b).
(4) Regulations—
   (a) may enable a person who has made an election under sub-paragraph (2) (including one that the person is treated by sub-paragraph (3) as having made) to change the election within a prescribed period and in a prescribed manner, if prescribed conditions are satisfied, and
   (b) if they enable a person to make an election under sub-paragraph (2)(b) in respect of a period of deferment after receiving any increase of pension under paragraph 4 by reference to that period, may for the purpose of avoiding duplication of payment—
      (i) enable an amount determined in accordance with the regulations to be recovered from the person in a prescribed manner and within a prescribed period, or
      (ii) provide for an amount determined in accordance with the regulations to be treated as having been paid on account of the amount to which the person is entitled under paragraph 7A.
(5) The making of an election under sub-paragraph (2)(b) does not affect the application of paragraphs 5 to 6 (which relate to an increase in pension where the pensioner's deceased spouse had deferred an entitlement to a guaranteed minimum pension)."

10 (1) Paragraph 4 (increase of pension where pensioner's deceased spouse has deferred entitlement) is amended as follows.
   (2) For sub-paragraph (1) substitute—
      "(1) Subject to paragraph 8, this paragraph applies where a widow or widower ("W") is entitled to a Category A or Category B retirement pension and was married to the other party to the marriage ("S") when S died and one of the following conditions is met—
         (a) S was entitled to a Category A or Category B retirement pension with an increase under this Schedule,

(b) W is a widow or widower to whom paragraph 3C applies and has made an election under paragraph 3C(2)(a), or

(c) paragraph 3C would apply to W but for the fact that the condition in sub-paragraph (1)(d) of that paragraph is not met.

(1A) Subject to sub-paragraph (3), the rate of W's pension shall be increased—

(a) in a case falling within sub-paragraph (1)(a), by an amount equal to the increase to which S was entitled under this Schedule, apart from paragraphs 5 to 6,

(b) in a case falling within sub-paragraph (1)(b), by an amount equal to the increase to which S would have been entitled under this Schedule, apart from paragraphs 5 to 6, if the period of deferment had ended immediately before S's death and S had then made an election under paragraph A1(1)(a), or

(c) in a case falling within sub-paragraph (1)(c), by an amount equal to the increase to which S would have been entitled under this Schedule, apart from paragraphs 5 to 6, if the period of deferment had ended immediately before S's death."

11 (1) After paragraph 7 insert—

*"Entitlement to lump sum where pensioner's deceased spouse has deferred entitlement*

7A (1) This paragraph applies where a person to whom paragraph 3C applies ("W") has made (or is treated as having made) an election under paragraph 3C(2)(b).

(2) W is entitled to an amount calculated in accordance with paragraph 7B (a "widowed person's lump sum").

*Calculation of widowed person's lump sum*

7B (1) The widowed person's lump sum is the accrued amount for the last accrual period beginning during the period which—

(a) began at the beginning of S's period of deferment, and

(b) ended on the day before S's death.

(2) In this paragraph—

"S" means the other party to the marriage;

"accrued amount" means the amount calculated in accordance with sub-paragraph (3);

"accrual period" means any period of seven days beginning with a prescribed day of the week, where that day falls within S's period of deferment.

**sch 11, Pensions Act 2004**

(3) The accrued amount for an accrual period for W is—

$$(A + P) \times 52 \sqrt{\left(1 + \frac{R}{100}\right)}$$

where—

A is the accrued amount for the previous accrual period (or, in the case of the first accrual period beginning during the period mentioned in sub-paragraph (1), zero);

P is—

(a) the basic pension, and

(b) half of the additional pension, to which S would have been entitled for the accrual period if his entitlement had not been deferred during the period mentioned in sub-paragraph (1);

R is—

(a) a percentage rate two per cent. higher than the Bank of England base rate, or

(b) if regulations so provide, such higher rate as may be prescribed.

(4) For the purposes of sub-paragraph (3), any change in the Bank of England base rate is to be treated as taking effect—

(a) at the beginning of the accrual period immediately following the accrual period during which the change took effect, or

(b) if regulations so provide, at such other time as may be prescribed.

(5) For the purposes of the calculation of the widowed person's lump sum, the amount of Category A or Category B retirement pension to which S would have been entitled for an accrual period—

(a) ncludes any increase under section 47(1) and any increase under paragraph 4 of this Schedule, but

(b) does not include—

(i) any increase under section 83A or 85 or paragraphs 5 to 6 of this Schedule,

(ii) any graduated retirement benefit, or

(iii) in prescribed circumstances, such other amount of Category A or Category B retirement pension as may be prescribed.

(6) The reference in sub-paragraph (5)(a) to any increase under subsection (1) of section 47 shall be taken as a reference to any increase that would take place under that subsection if subsection (2) of that section and section 46(5) of the Pensions Act were disregarded.

(7) In any case where—

(a) there is a period between the death of S and the date on which W becomes entitled to a Category A or Category B retirement pension, and

(b) one or more orders have come into force under section 150 of the Administration Act during that period,

the amount of the lump sum shall be increased in accordance with that order or those orders."

(2) In relation to any accrual period (within the meaning of Schedule 5 to the principal Act) ending before 6th April 2010 the reference in paragraph 7B(5)(b)

of that Schedule to section 83A of that Act is to be read as a reference to section 83 or 84 of that Act.

12 After paragraph 7B (inserted by paragraph 11 of this Schedule) insert—

*"Supplementary*

7C (1) Any lump sum calculated under paragraph 3B or 7B must be rounded to the nearest penny, taking any 1/2p as nearest to the next whole penny above.
   (2) In prescribing a percentage rate for the purposes of paragraphs 3B and 7B, the Secretary of State must have regard to—
      (a) the national economic situation, and
      (b) any other matters which he considers relevant."

13 For the heading immediately preceding paragraph 8 substitute "Married couples".

14 In paragraph 8 (married couples)—
   (a) in sub-paragraph (3) for "the reference in paragraph 2(3) above" substitute "the references in paragraphs 2(3) and 3B(3) and (5)", and
   (b) for sub-paragraph (4) substitute—
   "(4) The conditions in paragraph 3C(1)(c) and 4(1)(a) are not satisfied by a Category B retirement pension to which S was or would have been entitled by virtue of W's contributions.
      (5) Where the Category A retirement pension to which S was or would have been entitled includes an increase under section 51A(2) attributable to W's contributions, the increase or lump sum to which W is entitled under paragraph 4(1A) or 7A(2) is to be calculated as if there had been no increase under that section.
      (6) In sub-paragraphs (4) and (5), 'W' and 'S' have the same meaning as in paragraph 3C, 4 or 7A, as the case requires."

15 After Schedule 5 to the principal Act insert—

"SCHEDULE 5A

PENSION INCREASE OR LUMP SUM WHERE ENTITLEMENT TO SHARED ADDITIONAL PENSION IS DEFERRED

*Choice between pension increase and lump sum where entitlement to shared additional pension is deferred*

1 (1) Where a person's entitlement to a shared additional pension is deferred and the period of deferment is at least 12 months, the person shall, on claiming his pension or within a prescribed period after claiming it, elect in the prescribed manner either—
      (a) that paragraph 2 (entitlement to increase of pension) is to apply in relation to the period of deferment, or
      (b) that paragraph 4 (entitlement to lump sum) is to apply in relation to the period of deferment.
   (2) If no election under sub-paragraph (1) is made within the period prescribed under that sub-paragraph, the person is to be treated as having made an election under sub-paragraph (1)(b).
   (3) Regulations—

(a) may enable a person who has made an election under sub-paragraph (1) (including one that the person is treated by sub-paragraph (2) as having made) to change the election within a prescribed period and in a prescribed manner, if prescribed conditions are satisfied, and

(b) if they enable a person to make an election under sub-paragraph (1)(b) in respect of a period of deferment after receiving any increase of pension under paragraph 2 by reference to that period, may for the purpose of avoiding duplication of payment—

(i) enable an amount determined in accordance with the regulations to be recovered from the person in a prescribed manner and within a prescribed period, or

(ii) provide for an amount determined in accordance with the regulations to be treated as having been paid on account of the amount to which the person is entitled under paragraph 4.

*Increase of pension where entitlement deferred*

2 (1) This paragraph applies where a person's entitlement to a shared additional pension is deferred and either—

(a) the period of deferment is less than 12 months, or

(b) the person has made an election under paragraph 1(1)(a) in relation to the period of deferment.

(2) The rate of the person's shared additional pension shall be increased by an amount equal to the aggregate of the increments to which he is entitled under paragraph 3, but only if that amount is enough to increase the rate of the pension by at least 1 per cent.

*Calculation of increment*

3 (1) A person is entitled to an increment under this paragraph for each complete incremental period in his period of deferment.

(2) The amount of the increment for an incremental period shall be 1/5th per cent. of the weekly rate of the shared additional pension to which the person would have been entitled for the period if his entitlement had not been deferred.

(3) Amounts under sub-paragraph (2) shall be rounded to the nearest penny, taking any 1/2p as nearest to the next whole penny.

(4) Where an amount under sub-paragraph (2) would, apart from this sub-paragraph, be a sum less than 1/2p, the amount shall be taken to be zero, notwithstanding any other provision of this Act, the Pensions Act or the Administration Act.

(5) In this paragraph "incremental period" means any period of six days which are treated by regulations as days of increment for the purposes of this paragraph in relation to the person and pension in question.

(6) Where one or more orders have come into force under section 150 of the Administration Act during the period of deferment, the rate for any incremental period shall be determined as if the order or orders had come into force before the beginning of the period of deferment.

(7) The sums which are the increases in the rates of shared additional pension

*Lump sum where entitlement to shared additional pension is deferred*

4   (1) This paragraph applies where—
    (a) a person's entitlement to a shared additional pension is deferred, and
    (b) the person has made (or is treated as having made) an election under paragraph 1(1)(b) in relation to the period of deferment.
    (2) The person is entitled to an amount calculated in accordance with paragraph 5 (a "lump sum").

*Calculation of lump sum*

5   (1) The lump sum is the accrued amount for the last accrual period beginning during the period of deferment.
    (2) In this paragraph—
    "accrued amount" means the amount calculated in accordance with sub-paragraph (3);
    "accrual period" means any period of seven days beginning with a prescribed day of the week, where that day falls within the period of deferment.
    (3) The accrued amount for an accrual period for a person is—

$$(A + P) \times 52 \sqrt{\left(1 + \frac{R}{100}\right)}$$

where—
A is the accrued amount for the previous accrual period (or, in the case of the first accrual period beginning during the period of deferment, zero);
P is the amount of the shared additional pension to which the person would have been entitled for the accrual period if his entitlement had not been deferred;
R is—
(a) a percentage rate two per cent. higher than the Bank of England base rate, or
(b) if a higher rate is prescribed for the purposes of paragraphs 3B and 7B of Schedule 5, that higher rate.
    (4) For the purposes of sub-paragraph (3), any change in the Bank of England base rate is to be treated as taking effect—
    (a) at the beginning of the accrual period immediately following the accrual period during which the change took effect, or
    (b) if regulations so provide, at such other time as may be prescribed.
    (5) For the purpose of the calculation of the lump sum, the amount of the shared additional pension to which the person would have been entitled for an accrual period does not include, in prescribed circumstances, such amount as may be prescribed.
    (6) The lump sum must be rounded to the nearest penny, taking any 1/2p as nearest to the next whole penny."

## PART 2
## CONSEQUENTIAL AMENDMENTS

*Social Security Contributions and Benefits Act 1992 (c. 4)*

16 The Social Security Contributions and Benefits Act 1992 is amended as follows.

17 In section 62(1) (graduated retirement benefit)—
   (a) in paragraph (a), for "paragraphs 1 to 3" substitute "paragraphs A1 to 3B and 7C", and
   (b) after paragraph (b) insert—
      "(c) for amending that section in order to make provisions corresponding to those of paragraphs 3C, 4(1) and (1A) and 7A to 7C of Schedule 5 to this Act enabling a widowed person to elect to receive a lump sum, rather than an increase in the weekly rate of retirement pension, in respect of the graduated retirement benefit of his or her deceased spouse."

18 In section 122(1) (interpretation of Parts 1 to 6)—
   (a) before the definition of "beneficiary" insert—
      " "Bank of England base rate" means—
         (a) the rate announced from time to time by the Monetary Policy Committee of the Bank of England as the official dealing rate, being the rate at which the Bank is willing to enter into transactions for providing short term liquidity in the money markets, or
         (b) where an order under section 19 of the Bank of England Act 1998 is in force, any equivalent rate determined by the Treasury under that section;", and
   (b) for the definitions of "deferred" and "period of deferment" substitute—
      " "deferred" and "period of deferment"—
         (a) in relation to a Category A or Category B retirement pension, have the meanings given by section 55(3), and
         (b) in relation to a shared additional pension, have the meanings given by section 55C(3);".

19 In section 176 (parliamentary control of subordinate legislation) in subsection (1) (affirmative procedure), after paragraph (b) insert—
   "(bb) regulations prescribing a percentage rate for the purposes of—
      (i) paragraph 3B(3) or 7B(3) of Schedule 5, or
      (ii) paragraph 5(3) of Schedule 5A;".

*Social Security Administration Act 1992 (c. 5)*

20 The Social Security Administration Act 1992 is amended as follows.

21 In section 150 (annual up-rating of benefits)—
   (a) in subsection (1), after paragraph (d) insert—
      "(dza) which are lump sums to which surviving spouses will become entitled under paragraph 7A of that Schedule on becoming entitled to a Category A or Category B retirement pension;",
   (b) in subsection (1)(da), for "section 55C of" substitute "paragraph 2 of Schedule 5A to", and
   (c) in subsection (3)(b), after "(d)," insert "(dza),".

22 In section 151 (up-rating- supplementary) in subsection (2)—

(a) for "subsection (1)(d) or (e)" substitute "subsection (1)(d), (dza) or (e)", and
(b) after "apart from the order and" insert ", in the case of the sums mentioned in subsection (1)(d) or (e) of that section,".

*Welfare Reform and Pensions Act 1999 (c. 30)*

23  The Welfare Reform and Pensions Act 1999 is amended as follows.
24  In section 50, omit subsection (2) (which amends provisions relating to the deferment of shared additional pensions and is superseded by Part 1 of this Schedule).
25  In section 52(2) (power to make regulations preserving rights in respect of additional pensions), in paragraph (b)—
(a) after "increase of pension" insert "or payment of lump sum", and
(b) after "constituent element of an increase" insert "or of a lump sum".

## PART 3
## TRANSITIONAL PROVISIONS

*Widowers' entitlement to increase of pension or widowed person's lump sum*

26  In the case of a widower who attains pensionable age before 6th April 2010, paragraphs 3C, 4 and 7A of Schedule 5 to the Social Security Contributions and Benefits Act 1992 (c. 4) (entitlement to increase of pension or widowed person's lump sum) shall not apply unless he was over pensionable age when his wife died.

*Transitional provision*

27  (1) The Secretary of State may by regulations make such transitional provision as he thinks fit in connection with the coming into force of this Schedule.
(2) Regulations under this paragraph may, in particular, modify the preceding provisions of this Schedule in relation to cases where the retirement pension or shared additional pension of a person is deferred and the period of deferment begins before 6th April 2005 and continues on or after that day.
(3) In this paragraph "deferred" and "period of deferment" are to be read in accordance with section 55 or 55C of the Social Security Contributions and Benefits Act 1992, as the case requires.

## SCHEDULE 12

Section 319

### MINOR AND CONSEQUENTIAL AMENDMENTS

*Public Records Act 1958 (c. 51)*

1  In Schedule 1 to the Public Records Act 1958 (definition of public records), in Part 2 of the Table in paragraph 3 insert at the appropriate place—
"The Pensions Regulator."
"The Board of the Pension Protection Fund."
"The Ombudsman for the Board of the Pension Protection Fund."

*Superannuation Act 1972 (c. 11)*

2  (1) Schedule 1 to the Superannuation Act 1972 (kinds of employment in relation to which pension schemes may be made) is amended as follows.
(2) At the appropriate place in the list of "Other Bodies" insert—
"The Board of the Pension Protection Fund.",
"Employment by the Ombudsman for the Board of the Pension Protection Fund.", and
"The Pensions Regulator."
(3) At the appropriate place in the list of "Offices" insert—
"Chairman of the Board of the Pension Protection Fund.",
"Chairman of the Pensions Regulator.",
"A deputy to the Ombudsman for the Board of the Pension Protection Fund.",
"A deputy to the Pensions Ombudsman.", and
"The Ombudsman for the Board of the Pension Protection Fund."

*Matrimonial Causes Act 1973 (c. 18)*

3  After section 25D of the Matrimonial Causes Act 1973 (pensions: supplementary) insert—

**"25E The Pension Protection Fund**

(1) The matters to which the court is to have regard under section 25(2) include—
   (a) in the case of paragraph (a), any PPF compensation to which a party to the marriage is or is likely to be entitled, and
   (b) in the case of paragraph (h), any PPF compensation which, by reason of the dissolution or annulment of the marriage, a party to the marriage will lose the chance of acquiring entitlement to,
and, accordingly, in relation to PPF compensation, section 25(2)(a) shall have effect as if "in the foreseeable future" were omitted.
(2) Subsection (3) applies in relation to an order under section 23 so far as it includes provision made by virtue of section 25B(4) which—

(a) imposed requirements on the trustees or managers of an occupational pension scheme for which the Board has assumed responsibility in accordance with Chapter 3 of Part 2 of the Pensions Act 2004 (pension protection) or any provision in force in Northern Ireland corresponding to that Chapter, and
(b) was made before the trustees or managers of the scheme received the transfer notice in relation to the scheme.
(3) The order is to have effect from the time when the trustees or managers of the scheme receive the transfer notice—
  (a) as if, except in prescribed descriptions of case—
    (i) references in the order to the trustees or managers of the scheme were references to the Board, and
    (ii) references in the order to any pension or lump sum to which the party with pension rights is or may become entitled under the scheme were references to any PPF compensation to which that person is or may become entitled in respect of the pension or lump sum, and
  (b) subject to such other modifications as may be prescribed.
(4) Subsection (5) applies to an order under section 23 if—
  (a) it includes provision made by virtue of section 25B(7) which requires the party with pension rights to exercise his right of commutation under an occupational pension scheme to any extent, and
  (b) before the requirement is complied with the Board has assumed responsibility for the scheme as mentioned in subsection (2)(a).
(5) From the time the trustees or managers of the scheme receive the transfer notice, the order is to have effect with such modifications as may be prescribed.
(6) Regulations may modify section 25C as it applies in relation to an occupational pension scheme at any time when there is an assessment period in relation to the scheme.
(7) Where the court makes a pension sharing order in respect of a person's shareable rights under an occupational pension scheme, or an order which includes provision made by virtue of section 25B(4) or (7) in relation to such a scheme, the Board subsequently assuming responsibility for the scheme as mentioned in subsection (2)(a) does not affect—
  (a) the powers of the court under section 31 to vary or discharge the order or to suspend or revive any provision of it, or
  (b) on an appeal, the powers of the appeal court to affirm, reinstate, set aside or vary the order.
(8) Regulations may make such consequential modifications of any provision of, or made by virtue of, this Part as appear to the Lord Chancellor necessary or expedient to give effect to the provisions of this section.
(9) In this section—
"assessment period" means an assessment period within the meaning of Part 2 of the Pensions Act 2004 (pension protection) (see sections 132 and 159 of that Act) or an equivalent period under any provision in force in Northern Ireland corresponding to that Part;
"the Board" means the Board of the Pension Protection Fund;
"occupational pension scheme" has the same meaning as in the Pension Schemes Act 1993;

"prescribed" means prescribed by regulations;
"PPF compensation" means compensation payable under Chapter 3 of Part 2 of the Pensions Act 2004 (pension protection) or any provision in force in Northern Ireland corresponding to that Chapter;
"regulations" means regulations made by the Lord Chancellor;
"shareable rights" are rights in relation to which pension sharing is available under Chapter 1 of Part 4 of the Welfare Reform and Pensions Act 1999 or any provision in force in Northern Ireland corresponding to that Chapter;
"transfer notice" has the same meaning as in section 160 of the Pensions Act 2004 or any corresponding provision in force in Northern Ireland.

(10) Any power to make regulations under this section is exercisable by statutory instrument, which shall be subject to annulment in pursuance of a resolution of either House of Parliament."

*Matrimonial and Family Proceedings Act 1984 (c. 42)*

4 (1) The Matrimonial and Family Proceedings Act 1984 is amended as follows.
 (2) In section 18 (matters to which the court is to have regard in exercising its powers under section 17)—
  (a) in subsection (3A)—
   (i) in paragraph (a) after "have" insert "and any PPF compensation to which a party to the marriage is or is likely to be entitled,",
   (ii) in paragraph (b) after "include" insert "—
    (i)", and
   (iii) at the end of that paragraph insert ", and
    (ii) any PPF compensation which, by reason of the dissolution or annulment of the marriage, a party to the marriage will lose the chance of acquiring entitlement to", and
  (b) in subsection (7), after paragraph (b) insert ", and
   (c) "PPF compensation" means compensation payable under Chapter 3 of Part 2 of the Pensions Act 2004 (pension protection) or any provision in force in Northern Ireland corresponding to that Chapter."
 (3) In section 21 (application to orders under sections 14 and 17 of certain provisions of Part 2 of the Matrimonial Causes Act 1973), after subsection (1)(be) insert—
 "(bf) section 25E(2) to (10) (the Pension Protection Fund);".

*Companies Act 1985 (c. 6)*

5 (1) The Companies Act 1985 is amended as follows.
 (2) In section 449 (provision for security of information obtained by the Secretary of State under section 447), for subsection (1)(dg) substitute—
 "(dg) for the purpose of enabling or assisting the Pensions Regulator to exercise the functions conferred on it by or by virtue of the Pension Schemes Act 1993, the Pensions Act 1995, the Welfare Reform and Pensions Act 1999 or the Pensions Act 2004 or any enactment in force in Northern Ireland corresponding to any of those enactments;
  (dh) for the purpose of enabling or assisting the Board of the Pension Protection Fund to exercise the functions conferred on it by or by virtue of Part 2

of the Pensions Act 2004 or any enactment in force in Northern Ireland corresponding to that Part;".

(3) In Schedule 15D (permitted disclosures of information) (as inserted by Schedule 2 to the Companies (Audit, Investigations and Community Enterprise) Act 2004)—

(a) for paragraph 13 substitute—

"13 A disclosure for the purpose of enabling or assisting the Pensions Regulator to exercise the functions conferred on it by or by virtue of any of the following—

(a) the Pension Schemes Act 1993;
(b) the Pensions Act 1995;
(c) the Welfare Reform and Pensions Act 1999;
(d) the Pensions Act 2004;
(e) any enactment in force in Northern Ireland corresponding to any of those enactments.", and

(b) after that paragraph insert—

"13A A disclosure for the purpose of enabling or assisting the Board of the Pension Protection Fund to exercise the functions conferred on it by or by virtue of Part 2 of the Pensions Act 2004 or any enactment in force in Northern Ireland corresponding to that Part."

*Companies Act 1989 (c. 40)*

6 In section 87 of the Companies Act 1989 (exception from restriction on disclosure of information obtained from overseas regulatory authorities etc), in the table in subsection (4) for the entry relating to the Occupational Pensions Regulatory Authority substitute—

"*The Pensions Regulator*

Functions conferred by or by virtue of—

(a) the Pension Schemes Act 1993,
(b) the Pensions Act 1995,
(c) the Welfare Reform and Pensions Act 1999,
(d) the Pensions Act 2004,

or any enactment in force in Northern Ireland corresponding to an enactment mentioned in paragraphs (a) to (d) above.

*The Board of the Pension Protection Fund*

Functions conferred by or by virtue of Part 2 of the Pensions Act 2004 or any enactment in force in Northern Ireland corresponding to that Part."

*Social Security Administration Act 1992 (c. 5)*

7 In section 122AA of the Social Security Administration Act 1992 (disclosure of contributions etc information by Inland Revenue), in subsection (2)(d), for "Occupational Pensions Regulatory Authority" substitute "Pensions Regulator".

*Tribunals and Inquiries Act 1992 (c. 53)*

8 (1) The Tribunals and Inquiries Act 1992 is amended as follows.

sch 12, Pensions Act 2004

(2) In section 7 (concurrence required for removal of members of certain tribunals), in subsection (2) for "(g) or (h)" substitute "(i), (j), (k) or (l)".

(3) In section 14 (restricted application of Act in relation to certain tribunals), for subsection (1A) substitute—

"(1A) In this Act—
  (a) References to the working of the Pensions Regulator referred to in paragraph 35(i) of Schedule 1 are references to its working so far as relating to the exercise of its regulatory functions (within the meaning of section 93(2) of the Pensions Act 2004) or any corresponding function conferred by a provision in force in Northern Ireland, and
  (b) references to procedural rules for the Pensions Regulator are references to regulations under paragraph 19 of Schedule 1 to that Act (Secretary of State's powers to make regulations in respect of Regulator's procedure) so far as they relate to the procedure to be followed when exercising those functions."

(4) In Schedule 1, in Part 1, in paragraph 35, after paragraph (h) insert—

"(i) the Pensions Regulator established by section 1 of the Pensions Act 2004;
(j) the Pensions Regulator Tribunal established by section 102 of that Act;
(k) the Board of the Pension Protection Fund established by section 107 of the Pensions Act 2004 in respect of its functions under or by virtue of section 207 of that Act or any enactment in force in Northern Ireland corresponding to that section;
(l) the Ombudsman for the Board of the Pension Protection Fund in respect of his functions under or by virtue of section 213 of that Act or any enactment in force in Northern Ireland corresponding to that section."

*Pension Schemes Act 1993 (c. 48)*

9  The Pension Schemes Act 1993 is amended as follows.

10 In section 53 (supervision: former contracted-out schemes), after subsection (1B) insert—

"(1C) But where a direction under subsection (1) conflicts with a freezing order made by the Regulatory Authority under section 23 of the Pensions Act 2004 in relation to the scheme then, during the period for which the freezing order has effect, the direction to the extent that it conflicts with the freezing order—
  (a) is not binding as described in subsection (1), and
  (b) is not enforceable as described in subsection (1B)."

11 (1) Section 56 (provision supplementary to provision relating to payment of state scheme premiums) is amended as follows.

(2) In subsection (4) for the words from the beginning to "another scheme" substitute—

"(4) Where under the rules of the scheme, transfer credits have been allowed—
  (a) in respect of the earner's rights under another scheme, or
  (b) in respect of the earner by reference to the payment of a cash transfer sum (within the meaning of Chapter 5 of Part 4) to the trustees or managers of the scheme by the trustees or managers of another occupational pension scheme,".

# Pensions Act 2004, sch 12

(3) After subsection (6) insert—

"(7) Where a premium under section 55 is payable by the Board of the Pension Protection Fund by virtue of a transfer under section 161 of the Pensions Act 2004 (effect of the Board assuming responsibility for an occupational pension scheme), then, subject to subsection (8), sections 55 to 68 apply with such modifications as may be prescribed in relation to that premium.

(8) A premium under section 55 in respect of an earner ceases to be payable if—
(a) the liability to pay the premium is transferred to the Board of the Pension Protection Fund by virtue of section 161 of the Pensions Act 2004, and
(b) prescribed requirements are met."

12  In section 61 (deduction of contributions equivalent premium from refund of scheme contributions), after subsection (9) insert—

"(9A) Where under section 101AH the trustees or managers of an occupational pension scheme may pay a contribution refund to a member of the scheme, the member is to be treated for the purposes of this section as being entitled to the contribution refund."

13 (1) Section 94 (right to cash equivalent) is amended as follows.

(2) In subsection (2), for the definition of "the applicable rules" substitute—

" "the applicable rules" means—
(a) the rules of the scheme, except so far as overridden by a relevant legislative provision;
(b) the relevant legislative provisions, to the extent that they have effect in relation to the scheme and are not reflected in the rules of the scheme; and
(c) any provision which the rules of the scheme do not contain but which the scheme must contain if it is to conform with Chapter 1 of Part 4 of this Act;".

(3) After that subsection insert—

"(2A) For the purposes of subsection (2)—
(a) 'relevant legislative provision' means any provision contained in any of the following provisions—
  (i) Schedule 5 to the Social Security Act 1989 (equal treatment for men and women);
  (ii) this Chapter or Chapters 2, 3 or 5 of this Part of this Act or regulations made under this Chapter or any of those Chapters;
  (iii) Part 4A of this Act or regulations made under that Part;
  (iv) section 110(1) of this Act;
  (v) Part 1 of the Pensions Act 1995 (occupational pensions) or subordinate legislation made or having effect as if made under that Part;
  (vi) section 31 of the Welfare Reform and Pensions Act 1999 (pension debits: reduction of benefit);
  (vii) any provision mentioned in section 306(2) of the Pensions Act 2004;
(b) a relevant legislative provision is to be taken to override any of the provisions of the scheme if, and only if, it does so by virtue of any of the following provisions—
  (i) paragraph 3 of Schedule 5 to the Social Security Act 1989;
  (ii) section 129(1) of this Act;
  (iii) section 117(1) of the Pensions Act 1995;
  (iv) section 31(4) of the Welfare Reform and Pensions Act 1999;
  (v) section 306(1) of the Pensions Act 2004."

14  In section 99 (trustees' duties after exercise of option)—
    (a) in subsection (4) after "circumstances," insert "by direction", and
    (b) in subsection (4A) for "in relation to applications for extensions under subsection (4)" substitute "requiring applications for extensions under subsection (4) to meet prescribed requirements".
15  In section 101J (time for compliance with transfer notice)—
    (a) in subsection (2) after "circumstances," insert "by direction", and
    (b) in subsection (6)(a) for "in relation to applications under subsection (2)" substitute "requiring applications for extensions under subsection (2) to meet prescribed requirements".
16  In section 111A (monitoring of employers' payments to personal pension schemes) omit subsection (10).
17  In section 113 (disclosure of information about schemes to members etc), after subsection (2)(d) insert—
    "(e) persons of prescribed descriptions."
18  After that section insert—

    "113A  Disclosure of information about transfers etc

    Regulations may provide that, where—
    (a) a payment is made out of an occupational pension scheme to the trustees or managers of another occupational pension scheme, and
    (b) transfer credits are allowed to a member of that other scheme in respect of the payment,
    the trustees or managers of the first scheme must, in prescribed circumstances and in the prescribed manner, provide to the trustees or managers of the other scheme prescribed information relating to the payment."
19  In section 123 (interpretation of Chapter 2 of Part 7) omit—
    (a) the definition of "occupational pension scheme" in subsection (3), and
    (b) subsection (4).
20  In section 124 (duty of Secretary of State to pay unpaid contributions), after subsection (5) insert—
    "(6) In this section "on his own account", in relation to an employer, means on his own account but to fund benefits for, or in respect of, one or more employees."
21  In section 129(1) (overriding requirements),—
    (a) for "and IV" substitute, "IV and V", and
    (b) after "under" insert "any of those Chapters or".
22  In section 130(b) (extra-statutory benefits), for "or IV" substitute, "IV or V".
23  In section 145 (the Pensions Ombudsman), after subsection (1) insert—
    "(1A) Provisions conferring power on the Pensions Ombudsman to conduct investigations as mentioned in subsection (1) are to be read as conferring power that—
        (a) in a case of a prescribed description, or
        (b) in a case involving a scheme that is prescribed or is of a prescribed description,
    may be exercised whatever the extent of any connections with places outside the United Kingdom.
    (1B) In subsection (1A) "scheme" means occupational pension scheme or personal pension scheme.

Pensions Act 2004, sch 12

(1C) Subsection (1A) shall not be taken to prejudice any power of the Pensions Ombudsman apart from that subsection to conduct investigations in a case having connections with places outside the United Kingdom."

24   In section 146 (functions of the Pensions Ombudsman)—
   (a) for subsection (1)(f) substitute—
      "(f) any dispute, in relation to a time while section 22 of the Pensions Act 1995 (circumstances in which Regulatory Authority may appoint an independent trustee) applies in relation to an occupational pension scheme, between an independent trustee of the scheme appointed under section 23(1) of that Act and either—
         (i) other trustees of the scheme, or
         (ii) former trustees of the scheme who were not independent trustees appointed under section 23(1) of that Act, and",
   (b) after subsection (6) insert—
      "(6A) For the purposes of subsection (6)(c)—
         (a) a description of complaint may be framed (in particular) by reference to the person making the complaint or to the scheme concerned (or to both), and
         (b) a description of dispute may be framed (in particular) by reference to the person referring the dispute or to the scheme concerned (or to both).", and
      (c) in subsection (8), in paragraph (a) of the definition of "independent trustee" for the words from "section 23(1)(b)" to the end substitute "section 23(1) of the Pensions Act 1995 (appointment of independent trustee by the Regulatory Authority)".

25   In section 149 (procedure on investigation by Pensions Ombudsman), in subsection (6)—
   (a) for paragraph (b) substitute—
      "(b) the Board of the Pension Protection Fund,
      (ba) the Ombudsman for the Board of the Pension Protection Fund,", and
   (b) at the end insert—
      "(n) a person who, in a member State other than the United Kingdom, has functions corresponding to functions of the Pensions Ombudsman."

26   (1) Section 158A (other disclosures by the Secretary of State) is amended as follows.
   (2) In subsection (1), for the words from "any information" to "Pensions Act 1995" substitute "any regulated information".
   (3) In the Table in that subsection—
      (a) in the entry for the Regulatory Authority in the second column of the Table for the words from "or the" to the end substitute ", the Pensions Act 1995, the Welfare Reform and Pensions Act 1999 or the Pensions Act 2004 or any enactment in force in Northern Ireland corresponding to any of those enactments.", and
      (b) for the entry for the Pensions Compensation Board substitute—
      "*The Pensions Ombudsman.*
      Functions conferred by or by virtue of this Act or any enactment in force in Northern Ireland corresponding to it.
      The Board of the Pension Protection Fund.
      Functions conferred by or by virtue of Part 2 of the Pensions Act 2004 or

any enactment in force in Northern Ireland corresponding to that Part.

The Ombudsman for the Board of the Pension Protection Fund.

Functions conferred by or by virtue of Part 2 of the Pensions Act 2004 or any enactment in force in Northern Ireland corresponding to that Part."

(4) After that subsection insert—

"(1AA) In subsection (1), "regulated information" means information received by the Secretary of State in connection with his functions under—

(a) this Act,

(b) the Pensions Act 1995, or

(c) the Pensions Act 2004,

other than information supplied to him under section 235(2) of, or paragraph 2 of Schedule 10 to, the Pensions Act 2004 (supply of information for retirement planning purposes etc.)."

27 In section 168(4) (penalties for contravention of regulations) after "the provision" insert "to be required by notice in writing".

28 In section 175 (levies)—

(a) for subsection (8) substitute—

"(8) An amount payable by a person on account of a levy imposed under this section shall be a debt due from him to the Secretary of State, and an amount so payable shall be recoverable by the Secretary of State accordingly or, if the Secretary of State so determines, by the Regulatory Authority on his behalf.", and

(b) in subsection (9) for "subsections (1) and (4)" substitute "subsection (1)".

29 In section 178 (power to make regulations as to the persons to be regarded as trustees or managers of schemes for certain purposes), in paragraph (b) for "to 26C" substitute "to 26".

30 (1) Section 179 (linked qualifying service) is amended as follows.

(2) In subsection (1)(a)—

(a) for "the rules of a scheme" substitute "Chapter 4 or 5 of Part 4 or under the rules of a scheme",

(b) for sub-paragraph (i) substitute—

"(i) there was made a transfer of his rights (including any transfer credits allowed) under that scheme, or a transfer payment in respect of those rights, to, or to the trustees or managers of, another scheme applying to him in the later period of service;",

(c) for "and" at the end of sub-paragraph (ii), substitute "or", and

(d) after that sub-paragraph insert—

"(iii) a cash equivalent (within the meaning of Chapter 4 of Part 4) or cash transfer sum (within the meaning of Chapter 5 of that Part) was paid in respect of him to the trustees or managers of another scheme applying to him in the later period of service; and".

(3) In subsection (1)(b), after "second scheme," insert "or the payment to the trustees or managers of that scheme,".

31 In section 181(1) (general interpretation), in the definition of "transfer credits", for the words following "by reference to" substitute "—

(a) a transfer to the scheme of, or transfer payment to the trustees or managers of the scheme in respect of, any of his rights (including transfer credits allowed) under another occupational pension scheme or a personal pension scheme, other than rights attributable (directly or indirectly) to a pension credit, or

(b) a cash transfer sum paid under Chapter 5 of Part 4 in respect of him, to the trustees or managers of the scheme;".

32  In section 183(3) (sub-delegation), after "97(1)" insert, "101AF(1)".

33  In section 192(2) (provisions extending to Northern Ireland)—
    (a) for "section 145 (except subsections (4)" substitute "section 145 (except subsections (4A) to (4C)", and
    (b) at the appropriate place insert—
    "section 145A (except subsection (6)(b)),".

*Pensions Act 1995 (c. 26)*

34  The Pensions Act 1995 is amended as follows.

35  In section 4 (suspension orders), in subsections (3) and (5) for "class" substitute "description".

36  In section 7 (appointment of trustees)—
    (a) in subsection (1) omit "a trustee of such a scheme ceases to be a trustee", and
    (b) in subsection (2) for "section 23(1)(b)" in both places substitute "section 23(1)".

37  In section 9 (removal and appointment of trustees: property), after "exercise" insert "by order".

38  In section 10 (civil penalties), in subsection (5)(a) omit "as a trustee of a trust scheme".

39  In section 15(4) (failure to comply with Authority's direction) for "sections 3 and 10 apply" substitute "section 10 applies".

40  In section 22 (circumstances in which independent trustee provisions apply), in subsections (1) and (3) for "to 26A", in each place, substitute "to 26".

41  In section 25 (appointment and powers of independent trustees: further provisions)—
    (a) in subsection (1) for "section 23(1)(b)" substitute "section 23(1)",
    (b) in subsection (2)—
        (i) after "a scheme" insert "and there is an independent trustee of the scheme appointed under section 23(1)", and
        (ii) omit from "but if" to the end,
    (c) in subsection (3) for ", no independent trustee of the scheme may" substitute "and there is an independent trustee of the scheme appointed under section 23(1), the independent trustee may not", and
    (d) in subsection (4)—
        (i) for "section 23(1)(b)" substitute "section 23(1)", and
        (ii) after "person" insert "(within the meaning of section 23(3))".

42  In section 26 (insolvency practitioner or official receiver to give information to trustees), in subsection (1) after "a scheme" insert "by virtue of subsection (1) of that section".

43  Sections 26A to 26C are hereby repealed.

44  In section 28 (consequences of prohibition on trustee being auditor of scheme etc) omit subsection (4).

45  In section 29 (persons disqualified for being trustees), in subsection (5) for "class" substitute "description".

46  In section 30 (persons disqualified: consequences)—
    (a) in subsection (2), after "exercise" insert "by order", and
    (b) omit subsections (7) and (8).

47  Omit section 30A (accessibility of register of disqualified trustees).
48  In section 32 (decisions of trustees by a majority)—
    (a) in subsection (4) for, "16(3)(b) and 25(2)" substitute "and 25(2) of this Act and section 241(6) of the Pensions Act 2004", and
    (b) in subsection (5) for "sections 3 and 10 apply" substitute "section 10 applies".
49  In section 34 (powers of investment and delegation) in subsection (1) after "subject to" insert "section 36(1) and to".
50  (1) Section 38 (power to defer winding up) is amended as follows.
    (2) In subsection (2)—
        (a) in paragraph (a) after "scheme" insert "(other than those due to be paid before the determination is made)", and
        (b) in paragraph (b) omit "new".
    (3) After subsection (3) insert—
        "(4) This section also does not apply in relation to a trust scheme where the trustees are required to wind up, or continue the winding up, of the scheme under section 154(1) of the Pensions Act 2004 (requirement to wind up certain schemes with sufficient assets to meet protected liabilities)."
51  In section 40 (restriction on employer-related investments), in subsection (4) for "sections 3 and 10 apply" substitute "section 10 applies".
52  In section 41 (provision of documents for members)—
    (a) for subsection (3) substitute—
        "(3) The documents referred to in subsection (1)(b) are—
            (a) any statement of funding principles prepared or revised under section 223 of the Pensions Act 2004,
            (b) any valuation or report prepared by the actuary under section 224 of that Act,
            (c) any certificate given by the actuary under section 225 or 227 of that Act.", and
    (b) in subsection (5B) for "sections 3 and 10 apply to any trustee, and section 10 applies" substitute "section 10 applies to any trustee, and".
53  In section 47 (professional advisers), in subsections (3), (8) and (11) for "sections 3 and 10 apply to any trustee, and section 10 applies" substitute "section 10 applies to any trustee, and".
54  In section 49 (other responsibilities of trustees, employers, etc)—
    (a) in subsection (6) for "sections 3 and 10 apply" substitute "section 10 applies", and
    (b) in subsection (10)—
        (i) omit paragraph (a) and the word "and" immediately after it, and
        (ii) in paragraph (b) for "such steps" substitute "reasonable steps to secure compliance".
55  In section 49A (record of winding up decisions) omit subsection (4).
56  In section 68 (power of trustees to modify schemes by resolution), in subsection (2)—
    (a) in paragraph (b), for "section 16(1) or 17(2)" substitute "section 241 of the Pensions Act 2004", and
    (b) for paragraph (c) substitute—
        "(c) to enable the scheme to comply with such terms and conditions as may be imposed by the Board of the Pension Protection Fund in relation to any payment made by it under section 185 or 186 of the Pensions Act 2004,".

57 In section 69 (grounds for applying for modifications)—
- (a) in subsection (2) for "about the manner of dealing with applications under this section" substitute "requiring applications under this section to meet prescribed requirements",
- (b) in subsection (3) omit paragraph (a),
- (c) in subsection (4)(a) omit "(a) or", and
- (d) in subsection (5)(a) omit "either of" and for "subsection (3)(a) or (b)" substitute "subsection (3)(b)".

58 In section 71A(4)(d) (power to make provision in relation to applications for the purposes of that section)—
- (a) for "before such time as may be prescribed" substitute "before an application is made for the purposes of this section", and
- (b) for "an application for the purposes of this section" substitute "the application".

59 In section 72A (reports to Authority about winding up) omit subsection (9)(a) and "and" immediately after it.

60 In section 72C (duty to comply with directions for facilitating winding up) omit subsection (2).

61 In section 73 (preferential liabilities on winding up) in subsection (6), omit paragraph (a) and "and" immediately after it.

62 In section 76 (excess assets on winding up)—
- (a) in subsection (3), omit paragraph (c) (but not the word "and" immediately following it),
- (b) omit subsection (5), and
- (c) in subsection (6) for "sections 3 and 10 apply" substitute "section 10 applies".

63 In section 77 (excess assets remaining after winding up: power to distribute)—
- (a) omit subsections (2) and (3),
- (b) in subsection (4)—
  - (i) for the opening words substitute "Where this section applies-", and
  - (ii) in paragraph (a) for "those assets" substitute "the undistributed assets", and
- (c) in subsection (5) for "sections 3 and 10 apply" substitute "section 10 applies".

64 In section 87 (schedules of payment to money purchase schemes) omit subsection (5)(a) and "and" immediately after it.

65 In section 88 (provision supplementary to section 87) omit subsection (4)(a) and "and" immediately after it.

66 In section 89 (application of further provisions to money purchase schemes)—
- (a) in subsection (1)(a)—
  - (i) for "sections 56 to 60" substitute "Part 3 of the Pensions Act 2004", and
  - (ii) for "those sections" substitute "that Part", and
- (b) in subsection (2) omit "insolvency".

67 In section 118 (powers to modify Part 1 of the Pensions Act 1995)—
- (a) in subsection (2) for "to 26C" substitute "to 26", and
- (b) omit subsection (3).

68 In section 119 (calculations etc under regulations: sub-delegation), for "73(3)" substitute "73B(4)(a)".

69 (1) Section 124 (interpretation of Part 1) is amended as follows.
   (2) In subsection (1), in the definition of "transfer credits", for the words following "by reference to" substitute "—
   (a) a transfer to the scheme of, or transfer payment to the trustees or managers

of the scheme in respect of, any of his rights (including transfer credits allowed) under another occupational pension scheme or a personal pension scheme, other than pension credit rights, or

(b) a cash transfer sum paid under Chapter 5 of Part 4 of the Pension Schemes Act 1993 (early leavers) in respect of him, to the trustees or managers of the scheme,".

(3) In subsection (3A), after "(3E)" insert "and to sections 28, 154 and 219 of the Pensions Act 2004".

(4) In subsection (3B), after "(3E)" insert "and to sections 154 and 219 of the Pensions Act 2004".

*Bank of England Act 1998 (c. 11)*

70 In Schedule 7 to the Bank of England Act 1998 (restriction on disclosure of information), in the table in paragraph 3(1), for the entry relating to the Occupational Pensions Regulatory Authority substitute—
"*The Pensions Regulator*
Functions conferred by or by virtue of—
(a) the Pension Schemes Act 1993,
(b) the Pensions Act 1995,
(c) the Welfare Reform and Pensions Act 1999,
(d) the Pensions Act 2004, or
(e) any enactment in force in Northern Ireland corresponding to an enactment mentioned in paragraphs (a) to (d) above."

*Welfare Reform and Pensions Act 1999 (c. 30)*

71 The Welfare Reform and Pensions Act 1999 is amended as follows.

72 In section 1 (stakeholder pension schemes), in subsection (6), after "members etc)" insert "and of regulations under section 237 of the Pensions Act 2004 (combined pension forecasts)".

73 In section 2 (registration of stakeholder pension schemes)—
(a) in subsection (1) for "Occupational Pensions Regulatory Authority ("the Authority")" substitute "Authority",
(b) in subsection (3) after "may" insert "by direction", and
(c) in subsection (4) for the words from "Section 3" to "Act applies" substitute "Section 10 of the Pensions Act 1995 ("the 1995 Act") (civil penalties) applies to any trustee of a pension scheme which is or has been registered under this section, and".

74 In section 8(2)(a) (providing for stakeholder pension schemes to be treated as personal pension schemes), after "is" insert "prescribed or is".

75 In section 38 (treatment in winding up)—
(a) in subsection (2), for "section 56 of the Pensions Act 1995" substitute "this section", and
(b) after that subsection insert—
"(2A) This section applies to an occupational pension scheme other than—
(a) a money purchase scheme, or
(b) a prescribed scheme or a scheme of a prescribed description."

76 (1) Paragraph 1 of Schedule 1 (application of enactments relating to occupational schemes to certain stakeholder schemes) is amended as follows.
  (2) In sub-paragraph (2), in paragraph (b)—
    (a) in sub-paragraph (i) for the words from "except" to the end substitute "except sections 7(5A)(b), 8(1)(a) and (c) and (2), 11(3A) and (3B) and 15(1),
    (b) in sub-paragraph (ii) for "31" substitute "30",
    (c) in sub-paragraph (iii) omit the words from "except" to the end,
    (d) for sub-paragraph (v) substitute—
      "(v) section 47 (professional advisers);", and
    (e) in sub-paragraph (vii) for "section 50" substitute "sections 50 to 50B".
  (3) After that paragraph insert "; and
    (c) the following provisions of the Pensions Act 2004—
      (i) section 67 (accessibility of register of prohibited trustees);
      (ii) Chapters 4 and 5 of Part 2 (fraud compensation and information gathering);
      (iii) sections 247 to 249 (requirements for knowledge and understanding); and
      (iv) section 318 (interpretation)."
  (4) In sub-paragraph (5), after "1995 Act" insert, "and section 318(1) of the Pensions Act 2004,".
  (5) After sub-paragraph (5) insert—
    "(6) Chapters 4 and 5 of Part 2 of the Pensions Act 2004 (as applied by sub-paragraph (1)) shall have effect with such modifications as the Secretary of State may prescribe by regulations."

77 (1) Schedule 5 (pension credits: mode of discharge) is amended as follows.
  (2) In paragraph 8(1)(b), for the words from "section 56" to "related schemes)" substitute "Part 3 of the Pensions Act 2004 (scheme funding)".
  (3) After paragraph 13 insert—
    "13A The provisions of this Schedule are subject to—
      (a) section 73A(3) and (6) of the Pensions Act 1995 (prohibition on new members during winding up of scheme: exception for discharge of pension credit derived from the scheme), and
      (b) section 133(2) and (8) of the Pensions Act 2004 (prohibition on new members during an assessment period in relation to a scheme: exception for discharge of pension credit derived from the scheme)."

*Terrorism Act 2000 (c. 11)*

78 In Schedule 3A to the Terrorism Act 2000 (regulated sector and supervisory authorities), for paragraph 4(1)(f) substitute—
"(f) the Pensions Regulator;".

*Freedom of Information Act 2000 (c. 36)*

79 In Schedule 1 to the Freedom of Information Act 2000 (public authorities), in Part 6 insert at the appropriate place—
"The Pensions Regulator."

**sch 12, Pensions Act 2004**

"The Board of the Pension Protection Fund."
"The Ombudsman for the Board of the Pension Protection Fund."

*Proceeds of Crime Act 2002 (c. 29)*

80  In Schedule 9 to the Proceeds of Crime Act 2002 (regulated sector and supervisory authorities), for paragraph 4(1)(f) substitute—
"(f) the Pensions Regulator;".

## SCHEDULE 13

Section 320

## REPEALS AND REVOCATIONS

### PART 1
### REPEALS

| Short title and chapter | Extent of repeal |
| --- | --- |
| Parliamentary Commissioner Act 1967 (c. 13) | In Schedule 2, the entries relating to—<br>(a) the Occupational Pensions Regulatory Authority, and<br>(b) the Pensions Compensation Board. |
| House of Commons Disqualification Act 1975 (c.24) | In Schedule 1, in Part 2, the entries relating to—<br>(a) the Occupational Pensions Regulatory Authority, and<br>(b) the Pensions Compensation Board. |
| Northern Ireland Assembly Disqualification Act 1975 (c.25) | In Schedule 1, in Part 2, the entries relating to—<br>(a) the Occupational Pensions Regulatory Authority, and<br>(b) the Pensions Compensation Board. |
| Tribunals and Inquiries Act 1992 (c. 53) | Section 10(5)(ba) and the word "or" immediately preceding it.<br>In Schedule 1, in Part 1, paragraph 35(g) and (h). |
| Pension Schemes Act 1993 (c. 48) | Section 6.<br>In section 28—<br>(a) in subsection (4), paragraphs (a) and (b) and the word "and" in paragraph (c),<br>(b) subsections (4A) and (4B), and<br>(c) in subsection (8), the words, "which must not be earlier than the member's 60th birthday," in the definition of "the starting date".<br>In section 29(1)(aa)(ii), the words from "and is not" to "75th birthday,".<br>In section 34(1)(a)(ii), the words "or category".<br>Section 99(6).<br>Section 101J(3).<br>Section 111.<br>Section 111A(10).<br>Section 111B.<br>In section 123, the definition of "occupational pension scheme" in subsection (3), and subsection (4).<br>In section 129—<br>(a) in subsection (2) the words from "and Chapter IV" to the end, and<br>(b) subsection (3)(b).<br>In section 131(b), the words "payable at any earlier time or". |

| Short title and chapter | Extent of repeal |
|---|---|
| | In section 132, the words from "or the voluntary" to third "requirements".
Section 148(5)(ba) and (bb).
Section 149(1), (1A) and (1B).
In section 149(3)—
  (a) paragraph (ba), and
  (b) paragraph (d) and the word "and" immediately preceding it.
In section 149(6)—
  (a) paragraph (c), and
  (b) the word "and" at the end of paragraph (k).
Section 149(8).
In section 151(1), paragraph (c) and the word "and" immediately preceding it.
In section 151(3)—
  (a) paragraphs (ba) and (bb), and
  (b) in paragraph (c) the words "any of paragraphs (a) to (bb)".
In section 158—
  (a) in subsection (6), the words "Subject to subsection (7)", and
  (b) subsection (7).
Section 168A.
In section 175—
  (a) in subsection (1), paragraph (a) and the word "or" at the end of paragraph (b), and
  (b) subsections (4) to (7).
In section 177(5)—
  (a) the word "and" at the end of paragraph (a), and
  (b) paragraph (b).
In section 181—
  (a) in subsection (1), the definitions of "the register", "the Registrar", and "voluntary contributions requirements",
  (b) in subsection (3), the words "section 6,", and
  (c) in subsection (4), the word "6,".
In section 192(2), the words "section 6(1) and (2) (except paragraph (a)(ii)), (3), (4), and (8),".
In Schedule 9, paragraphs 5 and 7(2). |
| Pensions Act 1995 (c. 26) | Sections 1 and 2.
Section 5.
In section 7(1), the words "a trustee of such a scheme ceases to be a trustee".
Section 7(4).
In section 10(5)(a), the words "as a trustee of a trust scheme".
Section 11(3).
Section 13.
Sections 16 to 21.
In section 22(1)(b), the word "or" at the end of sub-paragraph (i).
In section 25(2), the words from "but if" to the end.
Sections 26A to 26C. |

| Short title and chapter | Extent of repeal |
|---|---|
| | Section 28(4). |
| | In section 29— |
| |    (a) subsections (3), (4) and (5)(b), and |
| |    (b) in subsection (6), the words "or revocation made". |
| | In section 30— |
| |    (a) in subsection (2), paragraph (b) and the word "or" immediately preceding it, and |
| |    (b) subsections (7) and (8). |
| | Section 30A. |
| | Section 31. |
| | Section 36(2). |
| | In section 38(2)(b), the word "new". |
| | Section 41(2)(c). |
| | Section 48. |
| | In section 49, subsection (10)(a) and the word "and" immediately after it. |
| | Section 49A(4). |
| | In section 51(1), the word "and" at the end of sub-paragraph (i) of paragraph (a). |
| | In section 54(3), the definition of "appropriate percentage". |
| | Sections 56 to 61. |
| | In section 63(4)(c), the words "or category". |
| | In section 69— |
| |    (a) subsection (3)(a), |
| |    (b) in subsection (4)(a), the words "(a) or", and |
| |    (c) in subsection (5)(a), the words "either of". |
| | In section 71A(4), paragraphs (f) and (g). |
| | Section 72A(9)(a) and the word "and" immediately after it. |
| | Section 72B(7) and (8)(b). |
| | Section 72C(2). |
| | Section 73(6)(a) and the word "and" immediately after it. |
| | In section 74— |
| |    (a) in subsection (2) the words "(including increases in pensions)", |
| |    (b) in subsection (4) the words "(including increases in pensions)", and |
| |    (c) subsection (5)(b) and the word "or" immediately preceding it. |
| | Section 75(9). |
| | In section 76— |
| |    (a) subsection (3)(c) (but not the word "and" immediately following it), and |
| |    (b) subsection (5). |
| | Section 77(2) and (3). |
| | Sections 78 to 86. |
| | Section 87(5)(a) and the word "and" immediately after it. |
| | Section 88(4)(a) and the word "and" immediately after it. |
| | In section 89(2), the word "insolvency". |
| | Sections 96 to 114. |
| | In section 117(2)— |
| |    (a) at the end of paragraph (b), the word "or", and |

sch 13, Pensions Act 2004

| Short title and chapter | Extent of repeal |
|---|---|
| | (b) paragraph (c). |
| | Section 118(3). |
| | In section 119, the word "56(3),". |
| | In section 124(1)— |
| |   (a) in the definition of "employer", the words "or category", |
| |   (b) the definitions of "member-nominated director", "member-nominated trustee" and "minimum funding requirement", and |
| |   (c) in the definition of "pensionable service", the words "or category". |
| | Section 134(3). |
| | Section 142(5). |
| | In section 162(1), the word "and" at the end of paragraph (a). |
| | In section 175(2), the word "or" at the end of paragraph (c). |
| | In section 178(2), the words "1, 2, 21(3)" and "78, 79, 80(4)". |
| | Schedules 1 and 2. |
| | In Schedule 3, paragraphs 12, 21, 23 and 44(a)(ii). |
| | In Schedule 4, paragraph 21(13) and (14). |
| | In Schedule 5— |
| |   (a) paragraph 20, and |
| |   (b) paragraph 77(b) (but not the word "and" immediately following it). |
| | In Schedule 6, paragraph 6(d). |
| Criminal Procedure (Consequential Provisions) (Scotland) Act 1995 (c. 40) | In Schedule 4, paragraph 98. |
| Employment Rights Act 1996 (c. 18) | In section 58(3)(b), the words "or category". |
| Bank of England Act 1998 (c. 11) | In Part 4 of Schedule 5, paragraph 71. |
| Social Security Contributions (Transfer of Functions, Etc.) Act 1999 (c. 2) | In Schedule 1, paragraphs 67 and 68. |
| Welfare Reform and Pensions Act 1999 (c. 30) | Section 2(5) and (6). |
| | Sections 4 and 5. |
| | Section 17. |
| | Section 38(1). |
| | In section 46(1), in the definition of "pensionable service", the words "or category". |
| | Section 50(2). |
| | In Schedule 1— |
| |   (a) paragraph 1(2)(a), |
| |   (b) in paragraph 1(2)(b)(i) the word ", 13", |
| |   (c) in paragraph 1(2)(b)(iii), the words from "except" to the end, |
| |   (d) paragraph 1(2)(b)(ix) and (xi) to (xiii), and |
| |   (e) paragraphs 2 and 3. |
| | In Schedule 2, paragraphs 3(1)(a), 9 and 13 to 16. |
| | In Schedule 12, paragraphs 39(3), 44, 45 to 49, 53, 55 and 60. |

| | |
|---|---|
| Child Support, Pensions and Social Security Act 2000 (c. 19) | In section 42(7), the word "and" at the end of paragraph (c).<br>Sections 43 to 46.<br>Section 47(1), (2) and (4).<br>Section 54.<br>In Schedule 5—<br>  (a) paragraph 3(3) and (4),<br>  (b) paragraph 10,<br>  (c) paragraph 11, and<br>  (d) paragraph 12(2), (3) and (4).<br>In Schedule 9, Part 3(10). |
| Freedom of Information Act 2000 (c. 36) | In Schedule 1, in Part 6 the entries for—<br><br>  (a) the Occupational Pensions Regulatory Authority,<br>  (b) the Pensions Compensation Board, and<br>  (c) the Registrar of Occupational and Personal Pension Schemes. |
| Anti-terrorism, Crime and Security Act 2001 (c. 24) | In Part 1 of Schedule 4, paragraph 37. |
| Employment Act 2002 (c. 22) | In Schedule 6, paragraph 1(a) and (b). |

The repeals in sections 148, 149 and 151 of the Pension Schemes Act 1993 (c. 48) relate to those provisions as amended by section 54 of the Child Support, Pensions and Social Security Act 2000 (c. 19) to the extent that those amendments have been brought into force for the purpose of making regulations and rules.

## PART 2
## REVOCATIONS

| *Title and number* | *Extent of revocation* |
|---|---|
| Pensions (Northern Ireland) Order 1995 (S.I. 1995/3213 (N.I. 22)) | Article 78(4). |

# APPENDIX 2

# Useful Addresses

**Association of Consulting Actuaries**
Warnford Court
29 Throgmorton Street
London
EC2N 2AT
Tel: 020 7382 4594
www.aca.org.uk

**Association of Corporate Trustees**
W J Stephenson (Secretary)
3 Brackerne Close
Cooden
Bexhill-on-Sea
East Sussex
TN39 3BT
Tel: 01424 844 144
www.trustees.org.uk

**Association of Pension Lawyers**
c/o Pensions Management Institute
PMI House
4–10 Artillery Lane
London
E1 7LS
Tel: 0870 240 6036
www.apl.org.uk

**Chartered Insurance Institute**
20 Aldermanbury
London
EC2V 7HY
Tel: 020 7417 4415/6
Fax: 020 7972 0110
www.cii.co.uk

# Useful Addresses

**Data Protection Registrar**
Wycliffe House
Water Lane
Wilmslow
Cheshire
SK9 5AF
Tel: 01625 545 745
Fax: 01625 524 510
www.dataprotection.gov.uk

**Department for Work and Pensions**
Pensions Division
The Adelphi
1–11 John Adam Street
London
WC2N 6HT
www.dwp.gov.uk
www.thepensionservice.gov.uk

**European Federation for Retirement Provision (EFRP)**
Koningsstraat 97 rue Royale
B–1000 Brussels
Tel: 00 32 2 289 14 14
Fax: 00 32 2 289 14 15
www.efrp.org

**Faculty of Actuaries**
Maclaurin House
18 Dublin Street
Edinburgh
EH1 3PP
Tel: 0131 240 1300
www.actuaries.org.uk

**Financial Ombudsman Service**
South Quay Plaza
183 Marsh Wall
London
E14 9SR
Tel: 020 7964 1000
Fax: 020 7964 1001

**Financial Services Authority**
25 The North Colonnade
Canary Wharf
London
E14 5HS
Tel: 020 7676 1000
www.fsa.gov.uk

# Useful Addresses

**HMSO**
St. Clements House
2–16 Colegate
Norwich
NR3 1BQ
Tel: 01603 723 011
www.hmso.gov.uk

**Institute of Actuaries**
Staple Inn Hall
High Holborn
London
WC1V 7QJ
Tel: 020 7632 2100
www.actuaries.org.uk

**Institute of Chartered Accountants in England and Wales**
Chartered Accountants Hall
PO Box 433
London
EC2P 2BJ
Tel: 020 7920 8100
www.icaew.co.uk

**Institute of Chartered Accountants in Scotland**
27 Queen Street
Edinburgh
EH2 1LA
Tel: 0131 225 5673
www.icas.org.uk

**Institute of Financial Planning**
Whitefriars Centre
Lewins Mead
Bristol
BS1 2NT
Tel: 0117 945 2470
www.financialplanning.org.uk

**Law Society**
113 Chancery Lane
London
WC2A 1PL
Tel: 020 7242 1222
www.lawsoc.org.uk

# Useful Addresses

**Occupational Pensions Regulatory Authority**
Invicta House
Trafalgar Place
Brighton
East Sussex
BN1 4DW
Tel: 01273 627 600
www.opra.gov.uk

**OPAS**
11 Belgrave Road
London
SW1V 1RB
Tel: 0845 601 2923
Fax: 020 7233 8016
email: enquiries@opas.org.uk

**National Association of Pension Funds**
NIOC House
4 Victoria Street
London
SW1H 0NX
Tel: 020 7808 1300
Fax: 020 7222 7585
email: membership@napf.co.uk
www.napf.co.uk

**Pensions Compensation Board**
6th Floor
11 Belgrave Road
London
SW1V 1RB
Tel: 020 7828 9794

**Pensions Management Institute**
PMI House
4–10 Artillery Lane
London
E1 7LS
Tel: 020 7247 1452
www.pensions-pmi.org.uk

**Pensions Ombudsman**
11 Belgrave Road
London
SW1V 1RB
Tel: 020 7834 9144
Fax: 020 7821 0065
email: enquiries@pensions-ombudsman.org.uk
www.pensions-ombudsman.org.uk

## Useful Addresses

**Pensions Policy Institute**
King's College
4th Floor, Waterloo Bridge Wing
Franklin-Wilkins Building
Waterloo Road
London
SE1 9NN
Tel: 020 7848 3744
Fax: 020 7848 3235
email: info@pensionspolicyinstitute.org.uk
www.pensionspolicyinstitute.org.uk

**Pensions Research Accountants Group (PRAG)**
The Secretary
David Slade
c/o Deloitte & Touche
4 Brindleyplace
Birmingham
B1 2HZ
Tel: 0121 632 6000
email: dslade@deloitte.co.uk

**Pensions Scheme Registry**
PO Box 1NN
Newcastle upon Tyne
NE99 1NN
Tel: 0191 225 6393/4/8
www.opra.co.uk

**SIPP Provider Group**
Martin Cadman (Chairman)
c/o MC Trustees Limited
Enterprise House
Meadow Drive
Hampton in Arden
West Midlands
B92 0BD
Tel: 01675 444 600
email: martin@mctrustees.co.uk

**Society of Pensions Consultants**
St Bartholomew House
92 Fleet Street
London
EC4Y 1DG
Tel: 020 7353 1688/9
Fax: 020 7353 9296

# Useful Addresses

**The Stationery Office (TSO)**
PO Box 29
St Crispins
Duke Street
Norwich
NR3 1GN
Tel: 0870 600 5522
Fax: 0870 600 5533
email: book.orders@tso.co.uk
www.tso.co.uk/bookshop

# APPENDIX 3

# Useful Web References

*UK government websites*

**Financial Assistance Scheme**
www.fas.gov.uk

**Her Majesty's Stationery Office**
www.hmso.gov.uk
Fully searchable database of legislation and statutory instruments.

**The Pension Protection Fund**
www.ppf.gov.uk

**The Pensions Regulator**
www.thepensionsregulator.gov.uk

**The United Kingdom Parliament**
www.parliament.uk

*US pensions websites*

**Pension Benefit Guaranty Corporation**
www.pbgc.gov

*UK case law websites*

**Daily law notes**
www.lawreports.co.uk
Free summaries of key cases from the House of Lords, the Court of Appeal, and the High Court.

**Casetrack**
www.casetrack.com
Subscription-based service; full access to judgments of the High Court and the Court of Appeal.

**Lawtel**
www.lawtel.com
Subscription based database providing full access to case summaries and judgments from the High Court and the Court of Appeal.

**British and Irish Legal Information Institute**
www.bailii.org
Powerful search engine providing access to British and Commonwealth case law.

# Useful Web References

*International case law websites*

**European Court of Human Rights**
www.echr.coe.int
Access to basic texts and to decisions of the Court through the HUDOC search engine.

**European Court of Justice**
www.curia.eu.int/en
Access to basic texts and decisions of the European Court of Justice.

**EUR-Lex**
www.europa.eu.int/eur-lex/en/index.html
Portal website providing access to texts of treaties, legislation, case law, the *Official Journal of the European Union*, and other public documents.

# Index

accounts
  Pension Protection Fund (PPF) Board 3.21
accrued rights and entitlements
  scheme modification 9.78, 9.79, 9.92
Acquired Rights Directive 9.46, 9.50
actuarial valuation
  Pension Protection Fund (PPF) 3.21, 3.93
  scheme modification 9.84, 9.85, 9.95, 9.96, 9.97
Additional Voluntary Contributions (AVC) 2.23
  implementation timetable 1.22, 9.174, 9.175
  removal of requirement 1.22
addresses, useful App 2
administration levy
  Pension Protection Fund (PPF) Board 3.33–3.35
administrative expenses
  Pension Protection Fund (PPF) Board 3.32
  stakeholder pensions 9.206
admissible rules 3.125
adoption leave 9.170–9.172
Alderney 12.33
annual increases
  occupational pension schemes 9.188–9.191
  pension credits 9.194, 9.195
  personal pension schemes 9.192–9.193
annual report
  Pension Protection Fund Ombudsman 6.25
annual reports
  Pension Protection Fund (PPF) Board 3.36, 3.37
  Pensions Regulator 2.16
anti-avoidance
  Pension Protection Fund (PPF) 3.96, 3.97
appeals
  disputes, pension 9.105
  Financial Assistance Scheme 10.12
  Pensions Regulator Tribunal 2.90
assessment period
  Pension Protection Fund (PPF) 3.42, 3.70–3.94
    accrual of benefits 3.73, 3.99
    commencement 3.71
    contributions 3.73, 3.74
    creditor of employer, Board to act as 3.84
    directions 3.77–3.79
    discharging scheme liabilities 3.81
    duration 3.71, 3.72
    ill health provisions, reviewable 3.87–3.92
    new members 3.73
    payment of scheme benefits 3.85, 3.86
    purpose 3.70
    restrictions during 3.70, 3.73–3.76, 3.80–3.83
    review of ill health provisions 3.87–3.92
    transfers 3.81
    valuation of assets and liabilities 3.93, 3.94
assistance, provision of
  Pensions Regulator 1.29
assumption of responsibility *see under* Pension Protection Fund (PPF)
Australia
  reciprocal agreement with Australia 12.03, 12.32, 12.33
authorized period
  Fraud Compensation Fund 4.16, 4.17

bank guarantees
  financial support directions 2.45
Bank of England base rate
  definition 12.30
board
  Pensions Regulator 2.08
bogus transfers 2.07, 2.31
  *see also* pension liberation
borrowing
  Pension Protection Fund (PPF) Board 3.31
  trustees 9.04, 9.16

cessation of involvement with a scheme 3.98, 3.99
Chairman
  Pensions Regulator 2.08, 2.09
chief executive
  Pensions Regulator 2.08, 2.10
clearance procedure
  moral hazard legislation 2.04
  Pensions Regulator 2.04
closed schemes
  Pension Protection Fund (PPF) 3.105, 3.106, 3.112–3.117
codes of practice
  early leavers 9.165
  knowledge and understanding of trustees 9.20

# Index

codes of practice—*contd.*
  Member Nominated Trustees (MNT) 9.35
  Pensions Regulator 2.02, 2.07, 2.78–2.80
    approval 2.80
    areas covered by codes 2.78
    breach 2.79
    consultation 2.80
    failure to observe codes 2.79
    issue of codes 2.78, 2.79
combined pension forecasts 8.09–8.13
commutation
  lump sum 3.127
  restrictions 9.201–9.204
compensation
  fraud *see* Fraud Compensation Fund
  maladministration 6.18
  Pension Protection Fund Ombudsman 6.32, 6.35
  Pension Protection Fund (PPF) *see* Pension Protection Fund (PPF)
  Pensions Compensation Board (PCB) *see* Pensions Compensation Board (PCB)
complaints to PPF Board 6.05–6.18
  maladministration complaints 6.15–6.18
    compensation 6.18
    decision-making 6.17
    initial decisions 6.16
    investigation 6.16
    procedure 6.15
    process for making complaints 6.17
    relevant complaints 6.15
    time limits 6.17
  review of Board determinations 6.05–6.14
    application process 6.13
    completion of review/reconsideration 6.11
    decision-making 6.14
    failure by Board to make determination 6.06
    interested person 6.10
    issues, dealing with 6.12
    notice of application 6.13
    powers of Board 6.11
    reconsideration decision 6.10
    review decision 6.10
    reviewable matter 6.05
    suspension of effect of decision of Board 6.07
    two-stage process 6.09
connected persons
  financial support directions 2.46, 2.47
consultation by employers 9.62–9.76
  active members 9.71
  background 9.62–9.66
  deferred members 9.71
  definition of employer 9.70
  exempt employers 9.70
  failure to comply with duties 9.74
  ICE Regulations 9.75

  implementation timetable 1.19
  inadequate 9.74
  individuals requiring consultation 9.71
  information 9.74
  limited alterations 9.69
  major significant changes 9.67, 9.68
  new duty 9.67–9.76
  occupational pension schemes 9.67–9.71
  pensioners 9.71
  personal pension schemes 9.72
  prospective members 9.71
  regulations 9.73
  relationship with other duties 9.75
  secondary legislation 9.73
  types of decision covered 9.68
contracting out 9.198–9.204
  age at which benefits may be received 9.201–9.204
  commutation, restrictions on 9.201–9.204
  implementation timetable 1.22
  Inland Revenue approval 9.200
  stakeholder pensions 9.207
  working life, meaning of 9.198, 9.199
contribution notices
  application 2.39
  apportionment of liability 2.36
  Avoidance of Employer Debt 2.35
  calculation of payment 2.34, 2.36
  deliberate act or omission 2.34, 2.35, 2.38
  exercise of powers 2.37
  good faith, absence of 2.37
  guidance 2.37
  impact 1.26
  imposing liability 2.37
  imposition 1.26
  limitation periods 2.39
  main purpose as avoidance of s 75 debt 2.37
  moral hazard legislation 1.26, 2.34
  party to act or deliberate failure 2.38
  purpose 2.34
  reasonable grounds 2.37
  reasonableness 2.37
  requirement to pay 2.35
  sum required 2.36
  test case 2.37
  time limits 2.39
contributions
  Additional Voluntary Contributions (AVC) *see* Additional Voluntary Contributions (AVC)
  employer 9.176–9.182
    enforcement by Pensions Regulator 2.19
    late payment 9.177, 9.178
    occupational pension schemes 9.179–9.182
    personal pension schemes 9.177, 9.178
    records 9.178
    unpaid 2.19

notices *see* contribution notices
occupational pension schemes 9.150–9.154, 9.179–9.182
personal pension schemes 9.177, 9.178
schedule of 1.29, 7.09
unpaid employer 1.29, 2.19
voluntary 9.174, 9.175
council tax 8.08
cross border pensions 11.01–11.30
  *see also* EU Pensions Directive
  commentary 11.29, 11.30
  European pensions institution 11.22
  European scheme of UK employer
    definition of UK employer 11.22
    duties of Regulator 11.16–11.22
    restrictions on disposal of UK-held assets 11.23–11.28
  Home State 11.02
  Host State 11.02
  implementation timetable 1.16
  meaning of cross border activity 11.02
  relevant legal requirements 11.22
  UK scheme with European employer
    authorization for particular employer 11.07–11.10
    conditions 11.03, 11.04
    general authorization 11.05, 11.06
    notification by Host State of legal requirements 11.11, 11.12
    ringfencing assets 11.15
    UK trustees to act in accordance with Host State's legal requirements 11.13, 11.14

death in service pensions
  scheme modification 9.93
defined benefits
  freezing orders 2.25
  winding up scheme 2.22
delegation
  Pension Protection Fund (PPF) Board 3.18–3.20
  Pensions Regulator 2.10
deposit taker
  meaning 3.31
Deputy Pension Protection Fund Ombudsman 6.20, 6.22
Deputy Pensions Ombudsman *see under* Pensions Ombudsman
design of scheme *see* scheme design
determination notice
  Pension Protection Fund (PPF) 3.53
  Pensions Regulator 2.86
Determinations Panel 2.12–2.15
  appointments 2.12
  decision-making 2.82
  duties 2.15
  establishment 2.12
  functions 2.13

membership 2.12
referrals to 2.13
remit 2.12, 2.13
reserved regulatory functions 2.14
responsibilities 2.15
role 2.06
structure 2.12, 2.13
detrimental modification 9.82
disclosure
  Pension Protection Fund Board 5.18–5.28
  Pensions Regulator 2.73–2.76
  State pensions 12.03, 12.31
disputes, pension 9.100–9.142
  appeals 9.105
  application for decision 9.108
  commencement of new regime 9.111
  definition 9.107
  disagreements 9.107
  employment law procedures 9.105
  every member of scheme is trustee, schemes where 9.112
  excluded disputes 9.113
  existing complaints 9.111
  generally 9.100
  IDRP Regulations 9.101, 9.102
  interest in scheme, person with 9.108, 9.115–9.117
  internal dispute resolution procedure 9.101–9.104
  minimum requirements 9.110
  new requirements 9.101–9.105
  non-dependant beneficiaries 9.104, 9.115, 9.116
  penalties 9.114
  Pensions Ombudsman *see* Pensions Ombudsman
  potential complainants 9.104
  practical impact of changes 9.105
  reasonable period 9.109
  reduction of two-stage procedure 9.104, 9.105
  requirement for dispute resolution 9.106–9.114
  review of existing procedures 9.105
  small schemes 9.105
  time limits 9.102, 9.109
disqualification
  trustees 2.28

early leavers
  calculation of refund of contributions 9.168
  cash transfer sum 9.165, 9.167
  code of practice 9.165
  immediate vesting of benefits 9.166
  information on options 9.165
  money purchase schemes 9.168
  reasonable period to exercise rights 9.165
  scheme design 9.164–9.169

# Index

early leavers—*contd.*
  statutory rights 9.164, 9.165
  waiting periods for entitlement to join scheme 9.169
early leavers, transfer options for
  implementation timetable 1.21
early retirement 9.47, 9.48
education
  Pensions Regulator 1.29, 2.01, 2.02, 2.07, 2.17–2.20
eligible scheme 3.58, 3.59, 4.07, 4.14
employer
  consultation *see* consultation by employers
  contributions 9.176–9.182
    enforcement by Pensions Regulator 2.19
    late payment 9.177, 9.178
    occupational pension schemes 9.179–9.182
    personal pension schemes 9.177, 9.178
    records 9.178
    unpaid 2.19
  obligations 9.45–9.76
    consultation *see* consultation
    generally 9.45
    transfer of employment, pension protection on *see* transfers
  payment of surpluses to 9.147–9.149
  transfer of employment, pension protection on *see* transfers
employer opt-out 9.31, 9.32, 9.34
Employer Task Force on Pensions 1.05
employment-related benefit schemes
  definition 9.172
entry of premises
  Pensions Protection Fund Board 5.04–5.07
equal treatment
  Pension Protection Fund (PPF) 3.140
EU Pensions Directive
  aim 11.02
  implementation 7.01, 9.06, 9.155
  investment power of trustees 9.06
  investment powers 9.06
  requirements 7.01
  statutory funding objective 7.05
European Convention on Human Rights
  financial planning for retirement 8.03
expenses
  Pension Protection Fund Ombudsman 6.19
  Pension Protection Fund (PPF) Board 3.32

final notice
  Pensions Regulator 2.87
final salary schemes
  Pensions Compensation Board (PCB) 4.02
Finance Act 2004 1.02
Financial Assistance Scheme 3.07, 10.01–10.17
  aim 1.12, 10.01

  appeals 10.12
  background 10.01, 10.02
  capped payments 10.07
  costs 10.05
  discretions 10.12
  eligibility 10.06
  establishment 10.03
  ethical duty to act 10.02
  fair distribution 10.07
  framework provision 10.03, 10.08–10.14
  funding 10.14
  government research 10.02
  grants 10.12
  implementation timetable 1.12, 10.04
  insufficient assets 10.11
  management 10.12
  OPRA guidance 10.16, 10.17
  payments 10.12
  Pensions Regulator 10.12
  PPF Board 10.12
  practical issues 10.15–10.17
  purpose 1.12, 10.01
  qualifying members 10.08, 10.09
  qualifying pension schemes 10.08, 10.10
  regulations 10.03, 10.12
  review of determinations 10.12
  scheme manager 10.12
  transfer of scheme property 10.12
financial planning for retirement 8.01–8.19
  combined pension forecasts 8.09–8.13
  employer information 8.14–8.19
  European Convention on Human Rights 8.03
  government-held information 8.06–8.08
  Green Paper *Simplicity, Security and Choice: Working and Saving for Retirement* 2.01
  information
    employers providing 8.14–8.19
    failure to provide 8.18
    government-held 8.06–8.08
    provision 8.05
    use of 8.06–8.08
  internet-based retirement planner 8.04
  legislation 8.04–8.19
  use of information 8.06–8.08
financial support directions 2.34, 2.40–2.47
  associated persons 2.46, 2.47
  bank guarantees 2.45
  connected persons 2.46, 2.47
  financial support 2.45
  funding arrangements 2.45
  inappropriate arrangements 2.47
  insufficiently resourced employer 2.40, 2.41
  joint and several liability 2.40, 2.45
  lapsed arrangements 2.47
  maximum liability 2.47
  Pensions Regulator 2.34
  policy 2.40–2.44

# Index

reasonableness 2.44, 2.47
service company 2.40, 2.42
top holding company taking liabilities 2.45
Fraud Compensation Fund 3.25
  administration of 4.04, 4.28
  application 4.15–4.17
  assets 4.28
  authorized period 4.16, 4.17
  cases where compensation payments can be made 4.05–4.17
    conditions 4.05
    eligible scheme 4.07, 4.14
    going concern, employer unlikely to continue as 4.13
    prescribed offences 4.09
    qualifying insolvency event 4.10, 4.11, 4.12
    relevant date 4.08
    s 182(2) 4.10, 4.11, 4.12
    s 182(3) 4.10, 4.13
    s 182(4) 4.10, 4.14
  Crown guarantee 4.07
  dishonesty 4.09
  eligible schemes 4.07
  establishment 4.01
  exercise of powers in relation to 3.29
  expenditure 4.29
  functions of PCB 4.04
  income 4.28
  levy 4.30–4.33
  liabilities 4.28
  payments *see* fraud compensation payments
  Pension Protection Fund, relationship with 3.141, 3.142, 4.25–4.27
  role 4.01
Fraud Compensation Levy 3.29, 4.30–4.33
fraud compensation payments
  *see also* Fraud Compensation Fund
  amount 4.22
  cases where compensation payments can be made 4.05–4.17
  definition 4.05
  interim payments 4.23, 4.24
  payment received 4.20
  receipt 4.21
  recoveries of value 4.19, 4.20
  recovery 4.19
  repayment terms 4.21
  settlement date 4.19
  terms on which paid 4.18–4.22
freezing orders
  ancillary orders 2.27
  defined benefits 2.25
  directions 2.25
  duration 2.27
  effect 2.26
  extending 2.27
  new order issued 2.27

notification 2.27
Pensions Regulator 2.03, 2.05, 2.07, 2.25–2.27
purpose 2.07, 2.26
revocation 2.27
suspension of terms 2.25
temporary nature 2.27
variation of terms 2.25
winding up scheme 2.27
fund managers
  Pension Protection Fund (PPF) Board 3.29
funding *see* scheme funding

Goode Committee 1.09, 9.77
Green Paper *Simplicity, Security and Choice: Working and saving for Retirement* 2.01
  financial planning for retirement 8.01
  Minimum Funding Requirement (MFR) 7.02
  OPRA 2.01
  Pension Protection Fund (PPF) 3.05, 3.06
  Pensions Regulator 2.01
  proposals 2.01
  scheme specific funding standard 7.03
  trustee duties 9.06
group actions
  Pensions Ombudsman 9.123, 9.138–9.142
group reorganizations 1.28
guaranteed minimum pension
  Pension Protection Fund (PPF) 3.134
Guernsey 12.33
guidelines
  Pensions Regulator 2.02

Herm 12.33
Home State
  cross border pensions 11.02
Host State
  cross border pensions 11.02
housing benefit 8.08

ICE Regulations 9.75
ill health provisions 3.87–3.92
implementation timetable 1.07–1.23
  Additional Voluntary Contributions (AVC) 1.22
  April 2005 1.08–1.13
  September 2005 1.14–1.16
  April 2006 1.17–1.23
  contracting out 1.22
  cross border pensions 1.16
  early leavers, transfer options for 1.21
  employer consultation 1.19
  financial assistance scheme 1.12, 10.04
  internal dispute resolution procedures 1.14
  knowledge and understanding of trustees 1.18, 9.28

# Index

implementation timetable—*contd.*
  Limited Price Indexation (LPI) 1.10
  Member Nominated Trustees (MNT) 1.17, 9.35
  Pension Protection Fund (PPF) 1.09, 3.01
  Pensions Regulator 1.08
  regulations 1.27
  scheme amendments 1.19
  scheme modification 1.20
  Statement of Funding Principles 1.15
  statement of investment principles 9.12
  Statutory Funding Objective (SFO) 1.15
  surpluses 1.22
  transfer, pension protection on 1.11, 9.61
  winding up, statutory order on 1.13
improvement notices
  directions 2.18
  guidance 2.18
  issue 2.07
  objective 2.18
  Pensions Regulator 1.29, 2.07, 2.18
  preventative steps 2.18
  remedies 2.18
  requirements 2.18
inalienability of occupational pension 9.173
incapacity
  Pensions Ombudsman 9.125
Independent Pensions Commission
  establishment 1.03
  long-term structure of private pensions 1.04
  role 1.03
  Turner Report 1.05
  voluntary UK pension provision regime 1.05
  work plan 1.03
independent trustee
  appointment 2.03, 2.30
information gathering
  penalties 5.08–5.17
  Pension Protection Fund Board 5.01–5.28
    altering documents 5.10
    concealing documents 5.10
    criminal sanctions 5.01
    destruction of documents 5.10
    disclosure of information by Board 5.18–5.28
    entry of premises 5.04–5.07
    failure to supply information 5.08–5.10
    false or misleading information, provision of 5.15–5.17
    generally 5.01
    issue of warrants 5.11–5.14
    notices requiring provision of information 5.03
    penalties 5.08–5.17
    powers to obtain information 5.03–5.07
    provision of information to members of scheme and others 5.23–5.27
    purpose of powers 5.01
    refusal to supply information 5.08–5.10
    requirement to disclose information to Board 5.02
    restricted information 5.18–5.22
    scheme premises 5.04, 5.06
    warrants, issue of 5.11–5.14
  Pensions Regulator 2.65–2.76
    confidentiality 2.73
    disclosure for tax purposes 2.74–2.76
    failure to comply 2.69
    misleading information 2.72
    premises, inspection of 2.66–2.68
    provision of false information 2.72
    provision of information 2.65
    restricted information 2.73, 2.75
    retention of documents 2.71
    warrants 2.70, 2.71
  reports 2.77, 5.28
information provision
  Pensions Regulator 1.29, 2.01, 2.02, 2.07, 2.17–2.20
initial levy 3.146–3.148
injunction application
  Pensions Regulator 2.19
insolvency
  date 3.48
  event 3.48, 4.10, 4.11, 4.12
  Pension Protection Fund (PPF) *see under* Pension Protection Fund (PPF)
insolvency practitioner
  Pension Protection Fund (PPF) 3.46, 3.49
Institute and Faculty of Actuaries 9.97
interim payments 4.23, 4.24
internal dispute resolution procedures
  implementation timetable 1.14
  simplification 1.14
intervention powers
  Pensions Regulator 1.29
investment powers
  Pension Protection Fund (PPF) Board 3.29–3.31
  Pensions Directive 9.06
  statement of investment principles 9.08–9.12
    balance between investments 9.09
    considerations affecting investments 9.09
    contents 9.09
    exempt schemes 9.09
    exercise of rights 9.09
    expected returns 9.09
    form 9.09
    implementation timetable 9.09, 9.12
    kind of investments 9.09
    maintenance 9.09
    penalties 9.11
    preparation 9.09

# Index

restrictions 9.10
review 9.08, 9.09
risk 9.09
trustees 9.04
  choice of investment 9.13–9.15
  Green Paper 9.06
  power to make regulations governing investment 9.13–9.15
  statement of investment principles 9.08–9.12

Jersey 12.33
Jethou 12.33

knowledge and understanding of trustees
  all members are trustees, schemes where 9.25
  case law 9.17
  code of practice 9.20
  corporate trustees 9.24
  degree of 9.20
  education 9.27
  enforcement 9.27
  funding/investment sub-committee 9.22
  implementation timetable 1.18, 9.28
  individual trustees 9.18–9.23
  irrelevant knowledge 9.21
  law 9.19
  matters requiring familiarity 9.18
  nature of duty 9.21
  newly appointed trustees 9.25
  Pensions Regulator 1.30
  prescribed circumstances in which requirements disapplied 9.25
  requirement 9.04, 9.17–9.28
  rules of law 9.26
  sole trustees 9.25
  training 9.23

lay trusteeship 9.07
Legal Assistance Scheme
  Pensions Regulator Tribunal 2.91
levies
  administration
    Pension Protection Fund (PPF) Board 3.33–3.35
  fraud compensation 4.30–4.33
  Pension Protection Fund (PPF) 1.25, 1.26, 3.01, 3.145–3.162
    calculation 3.151–3.162
    initial levy 3.146–3.148
    levy ceiling 3.151–3.162
    risk-based levy 3.149
    scheme-based levy 3.150
  Pensions Regulator 2.04
levy ceiling 3.151–3.162
limitation periods
  contribution notices 2.39

Limited Price Indexation (LPI) 9.147
  implementation timetable 1.10
  meaning 1.10
LPI *see* Limited Price Indexation (LPI)

maladministration
  compensation 6.18
  complaints to PPF Board *see under* complaints to PPF Board
  Pension Protection Fund Ombudsman 6.33
  Pensions Ombudsman 9.135
Member Nominated Directors of Corporate Trustees (MND)
  background 9.29–9.33
  employer opt-out 9.31, 9.32
  original provisions 9.30–9.32
Member Nominated Trustees (MNT) 1.24, 9.29–9.44
  background 9.29–9.33
  code of practice 9.35
  company as trustee 9.42
  definition 9.36
  employer opt-out 9.31, 9.32
    removal 9.34
  exempt schemes 9.40
  failure to take reasonable steps to comply 9.41
  implementation timetable 1.17, 9.35
  insufficient nominations 9.37
  new provisions 9.34–9.44
  nomination 9.36, 9.37
  not member of scheme, person 9.38
  original provisions 9.29–9.32
  penalties 9.41
  rationale 9.43
  reasonable period to ensure 9.35
  removal 9.39
  selection 9.36, 9.37
Minimum Funding Requirement (MFR)
  abolition 1.15, 1.28, 7.01, 7.03
  concerns raised by 7.02
  Green Paper 7.02
MND *see* Member Nominated Directors (MND)
MNT *see* Member Nominated Trustees (MNT)
modifications to schemes *see* scheme modification
money purchase schemes
  early leavers 9.168
  Pension Protection Fund (PPF) 3.139
moral hazard legislation 2.32–2.51
  ancillary powers 2.34
  clearance procedure 2.04
  contribution notices 1.26, 2.34
    *see also* contribution notices
  financial support directions 2.34
  interaction of measures 2.34
  overview 2.34

# Index

moral hazard legislation—*contd.*
  Pensions Regulator 1.29, 2.02, 2.04
  protection of PPF 1.29
  purpose 1.26, 1.29, 2.32, 2.33
  rationale 2.32, 2.33
  responsibility for provisions 1.28, 2.02
  restoration orders 2.34, 2.48–2.51
  supplemental provisions 2.34
multi-employer schemes
  Pensions Regulator 2.24
  s 75 debt 9.187
  winding up scheme 2.24
Myners Review 9.05, 9.05.9.06

National Association of Pension Funds 1.09
non-dependant beneficiaries
  disputes, pension 9.104, 9.115, 9.116
non-executive committee of the Regulator
  delegation 2.10
  functions 2.09, 2.10
  internal controls 2.10, 2.11
  membership 2.09
    remit 2.11
    sub-committees 2.09
notices *see* contribution notices; improvement notices; third party notices
notification
  freezing orders 2.27

occupational pension schemes
  activities of 9.155–9.158
  annual increases 9.188–9.191
  consultation by employers 9.67–9.71
  contributions 9.150–9.154, 9.179–9.182
  deficiency in assets 9.183–9.187
  establishment 9.150
  inalienability 9.173
  incentives to offer 1.28
  meaning 9.143, 9.144
  overpayments 9.173
  payment into
    non-European scheme 9.153, 9.154
    restrictions 9.150–9.154
    UK-based scheme 9.150–9.152
  personal pension schemes distinguished 9.143
  registration 2.54
  scheme design
    activities 9.155–9.158
    contributions 9.150–9.154
    payment into scheme 9.150–9.154
  withdrawal from existing arrangement 1.28
Occupational Pensions Regulatory Authority (OPRA)
  budget 1.29
  establishment 2.01, 3.04
  Financial Assistance Scheme, guidance on 10.16, 10.17
  Green Paper 2.01
  reactive nature 2.01
  replacement 1.08, 2.02
Ombudsman *see* Pension Protection Fund Ombudsman; Pensions Ombudsman

paternity leave 9.170–9.172
penalties
  disputes, pension 9.114
  information gathering 5.08–5.17
  investment powers 9.11
  Member Nominated Trustees (MNT) 9.41
  no indemnification for fines or civil penalties 9.159, 9.160
  scheme modification 9.89
  statement of investment principles 9.11
Pension Benefit Guaranty Corporation (PBGC) 3.07
pension credits 9.80, 9.194, 9.195
pension disputes *see* disputes, pension
pension liberation
  bogus transfers 2.31
  meaning 2.31
  Pensions Regulator 2.07, 2.31
  repatriation order 2.31
  restraining order 2.31
  restraining orders 2.31
Pension Protection Fund Ombudsman 6.19–6.42
  annual report 6.25
  appointment 6.19
  compensation 6.32, 6.35
  Deputy 6.20
  disqualifications 6.23
  establishment 6.19–6.25
  expenses 6.19
  fees 6.19
  financial year 6.25
  funding 6.19
  information powers 6.19
  obstruction in performance of duties 6.42
  recovery of debt 6.19
  references to 6.26–6.42
    appeals 6.40
    binding determination 6.31, 6.38
    categories of persons who can make reference 6.34
    compensation 6.32, 6.35
    death of original person 6.29
    evidence 6.28
    High Court, references to 6.39
    investigation 6.26
    maladministration complaints 6.33
    notification of 6.27
    obstruction in performance of duties 6.42

# Index

oral hearing 6.28
prescribed persons 6.29, 6.38
procedure 6.27
procedure for investigation of complaint 6.34
reports 6.41
representations 6.36
reviewable matter 6.26
stay of legal proceedings 6.30, 6.37
written representations 6.28
removal 6.19
remuneration 6.19
resignation 6.19
staff 6.19
terms and conditions of appointment 6.19
Pension Protection Fund (PPF) 3.01–3.162
abuse 2.02
actuarial valuation 3.21
administration of compensation payments 3.137
aim 3.01
anti-avoidance 3.96, 3.97
application for assistance 1.25
application by trustees 1.30
assessment of cases for entry to 1.34
assessment period 3.42, 3.70–3.94
  accrual of benefits 3.73, 3.99
  commencement 3.71
  contributions 3.73, 3.74
  creditor of employer, Board to act as 3.84
  directions 3.77–3.79
  duration 3.71, 3.72
  ill health provisions, reviewable 3.87–3.92
  new members 3.73
  payment of scheme benefits 3.85, 3.86
  purpose 3.70
  restrictions during 3.70
  review of ill health provisions 3.87–3.92
  transfers 3.81
  valuation of assets and liabilities 3.93, 3.94
  winding up, restrictions on 3.80–3.83
assets 3.143, 3.144
assumption of responsibility by 3.40, 3.41, 3.44
  applications 3.65–3.68
  duty to assume responsibility 3.60, 3.61
  insolvency of employer 3.62–3.64
  notifications 3.65–3.68
  payment of compensation 3.118–3.120
  protected liabilities 3.69
  refusal 3.63, 3.95–3.99
Board
  accounts 3.11, 3.21
  actuarial valuation 3.21
  administration levy 3.33–3.35
  administration of compensation payments 3.137

administrative expenses 3.32
annual reports 3.36, 3.37
appointments 3.10, 3.11, 3.12, 3.16
borrowing 3.31
chairman 3.10, 3.12
challenging decisions 6.01
Chief Executive 3, 3.10, 3.11, 3.15
committees 3.17
complaints to 6.02, 6.05–6.18
composition 3.10
costs 3.33–3.35
delegation powers 3.18–3.20
deposit taker 3.31
determination notice 3.53
discharge of liabilities 3.138, 3.139
disqualifications 3.23
entry of premises 5.04–5.07
establishment 3.09–3.16
exemption from liability 3.24
Financial Assistance Scheme 10.12
financial matters 3.29–3.32
functions 3.25, 3.26
fund managers 3.29
independence 3.22
information gathering *see* information gathering
investigation of complaints by *see* complaints to PPF Board
investment of funds 3.29
liability 3.11, 3.22
membership 3.10, 3.12
non-executive functions 3.27, 3.28
non-executive members 3.10, 3.14
obligations 3.09
ordinary members 3.10, 3.12, 3.14
powers 3.09
procedure 3.17–3.24
proceedings 3.11
purpose 3.09
records 3.21
removal from office 3.14
reports 5.28
resignations 3.14
responsibilities 3.09
reviewable matters 6.01
role 3.10
staff 3.15
statement of accounts 3.21
status 3.11, 3.22
sub-committees 3.17
tenure of members 3.14
terms and conditions 3.16
terms of appointment 3.13
vacancies 3.12
vacating office 3.14
validity of proceedings 3.12
written statement of investment principles 3.30

# Index

Pension Protection Fund (PPF)—*contd.*
  cash payments 3.138
  cessation of involvement with a scheme 3.98, 3.99
  closed schemes 3.105, 3.106, 3.112–3.117
  Commissioners of Inland Revenue, notification of 3.134
  death of member prior to assessment period 3.131, 3.135
  determination notice 3.53
  discharge of Board's liabilities 3.138, 3.139
  duty of Pensions Regulator to protect 1.34, 2.02, 2.05
  duty to notify events 3.47
  effect 1.26
  eligibility 3.39, 3.58, 3.59
  equal treatment 3.140
  essential function 3.07
  exclusions from scope 3.39
  fraud compensation regime, relationship with 3.141, 3.142, 4.25–4.27
  function 3.08
  fund 3.143, 3.144
  funding 1.25, 3.01
  going concern, employer unlikely to continue as 3.40, 3.60
  Green Paper 3.05, 3.06
  guaranteed minimum pension 3.134
  implementation timetable 1.09, 3.01
  income 3.143
  information gathering *see* information gathering
  initial cost 3.145
  insolvency of employer 3.45–3.57, 3.60
    assets of scheme 3.63
    binding scheme failure notice 3.62
    Board approval of notices 3.53
    circumstances in which notice becomes binding 3.55–3.57
    conditions for assumption of responsibility 3.62
    definitions 3.48, 3.49
    determination notice 3.53
    duty to assume responsibility for scheme 3.62–3.64
    duty to notify events 3.47
    failure to issue notice 3.54
    insolvency date 3.48
    insolvency event 3.48
    insolvency practitioner 3.46, 3.49
    non-compliance with s 122 duties 3.54
    notice confirming status of scheme 3.50–3.57
    qualifying insolvency event 3.40, 3.45, 3.64
    refusal to assume responsibility 3.63
    relevant time 3.63
    withdrawal event 3.62
  insolvency practitioner 3.46, 3.49
  insurance policies 3.138
  introduction 3.01
  investigation of complaints by Board *see* complaints to PPF Board
  level of compensation payable 3.44
  levies 1.25, 1.26, 3.01, 3.145–3.162
    calculation 3.151–3.162
    initial costs 3.145
    initial levy 3.146–3.148
    levy ceiling 3.151–3.162
    risk-based levy 3.149
    scheme-based levy 3.150
  maintenance 2.02
  money purchase benefits 3.139
  moral hazard provisions *see* moral hazard legislation
  notification that employer unlikely to continue as going concern 3.40, 3.60
  Ombudsman *see* Pension Protection Fund Ombudsman
  operation 1.26
  origins 1.09, 3.03, 3.04
  outgoings 3.143
  outstanding concerns 3.07
  payment of compensation 3.118–3.142
    adjustments where assumption of responsibility 3.131
    administration of compensation payments 3.137
    admissible rules 3.125
    annual increases 3.123, 3.130
    assessment date 3.124
    assumption of responsibility 3.118–3.120
    calculation of compensation 3.124, 3.137
    capping 3.123, 3.129
    Commissioners of Inland Revenue, notification of 3.134
    commutation of lump sum 3.127
    death of member prior to assessment period 3.131, 3.135
    definition of compensation 3.137
    duty to pay out amounts 3.135
    effect of transfer notice 3.121, 3.122
    entitlement before reaching normal pension age 3.128
    exceeding entitlement, payments 3.132, 3.137
    guaranteed minimum pension 3.134
    level of compensation payable 3.124
    lump sum payments 3.123
    method of payment 3.137
    normal pension age 3.124
    partial scheme rescues 3.136
    periodic compensation 3.123
    postponement of entitlement 3.133, 3.135
    relevant contract of insurance, modification of 3.122

# Index

revaluation 3.126
suspension 3.137
timing of payment 3.137
transfer notice 3.118–3.122
pension strategy 3.02
position prior to implementation 1.12
postponement of entitlement 3.133, 3.135
procedure
   assessment period 3.42
   assumption of responsibility 3.44
   eligibility 3.39
   qualifying conditions 3.40, 3.41
   summary 3.38–3.44
   valuation 3.43
protected liabilities 3.41, 3.69
purpose 1.25
qualification for compensation 3.07
qualifying conditions 3.40, 3.41
qualifying insolvency event 3.40
reconsideration 3.100–3.103
   application to Board for 3.100
   assumption of responsibility 3.102
   determination notice 3.103
   prescribed form 3.100
   protected benefits quotation 3.100, 3.101
refusal to assume responsibility 3.95–3.99
role 3.08
scheme rescue 3.41
schemes outside coverage 3.58, 3.59
subverting operation 1.28
transfer notice 3.118–3.122
valuation 3.43
White Paper 3.01, 3.05, 3.06
winding up 3.107–3.111
withdrawal notice 3.98
pension sharing order 9.80
pensionable age 12.01
Pensions Act 2004
   commentary 1.24–1.34
   context 1.06
   existing legislation 1.23, 1.27
   full text App 1
   implementation *see* implementation timetable
   overriding effect against conflicting provisions/practices 1.23
   regulations implementing 1.27, 1.28
   scheme of 1.27
Pensions Commission
   first report 9.175
Pensions Compensation Board (PCB) 3.04, 3.08, 4.01
   current compensation provision 4.02
   dissolution 4.28
   final salary schemes 4.02
   money purchase schemes 4.02
   transfer of property and rights from 4.28

Pensions Law Review Committee Report 1.09, 9.77
Pensions Ombudsman
   administrative acts 9.137
   administrator 9.135
   appointment 9.122
   delays 9.125
   delegation 9.123, 9.125–9.132
   deputies 9.123
      allowances 9.131
      appointment 9.124–9.132
      carrying out functions 9.129
      compensation for loss of office 9.131
      disqualifications 9.132
      gratuities 9.131
      interpretation of functions 9.130
      pension 9.131
      powers 9.127
      removal 9.128
      remuneration 9.131
      resignation 9.128
   disputes, pension 9.122, 9.123
   establishment of office 9.122
   extension of jurisdiction 9.122
   financing scheme, persons 9.137
   group actions 9.123, 9.138–9.142
   incapacity 9.125
   investigations 9.138–9.142
   jurisdiction 9.122, 9.133–9.137
   maladministration 9.135
   new requirements 9.122, 9.123
   persons concerned with administration of the scheme 9.133–9.136
   powers 9.122
   removal from office 9.124
   resignation 9.124
   resources 9.123
   workload 9.125
Pensions Registry
   maintenance 2.02
Pensions Regulator
   Annual Report 2.16
   assistance, provision of 1.29
   board 2.08
   bogus transfers 2.07
   budget 1.29
   Chairman 2.08, 2.09
   challenges facing 1.33.1.34
   chief executive 2.08
      remuneration 2.10
   clearance procedure 2.04
   codes of practice 2.02, 2.07, 2.78–2.80
      approval 2.80
      areas covered by codes 2.78
      breach 2.79
      consultation 2.80
      failure to observe 2.79
      issue of codes 2.78, 2.79

# Index

Pensions Regulator—*contd.*
  commentary on 2.04–2.06
  conduct of pension schemes 2.21–2.31
    closure 2.21–2.24
    freezing orders 2.25–2.27 *see also* freezing orders
    pension liberation 2.31
    trustees 2.28–2.30
    winding up 2.03, 2.05, 2.07, 2.21–2.24
  conflicting responsibilities 2.05, 2.06
  contribution notices *see* contribution notices
  creation 1.24
  determination notice 2.86
  Determinations Panel *see* Determinations Panel
  directions 2.07
  education 1.29, 2.01, 2.02, 2.07, 2.17–2.20
  exercise of regulatory function 2.81–2.87
    determination notice 2.86
    final notice 2.87
    procedure 2.81, 2.82
    publication of procedure 2.82
    regulatory functions 2.81
    special procedures 2.83–2.87
    standard procedure 2.83–2.87
    warning notices 2.83, 2.84
  final notice 2.87
  Financial Assistance Scheme 10.12
  financial controls 2.10
  financial support directions *see* financial support directions
  freezing orders 2.03, 2.05, 2.07 *see also* freezing orders
  funding 2.04
  Green Paper *Simplicity, Security and Choice: Working and Saving for Retirement* 2.01
  guidelines 2.02
  implementation timetable 1.08
  improvement notices 1.29, 2.07, 2.18
    *see also* improvement notices
  information gathering 2.65–2.76
    confidentiality 2.73
    disclosure for tax purposes 2.74–2.76
    failure to comply 2.69
    misleading information 2.72
    premises, inspection of 2.66–2.68
    provision of false information 2.72
    provision of information 2.65
    restricted information 2.73, 2.75
    retention of documents 2.71
    warrants 2.70, 2.71
  information provision 1.29, 2.01, 2.02, 2.07, 2.17–2.20
  injunction application 2.19
  inspection of premises 2.66–2.68
  internal financial controls 2.10
  intervention powers 1.29
  key objectives 2.02
  knowledge and understanding of trustees 1.30
  levy 2.04
  moral hazard legislation 1.29, 2.02, 2.04, 2.32–2.51
    *see also* contribution notices; financial support directions; moral hazard legislation; restoration orders
  multi-employer schemes 2.24
  non-executive committee
    delegation 2.10
    functions 2.09, 2.10
    internal controls 2.10, 2.11
    membership 2.09
    remit 2.11
    sub-committees 2.09
  notifying regulator 2.61–2.64
    breaches of the law 2.64
    prescribed events 2.61–2.63
  objectives 2.02
  operation 2.02, 2.03
  OPRA, replacement of 1.08, 2.02
  origins 2.01–2.06
  pension liberation 2.07, 2.31
  Pensions Registry, maintenance of 2.02
  powers 2.07
  PPF, duty to protect 1.34, 2.02, 2.05
  premises, inspection of 2.66–2.68
  prescribed events 2.61–2.63
  prevention of breaches of legislation 1.29
  proactive nature 1.02, 2.01, 2.21
  referrals to 2.07
  registration
    assimilation of data 2.55
    contents of register 2.52
    information held 2.53, 2.54
    inspection of data 2.55
    maintenance of the register 2.52
    manner of recording information 2.52
    notifying regulator 2.61–2.64
    occupational pensions 2.54
    prohibited trustees 2.59, 2.60
    registrable information 2.52, 2.53
    scheme returns 2.56–2.58
    winding up notices 2.52
  remit 2.02, 2.03
  repatriation order 2.31
  reports 2.77
  representations to 2.07
  resources 2.04, 2.20
  responsibilities 1.29–1.34, 2.04, 2.15
  restitution orders 2.07, 2.19
  restoration orders 2.34, 2.48–2.51
  restraining orders 2.07, 2.31
  role 1.29–1.34, 2.02, 2.03
  schedule of contributions 1.29
  scheme modification 1.29
  skill and knowledge of 1.33

# Index

Statement of Funding Principles 1.29
Statutory Funding Objective (SFO) 1.29
suspension order 2.28
third party notices 1.29, 2.07, 2.19
Tribunal *see* Pensions Regulator Tribunal
trustees 2.28–2.30
  disqualification 2.28
  independent trustee 2.03, 2.30
  jurisdiction over 1.30, 2.03
  new trustees, appointment of 2.29
  prohibition from acting in named scheme 2.28
  removal 2.03
  support 2.02
  suspension order 2.28
unauthorized transfers 2.07
unpaid employer contributions 2.19
unpaid employer contributions, recovery of 1.29
warning notices 2.83, 2.84
winding up scheme 2.03, 2.05, 2.07, 2.21–2.24
  circumstances 2.21
  defined benefits 2.22
  multi-employer schemes 2.24
  priority order on 2.23
  pro-active role 2.21
Pensions Regulator Tribunal 1.34, 2.88–2.91
  appeals 2.90
  decisions, effect of 2.89
  establishment 2.88
  lay members 2.88
  Legal Assistance Scheme 2.91
  permission for appeal 2.90
  purpose 2.88
  recommendations 2.89
permission for appeal
  Pensions Regulator Tribunal 2.90
personal pension schemes
  consultation by employers 9.72
  contributions 9.177, 9.178
  meaning 9.143, 9.145
  occupational pension schemes distinguished 9.143
personal pension schemes
  annual increases 9.192–9.193
Pickering Report 1.31
PPF *see* Pension Protection Fund (PPF)
premises, inspection of
  Pensions Regulator 2.66–2.68
prescribed events
  Pensions Regulator 2.61–2.63
prescribed offences
  Fraud Compensation Fund 4.09
priority order 2.23
prospective members
  consultation by employers 9.71
  transfer, pension protection on 9.52, 9.53

protected liabilities
  Pension Protection Fund (PPF) 3.41, 3.69
protected modification 9.81, 9.86

qualifying insolvency event 3.64, 4.10, 4.11, 4.12

reciprocal agreement with Australia 12.03, 12.32, 12.33
recovery of value 4.19
Reference Scheme Test 9.56
referrals
  Pensions Regulator, to 2.07
registration
  Pensions Regulator
    assimilation of data 2.55
    contents of register 2.52
    information held 2.53, 2.54
    inspection of data 2.55
    maintenance of the register 2.52
    manner of recording information 2.52
    notifying regulator 2.61–2.64
    occupational pensions 2.54
    prohibited trustees 2.59, 2.60
    registrable information 2.52, 2.53
    scheme returns 2.56–2.58
    winding up notices 2.52
remuneration
  chief executive of Pensions Regulator 2.10
  Deputy Pension Protection Fund Ombudsman 6.22
  Pension Protection Fund Ombudsman 6.19
repatriation order
  effect 2.31
  pension liberation 2.31
  Pensions Regulator 2.31
representations
  Pensions Regulator, to 2.07
reserved regulatory functions 2.14
resignation
  Pension Protection Fund Ombudsman 6.19
restitution orders
  Pensions Regulator 2.07, 2.19
restoration orders 2.34
  moral hazard legislation 2.34, 2.48–2.51
  non-compliance 2.50
  Pensions Regulator 2.34, 2.48–2.51
  undervalue, transactions at an 2.48–2.51
restraining orders
  effect 2.31
  pension liberation 2.31
  Pensions Regulator 2.07, 2.31
restricted information 5.18–5.22
Retail Prices Index 9.188, 9.189, 9.196
retirement, financial planning for *see* financial planning for retirement
revaluation 9.196, 9.197

# Index

reviews
  disputes, pension 9.105
  Financial Assistance Scheme 10.12
  ill health provisions 3.87–3.92
  PPF Board determinations 6.05–6.14
  statement of investment principles 9.08, 9.09
risk-based levy 3.149

schedule of contributions 7.09
  Pensions Regulator 1.29
scheme amendments
  implementation timetable 1.19
scheme design
  activities of occupational pension scheme 9.155–9.158
  adoption leave 9.170–9.172
  annual increases 9.188–9.195
  categories of pension scheme 9.143–9.146
  contracting out 9.198–9.204
    age at which benefits may be received 9.201–9.204
    commutation, restrictions on 9.201–9.204
    Inland Revenue approval 9.200
    working life, meaning of 9.198, 9.199
  deficiency in assets of occupational pension schemes 9.183–9.187
  early leavers 9.164–9.169
  inalienability of occupational pension 9.173
  no indemnification for fines or civil penalties 9.159, 9.160
  occupational pension schemes
    activities 9.155–9.158
    contributions 9.150–9.154
    payment into scheme 9.150–9.154
  paternity leave 9.170–9.172
  payment of surpluses to employer 9.147–9.149
  restrictions on payment into occupational pension schemes 9.150–9.154
  revaluation 9.196, 9.197
  safeguarding pension rights 9.170–9.173
  short service benefit 9.161–9.163
  stakeholder pensions 9.205–9.207
  voluntary contributions 9.174, 9.175
scheme failure notice 3.54, 3.62
scheme funding 7.01–7.14
  actuarial valuation 7.0
  advice to actuary 7.13
  agreement of employer 7.11, 7.12
  failure to comply with provisions 7.10
  Minimum Funding Requirement, abolition of 7.01
  powers for regulator 7.14
  schedule of contributions 7.09
  scheme specific funding standard 7.03
  statement of funding principles 7.07–7.10
  statutory funding objective 7.04–7.06

scheme modification 9.77–9.99
  accrued rights and entitlements 9.78, 9.79, 9.92
  actuarial equivalence 9.84, 9.85, 9.95, 9.96, 9.97
  areas of concern 9.90–9.99
  background 9.77, 9.78
  confirmation of willingness to exercise amendment powers 9.86
  consent 9.86
  costs, pension scheme 9.99
  death in service pensions 9.93
  detrimental modification 9.82
  failure to comply with requirements 9.98
  Goode Report 9.77
  implementation timetable 1.20
  information requirements 9.83, 9.94
  members, meaning of 9.78
  modification, meaning of 9.78
  modifying the modification 9.88
  new provisions 9.79–9.89
  notification of intention to exercise powers 9.87, 9.94
  opposition to change 9.97
  penalties 9.89
  Pensions Regulator 1.29
  prescribed schemes 9.79
  protected modification 9.81, 9.86
  purpose of new rules 9.90
  restriction on powers to alter schemes 9.77, 9.78
  subsisting rights 9.79
    definition 9.80
  survivor's benefits 9.93
  voidable exercise of powers 9.88
scheme rescue 9.186
  Pension Protection Fund (PPF) 3.41
scheme specific funding 7.03
scheme-based levy 3.150
service company
  financial support directions 2.40, 2.42
SFO *see* Statutory Funding Objective (SFO)
short service benefit
  scheme design 9.161–9.163
social security benefits 8.08
sole trustees
  knowledge and understanding of trustees 9.25
stakeholder pensions 9.169, 9.205–9.207
State Earnings Related Pension Scheme 12.30
State Graduated Pension 12.30
State pensions 12.01–12.35
  accrual period 12.21
  affirmative procedure 12.30
  choice of pension increments or lump sum 12.16
  commentary 12.34, 12.35
  consequential amendments 12.27–12.30

# Index

deferral 12.07–12.11, 12.30
disclosure of information 12.03, 12.31
entitlement to more than one Category B pension 12.04–12.06
lump sum 12.16, 12.19–12.22
lump sum alternative 12.12–12.15
payment 12.01
pension increments 12.16, 12.17, 12.18
pensionable age 12.01
qualifying years 12.01
reciprocal agreement with Australia 12.03, 12.32, 12.33
spouse, options for 12.23–12.26
Statement of Funding Principles 7.07–7.10
  implementation timetable 1.15
statement of investment principles 9.08–9.12
  balance between investments 9.09
  considerations affecting investments 9.09
  contents 9.09
  exempt schemes 9.09
  exercise of rights 9.09
  expected returns 9.09
  form 9.09
  implementation 9.09, 9.12
  maintenance 9.09
  penalties 9.11
  Pension Protection Fund (PPF) Board 3.30
  preparation 9.09
  restrictions 9.10
  review 9.08, 9.09
  risk 9.09
Statutory Funding Objective (SFO)
  implementation timetable 1.15
  minimum funding requirement replaced by 1.15
  Pensions Regulator, enforcement by 1.29
subsisting rights 9.79, 9.80
surpluses
  implementation timetable 1.22
  payment to employer 9.147–9.149
survivors' benefits 9.47
  scheme modification 9.93
suspension order
  trustees 2.28

third party notices
  Pensions Regulator 1.29, 2.07, 2.19
training
  knowledge and understanding of trustees 9.23
transactions at an undervalue
  restoration orders 2.48–2.51
transfer notice
  Pension Protection Fund (PPF) 3.118–3.122
transfers
  bogus 2.07, 2.31 *see also* pension liberation
  pension protection on 2.07, 2.31, 9.46–9.61
    background 9.46

case law 9.47
contracting out of requirements 9.60
form of protection 9.55
implementation timetable 1.11, 9.61
individuals covered 9.52–9.54
money purchase schemes 9.56
new protections 9.55–9.61
pensions exception 9.47
prospective members 9.52, 9.53
Reference Scheme Test 9.56
TUPE 9.46
unauthorized 2.07
Tribunal *see* Pensions Regulator Tribunal
trustees
  appointment of independent trustee 2.03
  borrowing 9.04, 9.16
  disqualification 2.28
  independent 2.03, 2.30
  investment powers 9.04
    principles 9.08–9.12
    statement of investment principles 9.08–9.12
  knowledge and understanding *see* knowledge and understanding of trustees
  lay trusteeship 9.07
  Member Nominated Trustee *see* Member Nominated Trustees (MNT)
  Myners Review 9.05.9.06
  new trustees, appointment of 2.29
  obligations 9.03–9.44
    borrowing 9.04, 9.16
    consequence of new rules 9.07
    existing standards 9.04
    focus of provisions 9.03
    Green Paper 9.06
    investment *see* investment powers
    knowledge and understanding *see* knowledge and understanding of trustees
    Member Nominated Trustee *see* Member Nominated Trustees (MNT)
    Myners Review 9.05, 9.06
    new trustee duties 9.04–9.07
    Pensions Directive 9.06
    power to make regulations governing investment 9.13–9.15
  Pensions Regulator 2.28–2.30
    disqualification 2.28
    independent trustee 2.03, 2.30
    jurisdiction 1.30, 2.03
    new trustees, appointment of 2.29
    prohibition from acting in named scheme 2.28
    removal of trustees by 2.03

535

trustees—*contd.*
  Pensions Regulator—*contd.*
    support for trustees 2.02
    suspension order 2.28
  perception of role 9.07
  prohibition from acting in named scheme 2.28
  support by Pensions Regulator 2.02
  suspension order 2.28

unauthorized transfers
  Pensions Regulator 2.07
undervalue, transactions at an
  restoration orders 2.48–2.51
unpaid employer contributions
  Pensions Regulator 2.19
  recovery by Pensions Regulator of 1.29

valuation
  Pension Protection Fund (PPF) 3.43
voluntary contributions 9.174, 9.175

warning notices
  Pensions Regulator 2.83, 2.84
web references, useful App 3
whistleblowing 2.07

White Paper
  Pension Protection Fund (PPF) 3.01, 3.05, 3.06
  transfer of employment, pension protection on 9.51
winding up scheme
  defined benefits 2.22
  freezing orders 2.27
  multi-employer schemes 2.24
  Pension Protection Fund (PPF) 3.107–3.111
  Pensions Regulator 2.03, 2.05, 2.07, 2.21–2.24
    circumstances of order 2.21
    defined benefits 2.22
    multi-employer schemes 2.24
    pro-active role 2.21
    statutory order on implementation timetable 1.13
    new order 2.23
    power to vary 2.23
withdrawal notice
  Pension Protection Fund (PPF) 3.98
working life
  meaning 9.198, 9.199